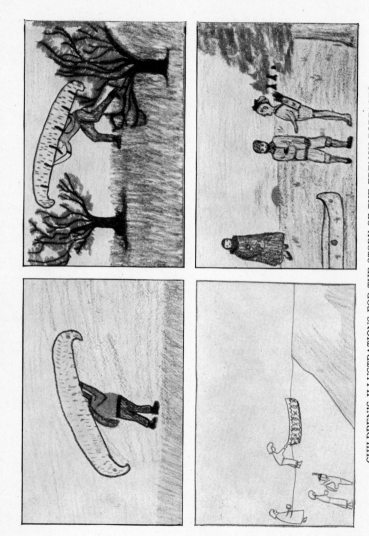

CHILDREN'S ILLUSTRATIONS FOR THE STORY OF THE FRENCH PORTAGES

In each case the child's undirected first attempt appears at the left, his directed drawing at the right.

See lesson on pages 690–696

TEACHING AMERICAN HISTORY
IN THE MIDDLE GRADES
OF THE ELEMENTARY SCHOOL

BY

MARY G. KELTY

SUPERVISOR OF HISTORY AND THE SOCIAL STUDIES IN THE TRAINING
DEPARTMENT, AND INSTRUCTOR IN THE TEACHING OF HISTORY
STATE TEACHERS COLLEGE, OSHKOSH, WISCONSIN

GINN AND COMPANY
BOSTON · NEW YORK · CHICAGO · LONDON
ATLANTA · DALLAS · COLUMBUS · SAN FRANCISCO

The Athenæum Press

GINN AND COMPANY · PRO-
PRIETORS · BOSTON · U.S.A.

TO THE MEMORY OF

THEODORE C. LUTZ

WHOSE FAITH IN EDUCATION
OPENED UP A NEW WORLD

PREFACE

The following study is offered as an aid to intermediate-grade teachers of American history, to junior-high-school teachers for use with "low ability" groups, to normal-school instructors giving a course in history for the intermediate grades, and to supervisors of the social studies. It is the result of many years of experimentation on the part of the author as a teacher in the grades, a critic in normal schools, an instructor of history in the academic department, and a supervisor of history in the training department, of normal schools. The earlier units have been tried out for seven years. The entire work has served for five years as the course of study in the fourth and fifth grades of the training departments in the teachers colleges at Oshkosh, Wisconsin, and Bloomsburg, Pennsylvania. It has been used for two years in the State Normal School at Ashland, Oregon. In Oshkosh it has constituted also the basis of the course in the teaching of history in intermediate grades. Selected units have been tried out over a period of five years in rural schools, in county normal schools, and in city grades.

Schools which have experimented with the materials have used them either in fourth and fifth grades or fifth and sixth grades, according to the reading ability and the general experience of the children.

The trend represented in the organization of material reflects the influence of Dr. R. M. Tryon of The University of Chicago. The general technique follows the principles enunciated by Dr. H. C. Morrison of the same institution, with, however, two very marked divergences from his views. These are, first, the use of minimal essentials and, secondly, the use of subpresentations.[1]

[1] See pages 5–6, 23–24.

v

Grateful acknowledgment is made to Miss Nelle E. Moore, Director of the Intermediate Department, State Normal School, Bloomsburg, Pennsylvania, for her advice and criticism; to the following members of the faculty of the Teachers College at Oshkosh, Wisconsin, for their illustrative lessons: Mrs. Laura T. Johnson, Training Department, Miss Lila M. Rose, Supervisor of Music, Miss Ethel J. Bouffleur, Art Department; and to Miss Clara A. Trotter, Director of the Intermediate Department, State Normal School, Ashland, Oregon.

MARY G. KELTY

Oshkosh, Wisconsin

CONTENTS

PART I. THE TECHNIQUE

PART II. UNIT TREATMENT OF AMERICAN HISTORY

PART III. ILLUSTRATIVE LESSONS

APPENDIXES

TEACHING AMERICAN HISTORY
IN THE MIDDLE GRADES
OF THE ELEMENTARY SCHOOL

PART I. THE TECHNIQUE

SECTION I

THE EDUCATIONAL TRENDS

1. The Objectives, General and Specific. Since no scientifically established objectives of history are available, it has been necessary, through an arbitrary process of opinion, to select from the aims proposed by various committees and individuals the general objectives which form the basis of the study. They are as follows: an understanding of present-day institutions,[1] the habit of weighing evidence and of seeing all sides of a question, "social experience,"[2] and the love of reading. For the general objectives to be attained in the intermediate grades the following have been selected: a love of the subject, "ability to comprehend a coherent narrative of successive events,"[3] a rudimentary understanding of the molding influence of geographic and economic forces, and the ability to use books. Specific subject-matter objectives[4] for each unit, based on the available scientific studies, are included in each story under the heading "Minimal Essentials."

2. The Organization as a Series of Large Units. The subject matter is organized[5] as a series of large units or projects. The whole story is a series of units each centering round one main idea or movement. An effort has been made to indicate in the subtitles the relationship existing between them and the

---

[1] Hill, H. C., "History for History's Sake." *The Historical Outlook*, XII: 310–315; see also text, p. 35.

[2] Bobbitt, Franklin, *How to make a Curriculum*, p. 115; Herriott, M. E., *How to make Courses of Study in the Social Studies*, Bureau of Educational Research, University of Illinois (Bulletin No. 5, 1926).

[3] Judd, C. H., *Psychology of High-School Subjects*, p. 456.

[4] Bobbitt, Franklin, *How to make a Curriculum*, p. 33.

[5] Morrison, H. C., *The Practice of Teaching in the Secondary School*, p. 182; Tryon, R. M., *The Teaching of History in Junior and Senior High Schools*, pp. 217–219.

3

unit as a whole. Irrelevant material has been rigidly excluded. Within the units the arrangement is usually chronological-topical, but psychological relationship[1] has been the dominating criterion. For example, the story of Marco Polo has been considered a better story approach to the problem of why the West wanted to reach the East than the story of the Crusades, though one would naturally expect the reverse order.

The basic movements or forces working in American history have been organized chiefly along social and economic lines, and have been told in simple narrative style. Constitutional and political questions have been avoided as far as possible. The following twelve units have been selected, five for completion in the fourth or fifth grade and the remaining seven in the fifth or sixth:

1. **Why Men wanted to reach the Countries of the Far East.**
2. **How the Nations tried to get Wealth from the New World.**
3. **Why English People came to live in the New World.**
4. **How England came to own most of North America.**
5. **How the English Colonies came to separate themselves from the Mother Country.**
6. **How the United States made itself respected among the Nations.**
7. **How the United States moved Westward to the Pacific.**
8. **How One Machine called for Another, until All our Methods of Living were Changed.**
9. **How the Slavery Question almost split the Nation into Two Parts.**
10. **How the United States became really united in Spirit.**
11. **How the United States became a Great Industrial Nation.**
12. **How the United States became a World Power.**

3. Developmental or Continuous Organization. The narrative is developmental or continuous, the biographical[2] element

---

[1] Gates, A. I., "The Psychological vs. the Chronological Order in the Teaching of History." *The Historical Outlook*, XI : 227–230.

[2] Johnson, Henry, *Teaching of History*, pp. 161–177; Wayland, John W., *How to Teach American History*, pp. 143–151; Kendall, C. N., and Stryker, F. E., *History in the Elementary School*, pp. 15–21; Klapper, Paul, *The Teaching of History*, pp. 4–8.

being subordinated to the thread of a movement, and the strictly chronological to the chronological-topical. The use of a time chart in each unit aids in keeping the perspective.[1]

4. Approach by the Method of Analysis rather than by that of Synthesis. A view of the whole is given before any detailed study of parts; for example, the overview of the entire unit, and the additional presentations for certain stories within a unit.[2]

5. Extensive Reading. Extensive rather than intensive reading is recommended. Readings are graded to provide as fully as possible for individual differences. The grading has been done after several years' experience with the reactions of groups toward the particular reading materials suggested, and with the aid of the American Library Association *Graded List of Books for Children*, the Winnetka *Graded Book List*, and Terman and Lima's *Children's Reading*.

6. Minimal Essentials based on Scientific Studies. Minimal essentials, while drawn from the story materials, are based so far as possible on the scientific studies available.[3]

a. Personages are selected from the lists presented by Bagley in his study of history texts,[4] from the report of the Committee to the Department of History and Other Social Studies of Academies and High Schools in Relation with the University of Chicago [5] (R. M. Tryon, chairman), and from Washburne's [6] list. Monroe and Herriott's *Objectives in United States History in Grades Seven and Eight* may be used as a summary of other studies.

b. Dates are chosen from Wooters's [7] list or from the committee report referred to in the preceding paragraph. Other

---

[1] An interesting study to determine whether or not fourth-grade pupils can appreciate change and development is reported by Clark, Marion G., "A Study in Testing Historical Sense in Fourth and Fifth Grade Pupils." *The Historical Outlook*, XIV : 147–150 (1923).

[2] See examples, text, pp. 52, 58.

[3] There are certain exceptions to this statement, noted in each case in footnotes.

[4] *The Fourteenth Yearbook of the National Society for the Study of Education*, Part I, p. 144.

[5] *The School Review*, XXVI : 473–485.

[6] *The Twenty-second Yearbook of the National Society for the Study of Education*, Part II, pp. 222–233.

[7] *School and Home Education*, XXXIV : 152–155; or *The Fourteenth Yearbook of the National Society for the Study of Education*, Part I, p. 140.

time expressions are based on Kelty's *Time Expressions comprehended by Children in the Elementary School.*[1]

c. Map study is adapted from the report of the committee referred to above, from Washburne's list, and from Rugg and Hockett's *Objective Studies in Map Location.*

d. Since no scientifically established materials on historical terms [2] are available (with the exception of Mrs. Pressey's *Technical Vocabularies of the Public-School Subjects*), those were selected which occurred over and over in the texts used and were fundamental to an understanding of the story. Study of these terms aims to develop the habit of thinking concretely "in terms of the realities involved." Cumulatively they build up a historical vocabulary.

e. A summary labeled "Things to Remember" is provided for use at the end of each story. It attempts to interpret the important points in the perspective of history, and forms the basis for the comprehension test at the end of each unit.

7. Drill. Drill games are suggested[3] for each unit.

8. Illustrative Material. The wealth of illustrative material[4] aims to insure concrete and objective imagery and to provide for the visual appeal.[5]

9. Objective Informal Tests. Objective informal tests are suggested for every story and provided for every unit. These are designed to test time-sense, place-sense, and knowledge of historical terms, dates-events, and personages. Special care has been used to cause the final test to measure comprehension rather than memory alone. Follow-up work is provided. The tests for the fourth grade are couched in the first two thousand words of the Thorndike word list [6] unless otherwise specifi-

[1] Master of Arts thesis, The University of Chicago, 1924.

[2] For the importance of a carefully considered vocabulary see Ayre, Adelaide, *Some Difficulties in Elementary-School History.*

[3] Wayland, John W., *How to Teach American History*, pp. 271–278; also text, pp. 40–43, 661–663.

[4] Kendall, C. N., and Stryker, F. E., *History in the Elementary School*, pp. 78–90; also text, Appendix B.

[5] Johnson, Henry, *Teaching of History*, pp. 202–224; Wayland, John W., *How to Teach American History*, pp. 161–168; Freeman, F. N., *Visual Education.*

[6] Thorndike, E. L., *The Teacher's Word Book.*

task is to see that the pupils do not become so lost in the sub-heads that they lose sight of the movement as a whole. One method of keeping the unit movement constantly in view is to record on the board during the period when it is under consideration the main title and the chief subdivision under which the work is being done. From time to time, as the class advances from one story to another, a new title is added, and the children tell how it bears on the subhead and on the title of the unit. For example, during the study of the discovery of gold in California, Unit VII,[1] the following outline is permanently and prominently displayed:

UNIT VII. HOW THE UNITED STATES MOVED WESTWARD TO THE PACIFIC

I. The First Great Addition was the Land just West of the Mississippi.
 1. Very early, people had begun to go over the mountains.
 2. The vast Louisiana country was bought.
 3. Roads and canals were necessary to reach unsettled parts of the country.
 4. Steamboats made travel easier and faster.
 5. Railroads reached parts of the country which steamboats could not.
 6. Huge farms in the new lands demanded new machinery and new

 was full of adventure.
 e first great man from the West.
 Spain.

 Trouble arose with Other Nations.
 t of the United States.
 ith Mexico over the question of Texas.
 vered in California.[2]

Another method used to preserve unity is to supply each child at the beginning with the outline of the new unit. He then checks off each story as studied, telling its relation to the subhead under which it stands and to the title of the unit.

The organization and recitation steps at the end of a unit [3] help to restore again the perspective which close consideration of details has warped. Therefore proper emphasis should be given to them as means of maintaining a view of the whole.

[1] See pages 348–394.
[2] When the next story is begun, the title is added to the outline, thus: 4. Oregon became part of the United States.
[3] See pages 43–49.

cally stated; and for the fifth grade, in the first three thousand words of the same list. The standard tests in the field are referred to at appropriate points.

10. Organization demanded of Pupils. Organization and generalization [1] suggestions are included for every story.

11. Provision for Children of Exceptional Ability. The creative and imaginative abilities of children are challenged.[2] Full provision is made for testing the capacities of the brightest members of the group through extensive reading and through the projects included in each story under the heading "Procedure during Assimilation." An attempt is made to discover special abilities through creative work.

12. Variety in Procedure. A variety of procedures is used.[3] These are listed in each story under the heading "Procedure during Assimilation."

13. Record Forms for the Study of the Individual Pupil. An adequate form of record is described to assist in the study of the reactions of the individual pupil.[4]

14. Pupil-Activity; Provision for supplying Experiences. Actual experiences are provided as a background for learning. Reaction members of the learning cycle are recognized in the organization and recitation steps and in the suggestions for things that children can do. Much project material is included. An attempt is made to overbalance teacher-activity by pupil-activity.[5]

15. Reading Materials couched in a Tested Vocabulary. A set of supplementary history-reading books based on the Thorndike word list and paralleling the organization given above [6] has been prepared by the author of this study for the use of lower-group pupils who cannot read the usual materials.

[1] Bobbitt, Franklin, *How to make a Curriculum*, pp. 58–59.
[2] See text, pp. 35–36; also Klapper, Paul, *The Teaching of History*, pp. 30–55.
[3] Morehouse, Frances M., "Forms of the History Recitation." *History Teacher's Magazine*, VII: 332–337.
[4] See text, pp. 20, 22, 26, 41.
[5] Woodburn, J. A., and Moran, T. F., *Introduction to American History*, p. 296; Parker, S. C., *General Methods of Teaching in Elementary Schools*, pp. 157–166; Tryon, R. M., *The Teaching of History in Junior and Senior High Schools*, pp. 24–25; Wayland, J. W., *How to Teach American History*, pp. 182–188.
[6] See text, p. 4, for the organization.

16. Combination of Materials[1] **from History, Geography, and Civics, studied by a Procedure which emphasizes Silent Reading.** Place geography has been emphasized throughout by the use of wall maps, globes, and sand-tables. Geographic influences are pointed out in the determining of trade routes, roads and railroads, in methods of frontier life, and in the connections between products and institutional life, for example in the development of slavery.

Materials usually considered in separate civics courses are here treated as parts of historical movements, such as the question of immigration, the formation of labor unions, and the growth of city problems. The method of mastery of historical, geographic, and civic materials is mainly through the medium of silent reading. School systems which were offering several silent-reading periods a day have found it easy and advantageous to give the following course in the place of at least one of those periods, and thus secure a double benefit from the same time and effort.

The sixteen educational trends enumerated above have determined the organization and the presentation of materials in this study.

[1] Klapper, Paul, *The Teaching of History*, pp. 82–90.

SECTION II

PRINCIPLES OF THE BASIC TECHNIQUE

Before considering the technique itself, attention must necessarily be directed to a preliminary step — the selection of the units.

The **selection of the units**[1] is of primary importance. Only by organizing material into large movements, unified and coherent, continuous and developmental, can the day-by-day, piecemeal memorization of unrelated facts be avoided. The organizing process may be compared to stringing a handful of beads. If one attempts to pick up a handful of loose beads, he finds that they run through his fingers and escape his grasp. The same thing happens in the learning of history through the day-by-day recitation: one small item of subject matter first (perhaps the acquisition of western lands), another small item of subject matter following (perhaps foreign relations at the same time), the next day the development of the same period, and then the story of such a study a review exercise has been the unrelated parts together into a coherent and organize them. It has failed to do so.

Suppose, instead, that the same number of beads is on twelve strong cords. When one attempts to pick up a bead, all those fastened on the same string follow at the same time and keep the same relative positions. They belong together, and it is easy to keep any part of a string in its proper position. Such is the contrast between history taught as a series of daily lessons and history organized into units.

The units included in the following study have been carefully organized so that all the material within a given division shall bear on an understanding of the topic. The teacher's

[1] Given on page 4; see also Morrison, H. C., *The Practice of Teaching in the Secondary School*, Part III, p. 182.

ing
nd
all
pe

ng

II.

The **basic technique** is the contribution of Dr. H. C. Morrison of The University of Chicago, but two features are included which are much at variance with his point of view; namely, the use of minimal essentials and of subpresentations.[1] These differences are emphasized so that the responsibility for failure may be rightly placed if unhappy results follow from the departures mentioned above.

The technique is based on the *mastery formula* [2] for science-type subjects; that is, *pre-test, teach, test, diagnose results, adapt procedure, and then reteach, and test again to the point of mastery.* Each part is explained in detail in the paragraphs immediately following. The successive *steps* used in applying this formula to a given unit are *preparation, presentation, assimilation, organization, and recitation,*[3] each of which is discussed in great detail in Section III, pp. 18–50. The basic procedure has been adapted herein to meet the interests and capacities of young children.

The purpose of the *preparation* step,[4] often called *exploration,* is twofold: (1) to find out what, if anything, the pupils already know about the new unit, so that time will not be wasted by repeating what they know, or, on the other hand, by assuming a knowledge which later experience proves they do not possess (thus the procedure orients the teacher); and (2) to motivate the study of the new unit, or awaken interest in the story. The step consists of the presenting of actual experiences or of oral questions asked by the teacher. The questions may be based on previous knowledge which she knows the class possesses, on moving pictures they may have seen, or on their general information. The exercise constitutes the *pre-test* part of the *mastery formula* referred to above; in terms of psychology it is a stimulus member of the learning

---

[1] See pages 5–6, 23–24.

[2] Morrison, H. C., *The Practice of Teaching in the Secondary School,* Part I, p. 79.

[3] Hill, H. C., "Curriculum in History." *Studies in Secondary Education,* I, (1923), Supplementary Educational Monographs, the University of Chicago Press, pp. 109–115; Morrison, H. C., *The Practice of Teaching in the Secondary School,* Part III, pp. 232–316.

[4] Morrison, H. C., *The Practice of Teaching in the Secondary School,* Part I, p. 80; Part III, pp. 232–243; also text, pp. 51, 57, 62, 66, 73.

cycle,[1] making provision for apperceptive approach[2] and favorable frame of mind. The conversation which constitutes this step will occupy possibly five minutes; it is followed immediately by the presentation.

The *presentation*[3] is given orally by the teacher, the class listening with concentrated attention. It is the *teaching* part of the *mastery formula* and a stimulus member of the learning cycle. The story sketches in bold and picturesque outline the main features of the unit, or states the problem, rigorously eliminating details of the action. Rather, it explains what the movement is about or in what direction it is driving. It is broad and interpretative, an extensive or bird's-eye view, not a recital of successive facts or an intensive scrutiny. The broad view of the whole precedes the analytical detailed study of any of the parts, the same principle as that utilized in the sentence method of beginning reading. Later, when the pupil acquires details, he knows how to frame them or how to place them in the proper perspective and proportion.

The presentations given in the following pages are merely suggestive. Teachers may find from their preparation step that children already know the particular material included, or that the language is too difficult for a specific group and hence must be simplified. Thus the story is improved from year to year. It should be told quite without notes and made as lively and interesting as possible. Much will depend upon the control technique,[4] as strict attention is necessary. Probably not over five minutes are employed with smaller children in presenting this step.

The presentation is followed immediately by the presentation test.[5] This is the *testing* part of the *mastery formula* and a reaction member of the learning cycle. Objective tests are

---

[1] Gates, A. I., *Psychology for Students of Education*, pp. 23–27, 31–33, 207–231; La Rue, D. W., *The Child's Mind and the Common Branches*, pp. 12–15, 68–84; Thorndike, E. L., *The Principles of Teaching*, pp. 39–41; Morrison, H. C., *The Practice of Teaching in the Secondary School*, Part III, pp. 154–157.

[2] Parker, S. C., *General Methods of Teaching in Elementary Schools*, pp. 168–199.

[3] Morrison, H. C., *The Practice of Teaching in the Secondary School*, Part III, pp. 243–256; also text, pp. 52, 58, 62, 66, 70, 74, 77, 90, 96, 100, 103, 106.

[4] Morrison, H. C., *The Practice of Teaching in the Secondary School*, Part II.

[5] Ibid. Part III, pp. 252–254.

herein provided for all units, but it is to be hoped that before finishing the fifth grade the form used will be a coherent composition embodying the reaction to the relationships stressed in the story. The tests are not timed. Words used for the fourth grade have been drawn from the first two thousand of the Thorndike word list [1] (except those specifically mentioned); and for the fifth grade, from the first three thousand of the same list.

It is of great importance, first, that the children be able to read the material in the test; secondly, that they grasp the *idea* of selecting the one right answer and checking it. Some children have difficulty in grasping the idea that the first part of the test sentence is to be tried out with the first answer and, if it does not make a correct statement, is to be repeated with the second answer, and so on until the correct answer is found, when it is to be checked.

The test papers are collected, scored, and the results recorded in a form [2] similar to the following:

PRESENTATION TEST FOR THE STORY OF THE NORTHMEN

NAMES	NUMBER OF ITEMS IN THE TEST				INDIVIDUAL SCORE	POSSIBLE SCORE
	1	2	3	4		
Abrams, John . .	V [3]	V	V	V	4	4
Bacon, Ada . . .	V	X [4]	X	V	2	4
Coe, Florence . .	V	V	X	V	3	4
Dahl, John	V	V	X	V	3	4
Etc.						
Total number of times each item is missed . . .	0	1	3	0	Total items missed 4	

[1] Thorndike, E. L., *The Teacher's Word Book.* The first two thousand words form the basis of choice for units one to five; the first three thousand words, for units six to twelve inclusive.

[2] Suggested by H. C. Morrison.

[3] V = item correctly answered.   [4] X = item incorrectly answered or omitted.

The closest study is given to these results, which study constitutes the *diagnosis* element of the *mastery formula*. Children who had all items correct are allowed to go on with the reading described in the step of assimilation. The papers which contained errors are returned. The children who had made mistakes take seats in a compact group and study their scores to ascertain on which points they failed. If only one point was missed, the teacher gives again the explanation of that point; if, however, there are scattering failures throughout all the points, it is economical in time to repeat the entire story to the reaching group.[1] Afterwards the test is taken as before, the scores are studied, the group is again divided on the basis of those who had learned and those who had learned only partly, and the story is repeated until all have a perfect score. This procedure carries out the mastery idea.

If more than two retellings are required for any pupils the cause must be diligently sought for. This study is also part of the diagnosis element of the mastery formula. The usual explanations are as follows:

1. Poor control technique; that is, pupils are inattentive.

2. The language of the story is poorly adapted to the particular group taught.

3. The children are not grasping the *idea* of how to select the correct test item.

4. A certain child may be distinctly a remedial problem. Naturally, when the teacher finds the cause of the difficulty, she applies curative measures for each case — the *adapting-of-procedure* part of the *mastery formula*.

The presentation test is not used as a basis for grading the pupil, but only for ascertaining whether he has grasped the idea. When the technique outlined above has been employed, many pupils who are not stupid but merely slow start the work of the unit with a clear idea of what it is about, and are therefore able to work intelligently. Under many types of procedure these pupils would be hopelessly confused from the beginning and hence almost preordained to failure.

[1] Morrison, H. C., *The Practice of Teaching in the Secondary School*, Part III, pp. 254–256.

The step of *assimilation*[1] is the time during which the child makes his own the story which he has just heard; he reads widely concerning it, he studies pictures, works out projects, and, in general, so considers and views it from various angles that an actual mental adaptation takes place. He develops a definite understanding-attitude toward it. Hereafter he may forget most of the details,[2] but the feeling-of-meanings[3] remains. The pupils who up to this point have been more or less passive now become active. The class periods consist largely of supervised study; there is not a recitation, in the usual sense of the word, every day.

Usually the first thing recommended in *assimilation* is reading.[4] In the studies which follow, the readings are given by groups, as those usually applicable for the upper group, the average, and the lower. The class is divided on the basis of reading ability, and each child is assigned to the set of readings appropriate to him, though the teacher may need to realign the references to suit the capacities of a certain group. Books needed should be kept in the room; history cannot be successfully taught by any method if only one text is provided.

In addition to readings, there are numerous other types of pupil-activity to be employed during assimilation.[5] Picture study (just as much as informational material given through the medium of language) must be *taught*.[6] It is not sufficient merely to expose the children to pictures. Construction work[7] adds an element of concreteness and objectivity and affords the children much pleasure.

[1] Morrison, H. C., *The Practice of Teaching in the Secondary School*, Part III, pp. 257–299.

[2] Bobbitt, Franklin, *How to Make a Curriculum*, p. 116.

[3] Parker, S. C., *Types of Elementary Teaching and Learning*, pp. 256–258.

[4] Stone, C. R., "Illustrative Silent-Reading Lessons." *Silent and Oral Reading*, pp. 125–131.

[5] For an exhaustive list see Parker, S. C., *Types of Elementary Teaching and Learning*, pp. 211–233; Bobbitt, Franklin, *How to Make a Curriculum*, pp. 44–62; also text, pp. 35–36.

[6] Johnson, Henry, *Teaching of History*, pp. 225–240; also illustrative lesson, text, pp. 699–706.

[7] Whitney, M. A., "Construction for History in the Grades." *History Teacher's Magazine*, VIII: 60–63.

Bulletin boards [1] for pictures and clippings, charts, booklets, moving pictures — all are helpful. Many times such exercises as these can be used to advantage in the case of superior students who have exhausted the supply of reading material and, in the opposite case, of pupils of such low reading ability that they can get nothing from even the simplest of the books. It helps the teacher little to suggest that in such serious remedial cases children ought not to be in the same group with the rest; all too often they are there, and the system makes no provision for them. Such work as is here suggested may be the means of their learning history when books absolutely fail. Specific suggestions as to projects are included in each story.

Drill exercises through games and flash cards are essential in rendering automatic the associations demanded [2] in the minimal essentials. Objective tests are provided for use before leaving a unit, in determining whether or not the main facts have been grasped. Special emphasis is put on the comprehension test, since it aims to ascertain whether or not actual mastery has been attained. If results show that it has not, there should be a redirection of teaching before leaving the unit. Study of test results enables the teacher to determine accurately whether or not each child in the class has mastered the unit and so is ready to go on. There should be no chance distribution in the scores.

The aim of the step of *organization* [3] is to reduce the mass of material which the pupil has gathered during the assimilative period to a systematized body of knowledge which he can get hold of and use. It consists ordinarily of the making of an outline. [4] Training is thus provided in one of our aims, the "ability to comprehend a coherent narrative of successive

---

[1] Burns, J. L., "The Bulletin Board." *The Twentieth Yearbook of the National Society for the Study of Education,* Part I, pp. 166–167.

[2] See pages 5–6 as to the method of determining these minimal essentials; see page 6 for reference to games.

[3] Morrison, H. C., *The Practice of Teaching in the Secondary School,* Part III, pp. 302–305.

[4] For other forms see pages 43–44.

events," [1] which is what Judd calls the first stage of history study. The work is, in the beginning, largely coöperative effort on the part of teacher and class, but tends to advance toward individual organization. So far as the learning cycle goes, this is a reaction member. One day is devoted to organization.

The *recitation* step [2] is introduced as the final reaction member of the learning cycle. At this time the pupil gives a connected, coherent account of the movement he has been studying, usually in the form of an oral story, beginning at the first of the unit and tracing its development straight through to the end. At intervals the story may be written. The step of organization guides this oral or written discussion.

The values of the recitation are these : (1) it clarifies thinking because of the necessity of clear expression and (2) it provides training in expression before an audience. It is thus seen to be the obverse side of the presentation. Different devices are used in the studies which follow, to insure the audience-situation.[3] Probably not more than one day should be used in recitation in the earlier part of the work ; but as the study progresses and the power of concentration improves, two or more days may be used and thus a larger proportion of the class enabled to take part each time.

[1] Judd, C. H., *Psychology of High-School Subjects*, pp. 456–457.

[2] To be sharply distinguished from the usual day-by-day lesson hearing. See Morrison, H. C., *The Practice of Teaching in the Secondary School*, Part III, pp. 306–316.

[3] See text, pp. 48–49.

SECTION III

DETAILS OF ADMINISTERING THE TECHNIQUE

PREPARATION

In the application of the technique to the units certain difficulties which are largely questions of management present themselves. While they will prove no stumblingblock to the experienced teacher, some suggestions may be appreciated by the novice.

Taking up the steps in order, we shall probably find the fewest difficulties in the preparatory step.[1] The questions used may or may not review the material of the previous units. Review just for its own sake is unnecessary, since the step of recitation, which had been completed just before taking up the new work, had proved the adequate mastery of old material. If, however, some of the work of the previous unit or story bears directly on the new unit, such points may well be brought into the foreground by a very few brief questions.

What is more urgently needed is to connect the new story, whenever possible, with real life-situations which are within the child's experience. An effort has been made in the following study to establish such connections so that concrete and objective thinking may be possible.[2] In case the necessary experience is lacking, the teacher in this step provides for it.

The amount of time which can be used for the preparation step should be kept in mind, since the presentation and the presentation test also are given in the same class period. The exploratory discussions, therefore, should not wander too far afield.

Materials to be used during the presentation — maps, globes, pictures, words written on the board, pointers, test papers, etc. — should be in readiness.

[1] See page 11.   [2] See note 1, p. 35.

Probably the most delicate problem of the preparation step is the teaching of new terms to be used in the presentation test. No new word is used in the test unless it is quite essential to the story. Those which the children do not know must be taught. When? Surely not in the presentation, for the story spirit would be lost. Not between the presentation and the presentation test, as such a break would blur the clear concept of the movement which had been described. Obviously, then, the words must be taught in the preparation step, not for spelling, but only for recognition in a context and for pronunciation.

In developing the meaning in the same context which is to be used later, great care must be exercised. Not so much discussion should be given as to interfere with the story which comes later; nor on the other hand, should the word be taught as an isolated term. Judgment must be used in steering a course between these two extremes.

PRESENTATION [1]

To the presentation should be given, so far as possible, the atmosphere of a real story-telling period. The teacher is seated; she uses a conversational tone quite different from the didactic tone of the usual lecture; she makes the story as dramatic as the material will permit. Children may not interrupt with questions; but when the story is finished, an opportunity is given for them to ask legitimate questions on points they did not hear or did not understand or about words they did not know. Here the teacher needs to exercise discrimination. It is very easy to wander off into an elaboration of points: children think of stories they wish to tell; one who did not listen while the story was being told now realizes that the testing period is upon him and tries to have most of the points repeated for his benefit. The standard for deciding what should be attended to here, and what eliminated, is that the purpose should be kept in mind; that is, the explanation of difficulties. Anything beyond that will mar the clearness

[1] See page 12.

of the concepts left by the story, the vividness and definiteness of which will determine success in the testing period.

The disastrous effect of interruptions from outside the classroom while the story is being told is illustrated by the following record. While test item No. 4 was being told to a 4-B class, another teacher entered the room bearing an armful of books. The teacher telling the story went over the point again, but the results speak for themselves.

PRESENTATION TEST FOR THE STORY OF THE NORTHMEN

NAMES OF PUPILS	NUMBER OF ITEMS IN THE TEST				INDIVIDUAL SCORE	POSSIBLE SCORE
	1	2	3	4		
Amy C.	V	V	V	V	4	4
Jean J.	V	V	V	X	3	4
Robert N.	V	V	V	X	3	4
Clarence M. . . .	V	V	V	X	3	4
Muriel O.	V	V	X	X	2	4
Jane T.	V	V	V	X	3	4
Etc.						
Total number of times each item was missed . . .	0	0	1	5		

Total items missed, 6.

Another such record, too long to be included here, shows the importance of being thoroughly prepared. The student teacher in this case had not the material well in hand, and so bolstered herself up with copious notes. As a result, in a class accustomed to a nearly perfect score, item 1 was missed twice, item 2 twice, item 3 six times, and item 4 once.

The importance of the teacher's being able to hold the attention of the group cannot be overestimated. No matter how well she may have prepared the story, pupils will fail on the presentation test unless they have been giving concentrated attention.[1]

[1] See page 14; also Morrison, H. C., *The Practice of Teaching in the Secondary School*. Part II.

The following directions are given to normal-school and college students to assist them in preparing their own over-views or presentation stories:

1. Familiarize yourself thoroughly with the material by wide reading.
2. Select the main movements, problems, forces, or points.
3. Decide which details to eliminate.
4. Introduce as few names, dates, and new terms as possible.
5. Outline the material.
6. Until quite expert, write out the story.
7. Summarize one point before going on to the next. Summarize the whole at the end.
8. For young children use direct quotations and include a few colorful details.
9. Time occupied in telling the story varies from about five minutes in 4-B grade to fifteen minutes in 6-A grade.

Presentation Test.[1] The presentation test must be made to conform to the particular presentation told. If the tests given herein are to be used, then the presentation preceding the test must follow closely the story as given. Whatever points the teacher decides to include in her test must be covered fully in the presentation; there can be no last-minute changes in the subject matter.

If hectographed copies are made by assistants the teacher should carefully check the original for errors.

For certain groups of children it probably is better not to call the presentation test a "test," but ask them to answer certain questions. They very soon learn what is expected of them. The best method of administration of the informal objective tests is to have copies mimeographed and distributed face downward before the presentation begins. The next best method is to have the copies hectographed. If neither method can be used, the questions may be written on the board and covered until time for the presentation test. The pupils are in this case to write the correct answer. Naturally, the results will not be as satisfactory from the third method as from the second; nor as satisfactory from the second as from the first.

[1] See examples on pages 54, 59, 70, 75, 78, 92, 97–98, 103.

If some children finish the presentation test before the close of the period, they may begin reading, as described in the step of *assimilation*.

Another form [1] of record is of value as indicating whether or not a child is improving in his ability to grasp the presentation, with fewer reteachings. Such a record assists in the study of the individual pupil.

RECORD OF NUMBER OF RETEACHINGS REQUIRED ON THE
PRESENTATIONS OF UNIT I

NAMES OF PUPILS	WHOLE UNIT	CRU-SADES	TRADE ROUTES	PRINCE HENRY AND HIS MEN	NORTH-MEN	GREAT INVEN-TIONS	COLUM-BUS'S GREAT IDEA
Abrams, John	1	1	1	1	1	1	1
Bacon, Ada	2	2	1	1	2	1	1
Coe, Florence	2	2	2	1	1	1	1
Deal, John	3	2	2	2	2	2	2

Figure 1 means that the child had his presentation test entirely correct at the first telling; figure 2, that he was told twice; figure 3, that he had to hear the story three times; and so on.

Reteaching the Presentation. After the teacher has corrected the test papers and made the records,[2] she returns the papers to the class at the beginning of the period the following day. Thereupon ensues a division of the group. Those whose papers were correct in every detail sit at one side of the room and begin reading quite without the teacher's help. It is understood that they are to ask no questions while the teacher is busy with the reteaching. Directions for the reading are found under the heading "Assimilation."

Those who marked some of the test items incorrectly sit at the other side of the room in a compact group. First they study their test papers to see just what their mistake was; any question as to the meaning of words in the items may be asked. Children must know what the questions in the test items call for.

[1] Also used by H. C. Morrison.　　　　[2] See table above, and page 20.

Then the teacher seats herself, again tells the presentation to the reteaching group, and they take the presentation test as before. Ordinarily it is wise to have all children who missed even one item hear the whole story over and take the entire test again. However, if only one or two children missed, and they missed only one item, it might be sufficient to reteach them that point only.

The procedure is continued until everyone has attained the point of mastery of the whole story.

If when the teacher looks over the papers the first time, she finds that a large number (perhaps one third of the class) have made an error on one point, she may have to change the wording of the test item. For example, it was found necessary to change the wording in item No. 1 [1] of the fourth question in the test on the Crusades, from "the Holy Land ought to belong to Christians" to "they thought that the Holy Land ought to belong to Christians." Or, it may be necessary to stress one item more than the original presentation did, or to explain it at greater length. If the teacher is inexperienced or a poor disciplinarian, she may well look to her control technique as a means of remedying the difficulty.

Whatever the cause of the difficulty may be, the presentation or presentation test is changed in order to remedy it.

Subpresentations. According to Dr. Morrison's point of view a whole unit such as Unit IX, "How the Slavery Question almost split the Nation into Two Parts," should be given in only one presentation. Our experience has been, however, that very young children have not worked successfully on a unit of such length. The reading periods especially extended over too many days at a time. Therefore the material within each unit has been organized into a series of stories. After the overview or presentation of the unit as a whole, additional subpresentations [2] are given for each story. It is to be noticed that the subpresentations for the early months of the fourth grade are long and complete. Oral presentation is in this case a very powerful supplement to reading.

[1] See page 59.
[2] For example, in Unit I, the stories on pages 57–59, 62–63, 66–67, 70, 74.

As the study progresses the subpresentations become shorter and shorter, until in Unit IX the emphasis has shifted to the child's getting most of his material directly from reading. By the last part of the fifth grade he is receiving little help from subpresentations.

In using subpresentations certain very obvious difficulties present themselves, such as losing sight of the unity of the movement because of the number of stories included. Methods of offsetting such disadvantages are detailed on page 10.

ASSIMILATION [1]

Reading: Method of Administration. The class is divided into upper, average, and lower groups on the basis of reading ability. For example, the following grouping was made for a 4-B class, according to the results of a standard achievement test: [2]

	Chrono-logical Age	Intelli-gence Ratio	Read-ing Age	Paragraph		Sentence		Word	
				Mean-ing	Grade Level	Mean-ing	Grade Level	Mean-ing	Grade Level
Pupil A . .	9–3	107	11	50	4–5	28	4–5	32	4–5
Pupil B . .	9–1	120	10–6	64	5–6	11	2–3	21	3–4
Pupil C . .	9–4	107	11–2	44	3–4	39	5–6	34	4–5
Pupil D . .	10–1	107	9–6	30	3–4	15	3–4	21	3–4
Pupil E . .	9–2	89	11–4	52	4–5	39	5–6	30	4–5
Pupil F . .	9–11	118	9–1	24	3–4	10	2–3	19	3–4
Pupil G . .	8–11	151	12–1	66	6	33	5–6	39	5–6

On the basis of these results the following division was made: Upper Group (known to the children as Group, or Section, I), Pupil G; Average Group (Group, or Section, II), Pupils A, C, E; Lower Group (Group, or Section, III), Pupils B, D, F. Numbers of sections are changed each semester so that Section III, for example, is not always the lower group.

A word of warning may be necessary: that the teacher is never to let children know or feel that they are in the lower group, average group, or upper group, as the case may be. A

[1] See pages 15–16. For examples see Part II, pp. 55–56, 60–61, 63–64.

[2] Data supplied by Miss Clara A. Trotter of the State Normal School, Ashland, Oregon. For an explanation of the scoring see the manual of directions accompanying the Stanford Achievement Test.

very ready excuse for the division may be found in the explanation (usually only too true!) that there are not enough books of each kind to supply everyone.

Either on mimeographed or hectographed sheets, or on one section of the board which may be reserved for several days, appear the readings for the various groups. For example, the readings in the text for "Upper Group" may be headed "For Section I"; those designated for "Average Group" may be headed "For Section II"; "Lower Group," "For Section III."

The reading is guided by questions. There may be one set of questions in mimeographed or hectographed form for the entire story in all the books, or they may be written on the board. Children test the success of their reading by these questions, or read to find specific points on which they have no information.

Another method of handling the questions is to place in each book a mimeographed or hectographed card asking a few questions that are to be answered from that particular book.[1] For example:

Southworth, Builders of Our Country, I, pp. 12-23.
Marco Polo.

1. What did the Polo Brothers want to see?
2. Why did the king send them home?
3. What happened to Marco on his journey to China?
4. What did Marco do in China?
5. Why were people interested in his book?

After two or three days' reading, these questions form the basis of the discussion. Children from the upper-ability groups may be required to answer the questions from only one book that they read; the average group, two; and the lower group, three.

The books for the different groups are kept in different places: Section I at one end of the desk, Section II at the

[1] See illustrations of directed reading in *The Twentieth Yearbook of the National Society for the Study of Education*, Part II, pp. 162–168.

other end, and Section III on a table in the corner — all so
far apart that no congestion occurs in securing them. Each
book contains the question card giving title, pages, and questions, as described above. There is also a sheet of paper left
with each pile of books, as follows:

BOOKS READ, SECTION I

SOUTHWORTH	TAPPAN	WOODBURN AND MORAN	BOURNE AND BENTON	HARDING, *Story of Europe*	HARDING, *Old World Background*
Amy (1)	Jean (1)	Robert (1)	Dorothy (1)	Clarence (2)	Robert (2)
Jean (3)	Amy (2)	Dorothy (2)	Jean (2)		
Dorothy (3)	Clarence (1)	Muriel (1)	Amy (3)		

Each child knows in what section he is; he goes to the place
where the books for his section are kept, takes one, and reads
it. When he returns the book he signs his name on the paper,
followed by the figure (1) if it is the first book he has read, by
(2) if the second, and by (3) if the third. After that he need
keep no record, but reads for pleasure. After he has read the
first, he selects another book, looks at the card or on his own
mimeographed sheet to ascertain what pages to read, returns
to his seat, and reads. Thus each proceeds at his own rate,
according to his ability.

Children in the lower group may try the books in the average
group after they have finished their own, but it usually is not
wise for them to try those of the upper group. Similarly,
children in the average group may try those in the upper-
group lists.

While reading, children may raise their hands for help if
they come to a difficulty, though they are encouraged to get
the meaning from the context if the teacher is very busy.
They are to read the story through once and then attempt to
answer the questions. If they cannot, they must re-read.

However, after a child has read one, two, or three references (depending on whether he is in the upper, average, or
lower group) in order to answer definite questions, any additional books that he may read are for his own pleasure without

being subject to test. A few minutes at the close of the hour given to the volunteering of bits of information not found in any of the "study references" may motivate this extensive reading habit.[1] Also a system of home reading with school credit may be set up.[2]

Positive encouragement is given to the habit of skipping over unfamiliar words on the first reading; often the context will reveal the meaning. Experience has shown that there is little danger of causing children to dislike history through reading books that are easy for them (provided there is range enough in the material), but that there is grave danger of causing them to dislike the subject if the reading matter is too difficult. Such a calamity is to be avoided at all costs.

The average and upper groups [3] proceed for two, three, or four days, each reading by himself at his own rate and coming to the teacher only when help is absolutely necessary, or to answer questions on the books. But the lower group may be so dependent [4] that she will have to gather them in one corner of the room while she teaches them to read the story. This procedure may be necessary, but is greatly to be deplored, since such incompetence will effectually hinder progress in all subjects throughout the entire school period. Strenuous training should then be given in remedial reading.

Thus the successful teacher of history in the intermediate grades must necessarily be an expert in the teaching of reading. All children should be made to feel that it is a great privilege and honor to be able to read for themselves, rather than to depend on the teacher's help. Since the presentation has already acquainted them with the vocabulary of the story, and they know the events in their main outline, they can read material of a more difficult grade [5] than would be possible under other circumstances.

[1] "A Reading Club." *The Twentieth Yearbook of the National Society for the Study of Education*, Part I, p. 157.

[2] Wheeler, J. L., "Home Reading with School Credit." *School and Society*, XIV: 210–214.

[3] Stone, C. R., *Silent and Oral Reading*, p. 291.

[4] Ibid. pp. 60–61.

[5] *The Twentieth Yearbook of the National Society for the Study of Education*, Part II, p. 55.

The teacher's chief work during the reading period is questioning children on the material read. She takes a seat at the front of the room near the book supplies. As a child comes to return his book, she selects one of the questions from the slip which guided his reading. He is to answer the question. If the pupil is one who ordinarily reads carelessly or whose comprehension score is low, she may ask him more than one question. If he answers satisfactorily, he signs his name on the above record and takes another book. If he cannot answer, he is sent to his seat to re-read the material and find the answer. The teacher gives him such help as she deems advisable in finding the answers. Members of the upper group are questioned on one book; of the average group, on two; and of the lower, on three.

There are certain difficulties for which the teacher must be prepared during the reading. (1) Some children skim through the material and want to change books without having comprehended. Firmness in rejecting unsatisfactory answers will help to remedy this situation. (2) Some children read so rapidly and well that they are constantly coming to the teacher to answer their questions, and she has no time to devote to those who have reading difficulties. If, however, the upper group answers questions only on the first book read, this difficulty will be minimized. (3) The lower group may loiter on one book and waste time while others are answering questions. A few judicious questions may keep them at the story until they finish. (4) A number of children may be ready to come to the teacher at once. In that case she indicates which one is next. By speeding up the questioning, by emphasizing the importance of having the answers ready before they leave their seats, and by choosing as test items, when other children are waiting, those questions which can be answered in a few words, the congestion may be relieved.

At the close of the reading period, monitors from each section collect the books from their sections, so that the readings for the various groups do not become mixed. Each child goes on, the next day, with the book he had not completed at the end of the preceding period.

Thus the reading part of the assimilation period consists of directed silent reading. Since at least three fifths of all the time of the course is so spent, it answers the modern demand for increased emphasis on silent reading of factual material.

Discussion after the Reading. With younger children it will probably be wise to allow one period of perhaps twenty minutes at the end of all the readings (not each day) to talk over the material read. The questions in the books form a convenient basis for discussion. This is not to be confused with the recitation step. It is a ·brief oral test to see whether or not the main thread of the story has been grasped, and is a great help in preparing for the objective test. If the group is a small one, this exercise may be quite unnecessary. Children who have read material which the rest of the class have not, especially enjoy this opportunity to offer their contributions.

Reading Materials. The reading lists which are given for each story make no pretense of including all the material available. Doubtless some very valuable books have been overlooked. Many more are given, however, than the average school possesses, in the hope that each may have access to at least some of the titles mentioned, and as a guide to further purchase. It is neither necessary nor desirable that full sets of every book be obtained; in fact, it is quite conceivable that each child in the average and upper groups reads from a different book.[1] For the lower groups, however, especially if the teacher must read [2] with them, uniformity is desirable. The assistance of the public library may be necessary in providing the requisite number of copies.[3] The list of readings for teachers is a strictly limited one, including references from two of the well-known and authoritative series of American histories, a few of the best books on each separate topic, source materials, and works on the social and economic phases. In case the other books are inaccessible, some standard secondary textbooks are given. An effort has been made to limit the number

[1] Stone, C. R., "Some Illustrative Silent-Reading Lessons." *Elementary School Journal*, XXI: 31–33.
[2] See page 27.
[3] Guilfoile, Elizabeth, "Using the Public Library in the Teaching of Reading." *Elementary School Journal*, XXII: 126–131.

to an amount that the average teacher might reasonably expect to read or to glance over.

For the guidance of school systems in buying materials the following study has been made, to determine which books have actually been used the greatest number of times in the stories included in Part II.

MINIMAL BOOK LIST, FOURTH GRADE

List of Books most widely used in Fourth-Grade Stories, with Number of Times Used

Upper Group [1]

	TIMES USED
GORDY, WILBUR F. Leaders in Making America. Charles Scribner's Sons	55
GORDY, WILBUR F. Stories of Early American History. Charles Scribner's Sons	46
TAPPAN, EVA M. An Elementary History of our Country. Houghton Mifflin Company	46
FOOTE, ANNA E., and SKINNER, AVERY W. Explorers and Founders of America. American Book Company	36
MONTGOMERY, DAVID H. The Beginner's American History. Ginn and Company	31
WOODBURN, JAMES A., and MORAN, THOMAS F. Finders and Founders of the New World. Longmans, Green & Co.	27
BEEBY, DANIEL J. and DOROTHEA. Community Life Today and in Colonial Times. Charles E. Merrill Company	26
EVANS, LAWTON B. America First. Milton Bradley Company.	26
BURNHAM, SMITH, and WHIPPLE, WAYNE. Hero Tales from History. John C. Winston Company	25
LOGIE, ALFRED E. From Columbus to Lincoln. Lyons and Carnahan	21
EGGLESTON, EDWARD. A First Book in American History. American Book Company	20

Average Group

GORDY, WILBUR F. Elementary History of the United States. Charles Scribner's Sons	54
McMASTER, JOHN B. Primary History of the United States. American Book Company	41
FORMAN, SAMUEL E. First Lessons in American History. The Century Co.	46
SOUTHWORTH, GERTRUDE V. Builders of our Country, I. D. Appleton and Company	44
MORRIS, CHARLES. Primary History of the United States. J. B. Lippincott Company	43
MACE, WILLIAM H. A Primary History. Rand McNally & Company	42
ELSON, HENRY W., and MacMULLAN, CORNELIA E. The Story of our Country, I. World Book Company	37
BEARD, CHARLES A., and BAGLEY, WILLIAM C. A First Book in American History. The Macmillan Company	34

[1] Blaisdell, Albert F., *The Story of American History*, and Guerber, Hélène A., *Story of the Thirteen Colonies*, ruled out because of brevity of treatment of many topics.

TIMES
USED

PERRY, ARTHUR C., and PRICE, GERTRUDE A. American History, I. American Book Company 32

NIDA, WILLIAM L. Following Columbus. The Macmillan Company 30

COE, FANNY E. Founders of our Country. American Book Company 24

Lower Group [1]

DAVIS, ANNA C. Stories of the United States. Educational Publishing Company 18

WAYLAND, JOHN W. History Stories for Primary Grades. The Macmillan Company 18

BLAISDELL, ALBERT F., and BALL, FRANCIS K. American History for Little Folks. Little, Brown & Company 14

BLAISDELL, ALBERT F., and BALL, FRANCIS K. Child's Book of American History. Little, Brown & Company 12

LUCIA, ROSE. Stories of American Discoverers for Little Americans. American Book Company 12

PRATT, MARA L. Stories of Colonial Children. Educational Publishing Company. Rev. Ed. 12

DODGE, NATHANIEL S. Stories of American History. Lothrop, Lee & Shepard Co. 11

BLAISDELL, ALBERT F., and BALL, FRANCIS K. Short Stories from American History. Ginn and Company 10

PRATT, MARA L. Beginners' Book (Vol. I of series America's Story for America's Children). D. C. Heath & Co. 8

MINIMAL BOOK LIST, FIFTH GRADE

List of Books most widely used in Fifth-Grade Stories, with Number of Times Used

Upper Group [2]

PERRY, ARTHUR C., and PRICE, GERTRUDE A. American History, II. American Book Company 65

GORDY, WILBUR F. Leaders in Making America. Charles Scribner's Sons 47

TAPPAN, EVA M. An Elementary History of our Country. Houghton Mifflin Company 38

GUERBER, HÉLÈNE A. Story of the Great Republic. American Book Company 32

LEFFERTS, WALTER. American Leaders, II. J. B. Lippincott Company . . 31

EVANS, LAWTON B. America First. Milton Bradley Company 30

GORDY, WILBUR F. Stories of Later American History. Charles Scribner's Sons 26

DARROW, FLOYD L. Thinkers and Doers. Silver, Burdett & Company . . . 25

WOODBURN, JAMES A., and MORAN, THOMAS F. The Makers of America. Longmans, Green & Co. 23

COE, FANNY E. Makers of the Nation. American Book Company 23

[1] Barnes (Donnelly, T. F.), *Primary History of the United States,* ruled out because of brevity of treatment of many topics.

[2] Blaisdell, Albert F., *The Story of American History,* ruled out because of brevity of treatment of many topics.

TIMES
USED

Average Group

GORDY, WILBUR F. Elementary History of the United States. Charles
Scribner's Sons 67

FORMAN, SAMUEL E. First Lessons in American History. The Century Co. 52

BEARD, CHARLES A., and BAGLEY, WILLIAM C. A First Book in American
History. The Macmillan Company. Rev. Ed. 49

ELSON, HENRY W., and MACMULLAN, CORNELIA E. The Story of our
Country, II. World Book Company 45

MORRIS, CHARLES. Primary History of the United States. J. B. Lippincott
Company 31

MOWRY, WILLIAM A. and ARTHUR M. First Steps in the History of our
Country. Silver, Burdett & Company. Rev. Ed. 28

NIDA, WILLIAM L. Following the Frontier. The Macmillan Company . . . 28

BARNES (BALDWIN J.). Elementary History of the United States. American
Book Company. Rev. Ed. 27

SOUTHWORTH, GERTRUDE V. Builders of our Country, II. D. Appleton and
Company 27

UHRBROCK, RICHARD S., and OWENS, ALBERT A. Famous Americans. The
Bobbs-Merrill Company 17

MACE, WILLIAM H. A Primary History. Rand McNally & Company . . . 16

Lower Group [1]

MCMASTER, JOHN B. Primary History of the United States. American
Book Company 36

DAVIS, ANNA C. Stories of the United States. Educational Publishing
Company 17

BALDWIN, JAMES. Fifty Famous People. American Book Company 8

CHAMBERLAIN, JAMES F. How we Travel. The Macmillan Company . . . 8

FAIRGRIEVE, JAMES, and YOUNG, ERNEST. The World. D. Appleton and
Company 8

WAYLAND, JOHN W. History Stories for Primary Grades. The Macmillan
Company 8

Few school systems will be able to buy duplicate copies of
all the books mentioned above. However, it is not necessary
that enough copies of each one be bought to supply the entire
class. A few copies of each, but many different titles, is greatly
superior to many copies of three or four books. For example,
a class of thirty-five children, instead of being supplied with
thirty-five copies of two basic texts, might be supplied with
one basic text and as follows: [2]

[1] Barnes (Donnelly, T. F.), *Primary History of the United States,* ruled out because
of brevity of treatment of many topics.

[2] Assuming that half the group is of average ability, 18; about one fourth in
the upper group, 9; about one fourth in the lower group, 8.

A MEANS OF SUPPLYING A CLASS OF THIRTY–FIVE CHILDREN WITH
DIFFERENT BOOKS TO READ

Fourth Grade [1]

LOWER GROUP	AVERAGE GROUP	UPPER GROUP
Copies	Copies	Copies
DAVIS. Stories of the United States 4	NIDA. Following Columbus 6	GORDY. Leaders in Making America 4
BLAISDELL and BALL. American History for Little Folks 4	McMASTER. Primary History of the United States 6	TAPPAN. An Elementary History of our Country 4
LUCIA. Stories of American Discoverers for Little Americans . . . 4	FORMAN. First Lessons in American History . 6	FOOTE and SKINNER. Explorers and Founders of America 4
PRATT. Beginners' Book . 4	SOUTHWORTH. Builders of our Country, I . . . 6	MONTGOMERY. The Beginner's American History 2
	ELSON and MacMULLAN. The Story of our Country, I 6	WOODBURN and MORAN. Finders and Founders of the New World . . 2
	BEARD and BAGLEY. A First Book in American History 6	BEEBY. Community Life Today and in Colonial Times 2

The following books may be borrowed from the fifth grade :

Extra copies of :	Extra copies of :	Extra copies of :
DAVIS. Stories of the United States	GORDY. Elementary History of the United States	WOODBURN and MORAN. The Makers of America
	McMASTER. Primary History of the United States	GORDY. Leaders in Making America
	FORMAN. First Lessons in American History	TAPPAN. An Elementary History of our Country
	BEARD and BAGLEY. A First Book in American History	COE. Makers of the Nation

These lists may be supplemented by the use of children's encyclopedias of various kinds. If reading materials are exhausted by the upper group, committees of children may work on projects, such as those listed on pages 35–36.

[1] See the list on pages 30–31.

Fifth Grade [1]

Lower Group	Average Group	Upper Group
Copies	Copies	Copies
McMaster. Primary History of the United States 6	Gordy. Elementary History of the United States 6	Perry and Price. American History, II 4
Davis. Stories of the United States 4	Forman. First Lessons in American History . 6	Gordy. Leaders in Making America 4
Baldwin. Fifty Famous People 2	Beard and Bagley. A First Book in American History 6	Tappan. An Elementary History of our Country 4
Chamberlain. How we Travel 2	Nida. Following the Frontier 6	Woodburn and Moran. Makers of America . . 4
Fairgrieve and Young. The World 2	Elson and MacMullan. Story of our Country, II 4	Coe. Makers of the Nation 2
	Southworth. Builders of our Country, II . . . 4	
	Uhrbrock and Owens. Famous Americans . . 4	

The following books may be borrowed from the fourth grade:

Extra copies of:	Extra copies of:	Extra copies of:
McMaster. Primary History of the United States	Gordy. Elementary History of the United States	Foote and Skinner. Explorers and Founders of America
Davis. Stories of the United States	Forman. First Lessons in American History	Gordy. Leaders in Making America
	Beard and Bagley. A First Book in American History	Montgomery. The Beginner's American History
		Tappan. An Elementary History of Our Country

Appendix A, 1,[2] gives a list of all books used more than ten times in the fourth grade; and Appendix A, 2, the same for the fifth grade. Appendix A, 3, gives lists of supplementary books for each unit, based on the number of times used. The series of readers written to accompany this study may also be used.

Projects used in Assimilation. All of the exercises suggested in all the stories under the heading "Procedure during Assimilation" are brought together and classified in the following:

[1] See the list on pages 31–32.   [2] See pages 711–715.

I. Use of present-day life-situations.
    1. Connecting the past with present institutions.[1]
    By questions and investigations.
    2. Actual performance of the function.[2]
    3. Performing experiments.
    4. Use of newspaper clippings.
    5. Trips to local industries.
II. Applied art.
    1. Drawing.
        a. Blackboard drawing.
        b. Imaginative drawing.
        c. Drawing from copy.
        d. Drawing plans.
        e. Design.
        f. Theme illustrations.
    2. Construction.
        a. For the school museum.
        b. For exhibits.
        c. For sand-table projects.
        d. For use with dramatization.
    3. Sand-table work.
        a. Modeling the outlines of various countries.
        b. Locating cities.
        c. Representing imaginative scenes.
    4. Use of pictures.
        a. Formal picture study.
        b. Slides.
        c. Moving pictures.
        d. Stereoscope and reflectoscope.
        e. Advertising-material and pictures from newspapers or magazines.
        f. Picture collections made by the teacher; by the pupils individually; by the class.
        g. A picture museum.
    5. Paper-cutting.
    6. Clay-modeling.
    7. Wood-carving.
    8. Making graphs, diagrams, charts, maps, cartoons.
    9. Setting up a miniature stage.

[1] See pages 64, 66, 73–74, 76, 99, 127, 129, 133, 138, 141, 147, 182, 189, 197, 211, 225, 230, 246, 248, 251, 273 (2), 277, 281 (2), 295, 296, 314, 317, 319, 322, 325, 330, 333, 334, 335, 348, 353, 363, 366, 367, 382, 388, 395, 396–397, 399, 401, 402, 403, 406, 408, 410, 411, 413, 416, 417, 418, 420 (2), 422, 424, 426, 436, 445, 470, 472, 475, 484, 486 (2), 488, 489, 491, 507, 511 (2), 512, 516, 519, 521, 528, 529, 530, 531, 532, 533, 534, 536, 550 (2), 551, 553, 555, 558 (2), 561, 564, 565–566, 567, 568, 569, 570, 572, 575 (2), 577, 579, 580, 582, 583, 585, 587, 588, 590, 608, 615, 637, 638. The large number of page references is given to suggest to the teacher other possibilities for connecting history with life.

[2] See pages 176, 182, 197, 208, 260, 325, 406, 416, 528.

    10. Dressing dolls in period costumes.
    11. Setting up ready-made illustrative material.
    12. Booklets.
    13. Correlation with household economics.

III. Oral work.
    1. Questions.
       Map questions.
    2. Book reports; reports of moving-picture incidents.
    3. Drill games: flash-card drill.
    4. Reading poems to the children.
    5. Giving quotations.
    6. Explaining cartoons.
    7. The teacher tells pupils additional material.
    8. An elementary form of debate.[1]

IV. Written work.
    1. Imaginative themes.
       a. Letters.
       b. Diaries.
       c. Editorials.
       d. Cables.
    2. Writing for the school newspaper.
    3. Correspondence with children in other lands.
    4. Original poems.
    5. Objective tests.

 V. Music.
    1. Phonograph records.
    2. Singing historical songs.
    3. Use of music to establish atmosphere.

VI. Dramatization and pageantry.
    1. Dramatization.
       a. Original.
          (1) Informal.
          (2) Formal.
       b. From books and magazines.
    2. Pageants.
    3. Planning programs.
    4. Tableaux.

VII. Miscellaneous activities.
    1. Observation of actual performance.
    2. Listening to the reports of travelers or other observers.
    3. Trips to the local museum.
    4. Planning trips.
    5. Problem-solving.
    6. Forming clubs.
    7. Collecting poems.
    8. Making a school museum.

---

[1] See pages 238, 273, 378, 465, 627, 636, 643.

Picture study is based at first on the pictures in the books. Each child shows a picture in his book and tells what he sees in it. The teacher may also have a collection of pictures with questions clipped to them, similar to the questions on the readings. Each child comes to the front of the room, shows his picture, and answers the questions. After all have had an opportunity to show their pictures, the copies are passed from one child to another to insure better study of them. Use of the slides and films listed in the illustrative material for each story [1] is strongly recommended. An occasional formal picture study,[2] in which the teacher presents material to the class, may be used to advantage.

Dramatization [3] is planned by having the class decide first how many scenes there shall be and what incidents are to be included in each scene. Several sets of characters are then chosen. Settings are decided upon. The characters choose one of their number as director. The class as a whole gives suggestions as to what each character might say in each scene. Then each cast of characters works by itself to plan its performance in detail. Each cast presents its performance to the group, and the group criticizes.

A sand-table project is carried out in the following way. First the class decides on the objects to be represented, and lists them. An executive committee is chosen to supervise arrangements. The members of the class choose the articles they wish to make. Sizes and materials are decided upon, and written on the board. Children then try to find pictures of the articles they have chosen, to serve as models for construction. In general, the use of actual materials — leather, silk, etc. — is much more interesting than are slips of paper with the words written on them. Often children find it necessary to read widely in order to gain information needed in construction work.

For theme illustration see the illustrative lesson, pp. 690–696.

---

[1] For example, see pages 56, 61 in Part. II.

[2] See the stenographic report of a picture-study lesson, p. 699, and also Freeman, Frank N., *Visual Education.*

[3] See the illustrative lesson, pp. 664–689.

Drill. The general principles of drill [1] should be observed. Data must be taught before there is any attempt to drill on them, especially the historical terms.[2] A small number of items is chosen at first and worked on until the reaction is perfect; after that the drill may be cumulative; that is, the items from previous lessons may be added also. Careful provision should be made for the correction of mistakes.[3] Eliminating the child who makes mistakes (sending him to his seat) is bad technique because it removes from the drill the very person who needs it most.

If the drill is in the form of a contest or game, all the rules must be clearly understood. What provision has been made for correcting mistakes? for scoring an incorrect answer? an answer which one child gives incorrectly, but which is answered correctly by an opponent or classmate?

One especially difficult matter is the reading of the centuries,[4] when such a case as the year 1000 is considered. Children must know how to read four-integer numbers by hundreds as well as by thousands; for example, fourteen hundred ninety-two as well as one thousand four hundred ninety-two; fourteen hundred fifty-three as well as one thousand four hundred fifty-three; ten hundred as well as one thousand. In naming centuries the hundreds method is used, and the centuries named one in advance of the hundreds; as, 1453, fourteen hundred fifty-three and therefore the fifteenth century. After drilling on such numbers as 1763, 1453, 1492, 1607, 1620, give more difficult exercises, such as 1000, 1066, 98, etc.

Music. For suggestions as to conducting the lessons involving music see the illustrative lesson on pages 707–709.

Minimal Essentials. For a complete list of minimal essentials see Appendix C and the drill lessons on pages 40–43.

Illustrative Material. For a complete list of the illustrative materials referred to and for addresses of the firms supplying them see Appendix B.

---

[1] Parker, S. C., *General Methods of Teaching in Elementary Schools*, pp. 255–267.
[2] See the lesson plan on page 697.
[3] See the lesson on individual drill, pp. 40–43.
[4] See text, pp. 657–660; also Chalmers, E. M., *Talks about our Country*, pp. 13–14.

Tests at the End of Each Story. The test should cover only the material which is of real importance to the understanding of the story, not details such as how many ships Columbus had, incidents and anecdotes of Magellan's voyage, dates of founding of all the colonies, etc. If the group is so large that the testing on the reading done in the books has not been very thorough, the test at the end is crucial in determining who is ready to go on to the next unit. Each child must correct every mistake he makes on these tests, just as he did on the presentation test.

The recognition form has been used so extensively in the lessons given that probably no teacher will have any trouble in devising such forms. Completion tests are easily made and effective. The true-false form presents many difficulties unless exceptionally well made. Another device is underlining, as used in the following test at the end of the story of the Northmen. Words used should be included in the first two thousand of the Thorndike word list or in the minimal essentials previously taught. One point to keep in mind is that these tests should prepare children to cope with the tests at the end of the unit. An example of the type of objective test suggested at the end of every story follows:

TEST QUESTIONS FOR USE AT THE END OF THE STORY OF THE NORTHMEN

Underline the word or words that correctly answer the question.

1. Where did Eric the Red go when he was sent away from his own country? (Germany, Iceland, Norway.)

2. What did Eric call the new country that he discovered? (Iceland, Greenland, Germany.)

3. What was Eric's son's name? (Joseph Johnson, Leif Ericson, John Hansen.)

4. When Leif Ericson went to Norway, what did he bring back with him? (Priests, merchants, food.)

5. Did Eric and most of the people become Christians? (Yes, no, didn't say.)

6. When Leif's men went out exploring the new country they had come to, what did one of them find? (Apples, grapes, potatoes.)

7. What did Leif Ericson name this new country? (Iceland, Vinland, Greenland.)

8. What did Leif and his men take back with them to Greenland? (Apples, dried grapes, wood, vegetables.)

9. Who was the first white man to set foot on the continent of America? (Marco Polo, Leif Ericson, Columbus.)

10. Why did the world forget that the Northmen discovered America? (They told nobody; they did not use the land; they did not want the land.)

The following procedure for conducting the drill on minimal essentials at the end of each unit was worked out and described by Miss Nelle E. Moore, director of the intermediate department of the Bloomsburg, Pennsylvania, State Normal School.

DRILL ON MINIMAL ESSENTIALS FOR UNIT II

The following plan for drill lessons shows the time required and the procedures used in bringing each pupil of a fourth-grade class up to mastery of the minimal essential list of characters given for Unit II of the course of study in history outlined on page 153. The same general plan has been followed in securing mastery of terms, places, and dates.

Care has been taken to make the drill fit the individual needs of the pupils. The mastery formula has been applied: teaching, testing, diagnosing difficulties, reteaching, retesting, diagnosing again, etc. The body of material used was necessarily added to as new stories of the unit were studied. The general plan has been to test on characters belonging to the story of the Spanish, from the test results to determine the individual mistakes, plan for individual help, and to play games using these characters in the correct association with events. After the stories of the English explorers were studied, new names were added to the list, and the list of Spanish and English was used for the next game period. As each new story of the unit was studied, the new names were added to the chart.

Chart I, p. 41, shows the results (1) after finishing the story, (2) at the end of the unit after all stories had been completed, and (3) after review games. From this chart, data were secured to guide the teacher in planning further drill. The games outlined below have been used.

The afternoon before the games were to be played, each child having made errors was given one name which he was to find out about before he came to class the next day. The teacher called these their "passwords" and no one was admitted to the room without his password. Any child failing on his password was given help immediately.

At the history period provision was made for both those who had difficulties and for those who had passed a perfect test. For each child having errors, the teacher had prepared sets of flash cards containing the names of the characters missed by him. She asked the group needing help to place these cards on their desks so that the names could be seen. Each child was then asked to select from the upper group a helper. These helpers sat by the pupils needing help and told them the stories of the characters whose names were on their cards. Upper-group children not chosen as helpers were given these instructions, "Look over the list of characters which are on the board and word one good question for each. If you can't think of a good question, take your text and

CHART I. DRILL ON MINIMAL ESSENTIALS

Fourth Grade Training School, State Normal School, Bloomsburg, Pennsylvania; class taught by student teachers

Names of Pupils	Hudson	Hawkins	Raleigh	Cortez	Drake	Champlain	Americus Vespucius	John Cabot	Ponce de Leon	Cartier	Magellan	De Soto	End of Story	End of Unit	After Special Drill
Henry	0	3	2				2	2	3 2		2	2	4	6	2
Edwin													0	0	0
Edward													0	0	0
Harold K.													1	1	0
Donald													0	0	0
Harold M.													0	0	0
Gordon													0	0	0
John													0	0	0
William R.													0	0	0
Robert			1		1								0	0	0
Kenneth		3	1		1		1	1	1 1	1 1		1	0	2	0
Paul													1	1	0
William N.													7	0	0
Robert O.													6	0	0
Susie			2						2				0	2	0
Edna			1 1	1 1	1 1	1	1	1	1	1	1	1	4	0	0
Edith													3	0	1
Gladys		2	2		1	1		1	2	1	1	1	0	0	0
Lela M.		2		1									9	0	0
Anna									2				0	4	0
Mary		2	1	1	1	1	1	1	1 1	1 1	1 1	1 1	1	0	0
Blanche		2	2 2		2 2				1				7	2	0
Vera													0	2	0
Jane			1	1	1	1	1	1	1	1	1	1	4	0	0
Emaline													7	0	0
Gene													8	0	0
Lillias													0	0	0
Betty													0	0	0
Total errors	0		5 7	6	6	4	4	6	8	7	5	7	62	20	3

1 = missed in test at end of story.   2 = missed in test at end of unit.   3 = missed in final test after reteaching and drill games.

look for that man's name in the index. Find the page from the index, read, and make a good question from the reading. You may use these questions in a game we shall play in a few minutes." (About five minutes were given for this exercise.)

In some game periods this exercise was changed and one child acted as helper and came to the front of the room. The pupils needing help took turns in asking him to tell one thing done by the character named. He easily answered all of the questions asked in the five minutes, as several children always held the same cards and got help through the same question.

After children had been helped in this way, the game "Guess who I Am"[1] was played. The first part of the play was planned to give the weaker pupils help. Each was asked to keep his cards out where he could see them and to question the leader about those which he had found hard in the test. A pupil who had a perfect score in the test was permitted to start the game. He came to the front of the room, selected one of the characters from the list on the board, whispered it to the teacher, then said, "I am thinking of one of the characters in our history stories. Which one do you think it is?" A pupil was called upon by the leader. This pupil asked, "Are you thinking of the man who _ _ _ _?" (*Then telling what the man did.*) The leader answered, "No, I am not thinking of _ _ _ _" (*character's name given here*), or, "Yes, I am thinking of _ _ _ _" (*names character*). The leader continued in the lead until the correct character was named, or until he failed to answer a question correctly. New leaders were selected from the group knowing all the characters as they were needed and the game proceeded as before. All the characters in the list could be reviewed in this way several times in five or six minutes.

The teacher changed the procedure at this point so that the pupils in the lower group might review their own difficulties. Correct associations had been given them by the preceding game. One child having a difficult name was sent from the room. The teacher named the characters that this child had missed on the test and the class selected one of them for use in the game. The child returned to the room and began questioning the class, "Are you thinking of _ _ _ _?" (*Telling something one character did.*) The class replied in concert, "No, we are not thinking of _ _ _ _" (*naming the character*), or, "Yes, we are thinking of _ _ _ _" (*naming character*). The game proceeds as in the previous game. The child guessing knew that the practice was to choose a name from his own hard list; hence he asked about those names first. This game was continued for a few minutes. The teacher sent from the room pupils who needed most help and selected them so that all characters were reviewed.

To give further drill to those needing practice on certain characters, the teacher had written on each slate of the board one statement telling some important thing one of these characters did. Each character was included in the list. She asked the pupils holding cards to go to the board and place each card below the statement which belonged to that name. Cards were placed with faces to the board so that each child had to think for himself. The pupils

[1] Woodburn, J. A., and Moran, T. F., *Introduction to American History*, pp. 298–299.

who had no cards to place then went to the board, turned the cards, and checked the mistakes. In case of mistakes, pupils were helped immediately. This game served as a test of the day's review.

The following day about five minutes of class time was used to test the effectiveness of the work. The completion form was used for this test. Chart I [1] shows the results. Twenty-seven children took these tests on twelve characters. Only three errors were made on the final test.

Similar results were obtained from drill on terms, places and dates.

ORGANIZATION [2]

Organization is one of the most difficult steps to handle. It is essential that every point included be known to the class beforehand. Whether or not they are known is ascertained by the tests at the end of the assimilation period.

All the methods used in organizing materials throughout the study have been collected and classified as follows:

I. Devices for arranging points in order.
   1. The teacher types the points on separate slips of paper. Each child receives a set, which he is to arrange on his desk in order.
   2. Sheets of worn-out textbooks are cut into sections corresponding to the points in the story. Children arrange in correct order.
   3. The teacher writes lists of points on the board, with the order confused. Children are to number them correctly.
   4. Children write their own slips, based on class work, and exchange to see if another can arrange the points properly.
   5. Children list their own points which they are to bring out in reports on special topics.
   6. Children decide how many points are necessary in order to cover the material adequately; these are then worded and arranged.

II. Use of outlines.
   1. Coöperative outlines made by teacher and pupils working together.
      a. Children suggest points; other children and the teacher suggest and criticize.
      b. The teacher makes the outline; children tell what details belong under each point.
      c. The teacher makes the outline; children write two or three subheads under each main point.
      d. The teacher makes the outline; children prepare to write a paragraph on each point.
      e. The teacher makes the outline; children substitute a complete sentence for each topic.

[1] P. 41.　　　　　　　　[2] See pages 16–17.

2. The class as a whole makes a coöperative outline without help from the teacher.
   Each row works out an outline of its own.
3. Children make their own outlines, each by himself.
    a. Each makes a list of points; the best are recorded on the board.
    b. Each pupil makes a list of points; each row then decides on its best list.
    c. Each works on his own outline until it is accepted by the teacher. (Brighter children are sometimes allowed to help the slower.)

III. Use of summary sentences.
   1. Coöperative.
   2. Individual.

IV. Use of questions.
   Each child makes out his own set of questions, adequately covering the material.

V. Graphic methods.
   1. A series of illustrations representing the steps in the story.
   2. Recording facts by:
    a. Making maps.
    b. Making charts and diagrams.
    c. Making graphs.

VI. Preparing imaginative material.
   1. Writing letters, diaries, editorials, cables.
   2. Writing or giving speeches.
   3. Preparing dramatizations.

A list of forms of organization arranged according to their simplicity is as follows: (1) The putting together of the cut-up story.[1] (2) The typing of the points and having the children arrange them in order.[2] (3) The teacher puts the points on the board and has children number them in the order in which they should occur. It may take a beginning class two months to develop to this point. (4) The teacher may write the points on the board and ask the class to tell what comes under each point. (5) After they have told the material, they decide how it could be written in a few words. As many of the contributions of the class should be used as is possible, though the teacher could furnish much better statements. One hard task is to help the class express the thought in the fewest words practicable. (6) The class works out its organization as a coöperative enterprise. One child proposes a point; and if the

[1] See page 62.
[2] See page 57.

class accepts it, it is written on the board. If it does not follow chronologically, it is written at one side and called into use later. (7) The children organize entirely by themselves,[1] the teacher either accepting or rejecting; if the latter, with constructive criticism.

The progress possible is shown by the following organizations, all made by classes who had used the basic technique herein described only three months, all made by method No. 5 above, and all taught by student teachers.

THE NORTHMEN
4-B Class

1. The Northmen traveled a great deal.
2. They discovered Iceland.
   Made a colony.
3. They discovered Vinland.
   Brought home wines and lumber.
4. People forgot the Northmen discovered Vinland.
   No colony made.

DE SOTO
4-A Class

1. His early life.
   Governor of Cuba and Florida.
2. Landing of the great expedition in Florida.
   a. Size of expedition.
   b. Searching for gold.
   c. Treatment of Indians.
   d. Hardships.
3. Discovery of Mississippi.
   Size of river.
4. Death of De Soto.
   a. Cause.
   b. Burial.
5. Return of explorers to Mexico.
   No gold found.

LA SALLE
5-B Class

1. Early life.
   a. Birth.
   b. Parents.
   c. Education.

[1] See page 148.

2. Early exploration.
   a. Trip down the Ohio.
   b. Trip down the Illinois.
   c. Fort Heartbreak.
3. Later exploration.
   a. Through the Great Lakes down the Mississippi.
   b. Entered the Gulf of Mexico.
4. Journey back to France.
   a. Permission to build a colony.
   b. Supplies.
5. Unsuccessful colonization.
   a. Supply boat lost.
   b. Texas instead of mouth of Mississippi.
6. Death.
   a. Journey back to Canada.
   b. Killed by his followers.
7. Results of his trip.
   Claimed for France all land drained by the Mississippi.

RECITATION [1]

The recitation step is based on the organization. At first the outline is left on the board, including subheads, and children tell the story one point at a time. Later there is added the telling of the whole story by certain individuals. If only the best students are called upon at first for the entire recitation, a high standard of performance is set and the class grasps the idea of what is involved in telling a whole story. Then, after considerable practice in this form, subheads are erased, and children recite from only the main points.

Other members of the group give corrections or additions after the speaker has finished, but on no account interrupt him while reciting. With younger children the same outline can be gone over several times before interest lags. At first there will probably have to be many suggestions in the form of questions, but as the exercise progresses more fluency develops.

The general rules for developing facility in English expression apply to the giving of the oral stories. By the time this step is reached, children have something to say on the subject; they are not at a loss for material. Thus one common difficulty is avoided.

[1] See page 17.

At intervals the recitation may be in the form of a written composition based on the outline. If children have great difficulty in handling written work, especially in the 4-B grade, one row may write on one point in the outline, another row on the second point, etc. Following are two compositions by *lower-group* 4-B children, based on two points in the outline of the story of Prince Henry.[1]

DIAS SAILED TO THE CAPE OF GOOD HOPE

Dias was the first man to sail to the Cape of Good Hope. When he got down there he called it the Cape of Storms because it was so stormy. After that, the king called it the Cape of Good Hope. Dias hoped they would get to India.   [JEAN]

VASCO DA GAMA WAS THE FIRST MAN TO SAIL TO INDIA

He sailed to India in 1498. He wasn't afraid that there were big monsters in the water. He was the bravest man. All the rest of the people thought there were big monsters in the sea that would take people off the boats and eat them. Vasco da Gama was from Prince Henry's country. He went farther than Dias. He went to India.   [JANE]

These stories were written in the history class and mistakes in subject matter corrected there. Then they were taken up in the English class and corrected as to errors in English.

By the time the children have used the same technique for a year there is great improvement. They progress from writing on one point to two, and so on to the whole story. Following is a story written by a 5-B pupil.

LA SALLE

La Salle was born in France. His father was a merchant. La Salle went to the best schools in France. His brother was in Canada, buying furs from the Indians. When La Salle was twenty years old he went to Canada. He started, went down the Ohio River, and then into the Illinois River.

He built a fort that he called "Heartbreak," and went back to Canada. Later he went to the Great Lakes and kept on till he got to Lake Michigan. Here he went across land to the Mississippi River and down to its mouth.

Then he returned to France for people and supplies to make colonies in America. When he started out for America, one ship was sunk with a lot of supplies. They landed in Texas and founded a colony, but his people became sick and died. He gave it up and started for Montreal. Before La Salle arrived at Montreal, one of his men shot him and he died.   [ROBERT]

[1] See page 69.

All of the different methods used throughout the study in order to motivate the step of recitation have been collected and classified as follows:

DIFFERENT METHODS OF MOTIVATING THE STEP OF RECITATION

I. Classroom situations: telling the stories under the following conditions.
  1. With only members of their own group present.
    a. Individual work.
      (1) Giving the summary sentences.
      (2) Giving the entire story based on their own outlines.
      (3) Telling the story to children who have been absent, as a help in make-up work.
      (4) Giving speeches impersonating certain characters.
      (5) Writing paragraphs for use in making their own booklets to take home.
      (6) Writing letters, diaries, editorials, cables.
    b. Group work.
      (1) Allowing those whose outlines were chosen to record on the board, to hear the others tell their stories.
      (2) Dividing the group into teams, and giving the winners a pennant to keep until defeated.
      (3) Dividing the class into groups of four, who hear each other's stories.
      (4) Answering each other's lists of questions on the story.
      (5) The child who makes a successful recitation on one point may call on another child to continue.
      (6) Use of parliamentary procedure.
      (7) A public-speaking club.
      (8) Giving dramatizations.
      (9) Grade programs.
      (10) Making booklets to be kept in the room library.
  2. In the presence of visitors.
    a. Principal or superintendent.
    b. Other teachers: high-school teachers of history, English, and science; teachers of other grades; special teachers; supervisors.
    c. Other citizens: war veterans; certain business and professional men; town officers.
    d. Pupils from other grades.
      Explaining posters, maps, diagrams, sand tables, charts, graphs, tables, and exhibits.
II. Extra-classroom situations: telling the stories under the following conditions.
  1. Telling the stories to persons outside the classroom, after sufficient preparation.
    a. To inmates of the Old Ladies' Home.
    b. To bedridden or unfortunate children who cannot go to school.
    c. To parents at home.

2. Giving programs at meetings of the Parent-Teacher Association.
3. Assembly programs.
4. Special-day programs.
5. Writing for the school newspaper.

GENERAL SUMMARY OF THE TECHNIQUE

In general, the procedure described above may be summarized as follows: preparation, presentation, presentation test, division of group and reteaching, readings, picture study, discussion based on the readings, project work, teaching the minimal essentials (especially the terms), drill on minimal essentials, objective test, organization, recitation.

As to time distribution, the 4-B usually requires about a week to a story, the higher sections moving a little faster. The time is distributed about as follows:

First day. Preparation, presentation, presentation test, beginning reading.
Second day. Re-presentation, reading, teaching terms.
Third day. Reading, picture study, drill, discussion.
Fourth day. Project (completed in art or language periods).
Fifth day. Organization and recitation.

MINIMAL BURDEN ON THE TEACHER

Some teachers upon first studying this technique exclaim that it may fit an experimental school but involves quite too much work for the overburdened grade teacher. The following outline is given to show which tasks may be delegated. Many times the teacher may secure the services of some high-school or upper-grade student who is interested in teaching to act as her assistant. In the following the star indicates work which must be done by the teacher; other details may be attended to by the assistant or by children in the class.

* 1. Dividing the class on the basis of reading ability.
2. Preparing materials for the preparation step.
* 3. Learning the presentation.
4. Preparing mimeographed or hectographed copies of the presentation test, or copying it on the board.
5. Correcting the test papers.

* 6. Diagnosing the difficulties and adapting the procedure accordingly.

7. Gathering all the books available.

8. Copying the reading lists on the board, or making mimeographed copies.

* 9. Making questions to guide the reading.

* 10. Planning drills and projects.

* 11. Making the objective test.

12. Making copies or writing the test on the board.

13. Correcting the papers. Many of these, when once done, can be used again year after year, so that the labor decreases with repetition.

ADAPTING THE TECHNIQUE TO A SYSTEM OF COMPLETELY INDIVIDUAL PROGRESS

The technique lends itself well to a system of individual progress.[1] A child comes to the teacher whenever ready for a new story. She discusses the preparatory step with him. He then reads the presentation, takes the presentation test, and begins his reading from the book lists, while the teacher corrects his presentation test. Projects may be individual or group. Each child drills on the minimal essentials for himself;[2] and when he has reached all his goals, he announces himself as ready for the objective test, which decides whether he may go on to the organization step. Recitation may be either oral or written.

In conclusion, the excellent results that have been achieved by the work carried on as outlined in the foregoing, even when taught by inexperienced student teachers, induces the belief that though the teacher should have to put more time on preparing her work, she will feel repaid by the thorough mastery obtained by the children. They grow in knowledge, in power, and in joy in the subject.

[1] *The Twenty-fourth Yearbook of the National Society for the Study of Education,* Part II, pp. 58–113.

[2] See the report of a lesson on individual drill, pp. 40–43.

PART II. UNIT TREATMENT OF AMERICAN HISTORY

UNIT I

WHY MEN WANTED TO REACH THE COUNTRIES OF THE FAR EAST

I. Marco Polo told the People about China.
II. Men who went on the Crusades learned to like New Things to Eat and Wear.
III. Some.went in Ships and Some on the Backs of Camels.
IV. Prince Henry wanted to go All the Way by Sea.
He sent Dias and Da Gama.
V. The Northmen went in the Opposite Direction.
VI. Men learned to use Things that made Travel Easier.
1. Compass.
2. Improvements in shipbuilding.
3. Influence of the printing press.
VII. Columbus's Great Idea was to go West and sail Clear around the World.

PREPARATION FOR THE OVERVIEW

The first exercise is the teaching of any words used in the presentation test which the children do not know. They need not be taught as spelling lessons, but for recognition only, and should be used in the same context in which they are to be found later. The following words of the presentation test do not appear in the first two thousand of the Thorndike word list:

camels   Marco Polo   rubies

The teacher asks, "Do you know what diamonds are? pearls? rubies?" She shows the children rings set with imitations of each precious stone mentioned; they add to the above list any others which they know. She mentions the fact that these stones cost a great deal of money and are called precious stones.

51

Children name spices they have seen used at home. Cloves and cinnamon bark may be displayed.

"What is perfume? Do you know of what it is made? Our lesson today is about precious stones and perfumes."

The exercise should not occupy more than five minutes.

PRESENTATION OR OVERVIEW

Long, long ago in a country far over the sea the people had very few diamonds, rubies, or pearls. Even the very rich did not own these beautiful precious stones. Neither did they have rare perfumes, nor spices for flavoring their food.

And worst of all, there was no sugar in the country! Since there was no sugar, there could be no candy, frosting, or sweetening of any kind but honey. Boys and girls a thousand years ago had to go without these good things.

After many years a man whose name was Marco Polo (*the teacher has previously written the name on the board, and points to it when she mentions him*) came back from a long journey. He said to his friends: "In the strange lands which I visited are many pearls and diamonds. Almost every rich man has a ruby ring. Spices are plentiful. And they have also a strange white sand which they call sugar. When they put in on cakes, it makes them taste sweet. The land is very wonderful. I liked it so well that some day I am going back."

The people looked doubtfully at each other. Sweet sand on cakes! They were not sure that the story could be true. However, a few men believed Marco Polo. They said, "Let us go on the long journey and find the sand that makes things sweet." They went; and when they came back they had all the sugar and spices they could carry.

Then everybody wanted sugar and spices. So the traders hired men to go to the sugar country and bring back bags of it, barrels of it, whole shiploads of it. Some men bought a hundred camels, loaded them with leather and wool, and rode all the long weary way on the camels' backs. It took two years to reach the strange country, two years of travel across deserts and over high mountains.

When they reached China (which was the name of the country) they unloaded the wool and the leather and traded them for pearls and rubies, sugar and perfumes and spices. They packed the sugar, pearls, rubies, perfume, and spices on the camels' backs and returned to their homes. There they sold their goods and made a great deal of money.

Other men built great ships and sailed away over the sea, for months at a time. When they reached the strange ports they landed, unloaded their ships, and left them at the sea-shore. Then they bought camels, which they loaded with the goods they had taken out of their ships, and rode away on their camels' backs until they arrived in China or India. There they also traded their leather and wool for diamonds, pearls, rubies, sugar, perfume, and spices. These they packed on the backs of their animals and, thus loaded, toiled back to the ships. How glad they were to put their goods into the ships and turn again toward their own country! After sailing many months they reached home, sold their goods, and became rich.

In these two ways a great trade grew up between China and the home country, some people going all the way by land; some, half by land and half by sea. Every year great bands of camels crossed the deserts and great fleets of ships sailed the seas. Traders grew rich, and the people of the West were satisfied because they had spices and perfumes.

But it cost a great deal of money to travel so far. To go all the way on camels was very slow. To unload the ships and pack the goods again on camels' backs was a great deal of trouble. How much better it would be if all the journey could be made by means of ships!

One man, Prince Henry (*this name also has been previously written on the board; the teacher now points to it*), began to send out his brave sailors to see if they could find a new way to go, a way entirely by sea without once unloading. Farther and farther away from home they sailed; but after many years they had not found any way to reach China by sea.

Then Columbus (*pointing to the name on the board*) came forward and said: "I have a new idea. I am going to sail clear around the world, and reach China that way." People laughed loudly and long. They thought Columbus's idea was very silly, but he waited his time. We shall now leave him, still waiting, but fully believing that one could sail clear around the world and reach China by sea.

PRESENTATION TEST

1. *Check the three right words in this list. Read carefully.*

At the time when our story began the people in the West did not have

_ _ _ rubies
_ _ _ houses
_ _ _ sugar

_ _ _ wool
_ _ _ pearls
_ _ _ kings

2. *Check the three right words in this list. Read carefully.*

Marco Polo told people he knew a country where they could get

_ _ _ sugar
_ _ _ pretty stones

_ _ _ horses
_ _ _ slaves

_ _ _ perfume

3. *Check the two right answers in this list. Read carefully.*

The two ways to travel to the new country were

_ _ _ on the backs of camels
_ _ _ on a train
_ _ _ part of the way by ship and the rest by camels
_ _ _ by walking

4. *Check the two right words in this list. Read carefully.*

The men took with them in order to trade

_ _ _ cows
_ _ _ wool

_ _ _ money
_ _ _ leather

5. *Check the one right answer in this list. Read carefully.*

Prince Henry wanted to find a way

_ _ _ to save money
_ _ _ to fight better than anyone else
_ _ _ to travel to China all the way by sea

6. *Check the one right answer in this list. Read carefully.*

Columbus's great idea was

_ _ _ to go to China all the way by land
_ _ _ to sail clear around the world and reach China by sea
_ _ _ to go part of the way by sea, then to ride on a camel

Procedure during Preparation and Presentation. The teacher asks the questions in the preparation step, which usually occupy about five minutes. Then she gives the presentation or overview of the whole unit,[1] followed immediately

[1] See pages 19–21.

by the presentation test.[1] As soon as a child finishes the test, he may begin to read the books mentioned in the step of assimilation.

After the teacher has scored the papers [2] she divides the class into two groups. Those whose test scores were perfect may go on with the reading for the story of Marco Polo; the other children will hear the overview again[3] and take the test. This procedure is repeated to the point of mastery.

I. MARCO POLO TOLD THE PEOPLE ABOUT CHINA

No additional preparation and presentation are required for the story of Marco Polo, these points having been adequately covered in the overview.

Assimilation

Readings

Upper Group (Difficult)

ATKINSON. Introduction to American History, 206–210.
BOURNE and BENTON. Introductory American History, 138–141.
BURNHAM. Our Beginnings in Europe and America, 214–217.
BURTON. Builders of our Nation, 14–22.
CROWE. Studies in American History, I : 1–17.
FARIS. Real Stories of the Geography Makers, 48–54.
FOOTE and SKINNER. Explorers and Founders of America, 18–23.
GORDY. American Beginnings in Europe, 229–230.
GREENWOOD. Our Heritage from the Old World, 325–327.
HAAREN and POLAND. Famous Men of the Middle Ages, 213–218.
HARDING. Old World Background to American History, 257–260.
HARDING. Story of Europe, 259–262.
JONES. Geography by Discovery, 16–34.
LAWLER. The Gateway to American History, 313–321.
NIDA. The Dawn of American History in Europe, 264–269.
O'NEILL. The World's Story, 303–304.
TERRY. History Stories of Other Lands, IV : 170–174.
VAN LOON. A Short History of Discovery, 52–57.
WHITCOMB. Heroes of History, 335–342.
WOODBURN and MORAN. Introduction to American History, 172–175.
Compton's Pictured Encyclopedia (Marco Polo).
World Book (Marco Polo).
Young Folks' Library, IX : 58–64.

Average Group

ELSON and MACMULLAN. The Story of our Country, I : 2–5.
MACE. Primary History, 3–7.
MILLER. My Bookhouse, II : 204–205.

[1] See pages 21–22.   [2] See page 20.   [3] See pages 22–23.

MOWRY. First Steps in the History of our Country, 17.
NIDA. Following Columbus, 20–22.
SHAW. Discoverers and Explorers, 16–22.
SOUTHWORTH. Builders of our Country, I : 10–23.
TAPPAN. European Hero Stories, 152–156.
TURPIN. Brief Biographies from American History, 13–20.

Lower Group

HANCOCK. Children of History : Later Times, 45–52.
McMANUS and HAAREN. Natural Method Readers, Third Reader, 40–43.

Teachers

Baltimore County Course of Study, 449–450, 467–472. (Contains a plan for teaching.)
BEAZLEY. Prince Henry the Navigator, 93–105.
BECKER. Beginnings of the American People, 8–12.
BROOKS. Story of Marco Polo.
CHEYNEY. European Background of American History, 46–50.
FISKE. The Discovery of America, I : 323–329.
KNOX. Travels of Marco Polo.
ROBINSON and BREASTED. Outlines of European History, I : 526.
TOWLE. Marco Polo.
WEBSTER. Early European History, 487–488, 616–618.
YULE. Book of Ser Marco Polo, the Venetian.

Minimal Essentials

Name of Person : **Marco Polo** (mär′kō pō′lō) [1]
Names of Places : **Venice** (vĕn′ĭs) ; **China** (chī′nà)
Date : **1300** (about) — Marco Polo's return from China
Historical Terms : **Far East; overland route**
Things to Remember
Marco Polo's story made people very eager to go to China.

Illustrative Material

GABRIEL (ED.). Pageant of America, I : 80–83.
Mentor, XII : 45–47 (November, 1924).
National Geographic Magazine, XXI : 289–319 (1910) ; XXIII : 996–1040 (1912) ; XXXVIII : 335–390 (1920).

Procedure during Assimilation

Reading as described on pages 24–29.
Picture study [2] based on the illustrative material listed above.
In the sand-box [3] model the Mediterranean countries and central, southern, and eastern Asia, using as large a scale as possible. Mark Venice and China. Chil-

---

[1] Webster's New International Dictionary is followed for pronunciations.

[2] Johnson, Henry, "The Use of Models and Pictures." *Teaching of History,* pp. 225–240.

[3] Williams, J., "A Sand Table Map." *The Twentieth Yearbook of the National Society for the Study of Education,* Part I, p. 69 ; Kendall, C. N., and Stryker, F. E., "Relation of History to Geography." *History in the Elementary School,* pp. 109–114.

dren construct ships and load them with the articles enumerated in the presentation. They unload the ships, repack the articles on camels' backs for the overland journey to China, and there exchange for the Chinese goods enumerated in the presentation story. Then the process [1] is reversed.

How far is it from Peking, China, to Venice?

Tell of someone who recently made a voyage to unknown lands, such as Stefansson, Scott, or Peary.

Use the helps suggested in the texts.

Flash-card drill on the minimal essentials.

Objective test.

Organization

The following points may be either mimeographed or hectographed, then cut so that only one point appears on each slip of paper. These are not numbered. Each child receives a complete package of the points and arranges them in the correct sequence.

MARCO POLO

1. Marco Polo's father and uncle first made the trip to China.
2. On the second trip Marco Polo went with his father and uncle.
3. Marco lived seventeen years in China.
4. At last the three Polos went home to Venice.
5. They told everybody of the wonders of the East.
6. Marco Polo made a book about his travels.

Recitation

Different children tell the story of each point in sequence. A few children tell the entire story.

Is there some bedridden or unfortunate child in the neighborhood who cannot go to school? Children may go to his home to tell stories and show the pictures.

II. MEN WHO WENT ON THE CRUSADES LEARNED TO LIKE NEW THINGS TO EAT AND WEAR

Preparation

First, it is necessary to teach in the same context in which they are to be used any words occurring in the presentation test which the children do not already know. The following words are not included in the first two thousand of the Thorn-

---

[1] See the map in Atkinson, A. M., *Introduction to American History*, p. 230.

dike word list and have not been taught in the previous
story :   Chinese   Jesus   Turks

"Have you ever heard of the Holy Land? Why do we call
it holy? Why did people think that a Christian nation ought
to own the Holy Land?" The teacher shows on the Marco
Polo sand table where the Holy Land is.

Presentation

(Additions needed after the general overview)

The land where Jesus lived and died is very dear to all
Christians. The old Bible names — Jerusalem, Bethlehem,
Galilee — are sacred to us because they are names of places
that Jesus knew and loved. For many hundreds of years after
his death people from Europe used to go to the Holy Land
just to see those places. Thousands went every year. For a
long time nobody interfered with them; they set out from
Europe, came to the Holy Land, and traveled about to see
where Jesus was born, where he preached, and where he was
crucified. Then they went home happy.

But at last a strong and fierce people conquered the Holy
Land. They came from a place near China. Marco Polo had
heard of them. They were called Turks (*pointing to the name
previously written on the board*). The Turks said : "If Christians
want to make journeys to the Holy Land, which now belongs
to us, they will have to pay us a great deal of money." And
sometimes the Turks even robbed and killed the travelers.

Of course, Christians did not like this. Some of them said :
"It is a shame that the Turks treat us so! They are not
Christians, and it is a shame that people who are not Christians should own the Holy Land. Let us make war on them
and thus win our sacred places back again."

So they did. Great armies and fleets of ships came from
Europe and fought the Turks. Sometimes the Turks would
win, sometimes the Christians; sometimes both stayed in
their camps for months at a time without fighting at all. The
war dragged on for hundreds of years. During this long time

the Christians often found it necessary to buy goods from the Turks. You remember that they came from a land near China, so they had the same goods as the Chinese. The Christians found that they could buy spices, silks, wines, fruit, ivory, and pearls, which the Turks had brought from the lands near India and China. Many of the men from the West had never known such products before, and learned to like them very much.

Finally, after many hundreds of years, the Christians gave up the struggle and went home to Europe without having taken the Holy Land. The Turks, in fact, continued to own it until the World War a few years ago. But when the Christians reached their homes they could not forget the beautiful silks and the rich wines they had had in the Holy Land. They kept saying: "Why doesn't someone go over to India or China and bring back a shipload of pretty things? We would pay him well."

After a while a few people did so, and trade was thus started between Europe and the East.

So we can see that Marco Polo's voyage and the wars for the Holy Land were alike in one way: they both made people want to trade with the East.

PRESENTATION TEST

1. *Check the best answer:*

   a. The Holy Land was

       _ _ _ the land Marco Polo found
       _ _ _ the land where Jesus lived
       _ _ _ the land where sugar grew

   b. For a long time people had gone to the Holy Land

       _ _ _ to get rich
       _ _ _ to trade
       _ _ _ to see where Jesus had lived

   c. The Holy Land was conquered by

       _ _ _ the Turks
       _ _ _ the Chinese
       _ _ _ the people of India

2. *Check the two best answers:*

   The Christians fought against the Turks because

       _ _ _ they thought the Holy Land ought to belong to Christians
       _ _ _ the Christians liked to fight
       _ _ _ the Turks would not let them travel freely in the Holy Land
       _ _ _ the Turks went to a different church from that of the Christians

3. *Check the best answer:*

    a. The Christians got most of their goods during the wars

         _ _ _ from America
         _ _ _ from the Turks in the Holy Land
         _ _ _ from China

    b. After the war the Christians wanted

         _ _ _ to go on fighting
         _ _ _ to live with the Turks
         _ _ _ to start trade with the East

    c. The story of Marco Polo and the wars for the Holy Land both

         _ _ _ made people want to trade with the East
         _ _ _ made people hate the Turks
         _ _ _ made people want to stay at home

Assimilation

Readings

Upper Group (*Difficult*)

ATKINSON. European Beginnings of American History, 143–156.
ATKINSON. Introduction to American History, 132–144.
BOURNE and BENTON. Introductory American History, 126–127.
CHURCH. Stories from English History, 165–187.
GORDY. American Beginnings in Europe, 203–228.
GREENWOOD. Our Heritage from the Old World, 290–307.
HARDING. Old World Background to American History, 231–256.
HARDING. The Story of the Middle Ages, 132–157.
NEWMAN. Beginners' Modern History, 27–33.
NIDA. The Dawn of American History in Europe, 201–231.
O'NEILL. The World's Story, 217–228, 245–247, 252–255.
SCALES. Boys of the Ages, 65–88.
STEIN. Our Little Crusader Cousin of Long Ago.
TAPPAN. When Knights were Bold, 123–148.
TERRY. History Stories of Other Lands, IV : 77–98.
WARREN. Stories from English History, 81–88.
WOODBURN and MORAN. Introduction to American History, 162–172.
Compton's Pictured Encyclopedia (Crusades).
World Book (Crusades).

Average Group

BUTTERWORTH. Zigzag Journeys in Classic Lands, 177–182.
TAPPAN. European Hero Stories, 136–151, 161–165.

Lower Group

PRATT. Exploration and Discovery, 11–16.
TERRY. History Stories of Other Lands, I : 49–57.

Teachers

ARCHER. The Crusades.
BECKER. Beginnings of the American People, 4.
COX. The Crusades.

DAY. History of Commerce, 86–88.
FISKE. Discovery of America, I : 312–315.
ROBINSON. Readings in European History, I : 312–345.
WEBSTER. General History of Commerce, 49–55.
The Twentieth Yearbook of the National Society for the Study of Education,
Part I, p. 44.

Minimal Essentials

Name of Persons: **Turks**
Names of Places: **Holy Land; Mediterranean Sea** (mĕd'ĭ tēr ā'nĕ ăn) ; **Constantinople**
Date: **1453** — capture of Constantinople by the Turks
Historical Terms: **pilgrim; siege; capture; conquer; crusade**
Things to Remember
The Crusades were fought to win the Holy Land.
Men who went on the Crusades learned to like the products of the East and
wanted to trade with the East.

Illustrative Material

ARNOLD. Historical Pictures : A. H. P. 14, Crusades, Richard and Saladin.
LEHMANN. Historical Pictures : L. H. 206, Siege of a City.
LONGMAN. Historical Wall Pictures : Richard Cœur de Lion's Sight of Jerusalem.
McKINLEY. Illustrated Topics : M. M. 5, The Crusades.

Procedure during Assimilation

Reading as described on pages 24–29.
Make a picture collection of Crusade subjects.
Show Jerusalem on the sand table.
Construct some of the medieval engines of siege warfare and use them as the nu-
cleus of a school historical museum.[1]
Do we today have anything resembling pilgrimages? Who uses the red cross as
an emblem today? Why were the Crusaders called "soldiers of the cross"?
See "A Christmas Trip to Palestine." *The Twentieth Yearbook of the National
Society for the Study of Education,* Part I, p. 44.
Use the following phonograph records to help in establishing a sympathetic at-
mosphere : "Crusaders' Hymn," "Pilgrims' Chorus."
Remember that the object of the study is to show the relationship of the holy wars
to the setting up of trade routes, not to give a detailed history of each of
the wars.
Use the helps suggested in the texts.
Drill on minimal essentials.[2]
Objective test.

[1] Salmon, Lucy, "The Historical Museum." *The Educational Review,* XLI :
144–160; Page, E. C., "How the Working Museum of History Works." *History
Teacher's Magazine,* VI : 307 ff. ; Briggs, T. H., "Public Museum and Art Gallery."
School and Society, XII : 259–260; Bach, R. F., "The Museum and the Teacher."
School and Society, XV : 597–599; Wilgus, A. C., "The High School History
Museum." *School and Society,* XIV : 461–463.
[2] See *History Teacher's Magazine,* VIII : 69, for a game of personages.

Organization

Worn-out copies of some of the texts describing the Crusades may be used: first cut into sections which will divide the story logically into four or five parts; then each part mounted on a fairly stiff cardboard. Children arrange the parts in the correct order.

Recitation

This story, illustrated by pictures, constitutes a good subject for an assembly program.

III. SOME WENT IN SHIPS AND SOME ON THE BACKS OF CAMELS

Preparation and Presentation

The story of the trade routes may be taken up as a problem lesson.[1] Gather the group about the sand table, which still shows all of Europe except the northeast, the northern rim of Africa, and all of western, southern, and central Asia.[2]

"What was one way in which the voyage of Marco Polo had the same effect as the Crusades?" The children study the map and suggest possible water routes that might be used. If one suggests going around the northern part of Europe, perhaps some member of the class can tell why that would be impracticable; that is, because of the ice. If not, the teacher may tell. If someone suggests going around Africa, accept the solution, adding: "That's the next story we shall hear about. People did try it after a while, but not for many years." Have ready long strings of colored yarn, and when one child selects a route that was actually followed lay it down on the sand table to mark the route. Use three routes: (1) northern, via the Ægean and Black seas and across the Caspian Sea, thence overland to China; (2) middle, via the Mediterranean, overland to the Tigris and Euphrates rivers (which must show very plainly on the sand table), and via the Persian Gulf to India; (3) southern, via the Mediterranean, up the Nile River, overland to the Red Sea, and thence across to India.

---

[1] Parker, S. C., *Types of Elementary Teaching and Learning*, pp. 263–330.

[2] Cheyney, *European Background of American History*, p. 55, has an excellent map to use as a model; see the list of teachers' references, text, p. 64.

Now use a slated map of the world.[1] Outline on it in heavy chalk lines the same map that is on the sand table. One child comes to the map and shows the northern route; the class judges whether he has traced it correctly. If he has, the teacher hastily traces the route on the map in the same color as the corresponding string on the sand table. The middle and southern routes are developed in the same way.

PRESENTATION TEST

Children draw the three trade routes on an outline map of the Eastern Hemisphere.

Assimilation

Readings

Upper Group (Difficult)

ATKINSON. European Beginnings of American History, 277–279.
ATKINSON. Introduction to American History, 219–220.
BLAISDELL. The Story of American History, 10–11.
BOURNE and BENTON. Introductory American History, 133–134.
CROWE. Studies in American History, I : 21–24.
DAVIDSON. Founders and Builders of our Nation, 7–9.
GORDY. American Beginnings in Europe, 220–222.
GORDY. History of the United States, 5–9.
GORDY. Leaders in Making America, 1–3.
GREENWOOD. Our Heritage from the Old World, 319–325.
HARDING. Old World Background to American History, 252.
LAWLER. The Story of Columbus and Magellan, 14–15.
NEWMAN. Beginners' Modern History, 68–69.
NIDA. The Dawn of American History in Europe, 269–270.
TAPPAN. An Elementary History of our Country, 2–3.
TAPPAN. Our European Ancestors, 142–144.
WOODBURN and MORAN. Finders and Founders of the New World, 23–27.
WOODBURN and MORAN. Introduction to American History, 177–178.

Average Group

ELSON and MacMULLAN. The Story of our Country, I : 5–6.
MACE. Primary History, 8.
GORDY. American Leaders and Heroes, 1–2.
NIDA. Following Columbus, 18–20.
SHAW. Discoverers and Explorers, 10–11.
SOUTHWORTH. Builders of our Country, I : 24–25.

Lower Group

BARROWS and PARKER. Geography : Journeys in Distant Lands, 10–14.
CHAMBERLAIN. How we Travel, 32–33, 122–130.
FAIRGRIEVE and YOUNG. Children of Many Lands, 79–96.
GRANT. Story of the Ship.

---

[1] See the catalogue of any map company.

Teachers

BARSTOW. Explorers and Settlers, 35–45.
BECKER. Beginnings of the American People, 5–8, 14–17.
CHEYNEY. European Background of American History, 3–40.
DAY. History of Commerce, 79–86.
FISKE. The Discovery of America, I : 316–322.
GRIFFIS. Romance of Discovery, 55–64.
OSGOOD. History of Industry, 152–159.
RICHMAN. Spanish Conquerors, 1–12.
ROBINSON and BREASTED. Outlines of European History, I : 502–509.
WEBSTER. Early European History, 47–48, 125, 134, 211, 540, 619–620.
WEBSTER. General History of Commerce, 41–48, 94–106.
Elementary School Journal, XVII : 550–552, 557–558. (Teaching suggestions.)

Minimal Essentials

Names of Places: India (ĭn′dĭ à) ; Genoa (jĕn′ō à) ; Europe (ū′rŭp) ; Asia (ā′shà)
Historical Terms: trade routes; caravan; products; water route; East; West
Things to Remember
People traded with the East by three main trade routes. (What were they?)
It cost a great deal of money to change from land routes to sea routes.
Everybody wanted to find a route entirely by water.

Illustrative Material

GABRIEL (ED.). Pageant of America, I : 84–86.
GRANT. Story of the Ship.
LEHMANN. Historical Pictures : L. H. 222, In the Harbor of a Hanseatic Town.
MCKINLEY. Illustrated Topics : M. M. 6, Rise of Towns and Growth of Commerce and Industry.
National Geographic Magazine, XXVII : 587–606 (1915), Venice.
Perry Pictures : 884, Turner, " Sun of Venice" Putting to Sea.
National Geographic Society Series : Sahara Life.
Travel, XLI : 28 (August, 1923) ; XLII : 9 (February, 1924).

Procedure during Assimilation

Reading as described on pages 24–29.
Picture study based on the illustrative material listed above.
Take a trip[1] to the local museum to see articles manufactured in India, China, and Japan.
Construct[2] a ship of the period and load it with articles to represent the products of the West. Unload just west of Antioch. Repack the goods on the backs of camels, to show why the broken route was so expensive. Reverse the process.[3]
Make an Oriental bazaar.[4]

[1] Stillman, B. W., "School Excursions." *Elementary School Journal*, XXII : 451–456.

[2] Whitney, M., "Construction for History in the Grades." *History Teacher's Magazine*, VIII : 60–63.

[3] For lists of the products see the following references in the reading lists above : Cheyney, pp. 18–19, 27 ; Becker, pp. 5–10 ; Woodburn and Moran, p. 178.

[4] *The Twentieth Yearbook of the National Society for the Study of Education*, Part I, pp. 72–73.

FIG. 1. Sand-Table Illustration of the Trade Routes, showing Europe, Northern Africa, and Eastern Asia

Ships and camels are loaded with the goods of the country from which they came

Why could traders not use the all-sea route via the Suez Canal? What things do
we get from the East today? [1]
Supply children with outline maps of the Eastern Hemisphere and have them
record the three trade routes. Make a key. [2] (These maps may be secured as
cheap as four fifths of a cent apiece if ordered in lots of five hundred.)
Use the helps suggested in the texts.
Drill on minimal essentials.
Objective test.

Organization

Pass outline maps and have the children record the routes
from memory.

Recitation

Children tell the complete story of each route, products
carried outbound, route, products carried homeward bound.
Invite the seventh-grade or eighth-grade teacher of history
to hear the stories.

IV. Prince Henry wanted to go All the Way by Sea

Preparation

If necessary teach the word *overland*, which does not occur
in the first two thousand words of the Thorndike list but which
was used in the story of Marco Polo.

"When we were trying to find out how people could go from
Europe to the East, someone mentioned a route which we said
we should hear of later. What was it?" (Around Africa.)

Presentation

Have ready a slated-cloth wall outline map of the Eastern
Hemisphere, with the world [3] as known before Prince Henry's
time outlined in chalk. As the teacher talks she outlines
further discovery of the coast of Africa.

One man, Prince Henry, was quite sure that the Indies
could be reached by going around Africa. This is the way he
thought he could go (*pointing on the map to southern Africa as*

---

[1] Barrows, H. H., and Parker, E. P., *Geography: Journeys in Distant Lands*, pp.
1–24.

[2] Johnson, Henry, "The Use of Maps." *Teaching of History*, pp. 241–268.

[3] Gordy, W. F., *American Beginnings in Europe*, p. 247, and Montgomery, D. H.,
Leading Facts of American History, p. 5, give maps that may be used as models.

shown there). He sent out sailors who sailed along the coast a little way, but became frightened and went back. Prince Henry said: "There is nothing to be afraid of. I will send another ship." And he did. They sailed a little farther (*each time the teacher says this, she sketches in a little more of the true coast line*), and stopped and traded with the black natives. Then they said: "We have been away from home a long time and have not yet come to India. Let us go back." Always Prince Henry was disappointed, and always he had to send out still another ship. At last he died, but the king of Portugal continued to send out ships.

When his sailors came to this part of the coast (*Gulf of Guinea; the teacher sketches it in as she talks*) they thought surely they would soon reach India because they were going in the right direction, but alas! the land began to stretch away south again. So it went, year after year and year after year. But at last one ship reached the end of the land (*sketching the coast to the Cape of Good Hope as the story proceeds*), and another which followed found the way clear to India (*show the route*). Prince Henry's dream had come true: his men could go all the way to India on ships without once unloading.

PRESENTATION TEST
Check the best answer:

Prince Henry wanted to go to India

_ _ _ by sea around Africa
_ _ _ overland
_ _ _ by camels

Assimilation
Readings
Upper Group

ATKINSON. European Beginnings of American History, 291–297.
ATKINSON. Introduction to American History, 210–212.
BOURNE and BENTON. Introductory American History, 142–144.
BURTON. Builders of our Nation, 23–28.
CROWE. Studies in American History, I : 25–35.
EGGLESTON. A First Book in American History, 3–4.
FARIS. Real Stories of the Geography Makers, 55–59, 81–86.
GORDY. American Beginnings in Europe, 246, 252–255.
GREENWOOD. Our Heritage from the Old World, 330–336.
GUERBER. Story of the Thirteen Colonies, 31–32, 35–36.
HARDING. Old World Background to American History, 262–264.

HARDING. Story of the Middle Ages, 252–253.
LAWLER. The Gateway to American History, 322–324.
LAWLER. The Story of Columbus and Magellan, 1–13.
NEWMAN. Beginners' Modern History, 70.
NIDA. The Dawn of American History in Europe, 271–278.
O'NEILL. The World's Story, 303, 305–309.
TAPPAN. Our European Ancestors, 151–154.
VAN LOON. A Short History of Discovery, 50–51, 58–59.
WHITCOMB. Heroes of History, 342–348.
WOODBURN and MORAN. Beginner's History of the United States, 20–21.
WOODBURN and MORAN. Finders and Founders of the New World, 27–28.
WOODBURN and MORAN. Introduction to American History, 181–187, 217.
Compton's Pictured Encyclopedia (Henry, Gama).
World Book (Henry, Gama).

Average Group

GOODALL. Peeps at Many Lands: Portugal, 14–15.
LUTHER. Trading and Exploring, 148–153, 174–191.
MACE. Primary History, 9.
NIDA. Following Columbus, 14–16, 25–41.
SHAW. Discoverers and Explorers, 40–43.
TAPPAN. European Hero Stories, 177–179.

Lower Group

Try MACE, NIDA, and SHAW.

Teachers

BEAZLEY. Prince Henry the Navigator.
BECKER. Beginnings of the American People, 17–22.
BOURNE. Spain in America, 3–7.
CHEYNEY. European Background of American History, 60–78.
DAY. History of Commerce, 128–132.
FISKE. The Discovery of America, I: 339–360, 364–384.
GRIFFIS. Romance of Discovery, 65–78.
ROBINSON and BREASTED. Outlines of European History, I: 528–529.
WEBSTER. Early European History, 620–622.
WEBSTER. General History of Commerce, 115–121.
Baltimore County Course of Study, 450–451.

Minimal Essentials

Names of Persons: **Prince Henry; Dias** (dē'äsh) ; **Vasco da Gama** (väs'kō dä gä'mä)
Names of Places: **Africa; Portugal** (pōr'tů gắl) ; **Cape of Storms; Cape of Good Hope**
Historical Terms: **navigator; continent; all-sea route; sea of darkness**
Date: **1498** — Vasco da Gama reached India.
Things to Remember
  The Portuguese were the first people who reached India by an all-sea route.
  Then trade shifted from the Mediterranean to the Atlantic coast.

Illustrative Material

BRADLEY. Village Series of Cut-Outs: African Village.
GABRIEL (ED.). Pageant of America, I: 88–93.
McKINLEY. Illustrated Topics for American History: S. 3.

Procedure during Assimilation

Use the pictures in the books.[1]

Reading as described on pages 24–29.

Picture study based on the illustrative material listed above.

Each child makes an illuminated copy of Prince Henry's motto, "Desire to do well."

Children draw imaginative reproductions of the terrors of the "green sea of darkness"; of the Cape of Storms.

Use Bradley's *African Village* (see Appendix B) to show the kind of people the sailors found in Africa. Read "The Congo Region," in Barrows and Parker's *Geography: Journeys in Distant Lands*, pp. 55–61.

Write a letter that Bartholomew Columbus, a member of Dias's crew, might have written to his older brother, Christopher, describing the voyage that changed the name from the Cape of Storms to the Cape of Good Hope.

How far is it from Lisbon to the Cape of Good Hope? Compare with the distance Marco Polo traveled.

Children trace the routes of Dias and Vasco da Gama on their outline maps.

Use the helps suggested in the texts.

Drill on minimal essentials. A game is suggested in Woodburn and Moran's *Introduction to American History*, p. 298.

Objective test.

Organization

As a coöperative class exercise pupils and teachers together make a list of the principal points [2] included in the story, somewhat like the following. This exercise is leading up to the making of outlines.

STORY OF PRINCE HENRY AND HIS MEN

1. Prince Henry studied the problems of sailing.
2. He sent his men down the coast of Africa.
3. Dias rounded the Cape of Good Hope.
4. Vasco da Gama finally reached India by an all-sea route around Africa.

Recitation

Divide the class into four groups. Each makes one section of a booklet to be kept in the school museum. The story of each section is written in several paragraphs. Illustrations may be added, and a cover designed in the art class.

---

[1] Young, F. D., "A Picture Museum." *The Twentieth Yearbook of the National Society for the Study of Education*, Part I, p. 83.

[2] Stone, C. R., *Silent and Oral Reading*, pp. 184–187, 192.

V. THE NORTHMEN WENT IN THE OPPOSITE DIRECTION

Preparation

Teach any words used in the presentation test which the children do not know. The context should be the same as in the story. The following words do not occur in the first two thousand of the Thorndike word list:

Iceland   Northmen   Vinland

Children tell what, if anything, they already know about the Northmen. Show on the map where the Northmen lived. Show pictures of their ships and their armor.

Presentation

All the time that the people of southern Europe were trading with the East, you may be sure that these brave, hardy Northmen (*pointing to the word on the board*) were not staying at home. No, indeed! They had poked the noses of their narrow black ships up almost every river in Europe; they had even come down to the Mediterranean Sea. They had found an island away out in the northern ocean which they liked well. They called it Iceland (*pointing to the name*) and built a town there. Once a Northman from Iceland was out on the sea in his ship when a great storm struck him. He was blown far out of his course, and when the storm was over found himself near a new land, different from any he had ever seen before. Many wild grapes grew there, so he called it Vinland (*pointing to the name*).

It really was North America; therefore the Northmen were the first to discover America, hundreds of years before Columbus. But they did not use this new-found land, and after a while the world forgot that they had ever seen Vinland.

PRESENTATION TEST

Check the best answer:

   a. The Northmen

      _ _ _ stayed at home
      _ _ _ traveled by land
      _ _ _ were great sailors

b. The Northmen found an island which they named

  _ _ _ Iceland

  _ _ _ England

  _ _ _ India

c. After the storm was over, the Northman found a new land. He called it

  _ _ _ Iceland

  _ _ _ Vinland

  _ _ _ Africa

d. The world forgot about Vinland

  _ _ _ because Columbus discovered America

  _ _ _ because the Northmen did not use their new land

  _ _ _ because Marco Polo reached China

Assimilation

Readings

Upper Group

ATKINSON. European Beginnings of American History, 106.

ATKINSON. Introduction to American History, 99–110.

BALDWIN. The Story of Roland.

BARSTOW. Explorers and Settlers, 3–14.

BLAISDELL. The Story of American History, 6–9.

BRADISH. Old Norse Stories.

COLUM. The Children of Odin.

EVANS. America First, 1–3.

FARIS. Real Stories of the Geography Makers, 42–47.

FOOTE and SKINNER. Explorers and Founders of America, 11–17.

FRENCH. The Story of Rolf and the Viking's Bow. (Difficult.)

GREENWOOD. Our Heritage from the Old World, 219–222.

HARDING. Story of Europe, 145–147.

HARDING. Story of the Middle Ages, 114–116, 123.

JOHONNOT. Stories of the Olden Time, 191–205.

JUDD. Classic Myths, 16–25, 70–75, 101–103, 174–180.

MORRIS. Heroes of Discovery in America, 9–13.

NEWMAN. Beginners' Modern History, 14–16.

PRICE. Wandering Heroes, 151–170.

SNEDDEN. Leif and Thorkel.

STEIN. Little Count of Normandy.

STEIN. Our Little Viking Cousin of Long Ago.

VAN LOON. A Short History of Discovery, 26–44.

WILMOT-BUXTON. Stories of Norse Heroes.

WOODBURN and MORAN. Beginner's History of the United States, 6–10.

WOODBURN and MORAN. Finders and Founders of the New World, 10–15.

WOODBURN and MORAN. Introduction to American History, 131–133.

WRIGHT. Children's Stories in American History, 27–37.

Compton's Pictured Encyclopedia (Northmen).

World Book (Northmen).

Young Folks' Library, VIII : 256–265; IX : 47–57.

Average Group

ELSON and MACMULLAN. The Story of our Country, I : 6–9.

KLINGENSMITH. Stories of Norse Gods and Heroes.

LEITH. Peeps at Many Lands: Iceland, 1–5.
LUTHER. Trading and Exploring, 95–147.
MABIE. Norse Stories.
MACE. Primary History, 1–3.
MILLER. My Bookhouse, IV: 436–448.
NIDA. Following Columbus, 1–10.
PERRY and PRICE. American History, I: 7–10.
PRATT. Exploration and Discovery, 1–10.
SHAW. Discoverers and Explorers, 13.
SOUTHWORTH. Builders of our Country, I: 1–9.
TERRY. History Stories of Other Lands, III: 177–181.
TURPIN. Brief Biographies from American History, 7–12.

Lower Group
DAVIS. Stories of the United States, 23–26.
HALL. Viking Tales.
KLUGH. Tales from the Far North.
PRATT. Beginners' Book, 1–22.
Flanagan Publishing Company. The Norse Seamen and Christopher Columbus, 2–7.

Teachers
BARSTOW. Explorers and Settlers, 3–14.
DU CHAILLU. Ivar the Viking.
FISKE. The Discovery of America, I: 175–225.
HART. American History Told by Contemporaries, I: 28–34.
ROBINSON. Readings in European History, I: 152–154.
UPTON. Life Stories for Young People: Eric the Red and Leif the Lucky.
WEBSTER. Early European History, 389–401.
Elementary School Journal, XVII: 417–422. (Teaching suggestions.)

Minimal Essentials

Names of Persons: **Leif Ericson** (lēf ĕr′ĭk sŭn) ; **Northmen; vikings** (vī′kĭngz)
Names of Places: **Iceland; Vinland** (vĭn′lănd)
Date: **1000** — discovery of America by the Northmen
Historical Terms: **found a colony; voyage**
Things to Remember
The Northmen discovered Iceland and Greenland.
They did not found colonies in Vinland, so their discovery of this land had no results.

Illustrative Material

GABRIEL (ED.). Pageant of America, I: 69–76.
GRANT. Story of the Ship.
LONGMAN. Historical Wall Pictures: A Danish Raid.
MCKINLEY. Illustrated Topics: M. M. 2, The Vikings: Funeral, Feast Hall.

Procedure during Assimilation

Reading as described on pages 24–29.
Picture study based on the illustrative material listed above.
The boys in their manual-training classes carve viking shields and decorate them. These are placed in the school museum. Girls dress dolls to represent Norse men and women.

A Norse ship may be modeled in clay or cut from wood.[1]
Music from the Nibelungen Ring.
Make a Norway book.[2]
The teacher may read to the class Longfellow's "Skeleton in Armor."
Remember that the story is to center on the discovery of America by the Northmen, rather than on Norse myths.
Suggestions for dramatization.[3]
Use the helps suggested in the texts.
Drill on minimal essentials.
Objective test.

Organization

A series of illustrations may be made, representing in sequence the development of the Norse story, from the time the vikings were in their homes in Norway until Vinland was discovered.

Recitation

The illustrations may be displayed and the oral story accompanying each one given at a Parent-Teacher Association meeting.

VI. MEN LEARNED TO USE THINGS THAT MADE TRAVEL EASIER

Preparation

Teach, first, any words in the presentation test which the children do not know. All are included in the first two thousand of the Thorndike word list.

Show the class a magnet; let them experiment with it. The children point to the north. Show them a compass; they carry it about the room and note how the needle always turns north. "Point to the south; to the east; to the west. Of what use would the compass be if you were lost in the woods? at sea?"

Have prepared an exhibit showing handwritten books, an outfit for block printing, and, if possible, a collection of mov-

---

[1] Parker, S. C., *Types of Elementary Teaching and Learning*, pp. 193–194.

[2] Williams, Jennie, "A Norway Book." *The Twentieth Yearbook of the National Society for the Study of Education*, Part I, p. 71.

[3] Clark, Ada B., "Dramatization of Norse Stories in the Fourth Grade." *School and Home Education*, XXXIV: 184–186, 292–294; Sims, Albert E., and Harry, M. L., *Dramatic Myths and Legends: Norse Legends*.

able type [1] and the trays into which they are fitted. The local
newspaper or printing office will probably be glad to supply
you. Have written on the board the expressions "block
printing"; "printing with movable type." Children print
their names with the block-printing outfit; they set up their
names from the movable type.

Discuss with children the meaning of the words *invent* and
invention.

Presentation

We shall find that one reason why Prince Henry's men were
so afraid to travel by sea was that they were sometimes out of
sight of land. Then how would they know which way to go?
At sea all directions look alike: there is no road to (*any place
of local importance*) to tell you that this is north; no road to
(*any place of local importance*) to tell you that this is south.
You remember the Northmen found Vinland only because a
storm blew them, not because they knew which way they
should go.

At about the time we are now studying people began to
use the compass. Then sailors were not so afraid as they had
been. They could sail for days out of sight of land and still
know they were going north or south or east or west, as the
case might be. Vasco da Gama had a compass. Naturally
from that time on many more voyages were made.

Long years ago, when people used to write books they wrote
them all out by hand or printed them with blocks such as we
used.[2] Of course this took a very long time, and not many
books could be written. But after the invention of movable
type, such as we wrote our names with, the work went much
faster and many more books were written. Marco Polo's
book, for example, was sent into many countries. Men then
knew much more than they used to, and if anybody found new
lands or new trade routes or had any new ideas he could let
the world know about it.

---

[1] Rubber type a little larger than typewriter size may be secured from school-
furnishing companies.

[2] See the step of preparation, above.

PRESENTATION TEST

Check the best answer:

a. A long time ago men were afraid to go far out to sea because
_ _ _ they were afraid of the water
_ _ _ they did not know which way was north and which way south
_ _ _ they liked to stay at home

b. The compass tells us
_ _ _ how far we are from land
_ _ _ how much longer we must sail
_ _ _ in what direction we are going

c. The invention of printing was important because
_ _ _ new ideas could spread faster
_ _ _ books were made by hand before that
_ _ _ the printers made more money

Assimilation

Readings

Upper Group (Difficult)

ATKINSON. European Beginnings of American History, 272–276.
ATKINSON. Introduction to American History, 293–298.
BACHMAN. Great Inventors and their Inventions, 187–207.
BOURNE and BENTON. Introductory American History, 127–128.
FORMAN. Stories of Useful Inventions, 218–221.
GREENWOOD. Our Heritage from the Old World, 353–357.
HAAREN and POLAND. Famous Men of the Middle Ages, 257–262.
HARDING. Old World Background to American History, 261.
HARDING. Story of the Middle Ages, 249–252.
HARTWELL. Story-Hour Readings, V: 367–372.
NIDA. The Dawn of American History in Europe, 272–274.
O'NEILL. The World's Story, 298–301.
ROCHELEAU. The Story of Printing.
TERRY. History Stories of Other Lands, V: 26–33.
VAN LOON. A Short History of Discovery, 46–49.
WOODBURN and MORAN. Introduction to American History, 179–180.
Compton's Pictured Encyclopedia (Compass, Printing).
World Book (Compass, Gunpowder).

Average Group

BALDWIN. Thirty More Famous Stories, 40–49.
NIDA. Following Columbus, 25–27.
PERRY and PRICE. American History, I: 46–47.
TAPPAN. European Hero Stories, 165–169.

Lower Group

BARNES. Primary History of the United States, 15–17.
CHAMBERLAIN. How we Travel, 156–158.
ETTINGER, SHIMER, and O'REGAN. Progressive Road to Silent Reading, IV: 204–207.
GRANT. Story of the Ship.
TERRY. History Stories of Other Lands, I: 80–88.

Teachers

CHEYNEY. European Background of American History, 55–59.
DAY. History of Commerce, 72–77.
FISKE. The Discovery of America, I : 360–363.
ROBINSON and BREASTED. Outlines of European History, I : 549–588.
WEBSTER. Early European History, 383, 572–579, 618–620.
WEBSTER. General History of Commerce, 108–112.
Pioneers of Progress. Samuel O. Kuhn, 3100 Broadway, New York.

Minimal Essentials

Name of Person: **John Gutenberg** (gōō′tĕn bĕrĸ)
Historical Terms: **compass; movable type; invention; inventor**
Things to Remember
    Before the invention of the compass sailors were afraid to sail out of sight of land.
    The compass showed in what direction they were sailing. Then men did not fear
        the sea so much.
    The invention of printing made it easier to print books.
    Then new ideas could spread faster.

Illustrative Material

ARNOLD. Historical Pictures : A. H. P. 23, Caxton showing his Printing Press to Edward IV.
BRADLEY. Modern Trade Pictures : The Printer.
GRANT. Story of the Ship.
LEHMANN. Historical Pictures : L. H. 219, Handwriting of a Monk ; L. H. 220, The Invention
    of Printing.
Mentor, X : 3–6 (March, 1922).

Procedure during Assimilation

Reading as described on pages 24–29.
If near any vessel which uses a compass, take the class to see it.
A trip to the local museum to see handmade manuscripts, or books.[1]
Boys in manual-training classes carve wooden blocks for use in printing words and
    pictures.
A trip to the local printing establishment.[2]
Use the helps suggested in the texts.
Drill on minimal essentials.
Objective test.

Organization

The class makes summary sentences similar to those given
under the heading "Things to Remember."

Recitation

Invite the manual-training teacher to hear the stories.

---

[1] Stockton, Helen, "A Book on Book-Making." *The Twentieth Yearbook of the
National Society for the Study of Education*, Part I, pp. 109–110.
[2] Briggs, Thomas H., "The Excursion as a Means of Education." *Teachers
College Record*, XXII : 415–419.

VII. COLUMBUS'S GREAT IDEA WAS TO GO WEST AND SAIL
CLEAR AROUND THE WORLD

Preparation

A slated globe is used, with the outlines of Europe, Africa,
and Asia appearing. Children tell why a globe is used to
represent the earth (a map will not serve the purpose nearly
so well). A large map of the world is in convenient position.
Children locate Portugal on the globe; they trace Da Gama's
route. They show which way is west and which east on the
globe; which is west and which east on the map.
"Who really did discover America?" Some child will
probably know. "This is the story of how it happened."

Presentation

During the years that some people were traveling to the
Indies overland (*running the pointer hastily over the route on
the map*), and Prince Henry's men were still trying to go
around Africa (*showing the route*), there was a man who had
long been studying and thinking and planning. He knew that
the earth is round like this globe; so did many of the other
wise men of his time. At last he said: "The best way to reach
the Indies is to sail right out into the ocean and go around this
way (*illustrating at the globe*) until one comes to China." How
simple the plan seemed to Columbus (*pointing to the word on
the board*), for he was the man who had the great idea!
But other people were very doubtful. They said: "We
never have gone that way. We have always traveled this
way." (*Showing the Mediterranean routes.*) Columbus answered: "I am sure my way is shorter and easier. Who will
furnish ships and men for me in order that I may reach the
East by sailing west?" (*Illustrating his route again.*) People
tapped their heads, looked at each other, and said: "The man
is crazy. Nobody has ever gone that way before, and anyway
it isn't reasonable to think that we can reach the East by
sailing west."
Nobody would help him. For years and years, until he was
a middle-aged man, bent and tired and almost discouraged,

he went about from one country to another asking kings to give him ships and men. No king would do so, but after many years a queen decided to help him. He was given three little boats and told to go and try his new idea of sailing straight out into the ocean.

Columbus thanked the queen warmly and said: "Great queen! You shall see that I am right. I shall sail west and thereby reach the East. Gold and precious stones and perfumes I will bring back to you. You will never be sorry that you helped me!"

Soon afterwards he set sail on his long journey. There we shall leave him, and wait to see whether or not he found the East by sailing west.

PRESENTATION TEST

Check the best answer:

a. Columbus's plan was

    _ _ _ to sail around Africa to India
    _ _ _ to go to China by land
    _ _ _ to sail west until he came to the East

b. Columbus went to many kings

    _ _ _ because he wanted ships and men
    _ _ _ because the kings liked him
    _ _ _ because he liked to travel

c. The person who first helped him was

    _ _ _ a king
    _ _ _ a queen
    _ _ _ Prince Henry

Assimilation

Readings

Upper Group

ATKINSON. European Beginnings of American History, 279–280.
ATKINSON. Introduction to American History, 212–214.
BARSTOW. Explorers and Settlers, 15–34.
BLAISDELL. The Story of American History, 12–15.
BOURNE and BENTON. Introductory American History, 146–148.
BURNHAM. Hero Tales from History, 78–82.
BURNHAM. Our Beginnings in Europe and America, 222–225.
BURTON. Builders of our Nation, 29–37.
CHANDLER and CHITWOOD. Makers of American History, 1–18.
DAVIDSON. Founders and Builders of our Nation, 6, 10–12.
DYER and BRADY. Merrill Fifth Reader, 110–113.
EGGLESTON. A First Book in American History, 1–3, 4–6.
ELLIS. Makers of our Country, 17–21.
FOOTE and SKINNER. Explorers and Founders of America, 24–29.

GORDY. American Beginnings in Europe, 234–240.
GORDY. Leaders in Making America, 4–8.
GORDY. Stories of Early American History, 1–8.
HARDING. Old World Background to American History, 265–269.
HARDING. Story of Europe, 269–273.
HARTWELL. Story-Hour Readings, V : 303.
HUBBARD. Little American History Plays, 3–12.
JOHNSON. World's Discoverers, 18–27.
LAWLER. The Story of Columbus and Magellan, 17–41.
LOGIE. From Columbus to Lincoln, 1–7.
MONTGOMERY. Beginners' American History, 1–6.
MORRIS. Heroes of Discovery in America, 14–15.
NIDA. The Dawn of American History in Europe, 279–287.
O'NEILL. The World's Story, 310–311.
PIERCY. Great Inventions and Discoveries, 92–99.
SEAWELL. Son of Columbus.
TAPPAN. Elementary History of our Country, 3–7.
TAPPAN. Our European Ancestors, 156–162.
TERRY. History Stories of Other Lands, V : 34–35.
TURPIN. Stories from American History, 7–20.
VAN LOON. A Short History of Discovery, 60–77.
WOODBURN and MORAN. Beginner's History of the United States, 14–17 22–26.
WOODBURN and MORAN. Finders and Founders of the New World, 17–23, 28–34.
WOODBURN and MORAN. Introduction to American History, 188–202.

Average Group

BALDWIN. Fourth Reader, 26–37.
BALDWIN. Thirty More Famous Stories, 7–9.
BEARD and BAGLEY. A First Book in American History, 1–9.
BLAISDELL and BALL. Log Cabin Days, 7–10.
COE. Founders of our Country, 7–16.
ELSON and MACMULLAN. The Story of our Country, I : 9–13.
FORMAN. First Lessons in American History, 14–16.
GORDY. American Leaders and Heroes, 1–9.
GORDY. Elementary History of the United States, 1–4.
MACE. Primary History, 9–14.
McMASTER. Primary History of the United States, 7–9.
MORRIS. Primary History of the United States, 9–16.
NIDA. Following Columbus, 29–35.
PERRY and PRICE. American History, I : 1–4.
PRATT. Exploration and Discovery, 17–22.
SHAW. Discoverers and Explorers, 9–15, 24–30.
SOUTHWORTH. Builders of our Country, I : 26–31.
SWAN. History and Civics, Grade 5 A, 1–3, 5–14.
TAPPAN. American Hero Stories, 1–5.
TAPPAN. European Hero Stories, 170–173.
TURPIN. Brief Biographies from American History, 20–25.

Lower Group

BLAISDELL and BALL. American History for Little Folks, 1–7.
BLAISDELL and BALL. Child's Book of American History, 1–3.
CALMERTON and WHEELER. Wheeler's Graded Readers, III : 197–207.
DAVIDSON and ANDERSON. Lincoln Readers, III : 31–33.
DAVIS. Stories of the United States, 27–37.

ELSON. Primary School Reader, III : 144–150.
FIELD. Second Reader, 52–59.
LUCIA. Stories of American Discoverers for Little Americans, 1–19.
PRATT. Beginners' Book, 23–29.
WAYLAND. History Stories for Primary Grades, 91–93.
WILSON. A History Reader, 33–42.
Flanagan Publishing Company. The Norse Seamen and Christopher Columbus, 9–17.

Teachers

BECKER. Beginnings of the American People, 22–29.
BOURNE. Spain in America, 8–19.
DAY. History of Commerce, 132–133.
DYNES. Socializing the Child, 226–252.
GRIFFIS. Romance of Discovery, 79–89.
IRVING. Life and Voyages of Christopher Columbus.
LAMPREY. Days of the Discoverers, 35–47, 50–64.
LANE and HILL. American History in Literature, 8–14.
MILLER. History in Story, Song, and Action, I : 47–52.
RICHMAN. Spanish Conquerors, 13–39.
WINSOR. Narrative and Critical History of America, II, Part I, 1–7.
Baltimore County Course of Study, 451.
Public School Methods, V : 166, 196–198. (The Methods Co., Chicago.)

Minimal Essentials

Names of Persons: **Ferdinand** (fûr′dĭ nănd) ; **Isabella** (ĭz′à bĕl′à) ; **Columbus** (kŏ lŭm′bŭs)
Names of Places: **Atlantic; Indies** (ĭn′dĭz) ; **France; Spain**
Historical Terms: **court** (royal) ; **charts** (for sailing)
Things to Remember
Wise men had known for a long time that the earth is round.
Columbus was the first man who had the courage to try to sail around it.

Illustrative Material

BROWN. Famous Pictures: 2248, Columbus Planning the Discovery of America.
GABRIEL (ED.). Pageant of America, I : 96–104.
GRANT. Story of the Ship.
McKINLEY. Illustrated Topics: M. M. 4, The Monastery.
Mentor, XI : 36–38 (October, 1923).
Perry Pictures: 1325, Columbus before the Council of Salamanca ; 1326-B, Portrait of Colum-bus ; 1327, Columbus at the Court of Ferdinand and Isabella.
Travel, XXXVI : 20 (March, 1921).

Procedure during Assimilation

Reading as described on pages 24–29.
Picture study of the monastery where Columbus left his son, his appearance at court, and the kinds of ships he was given.
Show copies of the maps and charts [1] he carried with him.
Use the dramatization "Columbus Story." Shoemaker, *Colonial Plays for the School-room,* pp. 9–17.

---

[1] Burnham, Smith, *The Making of our Country,* p. 6 ; Long, W. J., *America,* p. 35.

Make a list of the supplies that would be needed for a long sea voyage.
Children illustrate Columbus's idea with the slated globe.
Look over a large map of America and find places named for Columbus.
Drill on minimal essentials.
Objective test.

Organization

Compose a dramatization [1] of Columbus's request for aid before the king's court, his argument, his proofs, the objections raised, the incentives he held out to the rulers, their final decision.

Recitation

The giving of the dramatization.   .

MINIMAL ESSENTIALS OF UNIT I

PERSONS	PLACES	TERMS [2]	DATES [3]

Columbus
Dias
Leif Ericson
Ferdinand
Vasco da Gama
John Gutenberg
Prince Henry
Isabella
Northmen
Marco Polo
Turks
Vikings
	Africa
	Asia
	Atlantic
	Cape of Storms
	   (Good Hope)
	China
	Constantinople
	Europe
	France
	Genoa
	Holy Land
	Iceland
	India
		all-sea route
		capture
		caravan
		compass
		conquer
		continent
		court (royal)
		crusade
		East
		Far East
		found a colony
		invention
		inventor
			1000. Discovery
			   of America by
			   the Northmen
			1300 (about).
			   Marco Polo
			1453. Capture of
			   Constantinople
			   by the Turks
			1498. Vasco da
			   Gama reached
			   India

Make flash cards
   and use as a
   flash-card drill
See the game
   described in
   Woodburn and
   Moran, Intro-
   duction to
   American His-
   tory, p. 298
	Indies
	Mediterranean
	   Sea
	Portugal
	Spain
	Venice
	Vinland
		movable type
		navigator
		overland route
		pilgrim
		products
		route
		charts (for sailing)
			Drill with flash
			   cards
			Drill on placing
			   the persons in
			   the time chart

	Pupils pass to the
	   map and point
	   to places as read
	   by those at the
	   seats
		sea of darkness
		siege
		trade routes
		voyage
		water route
		West	

[1] Wayland, John W., "Dramatics as a Method of Teaching History." *How to Teach American History*, pp. 152–160; Kendall, C. N., and Stryker, F. E., "Dramatization." *History in the Elementary School*, pp. 91–102.

[2] Stone, C. R., *Silent and Oral Reading*, pp. 195–197, 210–215.

[3] Wayland, John W., *How to Teach American History*, pp. 235–243.

Drill on Terms

Pass slips of paper naming these terms. One half of the room plays against the other. A child on one side rises and says, "My word means ——" and then tells what the word means without naming it. The other side guesses. If one cannot give the meaning of his own word, the other side has a chance.

TIME CHART

Begin to make a time chart. For example, one board at the back of the room is selected as a starting point. A permanent border is selected, which may in time extend clear around the room. A yard to one hundred years will not be too much later. As each person or event is mentioned he or it is represented by a mountain rising from the base line, the height depending on the importance attached. A long strip of wall paper may be used if blackboard room is not available, but should be displayed permanently and prominently.

TESTS ON THE ENTIRE UNIT

(To be given after all the stories are completed)

Test of Place-Sense.[1] Pass outline maps of the world. Provide the children with colored crayons. Work is to be done in pencil except when color is specifically directed. Give the following directions:

1. Put a figure 1 where Venice should be.
2. Put a figure 2 where Genoa should be.
3. Write the word *China* in the right place.
4. Put a figure 3 where the Holy Land should be.
5. Put a figure 4 in the Mediterranean Sea.
6. Draw in green crayon the northern trade route.
7. Draw in red crayon the middle trade route.
8. Draw in blue crayon the southern trade route.
9. Write the word *India* in the right place.

[1] Washburne, C. W., *The Twenty-second Yearbook of the National Society for the Study of Education*, Part II, pp. 107–110; *History Teacher's Magazine*, VIII: 303.

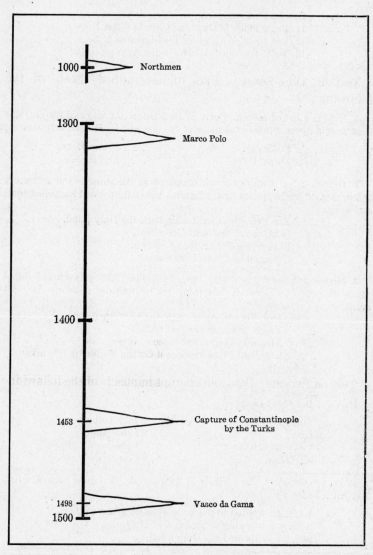

Time Chart — Unit I

10. Draw in yellow crayon Vasco da Gama's route.
11. Put a figure 5 where the Cape of Good Hope is.
12. Put the figure 6 where Portugal should be.
13. Write the word *Atlantic* in the right place.

Test of Time-Sense.[1] Pass mimeographed sheets of the following :

1. Here is a list of people. Put a figure 1 before the name of the one who lived first, a figure 2 before the name of the one who lived next, and so on.

  _ _ _ Columbus   _ _ _ Prince Henry
  _ _ _ Marco Polo   _ _ _ Leif Ericson

2. Here is a list of things which happened in the stories. Put a figure 1 before that which happened first, a figure 2 before that which happened next, and so on.
  _ _ _ The Crusades tried to win back the Holy Land.
  _ _ _ Northmen discovered Greenland.
  _ _ _ Dias reached the Cape of Storms.
  _ _ _ Columbus got help from Spain.

3. Here is a list of dates: *1000, 1300, 1453, 1498.* Below is a list of things which happened. Take each date from this list and put it before the right event.
  _ _ _ _ Discovery of America by the Northmen
  _ _ _ _ Vasco da Gama reached India
  _ _ _ _ Marco Polo returned home
  _ _ _ _ Capture of Constantinople by the Turks

Test on Persons. Pass mimeographed sheets of the following :

Here is a list of persons :

Turks   John Gutenberg
Dias   Ferdinand
Vasco da Gama   Isabella
Northmen   Columbus

Below are sentences which tell about these people. Take one name at a time and put it in the right place.

1. _ _ _ _ wanted to reach the East by going west.
2. _ _ _ _ was king of Spain.
3. _ _ _ _ captured the Holy Land.
4. _ _ _ _ was queen of Spain.
5. _ _ _ _ went as far as the Cape of Storms.

[1] Based on the minimal essentials of the stories in the unit. The children must have been given a good deal of practice in arranging such material. They may make up their own lists and submit them to each other as puzzles.

6. _ _ _ _ invented our kind of printing.
7. _ _ _ _ was the first to reach India by sea.
8. _ _ _ _ were the first to reach America.

Test on Historical Terms.[1] The teacher prepares descriptions such as the following, which may have been used previously, as the subject of drill games.[2]

I. Here is a list of words:

overland	conquers
sea route	capture
route	pilgrim
caravan	siege
trade route	Far East

Take one word at a time and put it in the right place in the sentences below:

1. This word means that people always travel over the same way. The word is _ _ _ _.

2. This word means that in traveling you go always by land, not by water. The word is _ _ _ _.

3. People used to call both China and India the _ _ _ _   _ _ _ _.

4. This word means a person who makes a voyage to a place he thinks is holy. The word is _ _ _ _.

5. When an army stays outside a town, will not let anyone out or in, and tries to take the town, we say the army is making a _ _ _ _.

6. When armies take a person or place that belongs to an enemy, we say they _ _ _ _ the person or place.

7. When one army or country beats another one so badly that it can do with the other one anything it wants to, we say the army _ _ _ _ the other one.

8. A number of camels loaded with goods and going on a journey is called a _ _ _ _.

9. A route that people travel over to trade with other people is called a _ _ _ _   _ _ _ _.

10. If the route is on the sea, so that people have to travel by boats, we call it a _ _ _ _   _ _ _ _.

II. Here is a list of words:

compass	founds a colony
products	voyage
court	invention
inventor	continent
crusade	sailing chart

[1] *The Twentieth Yearbook of the National Society for the Study of Education*, Part II, pp. 171–172.

[2] Based on historical terms in the minimal essentials of the stories included in the unit.

Take one word at a time and put it in the right place in the sentences below :

1. The things made or grown in a country we call its _ _ _ _.

2. A large body of land like Africa we call a _ _ _ _.

3. A long journey by water we call a _ _ _ _.

4. When somebody brings people to stay and live in a new land, we say
he _ _ _ _ _ _ _ _ _ _ _ _.

5. An object which looks somewhat like a clock and which is used to show
directions is a _ _ _ _.

6. A person who makes something that never was before is an _ _ _ _.
What he makes is an _ _ _ _.

7. All the people who live with a king or whose business it is to stay near
him make up his _ _ _ _.

8. A map for sailors that shows how deep the water is and where the rocks
are is called a _ _ _ _ _ _ _ _.

9. A war for a holy cause is called a _ _ _ _.

Or, the correct answers may be written on the board in
columns and the children be required to find the appropriate
word in each case, or the answers may be given entirely from
memory. These last two methods are less satisfactory than
using the hectographed or mimeographed sheets.

COMPREHENSION TEST[1] ON UNIT I

1. *Check the best answer :*

    a. Marco Polo was a great man

        _ _ _ because his story made people eager to find a way to China

        _ _ _ because he became rich

        _ _ _ because the king liked him

    b. The first people who knew that the earth is round were

        _ _ _ Prince Henry and his men

        _ _ _ wise men who lived long before Columbus

        _ _ _ the Northmen

    c. The invention of printing was a good thing for the world

        _ _ _ because new ideas could be spread faster

        _ _ _ because John Gutenberg was a great man

        _ _ _ because nobody knew how to read before that

    d. People wanted to find an all-sea route to the Indies

        _ _ _ because they did not like to ride camels

        _ _ _ because ships can go very fast

        _ _ _ because it cost a great deal of money to change from land routes
            to sea routes

[1] Based on "Things to Remember" in each division of the unit.

e. The first people who reached the Indies by sea were

_ _ _ men of Portugal
_ _ _ Columbus and his men
_ _ _ the Northmen

f. The world forgot about the discovery of Vinland by the Northmen

_ _ _ because they were always fighting
_ _ _ because they did not found any colonies in Vinland
_ _ _ because they lived so far north

g. The compass helped sailors

_ _ _ because they could see a long way with it
_ _ _ because it stopped the wind from blowing
_ _ _ because it showed in which direction they were going

h. We honor Columbus

_ _ _ because he had the courage to try to sail west to reach China
_ _ _ because many kings knew him
_ _ _ because he was the first man who knew that the earth is round

i. The men who went on the Crusades learned

_ _ _ to fight bravely
_ _ _ to like the products of the East, and they wanted to set up
trade to get them
_ _ _ that they were much better than the Turks

j. After Vasco da Gama sailed around Africa, the country which traded
most with the Indies was

_ _ _ Venice
_ _ _ Genoa
_ _ _ Portugal

2. *What is the title of Unit I?*

ORGANIZATION OF THE UNIT AS A WHOLE

The teacher may have the titles of the different stories comprising the unit printed on long slips of cardboard. A child
comes to the desk, selects the name of the first story, and
places the slip on the chalk tray, telling the main points of the
"things to remember" about it. The second slip is placed
next to it, and so on until all are arranged in sequence.

RECITATION OF THE UNIT AS A WHOLE

Each child then chooses which part he will tell. At a mothers' meeting divide the audience so that each group of seven children (stories I–VII) has an audience. Each child tells his story and shows one piece of illustrative material.

The oral exercise furnishes excellent motivation for review of points on which the child is not clear; it gives opportunity for English expression; and it gives the parents a closer contact with the actual work of the school than would a program prepared only for exhibition purposes.

UNIT II

HOW THE NATIONS TRIED TO GET WEALTH FROM THE NEW WORLD

I. Spain wanted Gold and Got It.
  1. Columbus found land which he thought was India.
  2. Magellan proved that it was a new world.
  3. Ponce de Leon helped to search out the coast.
  4. Cortez conquered the natives.
  5. De Soto explored the land far from the sea.
  6. The Spaniards built towns in their rich lands.
  Extra — for advanced group: Balboa, Pizarro, Coronado.

II. England was Slow in Starting and found Little Gold.
  1. John Cabot discovered North America.
  2. John Hawkins started the English slave trade.
  3. Francis Drake sailed around the world, but found no rich lands like Spain's.
  4. Walter Raleigh tried to build towns, but failed.
  5. At last England beat Spain at sea; then she could send out ships where she pleased
  Extra — for advanced group: Frobisher, Davis, Hudson's last voyage.

III. France, too, was Slow; she found No Gold, but Many Furs.
  1. Cartier found a great river leading into the country.
  2. Champlain built towns and made friends with the Indians.
  3. The Indians divided, some being friendly to the English and some to the French.
  Extra — for advanced group: Verrazano.

IV. Portugal had Little Land in the New World, but secured the Trade with the Real Indies.
  1. The name of Americus Vespucius was given to the new world.
  2. Portugal's trade with the Indies made her rich.
  3. Portugal founded a colony in Brazil.

V. The Dutch built on Land which the English thought was Theirs.
  1. Henry Hudson found a great river.
  2. They built a town on Hudson's river.

VI. Then they All claimed Land in the New World.
  1. Their claims overlapped.
  2. These were the days of the pirates.

PREPARATION FOR THE OVERVIEW

"In our story of Columbus we learned why people were so eager to go to the Indies. What was the reason?" (To get the rich products.) "What country finally helped him?"

(Spain.) Have written on the board *Countries which wanted to get Rich from Trade with the Indies*. List Spain under the heading. Children locate Spain on the map. "Where was Columbus about to go when the queen sent for him?" (France.) Add to the list and locate. "What country was Prince Henry from?" Add and locate. "There were two other countries that wanted a share in the riches: they were England and the country of the Dutch." The teacher adds these names. "All these countries (*running a pointer down the list*) wanted riches, and each one was eager to get ahead of the others. They were so afraid that someone else would reach the new lands first that they became very jealous of each other. The story we take up now is the story of each one's race to secure as much gold as possible before the others did."

Have ready a slated globe with the outline of the known world (1492).[1] There may be a very dimly stenciled outline of North and South America also, but this should be so dim that the children at their seats cannot see it.

Teach any words in the presentation test which the children do not know. All are included in the first two thousand of the Thorndike word list or were taught in Unit I.

PRESENTATION OR OVERVIEW

We found in our last story that Spain had at last helped Columbus. He set sail in three little vessels on which we would be afraid to sail across (Lake ____[2]), and at last reached land. (*Here the teacher draws on the globe just the small extent of coast line which Columbus ever touched.*) He thought this was the Indies (*showing the real Indies on the map*) and went back with great joy to tell the king. Spain was very proud because she had beaten all the other countries; but she was most interested in riches, so she sent out another man to bring back the gold and precious stones and perfumes. He came here (*and as the teacher tells of Magellan's route she sketches in all the eastern and southern coast line of South America*), and

---

[1] A useful model may be found in Muzzey, D. S., *An American History*, p. 9.

[2] Naming any local body of water.

thought at first that he had found some of Columbus's little islands. But he sailed and sailed and found only land. It wasn't at all like China, or India either. At last he reached here (*indicating Cape Horn*) and found, beyond, another ocean. Then he knew that this land was not India nor China (*pointing again to these*), but a new world. The king of Spain was sorry to hear that the land Columbus had found was not India, but he said, "We must see whether there is any gold in this new world." So he sent out thousands of men in hundreds of ships. They sailed up all the rivers and searched all the lands, and found more gold than they had ever dreamed of. Spain grew rich and powerful. She built forts and cities in the New World and held it for her own.

You may well believe that the other countries were very jealous of Spain because she was getting rich and they were not. England said: "We will send a man to a different part of the world, where Spain has not gone. Then we too may find gold." An Englishman did sail across here (*sketching in the shores of North America which Cabot touched*), and was the first man after the Northmen to discover North America. But he found no gold, no precious stones, no perfumes. It was a long time before England dared to send out any more men, because Spain was angry and captured many of England's ships. As long, then, as Spain had more ships than any other nation, England could not travel to the New World and did not secure its riches.

There was still another country jealous of Spain. France said: "Show me the will of Father Adam which says that all the wealth is to go to other countries. I must send ships to the New World, too, and see what I can find." So she sent ships to a place Spain had never seen, and farther inland than England had gone. The French captain found a great river, up which he sailed a long way (*sketching in the seacoast around the Gulf of St. Lawrence*). He went back and said to the king of France, "I found no gold in the strange lands, but there are furs, — hundreds, thousands, millions of them." The king replied: "Very well! Furs are as good as gold. We can sell them and make a great deal of money." So France sent over many men; they bought many furs, and were well satisfied with their part of the new lands. France was prospering.

There were still other countries which entered the race, but I shall not name them. However, you may picture to yourselves Spain, England, and France each claiming land in the New World and each jealous of the other. Trouble among them was bound to come, and trouble did come. But that is another story. What we now want to see is how all the countries tried to get wealth from the New World, and how each one sent out brave men to find it.

PRESENTATION TEST

1. *Check the best answer:*
   a. Columbus thought he had found

   _ _ _ the Indies
   _ _ _ Africa
   _ _ _ Venice

   b. The man who came after Columbus knew that the land was

   _ _ _ China
   _ _ _ Genoa
   _ _ _ a new world

   c. Spain came to the New World

   _ _ _ first
   _ _ _ second
   _ _ _ last

   d. The second nation to come to the New World was

   _ _ _ Spain
   _ _ _ England
   _ _ _ China

   e. England at this time

   _ _ _ found much gold in the New World
   _ _ _ did not get riches from the New World

   f. France found in the New World

   _ _ _ furs
   _ _ _ gold
   _ _ _ silver

   g. What all the nations wanted in the New World was

   _ _ _ land
   _ _ _ wealth
   _ _ _ slaves

2. *Check three answers this time:*
   Countries which had land in the New World were

   _ _ _ China   _ _ _ Venice
   _ _ _ France   _ _ _ England
   _ _ _ Spain   _ _ _ India

I. Spain Wanted Gold and Got It

1. *Columbus found Land which he thought was India*

No additional preparation and presentation are needed.

Assimilation

Readings

Upper Group

ATKINSON. Introduction to American History, 214–217.
BARSTOW. Explorers and Settlers, 34.
BLAISDELL. The Story of American History, 10–24.
BOURNE and BENTON. Introductory American History, 150–157.
BROOKS. True Story of Christopher Columbus.
BURNHAM. Hero Tales from History, 83–84.
BURNHAM. Our Beginnings in Europe and America, 225–230.
BURTON. Builders of our Nation, 37–45.
CHANDLER and CHITWOOD. Makers of American History, 18–23.
DAVIDSON. Founders and Builders of our Nation, 12–21.
DYER and BRADY. Merrill Fifth Reader, 113–116.
EGGLESTON. First Book in American History, 8–17.
ELLIS. Makers of our Country, 21–27.
FARIS. Real Stories of the Geography Makers, 68–74.
FOOTE and SKINNER. Explorers and Founders of America, 29–36.
GORDY. American Beginnings in Europe, 240–248.
GORDY. Leaders in Making America, 8–12.
GORDY. Stories of Early American History, 8–14.
GREENWOOD. Our Heritage from the Old World, 377–383.
HARDING. Old World Background to American History, 269–275.
HARDING. Story of Europe, 273–277.
HAZARD and DUTTON. Indians and Pioneers, 98–111.
HUBBARD. Little American History Plays, 6–12.
JOHNSON. The World's Discoverers, 18–92.
JONES. Geography by Discovery, 36–45.
LAWLER. The Gateway to American History, 326–328.
LAWLER. The Story of Columbus and Magellan, 41–65.
LOGIE. From Columbus to Lincoln, 8–9.
MONTGOMERY. Beginners' American History, 6–13.
MORRIS. Heroes of Discovery in America, 14–22.
NIDA. The Dawn of American History in Europe, 287–296.
OLCOTT. Good Stories for Great Birthdays, 2–27.
O'NEILL. The World's Story, 311–314.
PIERCY. Great Inventions and Discoveries, 99–107.
SEAWELL. Son of Columbus.
TAPPAN. Elementary History of our Country, 6–12.
TAPPAN. Our European Ancestors, 162–171.
TURPIN. Stories from American History, 20–37.
VAN LOON. A Short History of Discovery, 78–89.
WOODBURN and MORAN. Beginner's History of the United States, 26–35.
WOODBURN and MORAN. Finders and Founders of the New World, 1–9, 34–46.
WOODBURN and MORAN. Introduction to American History, 202–219.
Compton's Pictured Encyclopedia (Columbus).
World Book (Columbus).

Average Group

BALDWIN. Fourth Reader, 37–43.
BALDWIN. Thirty More Famous Stories, 8–9.
BEARD and BAGLEY. A First Book in American History, 10–20.
BLAISDELL and BALL. Log Cabin Days, 8–10.
COE. Founders of our Country, 16–35.
ELSON and MACMULLAN. The Story of our Country, I : 13–23.
FORMAN. First Lessons in American History, 16–20.
GORDY. American Leaders and Heroes, 9–20.
GORDY. Elementary History of the United States, 5–7.
HARTWELL. Story-Hour Readings, IV : 151–159.
MACE. Primary History, 14–20.
MCMASTER. Primary History of the United States, 9–14.
MORRIS. Primary History of the United States, 17–24.
MOWRY. First Steps in the History of our Country, 22–29.
NIDA. Following Columbus, 36–42.
PERRY and PRICE. American History, I : 4–7, 13–16, 37–46.
PRATT. Exploration and Discovery, 22–32.
SHAW. Discoverers and Explorers, 24–39.
SOUTHWORTH. Builders of our Country, I : 31–36.
SWAN. History and Civics, Grade 5 A, 15–22.
TAPPAN. American Hero Stories, 5–13.
TAPPAN. European Hero Stories, 173–176.
TURPIN. Brief Biographies from American History, 25–30.

Lower Group

BARNES. Primary History of the United States, 17–20.
BLAISDELL and BALL. American History for Little Folks, 7–11.
BLAISDELL and BALL. Child's Book of American History, 3–7.
CALMERTON and WHEELER. Wheeler's Graded Readers, III : 204–207.
CURTIS. Why we Celebrate our Holidays, 104–109.
DAVIS. Stories of the United States, 37–47.
ELSON. Primary School Reader, III : 144–150.
FIELD. Second Reader, 58–59.
LUCIA. Stories of American Discoverers for Little Americans, 19–32, 39–40.
PRATT. Beginners' Book, 29–36.
TERRY. History Stories from Other Lands, I : 89–96.
WAYLAND. History Stories for Primary Grades, 91–94.
WILSON. A History Reader, 42–49.
Flanagan Publishing Company. The Norse Seamen and Christopher Columbus, 17–29.

Teachers

See references for previous story.
In addition :
JONES. Geography by Discovery, 36–46.
MORRIS. Heroes of Discovery in America, 14–22.
MUZZEY. An American History, 4–8.
RICHMAN. The Spanish Conquerors, 39–63.
WEBSTER. Early European History, 624–627.
WETHERILL. The World and its Discovery, 182–209.
Old South Leaflets, II, 29, 33 (Letter of Columbus) ; III, 71.
Public School Methods, V : 199–206, 366–376. (The Methods Co., Chicago.)

Minimal Essentials

Name of Persons: **Indian** (ĭn'dĭ ăn)
Names of Places: **Spain; Canary** (kȧ nā'rĭ) **Islands**
Date: **1492** — Columbus discovered America.
Historical Terms: **discovery, discoverer, discover; mutiny**
Things to Remember
Columbus discovered America in 1492.
He never knew that it was a "new world"; he thought it was the Indies.

Illustrative Material

BRADLEY. Straight-Line Picture Cut-Outs: Landing of Columbus.
BROWN. Famous Pictures: 1921, Columbus received by Catholic Kings after the First Voyage; 704-M, Caravels of Columbus.
GABRIEL (ED.). Pageant of America, I: 105–110.
Chronicles of America Photoplays, Yale University Press: Columbus.
Educational Posters of the National Child Welfare Association: Columbus Day.
National Posters: Coming of Columbus.
Perry Pictures: 1323, Departure of Columbus; 1324, Departure of Columbus from Palos; 1326, 1269, Columbus Statue; 1328, Columbus on the Deck of the Santa Maria; 1329, Landing of Columbus; 658, Death of Columbus.

Procedure during Assimilation

Reading as described on pages 24–29.
Picture study based on the illustrative material listed above.
Children read orally the following dramatizations of the story of Columbus: "The Discovery of America." Hubbard, *Little American History Plays*, pp. 6–11; "The Columbus Story." Shoemaker, *Colonial Plays for the Schoolroom*, pp. 17–20.
Dramatize a story similar to those reported in *The Twentieth Yearbook of the National Society for the Study of Education*, Part I, pp. 50–51, 73–74, 97.
Members of the class draw [1] their ideas of a triumphal procession on Columbus's return.
Use the map in McMaster, J. B., *Primary History of the United States*, p. 13, to show what Columbus thought he had found. Muzzey, D. S., *An American History*, p. 5, gives a very illuminating map which compares what Columbus had found with what he thought he had found.
Read to the class Joaquin Miller's poem "Columbus." [2]
Begin making a cumulative map of Spanish explorations.
Each child traces Columbus's first voyage [3] on an outline map of the world. Give the map the name "Spanish Discoveries and Explorations."
How long would it take us today to make Columbus's voyage?
Use the helps in the books.
Drill with flash cards on the minimal essentials.
Objective test.

[1] Beale, H., "Illustrating Stories on the Blackboard." *The Twentieth Yearbook of the National Society for the Study of Education*, Part I, p. 55.

[2] See the reading described in *Graded List of Victor Records for Home and School*, p. 123.

[3] Woodburn, J. A., and Moran, T. F., *Introduction to American History*, p. 214; Long, W. J., *America*, p. 43.

Organization

Each child represents Columbus. He is to prepare a speech in which he (Columbus) reports to Ferdinand and Isabella the story of his journey. He writes down the points he will include in the speech.

Recitation

The speeches are given. The rest of the class may ask questions on points omitted from each speech, or parts not made clear.

2. *Magellan proved that it was a New World*

Preparation

"What was Columbus looking for? Did he find the riches he had expected? Have you ever heard of the Philippines?" All words used in the presentation test are found in the first two thousand of the Thorndike word list or have been taught in previous stories.

Presentation

Since Columbus had not brought her the jewels and spices she desired Spain decided to send out another man, to see if he would not be more successful. (*Turn to the slated globe used before in the overview story, on which was traced Magellan's route along the eastern coast of South America.*) Magellan, for that was his name (*pointing to the name previously written on the board*), sailed along the coast expecting constantly to reach India. Every time he came to a large river such as this (*pointing to the Plata*) he thought surely he could sail through it to reach India. But always there was land and more land.

He saw some Indians with very big feet, who amused him so much that some of his men wrote about them. After many adventures he finally passed through a very narrow place with high, stern mountains frowning down on his ships from both sides (*showing on the map*), a place which we still call the Strait of Magellan.

On the other side he saw a vast calm ocean. Then he knew that this land was not India, as Columbus (now long dead) had thought, but a whole new continent.

Of course he did not know how large the new ocean was. But he thought (and he was right) that off over here somewhere (*pointing toward Asia*) lay India. If he had known how very far away it was, he would never have started. But nobody knew the distance, so all set out bravely enough.

It was a terrible voyage. The ship ran out of food, and the men had to eat even the leather off from the yards of the vessel. They ran out of water. Men died by hundreds. That was one of the greatest voyages ever undertaken in the history of the world.

But they kept on westward, and finally came to the Philippines. In a great fight with the natives the brave leader Magellan was killed. The little band which was left sadly sailed away to the Spice Islands, where they loaded their ship with treasures. Then they started for Spain and reached home, having been gone three years.

The king of Spain was not pleased to hear that America was a whole continent by itself. He would much rather that it had been India! He was pleased, however, to think that his men had finally reached the Indies, even though it was much farther than he had thought. And, best of all, he was proud to think that his brave sailors under Magellan had been the very first people in all history who had sailed clear around the world and had finally come back to the same place from which they started. He gave them a globe on which was written "You first sailed around me."

PRESENTATION TEST

Check the best answer:

a. Magellan sailed for which country?

_ _ _ England
_ _ _ Portugal
_ _ _ Spain

b. He was trying to find

_ _ _ the Indies
_ _ _ America
_ _ _ islands

c. He found out that the land he passed was

_ _ _ an island
_ _ _ a new world
_ _ _ part of India

d. The new ocean he crossed was

_ _ _ large

_ _ _ small

_ _ _ stormy

e. The king was glad because his men had

_ _ _ had a fight

_ _ _ sailed clear around the world

_ _ _ left Magellan behind

Assimilation
Readings

Upper Group

ATKINSON. European Beginnings of American History, 298–305.

ATKINSON. Introduction to American History, 226–234.

BOURNE and BENTON. Introductory American History, 164–169.

BURNHAM. Hero Tales from History, 84–89.

BURNHAM. Our Beginnings in Europe and America, 233–236.

BUTTERWORTH. Story of Magellan and the Discovery of the Philippines.

CROWE. Studies in American History, I : 36–42.

FARIS. Real Stories of the Geography Makers, 87–92.

FOOTE and SKINNER. Explorers and Founders of America, 81–86.

GORDY. American Beginnings in Europe, 256–259.

GORDY. Leaders in Making America, 22–23.

GORDY. Stories of Early American History, 31–35.

GREENWOOD. Our Heritage from the Old World, 385–388.

HARDING. Old World Background to American History, 280–282.

JOHNSON. The World's Discoverers, 119–176.

JOHNSTON. Famous Discoverers and Explorers of America, 187–202.

JONES. Geography by Discovery, 47–61.

KNAPP. Story of the Philippines.

LAWLER. The Story of Columbus and Magellan, 94–144.

MCMURRY. Pioneers on Land and Sea, 161–185.

MORRIS. Heroes of Discovery in America, 57–67.

NIDA. The Dawn of American History in Europe, 301–305.

TAPPAN. Elementary History of our Country, 17–19.

TAPPAN. Our European Ancestors, 181–183.

VAN LOON. A Short History of Discovery, 98–99.

WOODBURN and MORAN. Beginner's History of the United States, 46–50.

WOODBURN and MORAN. Finders and Founders of the New World, 59–64.

WOODBURN and MORAN. Introduction to American History, 225–229.

Compton's Pictured Encyclopedia (Magellan).

World Book (Magellan).

Average Group

BARNES. Elementary History of the United States, 31–32.

BEARD and BAGLEY. A First Book in American History, 24–26, 29–32.

COE. Founders of our Country, 63–74.

MACE. Primary History, 21–24.

NIDA. Following Columbus, 49–57.

PERRY and PRICE. American History, I : 48–56.

SHAW. Discoverers and Explorers, 62–67.

SOUTHWORTH. Builders of our Country, I : 58–59.

SWAN. History and Civics, Grade 5 A, 33–39.
TAPPAN. American Hero Stories, 14–24.
TAPPAN. European Hero Stories, 179–183.
WADE. Our Little Philippine Cousin, 88–102.

Lower Group

BRAINE. Merchant Ships and What they Bring Us.
BURKS. Barbara's Philippine Journey, 42–49.
LUCIA. Stories of American Discoverers for Little Americans, 79–87.

Teachers

BOURNE. Spain in America, 115–132.
DAY. History of Commerce, 132–137.
FISKE. The Discovery of America, II : 419–450.
LONG. America, 40–42.
MUZZEY. An American History, 12–13.
WEBSTER. Early European History, 629–630.
Baltimore County Course of Study, 453.

Minimal Essentials

Name of Person: **Magellan** (mȧ jĕl′ăn)
Names of Places: **Pacific** (pȧ sĭf′ĭk) ; **Philippines** (fĭl′ĭ pēnz) ; **South America**
Dates: **1519–1522** — Magellan circumnavigated the globe.
Historical Terms: **circumnavigation; continent; natives**
Things to Remember
Magellan was the first man to circumnavigate the globe.
He proved that America was a separate continent.
He did not discover the Pacific Ocean, but he named it.

Illustrative Material

GABRIEL (ED.). Pageant of America, I : 117–119.
National Geographic Magazine, XXIV : 1161–1192 (1913).
Travel, XLIII : 13–17 (May, 1924).

Procedure during Assimilation

Reading as described on pages 24–29.
Picture study based on the illustrative material listed above.
Read in preparation for keeping a diary for Magellan : when he started, off the
coast of Patagonia, in the straits with Tierra del Fuego in the offing, in the mid-
dle of the Pacific, in the Philippines, Del Cano's return to Spain.[1]
Make a sand-table representation of a Philippine village.
Design an illuminated motto, "You first sailed around me."
Trace the voyage[2] of Magellan on the map entitled "Spanish Discoveries and
Explorations," each child making his individual copy.
Why do they call men who fly around the world in airships "air Magellans"?
Use the helps in the books.
Drill on minimal essentials.
Objective test.

[1] A model may be found in Tryon, R. M., *The Teaching of History in Junior and Senior High Schools*, p. 122.
[2] Atkinson, A. M., *Introduction to American History*, p. 231.

Organization

The writing of the diary referred to on page 99.

Recitation

Reading the diaries.

3. *Ponce de Leon helped to search out the Coast*

Preparation

"Has anyone ever heard of Florida? What? We are going to read today about how it was first found."

Presentation

We must remember that Columbus and Magellan both had sailed along the coast, but neither one knew much about the land far in from the ocean. Nobody knew. All sorts of wild tales were told. Some explorers came back and described the terrible animals; alligators, for example. People didn't know whether to believe that there could be any such creatures anywhere. Others described the Indians as neither white nor black, but red. People in Europe were not sure whether this could be true either; they had never seen any but white or black persons.

At last it came about that almost any story could be told about the New World, and somebody would believe it. It *might* be true. One wild tale about Florida reached the ears of Ponce de Leon (*pointing to the word on the board*), so he started to find out whether it was true. Now we shall read to find out what the wild tale was. (*The class practices the pronunciation of the words Ponce de Leon.*)

PRESENTATION TEST

Check the best answer:

People believed all sorts of wild stories about the new land

_ _ _ because nobody knew much about it
_ _ _ because they were not wise people
_ _ _ because they liked to hear strange tales

Assimilation
Readings

Upper Group

CHANDLER and CHITWOOD. Makers of American History, 35–37.
EVANS. America First, 15–18.
FOOTE and SKINNER. Explorers and Founders of America, 42–46.
GORDY. Leaders in Making America, 26–27.
GORDY. Stories of Early American History, 48–50.
HARDING. Old World Background to American History, 288.
JOHNSTON. Famous Discoverers and Explorers of America, 63–83.
LAWLER. The Story of Columbus and Magellan, 67–69.
McMURRY. Pioneers on Land and Sea, 222–226.
MONTGOMERY. Beginners' American History, 19.
MORRIS. Heroes of Discovery in America, 47–51.
NIDA. The Dawn of American History in Europe, 313–314.
TAPPAN. Elementary History of our Country, 16–17.
WOODBURN and MORAN. Beginner's History of the United States, 54–56.
WOODBURN and MORAN. Finders and Founders of the New World, 69–72.
WRIGHT. Children's Stories in American History, 71–75.
World Book (Ponce de Leon).

Average Group

BLAISDELL. Story of American History, 27–28.
BOURNE and BENTON. Introductory American History, 185.
COE. Founders of our Country, 36–40.
GORDY. Elementary History of the United States, 11–12.
McMASTER. Primary History of the United States, 24.
MORRIS. Primary History of the United States, 29–30.
NIDA. Following Columbus, 59–61.
PERRY and PRICE. American History, I : 77–78.
PRATT. Exploration and Discovery, 33–37.
SHAW. Discoverers and Explorers, 54–55.
SOUTHWORTH. Builders of our Country, I : 41–42.
SWAN. History and Civics, Grade 5 A, 25–27.

Lower Group

BALDWIN. Thirty More Famous Stories Retold, 23–28.
BARNES. Primary History of the United States, 22.
BLAISDELL and BALL. Child's Book of American History, 12–17.
FIRMAN and MALTBY. Winston Readers, III : 153–155.
LUCIA. Stories of American Discoverers for Little Americans, 41–44.
WAYLAND. History Stories for Primary Grades, 149–150.

Teachers

BOURNE. Spain in America, 133–136.
GRIFFIS. Romance of Discovery, 146–160.

Minimal Essentials

Name of Person: **Ponce de Leon** [1] (pŏn'thä dā lå ōn')
Name of Place: **Florida** (flŏr'ĭ då)
Historical Terms: **coast; governor**

---

[1] Not in the studies of personages referred to on page 5; included for its story value.

Things to Remember
> People knew so little about the New World that they were ready to believe any wild tale about it.
> Ponce de Leon discovered Florida.

Illustrative Material

Detroit Publishing Company. Little Phostint Journeys, XXXVI: Land of Ponce de Leon — Florida.
GABRIEL (ED.). Pageant of America, I: 127.

Procedure during Assimilation

Reading as described on pages 24–29.
Study pictures [1] of Porto Rico, over which Ponce de Leon was governor.
Use the "Largo" from Dvorák's *New World Symphony* to help to establish a sympathetic atmosphere.
Children read the dramatization "The Flowery Land," in Hubbard's *Little American History Plays*, pp. 13–17.
Trace the voyage [2] of Ponce de Leon on the map entitled "Spanish Discoveries and Explorations," [3] each child making his individual copy.
Use the helps in the books.
Drill on minimal essentials.
Objective test.

Organization

The teacher puts on the board the following outline. Children are to write in one sentence a summary of each part and substitute it for the corresponding part of the guidance outline.

PONCE DE LEON

1. As governor of Porto Rico
2. His explorations
3. His death

Recitation

Children organize a club to tell stories at the Old Ladies' Home, electing committees to go to the home and tell each story in the succeeding series. They take with them any illustrative material they have. These stories are practiced before the class group.

---

[1] *The National Geographic Magazine*, XLVI: 599–651 (December, 1924).
[2] Gordy, W. F., *American Beginnings in Europe*, p. 274.
[3] See page 95.

4. *Cortez conquered the Natives*

Preparation and Presentation

"Who is the only person we have studied about so far who has gone into the new country to see what it is like?" (Ponce de Leon.) "What story led him on?"

"The Spaniards wanted something else even more than a fountain of youth. What was it?" (Gold.)

"Our next story tells how a tale led another Spaniard, Cortez (*pointing to the name on the board*), to go to a place where he had heard there was gold." The class practices the pronunciation of the word *Cortez*.

"But there were people already living in the country — people to whom the gold belonged. Who?" (Indians.)

"Cortez knew this. How, then, could he get the gold for himself?

"What right would he have to take things which belonged to the Indians?

"But many times people and nations take things that belong to others, if only they are strong enough to do so. This story tells of one such time.

"Have you ever heard of Mexico?" (*Pointing to the word on the board*) "What have you heard about it? That is the country to which Cortez wished to go."

PRESENTATION TEST

Check the best answer:

a. Cortez wished to go to Mexico

    _ _ _ because he heard of a fountain of youth

    _ _ _ because he heard there was gold in Mexico

    _ _ _ because he liked to travel

b. The people living there were

    _ _ _ Indians

    _ _ _ Spanish

    _ _ _ English

c. Cortez had

    _ _ _ a right to take the gold because he was strong

    _ _ _ no right to take the Indians' gold

d. The country was called

    _ _ _ Mexico

    _ _ _ India

    _ _ _ China

Assimilation
Readings

Upper Group

ATKINSON. European Beginnings of American History, 306–313.
ATKINSON. Introduction to American History, 235–242.
BOURNE and BENTON. Introductory American History, 172–175.
BURNHAM. Hero Tales from History, 89–95.
BURNHAM. Our Beginnings in Europe and America, 244–250.
CROWE. Studies in American History, I : 47–99.
EVANS. America First, 3–9.
FOOTE and SKINNER. Explorers and Founders of America, 63–71.
GORDY. American Beginnings in Europe, 261–267.
GORDY. Leaders in Making America, 24–26.
GORDY. Stories of Early American History, 36–41.
HARDING. Old World Background to American History, 283–288, 290.
HENTY. By Right of Conquest.
JANVIER. Aztec Treasure House.
JOHNSTON. Famous Discoverers and Explorers of America, 109–187.
LANIER. The Book of Bravery, 113–145.
LAWLER. The Story of Columbus and Magellan, 73–81.
MORRIS. Heroes of Discovery in America, 68–76.
MUNROE. White Conquerors.
NIDA. The Dawn of American History in Europe, 307–309.
PLUMMER. Roy and Ray in Mexico, 132–145.
SWEETSER. Ten Great Adventurers.
TAPPAN. Our European Ancestors, 186–189.
VAN LOON. A Short History of Discovery, 104–105.
WADE. Ten Big Indians, 11–44.
WOODBURN and MORAN. Introduction to American History, 233–241.
WRIGHT. Children's Stories in American History, 103–113.
Compton's Pictured Encyclopedia (Cortez).
World Book (Cortez).

Average Group

CARROLL. Around the World, Second Book, 47–76.
COE. Founders of our Country, 41–51.
MACE. Primary History, 25–29.
PERRY and PRICE. American History, I : 59–68.
PRATT. Exploration and Discovery, 51–67.
SHAW. Discoverers and Explorers, 68–77.
SOUTHWORTH. Builders of our Country, I : 43–46.
SWAN. History and Civics, Grade 5 A, 40–52.

Lower Group

LUCIA. Stories of American Discoverers for Little Americans, 54–78.
PRATT. Beginners' Book, 37–52.

Teachers

BARSTOW. Explorers and Settlers, 111–115.
BOURNE. Spain in America, 152–158.
EGGLESTON and SEELYE. Montezuma and the Conquest of Mexico.
HART. American History told by Contemporaries, I : 49–53.

LAMPREY. Days of the Discoverers, 150–164.
RICHMAN. Spanish Conquerors, 91–138.
WALLACE. The Fair God.
Old South Leaflets, II, 35 (Cortez's description of the city of Mexico).

Minimal Essentials

Names of Persons: **Cortez** (kôr′tĕz) ; **Aztec** (ăz′tĕk)
Names of Places: **Gulf of Mexico; Mexico; Mexico City**
Historical Terms: **capital city; conquest; interpreter**
Things to Remember
　　Cortez conquered Mexico.
　　Spain became very rich because of the wealth of her new lands. Mexico belonged
　　　　to Spain until about a hundred years ago.

Illustrative Material

GABRIEL (ED.). Pageant of America, I : 128–136.
Society for Visual Education. Picturols: Mexico City ; A Trip through Old Mexico.

Procedure during Assimilation

Reading as described on pages 24–29.
Study pictures of Mexican life.
Construction projects.[1]
Children experiment with native designs.[2]
Trace the route [3] of Cortez on the map entitled "Spanish Discoveries and Explorations," each child making his own copy.
Use the helps suggested in the books.
Drill on minimal essentials.
Objective test.

Organization

　　The teacher writes the following outline on the board. Children are to write in one paragraph a summary of each part.

CORTEZ

　　　　1. His setting out from Cuba and landing in Mexico
　　　　2. His journey to the capital
　　　　3. His conquest of the city

Recitation

Continue the committee procedure described on page 102.

---

[1] Purcell, H. E., "Learning History by Doing." *History Teacher's Magazine,* VIII : 306–307.

[2] Dow, A. W., "Designs from Primitive American Motifs." *Teachers College Record,* XVI : 129–134.

[3] Gordy, W. F., *American Beginnings in Europe,* p. 266; see also text, p. 95.

5. *De Soto explored the Land far from the Sea*

Preparation

"What was Cortez seeking? Did he find it?
"Have you ever heard of the Mississippi River?"
New words in the presentation test not included in the first two thousand of the Thorndike word list nor taught in the preceding stories are

riches   Mississippi

Presentation

When news of the immense riches Cortez had found reached Spain, men were more eager than ever to go searching out the new lands. The king was very glad to let people go; he hoped they would bring him more wealth. So he gave permission to one man, De Soto (*pointing to the name previously written on the board*), to go and conquer all the land around Florida. With high hopes De Soto set out on his great expedition. It proved to be a long march, lasting throughout weary years.

Through jungle and forest and swamp they went, cutting their way through the thick underbrush, using up all their supplies, and going without food except berries and roots. Their journey reminds one strangely of Magellan's trials many years before, except that theirs was on land rather than at sea.

Worst of all, they found no gold — no wealth of any kind! To be sure, they found a great river which the Indians called the Mississippi, but what they wanted was riches. Bitterly disappointed, De Soto died in the wild land and was buried in the river he had discovered. His men made their way back to Mexico and reported that there was no gold. Therefore Spain was not interested in the great river and did not try to make settlements along its banks.

PRESENTATION TEST

Check the best answer:

  a. De Soto was looking for
    _ _ _ a great river
    _ _ _ new lands
    _ _ _ riches

b. His journey was like Magellan's
  _ _ _ because they both went by sea
  _ _ _ because they both had such a hard time
  _ _ _ because they both went around the world

c. De Soto discovered
  _ _ _ the Mississippi River
  _ _ _ Florida
  _ _ _ Mexico

d. Spain did not care much about the river
  _ _ _ because there was no gold near it
  _ _ _ because she liked land better
  _ _ _ because she had no ships

Assimilation
Readings

Upper Group

ATKINSON. European Beginnings of American History, 314.
ATKINSON. Introduction to American History, 243–244.
BASSETT. Plain Story of American History, 29–30.
BLAISDELL. Story of American History, 28–30.
BOURNE and BENTON. Introductory American History, 186–192.
BURNHAM. Hero Tales from History, 96–101.
BURNHAM. Our Beginnings in Europe and America, 253–255.
BURTON. Builders of our Nation, 56–60.
BUTTERWORTH. Zigzag Journeys in Classic Lands, 85–93.
CHANDLER and CHITWOOD. Makers of American History, 39–43.
DICKSON. New American History, 37–38.
ELLIS. Makers of our Country, 31–36.
EVANS. America First, 18–23.
FOOTE and SKINNER. Explorers and Founders of America, 47–56.
GORDY. American Beginnings in Europe, 270–274.
GORDY. Leaders in Making America, 27–29.
GORDY. Stories of Early American History, 50–54.
HARDING. Old World Background to American History, 289–290.
HART and HAZARD. Colonial Children, 16–19.
JOHNSTON. Famous Discoverers and Explorers of America, 251–270.
McMURRY. Pioneers of the Mississippi Valley, 202–218.
MORRIS. Heroes of Discovery in America, 108–118.
MONTGOMERY. Beginners' American History, 20.
NIDA. The Dawn of American History in Europe, 314–316.
TAPPAN. Elementary History of our Country, 21–23.
TAPPAN. Our European Ancestors, 191–194.
TURPIN. Brief Biographies from American History, 31–37.
VAN LOON. A Short History of Discovery, 108–109.
WETHERILL. The World and its Discovery, 224–226.
WOODBURN and MORAN. Beginner's History of the United States, 56–59.
WOODBURN and MORAN. Finders and Founders of the New World, 72–76.
WOODBURN and MORAN. Introduction to American History, 241–244.
WRIGHT. Children's Stories in American History, 172–198.
Compton's Pictured Encyclopedia (De Soto).
World Book (De Soto).

Average Group

    BALDWIN. Fourth Reader, 122–127.
    BARNES. Elementary History of the United States, 42–46.
    COE. Founders of our Country, 52–62.
    ELSON and MACMULLAN. The Story of our Country, I : 34–38.
    GORDY. American Leaders and Heroes, 22–29.
    GORDY. Elementary History of the United States, 13–15.
    HART and HAZARD. Colonial Children, 16–19.
    MACE. Primary History, 39–42.
    McMASTER. Primary History of the United States, 29, 231.
    MORRIS. Primary History of the United States, 31–33.
    MOWRY. First Steps in the History of our Country, 36–40.
    NIDA. Following Columbus, 63–73.
    PERRY and PRICE. American History, I : 78–82.
    PRATT. Exploration and Discovery, 77–83.
    SHAW. Discoverers and Explorers, 84–91.
    SOUTHWORTH. Builders of our Country, I : 50–53.
    SWAN. History and Civics, Grade 5 A, 53–61.

Lower Group

    BARNES. Primary History of the United States, 23–25.
    LUCIA. Stories of American Discoverers for Little Americans, 126–138.

Teachers

    BOURNE. Narratives of the Career of Hernando de Soto.
    BOURNE. Spain in America, 162–168.
    HART. American History told by Contemporaries, I : 57–59.
    KING. De Soto and his Men.
    Baltimore County Course of Study, 454–455.
    Old South Leaflets, II, 36 (Death of De Soto).

Minimal Essentials

Name of Person: **De Soto** (dĕ sō′tō)
Name of Place: **Mississippi** (mĭs′ĭ sĭp′ĭ) **River**
Historical Terms: **explore, explorer, exploration; score of years**[1] (after Cortez)
Things to Remember

    De Soto discovered the Mississippi River.
    His journey was "the most remarkable exploring expedition in the history of America."
    Spain did not settle in the region around the river, because there was no gold there.

Illustrative Material

BROWN. Famous Pictures : 97, De Soto discovering the Mississippi.
GABRIEL (ED.). Pageant of America, I : 143–144.
McKINLEY. Illustrated Topics for American History : S. 1, Early European Ideas of American Animals.
Perry Pictures : 1330, De Soto discovering the Mississippi.

    [1] Kelty, M. G., "Time Expressions Comprehended by Children of the Elementary School." *The Elementary School Journal*, XXV : 527, 615, 617.

Procedure during Assimilation

Reading as described on pages 24–29.

Picture study based on the illustrative material listed above.

Draw a series of three theme illustrations [1] representing (1) the setting out of the expedition, (2) the burial of De Soto, and (3) the return of the survivors to Mexico.

Do you wonder that the Indians came to hate the sight of any white man?

Add the route of De Soto [2] to the map entitled "Spanish Discoveries and Explorations," each child making his own copy.

Use the helps suggested in the books.

Drill on minimal essentials.

Objective test.

Organization

The guidance outlines of the two previous stories are placed on the board as models. With these as aids the class and teacher working together make an outline somewhat as follows:

DE SOTO

1. His early life
2. The landing of his great expedition in Florida
3. Their wanderings
4. Discovery of the Mississippi
5. Death of De Soto
6. Return of the expedition to Mexico

Recitation

Continue the committee procedure as suggested on page 102.

6. *The Spaniards built Towns in their Rich Lands*

No additional preparation and presentation are necessary.

Assimilation

Readings

Upper Group

ATKINSON. Introduction to American History, 244–247.

BEEBY. Community Life To-day and in Colonial Times, 341–342, 348–349.

BOURNE and BENTON. Introductory American History, 177–184.

BURNHAM. Our Beginnings in Europe and America, 242–244, 256–260.

---

[1] Suggestions in *The Twentieth Yearbook of the National Society for the Study of Education*, Part I, p. 112.

[2] Woodburn, J. A., and Moran, T. F., *Introduction to American History*, p. 241; Montgomery, D. H., *The Leading Facts of American History*, p. 23.

COE. Makers of the Nation, 278–282.
FORBES. Mission Tales in the Days of the Dons.
GORDY. American Beginnings in Europe, 274–277.
GORDY. Leaders in Making America, 128–135.
GREENWOOD. Our Heritage from the Old World, 391–392.
HARDING. Old World Background to American History, 290–293.
PRATT. Early Colonies, 15–24.
TAPPAN. Elementary History of our Country, 24–25.
TAPPAN. Our European Ancestors, 195–196.
WOODBURN and MORAN. Introduction to American History, 244–245.

Average Group

NIDA. Following Columbus, 73.
NIXON-ROULET. Our Little Spanish Cousin, 19–32.
PRATT. Exploration and Discovery, 115–126.

Lower Group

BASS. Stories of Pioneer Life, 13–20 (Relations with the Indians).
SNEDDEN. Docas, the Indian Boy, 57–114 (Life in a Mission).

Teachers

BOGART. Economic History of the United States, 20–21.
BOURNE. Spain in America, 202–219, 243–268, 282–301.
DAY. History of Commerce, 180–183.
HART. American History told by Contemporaries, I : 65–68.
MUZZEY. An American History, 14–15.
WEBSTER. Early European History, 635–638.
WEBSTER. General History of Commerce, 122–128.
Old South Leaflets, IV, 89 (Founding of St. Augustine).

Minimal Essentials

Names of Persons: **Spaniards; Spanish**
Names of Places: **St. Augustine** (sånt ô′gŭs tēn) ; **Santa Fe** (săn′tà fā′)
Historical Terms: **fort; galleon; Latin America**[1] **or Spanish America; mission; slaves; treasure fleet**
Things to Remember
The Spaniards built forts to protect their trade.
At first they made the Indians slaves.
Later they used negroes as slaves.
They tried to educate the Indians and make them Christians.
Descendants of the Spaniards live today in all Latin America.

Illustrative Material

GABRIEL (ED.). Pageant of America, I : 333–343 ; XIII : 19–26.
Compton's Pictured Encyclopedia (Central America, p. 681 : Treasure Trains).
Detroit Publishing Company. Little Phostint Journeys, XXIV : Missions of the Southwest.
National Geographic Magazine, XX : 119–141 ; XXIV : 228–250.
Travel, XXX : 12–15 (January, 1918) ; XL : 15–20 (November, 1922) ; XLIV : 22–26 (January, 1925).

[1] Burnham, Smith, *The Making of our Country*, pp. 12–13.

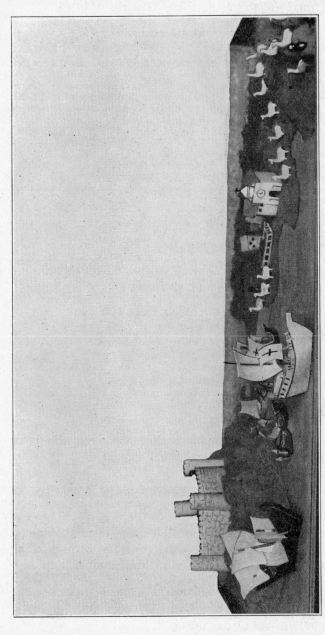

Fig. 2. Sand Table showing the Spanish Treasure Fleet

The picture shows the town of Nombre de Dios, with the Spanish galleons in the harbor. Notice the train of llamas bringing down the gold and silver from the mines. The main church of the mission is in the right foreground, and the fort at the left in the background

Procedure during Assimilation

Reading as described on pages 24–29.

Make a picture collection of scenes from Spanish America, especially those of forts and missions.

Show a Spanish town (for example, Nombre de Dios) on the sand table. On one side, coming down from the mountains, have a train of llamas loaded with bars of silver and gold. In the harbor place a fleet of Spanish galleons constituting the yearly treasure fleet. Make a mission and a fort.[1]

Find on the map Spanish names in the southwestern part of the United States. What do these names show?

What land does Spain possess in America today?

Use the following phonograph records for aid in the establishment of the right atmosphere: "Juanita," "La Paloma," "Tu Habanera."

Make a map [2] of the Western Hemisphere, showing in yellow Spain's possessions. Use the title "Spain in America."

Use the helps suggested in the books.

Drill on minimal essentials.

Objective test.

Organization

The teacher puts the following outline on the board, and the class plans the recitation on each step.

THE SPANIARDS BUILT TOWNS IN THEIR RICH LANDS

    1. The building of forts
    2. The sending of treasure back to Spain
    3. The treatment of the Indians
       a. At first slaves
       b. Missions and their work
    4. Spain in America: land owned

Recitation

The recitations based on the outline are given at a committee meeting as described on page 102.

DRILL LESSON ON THE TOPIC "SPAIN WANTED GOLD AND GOT IT"

Prepare flash cards for persons, dates, and terms, having on one side the name and on the other side the corresponding description. Use both sides for drill. For example:

[1] Bagley, W. C., "Make the Past Real." *School and Home Education,* XXXIV: 167.

[2] Fox, D. R., *Harper's Atlas of American History* (North America), p. 5; Shepherd, W. R., *Historical Atlas,* pp. 107–108.

PERSONS

DE SOTO	THE MAN WHO DISCOVERED THE MISSISSIPPI RIVER WAS _ _ _ _

DATES

1492	COLUMBUS DISCOVERED AMERICA IN _ _ _ _

TERMS

EXPLORE	TO TRAVEL IN A COUNTRY IN ORDER TO NOTE ITS FEATURES IS TO _ _ _ _

Places may best be drilled upon at the map.

For "things to remember" the class may be divided into baseball teams of nine each. The pitcher of each team is provided with a list of "things to remember" for each story. A pitcher then reads the list to the players on an opposing team to identify. Each player is given three strikes (that is, he may make two mistakes and go on, but at the third he is called out and another takes his place). Scores are counted for players who name correctly three successive "things to remember" (one score).

II. ENGLAND WAS SLOW IN STARTING AND FOUND LITTLE GOLD

1. *John Cabot discovered North America*

Preparation

"Do you remember from our overview story the next country after Spain to send out explorers?

"What was England looking for?

"Could she send men to the same places that the Spaniards had found? Why not?

"Can you find North America on this map?"

Teach any words used in the presentation test which the children do not know. All words used are either included in the first two thousand of the Thorndike word list or have been taught in previous stories.

Presentation

You remember that the king of England had been interested in Columbus's story and had been almost ready to help him. When Columbus discovered land which everybody thought was India, the king of England was probably sorry he had not furnished the ships. At any rate, only five years after Columbus's first voyage he let one of his own men, John Cabot (*pointing to the name on the board*), go to find India. Cabot came back soon and reported that he had found land. All England rejoiced, because they thought he had found the Indies.

There was no gold in the island (as they called it), so they claimed it as theirs, but soon lost interest. Many years later Magellan's voyage proved to them that their "island" was no island at all but a whole new continent. Were the English glad? No; they would rather have found the Indies. Nevertheless they said: "It is ours, anyway, no matter whether it is an island or a continent. John Cabot found it for us, so it is all ours, no matter how large it may be. He was the first man to touch North America."

England herself did not know how much land she was thus claiming for her own.

PRESENTATION TEST

Check the best answer:

  a. John Cabot sailed for which country?
    _ _ _ England
    _ _ _ Venice
    _ _ _ Spain
  b. He wanted to find
    _ _ _ an island
    _ _ _ a new world
    _ _ _ the Indies
  c. At first England thought that Cabot had found
    _ _ _ North America
    _ _ _ a new world
    _ _ _ an island of India

d. Later Magellan's voyage proved that the land was

　_ _ _ a separate continent
　_ _ _ part of India
　_ _ _ a small island

e. Because John Cabot had found it, England claimed

　_ _ _ some islands
　_ _ _ all of North America
　_ _ _ fishing grounds

Assimilation
Readings

Upper Group

ATKINSON. Introduction to American History, 217–219.
BLAISDELL. Story of American History, 26–27.
BOURNE and BENTON. Introductory American History, 159–160.
CHANDLER and CHITWOOD. Makers of American History, 30–33.
EGGLESTON. First Book in American History, 18–23.
FOOTE and SKINNER. Explorers and Founders of America, 87–90.
GORDY. American Beginnings in Europe, 250–252, 279–280.
GORDY. Leaders in Making America, 30–31.
GORDY. Stories of Early American History, 15–16.
HARDING. Old World Background to American History, 276–278.
HARDING. Story of Europe, 278–279.
LOGIE. From Columbus to Lincoln, 12–14.
MONTGOMERY. Beginners' American History, 14–18.
MORRIS. Heroes of Discovery in America, 32–38.
NIDA. The Dawn of American History in Europe, 297–298.
TAPPAN. Elementary History of our Country, 13–15.
TAPPAN. Our European Ancestors, 173–174.
VAN LOON. A Short History of Discovery, 90–91.
WOODBURN and MORAN. Beginner's History of the United States, 37–43.
WOODBURN and MORAN. Finders and Founders of the New World, 48–54.
WOODBURN and MORAN. Introduction to American History, 220–222.
WRIGHT. Children's Stories in American History, 61–64.
Compton's Pictured Encyclopedia (Cabot).
World Book (Cabot).

Average Group

BARNES. Elementary History of the United States, 25–29.
BEARD and BAGLEY. A First Book in American History, 26–29.
COE. Founders of our Country, 75–79.
ELSON and MACMULLAN. The Story of our Country, I : 27–29.
FORMAN. First Lessons in American History, 22–23.
GORDY. Elementary History of the United States, 17–18.
MACE. Primary History, 42–45.
McMASTER. Primary History of the United States, 44.
MORRIS. Primary History of the United States, 25–28.
MOWRY. First Steps in the History of our Country, 30–35.
NIDA. Following Columbus, 44–47.
SHAW. Discoverers and Explorers, 44–47.
SOUTHWORTH. Builders of our Country, I : 37–40.
SWAN. History and Civics, Grade 5 A, 63–69.
TURPIN. Brief Biographies from American History, 37–40.

Lower Group

BARNES. Primary History of the United States, 21.
BLAISDELL and BALL. Child's Book of American History, 8–11.
DAVIS. Stories of the United States, 53–55.
LUCIA. Stories of American Discoverers for Little Americans, 33–38.
WILSON. A History Reader, 58–61.
Flanagan Publishing Company. Henry Hudson and Other Explorers, 5–9.

Teachers

BOURNE. Spain in America, 54–66.
GRIFFIS. Romance of Discovery, 105–111.
HART. American History told by Contemporaries, I : 69–72.
LAMPREY. Days of the Discoverers, 81–93.
TYLER. England in America, 6–7, 8–9.
WOOD. Elizabethan Sea Dogs, 1–17.
American Citizenship Course in United States History, Book II : 140–157.
Baltimore County Course of Study, 452.
Elementary School Journal, XVII : 553. (Teaching suggestions.)
Old South Leaflets, II, 37 ; V, 115.

Minimal Essentials

Name of Person: **John Cabot** (kăb'ŭt)
Names of Places: **England; North America**
Date: **1497** — John Cabot discovered North America.
Historical Terms: **claims** (to land) ; **mainland**
Things to Remember
   John Cabot discovered the mainland of North America in 1497.
   Because of his voyages England later claimed all of the eastern coast of North America.

Illustrative Material

GABRIEL (ED.). Pageant of America, I : 112–113.
National Geographic Magazine, XL : 22–23 (1921), Fish from the Banks.

Procedure during Assimilation

Reading as described on pages 24–29.
Draw the English flag[1] which John Cabot planted on the shore of Labrador (see Webster's Dictionary).
Why is John Cabot said to have discovered North America when the Northmen had found it almost five hundred years before?
Begin a map entitled "England in America." Trace the route[2] of the Cabots. Each child should make his own map.
Use the helps suggested in the books.
Drill[3] on minimal essentials.
Objective test.

[1] *National Geographic Magazine*, XXXII : 338 (October, 1917).
[2] Atkinson, A. M., *Introduction to American History*, p. 231.
[3] Johnson, George E., *Education by Plays and Games*, p. 200, for character games.

Organization

The class is asked to pick out three important parts of the story of John Cabot and write a sentence about each. These are read in class and the best are selected to put on the board.

Recitation

Organize a public-speaking club[1] to meet during the step of recitation at the end of each story of the present unit. Elect officers, and have a formal program, announced by the president. This program should consist of oral stories based on the organization step.

2. *John Hawkins started the English Slave Trade*

Preparation

"When we studied about the Spanish towns, we learned that Spain would not let them trade with anybody but herself. How would England like that?

"We learned too that after a while the Indians were no longer made slaves. Who then would do the work?" (Negroes.) "The negroes lived in Africa. Our story today shows how they were brought over to the New World."

In the presentation test occurs a new word, *slavery*. It may need to be taught here.

Presentation

Spain was having a hard time to get people to work for her, now that the Indians could no longer be made slaves. All the traders knew it. The son of one of the English traders had a good idea. He decided that he would furnish people to work for Spain! He would go down to Africa where there were many black people, take them on board his vessel, sail away to the West Indies, and sell them to the Spaniards there at a very high price. What an adventure that would be! And at the same time he would grow rich. Of course it was against the law of Spain, but what cared he?

[1] Similar to the "Literary Society." *The Twentieth Yearbook of the National Society for the Study of Education*, Part I, p. 77.

The plan was carried out. John Hawkins, for that was his name (*pointing to the word previously written on the board*), did go to Africa and did sell the negroes he secured there to the Spaniards in the West Indies. The king of Spain was very angry, since he wanted all the trade for himself. But he could not catch John Hawkins.

So the king sent a message to the queen of England, saying: "Why do you let your people come to my country and trade when you know I do not want them to do so? You ought to make them stay at home. If I catch any of them I will hang them." The queen pretended that she was sorry, but she was not.

So year after year Spain kept getting angrier and angrier. Trouble was sure to come of it. And trouble *did* come, but not in today's story.

PRESENTATION TEST

Check the best answer:

a. The Spanish people in America at first used as slaves the

    _ _ _ English
    _ _ _ Indians
    _ _ _ black people

b. After they could not use the Indians, they wanted

    _ _ _ yellow people
    _ _ _ red people
    _ _ _ black people

c. John Hawkins got his slaves from

    _ _ _ Africa
    _ _ _ India
    _ _ _ Portugal

d. The king of Spain was angry at Hawkins

    _ _ _ because he did not believe in slavery
    _ _ _ because he did not like the English
    _ _ _ because he wanted the trade for himself

Assimilation

Readings

Upper Group

ATKINSON. European Beginnings of American History, 374–379.
ATKINSON. Introduction to American History, 270–275.
BOURNE and BENTON. Introductory American History, 230.
GORDY. American Beginnings in Europe, 287–288.

JONES. Geography by Discovery, 117–122.
SANFORD. Story of Agriculture in the United States, 54.
TAPPAN. In the Days of Queen Elizabeth, 208–212.
WALLING. A Sea Dog of Devon.
WOOD. Elizabethan Sea Dogs, 34, 74–94, 223–226.
WOODBURN and MORAN. Introduction to American History, 253.
World Book (Hawkins).

Average Group

BARNES. Elementary History of the United States, 48–50.
SOUTHWORTH. Builders of our Country, I : 54–57.

Lower Group

FAIRGRIEVE and YOUNG. The World, 157–160.
SCHWARTZ. Five Little Strangers, 72–102 (Slave Trade).

Teachers

BARSTOW. Explorers and Settlers, 84–96.
GRIFFIS. Romance of Discovery, 183–194.
HART. American History told by Contemporaries, I : 73–81.
PHILLIPS. American Negro Slavery, 9–66.
TILLINGHAST. Negro in Africa and America, 102–228.
TYLER. England in America, 9–10.
WOOD. Elizabethan Sea Dogs, 71–94.

Minimal Essentials

Name of Person: **John Hawkins** (hô′kĭnz) [1]
Name of Place: **west coast of Africa**
Historical Terms: **against the law; slave trade**
Things to Remember
　John Hawkins took negroes from Africa and sold them to the West Indies as
　　slaves.
　Spain was very angry at England for allowing him to do this.

Illustrative Material

GABRIEL (ED.). Pageant of America, I : 156.
MCKINLEY. Illustrated Topics for American History : S. 23, Pictures of a slave ship and a
slave market.

Procedure during Assimilation

Reading as described on pages 24–29.
Study the pictures in McKinley's *Illustrated Topics for American History* referred to
　above.
Make a speech to convince John Hawkins that he ought not to engage in the slave
　trade.
Did Spain have any right to object to Hawkins's expedition?
Use the helps suggested in the books.
Drill on minimal essentials.
Objective test.

[1] Not included in the standard lists mentioned on p. 5.

Organization

The teacher and the class together select the main points of the story somewhat as follows:

JOHN HAWKINS

1. Need of the Spanish settlers for laborers
2. Hawkins's successful trading trips
3. Spain's anger

Recitation

The public-speaking society as described on page 117.

3. *Francis Drake sailed around the World, but found No Rich Lands like Spain's*

Preparation

"Do you remember about the time that John Hawkins had his ships destroyed in the West Indies? Tell us about it. He had with him on that trip a young man who then and there vowed to get even with Spain. His name was Francis Drake." (*Pointing to the name already written on the board.*)

No words are included in the presentation test which are not in the first two thousand of the Thorndike word list or which have not been taught in previous stories. However, if there are any that the children do not know, they should be taught here.

Have ready a map of the world.

Presentation

Drake decided that the best way to get even with Spain was to stop the yearly treasure fleets and rob them; then the king of Spain would have no money. Today we would call him a pirate, but people looked on such things differently then. He sailed down this coast of South America (*tracing on a map the eastern coast*), and then up this coast (*west*), robbing ships and sacking towns as he went. It was a great life, exciting and interesting and dangerous. He went away up to here (*San Francisco*). By that time he had so much plunder that he was ready to go home. But how? If he went back around South America, the Spaniards would be watching and waiting for him. He could not surprise them again! He decided to sail clear around the world as Magellan had done. (*Show the route.*)

He reached home a very rich man. The queen was so much pleased that she knighted him on board his ship, and after that he was *Sir* Francis Drake. You may be sure that the king of Spain was furious. He kept saying to himself: "Those rascally Englishmen think they can rob my ships and kill my sailors any time they please. Just wait! Some day I will attack England and conquer and destroy them all!" But Sir Francis Drake only laughed.

PRESENTATION TEST

Check the best answer:

a. Drake got even with Spain by
 _ _ _ robbing her treasure ships
 _ _ _ fighting her army
 _ _ _ burning the king's house

b. He sailed around the coasts of
 _ _ _ Europe
 _ _ _ South America
 _ _ _ Africa

c. When he came to a Spanish ship he would
 _ _ _ go right by it
 _ _ _ stop for a visit
 _ _ _ rob it

d. Drake was the first
 _ _ _ man
 _ _ _ sailor
 _ _ _ Englishman
 who sailed around the world

e. Drake's voyage made the king of Spain
 _ _ _ angry
 _ _ _ happy
 _ _ _ sick

Assimilation

Readings

Upper Group

ATKINSON. European Beginnings of American History, 379–382.
ATKINSON. Introduction to American History, 275–278.
BOURNE and BENTON. Introductory American History, 229–234.
BURNHAM. Hero Tales from History, 102–109.
BURNHAM. Our Beginnings in Europe and America, 265–269.

BURTON. Builders of our Nation, 61–69, 72–73.
CROWE. Studies in American History, I : 120–127.
FARIS. Real Stories of the Geography Makers, 93–98.
FOOTE and SKINNER. Explorers and Founders of America, 91–102.
GORDY. American Beginnings in Europe, 287–293.
GORDY. Leaders in Making America, 31–34.
GORDY. Stories of Early American History, 58–62.
HARDING. Old World Background to American History, 302–303, 323.
HENTY. Under Drake's Flag.
JONES. Geography by Discovery, 82–97.
McMURRY. Pioneers of the Rocky Mountains, 201–224.
MILLER. My Bookhouse, IV : 11.
NIDA. The Dawn of American History in Europe, 360–361.
TAPPAN. In the Days of Queen Elizabeth, 212–226.
TAPPAN. Our European Ancestors, 204–207, 214, 226–235.
TERRY. History Stories of Other Lands, V : 141–145, 148–149.
WOODBURN and MORAN. Beginner's History of the United States, 69–72.
WOODBURN and MORAN. Finders and Founders of the New World, 78–84.
WOODBURN and MORAN. Introduction to American History, 253–256, 274–275.
Compton's Pictured Encyclopedia (Drake).
World Book (Drake).

Average Group

BARNES. Elementary History of the United States, 47–54.
BEARD and BAGLEY. A First Book in American History, 38–44, 47.
COE. Founders of our Country, 80–97.
ELSON and MacMULLAN. The Story of our Country, I : 39–44.
FORMAN. First Lessons in American History, 26–30.
GORDY. Elementary History of the United States, 18–20.
MACE. Primary History, 45–49.
MORRIS. Primary History of the United States, 35–36.
NIDA. Following Columbus, 107–117.
PRATT. Exploration and Discovery, 127–136.
SHAW. Discoverers and Explorers, 108–113.
SOUTHWORTH. Builders of our Country, I : 57–62.
SWAN. History and Civics, Grade 5 A, 69–79, 81–82.
TAPPAN. American Hero Stories, 24–37.
TURPIN. Brief Biographies from American History, 41–46.

Lower Group

BALDWIN. Thirty More Famous Stories Retold, 17–22.
DAVIS. Stories of the United States, 55–57.
LUCIA. Stories of American Discoverers for Little Americans, 139–150.

Teachers

BARSTOW. Explorers and Settlers, 122–123.
CORBETT. Drake and the Tudor Navy.
FRYER. Book of Boyhoods, 34–41.
GRIFFIS. Romance of Discovery, 195–206.
HART. American History told by Contemporaries, I : 81–88.
LAMPREY. Days of the Discoverers, 215–236.
TYLER. England in America, 10–13.
WOOD. Elizabethan Sea Dogs, 95–191, 223–229.
Old South Leaflets, V, 116.

Minimal Essentials

Names of Persons: **Sir Francis Drake** (drāk); **English**
Names of Places: **Pacific coast of North America; Spanish Main** [1] (northern coast
of South America); **South Sea; California**
Historical Terms: **confer knighthood; decade** [2] (six decades after Magellan);
pirate; sack (of a city); **attack**
Things to Remember
Sir Francis Drake was the first Englishman to circumnavigate the globe.
He made Spain angry by sacking her towns and capturing her fleets.

Illustrative Material

GABRIEL (ED.). Pageant of America, I: 162–164, 166.
PYLE. Book of the American Spirit, 4, 7.

Procedure during Assimilation

Reading as described on pages 24–29.
A special book report by some child who has read Henty's *Under Drake's Flag.*
Make a *Book of Sir Francis Drake,* containing pictures cut from old books, drawings
of the *Pelican,* a map, and the paragraphs written during the step of Organiza-
tion. The shape of the booklet may be that of the hull of a vessel.
Had Spain any cause to feel angry at Drake?
Add the route [3] of Sir Francis Drake to the map already begun, "England in
America," each child making his own copy.
Use the helps suggested in the books.
Drill on minimal essentials.
Objective test.

Organization

The teacher writes the following outline on the board. The
children are to make paragraphs about each point for their
booklets.

SIR FRANCIS DRAKE

1. Drake's trip with Hawkins
2. His voyage to plunder South America
3. His trip around the world
4. His return to England

Recitation

The writing and correcting of the paragraphs for the *Book
of Sir Francis Drake.*

---

[1] See the Century Cyclopedia of Names and the Century Dictionary.

[2] Kelty, M. G., "Time Expressions Comprehended by Children of the Elementary School," *The Elementary School Journal,* XXV: 527, 615, 617.

[3] Woodburn, J. A., and Moran, T. F., *Introduction to American History,* p. 255;
Montgomery, D. H., *The Leading Facts of American History,* p. 29.

4. *Walter Raleigh tried to build Towns, but Failed*

Preparation

"Have you ever heard of Virginia? Do you know how it came to be called Virginia?

"Who was queen of England during Drake's time?

"What had Drake wanted to get from the New World?"

If there are any unfamiliar words in the presentation test, teach them here.

Presentation

All the people we have heard about so far, English and Spanish alike, have been interested in the New World only because it could send out gold. They wanted to come to America, stay as short a time as possible, collect all the riches they could carry, and go back to the Old World to enjoy themselves.

Now we learn about a man who had a different idea. He said: "What we ought to do is to bring some of our English people over to the New World, give every one of them land enough for a farm, build towns, and tell them to plan to live there the rest of their lives. I, for one, will go there to live." His name was Walter Raleigh (*pointing to the name previously written on the board*).

But Queen Elizabeth (*the name also on the board*) loved Walter Raleigh very much. So she said: "No, we need you here at our court. You must not go, but you may send others."

Raleigh was disappointed, but he did not give up. He gathered together ships and men and sent them to' Virginia. They stayed a while and then came back. Instead of being discouraged he bought more ships and supplies and sent out more men. They disappeared. So it went, year after year, until Raleigh was an old man, with all his money spent. People thought he was a failure in life, but he was not; he was the father of a great idea. His idea was to make of the New World a home for English people, and not just a place from which to secure riches.

PRESENTATION TEST

Check the best answer:

a. The people before Walter Raleigh used the New World

    _ _ _ as a home

    _ _ _ as a place to get riches

    _ _ _ as a place to visit

b. Raleigh wanted to make the New World

    _ _ _ a home for English people

    _ _ _ a place to get riches

    _ _ _ a place to visit

Assimilation

Readings

Upper Group

ANDREWS. Ten Boys who lived on the Road from Long Ago to Now, 171–192.

ATKINSON. European Beginnings of American History, 382.

ATKINSON. Introduction to American History, 278–279.

BEEBY. Community Life Today and in Colonial Times, 222–225.

BLAISDELL. Story of American History, 31–34.

BOURNE and BENTON. Introductory American History, 241–248.

BURNHAM. Hero Tales from History, 109–114.

BURNHAM. Our Beginnings in Europe and America, 270–271.

CHANDLER and CHITWOOD. Makers of American History, 44–50.

CHURCH. Stories from English History, 412–420.

EVANS. America First, 23–31.

FOOTE and SKINNER. Explorers and Founders of America, 103–111.

GORDY. American Beginnings in Europe, 284–287, 323–328.

GORDY. American Leaders and Heroes, 31–40.

GORDY. Colonial Days, 4.

GORDY. Leaders in Making America, 34–39.

GORDY. Stories of Early American History, 63–69.

HARDING. Old World Background to American History, 300, 330–337.

JONES. Geography by Discovery, 99–111.

MARSHALL. An Island Story, 342–345.

MONTGOMERY. Beginners' American History, 22–25.

MORRIS. Heroes of Discovery in America, 166–175.

NIDA. The Dawn of American History in Europe, 361–363.

TAPPAN. Elementary History of our Country, 26–31.

TAPPAN. In the Days of Queen Elizabeth, 231–244.

TAPPAN. Our European Ancestors, 242–246.

TERRY. History Stories of Other Lands, V: 160–170.

VAN LOON. A Short History of Discovery, 116–117.

WARREN. Stories from English History, 242–247.

WOODBURN and MORAN. Beginner's History of the United States, 72–75, 77–78.

WOODBURN and MORAN. Finders and Founders of the New World, 84–92.

WOODBURN and MORAN. Introduction to American History, 250–252, 288–293.

Compton's Pictured Encyclopedia (Raleigh).

World Book (Raleigh).

Average Group

BARNES. Elementary History of the United States, 55–56, 58–62.

BEARD and BAGLEY. A First Book in American History, 47–48.

COE. Founders of our Country, 98–110.
ELSON and MACMULLAN. The Story of our Country, I: 45–50.
FORMAN. First Lessons in American History, 32–37.
GORDY. Elementary History of the United States, 20–23.
INGRAHAM. Story of Democracy, 146–148.
MACE. Primary History, 49–54.
MCMURRY. Pioneers on Land and Sea, 47–67.
MORRIS. Primary History of the United States, 36–37.
MOWRY. First Steps in the History of our Country, 41–47.
NIDA. Following Columbus, 146–156.
SOUTHWORTH. Builders of our Country, I: 64–72.
SWAN. History and Civics, Grade 5 A, 83–92.
TURPIN. Brief Biographies from American History, 46–51.
WRIGHT. Children's Stories in American History, 254–258.

Lower Group

BALDWIN. Fifty Famous Stories Retold, 54–57.
DAVIS. Stories of the United States, 59–61.
LEWIS and ROWLAND. Silent Readers, IV: 86–90.
WAYLAND. History Stories for Primary Grades, 13–14, 89–90.
WELSH. Colonial Days, 5–24.
WILSON. A History Reader, 90–92.

Teachers

BARSTOW. Explorers and Settlers, 78–81.
FRYER. Book of Boyhoods, 42–50.
GRIFFIS. Romance of Discovery, 207–216.
HART. American History told by Contemporaries, I: 96–101.
LAMPREY. Days of the Discoverers, 238–249.
TOWLE. Raleigh.
TYLER. England in America, 21–28, 32–33.
WOOD. Elizabethan Sea Dogs, 205–222.
Baltimore County Course of Study, 456–457.

Minimal Essentials

Name of Person: **Walter Raleigh** (rô′lǐ)
Names of Places: **eastern coast of North America; Virginia**
Historical Terms: **courtier; failure**
Things to Remember
   Walter Raleigh tried hard to found colonies for England in the New World.
He failed, but his idea lived on.

Illustrative Material

GABRIEL (ED.). Pageant of America, I: 7–8, 159–161.
LONGMAN. Historical Illustrations: Pictures of English Court Life.
Mentor, X: 26 (December, 1922): Queen Elizabeth.

Procedure during Assimilation

Reading as described on pages 24–29.
Picture study based on the illustrative material listed above.
Make a list of the things colonists would have to do when they tried to found a
   colony in America. Begin at the time they left the ship and chronicle every
   task confronting them. Do you wonder that they failed?

The class dresses dolls [1] in the costumes of an English court gentleman, a court lady, a serving man, a serving woman.
Find on the map the city of Raleigh, North Carolina.
Use the helps suggested in the books.
Drill on minimal essentials.
Objective test.

Organization

Children and teacher working together make an outline of the main points of the story somewhat similar to the following:

Sir Walter Raleigh

1. How he won the queen's favor
2. His first colony
3. His second colony
4. His later years

Recitation

The public-speaking club as described on page 117 gives the stories based on the outline.

5. *At last England beat Spain at Sea; then she could send out Ships where she Pleased*

Preparation

"How many reasons has Spain had so far to make her hate England?
"What do you suppose she will do about it?"

Presentation

While English ships had been thus constantly attacking Spain, you may be sure that the king of Spain was not idle. He set to work to build the greatest fleet that the world had ever known and to conquer England. It took years, but at last all his ships were ready. He sent this great Armada (*pointing to the word on the board*) to fight against the English, expecting to win an easy victory.

However, the English fought much better than he had expected, and a great storm came up, which wrecked many of

---

[1] Diez, W., *Zur Geschichte der Costüme*, pp. 1090–1091.

his vessels. Of all that great fleet which started so proudly from Spain only fifty limped home again with their story of failure.

Never again did Spain send ships to conquer England, and never again did England fear Spain at sea. Before this, Spain had been stronger on the ocean than any other country; but she was strongest no longer. England now might go where she pleased, and might send out ships to her lands in the New World without fear. We should expect soon to see many more English vessels sailing the seas than before the defeat of the great Spanish Armada.

PRESENTATION TEST

Check the best answer:

a. At the beginning of our story the country that was strongest on the sea was
- _ _ _ Spain
- _ _ _ England
- _ _ _ Portugal

b. The Armada was a fleet of a great many ships that belonged to
- _ _ _ Spain
- _ _ _ England
- _ _ _ Portugal

c. The great fight was won by
- _ _ _ Spain
- _ _ _ England
- _ _ _ Portugal

d. After that, England
- _ _ _ took away all the Spanish gold
- _ _ _ took Spanish towns for her own
- _ _ _ could send ships to the New World without fear

Assimilation

Readings

Upper Group

ATKINSON. Introduction to American History, 264–268.
BARSTOW. Explorers and Settlers, 68–77.
BOURNE and BENTON. Introductory American History, 236–238.
BURNHAM. Our Beginnings in Europe and America, 271–277.
BURTON. Builders of our Nation, 70–72.
CROWE. Studies in American History, I : 129–133.
EGGLESTON. Our First Century, 7–9.
GORDY. American Beginnings in Europe, 311–319.
GREENWOOD. Our Heritage from the Old World, 414–421.
HARDING. Old World Background to American History, 321–329.
MARSHALL. An Island Story, 338–341.
NIDA. The Dawn of American History in Europe, 340–345.

PYLE. Book of Pirates, 3–38.
TAPPAN. Elementary History of our Country, 30–31.
TAPPAN. In the Days of Queen Elizabeth, 263–279.
TAPPAN. Our European Ancestors, 229–237.
TERRY. History Stories of Other Lands, V : 150–159.
WOODBURN and MORAN. Introduction to American History, 270–281.
Compton's Pictured Encyclopedia (Armada).
World Book (Armada).

Average Group
BEARD and BAGLEY. A First Book in American History, 45–47.
FORMAN. First Lessons in American History, 30–31.
MACE. Primary History, 49–50.
NIDA. Following Columbus, 118–120.
SWAN. History and Civics, Grade 5 A, 79–81.
TAPPAN. European Hero Stories, 209–214.
TERRY. History Stories of Other Lands, II : 103–111.

Lower Group
Try MACE, NIDA, or TERRY (from the list for the Average Group).

Teachers
BARSTOW. Explorers and Settlers, 68–77.
ROBINSON and BREASTED. Outlines of European History, I : 644.
WEBSTER. Early European History, 677–679.
WOOD. Elizabethan Sea Dogs, 149–191.

Minimal Essentials

Name of Person: **Queen Elizabeth**
Names of Places: **the Channel; Scotland**
Date: **1588** — England defeated the Spanish Armada.
Historical Terms: **Armada** (är mä′dà); **fleet; defeat; naval**
Things to Remember
England defeated the Spanish Armada in 1588.
After that, England no longer feared Spain at sea, so she could send ships to the New World.

Illustrative Material

ARNOLD. Historical Pictures: A. H. P. 40, The Armada in the Channel.
GABRIEL (ED.). Pageant of America, I : 167–170.
LONGMAN. Historical Wall Pictures: The Armada in the Channel.
MCKINLEY. Illustrated Topics for Mediæval and Modern History: M. M. 14, The Spanish Armada.

Procedure during Assimilation

Reading as described on pages 24–29.
Picture-study lessons on the illustrative material listed above.
Add a paragraph to the *Book of Sir Francis Drake*, describing the part he took in the defeat of the Armada.
The class makes original poems on the story of the Armada.
What other fleet was recently sunk off the coast of Scotland (at Scapa Flow)?
Use the helps suggested in the books.
Drill on minimal essentials.
Objective test.

Organization

The teacher puts the following outline on the board and requires the pupils to substitute in each case a summary sentence for the topic suggested.

THE SPANISH ARMADA

1. Reasons why it was sent
2. Preparations in Spain
3. Preparations in England
4. The fight
5. Results

Recitation

Continue the public-speaking club as described on page 117.

A drill lesson should be given at this point, similar to that described on pages 112–113.

Example of an original poem by a 4-A child:

THE ARMADA

Sir Francis Drake was bowling
When the Armada came in sight,
The Great Armada floating, floating into sight.
Drake just calmly watched the sight
And then he got ready to fight.

The Spanish ships were longer
But the English ships were stronger.

HAMILTON

III. FRANCE, TOO, WAS SLOW; SHE FOUND NO GOLD, BUT MANY FURS

1. *Cartier found a Great River leading into the Country*

Preparation

"Do you remember from our overview story who it was that wanted to know whether Father Adam had said Spain and England could have all the land in the world?

"Do you know what Canada is? Our next story is about Canada many years ago."

Teach any unfamiliar words occurring in the presentation test.

Children practice the pronunciation of the name *Cartier*.

A wall map of the world will be needed.

Presentation

When John Cabot came home to England, you remember that he told about the great quantities of fish he saw, fish so plentiful that his ship could scarcely sail through the water! Ever since then France had been coming over to the New World and fishing. Her men built rude shelters on the little islands and dried their catch there. When winter came, they went back to France and stayed at home until the next spring. But catching fish is slow and uninteresting business when one hears all the time stories of the riches Magellan's men brought home and of Cortez's great wealth taken from the Aztecs.

The king of France wished very much to reach the Indies, which had so rich a trade. He knew by this time that South America stood in the way. Magellan had proved that. But couldn't he sail through here (*indicating the northwestern route*)? Nobody knew whether he could or not.

So he sent out a good sailor, Cartier (*pointing to the name previously written on the board*), who happened to reach here (*pointing to a map showing the St. Lawrence River*). He found that he could sail on and on far up into the land. Surely this must be the way to China! But alas, the farther he went the narrower grew the passage, until Cartier became convinced that it was only a river.

However, sailing up this river was a very easy way to go to any part of France's new land — much easier than walking overland, as Cortez and De Soto had had to do. So the king of France said: "Very well. I am sorry we did not find China; but since it is so easy to sail up the great river into any part of our new country, we will keep it all and call it New France."

PRESENTATION TEST

Check the right answer:

  a. For a long time France had been coming to the New World
  _ _ _ to find gold
  _ _ _ to fish
  _ _ _ to fight

  b. The king of France wanted to find a way
  _ _ _ to sail up into the country
  _ _ _ to find more fish
  _ _ _ to go to China

    c. Cartier thought his river was a way to go

         _ _ _ to China

         _ _ _ to America

         _ _ _ to France

    d. Finding the river was a good thing, because

         _ _ _ men could go to any part of the new land by water

         _ _ _ it kept all other people away

         _ _ _ it was the way to go to China

Assimilation

Readings

Upper Group

ATKINSON. Introduction to American History, 244.

BEEBY. Community Life Today and in Colonial Times, 316–317.

BOURNE and BENTON. Introductory American History, 204, 216–218.

FOOTE and SKINNER. Explorers and Founders of America, 187–193.

GORDY. American Beginnings in Europe, 259–260, 296–297.

GORDY. Leaders in Making America, 104.

GORDY. Stories of Early American History, 55–57.

GREENWOOD. Our Heritage from the Old World, 398–399.

HARDING. Old World Background to American History, 310–311.

JONES. Geography by Discovery, 63–70.

LOGIE. From Columbus to Lincoln, 16–18.

MORRIS. Heroes of Discovery in America, 129–136.

NIDA. The Dawn of American History in Europe, 348–350.

TAPPAN. Elementary History of our Country, 20–21.

TAPPAN. Our European Ancestors, 183–184.

WOODBURN and MORAN. Introduction to American History, 229–232.

WRIGHT. Children's Stories in American History, 210–227.

Compton's Pictured Encyclopedia (Cartier).

World Book (Cartier).

Average Group

BEARD and BAGLEY. A First Book in American History, 32–34.

GORDY. Elementary History of the United States, 103–104.

McMASTER. Primary History of the United States, 31–33.

MORRIS. Primary History of the United States, 33–34.

NIDA. Following Columbus, 75–81.

PRATT. Exploration and Discovery, 68–76.

SOUTHWORTH. Builders of our Country, I : 144–148.

SWAN. History and Civics, Grade 5 A, 106–112.

Lower Group

BARNES. Primary History of the United States, 23.

LUCIA. Stories of American Discoverers for Little Americans, 113–125 (story of Verrazano also).

Flanagan Publishing Company. Henry Hudson and Other Explorers, 10–11.

Teachers

BOURNE. Spain in America, 145–148.

GRIFFIS. Romance of Discovery, 134–145.

HART. American History told by Contemporaries, I : 107–112.
LAMPREY. Days of the Discoverers, 167–180.
MUNRO. Crusaders of New France, 15–31.
THWAITES. France in America, 7–10.

Minimal Essentials

Names of Persons: **Cartier** (kär'tyā') ; **French**
Names of Places: **France; Montreal** (mŏnt'rĕ ôl') ; **St. Lawrence River**
Historical Term: **attempt**
Things to Remember
  Cartier discovered the St. Lawrence River and claimed it for France.
  It was easy to sail up the St. Lawrence River into the new land.

Illustrative Material

GABRIEL (ED.). Pageant of America, I : 121, 287–290.
PYLE. Book of the American Spirit, 121.

Procedure during Assimilation

Reading as described on pages 24–29.
Model in the sand table North America east of the Mississippi. Plant Cartier's
  wooden cross [1] at the mouth of the St. Lawrence. Mark the site of Quebec and
  Montreal. Place stones to indicate the Lachine Rapids.
Write a letter that Cartier might have written to the king of France during the
  winter he stayed at Quebec. Describe his experiences.
In what way is the name *Lachine* the record of a mistake? The name *Indians?*
Begin a map entitled "France in America," using an outline map of North America.
  Trace on it Cartier's route.[2] Each child should make his own copy.
Drill on minimal essentials.
Objective test.

Organization

The teacher and the class working together select the
following points as the basis for recitation :

CARTIER

  1. His first trip : discovering the St. Lawrence
  2. His second trip : sailing up the river
  3. Attempt to build a colony at Quebec

Recitation

Divide the class into two teams. Award a pennant to the
team which gives the best speeches. High-school debaters
may be the judges. The pennant is to be kept by the winning
team until an adverse decision is made on a unit of work.

---

[1] Woodburn, J. A., and Moran, T. F., *Introduction to American History*, p. 229.
[2] Stephenson, N. W., *An American History*, p. 15.

2. *Champlain built Towns and made Friends with the Indians*

Preparation

"Do you remember what great idea Walter Raleigh had which no Englishman had had before?" (Bringing English people to America to live.)

"The Frenchman about whom we read today decided France ought to do the same thing. Why could he trade in furs better if he built towns?"

Presentation

You remember that Cartier had tried to build a town, but had failed. Many many years went by before anyone had the courage to try again. At last a wise Frenchman named Champlain (*pointing to the word previously written on the board*) said: "It would be better to build a town in some strong place on our great river. We could trade in furs with the Indians much better. Then they would always know where to find us; now they cannot tell when we are coming, nor just where we are to be. I know a good place on the top of a high hill."

So he came to this place (*showing on the sand-table map*) and built a town, which stands there to this day. Then he went farther and farther west and explored many lakes. He had exciting adventures on the way. One of his men led him hundreds of miles out of the way by a story that was not true. Later, in a battle with the Indians, he was badly hurt and had to be carried about in a big basket. Because of his work New France kept growing larger. Champlain did so much to make it grow that he is called the "father of New France."

PRESENTATION TEST

Check the best answer:

   a. Champlain wanted to build a town in order

      _ _ _ to fight the Indians better

      _ _ _ to make it easier to trade with the Indians

      _ _ _ to live with the Indians

   b. He is called the father of New France

      _ _ _ because he was the first Frenchman in America

      _ _ _ because he named New France

      _ _ _ because he did so much to make it grow

Assimilation
Readings

Upper Group

BEEBY. Community Life Today and in Colonial Times, 318–319.
BURNHAM. Hero Tales from History, 151–160.
CROWE. Studies in American History, I : 137–156, 162–166.
EGGLESTON. Our First Century, 160–164.
FOOTE and SKINNER. Explorers and Founders of America, 195–203, 205–206.
GORDY. Leaders in Making America, 105–106.
GORDY. Stories of Early American History, 121–122.
HARDING. Old World Background to American History, 311–312.
JOHNSTON. Famous Discoverers and Explorers of America, 273–280.
LOGIE. From Columbus to Lincoln, 41–46.
McMURRY. Pioneers on Land and Sea, 1–10, 21–34.
MORRIS. Heroes of Discovery in America, 198–208.
NIDA. The Dawn of American History in Europe, 350–351.
PRATT. Early Colonies, 76–81.
TAPPAN. Elementary History of our Country, 114–115.
WOODBURN and MORAN. Finders and Founders of the New World, 195–197.
Compton's Pictured Encyclopedia (Champlain).
World Book (Champlain).

Average Group

COE. Founders of our Country, 111–115, 120–122.
FIELD. Fourth Reader, 293–296.
FORMAN. First Lessons in American History, 47–49.
GORDY. Elementary History of the United States, 104.
McMASTER. Primary History of the United States, 33.
NIDA. Following Columbus, 83–86, 90–91, 94–95.
SOUTHWORTH. Builders of our Country, I : 153–156.
SWAN. History and Civics, Grade 5 A, 113–118, 120–122.
TAPPAN. American Hero Stories, 49–53, 55–59.
TURPIN. Brief Biographies from American History, 94–100.

Lower Group

LEWIS and ROWLAND. Silent Readers, IV : 137–144.
LUCIA. Stories of American Discoverers for Little Americans, 151–155.
Flanagan Publishing Company. Henry Hudson and Other Explorers, 13–16.

Teachers

GRANT (ED.). Voyages of Samuel de Champlain.
GRIFFIS. Romance of Discovery, 258–261, 265–268.
HART. American History told by Contemporaries, I : 125–129.
MUNRO. Crusaders of New France, 32–40, 43–54.
THWAITES. France in America, 12–22.
Baltimore County Course of Study, 465.

Minimal Essentials

Name of Person: **Champlain** (shăm′plān′)
Names of Places: **Canada; New France;** Quebec
Historical Term: **fur trade**
Something to Remember
  Champlain founded towns and explored many lakes, so he has been called the
  "father of New France."

Illustrative Material

Gabriel (Ed.). Pageant of America, I : 292, 296.
McKinley. Illustrated Topics for American History : S. 5, A French Fort.

Procedure during Assimilation

Reading as described on pages 24–29.
Use school film [1] "French Explorations in North America."
Visit the local museum to see relics of the French occupation and of the Indians.
On the sand-table map add a little log fort to represent Quebec.[2] Name Lake Ontario.
Are there any place names in your vicinity that show French occupation of the territory? List them.
Drill on minimal essentials.
Objective test.

Organization

Teacher and pupils together select the main points of the story to serve as an outline for the oral stories.

Story of Champlain

1. The founding of Quebec
2. Exploration in the West

Recitation

Leave the recitation of this story until the next story is finished ; then take the recitation of the two together.

3. *The Indians divided, Some being Friendly to the English and Some to the French*

Preparation and Presentation

"The French people would not sell any guns nor powder to the Indians. Why not?" (Danger of attack.)

"The Dutch people were willing to sell arms to the Indians. Why?" (Gain.)

"Therefore we are not surprised to find that the Iroquois, especially, became friendly to the Dutch and, later, to the English."

---

[1] Burgess, May Ayres, "Motion Pictures in the Public Schools." *Elementary School Journal*, XXIII : 676–682.

[2] Study the site from pictures.

Assimilation
Readings
Upper Group

BEEBY. Community Life Today and in Colonial Times, 319–322.

CROWE. Studies in American History, I : 157–161.

FOOTE and SKINNER. Explorers and Founders of America, 203–205.

GORDY. Stories of Early American History, 120–122.

JOHNSTON. Famous Discoverers and Explorers of America, 280–295.

MCMURRY. Pioneers on Land and Sea, 1–34.

MARSHALL. Story of Human Progress, 30–89. (Difficult.) (Has description of the Iroquois.)

NIDA. The Dawn of American History in Europe, 351–355.

PRATT. Early Colonies, 81–85.

TAPPAN. Elementary History of our Country, 115.

Average Group

COE. Founders of our Country, 116–119.

FIELD. Fourth Reader, 296–299.

FORMAN. First Lessons in American History, 48–49.

GORDY. Elementary History of the United States, 105.

MCMASTER. Primary History of the United States, 33–35.

NIDA. Following Columbus, 85–90.

SOUTHWORTH. Builders of our Country, I : 156–160.

SWAN. History and Civics, Grade 5 A, 118–120.

TAPPAN. American Hero Stories, 53–55.

Lower Group

LUCIA. Stories of American Discoverers for Little Americans, 155–160.

PRATT. Beginners' Book, 53–66.

Teachers

GRIFFIS. Romance of Discovery, 261–265.

MUNRO. Crusaders of New France, 40–43.

THWAITES. France in America, 35–38.

Minimal Essentials

Names of Persons: **Iroquois** (ĭr′ṓ kwoi′); **Algonquin** [1] (ăl gŏŋ′kĭn)

Name of Place: **Lake Champlain**

Historical Term: **battle**

Things to Remember

The Iroquois hated the French, so they became friends of the English and the Dutch.

They owned the land south of the lakes, [2] so the French had to travel inland by way of the Ottawa River and Lake Huron.

Illustrative Material

GABRIEL (ED.). Pageant of America, I : 298–299.

MCKINLEY. Illustrated Topics for American History : S. 9, Champlain's Attack on an Indian Fort.

[1] Not in the studies of persons referred to on page 5.

[2] Erie and Ontario.

Procedure during Assimilation

Reading as described on pages 24–29.

Picture study on the material listed on page 137.

On the sand-table map show Lakes Champlain, Ontario, and Huron. Cover the territory claimed by the Iroquois with tiny "long houses." Show how the French will have to pass from the St. Lawrence River via the Ottawa River and Lake Huron if they wish to travel to the other Great Lakes.

Construct an Iroquois long-house village.[1]

Add the routes of Champlain [2] to the map "France in America," each child making his own copy.

Drill on minimal essentials.

Objective test.

Organization

Repeat the organization of the preceding story and add the last two points.

STORY OF CHAMPLAIN

1. The founding of Quebec
2. Exploration in the West
3. Discovery of Lake Champlain and battle with the Iroquois
4. The Iroquois as enemies of the French and friends of the English

Recitation

Continue the contest for the pennant as described on page 133. A drill lesson [3] on France in the New World should be given at this point.

IV. PORTUGAL HAD LITTLE LAND IN THE NEW WORLD, BUT SECURED THE TRADE WITH THE REAL INDIES

1. *The Name of Americus Vespucius was given to the New World*

Preparation

"For whom are you named?" (*Ask several children.*) "Why did your parents name you for that person?

"When Columbus made his voyages, what did the people of Europe think he had found? How does the name *Indians* prove this?

"We are going to see today how America received its name. Why might we think that America should be called Columbia?"

---

[1] Marshall, L. C., *The Story of Human Progress*, pp. 25, 26.

[2] Muzzey, D. S., *An American History*, p. 76.

[3] Similar to that described on pages 112–113.

Presentation

Shortly after Columbus made his voyages Portugal was sorry that she had not helped him. France was sorry also, and England! Portugal decided to send out another man to see if he too couldn't find the Indies by sailing west, for everybody thought that was what Columbus had done.

The man she sent, Americus Vespucius (*pointing to the name on the board*), came to this part of the country (*showing Brazil*) and sailed along the coast for hundreds of miles. Quite delighted with the beauty of the land, he went home and wrote letters about it.

When people read Americus's letters they began to say to each other: "This cannot be the same land that Columbus found! Columbus found islands off the coast of India. Americus has sailed so far that his land must be a whole continent by itself." One of them, a teacher, said: "We have long known of three parts of the world — Europe, Asia, and Africa. Now Americus has found a fourth part. Let us name it after him and call it America." Many people agreed.

Years afterwards they found that Vespucius's land was the same as that Columbus had found. (*Run the pointer along the eastern and northern coasts of South America when naming Vespucius and Columbus.*) Then they knew they should have called it Columbia after Columbus, but by that time they were all so used to calling it America that they did not want to change. And *America* we call it to this day.

PRESENTATION TEST

Check the best answer:

a. Americus Vespucius sailed for which country?

    _ _ _ Portugal
    _ _ _ France
    _ _ _ England

b. When he went back home he

    _ _ _ called the new land America
    _ _ _ named the new land after himself
    _ _ _ wrote letters about what he had seen

c. People thought that

    _ _ _ he had found the same land that Columbus did
    _ _ _ he had found a different land from that found by Columbus
    _ _ _ he had not made any voyage at all

d. Later they knew that

    _ _ _ his land was part of what Columbus had found

    _ _ _ his land was not part of what Columbus had found

    _ _ _ his land was an island of India

Assimilation

Readings

Upper Group

ATKINSON. European Beginnings of American History, 313.

ATKINSON. Introduction to American History, 242–243.

BOURNE and BENTON. Introductory American History, 160–163.

BURNHAM. Our Beginnings in Europe and America, 232–233.

CHANDLER and CHITWOOD. Makers of American History, 24–28.

FARIS. Real Stories of the Geography Makers, 75–80.

FOOTE and SKINNER. Explorers and Founders of America, 38–41.

GORDY. American Beginnings in Europe, 249–250.

GORDY. Leaders in Making America, 12–13.

GORDY. Stories of Early American History, 16–17.

HARDING. Old World Background to American History, 278–279.

JOHNSTON. Famous Discoverers and Explorers of America, 45–59.

LOGIE. From Columbus to Lincoln, 10–12.

MARKWICK and SMITH. South American Republics, 13–15.

MONTGOMERY. Beginners' American History, 18–19.

MORRIS. Heroes of Discovery in America, 23–31.

NIDA. The Dawn of American History in Europe, 298–299.

TAPPAN. Elementary History of our Country, 15.

TAPPAN. Our European Ancestors, 175–177.

VAN LOON. A Short History of Discovery, 94–95.

WOODBURN and MORAN. Beginner's History of the United States, 44–45.

WOODBURN and MORAN. Finders and Founders of the New World, 57–59.

WOODBURN and MORAN. Introduction to American History, 222–224.

WRIGHT. Children's Stories in American History, 65–70.

World Book (Vespucius).

Average Group

BARNES. Elementary History of the United States, 22–24.

BEARD and BAGLEY. A First Book in American History, 21.

ELSON and MACMULLAN. The Story of our Country, I : 29–31.

FORMAN. First Lessons in American History, 23–24.

GORDY. Elementary History of the United States, 7–8.

MACE. Primary History, 20.

MORRIS. Primary History of the United States, 28.

NIDA. Following Columbus, 42.

PERRY and PRICE. American History, I : 48.

SHAW. Discoverers and Explorers, 48–53.

SWAN. History and Civics, Grade 5 A, 23–25.

Lower Group

BARNES. Primary History of the United States, 21–22.

DAVIS. Stories of the United States, 49–50.

WILSON. A History Reader, 49–50.

Teachers

BOURNE. Spain in America, 84–103.
GRIFFIS. Romance of Discovery, 112–125.
HART. American History told by Contemporaries, I : 49.
LAMPREY. Days of the Discoverers, 94–103.
LONG. America, 38–39.
MUZZEY. American History, 10–11.
WEBSTER. Early European History, 628.
Baltimore County Course of Study, 451–452.

Minimal Essentials

Name of Person: **Americus Vespucius** (*à* mĕr'ĭ kŭs vĕs pū'shŭs)
Name of Place: **America**
Historical Terms: **Old World; New World**
Things to Remember

Americus Vespucius described what he saw on his voyage.
The land did not seem to be like India, which people thought Columbus had found.
Therefore they called the new land America.
Later they learned that it was the same continent that Columbus had found.

Illustrative Material

GABRIEL (ED.). Pageant of America, I : 114.
Perry Pictures : 1270, Vespucci.

Procedure during Assimilation

Reading as described on pages 24–29.
Children look in the telephone book to see how many commercial companies in the city are named after Americus.
Should the name *America* be changed to *Columbia?* Is the name unjust to Columbus ?
Make a map [1] entitled "Portugal in America," using as a basis an outline map of the Western Hemisphere. Color the possessions of Portugal brown. Each child should make his own map. Compare with the map already made for "Spain in America."
What language do the people of Brazil speak today? the other people of South America?
Drill on minimal essentials.
Objective test.

Organization

The teacher puts the following outline on the board. Children are to substitute a sentence for each part of the outline.

THE NAME AMERICA

1. Americus's voyage
2. His letters
3. The name given

[1] Shepherd, W. R., *Historical Atlas*, pp. 107–108.

Recitation

Allow the class to criticize the stories based on the organization step on page 141.

2. *Portugal's Trade with the Indies made her Rich*

The teacher will have to tell the story orally to all groups (see the references below).

Assimilation
Readings

For Pupils
> LAWLER. The Gateway to American History, 335–337.
> LUTHER. Trading and Exploring, 192–202.

Teachers
> DAY. History of Commerce, 184–185.
> ROBINSON and BREASTED. Outlines of European History, I : 528–530.
> WEBSTER. Early European History, 622–623.
> WEBSTER. General History of Commerce, 115–121.

Minimal Essentials

Names of Places: West Indies; East Indies
Things to Remember
> Portugal built up a great trade with India after Vasco da Gama's return. Therefore she took little interest in the New World.

Illustrative Material

National Geographic Magazine. Pictures of India, XXIII : 118–192; XXXVIII: 245–282; XXXIX : 281–289; XL : 433–468, 481–496.

Procedure during Assimilation

Study the pictures of Indian life and industry.
Make a list of things Portugal can send to India ; of things she will receive in return.
Begin to make a booklet of *Trade with the Indies*, including pictures cut from the advertising pages of magazines.

Organization

Use "Things to Remember" as an outline.

Recitation

Children write paragraphs based on the outline, to include in their book of *Trade with the Indies*.

3. *Portugal founded a Colony in Brazil*

Preparation

"After a while the line of kings in Portugal died out, and the Spanish king made himself ruler there too. He lost all of Portugal's eastern empire. After a while Portugal again became independent, but her empire was lost to her forever.

"She had paid very little attention to Brazil before this. Why was she more interested in Brazil from that time on?" No additional presentation is needed.

Assimilation
Readings
Upper Group

MARKWICK and SMITH. South American Republics, 173–178.
NIXON-ROULET. Our Little Brazilian Cousin.
OLCOTT. Good Stories for Great Birthdays, 110–122.
SOUTHWORTH. Our South American Neighbors, 11–13.
TAPPAN. Our European Ancestors, 176.
WINSLOW. Our American Neighbors, 142–150.
WINSLOW. The Earth and its People, 133–136.
World Book (Brazil: History).

Average Group

BRIGHAM and McFARLANE. Essentials of Geography, First Book, 173.
FRYE. New Geography, Book One, 179, 182, 183, 190.
LAWLER. The Story of Columbus and Magellan, 91–93.
SMITH. Human Geography, Book One, 207–209.
TARR and McMURRY. New Geographies, First Book, 182–183.

Lower Group

The teacher will have to tell the story orally.
Descriptions of Brazil.
ALLEN. Children of the Palm Lands, 79–113.

Teachers

Encyclopædia Britannica, IV: 454–458.
New International Encyclopædia, III: 686–688.

Minimal Essentials

Name of Place: **Brazil**
Historical Terms: **emperor; independent**
Things to Remember
The Portuguese founded Brazil as a colony.
After a while Brazil became a country by itself.

Illustrative Material

Use the pictures in the geographies.

Procedure during Assimilation

Reading as described on pages 24–29.
Make a sand-table representation of Brazil: its people and native industries.
Drill on minimal essentials.

Organization

The teacher puts the following outline on the board. Pupils substitute sentences for the points in the outline.

BRAZIL

1. A colony of Portugal
2. An independent country

Recitation

Children criticize their own stories. The outline above serves as the basis for organizing the story. A drill lesson on section IV of Unit II is given at this point.

V. THE DUTCH BUILT ON LAND WHICH THE ENGLISH THOUGHT WAS THEIRS

1. *Henry Hudson found a Great River*

Preparation

"In our overview story you may remember that we made a list of countries which wanted to find riches. We have already had the stories about Spain, England, France, and Portugal. What was the other country?

"Have any of you ever seen or heard of the Hudson River? Do you know why it is called Hudson? Today we will find out why."

Teach the unfamiliar words in the presentation test; as, *Dutch.*

Have ready a map of the world.

Presentation

The Dutch people were great sailors, so they naturally wanted to have a share in that trade with the Indies which was making Portugal so rich. They dared not go this way (*pointing to the route around South America*), because that was Spain's route; nor did they want to go this way (*pointing to the route around Africa*), because that took such a long time.

But nobody knew yet just what was up here (*pointing to the northern parts of Europe and North America*), although England and France had both explored in this region. Perhaps ships could go around one way or the other and reach the Indies by a short route (*illustrating how this would be done*). At any rate, it would be worth trying.

So they sent out a man named Henry Hudson (*pointing to the name written on the board*). He came to this part of the country (*illustrating*) and sailed up a great river almost as beautiful as the one Cartier had found. Indians were everywhere. There seemed to be no gold, but all the natives had furs to trade. Henry Hudson went back and reported that much money could be earned in the fur trade.

The Dutch people were sorry not to have found the way to go to the Indies, but they said: "Since we have no gold we will build a town on our great river and make our fortunes by trading in furs with the Indians."

The English said: "But that land is ours. John Cabot found it for us years ago." The Dutch replied, "John Cabot did not find the particular place that Henry Hudson did; so we will build our town, anyway." England was not at all satisfied and threatened, "If you do, there will be trouble." Nevertheless the Dutch people built their town on the river, which they named in honor of Henry Hudson. Some of their children live there to this day.

PRESENTATION TEST

Check the best answer:

  a. Henry Hudson sailed for the
      _ _ _ English
      _ _ _ Dutch
      _ _ _ French

  b. He was looking for
      _ _ _ a route to the Indies
      _ _ _ fur trade
      _ _ _ a place to build a town

c. The land he found had
 _ _ _ precious stones
 _ _ _ gold
 _ _ _ furs

d. The English claimed the same land
 _ _ _ because they were stronger than the Dutch
 _ _ _ because John Cabot had found it first
 _ _ _ because Henry Hudson was an Englishman

Assimilation

Readings

Upper Group

BEEBY. Community Life Today and in Colonial Times, 247–250.
BLAISDELL. Story of American History, 88–92.
BURNHAM. Hero Tales from History, 115–120.
BURNHAM. Our Beginnings in Europe and America, 278–279, 321.
CHANDLER and CHITWOOD. Makers of American History, 75–77.
EGGLESTON. A First Book in American History, 42–48.
ELLIS. Makers of our Country, 37–40.
FOOTE and SKINNER. Explorers and Founders of America, 168–173.
GORDY. Leaders in Making America, 82–83.
GORDY. Stories of Early American History, 116–118.
JOHNSTON. Famous Discoverers and Explorers of America, 305–329.
McLEAN. Heroes of the Farthest North and Farthest South, 16–17.
McMURRY. Pioneers on Land and Sea, 35–46.
MONTGOMERY. Beginners' American History, 36–40.
MORRIS. Heroes of Discovery in America, 190–197.
NIDA. The Dawn of American History in Europe, 306–307, 356–357.
PRATT. Early Colonies, 86–88.
TAPPAN. Elementary History of our Country, 32–33, 88–89.
VAN LOON. A Short History of Discovery, 112–115.
WOODBURN and MORAN. Finders and Founders of the New World, 162–164.
Compton's Pictured Encyclopedia (Hudson).
World Book (Hudson).

Average Group

BARNES. Elementary History of the United States, 80–85.
BEARD and BAGLEY. A First Book in American History, 65–67.
COE. Founders of our Country, 123–128.
ELSON and MacMULLAN. The Story of our Country, I : 113–115.
FIELD. Fourth Reader, 276–282.
FORMAN. First Lessons in American History, 50–51.
GORDY. Elementary History of the United States, 10–11, 73–75.
GORDY. Our Patriots, 44–47.
LEWIS and ROWLAND. Silent Readers, V : 26–31.
LUTHER. Trading and Exploring, 232–235.
MACE. Primary History, 95–96.
McMASTER. Primary History of the United States, 14, 72–73.
MORRIS. Primary History of the United States, 51–55.
MOWRY. First Steps in the History of our Country, 75–77.
NIDA. Following Columbus, 100–106.
PERRY and PRICE. American History, I : 165–168.

PRATT. Exploration and Discovery, 137–143.
SHAW. Discoverers and Explorers, 114–120.
SOUTHWORTH. Builders of our Country, I : 123–129.
SWAN. History and Civics, Grade 5 A, 93–104.
TURPIN. Brief Biographies from American History, 80–84.
WRIGHT. Children's Stories in American History, 292–294.

Lower Group

BLAISDELL and BALL. American History for Little Folks, 38–42.
DAVIS. Stories of the United States, 115–119.
LUCIA. Stories of American Discoverers for Little Americans, 160–164.
WILSON. A History Reader, 110–112.

Teachers

BACON. Henry Hudson.
BARSTOW. Explorers and Settlers, 171–174.
GOODWIN. The Dutch and the English on the Hudson, **1–17.**
GRIFFIS. Romance of Discovery, 221–245.
JANVIER. Henry Hudson.
LAMPREY. Days of the Discoverers, 270–281.
TYLER. England in America, 291–294.
Baltimore County Course of Study, 459.

Minimal Essentials

Names of Persons: **Henry Hudson; Dutch**
Names of Places: **Holland; Hudson River**
Historical Term: **Northwest Passage**
Things to Remember
Henry Hudson discovered the Hudson River for the Dutch.
The English claimed the same land because of John Cabot's discovery years
before.

Illustrative Material

GABRIEL (ED.). Pageant of America, I : 227–228.
MCKINLEY. Illustrated Topics for American History: S. 4, Photograph of the replica of the
Half Moon.
PYLE. Book of the American Spirit, 69.

Procedure during Assimilation

Reading as described on pages 24–29.
Picture study based on the illustrative material listed above.
Children read the parts in the dramatization [1] "Henry Hudson" in Stevenson's
Children's Classics in Dramatic Form, IV : 116–128.
Try to act out a fur-trading scene in which neither party understands the language
of the other.
Begin a map entitled "The Dutch in America," each child making his own copy.
Trace Henry Hudson's voyage.
In what way may the building of the Panama Canal be considered as the continua-
tion of the search for the Northwest Passage?
Drill on minimal essentials.
Objective test.

[1] Crawford, C., "The Teaching of Dramatic Arts in the Kindergarten and Elementary School." *Teachers' College Record,* XVI : 366–383.

Organization

Copy on the board several organizations from previous stories to serve as models. Children now attempt making their own outlines.

Recitation

Wait for recitation until the following story also has been organized; then give the two together.

2. *They built a Town on Hudson's River*

No additional preparation and presentation are needed.

Assimilation

Readings

Upper Group

BEEBY. Community Life Today and in Colonial Times, 250–255.
BLAISDELL. Story of American History, 92–94.
CHANDLER and CHITWOOD. Makers of American History, 78.
FOOTE and SKINNER. Explorers and Founders of America, 175–180.
GORDY. Leaders in Making America, 83–87.
GORDY. Stories of Early American History, 118–120, 122–126.
MONTGOMERY. Beginners' American History, 40–42.
NIDA. The Dawn of American History in Europe, 357–358.
OTIS. Peter of New Amsterdam.
PRATT. Early Colonies, 88–98.
TAPPAN. Elementary History of our Country, 90–91.
VAN LOON. A Short History of Discovery, 120–121.
WOODBURN and MORAN. Finders and Founders of the New World, 164–166.
WRIGHT. Children's Stories in American History, 294–298.
Colonial Stories retold from *St. Nicholas*, 101–108.

Average Group

BARNES. Elementary History of the United States, 86–89.
BEARD and BAGLEY. A First Book in American History, 67–68.
COE. Founders of our Country, 218–222.
ELSON and MACMULLAN. The Story of our Country, I : 115–117.
FIELD. Fourth Reader. 282–285.
FORMAN. First Lessons in American History, 51–52.
GORDY. Elementary History of the United States, 75–76, 77.
LUTHER. Trading and Exploring, 235–240.
MACE. Primary History, 97–99.
McMASTER. Primary History of the United States, 73–74.
MORRIS. Primary History of the United States, 56.
MOWRY. First Steps in the History of our Country, 77.
NIDA. Following Columbus, 204–206.
SOUTHWORTH. Builders of our Country, I : 130–135.
SWAN. History and Civics, Grade 5 A, 157–163.

Lower Group

BLAISDELL and BALL. American History for Little Folks, 42.
DAVIS. Stories of the United States, 120–130.
PRATT. Beginners' Book, 101–107.
WAYLAND. History Stories for Primary Grades, 161–162.
WILSON. A History Reader, 112–114.

Teachers

BARSTOW. Explorers and Settlers, 174–180, 185–188.
GOODWIN. The Dutch and the English on the Hudson, 17–123.
TUCKER and RYAN. Historical Plays of Colonial Days, 50–55, 75–82, 92–100.

Minimal Essentials

Names of Places: **New York; Manhattan** (măn hăt′ăn)
Historical Terms: **trinkets; settlement; company** (a commercial)
Things to Remember

The Dutch built a town which they called New Amsterdam.
They bought the land from the Indians for a few trinkets.
New Amsterdam became a great trading center.

Illustrative Material

GABRIEL (ED.). Pageant of America, I: 229–231.
McKINLEY. Illustrated Topics for American History: S. 5, View of New Amsterdam about 1676.
Compton's Pictured Encyclopedia (Hudson).
Detroit Publishing Company. Little Phostint Journeys: XXXVII, The Hudson River.
Perry Pictures: 2106, Old Dutch Church, Tarrytown.

Procedure during Assimilation

Reading as described on pages 24–29.
Study the pictures for peculiarities of architecture.
The children read the dramatizations found in the following: "Manhattan Island."
Hubbard, *Little American History Plays*, pp. 42–45 (Act I); Tucker and Ryan, *Historical Plays of Colonial Days*, pp. 50–55, 75–82, 92–100; Stevenson, *Children's Classics in Dramatic Form*, IV: 128–135 (last act).
Construct a Dutch village on the sand table.
Find on a map of Europe the original Amsterdam and York for which New Amsterdam and New York were named.
Drill on minimal essentials.
Objective test.

Organization

This story is harder to organize; so the teacher had better put the following outline on the board:

DUTCH TOWNS IN THE NEW WORLD

1. The building of a fort at New Amsterdam
2. Purchase of Manhattan from the Indians
3. Slow growth of the town

Recitation

Complete the stories of Henry Hudson and of the building of the Dutch town. Hold a meeting of the public-speaking [1] society in which the two stories are told together.

A drill lesson [2] on the Portuguese and the Dutch in the New World is held at this point. Since the unit has been nearly completed, and the drill on all the minimal essentials is approaching, it is helpful for the teacher now to begin cumulative drill. The names of all the persons studied in Unit II are reviewed one day, the names of places the next day, dates the next day, and so on.

VI. THEN THEY ALL CLAIMED LAND IN THE NEW WORLD

1. *Their Claims Overlapped*

No additional preparation and presentation are needed.

Assimilation

Readings

Upper Group
  GORDY. American Beginnings in Europe, 328–329.

Average Group
  McMASTER. Primary History of the United States, 29–30.

Lower Group
  BARNES. Primary History of the United States, 25–27.

Teachers
  BOURNE. Spain in America, 190–201.
  COMAN. Industrial History of the United States, 8–19.

Minimal Essentials

Each child should be able to color from memory the lands claimed by Spain, England, France, Portugal, and the Netherlands about 1650. This work is done from the study of a colored map like those shown in the following works: *Harper's Atlas of American History*, p. 12; Perry and Price, *American History*, I : 245; Shepherd, *Historical Atlas*, p. 214; Thwaites, *The Colonies*, p. 298.

Use an outline map of the Western Hemisphere.

Things to Remember

Sometimes different countries claimed the same land.

They went to war about their claims.

[1] See page 117.   [2] See pages 112–113.

Procedure during Assimilation

Model in the sand table the entire Western Hemisphere. The children make many little flags (about $2 \times 1\frac{1}{2}$ inches) and mount them on toothpicks. Arrange these flags in rows around the territory of each country, using the appropriate flag in each case.[1]

Use a table similar to that in Perry and Price's *American History*, I: 236–237.

In what ways are the lives of the people who live in Europe different now than they were before America was discovered?

Organization

The making of the map referred to under "Minimal Essentials."

Recitation

Every child should be able to go to the map and point out the claims held by each country, stating the basis of each claim.

2. *These were the Days of the Pirates*

No preparation and presentation are necessary, since the term "pirate" was introduced in the story of Sir Francis Drake.

Assimilation

Readings

Upper Group

BARSTOW. The New Nation, 72–85.

EVANS. America First, 81–87, 118–121.

HART and HAZARD. Colonial Children, 34–37, 46–51.

LANG (ED.). Blue True Story Book, 136–142.

LANIER. The Book of Bravery, 97–102.

Compton's Pictured Encyclopedia (Pirate, Captain Kidd).

St. Nicholas, XIX: 600–603 (1892).

Possibly also the following (difficult):

BENNETT. Barnaby Lee.

HOLLAND. Blackbeard's Island.

INGERSOLL. The Book of the Ocean, 171–185.

PYLE. Boys' Book of Pirates.

VERRILL. Boys' Book of Buccaneers.

Average Group

EGGLESTON. Stories of American Life and Adventure, 48–52.

GUERBER. Story of the Thirteen Colonies, 163–164.

MCMASTER. Primary History of the United States, 84–87.

---

[1] See the *National Geographic Magazine*, XXXII: 338–339 (October, 1917), for the appropriate flags.

OBER. Storied West Indies, 140–155.
PIKE. Our Little Panama Cousin, 36–59.
PYLE. Stolen Treasure.
STOCKTON. Buccaneers and Pirates of our Coast.
SYLVESTER. Journeys through Bookland, IV: 350–359.

Lower Group

COE. Founders of our Country, 244–250 (Blackbeard).
FORMAN. First Lessons in American History, 75.

Teachers

FISKE. Old Virginia and her Neighbors, II: 361–369.
Americana Encyclopedia.
Encyclopædia Britannica.
New International Encyclopædia.

Minimal Essentials

Historical Terms: **black flag; walk the plank; piracy**
Things to Remember
Pirates robbed ships.
They were not sent out by any country.

Illustrative Material

GABRIEL (ED.). Pageant of America, I: 277–284.
Mentor, IX: 32–33 (August, 1921), Captain Kidd.
National Geographic Magazine, XLI: 154–155, 185, 187 (1923).
Travel, XLVI: 25–28 (January, 1926).

Procedure during Assimilation

Reading as described on pages 24–29.
Use sea songs to aid in establishing the necessary atmosphere.
Children design pirate flags.
Children prepare to tell to other members of the group the stories they have read.
Drill on minimal essentials.

Organization

Each child writes the main points of his own story.

Recitation

The telling of the stories to the group.
A drill lesson is held at this point, similar to those described on pages 112–113.

MINIMAL ESSENTIALS OF UNIT II

PERSONS	PLACES [1]	TERMS	DATES
Algonquin	America	against the law	*1492.* Columbus discovered America
Americus Vespucius	Brazil	Armada	
Aztecs	California	attack	*1497.* John Cabot discovered North America
John Cabot	Canada	attempt	
Cartier	Canary Islands	battle	*1519–1522.* Magellan circumnavigated the globe
Champlain	Channel	black flag	
Cortez	eastern coast of North America	capital city	
De Soto		circumnavigation	*1588.* England defeated the Spanish Armada
Francis Drake	East Indies	claims	
Dutch	England	coast	
Queen Elizabeth	Florida	company (a commercial)	
English	Gulf of Mexico		Drill on the placing of persons in the time chart
French	Holland	confer knighthood	
John Hawkins	Hudson River	conquest	
Henry Hudson	Lake Champlain	courtier	
Indians	Manhattan	decade	
Iroquois	Mexico	defeat	
Magellan	Mexico City	discover	
Ponce de Leon	Mississippi River	discoverer	
Walter Raleigh	Montreal	emperor	
Spaniards	New France	exploration	
Spanish	New York	explore	
	North America	explorer	
	Pacific	failure	
	Pacific coast of North America	fleet	
		fort	
	Philippines	fur trade	
	Quebec	galleon	
	St. Augustine	governor	
	St. Lawrence River	independent	
		interpreter	
	Santa Fe	Latin America	
	Scotland	mainland	
	South America	mission	
	South Sea	mutiny	
	Virginia	natives	
	west coast of Africa	naval	
	West Indies	New World	
		Northwest Passage	
		Old World	
		piracy	
		pirate	
		sack	
		score of years	
		settlement	
		slave trade	
		slaves	
		Spanish America	
		Spanish Main	
		treasure fleet	
		trinkets	

[1] For a game for places see Barrows, H. H., and Parker, E. P., *Geography: Journeys in Distant Lands,* "Review puzzles," "Making puzzles," p. 110.

TESTS ON THE ENTIRE UNIT

(To be given after all the stories are completed)

The following words may need explanation : *blank, sentence, Portuguese, anybody.* Illustrate at the board how to fill in blank spaces with words chosen from a specified list.

Test of Place-Sense. I. Pass outline maps [1] of the world. Words to be written on the maps may be placed on the board for assistance in spelling. Give the following directions:

1. Put the figure 1 where England is.
2. Put the figure 2 where Scotland is.
3. Write the word *Canada* in the right place.
4. Put the figure 3 where the English Channel is.
5. Write *eastern coast of North America* in the right place.
6. Write *Pacific coast of North America* in the right place.
7. Write *west coast of Africa* in the right place.
8. Put the figure 4 where the Mississippi River is.
9. Put the figure 5 where the Gulf of Mexico is.
10. Write *South America* in the right place.
11. Write *North America* in the right place.
12. Put the figure 6 where the Canary Islands are.
13. Put the figure 7 where the Philippine Islands are.
14. Write the word *Brazil* in the right place.
15. Put the figure 8 where the West Indies are.
16. Put the figure 9 where the East Indies are.
17. Put the figure 10 where Holland is.

II. Pass outline maps of North America. Give the following directions:

1. Write the word *Pacific* in the right place.
2. Put the figure 1 where Florida is.
3. Write the word *Mexico* in the right place.
4. Put the figure 2 where St. Augustine is.
5. Put the figure 3 where Santa Fe is.
6. Put the figure 4 where California is.
7. Put the figure 5 where Virginia is.
8. Put the figure 6 where the St. Lawrence River is.
9. Put the figure 7 where Montreal is.
10. Put the figure 8 where Quebec is.
11. Put the figure 9 where Lake Champlain is.
12. Put the figure 10 where the Hudson River is.

[1] Copies may be made very cheaply. See the Bishop and Robinson Historical Outline Maps (Ginn and Company).

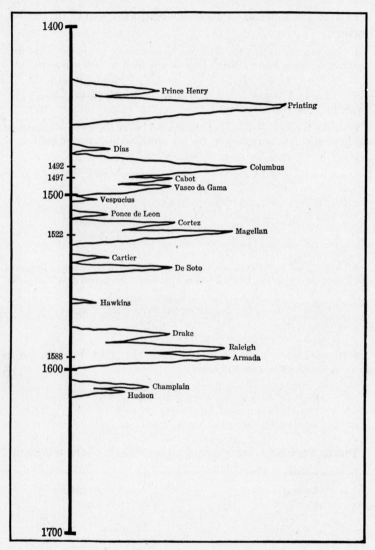

Time Chart — Unit II

Test of Time-Sense. Pass mimeographed sheets of the following:

1. Here is a list of persons. Put the figure 1 before the name of the man who lived first, the figure 2 before the one who lived second, and so on.

   _ _ _ John Cabot   _ _ _ Walter Raleigh
   _ _ _ Cartier   _ _ _ Magellan
   _ _ _ Henry Hudson

2. Here is a list of persons. Put the figure 1 before the name of the person who lived first, the figure 2 before the one who lived next, and so on.

   _ _ _ Ponce de Leon   _ _ _ Cortez
   _ _ _ Queen Elizabeth   _ _ _ Champlain
   _ _ _ Americus Vespucius

3. Here is a list of persons. Do the same.

   _ _ _ De Soto   _ _ _ Columbus
   _ _ _ John Hawkins   _ _ _ Prince Henry
   _ _ _ Francis Drake

4. Here is a list of things which happened. Put the figure 1 before the event which happened first, the figure 2 before that which happened next, and so on.

   _ _ _ England defeated the Spanish Armada.
   _ _ _ John Cabot discovered North America.
   _ _ _ Magellan sailed around the globe.
   _ _ _ Columbus discovered America.

5. Here is a list of dates: *1519–1522, 1492, 1497, 1588.* Put each date in the right blank in the sentences below:

   Columbus discovered America in _ _ _ _.
   England defeated the Spanish Armada in _ _ _ _.
   Magellan's trip around the world was made in _ _ _ _.
   John Cabot discovered North America in _ _ _ _.

Test on Persons. Pass mimeographed sheets of the following:

I. Here is a list of people:

   Indians   Americus Vespucius
   Dutch   Ponce de Leon
   John Cabot   Algonquins
   Henry Hudson   Magellan

Put each name in the right blank in the sentences below:

1. The first person to sail around the world was _ _ _ _.
2. The Indians who were friends of the French were _ _ _ _.
3. Columbus called the natives of America _ _ _ _.
4. America was named for _ _ _ _ _ _ _ _.

5. The man who discovered Florida was _ _ _ _ _ _ _ _ _ _ _ _.
6. The _ _ _ _ people sent out Henry Hudson to America.
7. North America was discovered by _ _ _ _ _ _ _ _.
8. The Dutch claimed land because of the voyage of _ _ _ _ _ _ _ _.

II. Here is a list of people:

Cortez	De Soto
French	Iroquois
Cartier	Aztecs
Champlain	Spaniards

Put each name in the right blank in the sentences below:

1. The _ _ _ _ people discovered the Great Lakes.
2. Mexico was conquered by _ _ _ _ _.
3. The _ _ _ _ built towns with missions and forts in them.
4. The _ _ _ _ Indians fought against Champlain.
5. _ _ _ _ discovered the St. Lawrence River.
6. The _ _ _ _ lived in Mexico before Cortez came.
7. The Mississippi River was discovered by _ _ _ _ _.
8. _ _ _ _ built Quebec.

III. Here is a list of people:

John Hawkins	Francis Drake
Queen Elizabeth	Spanish
English	

Put each name in the right blank in the sentences below:

1. The first Englishman to sail around the world was _ _ _ _ _ _ _ _.
2. The queen of England was _ _ _ _ _ _ _ _.
3. The _ _ _ _ people sent home a treasure fleet every year.
4. The English slave trade was begun by _ _ _ _ _ _ _ _.
5. The _ _ _ _ people defeated the Spanish Armada.

Test on Historical Terms.

I. Here is a list of words:

discover	native	circumnavigation
conquest	capital city	governor
coast	explore	interpreter
mutiny		

Put each word in the right blank in the sentences below:

1. This word means to travel over a country or sea in order to find out what kind of place it is. The word is _ _ _ _ _.
2. This word means sailing all around the world. The word is _ _ _ _ _.
3. A city which is the place where the king lives is called a _ _ _ _ _ _ _ _.
4. Any person who was born in a place is called a _ _ _ _ of that place.
5. To find any place and to tell the world about it is to _ _ _ _ the place.

6. Any person who explains in one language what has been said in another is an _ _ _ _.

7. Getting a country by force is called _ _ _ _.

8. When men in an army or on a ship refuse to do what their leaders say, it is called _ _ _ _.

9. The part of a country which is next to the sea is called the _ _ _ _.

10. A man whose duty is to control or govern is called the _ _ _ _.

II. Here is a list of words:

score of years	fort	Spanish America
missions	galleon	mainland
slaves	treasure fleet	claims
Latin America		

Put each word in the right blank in the sentences below:

1. The ships which once a year carried gold from the New World back to Spain were called the _ _ _ _ _ _ _ _.

2. Twenty years are a _ _ _ _ _ _ _ _ _ _ _ _.

3. The lands which the countries said belonged to them were their _ _ _ _.

4. All of America in which the Spanish and Portuguese lived was called _ _ _ _ _ _ _ _.

5. A large Spanish ship was called a _ _ _ _.

6. In the new lands the Spaniards built some churches for the Indians. These churches were _ _ _ _.

7. Another name for Latin America is _ _ _ _ _ _ _ _.

8. A large body of land, not an island, is called the _ _ _ _.

9. A strong building in which people can protect themselves is a _ _ _ _.

10. People who are owned by others are called _ _ _ _.

III. Here is a list of words:

slave trade	confers knighthood	decade
sack	courtier	pirate
attacks	armada	failure
Spanish Main		

Put each word in the right blank in the sentences below:

1. The Spanish call a fleet of warships an _ _ _ _.

2. Selling slaves to masters is called the _ _ _ _ _ _ _ _.

3. A man who robs on the sea is called a _ _ _ _.

4. What anybody tries to do and cannot is a _ _ _ _.

5. The northern coast of South America was called the _ _ _ _ _ _ _ _.

6. Anyone who spends much time in the king's court is called a _ _ _ _.

7. Ten years are a _ _ _ _.

8. When a king gives a man the title *Sir*, we say the king _ _ _ _ _ _ _ _ on him.

9. When an army tries to take a place by force, it _ _ _ _ the place.

10. Long ago when an army captured a city the soldiers used to take anything they saw which they wanted. When they do this they _ _ _ _ the city.

IV. Here is a list of words:

naval	defeat	emperor
fleet	Old World	New World
battle	fur trade	attempt
independent		

Put each word in the right blank in the sentences below:

1. When two armies fight, they are having a _ _ _ _.
2. Buying and selling furs is called the _ _ _ _ _ _ _ _.
3. Anything that has to do with ships is called _ _ _ _.
4. The part of the world which is not America is called the _ _ _ _ _ _ _ _.
5. America is called the _ _ _ _ _ _ _ _.
6. Whatever you try to do you _ _ _ _.
7. A country which can run its own affairs without asking help from anybody else is _ _ _ _.
8. Many ships of war together are a _ _ _ _.
9. The army which loses a battle suffers a _ _ _ _.
10. A man who rules over a country that has been conquered is called an _ _ _ _.

V. Here is a list of words:

Northwest Passage	trinkets
settlement	company
black flag	

Put each word in the right blank in the sentences below:

1. The flag of the pirates was the _ _ _ _ _ _ _.
2. The short way to India which France, England, and the Dutch hoped to find was called the _ _ _ _ _ _ _.
3. Any colony in a new place is called a _ _ _ _.
4. When men join together to do business, they make a _ _ _ _.
5. Pretty little things which are not worth much are _ _ _ _.

COMPREHENSION TEST ON UNIT II

1. *Check the best answer:*

   a. Columbus thought

       _ _ _ that he had discovered a new world

       _ _ _ that he had found India

       _ _ _ that he had sailed clear around the world back to Spain

   b. England claimed the eastern coast of North America

       _ _ _ because John Cabot discovered it

       _ _ _ because she had beaten the Spanish Armada

       _ _ _ because England was a strong country

   c. The French could go to their part of America easily

       _ _ _ because they had many ships

       _ _ _ because the Indians liked them

       _ _ _ because they found a great river leading into the country

d. America was named for Americus Vespucius
_ _ _ because he found it before Columbus
_ _ _ because people thought it was a different land from the one Columbus had found
_ _ _ because he was greater than Columbus

e. The Dutch claimed some of the same land that England did
_ _ _ because they hated England
_ _ _ because they did not know about the English claims
_ _ _ because Henry Hudson discovered a river for them in North America

f. When different countries claimed the same land, they usually
_ _ _ went to war about it
_ _ _ gave up their claims
_ _ _ gave the land to the church

g. Magellan's voyage around the world proved
_ _ _ that it is a long way around the world
_ _ _ that America was a continent, not part of Asia
_ _ _ that Magellan was a brave man

h. When John Hawkins started the slave trade, Spain
_ _ _ was glad he had found some people who would work
_ _ _ wanted her colonies to trade with him
_ _ _ did not want him to trade with her colonies

i. Champlain's great idea was
_ _ _ to go exploring
_ _ _ to fight with the Iroquois
_ _ _ to build towns and live in the new land

j. After Brazil became strong, it
_ _ _ made itself independent
_ _ _ was always a colony of Portugal
_ _ _ belonged to Spain

k. The Dutch people
_ _ _ did not care about having land in the New World
_ _ _ built a town on land which the English claimed
_ _ _ gave up and made no town

l. The pirates were sent out by
_ _ _ England
_ _ _ Spain
_ _ _ none of the countries

m. Francis Drake's voyage around South America
_ _ _ made England and Spain friends
_ _ _ made Spain very angry at England
_ _ _ made England very angry at Spain

n. The Iroquois Indians helped the English
_ _ _ because the French would not sell them guns
_ _ _ because the English people were so good to them
_ _ _ because they liked red coats

o. Portugal was not much interested in the New World at first
  _ _ _ because she did not have any ships
  _ _ _ because she would rather trade with the real Indies
  _ _ _ because she did not want to go far away from home

p. Walter Raleigh was the first Englishman
  _ _ _ who had the idea of building towns in the new land
  _ _ _ who sailed around the world
  _ _ _ who wore beautiful clothes

q. After Cortez conquered Mexico
  _ _ _ the Spaniards went back home
  _ _ _ the Spaniards killed all the Indians
  _ _ _ the Spanish people took the gold in Mexico

r. After the defeat of the Spanish Armada
  _ _ _ English ships could go where they pleased on the sea
  _ _ _ Spain would not let English ships sail the seas
  _ _ _ Spain and England were friends

s. The Spanish people did not build towns along the great river De Soto
    found
  _ _ _ because they liked to live on the sea
  _ _ _ because they were afraid
  _ _ _ because there was no gold there

t. Most of the people in South America today speak
  _ _ _ English
  _ _ _ Spanish
  _ _ _ Portuguese

2. *What is the title of the second unit?*

ORGANIZATION OF THE UNIT AS A WHOLE

The class makes a tabulation of the explorers and discoverers for each nation studied, including dates only if given in the lists of minimal essentials.

COUNTRY HE REPRESENTED	NAME	WHAT HE DID	DATE	IMPORTANCE OF

RECITATION OF THE UNIT AS A WHOLE

A pageant, "How America was Found," may be given.

UNIT III

WHY ENGLISH PEOPLE CAME TO LIVE IN THE NEW WORLD

I. Some People came to earn a Better Living.
  1. Virginia was the first English colony.
    a. John Smith helped the colony in the beginning.
    b. After a while it grew and prospered.
  2. How the people in the South lived.
    a. Houses and furniture.
    b. Food.
    c. Clothing.
    d. Work.
    e. Churches and schools.
    f. Amusements and social life.
    g. Punishments.
    h. Travel.
  3. Soon other colonies appeared along the coast.
  4. New Netherland became New York.
    a. Life in New Netherland.
    b. The war with the English.
II. Some People came so that they might go to their Own Churches.
  1. The Pilgrims came to Plymouth.
  2. The Puritans came to Boston.
  3. How the Puritans lived.
    a. Houses and furniture.
    b. Food.
    c. Clothing.
    d. Work.
    e. Churches and schools.
    f. Amusements and social life.
    g. Punishments.
    h. Travel.
  4. The Puritans spread out to many other colonies.
  5. They had trouble with the Indians.
  6. The Catholics came to Maryland.
  7. The Quakers came to Pennsylvania.
III. Very early Some of the Colonists began to wander into the Interior.
  Daniel Boone went across the mountains.

PREPARATION FOR THE OVERVIEW

"Where had the Spanish people built towns in the New World?

"Whom had the English sent out to explore?

162

"Did any Englishman try to make a colony?

"Why did he fail?

"Did the defeat of the Spanish Armada make it any easier for the English to colonize?"

Teach any new words in the presentation test. All are included in the first two thousand of the Thorndike word list.

PRESENTATION OR OVERVIEW

In our last unit we found that the Spanish people had built many cities in the New World and had founded many colonies. The English people had sent out Cabot and Hawkins and Drake to explore, and Walter Raleigh had tried to make colonies but had failed. There were no English people living in the New World.

After the defeat of the Spanish Armada the English were very happy and very proud of themselves. They began to say to each other: "Let us go over to America and build towns in our land there. Then we will be greater than the Spaniards."

It costs a great deal of money, however, to buy ships and supplies and to found colonies. The rich men remembered how Sir Walter Raleigh had spent all his money and died poor. Each one said: "No, I will not risk all my fortune. I might lose my money as Raleigh did, and my colony might fail." For a time it looked as if no English colonies could be made.

After a while, however, the problem was solved. Instead of any one man paying all the money, a collection was taken up. One rich man would pay $1000, another would pay $5000, another $2000, and soon there was money enough to buy ships and supplies and start a colony. These rich men formed a *company* (*pointing to the word on the board*).

But who would go to the New World, and cut down the forests and plant the crops and build the log cabins and fight the Indians? Surely not the rich men who had made the company and who had always had everything they wanted. They looked about, and after a while found many poor people who would be glad to go to the New World and build homes if

somebody would pay their way over. So the rich men stayed
at home in England and sent the poorer people out to America
to build a colony for them.

And what a hard time the colonists had! After they arrived in America they decided first to look for gold and silver,
as the Spaniards had done. They found none! Then they had
trouble with the Indians. Then they almost starved to death
because they had not raised enough food. For a long while it
looked as if this English colony would fail too.

Slowly, however, conditions became better. Each man was
given a farm. Settlers found they could make a great deal of
money by growing tobacco, and new people kept coming over.
So instead of only one colony, as there had been at first, there
were after a while many little towns dotted up and down the
coast. England felt very well satisfied with her colonies.

Then the English began to look about them, and they
noticed the Dutch people on the Hudson River. They said:
"Why are Dutch people living in this land? John Cabot found
it, and it all belongs to England." They sent word to the
Dutch to move, but their message had no result.

Then the English people gathered together an army and a
fleet from England and went over and conquered the Dutch.
The land along the coast (*show on a map from Florida to Connecticut*) after that was all in the hands of the English, and
there were many people there making a better living than
they ever had at home in the Old World.

In England at this same time lived some people who were
very unhappy. One could not go to the church he pleased. If
the king of the country did not like a certain church, he drove
the minister or priest away, nailed up the door, and would not
allow any services to be held. All people had to go to the same
church, and that was the one the king wanted.

Naturally, the people who did not believe as the king did
were very unhappy because their churches were closed. One
of them said: "Let us go to America. It is very far away, and
the king will not bother us there. We can have our own religion." The rest of the people consented joyfully, and one
hundred of them set out in the ship *Mayflower*.

When they came to America they had at first just as hard a time as the other colonists.   They were cold and hungry, and it was winter.   Many died, and all suffered greatly.   However, no one thought of going back to England.

When spring came they planted crops, built houses and a church, and were much better off.   Slowly they grew stronger, more people came from England, and they began to spread out to make other towns close by.   After a number of years all this part of the coast (*showing on the map Maine to New York, including also Pennsylvania and Maryland, though not by name*) was in the hands of the English who had come so that they might go to their own churches.

The rest of the English, who had come to earn a better living, were settled here (*showing on the map*) ; so together they had all the eastern coast.   And more kept coming and coming from England, until they found they would have to go back farther into the country.   The English had certainly come to stay, and it began to look as if they would in time possess most of the continent.

PRESENTATION TEST

1. *Check the best answer:*

    a. It was hard for the first English people to come to America

        _ _ _ because they were afraid of the Spaniards
        _ _ _ because their ships were not large enough
        _ _ _ because ships and supplies cost a great deal of money

    b. A company is

        _ _ _ many rich men, each one paying part of the necessary money
        _ _ _ a number of men who are having a good time
        _ _ _ one rich man who pays all the money

    c. The men who came to live in the colony were

        _ _ _ rich members of the company.
        _ _ _ poor people who wanted to earn a better living
        _ _ _ the sailors from the ships

    d. The English people who came to work for the company

        _ _ _ had a very hard time
        _ _ _ became rich quickly
        _ _ _ grew tired and went back to England

    e. The English claimed the land on which the Dutch people lived

        _ _ _ because they were stronger than the Dutch
        _ _ _ because they did not like the Dutch
        _ _ _ because John Cabot had discovered it

f. Some people did not like to remain in England
 _ _ _ because they did not like the king
 _ _ _ because all people had to go to the same church
 _ _ _ because they liked America better

g. All the land along the eastern coast belonged at last to
 \\ _ _ _ the English
 _ _ _ the Dutch
 _ _ _ the Spanish

h. When more and more people began to come over from England they had
 _ _ _ to go to the country of the Spanish
 _ _ _ to go farther back into the land
 _ _ _ to return to England

2. *Check the two best answers :*
The reasons why English people came to live in America were
 _ _ _ to find gold and silver
 _ _ _ to earn a better living
 _ _ _ to find a route to the Indies
 _ _ _ to trade with the Indians
 _ _ _ to be able to attend their own churches

I. Some People came to earn a Better Living
 1. Virginia was the first English colony
  a. John Smith helped the colony in the beginning

No additional preparation and presentation are needed.

Assimilation

Readings

Upper Group

BEEBY. Community Life Today and in Colonial Times, 225–238.
BLAISDELL. The Story of American History, 34–46.
BURNHAM. Hero Tales from History, 145–150.
BURTON. Builders of our Nation, 74–86.
EGGLESTON. A First Book in American History, 23–40.
EVANS. America First, 32–39.
FOOTE and SKINNER. Explorers and Founders of America, 112–135.
GORDY. Colonial Days, 7–24.
GORDY. Leaders in Making America, 40–46.
GORDY. Stories of Early American History, 71–83.
GUERBER. Story of the Thirteen Colonies, 87–101.
HAZARD and DUTTON. Indians and Pioneers, 138–148.
LOGIE. From Columbus to Lincoln, 18–39.
McMURRY. Pioneers on Land and Sea, 68–102.
MONTGOMERY. Beginners' American History, 25–33.
MORRIS. Heroes of Discovery in America, 181–189.

MOWRY. American Pioneers, 34–46.
OTIS. Richard of Jamestown.
PERSONS. Our Country in Poem and Prose, 33–34.
TAPPAN. Elementary History of our Country, 42–49.
TAPPAN. Letters from Colonial Children, 1–40 (selections).
TOMLINSON. Places Young Americans want to Know, 48–55.
TURPIN. Stories from American History, 38–83.
WADE. Ten Big Indians, 65–89.
WOODBURN and MORAN. Beginner's History of the United States, 80–93.
WOODBURN and MORAN. Finders and Founders of the New World, 93–114.
Compton's Pictured Encyclopedia (Smith, Jamestown).
World Book (Smith, Jamestown, Pocahontas, Powhatan, Virginia).

Average Group

BALDWIN. Fifty Famous Stories Retold, 58–59.
BEARD and BAGLEY. First Book in American History, 51–54.
COE. Founders of our Country, 132–152.
DYER and BRADY. Merrill Readers, IV : 36–47.
EGGLESTON. Stories of American Life and Adventure, 9–13.
ELSON and MACMULLAN. Story of our Country, I : 51–58.
FORMAN. First Lessons in American History, 38–43.
GORDY. American Leaders and Heroes, 42–54.
GORDY. Elementary History of the United States, 24–31.
GORDY. Our Patriots, 30–38.
INGRAHAM. Story of Democracy, 146–158.
MACE. Primary History, 56–63.
McMASTER. Primary History of the United States, 44–48.
MORRIS. Primary History of the United States, 38–48.
MOWRY. First Steps in the History of our Country, 48–55.
NIDA. Following Columbus, 158–169.
PERRY and PRICE. American History, I : 122–131.
PRATT. The Early Colonies, 33–65.
SOUTHWORTH. Builders of our Country, I : 73–81.
SWAN. History and Civics, Grade 5A, 124–142.
TAPPAN. American Hero Stories, 38–49.

Lower Group

BAKER and THORNDIKE. Everyday Classics, IV : 171–173.
BARNES. Primary History of the United States, 31–34.
BLAISDELL and BALL. American History for Little Folks, 12–17.
BLAISDELL and BALL. Child's Book of American History, 24–35.
BOLENIUS. Fourth Reader, 97–106.
DAVIS. Stories of the United States, 63–71.
DODGE. Stories of American History, 26–33.
FAIRGRIEVE and YOUNG. The World, 3–9.
FIELD. Fourth Reader. 263–276.
FOX. Indian Primer, 96–113.
WAYLAND. History Stories for Primary Grades, 151–154.
WELSH. Colonial Days, 25–70.
WILSON. A History Reader, 97–108.
YOUNG and FIELD. Literary Readers, IV : 238–249.

Teachers

BECKER. Beginnings of the American People, 54–64.
BOGART. Economic History of the United States, 23, 31–34.

COFFIN. Old Times in the Colonies, 90–92 (good illustrations).
COMAN. Industrial History of the United States, 22–26, 32–35, 37–39, 44–46.
FISHER. The Colonial Era, 30–41.
FISKE. Old Virginia and her Neighbors, I : 64–169.
JOHNSTON. Pioneers of the Old South, 10–72.
LAMPREY. Days of the Discoverers, 284–298.
MACDONALD. Documentary Source Book of American History, 1–19.
MUZZEY. An American History, 26–30.
SANFORD. Story of Agriculture in the United States, 12–15.
THWAITES. The Colonies, 65–72.
TYLER. England in America, 34–75.
TYLER. Narratives of Early Virginia, 25–71.
American Citizenship Course in United States History, III : 18–19, 43–54.
Baltimore County Course of Study, 447, 457–458.
Elementary School Journal, XVII : 631–633.

Minimal Essentials

Names of Persons: **John Smith; Pocahontas** (pō'k*à* hŏn't*à*s); **Powhatan** (pou'h*à* tăn')
Names of Places: **James River; Jamestown**
Date: **1607** — founding of Jamestown
Historical Terms: **permanent colony; colonization**
Things to Remember
Virginia was the first permanent English colony in the New World.
At first the colony had a very hard time.

Illustrative Material

BROWN. Famous Pictures: 115, Baptism of Pocahontas; 2251, Captain Smith rescued by Pocahontas.
GABRIEL (ED.). Pageant of America, I: 172–178, 183–186; V: 8; XI: 9–10, 33; XIII: 13–15.
McKINLEY. Illustrated Topics for American History: S. 6.
Keystone Views: 21, John Smith trading with the Indians; 22, John Smith and Pocahontas.
Perry Pictures: 1343-G, Captain John Smith; 1343-H, Marriage of Pocahontas.

Procedure during Assimilation

Reading as described on pages 24–29.
Picture study based on the illustrative material listed above.
Use the following dramatizations: "Gentlemen of Virginia." Tucker and Ryan, *Historical Plays of Colonial Days*, pp. 28–33; "A Narrow Escape." Ibid. pp. 131–136; "Pocahontas and Captain Smith."[1] Stevenson, *Children's Classics in Dramatic Form*, II : 99–107; "Pocahontas saves Jamestown." Ibid. pp. 107–115.
Children may manage their own library readings.[2]
Make a sand-table representation of the eastern coast and the first colony.[3]
Children make up a commercial company.

[1] Children should be told that the tale of Pocahontas saving Captain Smith's life is possibly not true; nevertheless it is an interesting tale.
[2] *The Twentieth Yearbook of the National Society for the Study of Education*, Part I, "Conducting a Real Library." pp. 92–93.
[3] Dobbs, E. V., *Primary Handwork*, pp. 76–101.

Children draw scenes representing John Smith's early life.

The class begins to make coöperatively a large wall map to be used throughout the study of colonization, and added to cumulatively.[1] Use the title "English Colonies in America." Mark Virginia, Jamestown, James River.

Special reports from Otis's *Richard of Jamestown.*

Drill on minimal essentials.

Objective test.

Organization

The teacher puts on the board an outline somewhat similar to the following. Children tell what details are to be included under each point.

THE COLONY OF VIRGINIA

1. Getting the people together
2. The voyage and the landing
3. Explorations and the search for gold
4. Hardships during the early years
5. What Smith did for the colony

Recitation

An oral language lesson based on the above outline.

---

b. After a while it grew and prospered

Preparation

A project is planned which will make clear the idea of representation; this should be begun long enough beforehand to have been carried to completion by the time this story is reached. It is desirable that the persons engaging in the project be separated far enough to show the difficulties caused by distance. For example, the fourth grades in all buildings in the city may decide to bring to the local moving-picture theater the Chronicles of America photoplay "Jamestown." First the project is discussed in each room, and the difficulties of carrying it out en masse brought forward. Each grade may elect two representatives (*carry on the election by the proper procedure, and call those elected "representatives"*). The children chosen, together with their teachers, then interview the

[1] Harris, Ruby M., "Making Maps." *The Twentieth Yearbook of the National Society for the Study of Education,* Part I, pp. 47–48.

manager of the theater and arrange the date and the price. Representatives may decide upon any other details necessary and report the results to their respective classes. All the way through the teacher calls attention to the machinery by which the object is achieved, as well as to the object itself. Introduce the word *representation* in connection with the system and discuss reasons why it is better than direct action by all.

No additional presentation is needed.

Assimilation

Readings

Upper Group

BEEBY. Community Life Today and in Colonial Times, 238–245.
BLAISDELL. The Story of American History, 37–38.
EGGLESTON. A First Book in American History, 79–85.
GORDY. Colonial Days, 26–38.
GORDY. Leaders in Making America, 46–49.
GORDY. Stories of Early American History, 83–85.
HAZARD and DUTTON. Indians and Pioneers, 149–157.
INGRAHAM. Story of Democracy, 159–160.
MONTGOMERY. Beginners' American History, 33–35.
OTIS. Richard of Jamestown.
TAPPAN. Elementary History of our Country, 49–51.
WOODBURN and MORAN. Beginner's History of the United States, 93–95.

Average Group

BEARD and BAGLEY. First Book in American History, 55.
ELSON and MACMULLAN. Story of our Country, I : 58–62.
FORMAN. First Lessons in American History, 43–44, 70–72.
GORDY. Elementary History of the United States, 31–36.
MACE. Primary History, 63–70.
McMASTER. Primary History of the United States, 48–52.
MORRIS. Primary History of the United States, 48–51.
NIDA. Following Columbus, 171–178.
PERRY and PRICE. American History, I : 131–135; II : 2–3.
SOUTHWORTH. Builders of our Country, I : 81–84, 201–207.
SWAN. History and Civics, Grade 5 A, 143–156.

Lower Group

BARNES. Primary History of the United States, 35–38.
WELSH. Colonial Days, 71–83.
WILSON. A History Reader, 108–109.

Teachers

BECKER. Beginnings of the American People, 65–80.
BOGART. Economic History of the United States, 36–50, 70–73.
CALLENDER. Economic History of the United States, 20–28.
COFFIN. Old Times in the Colonies, 97–110 (good illustrations).
COMAN. Industrial History of the United States, 54–61.
FISHER. The Colonial Era, 41–61.

FISKE. Old Virginia and her Neighbors, I : 223–298.
JOHNSTON. Pioneers of the Old South, 73–102.
MUZZEY. An American History, 30–33.
SANFORD. Story of Agriculture in the United States, 12–23.
THWAITES. The Colonies, 72–81.
TYLER. England in America, 76–117.
American Citizenship Course in United States History, III : 54–61.
Baltimore County Course of Study, 458.

Minimal Essentials

Name of Place: **Virginia** (vĕr jĭn′ĭ à)
Dates : **1619** — slavery introduced into Virginia ; **1619** — beginning of representation in America
Historical Terms: **representatives; plantations; making laws; colonists; vote**
Things to Remember

When each man was given a farm of his own, the colony grew.

In 1619 slaves were brought into Virginia.

In 1619 the colonists had the first representatives in America.

Illustrative Material

GABRIEL (ED.). Pageant of America, I : 187–192.
Chronicles of America Photoplays, Yale University Press : Jamestown.

Procedure during Assimilation

Reading as described on pages 24–29.
Picture study based on the illustrative material listed above.
On the sand-table map children apportion off farms for the settlers.
Make a sand-table representation of the beginning of tobacco-raising.[1]
Use the following dramatizations : "The Beginning of Negro Slavery." Tucker and Ryan, *Historical Plays of Colonial Days*, pp. 44–49 ; "Pocahontas in London." Ibid. pp. 68–74 ; "Virginia Children of Long Ago." Ibid. pp. 148–153.
Children draw pictures of the slave ships and a slave market.
Make a list of the subjects about which the plantation owners would need to come together for discussion. Hold a meeting of the House of Burgesses and make laws on the questions.
Drill on minimal essentials.
Objective test.

Organization

The teacher puts on the board an outline somewhat similar to the following. Children tell what details are included under each point.

THE GROWTH OF VIRGINIA

1. Land given to each settler
2. Tobacco raised
3. Representatives elected

[1] Holm, Johanna, *Poster and Sand-Table Work*.

Recitation

The recitation is based on the outline on page 171. Children are chosen to tell the story to members who have been absent, to help in their make-up work.

2. How the people in the South lived
   a. Houses and furniture
   b. Food
   c. Clothing
   d. Work
   e. Churches and schools
   f. Amusements and social life
   g. Punishments
   h. Travel

No additional preparation and presentation are necessary.

Assimilation

Readings

Houses and furniture

Upper Group

BEEBY. Community Life Today and in Colonial Times, 312–313.
EGGLESTON. Life in the Eighteenth Century, 10–15.
GORDY. Leaders in Making America, 55–56.
GORDY. Stories of Early American History, 149–150.
HART and HAZARD. Colonial Children, 149–152.

Average Group

McMASTER. Primary History of the United States, 52–54.
MORRIS. Primary History of the United States, 117–118.
NIDA. Following Columbus, 253–255, 272.
PRATT. Early Colonies, 66–67, 73–74.
SWAN. History and Civics, Grade 5 A, 255–256.

Lower Group

BLAISDELL and BALL. Short Stories from American History, 104–110.

Teachers

BURWELL. A Girl's Life in Virginia.
EGGLESTON. Life in the Eighteenth Century, 209–217.
FISKE. Old Virginia and her Neighbors, II : 220–228.
McMASTER. History of the People of the United States, I : 72, 80.
MUZZEY. An American History, 63–64.
PAGE. Social Life in Old Virginia before the War, 7–22.
SANFORD. Story of Agriculture in the United States, 65–67.
TYLER. England in America, 114–116.

FIG. 3. A Virginia Tobacco Plantation (before the Introduction of Cotton Culture)

Food

All Groups

HART and HAZARD. Colonial Children, 149–151.
NIDA. Following Columbus, 259–266, 268–271.
The teacher reads to the class the following reference:
FISKE. Old Virginia and her Neighbors, II : 228–231.

Clothing

Upper Group

EGGLESTON. Life in the Eighteenth Century, 141–143.
HART and HAZARD. Colonial Children, 151.

Average Group

MORRIS. Primary History of the United States, 119.
PRATT. The Early Colonies, 69–73.
SWAN. History and Civics, Grade 5 A, 256–257.

Lower Group

Try PRATT.

Teachers

FISKE. Old Virginia and her Neighbors, II : 274.

Work

All Groups

GORDY. Leaders in Making America, 56–57.
HART and HAZARD. Colonial Children, 63–64.
NIDA. Following Columbus, 255–256.
The teacher reads extracts from the following references:
BOGART. Economic History of the United States, 47–50.
CALLENDER. Economic History of the United States, 29–44.
FISKE. Old Virginia and her Neighbors, II : 232–235.
McMASTER. History of the People of the United States, I : 73–74, 96, 97.
OSGOOD. History of Industry, 338–346.
PAGE. Social Life in Old Virginia before the War, 22–46.
SANFORD. Story of Agriculture in the United States, 62–65.
THWAITES. The Colonies, 98–100, 102–104.

Churches and schools

Upper Group

GORDY. Leaders in Making America, 57.
GORDY. Stories of Early American History, 152.
HART and HAZARD. Colonial Children, 224–228.

Average Group

MORRIS. Primary History of the United States, 119–120.
PRATT. The Early Colonies, 68, 74–75.
SWAN. History and Civics, Grade 5 A, 255.

Lower Group

Try PRATT.

Teachers

EGGLESTON. Life in the Eighteenth Century, 224–243.
FISKE. Old Virginia and her Neighbors, II : 245–255.

McMASTER. History of the People of the United States, I : 26, 27, 79.
MUZZEY. An American History, 65–67.
THWAITES. The Colonies, 107–109.

Amusements and social life

Upper Group

BLAISDELL. The Story of American History, 136–138.
EGGLESTON. Our First Century, 235–239.
GORDY. Leaders in Making America, 57–58.
GORDY. Stories of Early American History, 153.
HART and HAZARD. Colonial Children, 228–232.

Average Group

NIDA. Following Columbus, 256–257.
PERRY and PRICE. American History, I : 225–229.

Lower Group

WILSON. A History Reader, 138–139.

Teachers

FISKE. Old Virginia and her Neighbors, II : 237–243.
McMASTER. History of the People of the United States, I : 74–78, 81, 82, 84.
PAGE. The Old South, 112–117, 129–139.
PAGE. Social Life in Old Virginia before the War, 46–109.
SANFORD. Story of Agriculture in the United States, 67–69.
THWAITES. The Colonies, 100–101, 106–108.

Punishments

All Groups

PRATT. The Early Colonies, 68–69.

Teachers

McMASTER. History of the People of the United States, I : 98–101.

Travel

All Groups

BALDWIN. Fourth Reader, 90–96.
NIDA. Following Columbus, 277–281.
SWAN. History and Civics, Grade 5 A, 257–258.
The teacher may read to the children "The Story of a New England Boy and his Visit to Virginia." *Elementary School Teacher*, II : 682–685.

Teachers

McMASTER. History of the People of the United States, I : 41–52.
THWAITES. The Colonies, 107.

Minimal Essentials

Name of Place: **Mount Vernon**
Historical Terms: **slave quarters; Church of England** (Episcopal); **coach; wharf**
Things to Remember
Each large plantation was a little world in itself.
The chief crop was tobacco.
The plantation owners were rich.

Illustrative Material

GABRIEL (ED.). Pageant of America, III: 29–31, 50–54, 60–68; V: 8–9; XIII: 43–49.
PYLE. Book of the American Spirit, 35, 37.
Keystone Views: 87, Home of Washington, Mount Vernon; 88, The Spinning Room at Mount Vernon; 90, The Slave Quarters at Mount Vernon.

Procedure during Assimilation

Reading as described on pages 24–29.
Picture study based on the illustrative material listed above.
Use the dramatization "Colonial Virginia." Shoemaker, *Colonial Plays for the School-room*, pp. 23–26.
Draw the plan of a plantation.
Construct on the sand table a plantation showing the "big house," kitchens, slave quarters, tobacco fields, drying-houses, smokehouses, wharf, etc. (Do not include cotton fields at this early date.)
For construction work see Clark's *On Early Transportation in America.*[1]
Make a museum collection on Southern life.[2]
Dress dolls to represent Southern gentlemen and ladies, poor whites, and slaves.
Play records of spinning songs, music of the cavaliers, the minuet.
Make hominy.[3]
Try to tan leather.[4]
Model in clay the dishes and furniture of the Old South.
Children list the advantages and disadvantages of pioneer life.[5]
Drill on minimal essentials.
Objective test.

Organization

The class makes a set of questions covering the entire study and sends it as a riddle book to an absent member.[6] Competition among members decides whose set of questions has covered the story best. The entire class then makes up an "answer sheet," allowing each child to word the answer to at least one question.

Recitation

The questions are arranged in order, and the children attempt to answer as many in the list as possible.

[1] Clark, Ada B., "Some Industrial Work done in the Harrisonburg State Normal Training School." *School and Home Education*, XXXIV: 26–28.
[2] Johnson, Beulah, "A Museum of Home Manufacture." *The Twentieth Year-book of the National Society for the Study of Education*, Part I, p. 68; Forsaith, Francis, "An Historical Museum." Ibid. p. 147.
[3] Baumgarten, Rose, "Making Old-fashioned Hominy." Ibid. p. 63.
[4] "A Fifth-Grade Pupil's Account of Tanning Leather." Ibid. p. 63.
[5] Morgan, Catherine, "Colonial Life." Ibid. p. 52.
[6] Robbins, Edith, "A Riddle Book made for an Absent Member." Ibid. p. 80.

3. Soon other colonies appeared along the coast

Preparation

"Have you ever heard of Georgia? of Carolina?
"What is a debt?" Introduce the word *debtor*.
Teach any new words in the presentation test.

Presentation

During all the time that Virginia was growing stronger, more and more people kept coming from England to start tobacco plantations for themselves. After a while most of the best land was taken, so they had to spread out along the seacoast and into the interior (*showing on the map*). Virginia might be thought of as the mother colony, and all these other little settlements as her daughters.

Other rich men in England said: "Why do we let the company which started Virginia have all the trade? Let us, too, start a colony in America, and we shall make a great deal of money trading with the West Indies." So eight of them went to the king, and he gave them some land south of Virginia (*showing on the map*).

They started a colony here. You can see how easy it would be for them to trade with the Spanish (*illustrating at the map*). In a very short time the colony was strong and prosperous. It was called Carolina (*pointing to the word on the board*).

You must not imagine that many of the people who lived in England were rich. Far from it! Some people were so poor that they had to borrow money from their neighbors. Then if they could not find work or if they were sick, when the time came to pay back the money they could not pay. What do you suppose happened? They were put in prison — not because they were bad, but just because they could not pay. This seems very silly to us. If they had not been put in prison they might after a while have been able to find work and pay back the money. If they were put in prison they surely could not earn any money. But in those days it was very common to put people in prison for debt.

One rich Englishman felt sorry for these debtors, so he decided to pay their expenses to America and to found a colony for them. You may be sure they were glad to leave the prisons. They came to America and settled just south of Carolina, very near to the Spanish people. This did not seem to be a very good place, but it was much better than being in prison. So grew up the colony of Georgia. Now we have studied three colonies in the south — Virginia, Carolina, and Georgia.

PRESENTATION TEST

Check the best answer:

  a. The people in Virginia had to spread out
     _ _ _ because they did not like to live near together
     _ _ _ because the best land had been taken
     _ _ _ because the king made a law

  b. The eight rich men wanted to make a colony
     _ _ _ to trade with the West Indies
     _ _ _ to help the poor people
     _ _ _ to help fight the Indians

  c. Their colony was named
     _ _ _ Virginia
     _ _ _ Georgia
     _ _ _ Carolina

  d. In England many people were put in prison
     _ _ _ because they were in debt
     _ _ _ because they would not fight
     _ _ _ because they would not work

  e. A kind man decided to bring them to
     _ _ _ Virginia
     _ _ _ Georgia
     _ _ _ Carolina

Assimilation

Readings

Upper Group

BEEBY. Community Life Today and in Colonial Times, 290–298.
EGGLESTON. Life in the Eighteenth Century, 39–51.
EGGLESTON. Wreck of the Redbird.
EVANS. America First, 72–75.
FOOTE and SKINNER. Explorers and Founders of America, 235–242.
GORDY. Leaders in Making America, 52–55.
GORDY. Stories of Early American History, 136–139.
MONTGOMERY. Beginners' American History, 84–89.
PENDLETON. King Tom and the Runaways.
TAPPAN. Elementary History of our Country, 109–114.
TAPPAN. Letters from Colonial Children, 296–319.
WOODBURN and MORAN. Beginner's History of the United States, 152–156.
WOODBURN and MORAN. Finders and Founders of the New World, 187–194.
Compton's Pictured Encyclopedia (Georgia).

Average Group

BEARD and BAGLEY. First Book in American History, 55–57, 77–78.
COE. Founders of our Country, 251–265.
EGGLESTON. Stories of Great Americans, 21–26.
ELSON and MACMULLAN. Story of our Country, I : 67–76.
FORMAN. First Lessons in American History, 83–87.
GORDY. Elementary History of the United States, 89–94.
GORDY. Our Patriots, 54–57.
MACE. Primary History, 111–114.
MCMASTER. Primary History of the United States, 83–89.
MORRIS. Primary History of the United States, 97–101.
NIDA. Following Columbus, 232–236.
PERRY and PRICE. American History, I : 193–199.
PRATT. The Early Colonies, 166–182.
SOUTHWORTH. Builders of our Country, I : 197–200.
STONE and FICKETT. Everyday Life in the Colonies, 103–114.

Lower Group

BARNES. Primary History of the United States, 62–67.
SHEPHERD. Geography for Beginners, 124–127.
WELSH. Colonial Days, 133–246.
WILSON. A History Reader, 325–326.

Teachers

COFFIN. Old Times in the Colonies, 337–356 (good illustrations).
FISHER. The Colonial Era, 76–81, 303–312.
HARRIS. Stories of Georgia.
JOHNSTON. Pioneers of the Old South, 199–244.
MACDONALD. Documentary Source Book of American History, 63–66, 95–103.
MUZZEY. An American History, 47–48, 55.
SANFORD. Story of Agriculture in the United States, 39–46.
THWAITES. The Colonies, 87–95.

Minimal Essentials

Names of Places: the South; Carolina; Georgia
Historical Term: debtors
Things to Remember
   Carolina grew because it could trade with the Spaniards.
   Georgia was founded as a home for debtors who had been in prison.

Illustrative Material

GABRIEL (ED.). Pageant of America, I : 264–275; III : 55–59.
Ford Educational Library (films) : 32, Landmarks of Early Explorations and Settlements in North America, Parts I and II.

Procedure during Assimilation

Reading as described on pages 24–29.
Picture study based on the illustrative material listed above.
Use the dramatization "Georgia Debtors." Shoemaker, *Colonial Plays for the Schoolroom*, pp. 49–50.

On the sand table make a South Carolina rice farm.[1]
Add Carolina and Georgia to the map "English Colonies in America."
Drill on minimal essentials.
Objective test.

Organization

Half of the class selects the main points in the story of Carolina, and the other half organizes the story of Georgia. Each child writes his points in sentences and cuts them so that only one sentence appears on one slip. They exchange bundles of slips and arrange them correctly. The child who made the slips in each case acts as judge of the correct arrangement.

Recitation

Each child prepares an oral story based on his own slips.

---

4. New Netherland became New York
    a. Life in New Netherland

Preparation

"Who had discovered land for the Dutch? Where? What did the Dutch people call their town at the mouth of the Hudson River? How did they get along with the Indians? Do you know anything about the way the Dutch people lived in Holland? Today we shall find out how they lived in the New World."

No additional presentation is needed.

Assimilation

Readings

Upper Group

BARSTOW. Explorers and Settlers, 177–181.
BEEBY. Community Life Today and in Colonial Times, 252–258.
BLAISDELL. The Story of American History, 92–95.
BROOKS. In Leisler's Times.
FOOTE and SKINNER. Explorers and Founders of America, 175–185.
GORDY. Colonial Days, 151–163.

---

[1] For pictures see Brigham, A. P., and McFarlane, C. T., *Essentials of Geography*, I : 120; Carpenter, F. G., *North America*, pp. 120, 122. For the teacher: Sutherland, W. J., and Sanford, C. M., *Practical Exercises in Geography*, Book One, pp. 41–44; Carpenter, F. G., *How the World is Fed*, pp. 56–66.

GORDY. Leaders in Making America, 87–89, 91–94.
GORDY. Stories of Early American History, 118–126, 153–156.
GUERBER. Story of the Thirteen Colonies, 142–145.
HAZARD and DUTTON. Indians and Pioneers, 233–239.
MONTGOMERY. Beginners' American History, 41–42.
OTIS. Peter of New Amsterdam.
TAPPAN. Elementary History of our Country, 90–95.
TAPPAN. Letters from Colonial Children, 188–217.
WOODBURN and MORAN. Beginner's History of the United States, 137–141.
WOODBURN and MORAN. Finders and Founders of the New World, 164–165, 167, 170–175.
World Book (New York, Patroons).

Average Group
BEARD and BAGLEY. First Book in American History, 68–69.
ELSON and MACMULLAN. Story of our Country, I : 115–119.
FORMAN. First Lessons in American History, 77–80.
GORDY. Elementary History of the United States, 77–80.
MACE. Primary History, 97–99.
MCMASTER. Primary History of the United States, 72–75.
MORRIS. Primary History of the United States, 58–60.
NIDA. Following Columbus, 206–210, 253.
PERRY and PRICE. American History, I : 170–175.
PRATT. The Early Colonies, 89–98.
SOUTHWORTH. Builders of our Country, I : 130–135.
SWAN. History and Civics, Grade 5A, 165–187 ; 249–254.

Lower Group
BARNES. Primary History of the United States, 38–40.
FAIRGRIEVE and YOUNG. The World, 9–10.
HARTWELL. Story Hour Readings, IV : 243–246.
PRATT. Beginners' Book, 101–107.
WAYLAND. History Stories for Primary Grades, 161.
WILSON. A History Reader, 137–138.

Teachers
COFFIN. Old Times in the Colonies, 143–146, 195–205 (good illustrations).
DAY. History of Commerce, 191.
FISHER. The Colonial Era, 177–187.
FISKE. Dutch and Quaker Colonies in America, I : 111–218.
GOODWIN. The Dutch and the English on the Hudson, 17–122.
HART. American History told by Contemporaries, I : 517–544.
MACDONALD. Documentary Source Book of American History, 26–31, 74–76.
SANFORD. Story of Agriculture in the United States, 34–37.
THWAITES. The Colonies, 196–202, 222–232.
American Citizenship Course in United States History, III : 86–93.
Baltimore County Course of Study, 447, 459.

Minimal Essentials

Names of Places: **New Amsterdam; New Netherland**
Historical Terms: **patroons; estates**
Things to Remember
  The Dutch people had large estates.
  The land belonged to only a few men.
  Most people could not own a farm.

Illustrative Material

BRADLEY. Village Series of Cut-Outs: Dutch Village.
GABRIEL (ED.). Pageant of America, I: 230–232; XI: 16; XIII: 36–40.
PYLE. Book of the American Spirit, 51, 57, 63, 67.
Keystone Views: 35, The *Half Moon* of Henry Hudson.

Procedure during Assimilation

Reading as described on pages 24–29.
Picture study based on the illustrative material listed above.
Use the following dramatizations: "Strategy of Director Kieft." Tucker and Ryan, *Historical Plays of Colonial Days*, pp. 50–55; "Easter Rabbit." Ibid. pp. 75–82; "Manhattan Island." Hubbard, *Little American History Plays*, pp. 42–49; "Life in New York." Shoemaker, *Colonial Plays for the Schoolroom*, pp. 45–47.
The class makes cheese.[1]
Model in clay some articles of furniture used by the Dutch.
Draw illustrations representing life under Dutch rule.[2]
Construct on the sand table a patroon's estate.
The teacher puts on the board a list of Dutch names prominent in American history, such as Roosevelt, Vanderbilt, etc.
Drill on minimal essentials.
Objective test.

Organization

Divide the class into groups. One group makes out a set of questions about the houses; another, clothing; another, work; and so on. These are submitted to the teacher for approval.

Recitation

Each group asks its questions of the other groups.

---

b. The war with the English

No additional preparation and presentation are needed.

Assimilation

Readings

Upper Group

BEEBY. Community Life Today and in Colonial Times, 258–262.
BLAISDELL. The Story of American History, 95–96.
EVANS. America First, 58–62.
FOOTE and SKINNER. Explorers and Founders of America, 181–186.
GORDY. Colonial Days, 163–169.

[1] Witherspoon, Helen, "A Fifth-Grade Pupil's Account of Making Cheese." *The Twentieth Yearbook of the National Society for the Study of Education*, Part I, p. 64.

[2] Dobbs, E. V., *Primary Handwork*, pp. 6–16.

GORDY. Leaders in Making America, 89–91.
GORDY. Stories of Early American History, 126–129.
GUERBER. Story of the Thirteen Colonies, 145–146.
HAZARD and DUTTON. Indians and Pioneers, 244–248.
MOWRY. American Pioneers, 58–67.
TAPPAN. Elementary History of our Country, 95–98.
TAPPAN. Letters from Colonial Children, 218–232.
WOODBURN and MORAN. Beginner's History of the United States, 133–137.
WOODBURN and MORAN. Finders and Founders of the New World, 165, 169–170.
Compton's Pictured Encyclopedia (Stuyvesant).
World Book (New York, Stuyvesant).

Average Group

BEARD and BAGLEY. First Book in American History, 69–72.
ELSON and MACMULLAN. Story of our Country, I : 120–121.
GORDY. Elementary History of the United States, 80–83.
GORDY. Our Patriots, 47–48.
MACE. Primary History, 100–104.
MCMASTER. Primary History of the United States, 75–77.
MORRIS. Primary History of the United States, 56–57.
MOWRY. First Steps in the History of our Country, 77–82.
NIDA. Following Columbus, 212–218.
PERRY and PRICE. American History, I : 176–179.
PRATT. The Early Colonies, 98–103.
SOUTHWORTH. Builders of our Country, I : 135–141.
SWAN. History and Civics, Grade 5 A, 188–192.
TAPPAN. American Hero Stories, 73–83.

Lower Group

BARNES. Primary History of the United States, 40–41.
BLAISDELL and BALL. American History for Little Folks, 42–44.
WAYLAND. History Stories for Primary Grades, 162.

Teachers

CALLENDER. Economic History of the United States, 16–20.
COFFIN. Old Times in the Colonies, 224–233 (good illustrations).
COMAN. Industrial History of the United States, 53–54.
FISHER. The Colonial Era, 187–190.
FISKE. Dutch and Quaker Colonies in America, I : 219–342.
GOODWIN. The Dutch and the English on the Hudson, 137–149.
MUZZEY. An American History, 48–52.
THWAITES. The Colonies, 202–207.
TYLER. England in America, 290–295.
Baltimore County Course of Study, 447, 459–460.

Minimal Essentials

Name of Person: **Peter Stuyvesant** (stī'vĕ sănt)
Name of Place: **New York**
Historical Term: **surrender**
Things to Remember
  The English claimed the land on which the Dutch had settled.
  The English conquered the Dutch.
  The name of the colony was changed from New Netherland to New York.

Illustrative Material

GABRIEL (ED.). Pageant of America, I: 233–238.
PYLE. Book of the American Spirit, 65, 71–76.
Chronicles of America Photoplays, Yale University Press: Peter Stuyvesant.

Procedure during Assimilation

Reading as described on pages 24–29.
Picture study based on the illustrative material listed above.
Use the dramatization "A Skirmish at Rensselaerswijck." Tucker and Ryan, *Historical Plays of Colonial Days*, pp. 92–100.
The class gives speeches which Stuyvesant might have used in attempting to stir his people to resistance.
Add New York and New Jersey to the map "English Colonies in America."
Find on the map York in England.
What is the title of the second son of the king of England today? Find a picture of him to show the class.
Drill on minimal essentials.
Objective test.

Organization

The teacher puts a topical outline on the board somewhat similar to the following:

THE WAR WITH THE ENGLISH

1. England's claim to the land
2. Stuyvesant's attempt at battle
3. The surrender

Recitation

Children write a paragraph on each of the topics above.
A drill lesson on section I of Unit III should be given at this point.

II. Some People came so that they might go to their Own Churches
    1. The Pilgrims came to Plymouth

Preparation

"From our overview story, do you remember why many people in England were unhappy about the religious conditions? What did the king want them to do?

"What did we call people who made a long journey for a

religious purpose?" (In the story of the Crusades.) "Today we shall hear about some other pilgrims."

Teach any new words in the presentation test. All are included in the first two thousand of the Thorndike word list or have previously been taught as minimal essentials.

Presentation

The people who wanted to go to their own churches were in a sad plight! The doors of their churches were nailed shut; many of their ministers were in prison; and when they tried to have services in barns or upstairs in their houses, soldiers would come and drive them away. It was an unhappy time.

At last they decided there was only one thing to do: that was to leave England. Where should they go? Not to Spain or France, because there people could not go to the church they liked, either. But just across the Channel, here in Holland (*showing on the map*), was a place where they could worship God as they pleased. They stole away to Holland, quietly, so that the king's soldiers would not see them.

There they lived happily for many years. Only one thing worried them. The neighbors were all Dutch. Their own children were learning the Dutch language, and they feared that after a while they would no longer seem English. What should they do? If they went back to England the same trouble would begin over again. Finally one of their number said: "I know what we can do. We can go to America. Part of America belongs to England, so we would still be English, and yet it is so far away that the king's soldiers could not come to close our churches."

That seemed a good idea, so all the people gathered together their trunks and boxes and some of their furniture, and set sail for America. They landed and founded a colony of their own. This was the first settlement made in order to allow people to go to their own churches. The others about which we studied — Virginia, Carolina, Georgia, and New York — were settled in order to earn a better living.

PRESENTATION TEST

1. *Check the best answer:*

   a. The king of England would not let his people

   _ _ _ come to America
   _ _ _ go to their own churches
   _ _ _ go to Holland

   b. The people decided to go to

   _ _ _ Holland
   _ _ _ Spain
   _ _ _ France

   c. They did not want to live there always

   _ _ _ because they liked to travel
   _ _ _ because the people of Holland were cruel
   _ _ _ because their children were becoming Dutch

   d. They decided to come to America

   _ _ _ because they wanted to make a long voyage
   _ _ _ because it was English land, but was far from the king
   _ _ _ because the king wanted them to go to America

   e. They made a new colony

   _ _ _ in order to make a better living
   _ _ _ in order to go to their own church

2. *Draw one line under the names of all the English colonies which were founded in order to earn a better living:*

   Virginia, New York, Mexico, Georgia, Spain, Carolina, India

Assimilation

Readings

Upper Group

BAILEY. Boys and Girls of Colonial Days, 11–21.
BARSTOW. Explorers and Settlers, 189–219.
BEEBY. Community Life Today and in Colonial Times, 173–206.
BLAISDELL. The Story of American History, 47–66.
BROOKS. Lem, a New England Village Boy.
BURNHAM. Hero Tales from History, 160–169.
BURTON. Builders of our Nation, 88–101.
BUTTERWORTH. Pilot of the Mayflower.
DIX. Soldier Rigdale.
DRAKE. On Plymouth Rock.
EGGLESTON. A First Book in American History, 49–59.
EVANS. America First, 40–51.
FARIS. Where our History was Made, Book One, 37–40.
FOOTE and SKINNER. Explorers and Founders of America, 136–148.
GORDY. Colonial Days, 53–71.
GORDY. Leaders in Making America, 59–68.
GORDY. Stories of Early American History, 93–108.
GUERBER. Story of the Thirteen Colonies, 105–122.
HAZARD and DUTTON. Indians and Pioneers, 167–193.
JENKS. Captain Myles Standish.

LOGIE. From Columbus to Lincoln, 47–57.
MATHEWS. Argonauts of Faith.
MONTGOMERY. Beginners' American History, 44–53.
MOORE. Pilgrims and Puritans, 22–91 (selections).
OTIS. Mary of Plymouth.
PERSONS. Our Country in Poem and Prose, 34–41.
TAPPAN. Elementary History of our Country, 52–60.
TAPPAN. Letters from Colonial Children, 85–127.
TERRY. History Stories of Other Lands, V : 182–185.
WARREN. Little Pioneers, 13–51, 100–140, 231–251 (select readings).
WOODBURN and MORAN. Beginner's History of the United States, 96–108.
WOODBURN and MORAN. Finders and Founders of the New World, 116–135.
Compton's Pictured Encyclopedia (Plymouth, Mayflower, Standish).
Colonial Stories retold from *St. Nicholas*, 27–55.
Indian Stories retold from *St. Nicholas*, 136–154.
World Book (Pilgrims, Mayflower, Plymouth Colony, Standish, Alden).

Average Group

BEARD and BAGLEY. First Book in American History, 57–59.
COE. Founders of our Country, 153–166, 214–217.
DICKINSON. Children's Book of Thanksgiving Stories, 26–40, 57–71, 86–105, 159–166.
EGGLESTON. Stories of American Life and Adventure, 21–26.
ELSON and MACMULLAN. Story of our Country, I : 77–88.
FIELD. Fourth Reader, 286–293.
FORMAN. First Lessons in American History, 53–58.
GORDY. American Leaders and Heroes, 64–79.
GORDY. Elementary History of the United States, 41–50.
GORDY. Our Patriots, 6–12.
INGRAHAM. Story of Democracy, 161–188.
MACE. Primary History, 75–87.
McMASTER. Primary History of the United States, 56–60.
MORRIS. Primary History of the United States, 60–70.
MOWRY. First Steps in the History of our Country, 56–62.
NIDA. Following Columbus, 179–192.
PERRY and PRICE. American History, I : 141–151.
PRATT. The Early Colonies, 113–120.
SOUTHWORTH. Builders of our Country, I : 89–98.
STONE and FICKETT. Everyday Life in the Colonies, 1–12.
SWAN. History and Civics, Grade 5 A, 194–208.
TAPPAN. American Hero Stories, 59–72.
TOMLINSON. Places Young Americans want to Know, 1–13.
USHER. Story of the Pilgrims for Children (selections).

Lower Group

BALDWIN. Stories of Old New England, 3–23.
BARNES. Primary History of the United States, 41–45.
BLAISDELL and BALL. American History for Little Folks, 18–29.
BLAISDELL and BALL. American History Story Book, 1–18.
BLAISDELL and BALL. Short Stories from American History, 1–21.
CURTIS. Why we celebrate our Holidays, 124–129, 130–141.
DAVIDSON and ANDERSON. Lincoln Readers, III : 56–61, 62–67.
DAVIS. Stories of the United States, 73–84.

DODGE. Stories of American History, 18–25.
FAIRGRIEVE and YOUNG. The World, 10–15.
FIELD. Second Reader, 112–115, 116–125.
NELSON. Our Pilgrim Forefathers.
PRATT. Beginners' Book, 89–100.
PRATT. Stories of Colonial Children, 7–12, 19–72.
PUMPHREY. Pilgrim Stories (selections).
WAYLAND. History Stories for Primary Grades, 15–20, 96–102.
WILSON. A History Reader, 65–83.
YOUNG and FIELD. Literary Readers, IV: 256–274.

Teachers

ANDREWS. Fathers of New England, 1–20.
BECKER. Beginnings of the American People, 80–90.
CALLENDER. Economic History of the United States, 12–15
COFFIN. Old Times in the Colonies, 111–140.
CRAWFORD. In the Days of the Pilgrim Fathers, 1–229.
FISHER. The Colonial Era, 82–100.
FISKE. Beginnings of New England, 59–106.
MACDONALD. Documentary Source Book of American History, 19.
MUZZEY. An American History, 33–36.
SANFORD. Story of Agriculture in the United States, 24–33.
THWAITES. The Colonies, 113–124.
TYLER. England in America, 149–162.
American Citizenship Course in United States History, III: 67–74.
Baltimore County Course of Study, 460–461.
Public School Methods, V: 221–224, 389–401. (The Methods Co., Chicago.)

Minimal Essentials

Names of Persons: **Governor William Bradford; Miles Standish; Massasoit** (măs′á soit′)**; Pilgrims**
Name of Place: **Plymouth**
Date: **1620** — settlement of Plymouth
Historical Terms: Mayflower ; **freedom of religion**
Things to Remember
 The Pilgrims came to America to have freedom of religion.
 The king had not given them the right to settle.

Illustrative Material

GABRIEL (ED.). Pageant of America, I: 194–225.
PYLE. Book of the American Spirit, 17.
Chronicles of America Photoplays, Yale University Press: The Pilgrims.
Educational Posters of the National Child Welfare Association: Thanksgiving.
Ford Educational Library (films): English Settlements — Plymouth.
Keystone Views: 25, Plymouth Rock; 27, Monument to Pilgrims; 28, Statue of Massasoit; 30, Grave of Captain Miles Standish.
National Posters: The Story of the Pilgrims.
Perry Pictures: 1331, Embarkation of the Pilgrims; 1331-B, The *Mayflower* in Plymouth Harbor; 1331-C, Departure of the Pilgrims from Delft Haven; 1332, Landing of the Pilgrims; 1332-B, Landing of the Pilgrims; 1334, Departure of the *Mayflower*; 1340, Miles Standish and his Soldiers.

Procedure during Assimilation

Reading as described on pages 24–29.

Picture study based on the illustrative material listed above.

Use the following dramatizations: "Massasoit's Illness." Tucker and Ryan, *Historical Plays of Colonial Days*, pp. 34–38; "Little Pilgrims." Ibid. pp. 39–43; "An Encounter in the Forest." Ibid. pp. 56–59; "The Pilgrims in Holland." Ibid. pp. 64–68; "The First Winter." Ibid. pp. 143–147; "The First Thanksgiving Day." Johnston and Barnum, *Book of Plays for Little Actors*, pp. 121–135; "The First Thanksgiving." Shoemaker, *Colonial Plays for the Schoolroom*, pp. 29–32; "The Courtship of Miles Standish." Parsons, *Red Letter Day Plays*, pp. 19–26; "The First Thanksgiving Day." Hubbard, *Little American History Plays*, pp. 23–28; "The Soul of Priscilla." McElroy, *A Dramatic and Musical Program for School Grades* (American Book Company series; free).

Set up a "Dutch Village." (See illustrative material in Appendix B.)

Play records of the landing of the Pilgrims.

Make a sand-table map showing Holland on one side, England in one corner, and Plymouth on the other side. Show the *Mayflower* returning.

The class plans a Thanksgiving program.[1]

Children attempt to make a frieze illustrating the story of the Pilgrims.[2]

Read parts of the governor's last Thanksgiving proclamation; the president's. Post them on the bulletin board.

Drill on minimal essentials.

Objective test.

Organization

One child is chosen from each row to put his own list of points on the board. The class judges which is best.

Recitation

Each child puts his own outline on the board and recites the entire story based on it.

---

2. The Puritans came to Boston

Preparation

"Have any of you ever heard of Boston? What do you know about it?

"There were many people in England who had not been allowed to go to their own churches, but who had not been able

---

[1] Kendall, C. N., and Stryker, F. E., "Concerning Holidays." *History in the Elementary School*, pp. 122–130.

[2] Juth, Emma C., "Making a Frieze illustrating the Story of Miles Standish." *The Twentieth Yearbook of the National Society for the Study of Education*, Part I, pp. 112–113; Boylston, E. R., "A Thanksgiving Thought." *School Arts Magazine*, XXV: 152–155 (November, 1925); Hubbard, Priscilla, "The Story of the Pilgrims." *School Arts Magazine*, XXV: 178–180 (cut-outs).

to go to Holland. Some had been sick, others had had old people to care for, others were too young. They had had to stay in England. What do you suppose they would think when they heard that the Pilgrims were getting along so well in America?

"Many of them did decide to come too. We shall now read about how they made their settlement in America."

No additional presentation is needed.

Assimilation
Readings

Upper Group

ANDREWS. Ten Boys who lived on the Road from Long Ago to Now, 193–209.
BEEBY. Community Life Today and in Colonial Times, 264–273.
BURNHAM. Hero Tales from History, 170–175.
FOOTE and SKINNER. Explorers and Founders of America, 150–159.
GORDY. Colonial Days, 73–78.
GORDY. Stories of Early American History, 108–110.
GUERBER. Story of the Thirteen Colonies, 122–125.
HAZARD and DUTTON. Indians and Pioneers, 194–202.
LOGIE. From Columbus to Lincoln, 57–62.
MONTGOMERY. Beginners' American History, 53–54.
MOORE. Pilgrims and Puritans, 115–152 (selections).
OTIS. Ruth of Boston.
PERKINS. Puritan Twins.
TAPPAN. Elementary History of our Country, 61–68.
WOODBURN and MORAN. Beginner's History of the United States, 110–115.
WOODBURN and MORAN. Finders and Founders of the New World, 136–142.
Compton's Pictured Encyclopedia (Puritans, Massachusetts).
World Book (Puritans, Massachusetts: History).

Average Group

BEARD and BAGLEY. First Book in American History, 59–65.
EGGLESTON. Stories of Great Americans, 9–11.
ELSON and MACMULLAN. Story of our Country, I: 88–91.
FORMAN. First Lessons in American History, 59–63.
GORDY. Elementary History of the United States, 51–54.
GORDY. Our Patriots, 13–18.
MACE. Primary History, 87–88.
McMASTER. Primary History of the United States, 60.
MORRIS. Primary History of the United States, 70–71.
MOWRY. First Steps in the History of our Country, 64–68.
NIDA. Following Columbus, 194–196.
PERRY and PRICE. American History, I: 151–154.
SOUTHWORTH. Builders of our Country, I: 101–106.
SWAN. History and Civics, Grade 5 A, 208–216.

Lower Group

BARNES. Primary History of the United States, 45–46.
DAVIS. Stories of the United States, 85–106.
PRATT. Stories of Colonial Children, 73–76.

Teachers

ANDREWS. The Fathers of New England, 21–44.
BECKER. Beginnings of the American People, 86–102.
COFFIN. Old Times in the Colonies, 152–176.
COMAN. Industrial History of the United States, 35, 63–66, 66–72.
FISHER. The Colonial Era, 101–114.
FISKE. Beginnings of New England, 107–169.
MACDONALD. Documentary Source Book of American History, 22–26.
MUZZEY. An American History, 36–38.
THWAITES. The Colonies, 124–132.
TYLER. England in America, 183–209.
American Citizenship Course in United States History, III: 75–80.
Public School Methods, V: 222–233. (The Methods Co., Chicago.)

Minimal Essentials

Names of Persons: **John Winthrop; Puritans**
Names of Places: **Massachusetts; Boston**
Date: **1630** — settlement of Boston
Historical Term: **settled**
Things to Remember
　The Puritans settled in Boston.
　They were better off than the Pilgrims.
　After a while Boston and Plymouth joined as one colony, and were called
　　Massachusetts.

Illustrative Material

GABRIEL (ED.). Pageant of America, I: 210–216.
Chronicles of America Photoplays, Yale University Press: The Puritans.

Procedure during Assimilation

Reading as described on pages 24–29.
Picture study based on the illustrative material listed above.
Use the following dramatizations: "The Settling of Boston." Hubbard, *Little Amer-
　ican History Plays*, pp. 34–41; "Saturday Night in New England." Tucker and
　Ryan, *Historical Plays of Colonial Days*, pp. 154–157; "A Christmas Tree in New
　England." Ibid. pp. 115–121; "How the Indians planted Powder." Ibid. pp. 101–
　105; "The Quakers in New England." Ibid. pp. 20–27; "The Departure." Ibid.
　pp. 1–6.
Add Boston to the sand-table representation of Plymouth.
Play the record "Music of the Puritans."
Add Massachusetts to the map "English Colonies in America," showing both
　Plymouth and Boston.
Drill on minimal essentials.
Objective test.

Organization

Other children than those chosen for the last story put
their lists of points on the board. The class decides which
is best.

Recitation

Each child puts his own outline on the board and gives the complete story based on it.

---

3. How the Puritans lived
   a. Houses and furniture
   b. Food
   c. Clothing
   d. Work
   e. Churches and schools
   f. Amusements and social life
   g. Punishments
   h. Travel

No additional preparation and presentation are needed.

Assimilation

Readings

Houses and furniture

Upper Group

BEEBY. Community Life Today and in Colonial Times, 208–217.
BLAISDELL. The Story of American History, 66–70.
GORDY. Colonial Days, 78–80.
GORDY. Leaders in Making America, 72–74.
GORDY. Stories of Early American History, 140–142.
MOWRY. American Inventions and Inventors, 24–33.
PRESCOTT. A Day in a Colonial Home, 1–5.
TAPPAN. Elementary History of our Country, 83–86.
WARREN. Little Pioneers, 52–63, 86–99.

Average Group

FORMAN. First Lessons in American History, 88–89.
GORDY. Elementary History of the United States, 66–67.
McMASTER. Primary History of the United States, 64–66.
MORRIS. Primary History of the United States, 110–111.
NIDA. Following Columbus, 237–240.
PRATT. The Early Colonies, 129–130.
SOUTHWORTH. Builders of our Country, I : 98–99.
SWAN. History and Civics, Grade 5 A, 244–245.

Lower Group

HARTWELL. Story-Hour Readings, IV : 239–242.
WILSON. A History Reader, 130–133.

Teachers
- ANDREWS. Colonial Folk Ways, 45–69.
- EARLE. Home Life in Colonial Days, 1–75.
- McMASTER. History of the People of the United States, I : 13–14.
- Baltimore County Course of Study, 460.

Food

Upper Group
- BEEBY. Colonial Life Today and in Colonial Times, 217–218.
- BLAISDELL. The Story of American History, 70–72.
- GORDY. Leaders in Making America, 74.
- GORDY. Stories of Early American History, 142–143.
- PRESCOTT. A Day in a Colonial Home, 7–13.
- WARREN. Little Pioneers, 64–75, 141–154.

Average Group
- FORMAN. First Lessons in American History, 90–92.
- GORDY. Elementary History of the United States, 67–68.
- HARTWELL. Story-Hour Readings, IV : 239–240.
- McMASTER. Primary History of the United States, 66–67, 70–72.
- MORRIS. Primary History of the United States, 111–112.
- NIDA. Following Columbus, 241.
- SWAN. History and Civics, Grade 5 A, 245.
- USHER. Story of the Pilgrims for Children, 130.

Lower Group
- Try McMASTER and NIDA.

Teachers
- EARLE. Home Life in Colonial Days, 76–165.
- McMASTER. History of the People of the United States, I : 17.

Clothing

Upper Group
- MOWRY. American Inventions and Inventors, 143–147.

Average Group
- MORRIS. Primary History of the United States, 112.
- NIDA. Following Columbus, 241–243.
- PRATT. Early Colonies, 127–128.
- SWAN. History and Civics, Grade 5 A, 245–246.

Lower Group
- HARTWELL. Story-Hour Readings, IV : 241–242.
- PRATT. Stories of Colonial Children, 155–159, 161, 163.

Teachers
- ANDREWS. Colonial Folk Ways, 70–95.
- EARLE. Child Life in Colonial Days, 34–62.
- EARLE. Home Life in Colonial Days, 281–299.
- McMASTER. History of the People of the United States, I : 18, 19.

Work

Upper Group
- ALLEN. The United States, 307–311.
- BAILEY. Boys and Girls of Colonial Days, 33–44, 101–109.

BEEBY. Community Life Today and in Colonial Times, 305–312.
EGGLESTON. Stories of American Life and Adventure, 66–74.
GORDY. Leaders in Making America, 75–78.
GORDY. Stories of Early American History, 143–144.
HART and HAZARD. Colonial Children, 55–57.
MOWRY. American Inventions and Inventors, 67–76.
PRESCOTT. A Day in a Colonial Home, 13–48.
TAPPAN. Elementary History of our Country, 86–88.
WARREN. Little Pioneers, 209–230.
Lessons in Community and National Life, Series B, 17–24.

Average Group

EDSON-LAING. Readers, IV : 102–108, 170–172, 173–177.
FORMAN. First Lessons in American History, 92–93.
GORDY. Elementary History of the United States, 69–70.
McMASTER. Primary History of the United States, 68–70.
MORRIS. Primary History of the United States, 115–116.
NIDA. Following Columbus, 243–245.
SOUTHWORTH. Builders of our Country, I : 108–109.
STONE and FICKETT. Everyday Life in the Colonies, 36–41, 61–68.
SWAN. History and Civics, Grade 5 A, 242–243.
USHER. Story of the Pilgrims for Children, 78–84.
Lessons in Community and National Life, Series C, 17–24.

Lower Group

BALDWIN. Stories of Old New England, 27–29.
BOLENIUS. Fourth Reader, 129–133.
DAVIDSON and ANDERSON. Lincoln Readers, III : 71–77 (storing food) ; 250–254 (soap-making).
PRATT. Stories of Colonial Children, 13–18.
WILKINS. Weavers' Children.

Teachers

ANDREWS. Colonial Folk Ways, 178–203.
ANDREWS. Fathers of New England, 72–80, 85–87.
BOGART. Economic History of the United States, 53–63, 82–84.
CALLENDER. Industrial History of the United States, 50–53.
EARLE. Child Life in Colonial Days, 305–341.
EARLE. Home Life in Colonial Days, 166–280, 300–324.
McMASTER. History of the People of the United States, I : 10, 16, 27–30, 62, 63.
OSGOOD. History of Industry, 318–331, 351–360.
SANFORD. Story of Agriculture in the United States, 51–62.
SPEARS. The Story of the New England Whalers.
THWAITES. The Colonies, 184–186.
TRYON. Household Manufactures in the United States.
Elementary School Journal, XVII : 163–177, 234–249.

Churches and schools

Upper Group

BAILEY. Tell me Another Story, 123–127.
EVANS. America First, 125–134.
GORDY. Colonial Days, 81, 82–83.
GORDY. Leaders in Making America, 78–80.
GORDY. Stories of Early American History, 145–147.

HART and HAZARD. Colonial Children, 194–196, 220–221.
LOGIE. From Columbus to Lincoln, 63–64.
WARREN. Little Pioneers, 172–182.

Average Group
EDSON-LAING. Readers, IV : 114–118.
ELSON and MACMULLAN. Story of our Country, I : 91–94.
FORMAN. First Lessons in American History, 95–97, 99–102.
GORDY. Elementary History of the United States, 68–69, 70–72.
MORRIS. Primary History of the United States, 113–115.
NIDA. Following Columbus, 245–247, 250–251.
PRATT. The Early Colonies, 120–124.
SOUTHWORTH. Builders of our Country, I : 106–107.
STONE and FICKETT. Everyday Life in the Colonies, 13–35.
SWAN. History and Civics, Grade 5 A, 243–244.
USHER. Story of the Pilgrims for Children, 135–137.

Lower Group
BALDWIN. Stories of Old New England, 23–27, 29.
PRATT. Stories of Colonial Children, 77–91, 92–104.

Teachers
ANDREWS. Colonial Folk Ways, 130–177.
COFFIN. Old Times in the Colonies, 303–317.
EARLE. Child Life in Colonial Days, 63–210, 227–304.
EARLE. Home Life in Colonial Days, 364–387.
McMASTER. History of the People of the United States, I : 14–15, 20–26, 31–39.
MUZZEY. An American History, 61–62.
THWAITES. The Colonies, 188–192.
Baltimore County Course of Study, 460–461.

Amusements and social life

Upper Group
GORDY. Leaders in Making America, 80–81.
GORDY. Stories of Early American History, 148–149.
HART and HAZARD. Colonial Children, 152–155.

Average Group
FORMAN. First Lessons in American History, 94–95, 102–103.
GORDY. Elementary History of the United States, 70.
MORRIS. Primary History of the United States, 113.
NIDA. Following Columbus, 247–249.
PRATT. The Early Colonies, 126.
SWAN. History and Civics, Grade 5 A, 247–248.
USHER. Story of the Pilgrims for Children, 133–134.

Lower Group
BALDWIN. Stories of Old New England, 47–48.

Teachers
ANDREWS. Colonial Folk Ways, 96–129.
CRAWFORD. In the Days of the Pilgrim Fathers, 258–278.
EARLE. Child Life in Colonial Days, 211–226, 342–376.
EARLE. Home Life in Colonial Days, 388–451.
McMASTER. History of the People of the United States, I : 62.
THWAITES. The Colonies, 181–184, 186–188.

Punishments

Upper Group

GORDY. Colonial Days, 83.
LOGIE. From Columbus to Lincoln, 64–66.
World Book (Pillory).

Average Group

ELSON and MACMULLAN. Story of our Country, I : 94–95.
GORDY. Elementary History of the United States, 72.
NIDA. Following Columbus, 249–250.
PRATT. The Early Colonies, 125.
SOUTHWORTH. Builders of our Country, I : 107.
SWAN. History and Civics, Grade 5 A, 247.

Lower Group

Try NIDA and PRATT.

Teachers

MCMASTER. History of the People of the United States, I : 98–101.

Travel

Upper Group

BEEBY. Community Life Today and in Colonial Times, 300–304.
EVANS. America First, 134–139.
GORDY. Colonial Days, 81.
HART and HAZARD. Colonial Children, 67–70.
LOGIE. From Columbus to Lincoln, 114–122.
MOWRY. American Inventions and Inventors, 187–206.
ROCHELEAU. Great American Industries : Transportation, 34–37.

Average Group

FORMAN. First Lessons in American History, 97–98.
INGRAHAM. Story of Democracy, 205–209.
STONE and FICKETT. Everyday Life in the Colonies, 94–102.

Lower Group

Try STONE and FICKETT.

Teachers

ANDREWS. Colonial Folk Ways, 204–237.
BOGART. Economic History of the United States, 79–81.
COMAN. Industrial History of the United States, 73–76.
EARLE. Home Life in Colonial Days, 325–363.
MCMASTER. History of the People of the United States, I : 44–52.
RUGG and SCHWEPPE. The Westward Movement and the Growth of Transportation, 12–16.

Minimal Essentials

Historical Terms: **stocks; pillory; hourglass; town meeting**
Things to Remember
 The Puritans lived a very simple life.
 They lived in towns, not on plantations.
 They manufactured most of their goods at home.

Illustrative Material

BRADLEY. Village Series of Cut-Outs: Pilgrim Village.

BROWN. Famous Pictures: 1497, First Sunday in New England; 2069, 2070, Plymouth in 1622; 1444, Priscilla Spinning.

GABRIEL (ED.). Pageant of America, III: 24–28, 32–40, 69–89, 298–306, 314–324; V: 9–13; XI: 12–15; XIII: 29–36.

Mentor, XI: 7–8, 14–20, 38 (July, 1923); XIII: 26–36 (October, 1925).

Perry Pictures: 1333-E, First Houses in Plymouth; 1337, Puritans going to Church.

Society for Visual Education. Schoolfilm: English Settlements in North America.

Travel, XXXVII: 21–25 (June, 1921).

Procedure during Assimilation

Reading as described on pages 24–29.

Picture study based on the illustrative material listed above.

Use the following dramatizations: "Soft-Soap Day." Hubbard, *Little American History Plays*, pp. 29–33; "Fire Spirits." Parsons, *Red Letter Day Plays*, pp. 5–14; "A Witchcraft Story." Shoemaker, *Colonial Plays for the Schoolroom*, pp. 35–39; "First Thanksgiving." White, Amelia, *School Arts Magazine*, XXIV: 167–173.

Invite an old lady of the community to come to school and show the children how to spin.[1]

Observe weaving if possible.

Take a trip to the local museum to see articles of colonial days.

Make candles.[2]

Make soap.[3]

Girls begin to piece a quilt in the sewing class.

If there is a log house in the vicinity, take the children to see it.

The children represent a New England village on the sand table,[4] showing fort, church, houses, palisade, stocks, ducking-stool, pillory, Indian village in the distance, the common, corn fields.

Make a log cabin; carve pieces of furniture from soft wood. Furnish completely with furniture, dishes, and implements.

Dress dolls to represent a Puritan lady, a gentleman, an elder, a soldier, a servant.[5]

Make a Puritan church.

Set up a cut-out of a Pilgrim village.

Make a booklet about *The Pilgrim Fathers*.[6]

Make a picture museum.[7]

Children compose original poems about the Pilgrims or Puritans.

Use the suggestions for cut-outs in "A Thanksgiving Cut-Out." Robbins, Grace, *School Arts Magazine*, XXIV: 183–185.

Drill on minimal essentials.

Objective test.

---

[1] Parker, S. C., *General Methods of Teaching in Elementary Schools*, pp. 14–15.

[2] King, Florence, "Making a Candle as Primitive Man Did." *The Twentieth Yearbook of the National Society for the Study of Education*, Part I, p. 60.

[3] Hubbard, E., *Little American History Plays*, pp. 29–33.

[4] Yount, Ethelyn, "History of Pioneer Life." *The Twentieth Yearbook of the National Society for the Study of Education*, Part I, p. 49.

[5] McLaughlin, K., and Troxell, E., "Dressing the Pilgrims." *Number Projects for Beginners*, pp. 52–60.

[6] Van der Kar, Alma, "Our Pilgrim Fathers — A Booklet." *The Twentieth Yearbook of the National Society for the Study of Education*, Part I, p. 51.

[7] Young, Francis D., "A Picture Museum." Ibid. p. 83.

Organization

Divide the class into groups and assign a subject to each group to organize.

Recitation

Each child chooses from the list one topic and recites on that in detail.

---

4. The Puritans spread out to many other colonies

Preparation

"Have you ever heard of Connecticut? Rhode Island?" (*Write the words on the board.*) "What do you know about them?

"What was the reason why the Puritans had left England?

"Have you ever heard of Quakers?"

Teach here any new words in the presentation test.

Presentation

We must remember that the Puritans had left England because they were not allowed to go to their own church. We should expect, then, that when they came to America they would be good to others. Suppose that somebody wanted to come to Boston, but did not believe quite the same as the Puritans. Did the Puritans say, "Let us remember how badly we were treated in England, and not treat anyone that way ourselves?" No, indeed, they did not. They said: "We have come a long way in order to have our own church. Now we will not have any other church among us. If any person does not believe as we do, let him leave our colony." And sometimes they did not wait for such a person to leave; they drove him out.

Since all of us do not believe the same things, it was natural that some people would come to Boston who did not want to go to the Puritans' church. They had to leave, so they went a little way off and founded colonies of their own. In this way new colonies began to spring up all around Massachusetts. Also, in time there were so many Puritans in America that some of them, too, went to the new colonies to live. The names of some of the new colonies were Connecticut and Rhode Island.

PRESENTATION TEST

1. *Check the best answer:*

   a. When the Puritans came to America

     _ _ _ they would not let anyone stay in their colony if he went to a different church

     _ _ _ they let everybody come who wanted to

     _ _ _ they did not care whether or not anybody came

   b. In the Puritan colony

     _ _ _ none but Puritans ever came

     _ _ _ some people who believed differently came and wanted to stay in Boston

     _ _ _ the people who were not Puritans drove out the Puritans

   c. The Puritans

     _ _ _ paid no attention to the other people

     _ _ _ let the other people stay

     _ _ _ drove the other people out

2. *Draw one line under the two correct answers in the following list:*

   The other people founded the colonies of

          Virginia, Rhode Island, Connecticut, Georgia

Assimilation

Readings

Upper Group

BEEBY. Community Life Today and in Colonial Times, 273–277.
BURNHAM. Hero Tales from History, 176–180.
CROWE. Studies in American History, I : 217–241.
EVANS. America First, 54–58.
FOOTE and SKINNER. Explorers and Founders of America, 160–166.
GORDY. Colonial Days, 83–88, 98–111.
GORDY. Stories of Early American History, 110–115.
GUERBER. Story of the Thirteen Colonies, 126–132.
HALL. The Golden Arrow.
LOGIE. From Columbus to Lincoln, 70–71, 76–81.
MONTGOMERY. Beginners' American History, 60–65.
PERSONS. Our Country in Poem and Prose, 41–42.
TAPPAN. Elementary History of our Country, 70–82.
TAPPAN. Letters from Colonial Children, 175–187.
Compton's Pictured Encyclopedia (Roger Williams, Connecticut).
World Book (Roger Williams, Rhode Island: History, Connecticut).

Average Group

ELSON and MACMULLAN. Story of our Country, I : 95–102.
FORMAN. First Lessons in American History, 64–69.
GORDY. American Leaders and Heroes, 81–91.
GORDY. Elementary History of the United States, 57–65.

GORDY. Our Patriots, 19–29.
MACE. Primary History, 89–93.
McMASTER. Primary History of the United States, 60–61.
MORRIS. Primary History of the United States, 71–75, 80–86.
MOWRY. First Steps in the History of our Country, 69–74.
NIDA. Following Columbus, 196–199.
PERRY and PRICE. American History, I : 154–158.
PRATT. The Early Colonies, 138–147, 152–157.
SOUTHWORTH. Builders of our Country, I : 110–114.
SWAN. History and Civics, Grade 5 A, 217–221.

Lower Group

BARNES. Primary History of the United States, 51–53.
DODGE. Stories of American History, 34–39.
WAYLAND. History Stories for Primary Grades, 172–174.

Teachers

COFFIN. Old Times in the Colonies, 184–194.
FISHER. The Colonial Era, 114–133.
MacDONALD. Documentary Source Book of American History, 36–45.
MUZZEY. An American History, 38–45.
THWAITES. The Colonies, 140–153.
TYLER. England in America, 229–281.
American Citizenship Course in United States History, III : 80–86.

Minimal Essentials

Name of Person: **Roger Williams**
Names of Places: **Rhode Island; Connecticut; New England**
Historical Term: **exile**
Things to Remember
The Puritans did not want to give religious freedom to other people.
Roger Williams founded a colony where everyone could worship as he chose.

Illustrative Material

GABRIEL (ED.). Pageant of America, I : 217–225; XI : 24.
Educational Posters of National Child Welfare Association : Freedom of Conscience : Roger Williams.
Perry Pictures : 1353, Charter Oak.

Procedure during Assimilation

Reading as described on pages 24–29.
Picture study based on the illustrative material listed above.
Use the dramatization [1] "The First Crop of Apples." Tucker and Ryan, *Historical Plays of Colonial Days*, pp. 83–91.
Add Connecticut and Rhode Island to the sand-table map; to the map entitled "English Colonies in America." Color New England red.
Drill on minimal essentials.
Objective test.

[1] For stage settings see Todd, Jessie, "Stage Scenery and Color." *School Arts Magazine*, XXIV : 364–367.

Organization

The teacher writes the following topical outline on the board. Children write summary sentences for each point.

THE PURITANS SPREAD TO OTHER COLONIES

1. Roger Williams in Boston
2. The founding of Rhode Island
3. Hooker's people leaving Massachusetts
4. The beginning of Connecticut

Recitation

Each child chooses the first two topics or the second two and prepares a three-minute speech on them.

> 5. They had trouble with the Indians

Preparation

"How had the Indians treated the first Spanish explorers?
"How had the Spaniards treated the Indians at first?
"How did the Indians treat the people of Jamestown? of Plymouth?"

Discuss the meaning of the expression "back into the interior."

Presentation

We must remember that the Indians made their living largely by hunting the herds of deer that traveled over the vast plains and in the great forests. The deer were afraid of men and ran away whenever they saw human beings.

Now the white men were beginning to come in great numbers; at first there were only a few, then a hundred, then several hundred, then a thousand, then several thousand. They had to have a large farm for each family, so they kept spreading out — first along the coast and up the rivers (*showing on the map*), and then back into the interior.

The Indians began to be alarmed: not because of the land, for there was land enough for all; but as the settlers moved farther inland, the wild animals, which were afraid of people, kept moving farther and farther west, and so the Indians were left without food.

Some of the wiser Indians knew that if the white men continued to spread out, they would all have to move west. One of their wisest men said: "There is only one thing for us to do. We shall have to make war upon the white people and drive them back to the country from which they came. Then the wild animals will come back, and we can live as we have always done in the land of our fathers."

So they started a great war against the colonists, but it was a sad failure. The Indians were too few; they had to secure their guns and ammunition from other white colonists, and so the newcomers won. It was plain that white people had come to America to stay.

However, the English did not feel that they were stealing the Indians' homes. They said: "All those square miles of land on which only wild animals feed are being wasted. They furnish food enough for only a few thousand Indians. Now, when we take the land, we divide it into farms; each farm grows rich crops, and we can then feed many, many more people. Let the land belong to whoever will make the best use of it." So the stronger people took the land, and the weaker had to move on.

PRESENTATION TEST

Check the best answer:

a. The Indians needed a great deal of land
  _ _ _ because there were so many of them
  _ _ _ because the wild animals, which were their food, needed much room
  _ _ _ because they did not want the white people to have it

b. To keep the white people from getting the land, the Indians
  _ _ _ made a fence around it
  _ _ _ ran away
  _ _ _ made war

c. The war was won by the
  _ _ _ Indians
  _ _ _ white people

d. The English people thought they had a right to the land
  _ _ _ because they could make better use of it
  _ _ _ because they were strong enough to take it
  _ _ _ because they were white

Assimilation
Readings
Upper Group

BAILEY. Boys and Girls of Colonial Days, 45–57.
EGGLESTON. A First Book in American History, 67–79.
FOOTE and SKINNER. Explorers and Founders of America, 243–252.
GORDY. Colonial Days, 114–137.
GORDY. Stories of Early American History, 172–176.
GUERBER. Story of the Thirteen Colonies, 132–134, 138–142.
HART and HAZARD. Colonial Children, 112–115.
LOGIE. From Columbus to Lincoln, 72–76.
MONTGOMERY. Beginners' American History, 66–76.
MOWRY. American Pioneers, 318–325 (Eliot).
PERSONS. Our Country in Poem and Prose, 14–15.
TAPPAN. Elementary History of our Country, 68–69.
WADE. Ten Big Indians, 91–123.
WOODBURN and MORAN. Beginner's History of the United States, 119–130.
WOODBURN and MORAN. Finders and Founders of the New World, 143–160.
World Book (King Philip, Pequot, Eliot).

Average Group

COE. Founders of our Country, 187–201.
EGGLESTON. Stories of American Life and Adventure, 26–31.
ELSON and MacMULLAN. Story of our Country, I : 103–112.
GORDY. Elementary History of the United States, 54–56, 62–63, 101–102.
McMASTER. Primary History of the United States, 61–63.
MORRIS. Primary History of the United States, 76–80.
MOWRY. First Steps in the History of our Country, 95–100.
NIDA. Following Columbus, 199–202.
PERRY and PRICE. American History, I : 158–162.
PRATT. The Early Colonies, 148–151.
SOUTHWORTH. Builders of our Country, I : 115–122.
STONE and FICKETT. Everyday Life in the Colonies, 42–60.
TAPPAN. American Hero Stories, 84–95.

Lower Group

BARNES. Primary History of the United States, 46–47, 53–55.
BLAISDELL and BALL. American History for Little Folks, 30–37, 53–58.
PRATT. Stories of Colonial Children, 105–154.
WILSON. A History Reader, 21–25, 121–129.

Teachers

BURTON. The Story of the Indians of New England.
COFFIN. Old Times in the Colonies, 176–183, 241–250.
FISHER. The Colonial Era, 153–157.
FISKE. Beginnings of New England, 211–216, 220–233, 235–237.
THWAITES. The Colonies, 136–137, 170–172.
Baltimore County Course of Study, 461.
Public School Methods, V : 144–147. (The Methods Co., Chicago.)

Minimal Essentials

Name of Person: **King Philip**
Historical Terms: **ambush; betray**
Things to Remember
> The Indians began to see that the white people were fast taking the land.
> The Indians tried to stop them, but failed.
> The white people thought they had a right to the land because they could make
> it produce more.

Illustrative Material

GABRIEL (ED.). Pageant of America, XI : 16–19, 40–41.
PYLE. Book of the American Spirit, p. 47.
Perry Pictures : 1341-B, John Eliot Preaching.

Procedure during Assimilation

Reading as described on pages 24–29.
Picture study based on the illustrative material listed above.
Use the following dramatizations : "An Indian Story." Shoemaker, *Colonial Plays
for the Schoolroom,* pp. 53–57 ; "Wampum Belts." Tucker and Ryan, *Historical
Plays of Colonial Days,* pp. 60–63.
Children draw scenes of Indian warfare.
Construct on the sand table Philip's stronghold.
Drill on minimal essentials.
Objective test.

Organization

The teacher puts an outline of the story on the board.
Each child is to write two subheads under each main point.

Recitation

Give the recitation step as a socialized recitation.[1]

---

6. The Catholics came to Maryland

No additional preparation and presentation are needed.

Assimilation

Readings

Upper Group
> BEEBY. Community Life Today and in Colonial Times, 286–291.
> BURNHAM. Hero Tales from History, 180–185.
> FOOTE and SKINNER. Explorers and Founders of America, 219–224.
> GORDY. Colonial Days, 40–51.

[1] Havighurst, H. C., "A Plan for a Socialized History Recitation." *The Historical Outlook,* XII : 293–295.

GORDY. Leaders in Making America, 49–52.
GORDY. Stories of Early American History, 87–92.
GUERBER. Story of the Thirteen Colonies, 152–154.
HART and HAZARD. Colonial Children, 143–144.
LOGIE. From Columbus to Lincoln, 71–72.
MONTGOMERY. Beginners' American History, 55–60.
OTIS. Calvert of Maryland.
TAPPAN. Elementary History of our Country, 104–108.
TAPPAN. Letters from Colonial Children, 128–155.
World Book (Maryland, Lord Baltimore).

Average Group

ELSON and MACMULLAN. Story of our Country, I : 63–66.
FORMAN. First Lessons in American History, 72–75.
GORDY. Elementary History of the United States, 37–41.
GORDY. Our Patriots, 39–43.
MACE. Primary History, 70–74.
McMASTER. Primary History of the United States, 54–55.
MORRIS. Primary History of the United States, 86–89.
MOWRY. First Steps in the History of our Country, 83–87.
NIDA. Following Columbus, 220–224.
PERRY and PRICE. American History, I : 135–137, 193.
PRATT. The Early Colonies, 132–137.
SOUTHWORTH. Builders of our Country, I : 179–186.
SWAN. History and Civics, Grade 5 A, 222–232.

Lower Group

BARNES. Primary History of the United States, 50–51.
DODGE. Stories of American History, 40–45.
WELSH. Colonial Days, 84–132.

Teachers

COFFIN. Old Times in the Colonies, 293–296.
FISHER. The Colonial Era, 62–75.
FISKE. Old Virginia and her Neighbors, I : 255–285.
GAMBRILL. Leading Events of Maryland History.
HALL. Narratives of Early Maryland, 25–43, 277–304.
JOHNSTON. Pioneers of the Old South, 116–131.
MACDONALD. Documentary Source Book of American History, 31–35.
MUZZEY. An American History, 45–47.
SANFORD. Story of Agriculture in the United States, 38–39.
THWAITES. The Colonies, 81–87.
TYLER. England in America, 118–132.
American Citizenship Course in United States History, III : 61–67.
Baltimore County Course of Study, 448, 461–463.

Minimal Essentials

Names of Persons: **Catholics; Lord Baltimore**
Name of Place: **Maryland**
Historical Terms: **persecution; proprietor**
Things to Remember
    Lord Baltimore founded Maryland as a home for persecuted Catholics.
He allowed all Christians to come and settle there.

Illustrative Material

GABRIEL (ED.). Pageant of America, I: 257–262.
Perry Pictures: 1414-F, Landing of Lord Baltimore.

Procedure during Assimilation

Reading as described on pages 24–29.
Picture study based on the illustrative material listed above.
Dramatize scenes from Otis's *Calvert of Maryland*.
Model in clay Father White's wigwam church.
Add Maryland to the map [1] "English Colonies in America."
Drill on minimal essentials.
Objective test.

Organization

Each child makes his own outline of the main points in the story. Brighter children and the teacher assist the slower.

Recitation

Continue as a socialized recitation.[2]

---

7. The Quakers came to Pennsylvania

No additional preparation and presentation are needed.

Assimilation

Readings

Upper Group

BEEBY. Community Life Today and in Colonial Times, 278–285.
BLAISDELL. The Story of American History, 96–105.
BURNHAM. Hero Tales from History, 185–189.
BURTON. Builders of our Nation, 129–140.
EGGLESTON. A First Book in American History, 59–66.
EVANS. America First, 63–67.
FOOTE and SKINNER. Explorers and Founders of America, 225–233.
GORDY. Colonial Days, 88–92, 173–183.
GORDY. Leaders in Making America, 95–103.
GORDY. Stories of Early American History, 130–135.
GUERBER. Story of the Thirteen Colonies, 134–136, 147–152.
HAZARD and DUTTON. Indians and Pioneers, 252–262.
LEWIS and ROWLAND. Silent Readers, V: 171–186.
MONTGOMERY. Beginners' American History, 76–83.
MOWRY. American Pioneers, 68–80.
OTIS. Stephen of Philadelphia.

---

[1] Helpful suggestions for map-making are found in Forsee, Corinne, "Helps for History Teachers." *The Historical Outlook*, XV: 402–405, especially page 403.
[2] See page 204.

PERSONS. Our Country in Poem and Prose, 44–48.
TAPPAN. Elementary History of our Country, 99–104.
TAPPAN. Letters from Colonial Children, 249–288.
WOODBURN and MORAN. Beginner's History of the United States, 142–151.
WOODBURN and MORAN. Finders and Founders of the New World, 176–186.
Compton's Pictured Encyclopedia (William Penn).
World Book (Pennsylvania, William Penn, Quakers, Philadelphia).

Average Group

BEARD and BAGLEY. First Book in American History, 73–76.
COE. Founders of our Country, 233–243.
EGGLESTON. Stories of Great Americans, 17–21.
ELSON and MacMULLAN. Story of our Country, I : 122–128.
FORMAN. First Lessons in American History, 80–82.
GORDY. American Leaders and Heroes, 92–101.
GORDY. Elementary History of the United States, 83–87.
GORDY. Our Patriots, 49–53.
MACE. Primary History, 104–111.
McMASTER. Primary History of the United States, 78–82.
MORRIS. Primary History of the United States, 90–97, 116.
MOWRY. First Steps in the History of our Country, 88–94.
NIDA. Following Columbus, 225–230.
PERRY and PRICE. American History, I : 183–192.
PRATT. The Early Colonies, 158–165.
SOUTHWORTH. Builders of our Country, I : 187–196.
SWAN. History and Civics, Grade 5 A, 233–240.
TAPPAN. American Hero Stories, 108–117.

Lower Group

BARNES. Primary History of the United States, 59–62.
BLAISDELL and BALL. American History for Little Folks, 45–52.
DAVIS. Stories of the United States, 107–113.
DODGE. Stories of American History, 46–51.
WAYLAND. History Stories for Primary Grades, 169–171.

Teachers

COFFIN. Old Times in the Colonies, 216–223, 297–302.
FISHER. The Colonial Era, 199–206.
MacDONALD. Documentary Source Book of American History, 80–84.
MUZZEY. An American History, 52–55.
SANFORD. Story of Agriculture in the United States, 37–38.
THWAITES. The Colonies, 215–217.
American Citizenship Course in United States History, III : 93–97.
Baltimore County Course of Study, 448, 463–464.

Minimal Essentials

Names of Persons : **Quakers; William Penn**
Names of Places : **Philadelphia; Pennsylvania**
Date : **half century** — after Maryland
Historical Term : **treaty**
Things to Remember
  William Penn founded Pennsylvania.
  The Quakers lived there.
  They got along well with the Indians.

Illustrative Material

GABRIEL (ED.). Pageant of America, I: 247–255; XI: 36.
McKINLEY. Illustrated Topics for American History: S. 10.
PYLE. Book of the American Spirit, 92, 93, 95, 96, 97.
Educational Posters of National Child Welfare Association: Justice to Weaker Races: William Penn.
Keystone Views: 37, William Penn's House.
Perry Pictures: 1395-A, Penn's Treaty with the Indians.

Procedure during Assimilation

Reading as described on pages 24–29.
Picture study based on the illustrative material listed above.
Use the following dramatizations: "William Penn's Treaty with the Indians." Tucker and Ryan, *Historical Plays of Colonial Days*, pp. 7–9; "A Pennsylvania Incident." Shoemaker, *Colonial Plays for the Schoolroom*, pp. 41–43.
A trip to the museum to see wampum designs.
The children try to make a wampum belt of beads.
Dress dolls in Quaker costume. Use them in the making of a little theater.[1]
Drill on minimal essentials.
Objective test.

Organization

Each child makes his own outline of the main points in the story.

Recitation

Continue as a socialized recitation.[2]

A drill lesson on section II of Unit III should be given at this point.

III. Very early Some of the Colonists began to wander into the Interior

Daniel Boone went across the mountains

Preparation and Presentation

"We have now reached the time in our history studies when most of the very good land along the coast had been taken up by farms. Suppose that a farmer had five sons. If he divided his land up into five farms, none of them would be very large. Many of the younger boys, then, went out to seek their fortunes and to find other farms for themselves.

---

[1] Forsee, Corinne, "Helps for History Teachers." *The Historical Outlook*, XV: 402–405, especially page 405.   [2] See page 204.

Where would they go?" (*Children show on the map. Use a relief map of the United States east of the Mississippi.*)

"How could they travel over the mountains?" (*Children find the water gaps. Show pictures of gaps through mountains.*)[1]

"When they had crossed the mountains, they could no longer get their supplies of clothing, food, etc. from England. How would they earn their living?" (*Children decide how they could satisfy their wants.*)

"The people who kept coming from England would either have to buy at a good price farms from the settlers along the coast, or they too would have to go away back into the country. Why did they not stay in the towns and work there?

"Our new story is about the people who had to go away back into the country in order to obtain good land."

PRESENTATION TEST

1. *Check the best answer:*

   a. Newcomers had to go away back into the country
   _ _ _ because all the land along the coast had been taken
   _ _ _ because all the *good* land along the coast had been taken
   _ _ _ because it was too crowded near the coast

   b. The best way to go over the mountains was
   _ _ _ to climb over
   _ _ _ to go around the mountains
   _ _ _ to go through the gaps

   c. After they had crossed the mountains, they would have to get their supplies
   _ _ _ by making them all
   _ _ _ by bringing supplies from England
   _ _ _ by going without food

2. *Check the two best answers:*

   New people who came from England could obtain farms in *two* ways
   _ _ _ by buying farms from the settlers at a high price
   _ _ _ by taking farms away from the settlers
   _ _ _ by going to the Spanish colonies
   _ _ _ by going back into the country for farms

Assimilation

Readings

Upper Group

BAILEY. Boys and Girls of Colonial Days, 132–142.
BARSTOW (ED.). Westward Movement, 75–81.
BURNHAM. Hero Tales from History, 232–240.

[1] See the advertising material of the Beechnut Co., Canajoharie, New York: "Farm Slopes of the Mohawk Valley."

DICKSON. Pioneers and Patriots in Early American History, 79–90.
EGGLESTON. A First Book in American History, 134–140.
EVANS. America First, 121–124, 226–231.
FARIS. Where our History was Made, 119–123.
FORBES-LINDSAY. Daniel Boone, Backwoodsman.
GORDY. Leaders in Making America, 213–225.
GORDY. Stories of Later American History, 94–106, 107–121 (Robertson).
GUERBER. Story of the Thirteen Colonies, 288–293.
JOHNSTON. Famous Scouts, 38–74.
LEFFERTS. American Leaders, I : 260–275.
LOGIE. From Columbus to Lincoln, 105–113.
McMURRY. Pioneers of the Mississippi Valley, 68–83.
MONTGOMERY. Beginners' American History, 132–139.
MOWRY. American Heroes and Heroism, 117–124.
MOWRY. American Pioneers, 103–116, 117–126 (Kenton).
OTIS. Hannah of Kentucky.
PERRY and BEEBE. Four American Pioneers, 11–68.
PERRY and PRICE. American History, II : 237–238.
ROOSEVELT. Stories of the Great West, 3–12.
RUGG and SCHWEPPE. The Westward Movement and the Growth of Trans-
    portation, 44–50.
TOMLINSON. Scouting with Daniel Boone.
VOLLINTINE. The Making of America, 54–62, 63–72.
WOODBURN and MORAN. Beginner's History of the United States, 250–264.
Compton's Pictured Encyclopedia (Boone).
World Book (Boone).

Average Group

BASS. Stories of Pioneer Life, 29–32, 33–45, 51–53, 103–136.
COE. Makers of the Nation, 131–150.
EGGLESTON. Stories of Great Americans, 76–83.
FORMAN. First Lessons in American History, 125–129.
GORDY. American Leaders and Heroes, 222–233.
GORDY. Elementary History of the United States, 198–201.
MACE. Primary History, 241–247.
McMASTER. Primary History of the United States, 134–136.
MORRIS. Primary History of the United States, 170–176.
NIDA. Following the Frontier, 48–52.
SOUTHWORTH. Builders of our Country, II : 116–121.
TAPPAN. American Hero Stories, 200–207.

Lower Group

BLAISDELL and BALL. American History for Little Folks, 109–114.
BLAISDELL and BALL. Short Stories from American History, 92–98 (Robertson).
DAVIDSON and ANDERSON. Lincoln Readers, V : 131–137.
GROVE. Story of Daniel Boone.
WAYLAND. History Stories for Primary Grades, 106–108.

Teachers

BOLTON and MARSHALL. Colonization of North America, 96–97, 309–310,
    317–323.
COMAN. Industrial History of the United States, 124–126.
DUNBAR. A History of Travel in North America, I : 24–135, 136–150.
HART. Formation of the Union, 3–5.

HULBERT. The Paths of Inland Commerce, 1–43.
SANFORD. Story of Agriculture in the United States, 70–75.
TURNER. Rise of the New West.
WEST. History of the American People, 142–144.

Minimal Essentials

Name of Person: **Daniel Boone** [1] (bo͞on)
Names of Places: **Kentucky; Appalachian** (ăp′*à* lăch′ĭ ăn; ăp′*à* lā′chĭ ăn) **Mountains**
Date: **eighteenth century**
Historical Terms: **colonial period; pioneer; interior**
Things to Remember
  Some colonists went far away from the sea, because they wanted cheap land.
  They had a hard time going over the mountains.
  They wished still to be English.

Illustrative Material

PYLE. Book of the American Spirit, 153–157.
Chronicles of America Photoplays, Yale University Press: Daniel Boone.
Society for Visual Education. Schoolfilm: Breaking through the Appalachians.

Procedure during Assimilation

Reading as described on pages 24–29.
Picture study based on the illustrative material listed above.
Make a trip to the local museum to see articles used by the pioneers.
Use the following dramatizations: "Daniel Boone." Stevenson, *Children's Classics in Dramatic Form*, IV: 142–154; "Daniel Boone's Snuff Box." Hubbard, *Little American History Plays*, pp. 125–129.
Construct Boonesboro on the sand table.[2]
Dress dolls to represent pioneers.[3]
Use the helps suggested in the books.
Drill on minimal essentials.
Objective test.

Organization

The teacher and the class together make a coöperative outline of the story.

Recitation

Write the story based on the outline above.

---

[1] Not included in the studies of personages referred to on page 5.

[2] Excellent suggestive material for pioneer life is found in Fitzpatrick, Mary, "History Project for the Grades." *The Historical Outlook*, XIV: 68–71.

[3] Dobbs, E. V., "A Colonial Kitchen," p. 56, and "Two Little Knights of Kentucky," p. 94, in *Primary Handwork*; also Hill, H. C., *Community Life and Civic Problems*, pp. 114–121 (picture on page 116).

Minimal Essentials of Unit III

Persons	Places	Terms	Dates
Lord Baltimore	Appalachian Mountains	ambush	*1607.* Founding of Jamestown
Daniel Boone	Boston	betray	*1619.* Slavery introduced into Virginia
Governor Bradford	Carolina	Church of England	
Catholics	Connecticut	coach	
Massasoit	Georgia	colonial period	*1619.* Beginning of representation in America
William Penn	James River	colonists	
King Philip	Jamestown	colonization	*1620.* Settlement of Plymouth
Pilgrims	Kentucky	permanent colony	
Pocahontas	Maryland	debtors	*1630.* Settlement of Boston
Powhatan	Massachusetts	estates	
Puritans	Mount Vernon	exile	
Quakers	New Amsterdam	freedom of religion	Drill on the peaks represented in the time chart
John Smith	New England	hourglass	
Miles Standish	New Netherland	making laws	
Peter Stuyvesant	Pennsylvania	*Mayflower*	
Roger Williams	Philadelphia	patroons	
John Winthrop	Plymouth	persecution	
	Rhode Island	pillory	
Children write paragraphs such as the following, and read to the class as puzzles:	the South	pioneer	
		plantations	
		proprietor	
I am an Indian who lived in Virginia. My daughter married one of the colonists and went to England. My name is		representatives	
		settled	
		slave quarters	
		stocks	
		surrender	
- - - -		town meeting	
		treaty	
		wharf	

Drill on the minimal essentials of the entire unit with flash cards, as described on pages 112–113.

DRILL ON THE UNIT AS A WHOLE

The children decide upon some event in history which they wish to pantomime; each gives his topic to the teacher so that there will not be too much duplication. Two or three may plan an act together. The rest of the class guesses what event has been acted by each group.

Give the tests described in the *Historical Outlook,* XV: 128–130.

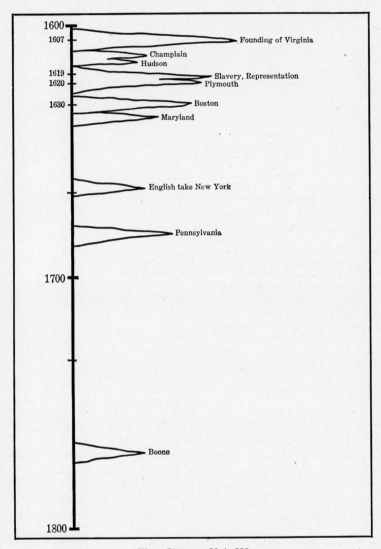

1600
1607 — Founding of Virginia
Champlain
Hudson
1619
1620 — Slavery, Representation
Plymouth
1630 — Boston
Maryland

English take New York

Pennsylvania

1700

Boone

1800

Time Chart — Unit III

TESTS ON THE ENTIRE UNIT

(To be given after all the stories are completed)

Test of Place-Sense. I. Pass outline maps of North America and give the following directions:

1. Draw a line with pencil to represent the Appalachian Mountains.
2. Put the figure 1 where Philadelphia is.
3. Put the figure 2 where Boston is.
4. Put the figure 3 where Plymouth is.
5. Color New England red.
6. Put the figure 4 where Jamestown was.
7. Draw a wavy line to represent the James River.
8. Color the South yellow.

II. Pass outline maps of the United States on which the boundaries of the states are shown. Give the following directions:

1. Put a capital *K* in Kentucky.
2. Put a capital *P* in Pennsylvania.
3. Put a capital *C* in North Carolina and another in South Carolina.
4. Put a capital *M* in Maryland. |
5. Put a capital *G* in Georgia.
6. Write *Conn.* in Connecticut.
7. Put a capital *R* in Rhode Island.
8. Write *Mass.* in Massachusetts.

Test of Time-Sense. Pass mimeographed sheets of the following:

1. Here is a list of people. Put a figure 1 before the name of the man who lived first, a figure 2 before the name of the one who lived next, and so on.

        _ _ _ John Smith
        _ _ _ William Penn
        _ _ _ Peter Stuyvesant
        _ _ _ Governor Bradford
        _ _ _ Lord Baltimore

2. Here is another list of people. Put a figure 1 before the name of the person who lived first, a figure 2 before the name of the one who lived next, and so on.

        _ _ _ Miles Standish
        _ _ _ Roger Williams
        _ _ _ Pocahontas
        _ _ _ King Philip
        _ _ _ Daniel Boone

3. Here is a list of things which happened in the stories. Put a figure 1 before that which happened first, a figure 2 before that which happened next, and so on.

_ _ _ settlement of Plymouth
_ _ _ founding of Jamestown
_ _ _ settlement of Boston
_ _ _ first representatives in America met

4. Here is a list of dates: *1619, 1607, 1630, 1620.* Below is a list of things which happened. Take each date from this list and put it before the right event.

_ _ _ _ founding of Jamestown
_ _ _ _ settlement of Boston
_ _ _ _ slavery begun in Virginia
_ _ _ _ settlement of Plymouth

Test on Persons. Pass mimeographed sheets of the following:

I. Here is a list of persons:

John Smith	Pocahontas	John Winthrop	Catholics
Daniel Boone	William Penn	Puritans	Peter Stuyvesant

Take one name at a time and put it in the right place in the sentences below:

1. _ _ _ _ _ _ _ _ founded Pennsylvania as a home for Quakers.
2. _ _ _ _ _ _ _ _ went over the mountains into Kentucky.
3. _ _ _ _ _ _ _ _ wanted his people to fight against the English.
4. _ _ _ _ came to live in Maryland.
5. _ _ _ _ _ _ _ _ helped to found Virginia.
6. _ _ _ _ _ _ _ _ was a governor of Massachusetts Bay Colony.
7. _ _ _ _ helped the English in Jamestown.
8. _ _ _ _ came to live in Boston.

II. Here is a list of persons:

Powhatan	Lord Baltimore	Roger Williams
Quakers	King Philip	Pilgrims
Miles Standish	Massasoit	Governor Bradford

Take one name at a time and put it in the right place in the sentences below:

1. _ _ _ _ was the Indian chief who was a friend of the Pilgrims.
2. _ _ _ _ _ _ _ _ founded Maryland as a home for the Catholics.
3. _ _ _ _ _ _ _ _ was driven out of Massachusetts.
4. _ _ _ _ _ _ _ _ was the brave soldier of Plymouth.
5. _ _ _ _ was the Indian chief who was a friend to Virginia.
6. _ _ _ _ went from England to Holland and then to America.
7. _ _ _ _ _ _ _ _ tried to keep the English from taking more land.
8. _ _ _ _ came to live in Pennsylvania.
9. _ _ _ _ _ _ _ _ was a governor of Plymouth.

Test on Historical Terms.

I. Here is a list of words:

permanent colony   colonial period
pioneer   plantations
colonization   proprietor
treaty   persecution
representatives   colonists

Take one word or expression at a time and put it in the right place in the sentences below:

1. Persons who are chosen by vote of the people to make laws for them are _ _ _ _.

2. Settlers in a colony are called _ _ _ _.

3. A leader in exploring or settling a country is called a _ _ _ _.

4. The years during which many new colonies were being made are called the _ _ _ _ _ _ _ _.

5. Punishing people because they have a certain belief is _ _ _ _.

6. Large farms where a great deal of one crop is raised are called _ _ _ _.

7. A settlement in which the people stay is a _ _ _ _ _ _ _ _.

8. A man who owned all the land of a colony was called a _ _ _ _.

9. When two nations agree to do a certain thing, we call it making a _ _ _ _.

10. Making colonies is called _ _ _ _.

II. Here is another list of words:

making laws   Church of England
betray   town meeting
slave quarters   coach
ambush   hourglass
exile   wharf

Take one word or expression at a time and put it in the right place in the sentences below:

1. The place where a ship ties up near the shore is called a _ _ _ _.

2. A person who is forced by law to leave his home is an _ _ _ _.

3. The church which the king wanted all people to attend was the _ _ _ _ _ _ _ _ _ _ _ _.

4. When the people or their representatives make a rule which all must obey, they are _ _ _ _ _ _ _ _.

5. The houses where the slaves lived were called _ _ _ _ _ _ _ _.

6. A large carriage drawn by many horses is a _ _ _ _.

7. When people lie hidden to attack their enemies, we say they are in _ _ _ _.

8. An article used to tell time by means of sand running from one part to the other is an _ _ _ _.

9. To give anyone up to his enemies when he does not know about it is to _ _ _ _ him.

10. When all the people of a town come together to make their laws, they form a _ _ _ _ _ _ _ _.

III. Here is another list of words:

pillory	settled	freedom of religion
debtors	patroon	surrender
stocks	estate	*Mayflower*

Take one word or expression at a time and put it in the right place in the sentences below:

1. When new people began to live in a town or colony they _ _ _ _ there.

2. A large amount of land owned by anyone is an _ _ _ _.

3. The name of the ship in which the Pilgrims came to America was the _ _ _ _.

4. The block of wood in which one's head and hands were held to punish him was a _ _ _ _.

5. To give up to an enemy is to _ _ _ _.

6. People who owe money are _ _ _ _.

7. A Dutchman who owned a large estate in New Netherland was a _ _ _ _.

8. The block of wood in which one's legs were held to punish him was called the _ _ _ _.

9. The right to go to the church one chooses is _ _ _ _ _ _ _ _ _ _ _ _.

COMPREHENSION TEST ON UNIT III

1. *Check the best answer:*

    a. The first lasting English colony in the New World was

        _ _ _ Plymouth
        _ _ _ Virginia
        _ _ _ Maryland
        _ _ _ Boston

    b. The Pilgrims came to America

        _ _ _ to win freedom of religion for themselves
        _ _ _ to trade with the Indians
        _ _ _ to find a new route to the Indies

    c. The reason why people began to cross the mountains was

        _ _ _ because they wanted to be near the French
        _ _ _ because they wanted to get away from their neighbors
        _ _ _ because they wanted cheap land

d. Virginia did not grow well

_ _ _ until John Smith left the colony

_ _ _ until each man had his own farm

_ _ _ until Catholics came to Maryland

e. The first representatives in America met in

_ _ _ Virginia

_ _ _ Massachusetts

_ _ _ Rhode Island

f. The Quakers got along well with the Indians

_ _ _ because they would not fight

_ _ _ because the Indians liked them

_ _ _ because they treated the Indians fairly

g. After many years

_ _ _ Boston and Plymouth fought each other

_ _ _ Boston and Plymouth joined as one colony

_ _ _ Boston and Plymouth both disappeared

h. Georgia was founded

_ _ _ as a neighbor to Florida

_ _ _ as a good place to trade with Mexico

_ _ _ as a home for debtors

i. The Puritans lived

_ _ _ in small towns

_ _ _ on large plantations

_ _ _ in large cities

j. They got most of their goods in this way:

_ _ _ they sent back to England

_ _ _ they got them from the Spanish colonies

_ _ _ they made them for themselves

k. The Dutch people would not fight for their town

_ _ _ because they wanted to be English

_ _ _ because only rich men had been able to own a farm there

_ _ _ because their rulers were cruel

l. The Indians did not want more white people to come

_ _ _ because there would not be enough land for hunting-grounds

_ _ _ because there would be more white people than Indians

_ _ _ because there would be war

2. *What is the title of the third unit?*

ORGANIZATION OF THE UNIT AS A WHOLE

Make a chart somewhat similar to this; children fill in the blanks for all the colonies studied.

NAME OF COLONY	WHERE IT IS	WHEN SETTLED	WHY SETTLED	NAMES OF PROMINENT PERSONS
		(If in the list of minimal essentials)		(If in the list of minimal essentials)

RECITATION OF THE UNIT AS A WHOLE

One child tells all the factors above for one colony; another child, for another colony; and so on.

UNIT IV

HOW ENGLAND CAME TO OWN MOST OF NORTH AMERICA

I. The French People went into the Heart of the Country.
   1. The fur traders went far into the forests and set up fur-trading posts.
   2. The missionaries followed and built missions.
   3. Marquette and Joliet looked for a passage to India.
   4. La Salle went down the Mississippi.
II. The English People were fast spreading over the Mountains.
    They settled along the Ohio River.
III. The French and the English wanted the Same Land.
   1. Each built a line of forts.
   2. Early life of George Washington (to the Revolution).
   3. The English sent George Washington to warn the French away.
IV. Three Early Wars did not decide which Nation was going to Win.
   1. How the early wars were carried on.
   2. Life of Benjamin Franklin (to the Revolution).
   3. Benjamin Franklin tried to make the colonies work together.
V. The French and Indian War decided that England should rule Most of North America.
   1. For a long time the English failed to drive the French away from the Ohio.
   2. General Wolfe took Quebec.
   3. Pontiac tried to push back the English people.
   4. England now owned almost all of North America.

PREPARATION FOR THE OVERVIEW [1]

Model in the sand table the eastern part of North America, showing with great care the St. Lawrence River, the Great Lakes, and the Mississippi and Ohio rivers. Show the Wisconsin River, Green Bay, and the Fox River plainly, but do not allude to them by name.

Place in the St. Lawrence River, opposite Montreal, a tiny canoe. Children find out how far into the interior they can go entirely by water; how far by making short portages.

Children show on the sand-table map the parts that have already been explored by French explorers.

Show how the English people could reach the Ohio River.

[1] The following words may need explanation: *messenger, party* (group).

220

PRESENTATION OR OVERVIEW

After Champlain had discovered many interesting places, he died. So the French king chose another great man to be governor of New France. This governor sent out fur traders to buy skins of beaver, fox, otter, and mink from the Indians. Then he would send the furs to France and sell them at a high price. The fur traders traveled far and wide; they went up strange rivers and into forests where never a white man had been before. When they came back to the governor they said, "We have heard from the Indians of lands still farther away — lands to which none of our people have ever traveled!" Then the governor would send out other fur traders to the strange lands. In this way they kept exploring more and more land and going farther and farther away from home. New France was growing fast.

Some good priests heard from the fur traders about the Indians who lived in the wild places. They said: "These poor Indians are not Christians. Let us ask the governor to allow us to go with the fur traders. We will build up missions in the far-off places and teach the Indians our religion." The governor listened to this request with attention and answered, "Wherever the fur traders go, the priests may go with them." So, together, priest and fur trader explored far and wide.

One such party went down the St. Lawrence through the Great Lakes, carried their canoes some little distance, and then drifted down the Mississippi just as we showed on the sand-table map. The first people did not go clear to the mouth of the river, but a second party did, and claimed all these vast lands for France (*illustrating at the map*).

The English people were watching with jealous eyes. Some said to their friends, "If we do not hurry, the French will have all the land along the great rivers, and there will be none left for us." Others urged: "Let us get together a company of people, go over the mountains to the Ohio River, and make a colony there. Then England also will have a claim to the land."

That seemed a good idea; so many Englishmen went over the mountains by the route that we once showed on the sand table. After that both England and France were making forts and trading posts along the rivers as fast as they could. Each side thought it could protect its colonies better if it built forts; so we see quickly rising on one side a line of French forts, and on the other side a line of English forts. Surely there would be trouble between the two!

The English said: "We know that the French people are making colonies and building forts in the land beyond the mountains. That land belongs to us. What shall we do about it?" One Englishman suggested, "Let us send a messenger to the French and tell them that they must go away from our land." Others agreed, "Yes; that is the thing to do." Whom do you suppose they sent? *George Washington*. This is the first time he has come into our history story, but it will not be the last.

Do you suppose the French people paid any attention to George Washington's message? No, indeed. They replied: "This land is ours, and we shall not leave it. The English are very foolish if they think we will go away. Frenchmen were the first to explore this region."

There seemed to be only one way to settle the question of ownership: that was *war*. And wars did come, one after the other, dragging on for long weary years. There were four in all. The first three did not decide whether France should have the land, or whether England should. First one side was ahead and then the other. At last, however, in the fourth war, the English won the victory. France had to give up all her land. What a sad day for France—to see her forts, her colonies, her claims, south to the Gulf of Mexico, north to the ocean, and west to the great river, all given to England! The French people wept with grief, but they could do nothing. They had lost the war.

How England had grown since her beginning in the New World! There had been Dutch people along the Hudson, and England had driven them away. There had been French people along the St. Lawrence, the Great Lakes, and the Mississippi, and England had defeated them and taken their land. English people had begun to cross the mountains and make colonies beyond. Would they keep on moving farther and farther inland? Only time would tell. The French people could not stop them, for France had been beaten.

PRESENTATION TEST

1. *Check the best answer:*

   a. The fur traders told the French governor
      _ _ _ that there were many other unknown rivers
      _ _ _ that there was gold in the land
      _ _ _ that he must not go farther inland

   b. The priests went with the fur traders
      _ _ _ because they wanted to make the Indians angry
      _ _ _ because they wanted to make the Indians Christians
      _ _ _ because they wanted to travel

   c. One French party went to
      _ _ _ the Indies
      _ _ _ the Pacific Ocean
      _ _ _ the mouth of the Mississippi

   d. The English people
      _ _ _ did not want the French to fish
      _ _ _ did not want the French to build colonies on the rivers
      _ _ _ did not want the French to travel in canoes

   e. The English people decided
      _ _ _ to tell the French to go back to France
      _ _ _ to tell the French to stay where they were
      _ _ _ to tell the French to go away from the Ohio River

   f. Each side built a line of forts so that
      _ _ _ it could protect its claims
      _ _ _ it could keep soldiers in the forts
      _ _ _ it could fight against the Indians

   g. The way they settled the question was by
      _ _ _ doing nothing
      _ _ _ war
      _ _ _ talking

   h. The first three wars
      _ _ _ decided that the French would win
      _ _ _ decided that the English would win
      _ _ _ did not decide who would win

   i. The fourth war was won by
      _ _ _ France
      _ _ _ England
      _ _ _ the Indians

   j. Because of the fourth war
      _ _ _ France had to give up almost all her land in America
      _ _ _ England had to give up almost all her land in America
      _ _ _ Spain had to give up almost all her land in America

2. Check two answers:

> The English people have now taken away all the land in North America which belonged to the

    _ _ _ Spanish   _ _ _ Portuguese
    _ _ _ French   _ _ _ Indians
    _ _ _ Dutch

I. The French People went into the Heart of the Country

1. *The Fur Traders went far into the Forests and set up Fur-Trading Posts*

No additional preparation and presentation are needed.

Assimilation

Readings

Upper Group

 BALDWIN. Conquest of the Old Northwest, 17–23.
 BALDWIN. Discovery of the Old Northwest, 243.
 BEEBY. Community Life Today and in Colonial Times, 324–325.
 CARPENTER. How the World is Clothed, 176–192.
 GORDY. Colonial Days, 188.
 GORDY. Stories of Early American History, 158.
 GRINNELL. Jack, the Young Trapper.
 GUERBER. Story of the Thirteen Colonies, 176.
 HASBROUCK. Boys' Parkman, 96–109 (difficult).
 LAUT. The Story of the Trapper, 50–64, 102–116, 181–205.
 MORRIS. Heroes of Discovery in America, 254–262.
 OTIS. Antoine of Oregon, 9–13.
 SPARKS. Expansion of the American People, 239.
 THWAITES. Stories of the Badger State, 81–86, 87–91.
 VOLLINTINE. The Making of America, 12–13.
 WILSON and DRIGGS. White Indian Boy, 197–201.
 Compton's Pictured Encyclopedia (Furs).
 World Book (Fur, Fur Trade).

Average Group

 COE. Founders of our Country, 288–295.
 GEORGE. Little Journeys to Alaska and Canada, 21–23 (Canada).
 GORDY. Elementary History of the United States, 105–106.
 McMASTER. Primary History of the United States, 35–37.
 NIDA. Following the Frontier, 19.
 SOUTHWORTH. Builders of our Country, I : 160, 161.

Lower Group

 BASS. Stories of Pioneer Life, 29–32.
 CHAMBERLAIN. How we are Clothed, 129–153.
 FAIRGRIEVE and YOUNG. The World, 90–99.
 SHEPHERD. Geography for Beginners, 91–95.
 Flanagan Publishing Company. Henry Hudson and Other Explorers, 18–19, 22–24.

Teachers

BOLTON and MARSHALL. Colonization of North America, 90, 100, 257.
COMAN. Industrial History of the United States, 10–13.
HART. American History told by Contemporaries, II : 320–324, 327–330.
MUNRO. Crusaders of New France, 95–96, 161–179.
MUZZEY. An American History, 72–73.
THWAITES. The Colonies, 247–250.
THWAITES. France in America, 10, 12, 17, 38, 60–63, 126–127, 134.
"How Furs came down from the North Country." *The Historical Outlook*, VII : 44–46.

Minimal Essentials

Name of Place : **Mackinac** (măk′ĭ nô)
Historical Terms : **fur traders; trading posts; woodrangers**
Things to Remember
The woodrangers explored far into the forests.
They made many of the Indians friendly to the French.

Illustrative Material

GABRIEL (ED.). Pageant of America, I : 301.
PYLE. Book of the American Spirit, 129.
SCHMEIL. Animal Pictures : S. Z. 17, Beaver Colony at Work.
Mentor, XI : 1–16 (April, 1923).

Procedure during Assimilation

Reading as described on pages 24–29.
Picture study based on the illustrative material listed above.
Name the animals whose skins were most valuable. Make a picture collection of them. Take a trip to the local fur store to see the skins.
Children describe fur-trading posts they have seen in moving pictures.
Construct on the sand table a fur-trading post representing the annual fair.
Children attempt to barter furs by signs.
Drill on minimal essentials.
Objective test.

Organization

The teacher writes the following outline on the board. Children tell what points are included under each.

FUR TRADERS AND FUR-TRADING POSTS

1. Life of the fur traders
2. Their work as explorers

Recitation

Divide the class into groups, two children working together in a group. Try to have as partners one child who will do well and one who is not so strong. Each hears the other give the recitation based on the organization above.

2. *The Missionaries followed and built Missions*

No additional preparation and presentation are needed.

Assimilation
Readings

Upper Group

BALDWIN. Discovery of the Old Northwest, 96–99.
BEEBY. Community Life Today and in Colonial Times, 322–324, 326.
GORDY. Leaders in Making America, 106.
GORDY. Stories of Early American History, 158–159.
GUERBER. Story of the Thirteen Colonies, 176–177.
HARDING. Story of Europe, 295.
MOWRY. American Pioneers, 81–84.
TAPPAN. Elementary History of our Country, 116.
THWAITES. Stories of the Badger State, 51–58.
VOLLINTINE. The Making of America, 10–12.
World Book (Jesuits, as Educators and Missionaries).

Average Group

COE. Founders of our Country, 279–287.
FORMAN. First Lessons in American History, 104–105.
GORDY. Elementary History of the United States, 106–107.
McMASTER. Primary History of the United States, 34–35.
SOUTHWORTH. Builders of our Country, I : 161.

Lower Group

Flanagan Publishing Company. Henry Hudson and Other Explorers, 19–20.

Teachers

HART. American History told by Contemporaries, I : 129–133.
LAWLER. Essentials of American History, 121–122.
MUNRO. Crusaders of New France, 54–55, 115–158.
MUZZEY. An American History, 74.
NICOLINI. History of the Jesuits.
PARKMAN. Jesuits in North America.
THWAITES. France in America, 21, 22, 137.
THWAITES (ED.). Jesuit Relations (Fur Trading).

Minimal Essentials

Name of Person: **Jesuit** (jĕz′ủ ĭt)
Historical Term: **mission stations**
Things to Remember
The missionaries went into the interior with the fur traders.
They explored for France.

Illustrative Material

GABRIEL (ED.). Pageant of America, I : 301.
PYLE. Book of the American Spirit, 135.
Ford Educational Library (films) : 32, Landmarks of Early Exploration and Settlement in North America, Part II.

Procedure during Assimilation

Reading as described on pages 24–29.

Picture study based on the illustrative material listed above.

Represent on the sand table a mission station.

Are there any places near your home which were visited by the early Jesuits? If so, are they adequately marked?

Write a report which a Jesuit might have sent back to his superior.

Dress a doll as a Jesuit missionary.

Drill on minimal essentials.

Objective test.

Organization

The teacher puts on the board an outline somewhat similar to the following. Children tell what points belong under each.

MISSIONARIES AND MISSION STATIONS

1. Ways in which the missionaries' work was not pleasant
2. Ways in which the missionaries' work was pleasant
3. The missionaries as explorers

Recitation

Continue the same procedure, having one child in a group hear the other.

3. *Marquette and Joliet looked for a Passage to India*

Preparation

"Do you remember from our overview story how people could travel from the Great Lakes to the Mississippi?" (*One child illustrates at the sand table; another, at the wall map.*)

"What was Columbus looking for? Cartier?"

Introduce the term "portage" and illustrate it on the sand table.[1]

Presentation

The French people could not forget their dream of a short route to India, even though many explorers had tried to find it, and all had failed. At last two Frenchmen, Joliet, a fur trader, and Marquette, a priest, set out together to see if they might not meet with better success than the others. They paddled along through the Great Lakes, carried all their

[1] See the illustrative lesson on pages 690–696.

goods and canoes over the portage, and drifted down the broad waters of the Mississippi.

I shall not tell you now all their experiences with the Indians, nor of the wonderful pictures they saw on the banks of the river, nor how they ate roast dog at a feast. You will read all that in your books. They journeyed on and on and still did not come to the Pacific Ocean. Finally Joliet said: "I am sure we are going the wrong way. The Pacific Ocean is far over to the west. If we keep on going in the same direction as we now are, we shall reach the Gulf of Mexico. That is not what we want. We want to reach India."

The rest agreed that he was right, so they turned around and went back to New France. They had not found India, but they had good news. It was that a boat could travel from the St. Lawrence to the Great Lakes and down the Mississippi, making only a few portages. What an easy way to go into the interior of the country!

PRESENTATION TEST

Check the best answer:

   a. Marquette and Joliet were looking for

      _ _ _ the gulf south of the Mississippi River

      _ _ _ a short route to India

      _ _ _ a portage

   b. They did not go all the way to the Gulf of Mexico

      _ _ _ because they decided that was not the way to India

      _ _ _ because the Indians were cruel to them

      _ _ _ because they became tired

   c. They brought back good news. It was

      _ _ _ that the world is round

      _ _ _ that they had found a short route to India

      _ _ _ that a boat could easily travel through the Great Lakes and down the Mississippi

Assimilation

Readings

Upper Group

   BEEBY. Community Life Today and in Colonial Times, 326–331.

   CATHERWOOD. Heroes of the Middle West, 1–43 (difficult).

   CHANDLER and CHITWOOD. Makers of American History, 103–105.

   EGGLESTON. Our First Century, 165.

   FARIS. Real Stories of the Geography Makers, 230–236.

   GORDY. Leaders in Making America, 106–108.

   GORDY. Stories of Early American History, 159–162.

GUERBER. Story of the Thirteen Colonies, 177–179.
HASBROUCK. Boys' Parkman, 26–37 (difficult).
McMURRY. Pioneers of the Mississippi Valley, 1–15.
MORRIS. Heroes of Discovery in America, 209–215.
MOWRY. American Pioneers, 84–93.
PRATT. Later Colonial Period, 1–14.
TAPPAN. Elementary History of our Country, 117.
THWAITES. Stories of the Badger State, 42–50.
WOODBURN and MORAN. Beginner's History of the United States, 160–165.
WOODBURN and MORAN. Finders and Founders of the New World, 197–207.
Compton's Pictured Encyclopedia (Marquette, Joliet).
World Book (Marquette, Joliet).

Average Group

BARNES. An Elementary History of the United States, 130–137.
COE. Founders of our Country, 266–268.
EGGLESTON. Stories of Great Americans, 11–17.
FIELD. Fourth Reader, 300–317.
FORMAN. First Lessons in American History, 105–106.
GORDY. Elementary History of the United States, 107–109.
MACE. Primary History, 119–124.
McMASTER. Primary History of the United States, 37–39.
PERRY and PRICE. American History, I : 99–103.
SOUTHWORTH. Builders of our Country, I : 161–169.
TAPPAN. American Hero Stories, 96–103.

Lower Group

BARNES. Primary History of the United States, 69–71.
BASS. Stories of Pioneer Life, 21–28.
Flanagan Publishing Company. Father Marquette.

Teachers

DOUDNA. Our Wisconsin, 45–52.
HART. American History told by Contemporaries, I : 136–140.
KELLOGG. Early Narratives of the Northwest, 227–280.
MUNRO. Crusaders of New France, 103, 164.
MUZZEY. An American History, 74–75.
THWAITES. Father Marquette.
THWAITES. France in America, 56–57.
Baltimore County Course of Study, 465.
Public School Methods, IV : 204–209. (The Methods Co., Chicago.)

Minimal Essentials

Names of Persons: **Marquette** (mär′kĕt′); **Joliet** (zhȯ′lyā′)
Name of Place: **Lake Michigan**
Historical Terms: **pipe of peace; portage**
Things to Remember
 Marquette and Joliet were looking for a passage to India.
 They were the first people to discover the middle part of the Mississippi River.

Illustrative Material

GABRIEL (ED.). Pageant of America, I : 317.
Society for Visual Education. Schoolfilm : French Explorations in North America.

Procedure during Assimilation

Reading as described on pages 24–29.
Picture study based on the illustrative material listed on page 229.
Use the dramatization "The Father of the Waters." Hubbard, *Little American History Plays*, pp. 50–57.
Children draw or cut illustrations of the expedition making a portage.[1]
On a large map of the United States find places named for Marquette; for Joliet.
To the map "French Explorations in the New World" (begun in Unit II) add the route of Marquette and Joliet. Mark portages in red thus (======).[2]
Drill on minimal essentials.
Objective test.

Organization

The class selects the main points and then gives two sub-heads under each.

Recitation

Continue the procedure described for the previous story.

4. *La Salle went down the Mississippi*

Preparation

"Did Marquette and Joliet ever reach the mouth of the Mississippi? Why would it be a good thing for a country to own the land here at the mouth of the river?" (*Pointing it out at the map.*) Show a picture of sailboats in use about 1680.

Presentation

Marquette and Joliet were looking for a way to the Indies, and when they found that the Mississippi was not the way they turned around and went back. Another Frenchman, however, kept thinking what a good thing it would be for France to build a colony at the mouth of the Mississippi River. Then she could decide who should go up the river and who should not. In that way she could control all the heart of the country.

---

[1] Similar to those described in *The Twentieth Yearbook of the National Society for the Study of Education*, Part I, p. 55, and the illustrative lesson, pp. 690–696 of text.

[2] Muzzey, D. S., *An American History*, p. 76.

Fig. 4. Children's Illustrations of Incidents in the Story of Making a Portage (see pages 690–696) In each case the child's undirected first attempt is at the left and his directed drawing at the right

This man was La Salle (*pointing to the name on the board*). He had had a very interesting life, about which we shall read later. He had been nobleman, soldier, and explorer. He built a sailing vessel, the first one ever seen on the Great Lakes. All the earlier explorers in this region had used canoes, but La Salle wanted to carry with him such quantities of supplies that a canoe would not hold them. Many times he started on his great expedition and many times he failed. Once he was so discouraged that he named a fort which he was building "Heartbreak," but always he kept on with his work. At last he reached the mouth of the Mississippi, and there set up a great wooden cross and claimed the country round about for France.

Then he tried to found a colony, but again he had a very hard time. He could not find the mouth of the river a second time. Ships which were bringing supplies were wrecked. The people who were to stay in the colony became sick, and at last one of La Salle's own men shot him; so he found only a grave in the wild land in which he had hoped to build a town.

But though La Salle died, his work lived on. France claimed all the land of which La Salle had taken possession, and called it Louisiana. She held the land for many years. Some of the children of the Frenchmen live there even now.

PRESENTATION TEST

Check the best answer:

  a. La Salle wanted

     _ _ _ to fight with the English

     _ _ _ to make a colony at the mouth of the Mississippi

     _ _ _ to go back to France

  b. Whoever owned the land at the mouth of the river

     _ _ _ could decide who should go up and down the river

     _ _ _ could have many boat rides

     _ _ _ could take the land away from the Spanish

  c. La Salle built for his trip a

     _ _ _ canoe

     _ _ _ steamboat

     _ _ _ sailing vessel

  d. He found the work of exploring

     _ _ _ very hard

     _ _ _ very easy

     _ _ _ much fun

e. His colony near the mouth of the Mississippi

＿ ＿ ＿ lasted a long time

＿ ＿ ＿ did not last

f. What La Salle had done for France was

＿ ＿ ＿ to drive the Spanish away from the river

＿ ＿ ＿ to fight the Indians

＿ ＿ ＿ to claim the land along the Mississippi for France

Assimilation

Readings

Upper Group

ABBOTT. La Salle.

BEEBY. Community Life Today and in Colonial Times, 331–335.

BLAISDELL. The Story of American History, 107–109.

BURNHAM. Hero Tales from History, 120–126.

BURTON. Builders of our Nation, 115–128.

CATHERWOOD. Story of Tonty.

CHANDLER and CHITWOOD. Makers of American History, 105–110.

CROWE. Studies in American History, I : 169–212.

FOOTE and SKINNER. Explorers and Founders of America, 208–218.

FRYER. Book of Boyhoods, 51–61.

GORDY. Leaders in Making America, 108–113.

GORDY. Stories of Early American History, 164–171.

GUERBER. Story of the Thirteen Colonies, 180–183.

HASBROUCK. Boys' Parkman, 38–54, 71–95 (difficult).

McMURRY. Pioneers of the Mississippi Valley, 16–53.

MORRIS. Heroes of Discovery in America, 217–227.

PRATT. Later Colonial Period, 15–28.

TAPPAN. Elementary History of our Country, 117–118.

WOODBURN and MORAN. Beginner's History of the United States, 165–173.

WOODBURN and MORAN. Finders and Founders of the New World, 209–212, 217–224.

Compton's Pictured Encyclopedia (La Salle).

World Book (La Salle).

Average Group

BARNES. An Elementary History of the United States, 137–139.

BEARD and BAGLEY. A First Book in American History, 83–91.

COE. Founders of our Country, 268–278.

ELSON and MacMULLAN. The Story of our Country, I : 130–131.

FORMAN. First Lessons in American History, 106–108.

GORDY. American Leaders and Heroes, 103–114.

GORDY. Elementary History of the United States, 109–112.

MACE. Primary History, 124–130.

McMASTER. Primary History of the United States, 39–41.

PERRY and PRICE. American History, I : 103–109.

SOUTHWORTH. Builders of our Country, I : 169–178.

TAPPAN. American Hero Stories, 103–107.

Lower Group

BARNES. Primary History of the United States, 71–72.

Flanagan Publishing Company. The Story of La Salle.

Teachers

GRIFFIS. Romance of Discovery, 269–282.
HART. American History told by Contemporaries, I : 140–144.
KELLOGG. Early Narratives of the Northwest, 286–322.
MUNRO. Crusaders of New France, 100–112.
MUZZEY. An American History, 74–75.
PARKMAN. La Salle and the Discovery of the Great West.
THWAITES. France in America, 58–71.
Baltimore County Course of Study, 465–466.

Minimal Essentials

Name of Person: **La Salle** (là sȧl′)
Names of Places: **mouth of the Mississippi River; Great Lakes; Louisiana** (lōō ē′zē ăn′ȧ)
Date: **near the end of the seventeenth century**
Historical Term: **the *Griffin*** (the first sailing vessel on the Great Lakes)
Things to Remember
La Salle went down the Mississippi River to its mouth and claimed the land for France.
He built some forts along the river.
He wanted to found a colony at the mouth of the Mississippi, but failed.

Illustrative Material

GABRIEL (ED.). Pageant of America, I : 318–322.
McKINLEY. Illustrated Topics : M. M. 16, Palace of Versailles.
PYLE. Book of the American Spirit, 131, 134.

Procedure during Assimilation

Reading as described on pages 24–29.
Picture study based on the illustrative material listed above.
Children dramatize the scene in which La Salle, coming from France, fails to find the mouth of the Mississippi.
Children draw blackboard illustrations of scenes from the life of La Salle ; the rest of the class is to tell what incident each represents.   The best drawing is preserved on the board.
Do you know of anything which has been named for La Salle?
To the map "French Explorations in America" add the route of La Salle.
Drill on minimal essentials.
Objective test.

Organization

The children work out coöperatively an outline, the teacher giving as little help as possible.[1]

Recitation

A written composition following the outline.

A drill lesson on section I of Unit IV should be given at this point.

[1] See pages 43–46.

II. THE ENGLISH PEOPLE WERE FAST SPREADING OVER THE MOUNTAINS

They settled along the Ohio River

Preparation

"Do you remember from our overview story at what places the English people had at last managed to go over the mountains?" (*Children show on the map.*)

"Why had they been so eager to cross the mountains when there was still land along the seacoast?"

Presentation

One group of English people said: "The best thing for us to do is to make up a company. Everybody who wants to go may join us. Since we wish to settle along the Ohio River, let us call ourselves the Ohio Company."

Already there were many families who had gone on by themselves, and now that a company had been formed too, there soon would be many English people in the Ohio country.

PRESENTATION TEST

Check the best answer:

The Ohio Company was formed

_ _ _ to sell goods in Ohio
_ _ _ to settle along the Ohio
_ _ _ to travel in Ohio

Assimilation

Readings

Upper Group

ATKINSON. Johnny Appleseed.
BLAISDELL. The Story of American History, 116.
BRIGHAM. From Trail to Railway, 111–114 (difficult).
FARIS. Where our History was Made, 141–145.
FOOTE and SKINNER. Explorers and Founders of America, 274–275.
GORDY. Leaders in Making America, 114.
GORDY. Stories of Early American History, 185.
MILLER. My Bookhouse, II : 323.
MOWRY. American Pioneers, 141–149.
OTIS. Benjamin of Ohio.
VOLLINTINE. The Making of America, 14–16.

Average Group

BARNES. An Elementary History of the United States, 195–196.
EDSON-LAING. Readers, IV : 71–77.

FORMAN. First Lessons in American History, 80–81 (map), 84–85, 86.
GORDY. Elementary History of the United States, 119.
NIDA. Following the Frontier, 24–25, 96–104.
PERRY and PRICE. American History, I : 208–209.

Lower Group
GORDON. Readers, III : 136–139 (Appleseed John).
MAGEE. Readers, III : 112–113 (Appleseed John).

Teachers
GREGORY and GUITTEAU. History and Geography of Ohio, 6–7.
MUZZEY. An American History, 77–78, 80–82.
Elementary School Journal, XVII : 634.

Minimal Essentials

Name of Person: **Johnny Appleseed**[1]
Names of Places: **Ohio River; "the West"**
Date: **about the middle of the eighteenth century**
Historical Term: **Ohio Company**
Things to Remember
The English did not want the French to get possession of all the land west of the mountains.
They formed the Ohio Company.
The Ohio Company was to make settlements along the Ohio River.

Illustrative Material

Society for Visual Education. Picturol : First Westward Movement.
Society for Visual Education. Schoolfilm : Settling the Ohio Valley.

Procedure during Assimilation

Reading as described on pages 24–29.
Picture study based on the illustrative material listed above.
Give a speech which the leader of the Ohio Company might have made in order to persuade settlers to go over the mountains.
On the sand table show the routes by which the English would have to approach the upper Ohio.[2]
Show the influence of the Appalachian barrier on colonization.
Drill on minimal essentials.
Objective test.

Organization

The teacher chooses the best of the outlines made by the children to serve as a basis for the recitation. It is put on the board, and the class discusses the points to include under each part.

Recitation

By two's as before.[3]

---

[1] Not in the lists of personages referred to on page 5.
[2] *To the teacher:* see the maps in Woodburn, J. A., and Moran, T. F., *Elementary American History and Government*, pp. 48, 91.   [3] See page 225.

III. The French and the English wanted the Same Land

1. *Each built a Line of Forts*

Preparation

"Show on the map where the English people had crossed the mountains.

"Show the land that the French claimed.

"Do you remember from our overview story what each side did to protect its settlements?"

Here is a list of names of the forts built. Try to select the French names.

Fort St. Louis	Fort William Henry
Fort Crèvecœur	Fort Frontenac
Fort Cumberland	Fort Duquesne
Fort Vincennes	Fort Edward
Fort Le Bœuf	Fort Venango

No additional presentation is needed.

Assimilation

Readings

Upper Group

BURNHAM. The Making of our Country, 93, 98–100.
FOOTE and SKINNER. Explorers and Founders of America, 274–275.
GORDY. Colonial Days, 200–201.
PRATT. Later Colonial Period, 39–42.
VOLLINTINE. The Making of America, 16–19.

Average Group

BARNES. An Elementary History of the United States, 196–197.
BEARD and BAGLEY. A First Book in American History, 83, 91–92.
ELSON and MACMULLAN. The Story of our Country, I : 130.
FORMAN. First Lessons in American History, 108–109, 112.
GORDY. Elementary History of the United States, 113–114, 118–119.
MACE. Primary History, 131–132.
MCMASTER. Primary History of the United States, 99–102.
MORRIS. Primary History of the United States, 133.
NIDA. Following the Frontier, 19–22, 25–26.
TAPPAN. American Hero Stories, 117–118.

Lower Group

BASS. Stories of Pioneer Life, 51–53.

Teachers

FINLEY. The French in the Heart of America, 216–245.
HART. Formation of the Union, 25–26.

MUZZEY. An American History, 75.
MUZZEY. The United States of America, I : 47–48.
PARKMAN. A Half Century of Conflict, II : 63–78.
PARKMAN. The Struggle for a Continent, 301–459.
THWAITES. The Colonies, 255–257.
THWAITES. France in America, 157–158.

Minimal Essentials

Name of Place: **Mohawk River**
Historical Terms: **leaden plates; blockhouse**
Things to Remember
>   The French people came down from Lake Erie to the Ohio River.
>   The English people went up the Hudson River, up the Mohawk River, and then
>   to the Ohio.
>   Both sides built forts so that they might hold their lands.

Illustrative Material

Keystone Views: 44, Blockhouse at Fort Pitt; 45, Fort Niagara; 46, Blockhouse at Fort
Presque Isle; 49, Old Hudson Bay Company Blockhouse.

Procedure during Assimilation

Reading as described on pages 24–29.
Picture study based on the illustrative material listed above.
Model in clay the leaden plates which the French buried along the line of their
    claims.
Make a map, "Rival Claims of France and England."[1] Color the territory of
    France blue and that of England red. Make crosses (X) for the French forts,
    and circles (O) for the English forts.
Model in the sand table the same map. Designate English forts by small British
    flags, and French forts by French flags.
Make a graph to show the comparative numbers of French and English in America.[2]
Draw pictures of a fort and a blockhouse.
Divide the class into two parts: one gives an argument as to England's right to
    the land; the other, France's.
Drill on minimal essentials.
Objective test.

Organization

The modeling of the sand-table map referred to above.

Recitation

The drawing of the map referred to above, and an explanation by each child of what his map shows.

---

[1] Muzzey, D. S., *An American History*, pp. 76, 85; Sanford American History
Maps, No. 6.

[2] Hart, A. B., *Formation of the Union*, p. 27.

2. *Early Life of George Washington* (*to the Revolution*)

Preparation and Presentation

Now we shall have to stop our story of the struggle between the French and the English long enough to go back and learn about the life of a boy who had been growing up during these years. He was born about the time that the colony of Georgia was founded, has lived always in Virginia, and now is old enough to take his part as a good Englishman against the French. His name is — George Washington!

Assimilation

Readings

Upper Group

BROOKS. True Story of George Washington.
BURNHAM. Hero Tales from History, 296–301.
CHANDLER and CHITWOOD. Makers of American History, 144–146.
DAVIDSON. Founders and Builders of our Nation, 56–59.
EGGLESTON. A First Book in American History, 102–106.
EVANS. America First, 94–99.
FRYER. Book of Boyhoods, 70–81.
GERWIG. Washington the Young Leader, 1–39.
GORDY. Colonial Days, 202–206.
GORDY. Leaders in Making America, 114–117.
GORDY. Stories of Early American History, 186–189.
GUERBER. Story of the Thirteen Colonies, 191–196.
LEFFERTS. American Leaders, I : 65–69.
MONTGOMERY. Beginners' American History, 103–108.
O'NEILL. World's Story, 427–428.
WOODBURN and MORAN. Finders and Founders of the New World, 226–234.
Colonial Stories retold from *St. Nicholas*, 172–182.
Compton's Pictured Encyclopedia (Washington).
World Book (Washington).

Average Group

BALDWIN. Four Great Americans, 9–34.
BARNES. Elementary History of the United States, 193–195.
BEARD and BAGLEY. A First Book in American History, 92–94.
COE. Founders of our Country, 296–302.
EGGLESTON. Stories of Great Americans, 54–55.
ELSON and MACMULLAN. Story of our Country, I : 132–134.
FIELD. Fourth Reader, 337–342.
FORMAN. First Lessons in American History, 112–114.
GORDY. American Leaders and Heroes, 116–127.
GORDY. Elementary History of the United States, 119–120.
HARTWELL. Story-Hour Readings, IV : 160–161, 162–167.
MACE. Primary History, 159–164.
MORRIS. Primary History of the United States, 131–132.
SOUTHWORTH. Builders of our Country, II : 24–31.

Lower Group

BALDWIN. Fifty Famous People, 60–62.
BALDWIN. Fifty Famous Stories Retold, 59–61.
BLAISDELL and BALL. Child's Book of American History, 77–85.
BOLENIUS. Fourth Reader, 107–109.
CURTIS. Why we celebrate our Holidays, 24–30.
DAVIS. Stories of the United States, 139–151.
ELSON. Primary School Readers, III : 156–157.
HUSTED. Stories of '76, 16–20.
MCMANUS. Natural Method Readers, III : 206–212.
VAN SICKLE and SIEGMILLER. Riverside Readers, III : 99–103.
WAYLAND. History Stories for Primary Grades, 21–23, 109–115, 155–157.
WILSON. A History Reader, 199–207.
Flanagan Publishing Company. Story of the Revolution, 23–25.

Teachers

BROOKS. The True Story of George Washington.
LODGE. George Washington.
OLCOTT. Good Stories for Great Birthdays, 190–234.
Public School Methods, V : 234–246, 457–469. (The Methods Co., Chicago.)

Minimal Essentials

Names of Persons: **George Washington; Martha Washington**[1]
Name of Place: **Mount Vernon**
Date: **born the same year that the colony of Georgia was planned**
Historical Term: **surveyor**
Things to Remember
George Washington knew a great deal about life in the forests.
He was patient, honest, and brave.

Illustrative Material

BRADLEY. Straight-Line Picture Cut-Outs: George Washington: his Mount Vernon Home.
Educational Posters of the National Child Welfare Association: Washington's Birthday.
National Posters: The Story of George Washington.

Procedure during Assimilation

Reading as described on pages 24–29.
Picture study based on the illustrative material listed above.
Use the dramatization "George Washington and the Cherry Tree." Johnston and
 Barnum, *Book of Plays for Little Actors*, pp. 82–86.
Tell the class how and why myths grow up about great personages. (Cherry tree,
 "never told a lie," etc.)
A person who has visited Mount Vernon describes it to the class.
Children plan the Washington's Birthday program.
Drill on minimal essentials.
Objective test.

[1] Not included in the lists of personages referred to on page 5.

Organization

The teacher and the class working together plan an outline somewhat similar to the following:

EARLY LIFE OF GEORGE WASHINGTON

     1. His early boyhood and school days
     2. His work as a surveyor

Recitation

Each child in the room selects a different anecdote or incident in Washington's life. These are related in a general assembly.

3. *The English sent George Washington to warn the French away*

No additional preparation and presentation are needed.

Assimilation

Readings

Upper Group

     BALDWIN. Conquest of the Old Northwest, 76–83.
     BLAISDELL. The Story of American History, 116–118.
     CHANDLER and CHITWOOD. Makers of American History, 146.
     DAVIDSON. Founders and Builders of our Country, 59–62.
     EGGLESTON. A First Book in American History, 106–108.
     EVANS. America First, 99–104.
     FOOTE and SKINNER. Explorers and Founders of America, 275–276.
     GERWIG. Washington the Young Leader, 40–80.
     GORDY. Colonial Days, 206–208.
     GORDY. Leaders in Making America, 117–118.
     GORDY. Stories of Early American History, 189–191.
     GUERBER. Story of the Thirteen Colonies, 196–199.
     MONTGOMERY. Beginners' American History, 108–110.
     MORRIS. Heroes of Discovery in America, 263–272.
     PRATT. Later Colonial Period, 43–48.
     TAPPAN. Elementary History of our Country, 122–123.
     VOLLINTINE. The Making of America, 19–23.
     WOODBURN and MORAN. Beginner's History of the United States, 179–182.
     WOODBURN and MORAN. Finders and Founders of the New World, 235–238.
     Compton's Pictured Encyclopedia (Washington).
     World Book (Washington).

Average Group

     BARNES. Elementary History of the United States, 197–198.
     BALDWIN. Four Great Americans, 35–40.
     BEARD and BAGLEY. First Book in American History, 94–96.
     COE. Founders of our Country, 302–306.
     ELSON and MACMULLAN. Story of our Country, I : 131–132, 134–135.

FORMAN. First Lessons in American History, 114–116.
GORDY. American Leaders and Heroes, 127–131.
GORDY. Elementary History of the United States, 120–122.
HARTWELL. Story-Hour Readings, V : 326–331.
MACE. Primary History, 164–167.
McMASTER. Primary History of the United States, 102–103.
MORRIS. Primary History of the United States, 133–136.
NIDA. Following the Frontier, 27–30.
PERRY and PRICE. American History, I : 209–210.
SOUTHWORTH. Builders of our Country, II : 31–39.
TAPPAN. American Hero Stories, 118–123.

Lower Group

BARNES. Primary History of the United States, 76–78.
BLAISDELL and BALL. Child's Book of American History, 86–90.
WILSON. A History Reader, 207–212.

Teachers

THWAITES. France in America, 158–168.

Minimal Essentials

Name of Person: governor of Virginia
Name of Place: Fort Duquesne (dōō kān′)
Historical Term: forks of the Ohio
Things to Remember
　Washington's journey showed that the French would not leave the Ohio.
　War between France and England would surely come.

Illustrative Material

Chronicles of America Photoplays,[1] Yale University Press : The Gateway to the West.

Procedure during Assimilation

Reading as described on pages 24–29.
Picture study based on the illustrative material listed above.
Write a letter describing his journey that George Washington might have sent to
　Lord Fairfax.
Show on the sand table where he had to go.
Drill on minimal essentials.
Objective test.

Organization

The teacher puts these points on the board in an order different from the correct one. Children are to number them correctly.

WASHINGTON SENT TO WARN THE FRENCH

　　1. Washington chosen for the mission
　　2. The journey to the fort
　　3. The return home

　[1] Fox, D. R., " Chronicles of America in Motion Pictures." *The Historical Outlook*, XV: 12–17.

Recitation

One child recites on point one, another on point two, and so on.

A drill lesson on sections II and III of Unit IV should be given at this point.

IV. THREE EARLY WARS DID NOT DECIDE WHICH NATION WAS GOING TO WIN

1. *How the Early Wars were carried on*

Preparation

"About what are the French and the English ready to go to war?

"Which should you expect to win? Why?

"How long is three quarters of a century?"

Explain the word *ammunition*.

Presentation

The struggle between the French and the English, to decide which should take North America away from the other, lasted a very long time — three quarters of a century, to be exact. During this time four different wars were fought. Our story today is about the first three, which we shall call the early wars.

In each of the three France and England began fighting in Europe. Then the French colonies in America said: "France is fighting England across the ocean. Let us help France by attacking the English colonies here." The English colonies said: "England is fighting France across the ocean. Let us help England by attacking the French colonies here." And they did.

There were no great armies in America as there were in Europe. How, then, could the French colonies attack the English? One way was to persuade the Indians to make war. So the French bought guns and ammunition for the Algonquins and sent them out against the English. The English bought guns and ammunition and sent the Iroquois out against the French. This was a very terrible way to carry on war. You already know the methods that the Indians used.

No great battles took place, and at the end of the third war one could not yet tell which side would finally win.

PRESENTATION TEST

Check the best answer:

 a. There were how many wars between the English and the French?
  _ _ _ Two
  _ _ _ Three
  _ _ _ Four

 b. In the early wars the fighting began in
  _ _ _ Europe
  _ _ _ America
  _ _ _ Asia

 c. The colonies joined in the fighting by using
  _ _ _ Spaniards
  _ _ _ Indians
  _ _ _ Portuguese

 d. Those who helped the French were the
  _ _ _ Algonquins
  _ _ _ Iroquois
  _ _ _ Aztecs

 e. Those who helped the English were the
  _ _ _ Algonquins
  _ _ _ Iroquois
  _ _ _ Aztecs

 f. At the end of the third war
  _ _ _ the English were winning
  _ _ _ the French were winning
  _ _ _ no one could tell who would win

Assimilation

Readings

Upper Group

BLAISDELL. The Story of American History, 110–116.

EVANS. America First, 87–91, 112–117.

FOOTE and SKINNER. Explorers and Founders of America, 296–306 (Sir William Johnson).

GORDY. Colonial Days, 188–199.

GORDY. Stories of Early American History, 178–184.

GRINNELL. Beyond the Old Frontier.

GUERBER. Story of the Thirteen Colonies, 183–191.

PRATT. Later Colonial Period, 29–38.

SMITH. The Boy Captive of Old Deerfield.

TAPPAN. Elementary History of our Country, 119–122.

VOLLINTINE. The Making of America, 8–9.

World Book (French and Indian Wars).

Average Group

BARNES. Elementary History of the United States, 184–187 (Sir William Johnson).

EGGLESTON. Stories of American Life and Adventure, 26–31, 110–122.

EGGLESTON. Stories of Great Americans, 39–43.

FORMAN. First Lessons in American History, 110–112.

GORDY. Elementary History of the United States, 114–117.

MCMASTER. Primary History of the United States, 92–99.

NIDA. Following the Frontier, 10.

PERRY and PRICE. American History, I : 203–208.

Lower Group

BARNES. Primary History of the United States, 72–76.

BLAISDELL and BALL. American History for Little Folks, 53–58.

BLAISDELL and BALL. American History Story Book, 19–27.

BLAISDELL and BALL. Child's Book of American History, 64–76.

BLAISDELL and BALL. Short Stories from American History, 22–29.

BURCHILL, ETTINGER, and SHIMER. Progressive Road to Reading, IV : 225–243.

PRATT. Stories of Colonial Children, 121–129, 136–154.

Teachers

COFFIN. Old Times in the Colonies (good illustrations).
  King William's War, 271–288.
  Queen Anne's War, 318–327.

DRAKE. Border Wars of New England.

FISKE. New France and New England, 233–236.

HART. American History told by Contemporaries, II : 331–334, 337–340, 346–349.

MUZZEY. An American History, 79–80.

RUGG and SCHWEPPE. The Westward Movement and the Growth of Transportation, 48–50.

STABLETON, J. K. "Thrilling Encounters with Indians." *School and Home Education*, XXXIV : 188–192.

THWAITES. The Colonies, 253–255.

THWAITES. France in America, 26–27, 28, 106–122.

WRONG. The Conquest of New France, 1–97.

American Citizenship Course in United States History, General Course, 78–80; III : 103–117.

Minimal Essentials

Name of Person: **Sir William Johnson**
Name of Place: **Canada**
Historical Terms: **stockade; war whoop; outlying settlements**
Things to Remember
  The early wars with the French were for the possession of the land around the St. Lawrence River.
  It was hard to tell which side would win.

Illustrative Material

MCKINLEY. Illustrated Topics for American History : S. 11, Intercolonial Wars.

PYLE. Book of the American Spirit, 137.

Procedure during Assimilation

Reading as described on pages 24–29.

Picture study based on the illustrative material listed on page 245.

Use the dramatization "An Indian Story." Shoemaker, *Colonial Plays for the Schoolroom*, pp. 53–57.

The teacher may read to the class selections from Cooper's *Last of the Mohicans*, describing the methods of Indian warfare.

Compare firearms used then with those of the present day. Use pictures. A child may illustrate the differences by drawings on the blackboard.

Visit the local museum.[1]

Drill on minimal essentials.

Objective test.

Organization

The teacher puts the following outline on the board. Children are to substitute a summary-sentence for each point.

EARLY WARS BETWEEN FRENCH AND ENGLISH

1. Attacks on outlying settlements
2. Warfare of the Indians
3. The attack on the great island fort

Recitation

Children are to prepare a paragraph on each of the points above.

2. *Life of Benjamin Franklin (to the Revolution)*

Preparation

"Again we must stop our story of the struggle between the French and the English in order to read about the life of a boy who had been growing up in the English colonies. He is now old enough to take part in the struggle; in fact, he is much older than George Washington. His name is Benjamin Franklin.

"Is there anything in your town that is named for Franklin? Do you know anything about him?"

No additional presentation is needed.

---

[1] Poole, Earl L., "A City that includes a Museum and Art Gallery in its Public School System." *School Arts Magazine*, XXIV : 553–555 (May, 1925).

Assimilation
Readings

Upper Group

BAILEY. Boys and Girls of Colonial Days, 71–80.
BROOKS. The True Story of Benjamin Franklin, 1–82.
BURNHAM. Hero Tales from History, 292–296.
DAVIDSON. Founders and Builders of our Nation, 35–45.
EGGLESTON. A First Book in American History, 86–99.
EVANS. America First, 221–226.
FARIS. Real Stories of the Geography Makers, 213–216.
FOOTE and SKINNER. Explorers and Founders of America, 261–267.
GORDY. Leaders in Making America, 120–121.
GORDY. Stories of Early American History, 191–193.
GUERBER. Story of the Thirteen Colonies, 199–205.
HART and HAZARD. Colonial Children, 197–199.
LEFFERTS. American Leaders, I : 1–18.
LOGIE. From Columbus to Lincoln, 81–88.
MONTGOMERY. Beginners' American History, 89–101.
TURPIN. Stories from American History, 84–109.
WOODBURN and MORAN. Beginner's History of the United States, 185–193.
WOODBURN and MORAN. Finders and Founders of the New World, 244–259.
Compton's Pictured Encyclopedia (Franklin).
World Book (Franklin).

Average Group

BALDWIN. Four Great Americans, 69–104, 106–117.
BARNES. Elementary History of the United States, 172–179.
BEARD and BAGLEY. First Book in American History, 136–140.
COE. Founders of our Country, 310–319.
EGGLESTON. Stories of Great Americans, 26–38.
FORMAN. First Lessons in American History, 117–118.
MORRIS. Primary History of the United States, 121–130.
SOUTHWORTH. Builders of our Country, I : 208–221.

Lower Group

BAKER and THORNDIKE. Everyday Classics, IV : 179–189.
BALDWIN. Fifty Famous People, 21–24.
DAVIDSON and ANDERSON. Lincoln Readers, IV : 120–123.
HARTWELL. Story-Hour Readings, IV : 230, 302–303.
WILSON. A History Reader, 141–152.

Teachers

FISHER. The True Benjamin Franklin.
MORSE. Benjamin Franklin.
OLCOTT. Good Stories for Great Birthdays, 165–172.
Baltimore County Course of Study, 464.

Minimal Essentials

Name of Person: **Benjamin Franklin**
Historical Term: *Poor Richard's Almanac*
Things to Remember
Franklin became a learned man.
He made many inventions.

Illustrative Material

GABRIEL (ED.). Pageant of America, XI: 61–66.
Educational Posters of the National Child Welfare Association: Service of City and Nation: Benjamin Franklin.
National Posters: The Story of Benjamin Franklin.

Procedure during Assimilation

Reading as described on pages 24–29.
Picture study based on the illustrative material listed above.
Each child chooses an adage from *Poor Richard's Almanac* and makes an illuminated motto. [1]
Consult the index of an atlas of the United States to see how many places have been named after Franklin.
The class plans a program for Franklin's birthday (January 17).
Drill on minimal essentials.
Objective test.

Organization

Children select their own points by which to organize the story. Those whose lists are approved by the teacher write them on the board, changing the order of the points. They may then call on other members of the class to come to the board and number the points correctly.

Recitation

One child may call on another to tell the story of his outline. Combine this recitation with that of the story which follows.

3. *Benjamin Franklin tried to make the Colonies work together*

Preparation

"About how many wars between France and England have we read?
"Which side seems to be ahead?"

Presentation

Benjamin Franklin was troubled to think that the colonies had fought three long wars and had not yet defeated the French. He said to himself, "What can be the reason?" He studied the question, and this is what he noticed.

[1] Foote, A. E., and Skinner, A. W., *Explorers and Founders of America*, p. 265.

Let us suppose that Massachusetts was ready to fight the French. She would send an army to the St. Lawrence region and fight very hard. But what might Carolina be doing? Perhaps at that very time she was trading peaceably with the French colonies.

Or, again, Virginia might decide to send an army to the Ohio country and might send to New York for help. Perhaps New York would say: "No; I need my soldiers at home to protect my own people. I will not send them to the Ohio country. Instead, you should send your army here and help me to fight the French around Lake Champlain."

So it went. The colonies would not help each other and would not work together. If one wanted to carry out a certain plan, the others wanted to do something different.

Benjamin Franklin said: "This is not right. We will never win from the French in this way. What we ought to do is all work together. We ought to have one leader; and then whatever we decide to do, we should all do it at the same time."

The idea was a very wise one; but when Franklin explained it to the colonies, they said: "No indeed; nobody can order us to fight. We will not have a leader. We want to decide for ourselves what we shall do." Franklin said, "We should let the king decide who might be governor over all the colonies." The others answered, "No, the king would then have too much power." Franklin said, "Some representatives could be sent by each colony to help make the laws." The king cried, "No, the colonies would then have too much power."

Therefore Franklin's wise plan failed, but many years afterwards people remembered what he had said.

PRESENTATION TEST

Check the best answer:

a. The reason why the English colonies had not won the first three wars was

_ _ _ because the French were too strong for them

_ _ _ because they did not have a big army

_ _ _ because they would not work together

b. Franklin wanted them

_ _ _ to unite

_ _ _ to give up

_ _ _ to fight on

Assimilation
Readings
Upper Group

BROOKS. True Story of Benjamin Franklin, 83–95.
FOOTE and SKINNER. Explorers and Founders of America, 267.
GORDY. Leaders in Making America, 121–122.
GORDY. Stories of Early American History, 193–194.
LEFFERTS. American Leaders, I : 18–19.
PRATT. Later Colonial Period, 48–49.

Average Group

BALDWIN. Four Great Americans, 104–105.
BARNES. Elementary History of the United States, 180.
COE. Founders of our Country, 319–320.
FORMAN. First Lessons in American History, 117, 118–119.
PERRY and PRICE. American History, I : 214.
SOUTHWORTH. Builders of our Country, I : 221–222.

Lower Group

MCFEE. Story of Benjamin Franklin.

Teachers

FISKE. New France and New England, 279–280.
HART. American History told by Contemporaries, II : 229–235, 381–382.
HART. Formation of the Union, 28–30.
MUZZEY. An American History, 82–83.
THWAITES. France in America, 168–172.

Minimal Essentials

Name of Place: **Albany** (ôl′ba̤ nĭ)
Historical Terms: **Franklin's plan of union; unite**
Things to Remember

Franklin wanted the colonies to unite to fight against the French.
They would not unite.
Years afterwards they remembered Franklin's advice.

Procedure during Assimilation

Reading as described on pages 24–29.
Use the helps suggested in the books.
The class draws Franklin's flag.[1]

Organization

To the preceding organization, add one point for this story.

Recitation

Give the recitations at an assembly program on Franklin's birthday, January 17.

---

[1] Tappan, E. M., *An Elementary History of our Country*, p. 136; or Lawler, T. B., *Essentials of American History*, p. 137.

V. The French and Indian War decided that England should rule Most of North America

1. *For a Long Time the English failed to drive the French away from the Ohio*

Preparation

"What was the name of the fort that was built where two rivers come together to make the Ohio? Show it on the map. What city is there today?

"Why were both England and France so eager to possess this place?

"What is a general in an army?"

Presentation

In our last story we found that the fighting in the first three wars had been done mainly by the colonists and the Indians. At that time, however, a new leader appeared in England. He said to his followers: "England has not done her share in fighting the French in America. We have left the colonists to carry on the war by themselves. No wonder they have not conquered the French! We must help them by sending great armies, our best generals, many ships, and all the supplies they need."

England agreed. Great armies began to pour into America. Do you suppose, though, that the English generals knew how to fight as the Indians did — behind trees and from ambush? No, they did not. So at first the French and the Algonquins kept on winning, but after a while the English generals learned the new method of fighting. Then England, with her splendid generals and her much larger armies, finally won the victory. Our story today is about one of the English generals who did not know how to fight in the Indian way.

PRESENTATION TEST

Check the best answer:

> *a.* The fighting in the first three wars had been done mainly by
>
> _ _ _ English armies
> _ _ _ the English navy
> _ _ _ the colonies

b. The new ruler in England decided

   _ _ _ that England should give the colonies more help

   _ _ _ that England should leave the colonies alone

   _ _ _ that England should let France have the land

c. At first the English generals did not win

   _ _ _ because they were afraid of the French

   _ _ _ because they did not know the Indian method of fighting

   _ _ _ because their armies were not large enough

Assimilation

Readings

Upper Group

BALDWIN. Conquest of the Old Northwest, 83–91 (difficult).

BLAISDELL. The Story of American History, 118–122.

CHANDLER and CHITWOOD. Makers of American History, 146–149.

EGGLESTON. A First Book in American History, 109–114.

FOOTE and SKINNER. Explorers and Founders of America, 276–280.

GERWIG. Washington the Young Leader, 90–125.

GORDY. Colonial Days, 208–213.

GORDY. Leaders in Making America, 118–119, 122–124.

GORDY. Stories of Early American History, 194–198.

GUERBER. Story of the Thirteen Colonies, 206–209.

LOGIE. From Columbus to Lincoln, 88–105.

MONTGOMERY. Beginners' American History, 110–112.

PRATT. Later Colonial Period, 51–62.

TAPPAN. Elementary History of our Country, 124–126.

VOLLINTINE. The Making of America, 22–29.

WOODBURN and MORAN. Beginner's History of the United States, 182–184.

WOODBURN and MORAN. Finders and Founders of the New World, 238–242.

Compton's Pictured Encyclopedia (French and Indian War).

World Book (French and Indian War).

Average Group

BALDWIN. Four Great Americans, 40–46.

BARNES. Elementary History of the United States, 188–190, 198–200.

BEARD and BAGLEY. First Book in American History, 96–97.

COE. Founders of our Country, 306–309.

ELSON and MacMULLAN. Story of our Country, I : 136–141.

FORMAN. First Lessons in American History, 119–122.

GORDY. American Leaders and Heroes, 132–134.

GORDY. Elementary History of the United States, 122–126.

MACE. Primary History, 167–168.

McMASTER. Primary History of the United States, 103–105.

MORRIS. Primary History of the United States, 136–143.

NIDA. Following the Frontier, 31–33.

PERRY and PRICE. American History, I : 210–214, 215–216.

SOUTHWORTH. Builders of our Country, II : 36–43.

TAPPAN. American Hero Stories, 123–125.

Lower Group

BARNES. Primary History of the United States, 78–81.

BLAISDELL and BALL. Child's Book of American History, 97–103.

DAVIS. Stories of the United States, 131–134.
DODGE. Stories of American History, 52–59.
WILSON. A History Reader, 212–215.

Teachers

COFFIN. Old Times in the Colonies, 363–388.
FISKE. New France and New England, 281–293.
HART. American History told by Contemporaries, II : 365–369.
HART. Formation of the Union, 30–33.
MUZZEY. An American History, 83–86.
MUZZEY. The United States of America, I : 46–54.
PARKMAN. The Struggle for a Continent, 297–513.
THWAITES. France in America, 173–181.
WRONG. The Conquest of New France, 145–164.

Minimal Essentials

Name of Person: **General Braddock** (brăd'ŭk)
Name of Place: **Pittsburgh** (Fort Duquesne; Fort Pitt)
Historical Terms: **aide; regiments; retreat**
Things to Remember

The last war in America between the English and the French was called the French and Indian War.

This war was fought to obtain possession of the Ohio River and of Quebec.

For a long time the English could not drive the French away from the Ohio River.

Illustrative Material

BROWN. Famous Pictures: 2133, Braddock's Defeat.
PYLE. Book of the American Spirit, 171, 173.
Society for Visual Education. Picturol: The French and Indian War.

Procedure during Assimilation

Reading as described on pages 24–29.
Picture study based on the illustrative material listed above.
On the sand-table map show the forks of the Ohio. Place a line of little tin soldiers along the route that Braddock followed. See the map in W. J. Long's *America,* p. 137.
Dress dolls in the uniforms of a British soldier; of a British officer; of a colonial soldier.
Dramatize Braddock's expedition.
Collect pictures of the British Parliament and of the Prime Minister. Explain to the children that it was a body such as this which sent help to the colonies.
Drill on minimal essentials.
Objective test.

Organization

The teacher puts the following outline on the board, changing the order of the topics. Children are to number the points correctly.

Recitation

Children write the stories, add cut-out pictures or illustrations they themselves draw, trace a map, design a cover (the British flag), and make a booklet of *The French and Indian War.*

2. General Wolfe took Quebec

Preparation

"Why did the English generals lose their battles when they first came to America to fight the French? Name one general who lost his life also."

Show a picture of the fort at Quebec. Discuss the meaning of the word *cliff*.

"Why would both France and England be eager to have Quebec?"

Presentation

We found in our last story that after the English generals learned the methods of fighting used by the Indians they had much better success. They began to win from the French; one by one they took the French forts, even Fort Duquesne at last. Bit by bit they drove the French back, until of all the great French strongholds in the New World only Quebec was left.

The English king said: "We must have Quebec. If it were ours, we could prevent anybody from sailing up the St. Lawrence River; and if people couldn't sail up the St. Lawrence they couldn't go to the Great Lakes, either. So whoever has Quebec can command all the region called New France."

The king then chose his very bravest generals and sent them over to take Quebec. You saw in the picture that Quebec is built away up on the top of a hill. How could an army ever climb those steep cliffs? It looks as if it could not be done, but an English army did it. Our story today is about how they took Quebec.

PRESENTATION TEST

Check the best answer:

a. After the English generals learned the Indian ways of fighting

_ _ _ they liked the Indian ways better than their own
_ _ _ they captured all the French forts
_ _ _ they went back to England

b. Both sides wanted to have Quebec

_ _ _ because Quebec is a beautiful city
_ _ _ because Quebec is built or a hill
_ _ _ because Quebec commands all the land along the river

c. The English army

_ _ _ took Quebec
_ _ _ failed to take Quebec
_ _ _ ran away from the Indians

Assimilation

Readings

Upper Group

BLAISDELL. The Story of American History, 122–125.
BURNHAM. Hero Tales from History, 224–232.
CHANDLER and CHITWOOD. Makers of American History, 112–120.
EVANS. America First, 104–108.
FOOTE and SKINNER. Explorers and Founders of America, 281–295.
GORDY. Colonial Days, 222–233.
GORDY. Leaders in Making America, 124–128.
GORDY. Stories of Early American History, 198–203.
GUERBER. Story of the Thirteen Colonies, 210–213.
LANIER. The Book of Bravery, 240–253.
O'NEILL. World's Story, 429–431.
PLUMMER. Roy and Ray in Canada, 175–179.
PRATT. Later Colonial Period, 73–88.
TAPPAN. Elementary History of our Country, 126–127.
TERRY. History Stories of Other Lands, VI : 109–113 (difficult).
VOLLINTINE. The Making of America, 25–34.
Compton's Pictured Encyclopedia (Wolfe, Quebec, Montcalm).
World Book (French and Indian War ; Wolfe ; Quebec, Battle of).

Average Group

BEARD and BAGLEY. First Book in American History, 97–101.
ELSON and MACMULLAN. Story of our Country, I : 141–146.
FORMAN. First Lessons in American History, 122–123.
GORDY. American Leaders and Heroes, 136–144.
GORDY. Elementary History of the United States, 126–129.
MACE. Primary History, 133–138.
MCMASTER. Primary History of the United States, 105–106.
NIDA. Following the Frontier, 33–36.

PERRY and PRICE. American History, I: 216–220.
SOUTHWORTH. Builders of our Country, I: 226–243.
TAPPAN. American Hero Stories, 126–134.

Lower Group

BARNES. Primary History of the United States, 82–83.
DAVIS. Stories of the United States, 136–137.
WAYLAND. History Stories for Primary Grades, 158–160.

Teachers

COFFIN. Old Times in the Colonies, 389–453.
FISKE. New France and New England, 349–359.
HART. American History told by Contemporaries, II: 369–372.
HART. Formation of the Union, 33–34.
MACDONALD. Documentary Source Book of American History, 109–116.
MUZZEY. An American History, 86–87.
PARKMAN. Montcalm and Wolfe, II: 259–325.
THWAITES. France in America, 241–254.

Minimal Essentials

Names of Persons: **General Wolfe; General Montcalm** (mŏnt käm')
Name of Place: **Plains of Abraham**
Things to Remember

The English wanted to take Quebec because it was the strongest place along the
St. Lawrence River.
General Wolfe took Quebec.

Illustrative Material

ARNOLD. Historical Pictures: A. H. P. 71, Wolfe at Quebec.
BROWN. Famous Pictures: 1421, Death of Wolfe.
LONGMAN. Historical Wall Pictures: Wolfe on the Plains of Abraham (very beautiful).
Chronicles of America Photoplays, Yale University Press: Wolfe and Montcalm.
Keystone Views: 47, Common Monument to Wolfe and Montcalm.
Society for Visual Education. Schoolfilm: Struggle of the French and the English for North
America.

Procedure during Assimilation

Reading as described on pages 24–29.
Picture study based on the illustrative material listed above.
On the sand table show the St. Lawrence River, Quebec, the Plains of Abraham,
and Wolfe's Cove.
Stage a toy scene of the battle of Quebec.[1]
Make a series of illustrations[2] representing Wolfe's army coming up the river, the
ascent to the Plains of Abraham, the battle of Quebec.
Place the Montcalm-Wolfe monument.
Drill on minimal essentials.
Objective test.

[1] Similar to that described in *The Twentieth Yearbook of the National Society for
the Study of Education*, Part I, p. 82.
[2] Birtwistle, A., "A Problem in Wall Decoration." *School Arts Magazine*, XXIV:
436–438.

Organization

Use the series of illustrations as the organization points.

Recitation

Each child copies the illustrations for his booklet of *The French and Indian War*, describing the pictures by short paragraphs.

3. *Pontiac tried to push back the English People*

Preparation

"Do you remember, from the story of Champlain, which Indians were friendly to the French? which were friendly to the English?

"Show the great amount of territory occupied by the Algonquins.[1]

"How do you suppose the Algonquins will feel when their friends, the French, are beaten by their enemies, the English?"

Presentation

One of the greatest chiefs was Pontiac (*pointing to the name on the board*). His tribe lived in this territory (*showing on the map*).

Pontiac was very sad indeed when the news came that the French had lost Quebec. He said to his Indian friends: "Our enemies, the English, have beaten the French. That is very bad for us. The French only traded with us for furs, but the English always want to cut down our trees and make farms. The game will all be driven away, our beautiful forests will be destroyed, and the Indians will be driven out. There is only one thing for us to do, and we must do that quickly. We must drive the English out of all our part of the country."

His friends listened gravely and agreed that there must be war. How the Indians planned to get into the English forts, and how their plans almost succeeded, is our story for today.

[1] Sanford American History Maps, No. 3.

PRESENTATION TEST

Check the best answer:

    a. The Algonquin Indians were friendly to

         _ _ _ the French   _ _ _ the English   _ _ _ the Spanish

    b. The Algonquins did not like the English

         _ _ _ because the English wore red coats

         _ _ _ because the English cut down the trees to make farms

         _ _ _ because the English were friends of the Iroquois

    c. The Indians decided

         _ _ _ to join the English   _ _ _ to make war

         _ _ _ to leave the country

    d. Their leader was

         _ _ _ Pontiac   _ _ _ Philip   _ _ _ Powhatan

Assimilation

Readings

Upper Group

    BALDWIN. Conquest of the Old Northwest, 92–116 (difficult).

    EVANS. America First, 109–112.

    GORDY. Colonial Days, 235–245.

    GUERBER. Story of the Thirteen Colonies, 214.

    HASBROUCK. Boys' Parkman, 135–165 (difficult).

    PRATT. Later Colonial Period, 89–116.

    WADE. Ten Big Indians, 125–151.

    WRIGHT. Children's Stories in American History, 337–347.

    World Book (Pontiac).

Average Group

    EGGLESTON. Stories of American Life and Adventure, 79–90.

    FORMAN. First Lessons in American History, 124–125.

    GORDY. Elementary History of the United States, 129–132.

    McMASTER. Primary History of the United States, 107–109.

    NIDA. Following the Frontier, 37–38.

    TAPPAN. American Hero Stories, 135–143.

Lower Group

    BLAISDELL and BALL. Short Stories from American History, 30–37.

Teachers

    JOHNSTON. Famous Indian Chiefs, 151–208.

    PARKMAN. Conspiracy of Pontiac, I, II.

    THWAITES. France in America, 278–279.

Minimal Essentials

Name of Person: **Pontiac** (pŏn'tĭ ăk)

Name of Place: **Detroit**

Historical Terms: **conspiracy; council; plot**

Things to Remember

    The Indians did not like the English, because they were settlers rather than fur traders.

    Pontiac tried to drive the English out of the West.

Illustrative Material

PYLE. Book of the American Spirit, 143.

Procedure during Assimilation

Reading as described on pages 24–29.

Picture study based on the illustrative material listed above.

Write the speech Pontiac might have made to the Indians of Michigan, persuading them to rise against the English.

Construct on the sand table the fort at Detroit and the stockade.

Dramatize the attack on Detroit.

Drill on minimal essentials.

Objective test.

Organization

Children and teacher together select the main points of the story, somewhat as follows:

PONTIAC TRIED TO DRIVE BACK THE ENGLISH

1. The feeling of the Indians toward the English
2. The conspiracy
3. The council
4. Siege of Detroit
5. War at other forts
6. Failure of Pontiac

Recitation

Children complete their booklets of *The French and Indian War* by adding the story of Pontiac, with any illustrations they choose.

4. *England now owned Almost All of North America*

No additional preparation and presentation are needed.

Assimilation

Readings

Upper Group

BLAISDELL. The Story of American History, 125.

GORDY. Stories of Early American History, 203.

GUERBER. Story of the Thirteen Colonies, 213.

TAPPAN. Elementary History of our Country, 127–128.

VOLLINTINE. The Making of America, 35, 37–53.

Average Group

FORMAN. First Lessons in American History, 123.

GORDY. Elementary History of the United States, 129.

MCMASTER. Primary History of the United States, 106.

PERRY and PRICE. American History, I : 221.

Lower Group
> BARNES. Primary History of the United States, 83.

Teachers
> HART. Formation of the Union, 34–41.
> MacDONALD. Documentary Source Book of American History, 109–112.
> MUZZEY. An American History, 88–89.
> NEWMAN. Beginners' Modern History, 89–95.
> THWAITES. France in America, 272–276.

Minimal Essentials

Name of Place: **land east of the Mississippi River**
Date: **1763** — end of French and English Wars
Historical Term: **treaty of peace**
Things to Remember
> In the treaty of peace (1763) France gave up all her claims to land east of the
> Mississippi, except two small islands for fishing.
> England was then the strongest nation in North America.

Procedure during Assimilation

Reading as described on pages 24–29.
One group of children representing the French and another group representing
the English meet and make a treaty.[1] After reading it to the class for approval,
both sides sign the treaty.
Make a map showing the English territory and the French territory after the war.[2]
Compare it with the "Rival Claims" map.[3]

Organization
Making the map.

Recitation .

An explanation of what the map tells.

Play a game of *Personages* similar to the game of *Authors*.[4]
Give a standardized test on all units covered so far.[5]
The teacher may give the class Test I, "Exploration and
Settlement," of the *Informational Tests in United States History*
to accompany Beard and Bagley's *History of the American
People*.[6] Children are not expected to answer all the items,
but they may be interested in seeing how many they know.

---

[1] MacDonald, W., *Documentary Source Book of American History*, pp. 109–112.

[2] Muzzey, D. S., *An American History*, p. 88.

[3] See page 238.

[4] Johnson, G. E., *Education by Plays and Games*, p. 199.

[5] *The Van Wagenen American History Scales*, Revised Edition, Information
Scale C 1. Teachers College, "Discovery to Revolutionary War," Grades 5 and 6.

[6] The Macmillan Company.

MINIMAL ESSENTIALS OF UNIT IV

PERSONS	PLACES	TERMS	DATES
Johnny Appleseed	Detroit	aide	*1763.* End of
General Braddock	Fort Duquesne	blockhouse	French and Eng-
Benjamin Frank-	Great Lakes	conspiracy	lish Wars
lin	Louisiana	council	Near the end of
governor of Vir-	Mackinac	forks of the Ohio	the seventeenth
ginia	Lake Michigan	Franklin's plan of	century
Jesuits	Mohawk River	union	About the middle
Sir William John-	mouth of Missis-	fur traders	of the eighteenth
son	sippi River	the *Griffin*	century
Joliet	Ohio River	leaden plates	
La Salle	Pittsburgh (Fort	mission stations	Drill on the peaks
Marquette	Pitt)	Ohio Company	represented in
General Montcalm	Plains of Abraham	outlying settle-	the time chart
Pontiac	"the West"	ments	
George Washing-		pipe of peace	
ton		plot	
Martha Washing-		*Poor Richard's Al-*	
ton		*manac*	
General Wolfe		portage	
		regiment	
		retreat	
		stockade	
		surveyor	
		trading posts	
		treaty of peace	
		unite	
		war whoop	
		woodrangers	

TESTS ON THE ENTIRE UNIT

(To be given after all the stories are completed)

Test of Place-Sense. Pass outline maps of North America, double size. Give the following directions:

1. Put the initials *G L* in each one of the Great Lakes.
2. Put the letter *M* in Lake Michigan.
3. Put the letter *D* where Detroit is.
4. Write *Miss.* at the mouth of the Mississippi River.
5. Write *La.* where Louisiana is.
6. Put the figure 1 where Mackinac is.
7. Put the figure 2 where the Mohawk River is.
8. Put the figure 3 where Fort Duquesne was.
9. Write *Ohio* where the Ohio River is.

Test of Time-Sense. Pass mimeographed sheets of the following:

1. Here is a list of people. Put the figure 1 before the name of the man who lived first, a figure 2 before the name of the one who lived next, and so on.

   _ _ _ Marquette   _ _ _ Benjamin Franklin
   _ _ _ La Salle   _ _ _ De Soto

2. Here is a list of people. Put the figure 1 before the name of the man who lived (or did his great work) first, a figure 2 before the name of the one who lived next, and so on.

   _ _ _ John Hawkins   _ _ _ Joliet
   _ _ _ George Washington   _ _ _ Pontiac

3. Here is a list of people. Put the figure 1 before the name of the person who lived first, a figure 2 before the name of the one who lived next, and so on.

   _ _ _ Montcalm   _ _ _ Braddock
   _ _ _ Martha Washington   _ _ _ Drake

4. Here is a list of things which happened in the stories. Put the figure 1 before that which happened first, the figure 2 before that which happened next, and so on.

   _ _ _ La Salle sailed down to the mouth of the Mississippi.
   _ _ _ Pontiac tried to drive back the English.
   _ _ _ The governor of Virginia sent George Washington to drive the French away.
   _ _ _ Benjamin Franklin tried to get the colonies to work together.

5. Here is a list of things which happened. Number in the same way.

   _ _ _ General Wolfe took Quebec.
   _ _ _ The French drove Braddock back.
   _ _ _ Marquette and Joliet explored the upper part of the Mississippi.
   _ _ _ The French lost all their land east of the Mississippi River except two little islands.

6. Here is a list of dates: *1607, 1620, 1763, 1754, 1492.* Choose the right one and place it before the event below:

   _ _ _ _ end of the French and Indian War

Test on Persons. Pass mimeographed sheets of the following:

I. Here is a list of names:

       Jesuits   Marquette
       Pontiac   Sir William Johnson
       General Montcalm   General Braddock
       Johnny Appleseed

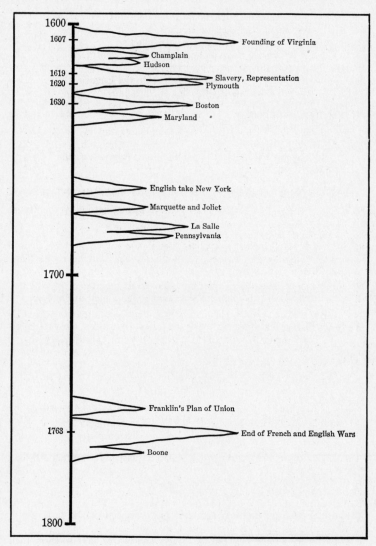

1600
1607 — Founding of Virginia
Champlain
Hudson
1619 — Slavery, Representation
1620 — Plymouth
1630 — Boston
Maryland

English take New York
Marquette and Joliet
La Salle
Pennsylvania

1700

Franklin's Plan of Union
1763 — End of French and English Wars
Boone

1800

Time Chart — Unit IV

Take one name at a time and put it in the right place in the sentences below:

1. _ _ _ _   _ _ _ was the Frenchman who fought at Quebec.
2. _ _ _ _ were missionaries to the Indians.
3. _ _ _ _ sailed down the Mississippi with Joliet.
4. _ _ _ _   _ _ _ was an early pioneer in the Ohio country.
5. _ _ _ _   _ _ _ was killed near Fort Duquesne.
6. _ _ _ _   _ _ _   _ _ _ made the Iroquois help the English.
7. _ _ _ _ tried to drive the English out of Michigan.

II. Here is a list of names:

Joliet	Benjamin Franklin
General Wolfe	George Washington
La Salle	The governor of Virginia
Martha Washington	

Take one name at a time and put it in the right place in the sentences below:

1. _ _ _ _   _ _ _   _ _ _ _   _ _ _ sent George Washington to warn the French away.
2. _ _ _ _ sailed on the upper Mississippi.
3. _ _ _ _   _ _ _ was with General Braddock.
4. _ _ _ _   _ _ _ was the wife of George Washington.
5. _ _ _ _   _ _ _ was a great inventor.
6. _ _ _ _   _ _ _ sailed down the Mississippi to its mouth.
7. _ _ _ _   _ _ _ was the great English soldier who fought at Quebec.

Test on Historical Terms. The teacher prepares descriptions such as the following, which may have been used previously as the subject of drill games.

I. Here is a list of words:

fur traders	woodrangers	*Griffin*
treaty of peace	council	*Poor Richard's Almanac*
trading post	forks of the Ohio	war whoop
plot	portage	leaden plates

Take one word at a time and put it in the right place in the sentences below:

1. A secret plan to harm somebody is a _ _ _ _.
2. A loud shout used as a call to war is a _ _ _ _   _ _ _ _.
3. A meeting called to think things over is a _ _ _ _.
4. Men who traveled around in the forests were called _ _ _ _.
5. When nations agree to stop fighting they make a _ _ _ _   _ _ _ _   _ _ _ _.
6. Where there is land between two rivers and people have to carry their boats from one to the other, the land is a _ _ _ _.
7. A book made by Benjamin Franklin was called _ _ _ _ _   _ _ _ _   _ _ _ _.
8. People who bought furs from the Indians and then sold them were _ _ _ _   _ _ _ _.

9. The place where two rivers come together to make the Ohio is called the ____ ____ ____ ____.

10. A settlement made in order to trade is a ____ ____.

11. The pieces of metal the French buried to show that the land was theirs were ____ ____.

12. The first sailing ship on the Great Lakes was the ____.

II. Here is a list of words:

conspiracy	retreat	surveyor
mission station	pipe of peace	regiment
aide	unite	blockhouse
Franklin's plan of union	stockade	Ohio Company

Take one word at a time and put it in the right place in the sentences below:

1. To go back, away from an enemy, is to ____.

2. A high fence around a place to protect it is a ____.

3. A heavy fort made of logs with little holes to shoot from is a ____.

4. When people secretly agree to do an evil act, they make a ____.

5. An Indian sign of peace was to smoke a ____ ____ ____.

6. A man who helps a general to give his orders is an ____.

7. A man who measures land is a ____.

8. Part of an army is a ____.

9. To join together is to ____.

10. Franklin's idea that all the colonies should join as one is called ____ ____ ____ ____.

11. A place where missionaries stay is a ____ ____.

12. The people who lived along the Ohio were the ____ ____.

COMPREHENSION TEST ON UNIT IV

1. *Check the best answer:*

   a. The wars between the French and the English

      ___ left the French half of the land

      ___ drove the French out of North America

      ___ drove the English out of North America

   b. Benjamin Franklin's plan was

      ___ for all the colonies to join to fight the French

      ___ for each colony to fight the French alone

      ___ for all the colonies to stop fighting

   c. When Washington made his journey to the Ohio River the French told him

      ___ that they would leave the Ohio River

      ___ that they would share the land with the English

      ___ that they would not leave the Ohio River

   d. The English people wanted to settle along the Ohio River

      ___ because they did not like to live by the sea

      ___ because they did not want the French to hold the land

      ___ because they could have boat rides

e. La Salle's great idea was

     _ _ _ to build forts along the rivers in the French claims

     _ _ _ to discover the Mississippi

     _ _ _ to go back to France

f. When Pontiac failed to drive the English out

     _ _ _ the English still had to fight the French

     _ _ _ the English were masters of most of North America

g. Both the French and the English built a line of forts

     _ _ _ in order to protect the land they claimed

     _ _ _ because they were afraid of the Indians

     _ _ _ in order to show how strong they were

h. Marquette and Joliet showed the French people

     _ _ _ that all Indians were friendly

     _ _ _ that the Mississippi was a route to India

     _ _ _ that they could travel most of the way by water through the Great Lakes and down the Mississippi

i. The English wanted to take Quebec

     _ _ _ because it was a beautiful city

     _ _ _ because it was the strongest city along the St. Lawrence

     _ _ _ because it was on a great river

j. The first three wars between the French and the English

     _ _ _ did not show which was going to win

     _ _ _ showed that the English would win

     _ _ _ showed that the French would win

k. The missionaries and fur traders helped France

     _ _ _ to fight the Indians

     _ _ _ to explore the land

     _ _ _ to fight the English

2. *What is the title of the fourth unit ?*

ORGANIZATION OF THE UNIT AS A WHOLE

Children make from memory a list of the principal stories in the unit.

RECITATION OF THE UNIT AS A WHOLE

Divide the stories among the different rows in the class, each row being held responsible for at least three stories. Each child should prepare to tell briefly all the stories assigned to his row, one after the other, as a continuous recitation.

UNIT V

HOW THE ENGLISH COLONIES CAME TO SEPARATE THEMSELVES FROM THE MOTHER COUNTRY

I. Why the Colonies and England could not Agree.
II. How the Revolution was Fought.
    1. In the north the colonists won.
    2. In the middle states England held New York.
    3. In the back-country the Americans won much land.
    4. Not many battles were fought at sea.
    5. In the south the Americans captured the British army and the war was won.
III. Making a New Nation.
    1. The Declaration of Independence made the colonies the United States.
    2. The first governments were poor and weak.
    3. A strong government was made after several years.

PREPARATION FOR THE OVERVIEW

"Why do we celebrate the Fourth of July? What happened on that day?

"In our unit about colonization which nation did we find settled here?" (*Showing the eastern seacoast.*)

"In our unit about how England came to own most of North America, we found that she had driven out what other people?

"What do we mean by the expression 'mother country'?

"Now we find that since there were no enemies to face, colonies and mother country began quarreling among themselves.

"What is a tax? Why do people pay taxes? Who says that they must?" Show a tax receipt.

"Our new unit tells how the English colonies came to separate themselves from the mother country."

PRESENTATION OR OVERVIEW

We must remember that the colonies had been settled chiefly by England. Of course, founding colonies costs a great deal of money and a great deal of trouble. So after the colonies became strong and prosperous, England said: "I should be paid back in some way for all my trouble. I will make a law that the colonies may trade with no other country. They must sell their goods to me and must buy from me." The United States does much the same thing today, in regard to where its possessions must buy their goods.

The colonies did not like the plan at all. They replied: "That is not fair. We have worked hard to build our homes in the New World, and should be allowed to buy our goods wherever we can buy them cheapest." You may see that both sides became angry over the question of trade.

Then again England said: "You are English people. All English people pay taxes to support the government; so you must pay your share." The colonies answered: "You have let us alone now for a long time; so we do not take kindly to the idea of taxation. However, if you will let us decide how much we will pay, we will agree. We are your children, and, of course, we must pay our share. But we wish to decide for ourselves how much it is to be." Here was another question on which they could not agree — that of taxation.

From quarreling, both sides advanced to fierce anger, and finally to open war. At first the colonies had no thought of making themselves a separate country — they wanted only to govern themselves completely; but after there had been a year of desperate fighting, after many men had been killed, and after each side had learned to hate the other, it seemed best to make the colonies a separate country altogether.

Thus was born the United States. We should no longer call Massachusetts, Virginia, and the rest *colonies*; they were *states*. We should no longer call them *English* or *British*; they were *American*. For better or for worse they had made themselves independent. No more could they look to England for help or protection. They had to stand on their own feet.

Naturally England did not like this step. She did not intend to let her colonies go without a struggle. A long war followed. For eight years the colonies fought and suffered. It was very hard to get men and supplies; there was very little money; they had few ships; and for a long time it seemed as if England must win. In fact, if France had not helped them they might never have been able to keep up.

France did help them, and at last, eight years after the war began, England and the United States made peace. England agreed that the United States was to be a country by itself.

The new nation had to face several very puzzling questions. What kind of nation should it be? Should it have a king? Who should make the laws? Should the people have to pay taxes? What should the nation do with a state if it refused to pay a tax? You see, it is not easy to make a new nation.

If you have ever tried to learn to skate, you know that at first you made very hard work of it. You fell down again and again. That is just what the United States did when it tried to plan a new government. The first plan was very poor; it could not work well. The nations of Europe, who were watching us, said to each other: "The United States cannot last. They will have to ask England to take them back. They do not know how to make a good plan for a nation."

But just as you kept on and kept on while you were learning to skate, so the United States kept on making plan after plan until at last it had a very good one. Then the great men wrote down that plan on paper, and the states liked it well enough to accept it. We call that plan the *Constitution of the United States* (*pointing to the words written on the board*), and it is the plan of government we have today for all our United States.

PRESENTATION TEST

Check the best answer:

   a. England thought she should be paid back for all her trouble in founding the colonies

     _ _ _ by having the colonies trade only with herself
     _ _ _ by taking all the gold found in the colonies
     _ _ _ by capturing French ships

   b. The colonies were willing to pay a tax, but they wanted

     _ _ _ to have all the money kept in the colonies
     _ _ _ to decide for themselves what they should pay
     _ _ _ to pay very little

c. At the beginning of the war the colonies

 _ _ _ wanted to be a separate country
 _ _ _ wanted to conquer England
 _ _ _ wanted what they thought were their rights

d. After a while the colonies became

 _ _ _ colonies of France
 _ _ _ a separate country
 _ _ _ part of England

e. We might not have won the war

 _ _ _ if France had not helped us
 _ _ _ if England had not become tired
 _ _ _ if the English soldiers had not been lazy

f. The new nation had to decide

 _ _ _ what to call itself
 _ _ _ what kind of a flag to have
 _ _ _ what kind of government to have

g. The first plans of government were

 _ _ _ not good enough
 _ _ _ very good
 _ _ _ not tried

h. After a while the United States made a very good plan. It was

 _ _ _ the Declaration of Independence
 _ _ _ the treaty of peace
 _ _ _ the Constitution of the United States

I. Why the Colonies and England could not Agree

Preparation and Presentation

On the board is a list of the colonies and the population of each. Each child chooses what colony he wishes to represent. Present to the class a bill for $200,000,000 (*write* $200 million) for the French wars. The representatives discuss the matter, argue back and forth as to whether they will pay, and finally vote on the measure. Then they decide how much each colony will pay, judging by its population.

"This is what happens when people tax themselves. Suppose, however, that you had voted here to tax another school in the city instead. Do you think they would like that? Why not?

"The trouble between the colonies and England was over a matter very similar to that we have talked about."

Assimilation
Readings

Upper Group

BAILEY. Boys and Girls of Colonial Days, 81–91.

BLAISDELL. The Story of American History, 139–157.

BLAISDELL and BALL. Heroic Deeds of American Sailors, 15–29.

BROOKS. Stories of the Old Bay State, 109–126.

BURNHAM. Hero Tales from History, 190–194 (Henry).

CHANDLER and CHITWOOD. Makers of American History, 130–134 (Otis), 135–143 (Henry).

CHURCH. Stories from English History, 580–581.

DICKINSON. Children's Book of Patriotic Stories, 189–191, 225–226.

EGGLESTON. A First Book in American History, 115–117.

EVANS. America First, 139–148.

FOOTE and SKINNER. Makers and Defenders of America, 9–30.

GORDY. Leaders in Making America, 137–146 (Henry), 147–158 (Adams).

GORDY. Stories of Later American History, 1–13 (Henry), 15–28 (Adams).

GUERBER. Story of the Thirteen Colonies, 214–232.

LEFFERTS. American Leaders, I : 38–54 (Adams), 55–64 (Henry).

LOGIE. From Columbus to Lincoln, 122–145.

MARSHALL. An Island Story, 442–447.

MONTGOMERY. Beginners' American History, 113–115.

PERRY and PRICE. American History, II : 1–12.

TAPPAN. Elementary History of our Country, 132–140.

TERRY. History Stories of Other Lands, VI : 138–139.

TURPIN. Brief Biographies from American History, 142–180.

WOODBURN and MORAN. Beginner's History of the United States, 193–205.

WOODBURN and MORAN. Makers of America, 8–17 (Otis), 18–32 (Henry).

WRIGHT. Children's Stories in American History, 348–351.

Compton's Pictured Encyclopedia (Revolution, Adams, Henry, Otis, Stamp Act).

World Book (Revolution).

Average Group

BARNES. Elementary History of the United States, 201–204.

BEARD and BAGLEY. A First Book in American History, 103–118.

COE. Makers of the Nation, 9–18 (Henry), 19–29 (Adams).

ELSON and MacMULLAN. Story of our Country, I : 147–152.

FORMAN. First Lessons in American History, 130–136.

GORDY. American Leaders and Heroes, 146–154 (Henry), 156–163 (Adams).

GORDY. Elementary History of the United States, 133–144.

GORDY. Our Patriots, 58–76.

MACE. Primary History, 141–155, 172–176.

McMASTER. Primary History of the United States, 110–120.

MORRIS. Primary History of the United States, 144–150.

MOWRY. First Steps in the History of our Country, 114–121.

PRATT. Foundations of the Republic, 1–61.

SOUTHWORTH. Builders of our Country, II : 1–8 (Henry), 9–18 (Adams).

Lower Group

BARNES. Primary History of the United States, 85–93.

BLAISDELL and BALL. American History for Little Folks, 59–79.

BLAISDELL and BALL. Child's Book of American History, 104–119.

BLAISDELL and BALL. Short Stories from American History, 38–44, 51–57.

DAVIDSON and ANDERSON. Lincoln Readers, IV: 117–119.
DAVIS. Stories of the United States, 153–159.
DODGE. Stories of American History, 60–78 (read by sections).
HUSTED. Stories of '76, 3–11.
PRATT. Stories of Colonial Children, 165–188.
WILSON. A History Reader, 223–225.
Flanagan Publishing Company. Story of the Revolution, 3–5.

Teachers

BECKER. Beginnings of the American People, 202–247.
BECKER. Eve of the Revolution, 1–97, 98–256.
BOGART. Economic History of the United States, 90–111.
CALLENDER. Economic History of the United States, 122–140.
COMAN. Industrial History of the United States, 89–106.
FISKE. The American Revolution, I: 1–36, 76–117.
GREENE. Provincial America, 283–300.
HART. American History told by Contemporaries, II: 373–382, 394–433, 434–451.
HART. Formation of the Union, 43–68.
HOWARD. Preliminaries of the Revolution, 47–67, 121–192, 259–295.
LODGE. Short History of the English Colonies in America, 476–491.
MACDONALD. Documentary Source Book of American History, 55–60, 103–109, 117–136, 150–154, 162–166.
MUZZEY. An American History, 90–104.
WILSON. History of the American People, IV: 1–50.
American Citizenship Course in United States History, III: 118–157.
Baltimore County Course of Study, 501–503.

Minimal Essentials

Names of Persons: **Samuel Adams; Patrick Henry; George III**
Date: **1765 — the Stamp Act**
Historical Terms: **Yankee; tax; Tory; Continental Congress; "Yankee Doodle"**
Things to Remember
  The mother country thought that the colonies were made for her benefit.
  The colonies did not want England to interfere with their trade. They wanted to govern themselves completely.
  The First Continental Congress asked England not to pass the tax laws.

Illustrative Material

GABRIEL (ED.). Pageant of America, XI: 51–53.
Chronicles of America Photoplays, Yale University Press: The Eve of the Revolution.
Keystone Views: 307, James Otis; 309, Samuel Adams. (Slides only.)
Perry Pictures: 1383-F, Patrick Henry delivering his Great Speech; 1384-C, Boston Massacre.

Procedure during Assimilation

Reading as described on pages 24–29.
Picture study based on the illustrative material listed above.
Use the following phonograph records: "Patrick Henry's Speech," "The Rising of '76."
Use the following dramatizations: "The Boston Tea Party." Hubbard, *Little American History Plays*, pp. 61–65; "The Boston Tea Party." Stevenson,

Dramatized Scenes from American History, pp. 145–175; "When Courage was Needed." Ibid. pp. 177–215; "Patrick Henry." Hand, *Historical Studies in Dramatic Form*; "George Washington." Ibid.; "Boston Tea Party." Ibid.; "Boston Tea Party." *Drama of American Independence*, National Education Association Bulletin, pp. 92–96 (1926).

Sing "Yankee Doodle."

Show the class internal-revenue stamps in use today. How do they compare with the stamps of the Stamp Act?

Some children represent England, and others the colonies. Each side tries to persuade the other that it is right in regard to taxation.

Original poems on the Revolution.

Drill on minimal essentials.

Objective test.

Organization

The teacher puts the following outline on the board. Children tell what points belong under each.

CAUSES OF THE REVOLUTION

1. What England thought that the colonies should do
2. What the colonies thought that England should do
3. The acts passed by England
4. Things the colonies did which England did not like

Recitation

The points are divided, each row preparing as extensive a discussion as possible of its own point.

Each row calls itself a Committee of Correspondence of Massachusetts, of Virginia, and so on, and makes its point the subject of a circular letter.

II. How the Revolution was Fought

1. *In the North the Colonists Won*

Preparation

"Have you ever heard of Paul Revere's ride? of minutemen?

"Which of the colonies had seemed to have the most to say against England's acts? Then the war will probably begin where? By *the north* we mean this section (*showing on the map*) east of the Hudson River."

If possible, children watch the local units of the National Guard drilling.

Discuss the meaning of the terms "ammunition," "siege."

Presentation

The king's generals knew that some of the colonists were secretly drilling, were collecting all the guns and shot and powder that they could buy anywhere, and were hiding them in a secret place. So they decided to send out a number of British soldiers to capture the leaders of the colonists and to destroy the ammunition.

The British troops started out from Boston to go to some small towns close by. The minutemen met them, and two small battles were fought. Then the British soldiers went back to Boston, and were glad indeed to be with their friends once more.

After that both sides settled down to a real war. The colonists could not beat the British in battle, so they lined up their army all around Boston and prepared for a siege. In the meantime Washington had been given command of the American army. The British, who could see that they had few friends in the New England region, decided to leave Boston and go to New York instead. They did so, and the colonists were left in possession of the north. So far the war seemed to have resulted in favor of the colonists, but we must remember that it had only begun.

PRESENTATION TEST

Check the best answer:

  a. The king's generals went out from Boston

    _ _ _ to fight the colonists
    _ _ _ to destroy the guns and powder
    _ _ _ to take towns

  b. The colonists could not beat the British in battle, so they

    _ _ _ gave up fighting
    _ _ _ became friends of the British
    _ _ _ laid siege to Boston

  c. The British left Boston and went to New York

    _ _ _ because they had more friends around New York than in Boston
    _ _ _ because New York was a nicer city
    _ _ _ because winter was coming on

  d. In the north which side came out ahead?

    _ _ _ British
    _ _ _ colonists
    _ _ _ neither

Assimilation

Readings

Upper Group

BLAISDELL. The Story of American History, 158–183.
BLAISDELL and BALL. Hero Stories from American History, 18–35.
BROOKS. Stories of the Old Bay State, 127–135.
CHURCH. Stories from English History, 580–585.
DICKINSON. Children's Book of Patriotic Stories, 64–78, 102–110, 111–116, 256–259.
EGGLESTON. A First Book in American History, 117–121.
EVANS. America First, 91–94, 149–160.
FOOTE and SKINNER. Makers and Defenders of America, 31–37, 51–56.
GORDY. Leaders in Making America, 159–175.
GORDY. Stories of Later American History, 30–55.
GUERBER. Story of the Thirteen Colonies, 233–248.
LEFFERTS. American Leaders, I : 68–73.
MONTGOMERY. Beginners' American History, 115–120.
MOSES. Paul Revere (difficult).
PERRY and PRICE. American History, II : 12–22.
SMITH. Boys and Girls of '77.
TAPPAN. Elementary History of our Country, 141–148.
TERRY. History Stories of Other Lands, VI : 139–140.
WRIGHT. Children's Stories in American History, 351–355.
Compton's Pictured Encyclopedia (Revolution, Putnam, Allen, Lexington, Concord, Bunker Hill).
Revolutionary Stories retold from *St. Nicholas*, 3–14.
World Book (Revolution).

Average Group

BARNES. Elementary History of the United States, 204–205.
BEARD and BAGLEY. A First Book in American History, 121–123.
COE. Makers of the Nation, 37–61.
EGGLESTON. Stories of Great Americans, 49–53.
ELSON and MacMULLAN. Story of our Country, I : 152–164, 169–170.
FORMAN. First Lessons in American History, 137–144.
GORDY. American Leaders and Heroes, 165–175, 193–195.
GORDY. Elementary History of the United States, 144–153.
GORDY. Our Patriots, 77–83.
INGRAHAM. Story of Democracy, 190–209.
MACE. Primary History, 155–157.
McMASTER. Primary History of the United States, 120–126.
MORRIS. Primary History of the United States, 150–154.
MOWRY. First Steps in the History of our Country, 124–134.
PRATT. Foundations of the Republic, 62–83.
SOUTHWORTH. Builders of our Country, II : 19–23, 44–58.
TAPPAN. American Hero Stories, 143–157.

Lower Group

BALDWIN. Fifty Famous People, 37–42.
BALDWIN. Fifty Famous Rides and Riders, 104–107.
BARNES. Primary History of the United States, 93–100.
BLAISDELL and BALL. Child's Book of American History, 120–129.
DAVIS. Stories of the United States, 161–170.

DODGE. Stories of American History, 79–117.
HARTWELL. Story-Hour Readings, IV : 168–173.
HOWE. Readers, Fifth Reader, 270–274.
HUSTED. Stories of '76, 11–15.
PRATT. Stories of Colonial Children, 195–207.
WAYLAND. History Stories for Primary Grades, 175–178.
Flanagan Publishing Company. Story of the Revolution, 5–11.

Teachers

CONKLIN. American Political History, 85–97.
FISKE. American Revolution, I : 100–207.
HART. American History told by Contemporaries, II : 546–574.
HART. Formation of the Union, 70–87.
LODGE. Story of the Revolution, 34–122.
MUZZEY. An American History, 104–113.
MUZZEY. The United States of America, I : 70–71.
VAN TYNE. The American Revolution, 25–87.
WRONG. Washington and his Comrades in Arms, 1–80.
Baltimore County Course of Study, 503–505.
Elementary School Journal, XVII : 635.

Minimal Essentials

Name of Person: **British** (brĭt′ĭsh)
Names of Places: **Lexington; Bunker Hill; Concord**
Date: **1775** — battles of Lexington and Concord
Historical Terms: **the Revolution; the north**
Things to Remember
　　England punished Massachusetts; so the rest of the colonies helped their sister
　　　　colony.
　　The actual fighting began at Lexington.
　　The colonists drove the British out of Boston.
　　In the north the Americans were successful.

Illustrative Material

GABRIEL (ED.). Pageant of America, XI : 55–60.
MCKINLEY. Illustrated Topics for American History : S. 14, Burning of Charlestown.
Ford Educational Library (films) : Boston and Lexington; Landmarks of the American
　　Revolution, Part I.
Keystone Views: 60, Lexington Common; 61, Statue of Captain Parker; 62, North Bridge
　　and Statue of the Minute Man; 63, Bunker Hill Monument; 311, First Battle of the
　　Revolution (slide only) ; 312, Battle of Bunker Hill (slide only) ; 313, Spirit of '76 (slide
　　only) ; 314, Washington taking Command of the Army (slide only).
Little Phostint Journeys: Historic Boston and Vicinity.
Mentor, IX : 36–37 (July, 1921).

Procedure during Assimilation

Reading as described on pages 24–29.
Picture study based on the illustrative material listed above.
Use the following dramatizations : "Paul Revere's Ride." Hubbard, *Little American
　　History Plays*, pp. 66–71 ; "The First in War." Ibid. pp. 72–76 ; "Paul Revere's
　　Ride." *Drama of American Independence*, National Education Association Bul-
　　letin, pp. 40–43 (1926) ; "Paul Revere." Hand, *Historical Stories in Dramatic
　　Form* ; "Battle of Lexington." Ibid. ; "Israel Putnam." Ibid.

Stage the scene of Paul Revere's ride for the toy theater.[1]
Use these phonograph records: "Paul Revere's Ride," "Yankee Doodle."
Show United States postage stamps "Lexington and Concord."
Draw a blackboard illustration of the siege of Boston. Draw the Bunker Hill flag.[2]
Make a sand-table representation of the northern theater of war.[3]
What is the origin of the expression "Go to Halifax"?
Drill on minimal essentials.
Objective test.

Organization

The children make coöperatively an outline of the action in the north, somewhat similar to the following:

THE WAR IN THE NORTH

1. Lexington, Concord, and the retreat to Boston
2. Battle of Bunker Hill
3. Washington made commander in chief
4. Siege of Boston

Recitation

Draw on the board a large-scale map of the northern theater of war. Each child comes to the map and tells all the story of the war in the north.

2. *In the Middle States England held New York*

Preparation

"Have you ever heard of the flag which Betsy Ross made? Have you ever heard of Lafayette?

"In what city did the British army decide to stay when it left Boston?"

Show on a map what territory was included in the middle states.

Presentation

When the British army reached New York it found conditions very different from those around Boston. Many people were Tories, and felt honored to have the British officers as

---

[1] *The Twentieth Yearbook of the National Society for the Study of Education,* Part I, p. 82.

[2] *The National Geographic Magazine,* XXXII: 338.

[3] Perry, A. C., and Price, G. A., *American History,* II: 20; Stephenson, N. W., *An American History,* p. 176; Montgomery, D. W., *Leading Facts of American History,* p. 143.

their friends. The British general decided to stay in New York and send his armies out from there to fight battles.

Washington and the American army did not dare attack New York, for the British had a much larger force; so they stayed in the country round about and had a very hard time indeed. Often there was no money to pay the soldiers, and they even had to walk barefoot in the snow. The colonists were very much discouraged.

There was another large town in the middle states — Philadelphia. Both sides wanted it and fought over it continually. Sometimes it belonged to the British and sometimes to the Americans.

Finally the British king said: "I believe that most of the trouble comes from the northern states. If we could only find some way to separate the northern states from the middle states, the middle states would give up." Some of his friends said: "We ought to be able to do that. Look at this map. If we should send one army down Lake Champlain (*showing at the map*) and then another up the Hudson, we could cut the United States right in two (*illustrating with a ruler*). That ought to end the war."

The king was delighted with the plan. He sent an army to do as his friends had said, and was disappointed indeed when the Americans defeated it in the greatest battle of the war.

All this time the Americans had been asking the king of France to help them, for they knew he hated the British. After the great battle the French king said to his followers: "I believe the Americans have a good chance to win after all. So now I am going to help them." And he did. He sent armies, which Washington needed very badly; he lent money; and, best of all, he sent his fleet, for the Americans had very few ships of their own.

Things now looked much brighter for the Americans, but still the British held New York, down to the very end of the war. On the whole, while the Americans were ahead in the north the British were ahead in the middle states. They had not been strong enough, however, to bring the war to an end.

PRESENTATION TEST

Check the best answer:

a. The British army liked to stay in New York

_ _ _ because they had many friends there
_ _ _ because New York was farther south
_ _ _ because they did not have to fight

b. The American army suffered a great deal

_ _ _ because the weather was cold
_ _ _ because the British fought them
_ _ _ because there was not enough money for supplies

c. The British king's plan was

_ _ _ to fight the Americans at sea
_ _ _ to take Philadelphia
_ _ _ to cut the northern states away from the middle states

d. After the British king's plan failed

_ _ _ the British army gave up
_ _ _ the king of France decided to help us
_ _ _ the Americans did not fight any more

Assimilation

Readings

Upper Group

BAILEY. Boys and Girls of Colonial Days, 110–131, 143–150.
BLAISDELL. The Story of American History, 198–221, 230–241, 270–285.
BLAISDELL and BALL. Hero Stories from American History, 50–61, 77–89.
BROOKS. The True Story of Lafayette.
BURNHAM. Hero Tales from History, 194–208.
BURTON. Lafayette, the Friend of American Liberty, 15–59.
CHURCH. Stories from English History, 585–587.
CROWE. Studies in American History, I : 245–264.
DAVIDSON. Founders and Builders of our Nation, 74–82.
DICKINSON. Children's Book of Patriotic Stories, 55–63, 145–188.
DICKSON. Pioneers and Patriots, 1–63, 99–129.
EGGLESTON. A First Book in American History, 119–121.
EVANS. America First, 161–164, 169–184, 200–212.
FARIS. Where our History was Made, Book II, 259–261.
FOOTE and SKINNER. Makers and Defenders of America, 56–68, 74–87, 98–102.
GORDY. Leaders in Making America, 177–194.
GORDY. Stories of Later American History, 53–71.
GUERBER. Story of the Thirteen Colonies, 253–286, 304–312.
LANIER. The Book of Bravery, 254–259.
LEFFERTS. American Leaders, I : 74–83, 123–135, 145–175.
LOGIE. From Columbus to Lincoln, 147–165.
MASON. Tom Strong, Washington's Scout.
MONTGOMERY. Beginners' American History, 121–122.
NICHOLAY. The Boys' Life of Lafayette (difficult).
PERRY and PRICE. American History, II : 26–43, 45–50.
TAPPAN. Elementary History of our Country, 151–162.
TERRY. History Stories of Other Lands, VI : 141–142.

TURPIN. Stories from American History, 109–116.
WOODBURN and MORAN. Makers of America, 108–111 (Hale).
Compton's Pictured Encyclopedia (Revolution, Hale, Flag, Lafayette, Arnold).
Revolutionary Stories retold from *St. Nicholas*, 32–80, 87–107, 166–179.
World Book (Revolution).

Average Group

BEARD and BAGLEY. A First Book in American History, 124–127, 136–142.
COE. Makers of the Nation, 71–77, 88–94, 120–130.
EGGLESTON. Stories of American Life and Adventure, 54–59.
EGGLESTON. Stories of Great Americans, 39–43, 61–66.
ELSON and MacMULLAN. Story of our Country, I : 170–196.
FORMAN. First Lessons in American History, 145–153.
GORDY. American Leaders and Heroes, 175–189, 195–206.
GORDY. Elementary History of the United States, 155–168.
GORDY. Our Patriots, 91–113.
MACE. Primary History, 176–180, 187–198, 225–228, 230–239.
McMASTER. Primary History of the United States, 127–134.
MORRIS. Primary History of the United States, 157–161, 165–170.
MOWRY. First Steps in the History of our Country, 134–139.
PRATT. Foundations of the Republic, 95–142.
SOUTHWORTH. Builders of our Country, II : 51–60, 63–74, 93–96.
TAPPAN. American Hero Stories, 158–178.
TURPIN. Brief Biographies from American History, 169–176.

Lower Group

BALDWIN. Fifty Famous People, 43–47.
BALDWIN. Fifty Famous Rides and Riders, 111–119.
BARNES. Primary History of the United States, 101–110.
BLAISDELL and BALL. American History for Little Folks, 86–92, 98–102.
BLAISDELL and BALL. American History Story Book, 37–58.
BLAISDELL and BALL. Short Stories from American History, 58–63, 72–79, 80–85, 122–129.
DAVIDSON and ANDERSON. Lincoln Readers, III : 243–249 (first flag).
DODGE. Stories of American History, 125–147 (read by sections).
SMITH. Easy Road to Reading, IV : 286–290.
WAYLAND. History Stories for Primary Grades, 28–30 (flag), 184–187.
YOUNG and FIELD. Literary Readers, IV : 283–293 (a play).
Flanagan Publishing Company. Story of the Revolution, 11–19.

Teachers

CALLENDER. Economic History of the United States, 142–167.
CONKLIN. American Political History, 97–106.
FISKE. The American Revolution, I : 199–403.
HART. American History told by Contemporaries, II : 574–578.
HART. Formation of the Union, 87–92.
LODGE. Story of the Revolution, 123–215.
MUZZEY. An American History, 116–120.
MUZZEY. The United States of America, I : 84–93.
VAN TYNE. The American Revolution, 88–124, 203–247.
WRONG. Washington and his Comrades in Arms, 81–210.
Baltimore County Course of Study, 506–507, 513–514.
Public School Methods, V : 257–262. (The Methods Co., Chicago.)

Minimal Essentials

Names of Persons: **Lafayette** (lä′ fȧ yĕt′); **General Burgoyne** (bûr goin′); **Robert Morris; Nathan Hale**

Names of Places: **Saratoga; West Point; Valley Forge**

Date: **1777** — battle of Saratoga

Historical Terms: **retreat; traitor; surrender**

Things to Remember

    The British held New York throughout the war.

    Burgoyne could not cut the colonies in two.

    Washington's army suffered a great deal.

    It was very hard to find money enough to buy supplies for the army.

    France helped the colonies when she knew that the British had failed at Saratoga.

Illustrative Material

Educational Posters of the National Child Welfare Association: Freedom of a Nation: George Washington.

Ford Educational Library (films): Historic Philadephia and Valley Forge.

Keystone Views: 73, Continental Paper Money; 79, West Point from across the Hudson; 306, Nathan Hale (slide only); 315, Washington crossing the Delaware (slide only); 316, Lafayette (slide only).

Mentor, IX: 2–5, 6–8 (September, 1921); XII: 1–17, 29–40 (September, 1924); XIII: 45–48 (October, 1925).

Perry Pictures: 1386, Battle of Princeton; 1387, Surrender of Burgoyne; 1414, Washington crossing the Delaware; 1415, Washington at Trenton; 1416-F, Washington at Valley Forge.

Procedure during Assimilation

Reading as described on pages 24–29.

Picture study based on the illustrative material listed above.

Use the following dramatizations: "Our First Flag." Hubbard, *Little American History Plays,* pp. 81–88; "The Great General's Lesson to the Little Corporal." Ibid. pp. 89–91; "Lafayette, the Friend of America." Ibid. pp. 92–98; "Robert Morris and the Revolution." Tucker and Ryan, *Historical Plays of Colonial Days,* pp. 122–125; "Mrs. Murray's Dinner Party." Walker, *Little Plays from American History for Young Folks,* pp. 57–120; "Revolutionary Days." Shoemaker, *Colonial Plays for the Schoolroom,* pp. 59–64; "Nathan Hale." Stevenson, *Children's Classics in Dramatic Form,* V: 1–23; "Washington, the Commander at Valley Forge." Hand, *Historical Stories in Dramatic Form;* "Nathan Hale." Ibid.; "Robert Morris." *The Historical Outlook,* XVII: 131–132.

Draw a picture of the first flag; compare with our present flag.

Girls in the sewing class make a flag like Betsy Ross's.

A trip to the local museum to see objects connected with the Revolution: arms, currency, uniforms.

Make a sand-table representation of the middle theater of war showing New York, Trenton, West Point, Philadelphia, Valley Forge, Saratoga. Show by red-paper arrows Burgoyne's plan.

Give the speech which Benjamin Franklin might have made to the king of France when persuading him to help the United States.

In what other war have France and the United States fought side by side?

What does the expression "not worth a Continental" mean?

Drill on minimal essentials.

Objective test.

Organization

The teacher and the class working together make an outline somewhat similar to the following:

The War in the Middle States

1. England held New York.
2. Washington kept the British busy around Philadelphia.
3. Burgoyne was beaten at Saratoga.
4. Then France decided to help the United States.

Recitation

Continue the procedure indicated on page 277.

3. *In the Back-Country the Americans won Much Land*

Preparation

"Why did the colonists stay along the seacoast at first?

"When they began to go over the mountains what routes did they follow?

"What other nation also had wanted the same land? What were the names of some of their forts?

"What Indian chief had tried to keep it for his people?"

Presentation

After the French and Indian War was over, all this land (*showing at the map*) belonged to the British. There were not enough British people to settle such a vast territory; so they decided that the best thing to do was to station British soldiers in all the forts. These soldiers could keep the French from coming back.

When the Revolution began, of course the British soldiers took the side of England. Then Virginia, who claimed much of the land beyond the mountains, thought she saw a great opportunity. She explained: "There are really very few British soldiers in those forts, and the British army along the coast (*illustrating at the map*) has its hands full. The generals could not afford to send troops into the interior. So now if we can get together a small army of our own and send it secretly over the mountains, nobody will know it is coming, and it can take all the forts by surprise. Then they will be American instead of British."

The Virginians carried out their plan. An army was brought together, and started on its long march. We shall read today about what a hard time the soldiers had, sometimes wading in icy water up to their waists and holding their guns over their heads. Their plan succeeded. They took the forts without having to fight very hard.

Then the United States could and did claim all this land west of the mountains and north of the Ohio River (*showing at the map*) and raised the American flag over the forts. Best of all, they had not had to fight many battles to win it.

PRESENTATION TEST

Check the best answer:

a. The British generals put soldiers in the forts

     _ _ _ because there were not enough British people to settle the country

     _ _ _ because they wanted to fight the Indians

     _ _ _ because they did not trust the Americans

b. When the Revolution began, these soldiers sided with

     _ _ _ the colonies

     _ _ _ England

c. Virginia thought she could capture the forts

     _ _ _ because she owned the land

     _ _ _ because the British generals could not send help to the forts

     _ _ _ because she had braver soldiers than England had

d. When the army had taken the forts, they claimed all the land in that part

     _ _ _ for Spain

     _ _ _ for England

     _ _ _ for the United States

Assimilation

Readings

Upper Group

BALDWIN. Conquest of the Old Northwest, 145–178 (difficult).

BLAISDELL and BALL. Hero Stories from American History, 1–17.

BURNHAM. Hero Tales from History, 240–247.

CHANDLER and CHITWOOD. Makers of American History, 158–164.

CROWE. Studies in American History, I : 277–297.

DAVIDSON. Founders and Builders of our Nation 101–108.

DICKSON. Pioneers and Patriots, 91–98.

EVANS. America First, 165–169, 216–221.

GORDY. Leaders in Making America, 226–236.

GORDY. Stories of Later American History, 132–150.
GUERBER. Story of the Thirteen Colonies, 287–288, 290–293.
LEFFERTS. American Leaders, I : 135–144.
McMURRY. Pioneers of the Mississippi Valley, 124–149.
MONTGOMERY. Beginners' American History, 143–150.
MOWRY. American Pioneers, 127–137.
OTIS. Hannah of Kentucky, 76–184.
PERRY and BEEBE. Four American Pioneers, 73–128.
PERRY and PRICE. American History, II : 50–51.
ROOSEVELT. Stories of the Great West, 55–65.
WOODBURN and MORAN. Makers of America, 150–168.
Compton's Pictured Encyclopedia (Clark).
Revolutionary Stories retold from *St. Nicholas*, 141–143.

Average Group

BARNES. Elementary History of the United States, 221–228.
COE. Makers of the Nation, 158–178.
EGGLESTON. Stories of American Life and Adventure, 128–132.
EGGLESTON. Stories of Great Americans, 72–76.
FORMAN. First Lessons in American History, 153–155.
GORDY. Elementary History of the United States, 169–173.
GORDY. Our Patriots, 120–126.
MACE. Primary History, 258–266.
McMASTER. Primary History of the United States, 134–138.
MORRIS. Primary History of the United States, 176–182.
MOWRY. First Steps in the History of our Country, 159–166.
NIDA. Following the Frontier, 78–84.
PRATT. Foundations of the Republic, 143–150.
TAPPAN. American Hero Stories, 185–192.

Lower Group

BLAISDELL and BALL. Short Stories from American History, 64–71, 99–103.
PRATT. Stories of Colonial Children, 189–194.

Teachers

DUNBAR. History of Travel in America, I : 151–170.
LODGE. Story of the Revolution, 216–236.
MUZZEY. An American History, 123–127.
OGG. The Old Northwest, 41–75.
VAN TYNE. The American Revolution, 269–288.
Baltimore County Course of Study, 512.

Minimal Essentials

Name of Person: **George Rogers Clark**
Name of Place: **the Northwest**
Historical Term: **expedition**
Things to Remember
    George Rogers Clark took some British forts in the back-country north of the
        Ohio River.
    Later the United States claimed all this land as hers.

Illustrative Material

Chronicles of America Photoplays, Yale University Press : Vincennes.

Procedure during Assimilation

Reading as described on pages 24–29.

Picture study based on the illustrative material listed above.

Use the following dramatizations: "One Way to capture a Fort." Hubbard, *Little American History Plays*, pp. 111–114; "Only a Girl." Ibid. pp. 115–119; "A Lucky Halloween." Ibid. pp. 120–124.

Show on the sand table the route of George Rogers Clark and the forts taken by him.[1]

Children draw their own ideas of the difficulties of Clark's expedition.[2]

Drill on minimal essentials.

Objective test.

Organization

Each child makes his own outline of the story.

Recitation

Each child recites to the class the story based on his own outline.

4. *Not Many Battles were fought at Sea*

Preparation

"What is a warship? a merchant ship?

"When did France decide to help us? Why?

"What event had made it possible for England to become the greatest power in the world at sea?"

Presentation

We know that England was the greatest power in the world at sea, and that her navy was feared by all other countries. Naturally, then, most of the fighting in the Revolution would have to be done on land, since the Americans would be no match for the British at sea.

In fact, when the war began the colonies had no navy at all. They had no warships, but had mounted some guns on merchant vessels and used these. After a while Congress did build a few war vessels, but they did not have very many even then.

---

[1] Mowry, W. and B., *American Pioneers*, p. 129; Stephenson, N. W., *An American History*, p. 201.

[2] Lemos, Pedro, *School Posters* (Davis Press, Worcester, Massachusetts).

Since the advantage at sea was on England's side, it is all the more interesting to hear of the brave deeds of the first great American sailor. We shall read today about the great and thrilling adventures of John Paul Jones.

Being so poor in ships, you may be very sure that the United States appreciated all the more the help that France gave. For she sent not only an army and supplies, but her navy as well.

PRESENTATION TEST
Check the best answer:

a. One reason why the United States did not try to fight much at sea was
_ _ _ because we were afraid
_ _ _ because England was the greatest sea power in the world
_ _ _ because we let France do it

b. When the war began the only ships the colonies had were
_ _ _ merchant ships
_ _ _ warships
_ _ _ rowboats

c. They owed their victory over the British partly to the fact
_ _ _ that their sailors were braver
_ _ _ that Americans knew how to fight at sea better than the British
_ _ _ that France sent some ships to America

Assimilation
Readings
Upper Group

BEEBE. Four American Naval Heroes, 17–68.
BLAISDELL. The Story of American History, 286–295.
BURNHAM. Hero Tales from History, 208–216.
DAVIDSON. Founders and Builders of our Nation, 83–90.
DICKINSON. Children's Book of Patriotic Stories, 295–305.
DICKSON. Pioneers and Patriots, 140–157.
FOOTE and SKINNER. Makers and Defenders of America, 103–110.
GORDY. Leaders in Making America, 207–212.
GORDY. Stories of Later American History, 87–93.
GUERBER. Story of the Thirteen Colonies, 293–297.
HUMPHREY. Heroes of Liberty, 1–14.
LANIER. The Book of Bravery, 315–335.
MORRIS. Heroes of the Navy in America, 22–64.
TAPPAN. Elementary History of our Country, 163–164.
WOODBURN and MORAN. Makers of America, 113–117 (Jones).
Compton's Pictured Encyclopedia (Jones).

Average Group

BEARD and BAGLEY. A First Book in American History, 128–131.
BLAISDELL and BALL. Heroic Deeds of American Sailors, 1–14.
COE. Makers of the Nation, 110–119.
ELSON and MacMULLAN. Story of our Country, I : 196–198.

FORMAN. First Lessons in American History, 155–156.
GORDY. Elementary History of the United States, 173–175.
GORDY. Our Patriots, 115–119.
MACE. Primary History, 211–219.
SOUTHWORTH. Builders of our Country, II : 84–92.
TAPPAN. American Hero Stories, 193–200.
TURPIN. Brief Biographies from American History, 181–186.

Lower Group

DODGE. Stories of American History, 148–153.
GROVE. American Naval Heroes, 3–12.
PRATT. Stories of Colonial Children, 195–207.
WILSON. A History Reader, 308–309.

Teachers

HAPGOOD. Paul Jones.
HART. American History told by Contemporaries, II : 612–615.
Baltimore County Course of Study, 509–512.

Minimal Essentials

Name of Person: **John Paul Jones**
Name of Place: **Annapolis** (ă năp′ô̆ lĭs)
Historical Term: **high seas**
Things to Remember
  The American navy was very small.
  Much of the fighting at sea was done for the Americans by the French.
  John Paul Jones was a great American hero.

Illustrative Material

PYLE. Book of the American Spirit, 241, 243.
Keystone Views: 320, John Paul Jones (slide only).
Mentor, XII : 18–28, 41–52 (September, 1924) : Naval Academy at Annapolis.

Procedure during Assimilation

Reading as described on pages 24–29.
Picture study based on the illustrative material listed above.
Use the dramatization "John Paul Jones." Hand, *Historical Stories in Dramatic Form.*
Draw a picture of the first navy jack [1] with the legend "Don't tread on me"; of Washington's cruisers.[2]
In manual-training class the boys may make a replica of one of John Paul Jones's ships.
Some person who has been in Annapolis describes John Paul Jones's grave.
Play a game of "assumed characters." [3]
Drill on minimal essentials.
Objective test.

[1] *The National Geographic Magazine*, XXXII : 338.
[2] Ibid. 339.
[3] Johnson, George E., *Education by Plays and Games*, p. 200.

Organization

The teacher puts the following outline on the board. The
children tell what belongs under each point.

WAR ON THE SEA

1. Size of the American navy
2. Work of John Paul Jones
3. What the French fleet did for the United States

Recitation

Children are allowed to choose partners and to tell their
stories to their partners.

5. *In the South the Americans captured the British Army, and the War was Won*

Preparation

"Which side had the best of it in the north? in the middle
states?

"Which states do we call *the south*?" (*Show on the map.*)

"What do nations do when they agree to stop fighting after
a war is over?"

Presentation

Since the Americans had won in the northern states, and
England seemed to have the best of it in the middle states, a
great deal depended on what happened in the south. The
British decided to begin away down here in Georgia (*showing
at the map*) and plow right through from there up to New York,
conquering each state in turn. And at first they succeeded.

Things looked bad for the Americans. Their army was
beaten in the south, and it seemed as if nobody could stop
the British from coming on toward New York.

However, the brave southern fighters were not discouraged.
They couldn't fight the whole British army; but wherever
they found a few men together, they attacked. They captured
the wagons that were bringing up supplies, they attacked at
night, and by the time the British could come out to find and
fight them they would be far away.

After a while the British became tired of this kind of fighting and went to the seacoast. That gave Washington the great chance for which he had been waiting so long. He placed his men completely around the British, so that no way of escape was open. There was only one thing left them to do — that was to surrender. The British general did surrender to Washington, and the long war was over. The Americans had won.

People were so overjoyed to hear the war was ended that they could scarcely believe the good news. It seemed too good to be true. They had been fighting for six years.

When the two sides finally came together to sign the treaty of peace, England admitted that the United States had won the right to be considered a country by itself. Both nations turned their attention once more to ways of peace, and the Revolution was over.

PRESENTATION TEST

Check the best answer:

a. The British plan in the south was

   _ _ _ to fight from the sea
   _ _ _ to begin at Georgia and conquer each state in turn
   _ _ _ to fight great battles around New York

b. The American plan of fighting was

   _ _ _ to capture a few men at a time and then hide
   _ _ _ to fight great battles around New York
   _ _ _ to wait for the French

c. The British general had to surrender

   _ _ _ because his troops were tired
   _ _ _ because the Americans had more men than he had
   _ _ _ because the Americans had surrounded his army

d. In the treaty of peace England

   _ _ _ wanted to keep America as a colony
   _ _ _ admitted that the United States was a separate country
   _ _ _ said nothing about the United States

Assimilation

Readings

Upper Group

BLAISDELL. The Story of American History, 242–245, 250–270.
BLAISDELL and BALL. Hero Stories from American History, 36–49, 90–104, 123–137.
BURNHAM. Hero Tales from History, 217–223.
CHURCH. Stories from English History, 587.

CROWE. Studies in American History, I : 265–273.
DICKINSON. Children's Book of Patriotic Stories, 260–269, 279–294.
DICKSON. Pioneers and Patriots, 64–78, 130–139.
EGGLESTON. A First Book in American History, 122–124.
EVANS. America First, 184–200.
FOOTE and SKINNER. Makers and Defenders of America, 68–71, 89–97.
GORDY. Leaders in Making America, 195–206.
GORDY. Stories of Later American History, 73–86.
GUERBER. Story of the Thirteen Colonies, 297–301, 312–326.
LEFFERTS. American Leaders, I : 83–85.
LOGIE. From Columbus to Lincoln, 165–167.
MONTGOMERY. Beginners' American History, 122–129.
PERRY and PRICE. American History, II : 23, 52–59.
TAPPAN. Elementary History of our Country, 164–168.
TERRY. History Stories of Other Lands, VI : 143–144.
WOODBURN and MORAN. Makers of America, 88–96 (Greene), 96–101 (Morgan), 101–106 (Marion), 107–108 (Sumter).
Compton's Pictured Encyclopedia (Revolution, Marion).
Revolutionary Stories retold from *St. Nicholas*, 131–140, 180–183, 190–194.
World Book (Revolution).

Average Group

BEARD and BAGLEY. A First Book in American History, 127–128, 145.
COE. Makers of the Nation, 78–87, 95–109.
EGGLESTON. Stories of American Life and Adventure, 104–110.
EGGLESTON. Stories of Great Americans, 67–72.
ELSON and MACMULLAN. Story of our Country, I : 199–203, 205–209.
FORMAN. First Lessons in American History, 156–159.
GORDY. American Leaders and Heroes, 206–209, 211–221 (Greene).
GORDY. Elementary History of the United States, 176–185.
GORDY. Our Patriots, 127–131.
INGRAHAM. Story of Democracy, 209–214.
MACE. Primary History, 181–183, 200–210.
McMASTER. Primary History of the United States, 138–142.
MORRIS. Primary History of the United States, 162–164.
MOWRY. First Steps in the History of our Country, 142–147.
PRATT. Foundations of the Republic, 151–172.
SOUTHWORTH. Builders of our Country, II : 60–62, 75–83.
TAPPAN. American Hero Stories, 179–184.
TURPIN. Brief Biographies from American History, 176–181.

Lower Group

BALDWIN. Fifty Famous Rides and Riders, 120–129.
BARNES. Primary History of the United States, 110–116.
BLAISDELL and BALL. American History for Little Folks, 80–85, 103–108.
BLAISDELL and BALL. American History Story Book, 59–72, 86–91.
BLAISDELL and BALL. Short Stories from American History, 45–50, 86–91.
DODGE. Stories of American History, 154–170 (read by sections).
ELSON. Primary School Reader, III : 151–156.
HARTWELL. Story-Hour Readings, IV : 174–176.
McMANUS. Natural Method Reader, III : 257–266.
SMITH. Easy Road to Reading, IV : 179–187.
WAYLAND. History Stories for Primary Grades, 26–27, 179–181, 188–191.
Flanagan Publishing Company. Story of the Revolution, 19–22.

Teachers

HART. American History told by Contemporaries, II : 606–612.
LODGE. Story of the Revolution, 237–414.
MUZZEY. An American History, 120–123, 127–132.
MUZZEY. The United States of America, I : 94–103.
VAN TYNE. The American Revolution, 289–333.
WRONG. Washington and his Comrades in Arms, 211–276.
Baltimore County Course of Study, 507–509, 514–517.

Minimal Essentials

Names of Persons: **Cornwallis; Nathanael Greene**
Names of Places: **Paris; Yorktown**
Date : **1783** — Treaty of Paris (end of the Revolutionary War)
Historical Term: **"swamp fox"**
Things to Remember
Most of the fighting in the south was done by small American forces.
The British general was shut up in Yorktown.
The French fleet would not let any more British troops come in to help him.
Cornwallis surrendered, and the war was over.

Illustrative Material

Chronicles of America Photoplays, Yale University Press : Yorktown.
Ford Educational Library (films) : Landmarks of the American Revolution, Part II.
Perry Pictures : 1388, Surrender of Cornwallis.
Society for Visual Education. Picturols : Campaigns of the Revolution ; George Washington ;
    War of the Revolution.
Society for Visual Education. Schoolfilm : War of the American Revolution.

Procedure during Assimilation

Reading as described on pages 24–29.
Picture study based on the illustrative material listed above.
Dramatize the surrender of Cornwallis.
Why did the band play "The World's Upside Down"?
See in the Standard Dictionary (under Revolution) the uniforms used during the
    Revolution.
Show on the sand table Yorktown, Cornwallis's army, the French fleet, Lafayette's
    army, Washington's army.
The children arrange a series of tableaux representing different scenes from the period.
Drill on minimal essentials.
Objective test.

Organization

The teacher and the class working together make an outline somewhat similar to the following :

THE WAR IN THE SOUTH

1. For a long time the British held the south.
2. The Americans fought by "swamp fox" methods.
3. Cornwallis was shut up in Yorktown.
4. The end of the war came when Cornwallis surrendered.
5. The treaty of peace was signed in 1783.

Recitation

Continue the procedure used for the previous story.

At this point a drill lesson should be given on sections I and II of Unit V.

III. MAKING A NEW NATION

1. *The Declaration of Independence made the Colonies the United States*

Preparation

"You may have noticed that as we went through our story of the war, part of the time we called Massachusetts, Virginia, New York, and the rest *colonies*, and part of the time we called them *states*. Do you know just when they ceased being colonies and became states instead?

"What is the meaning of the word *independent*?"

Presentation

You remember when the war began that very few people wished to separate from England : almost everybody in the colonies wished to remain British. What they wanted was to have just the same rights as had their British brothers who had remained in England. These rights they believed had been taken away from them, whereas England claimed that the colonists had just as many rights as anyone in the mother country.

The first plan the Americans tried was to send long letters to the king explaining their ideas about their rights, but the king paid no attention. What should they do next? They went to war, because they thought surely the king would then know that they were in earnest and would pay attention to what they said. But still they were disappointed.

When people start fighting, even if they are not very angry at first, after a while they become angry. So, after the Revolution had been going on for more than a year and many men on both sides had been killed, the colonists' feelings were quite changed. They began to hate Great Britain in deadly earnest.

Some of the colonists began saying: "We have been fighting over a year now, and are no nearer to getting our rights than we were in the beginning. We do not believe the king will ever give in." They were so much troubled that they had a meeting, or *congress*, in order to talk things over.

After talking a long time they decided that there was no longer any use in asking the king for their rights. He would not listen. In order to be able to govern themselves, they would have to separate from England and would have to make a new nation of their own. Many people gave their consent very unwillingly; they had been born in England, their relations lived there, and all their ancestors were buried there. But no other satisfactory method presented itself.

One of the leaders of the Americans said, "If we have to separate from England, I believe we ought to write down on paper all the reasons why." The suggestion pleased them; so one of them sat down to write. "The king has kept soldiers here when we didn't want them," began a bystander. Another added, "He has made us pay taxes which we did not vote for." A third, "He has taken away the charters of many of our colonies." And so they went on, until they had a long list of things they did not like. Then another said: "At the end I think we ought to add a sentence saying that we are going to separate from England and make a new nation called the United States. Then everybody will know exactly what we intend to do." The sentence was added.

After the paper had been copied over and over, until it suited the representatives, fifty-six of them signed their names to it. We call this paper the *Declaration of Independence* (*pointing to the words written on the board*). The United States of America began when that paper was signed.

PRESENTATION TEST

Check the best answer:

a. When the Revolution began, the colonies were fighting

_ _ _ to make a new nation

_ _ _ to obtain the same rights that other Englishmen had

_ _ _ to get even with the king

b. The first thing they tried was

   _ _ _ to send letters to the king

   _ _ _ to make war

   _ _ _ to make a new nation

c. After the war had gone on for a year the colonists decided

   _ _ _ that they could beat the king's army

   _ _ _ that they would fight no more

   _ _ _ that the king would never listen to them

d. The only thing left to do was

   _ _ _ to separate from England

   _ _ _ to give up

   _ _ _ to go on fighting for their rights

e. They wrote down

   _ _ _ the reasons why they thought they would win

   _ _ _ the reasons why they were separating from England

   _ _ _ the reasons why the king did not like them

f. This paper was called

   _ _ _ the charter of Massachusetts

   _ _ _ the Declaration of Independence

   _ _ _ the Albany plan

g. The United States began

   _ _ _ when the king would not listen to the colonists

   _ _ _ when the Revolution began

   _ _ _ when the Declaration of Independence was signed

Assimilation

Readings

Upper Group

BLAISDELL. The Story of American History, 184–197.

DICKINSON. Children's Book of Patriotic Stories, 241–255.

GORDY. Leaders in Making America, 175–177.

GORDY. Stories of Later American History, 51–52.

GUERBER. Story of the Thirteen Colonies, 248–253.

HARTWELL. Story-Hour Readings, V: 381–384.

MONTGOMERY. Beginners' American History, 120–121.

MOWRY. American Pioneers, 217–229 (Thomas Jefferson).

PERRY and PRICE. American History, II: 24–26.

SMITH. Easy Road to Reading, V: 316–317.

TAPPAN. Elementary History of our Country, 148–150.

WRIGHT. Children's Stories in American History, 353–354.

Compton's Pictured Encyclopedia (Declaration of Independence).

World Book (Declaration of Independence).

Average Group

BALDWIN. Fifty Famous Rides and Riders, 108–110.

BALDWIN. Fourth Reader, 67–73.

BARNES. Elementary History of the United States, 231–233.

BEARD and BAGLEY. A First Book in American History, 131–136.

COE. Makers of the Nation, 62–69.

ELSON and MACMULLAN. Story of our Country, I : 165–169.
FORMAN. First Lessons in American History, 143–144.
GORDY. Elementary History of the United States, 153–154.
GORDY. Our Patriots, 84–90.
MACE. Primary History, 158.
McMASTER. Primary History of the United States, 126–127.
MORRIS. Primary History of the United States, 155–156.
MOWRY. First Steps in the History of our Country, 121–123.
PRATT. Foundations of the Republic, 84–94.

Lower Group

BARNES. Primary History of the United States, 100.
BLAISDELL and BALL. American History Story Book, 28–36.
CURTIS. Why we celebrate our Holidays, 93–99.
DODGE. Stories of American History, 118–124.
HUSTED. Stories of '76, 28–32.
WAYLAND. History Stories for Primary Grades, 24–25, 182–183.

Teachers

HART. American History told by Contemporaries, II : 519–539.
MUZZEY. An American History, 113–116.
MUZZEY. The United States of America, I : 71–83.

Minimal Essentials

Name of Person: **John Hancock**
Name of Place: **Independence Hall**
Date: **July 4, 1776** — Declaration of Independence
Historical Terms: **Declaration of Independence; Fourth of July; state; independent**
Things to Remember
At first the colonies were fighting for their rights as Englishmen.
Later they decided to make a nation of their own.
The history of the *United States* begins with the Declaration of Independence.

Illustrative Material

McKINLEY. Illustrated Topics for American History : S. 15, The Declaration of Independence.
Chronicles of America Photoplays, Yale University Press : The Declaration of Independence.
The Drama of American Independence, Bulletin of the National Education Association (1926).
Keystone Views : 68, Independence Hall ; 69, Interior of Independence Hall ; 70, Liberty Bell ; 72, Signing of the Declaration of Independence ; 308, John Hancock (slide only).

Procedure during Assimilation

Reading as described on pages 24–29.
Picture study based on the illustrative material listed above.
Use the following dramatizations : "Independence Day." Hubbard, *Little American History Plays*, pp. 77–80; "The Fourth of July." Johnston and Barnum, *Book of Plays for Little Actors*, pp. 165–171; "A Brave Deed by Brave Men." Stevenson, *Dramatized Scenes from American History*, pp. 217–262; "Independence Day." *Drama of American Independence*, National Education Association Bulletin, pp. 44–46 (1926).
Is shooting firecrackers the best way to celebrate the Fourth of July?

The class plans for the Fourth of July a program which each member can carry
out in his own home.

The children run through the list of grievances given in the Declaration and explain those they know. Read to them the one sentence which actually de-
clares the colonies independent.[1]

What does the expression "I'll put my John Hancock on that" mean?

Drill on minimal essentials.

Objective test.

Organization

The teacher puts the following outline on the board. Children tell what belongs under each point.

THE DECLARATION OF INDEPENDENCE

1. What the colonies were fighting for at first
2. Why they decided to be independent
3. The Declaration of Independence

Recitation

Invite the eighth-grade teacher of history to hear the stories.

2. *The First Governments were Poor and Weak*

Preparation

"How many colonies were there?

"What was Franklin's plan of union? Why had it failed?"

Presentation

After the Declaration of Independence was signed, there
were thirteen states, each one independent. But there was no
plan for their working together. New York did as it pleased,
Georgia did as it pleased, and New Hampshire did something
different from either.

Have you ever seen nine boys playing ball without an
umpire? If so, you can imagine what confusion resulted in
the states because of lack of union. If South Carolina wanted
to do one thing, Maryland would be sure to want to do another. Who could decide whether the United States should
go to war? Certainly if Massachusetts should want to, Rhode
Island would not.

[1] MacDonald, W., *Documentary Source Book of American History*, pp. 190–194.

It was very plain that there must be one government instead of thirteen. Again the representatives came together and made a plan for one government over all the thirteen states. But how afraid the states were that they were going to lose some of their own power! They said, "Let us not give this one government over us very much power." North Carolina said, "We will not let the United States government force us to pay taxes." Delaware said, "We will not let the United States government have anything to say about our commerce." Connecticut said, "We will not let the United States government make any of our people fight in its army unless they wish to." And all together they said: "Let us not have any president. He would have too much power. He would be almost as bad as a king."

Poor United States government! About the only thing the states would allow it to do was to sign the treaty of peace with Great Britain. It was weak as well as new. The name of the paper which described this weak United States government was the *Articles of Confederation* (*pointing to the words written on the board*). It was perhaps a good beginning to make, but we know without being told that such a government could not last. And it did not last very long.

PRESENTATION TEST

1. *Check the best answer:*

   a. When the Declaration of Independence was signed, the government was

       _ _ _ thirteen separate states

       _ _ _ one strong government

       _ _ _ no government at all

   b. The states got together and made

       _ _ _ thirteen independent states

       _ _ _ one government for all the United States

       _ _ _ no government at all

2. *Check three answers:*

   The government of the Articles of Confederation *could not*

       _ _ _ collect taxes

       _ _ _ make new roads

       _ _ _ make people join the army

       _ _ _ sign treaties

       _ _ _ make speeches

       _ _ _ govern the commerce between the states

3. *Check the best answer:*

One thing the government of the Articles of Confederation did was

_ _ _ to sign the treaty of peace with Great Britain

_ _ _ to fight France

_ _ _ to buy land from Spain

Assimilation

Readings

Upper Group

BLAISDELL and BALL. Hero Stories from American History, 138–145.
FOOTE and SKINNER. Makers and Defenders of America, 111–116.
GORDY. Leaders in Making America, 237–238.
PERRY and PRICE. American History, II : 63–66.
TAPPAN. Elementary History of our Country, 168–170.

Average Group

BARNES. Elementary History of the United States, 206–207.
BEARD and BAGLEY. A First Book in American History, 149–150.
COE. Makers of the Nation, 179.
ELSON and MacMULLAN. Story of our Country, II : 1.
FORMAN. First Lessons in American History, 161–164.
GORDY. Elementary History of the United States, 186–189.
McMASTER. Primary History of the United States, 147–148.

Lower Group

BARNES. Primary History of the United States, 117–120.

Teachers

CALLENDER. Economic History of the United States, 180–235.
CONKLIN. American Political History, 107–130.
DUNBAR. History of Travel in America, I : 171–192.
ELSON. Side Lights on American History, 25–33.
FARRAND. Fathers of the Constitution, 35–107.
HART. Formation of the Union, 93–119.
McLAUGHLIN. The Confederation and the Constitution, 35–183.
McMASTER. History of the People of the United States, I : 103–389.
MUZZEY. An American History, 135–141.
MUZZEY. The United States of America, I : 104–133.
VAN TYNE. The American Revolution, 175–202.
American Citizenship Course in United States History, III : 158–170.

Minimal Essentials

Historical Terms: **government** [1] ; **Second Continental Congress; Articles of Confederation**

Things to Remember

The first two times that the states tried to make a government they did not have much success.

They were afraid to let the United States government have power over them.

Illustrative Material

McKINLEY. Illustrated Topics for American History : S. 16.

[1] See the lesson plan on page 697.

Procedure during Assimilation

Reading as described on pages 24–29.

Picture study based on the illustrative material listed above.

Children and teacher working together make a list of things a government must be able to do if it is to be a real government, such as

> make war
> make peace
> coin money
> collect taxes
> send representatives to other countries

The children look through their readings to find out whether the Articles of Confederation allowed the United States government to do these things.

Drill on minimal essentials.

Objective test.

Organization

The teacher puts the following outline on the board:

THE FIRST WEAK GOVERNMENTS OF THE UNITED STATES

1. What a government must do to be strong
2. Our early governments

Recitation

Children tell what points belong under each of the topics above.

3. *A Strong Government was made after Several Years*

Preparation

"Name the things which the states, under the Articles of Confederation, would not let the United States do. Why would such a weak government be sure to fail?"

Presentation

After six years of experience under the Articles of Confederation the states could see that they had made a mistake. They had been selfish and had not been willing to give up enough power to the United States. During these six years things had gone badly. The states were unfriendly to each other, and foreign countries laughed at the United States and said: "They do not know how to make a government. They will never last. Some other nation will come along and gobble them up."

Those years were the hardest years that the United States has ever had — worse even than any war.   At last the states saw that they would have to do better.   They would have to make a new plan ; and the things that before they had not let the United States government do, they would have to allow.

Again the representatives met.   For months they worked and worked.   Many times they became discouraged, for it seemed that the selfishness of some states had no limit.   But at last they succeeded.   They had written down on paper a wonderful new plan of government.   You may be sure that this time they had given the United States power to collect taxes, power to make people join the army, power to look after the commerce between the states, and many other powers besides.

Their plan pleased many people.   One by one the states agreed to accept it as the government of the United States. It was such a good plan that it has lasted from that day to this.   We call it the *Constitution of the United States* (*pointing to the words on the board*).

PRESENTATION TEST

Check the best answer :

a. The Articles of Confederation failed

     _ _ _ because not enough power was given to the United States
     _ _ _ because foreign countries laughed at them
     _ _ _ because their plan was never tried

b. The new plan made by the representatives

     _ _ _ gave the United States less power
     _ _ _ gave the United States the same power
     _ _ _ gave the United States more power

c. The name of the new plan was

     _ _ _ the Declaration of Independence
     _ _ _ the Constitution of the United States
     _ _ _ the Articles of Confederation

Assimilation

Readings

Upper Group

BLAISDELL. The Story of American History, 245–246.
BLAISDELL and BALL. Hero Stories from American History, 62–76, 145–155.
EGGLESTON. A First Book in American History, 124–126.
FOOTE and SKINNER. Makers and Defenders of America, 114–116.
GORDY. Leaders in Making America, 238–246.

GORDY. Stories of Later American History, 151–156.
GUERBER. Story of the Great Republic, 21–25.
LEFFERTS. American Leaders, I : 85–90.
MONTGOMERY. Beginners' American History, 129–130.
MOWRY. American Pioneers, 230–238 (James Madison).
PERRY and PRICE. American History, II : 66–74.
STONE and FICKETT. Days and Deeds a Hundred Years Ago, 36–52.
TAPPAN. Elementary History of our Country, 170–171.
WOODBURN and MORAN. Makers of America, 169–174.

Average Group

BARNES. Elementary History of the United States, 206–208.
BEARD and BAGLEY. A First Book in American History, 150–157.
COE. Makers of the Nation, 180–185.
ELSON and MACMULLAN. Story of our Country, II : 2–11.
FORMAN. First Lessons in American History, 165–168.
GORDY. Elementary History of the United States, 190.
INGRAHAM. Story of Democracy, 221–225.
MACE. Primary History, 183–185.
McMASTER. Primary History of the United States, 148–150.
MOWRY. First Steps in the History of our Country, 139–141, 154–155, 168–174
(Hamilton).

Lower Group

BARNES. Primary History of the United States, 119–120.
PRATT. Stories of Colonial Children, 217–221.
WAYLAND. History Stories for Primary Grades, 116–118.

Teachers

CALLENDER. Economic History of the United States, 221–238.
COMAN. Industrial History of the United States, 132–146.
CONKLIN. American Political History, 133–146.
FISH. Development of American Nationality, 31–43.
HART. American History told by Contemporaries, III : 177–254.
HART. Formation of the Union, 121–135.
McLAUGHLIN. The Confederation and the Constitution, 168–220, 253–317.
MUZZEY. An American History, 141–153.
SCHOULER. History of the United States, I : 39–83.
Baltimore County Course of Study, 519.

Minimal Essentials

Date: 1789 — the Constitution went into effect.
Historical Term: **Constitution of the United States**
Things to Remember
The Constitution provided for a much stronger government.
We still have the same government in the United States today.
George Washington was elected the first president.

Illustrative Material

Keystone Views: 85, The First President; 322, Washington inaugurated First President
(slide only).
World Book (Constitution).

Procedure during Assimilation

Reading as described on pages 24–29.

Picture study based on the illustrative material on page 301.

Children turn to the enumerated powers of Congress in the Constitution, and find out whether the Constitution gives the government the powers that were mentioned in the preceding story.

Each child makes a speech telling why he would have signed the Constitution if he had been there.

The class may plan a simple pageant of the period.[1]

Under what government do we live today?

Use the dramatization "Three Compromises of the Constitution." Shoemaker, *Colonial Plays for the Schoolroom*, pp. 65–72.

Show children copies of the Constitution. (The advertising material of certain life-insurance companies furnishes full-sized models.)

Children select the names of the signers whom they know.

Drill on minimal essentials.

Objective test.

Organization

The teacher makes the following outline:

THE GOVERNMENT UNDER THE CONSTITUTION

1. Trying to make a new government
2. Ways in which the new government was better than the old
3. The first president

Recitation

Children tell which points belong under each of the topics above.

A drill lesson on section III of Unit V should be given at this point, followed by a drill lesson[2] on Unit V.

The teacher may give the class Test II, "The Struggle for Independence and the Founding of the New Nation," of the *Informational Tests in United States History* to accompany Beard and Bagley's *History of the American People*.[3] Children are not expected to answer all the items, but they may be interested in seeing how many they know.

[1] *The Twentieth Yearbook of the National Society for the Study of Education,* Part I, pp. 52, 81.

[2] See pages 40–43, 112–113.

[3] The Macmillan Company.

MINIMAL ESSENTIALS OF UNIT V

PERSONS	PLACES	TERMS	DATES

Samuel Adams
British
General Burgoyne
George Rogers
  Clark
Cornwallis
George III
Nathanael Greene
Nathan Hale
John Hancock
Patrick Henry
John Paul Jones
Lafayette
Robert Morris
	Annapolis
	Bunker Hill
	Independence Hall
	Lexington
	the Northwest
	Paris
	Saratoga
	Valley Forge
	West Point
	Yorktown
		Articles of Confed-
		  eration
		Constitution of the
		  United States
		Continental Con-
		  gress
		Declaration of In-
		  dependence
		expedition
		Fourth of July
		government
		high seas
		the north
		the Revolution
		state
		"swamp fox"
		tax
		Tory
		traitor
		Yankee
		"Yankee Doodle"
			1765. Stamp Act
			1775. Battles of
			  Lexington and
			  Concord
			July 4, 1776. The
			  signing of the
			  Declaration of
			  Independence
			1777. Battle of
			  Saratoga
			1783. Treaty of
			  Paris ended the
			  Revolution
			1789. The Con-
			  stitution went
			  into effect
			
			Drill on the peaks
			  of the time chart

TESTS ON THE ENTIRE UNIT

(To be given after all the stories are completed)

Test of Place-Sense. Trace an outline of the United States east of the Mississippi. Make it on as large a scale as possible. Supply each child with a copy. Give the following directions:

1. Put the figure 1 where Lexington is.
2. Put the figure 2 where Bunker Hill is.
3. Put the figure 3 where Saratoga is.
4. Put the letter *W* where West Point is.
5. Put the figure 4 where Valley Forge is.
6. Put the letter *A* where Annapolis is.
7. Put the figure 5 where Yorktown is.
8. Write the word *Northwest* in the right place.
9. Show Paris on a wall map at the front of the room.
10. In what city is Independence Hall? _ _ _ _

Test of Time-Sense. Pass mimeographed sheets of the following:

1. Here is a list of things which happened. Put the figure 1 before that which happened first, the figure 2 before that which happened next, and so on.

    _ _ _ George III decided to tax the colonies.
    _ _ _ General Burgoyne surrendered at Saratoga.
    _ _ _ The Declaration of Independence was signed.
    _ _ _ Robert Morris collected money to pay for the war.
    _ _ _ Samuel Adams made speeches against the tax.

2. Here is a list of things. Proceed as in the exercise above.

    _ _ _ Boston Tea Party.
    _ _ _ A strong government was made.
    _ _ _ The British had to leave Boston.
    _ _ _ The first governments were poor and weak.
    _ _ _ The British surrendered at Yorktown.

3. Here is a list of dates: *1789; 1765; July 4, 1776; 1783; 1775; 1777.* Put each date in the right blank in the sentences below:

    The Stamp Act was passed in _ _ _ _.
    The battle of Saratoga was fought in _ _ _ _.
    The treaty which ended the war was signed in _ _ _ _.
    The Constitution went into effect in _ _ _ _.
    The Declaration of Independence was made on _ _ _ _.
    The first battle of the Revolution was fought in _ _ _ _.

Test on Persons. Pass mimeographed sheets of the following:

I. Here is a list of people:

Robert Morris	John Hancock	British
John Paul Jones	George III	Nathan Hale

Put each name in the right blank in the sentences below:

1. A great hero of the American navy was _ _ _ _ _ _ _ _ _ _ _ _.
2. _ _ _ _ _ _ _ _ said, "I only regret that I have but one life to give for my country."
3. The king of England at the time of the Revolution was _ _ _ _.
4. The man who helped to collect money for the army was _ _ _,_ _ _ _ _.
5. The first man to sign the Declaration of Independence was _ _ _ _ _ _ _ _.
6. People who are under the government of England are called _ _ _ _.

II. Here is another list of people:

Samuel Adams	Lafayette	General Burgoyne
Patrick Henry	George Rogers Clark	Cornwallis
Nathanael Greene		

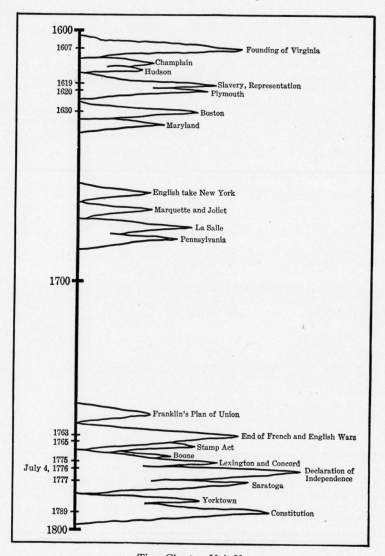

1600
1607 — Founding of Virginia
Champlain
Hudson
1619 — Slavery, Representation
1620 — Plymouth
1630 — Boston
Maryland

English take New York
Marquette and Joliet
La Salle
Pennsylvania

1700

Franklin's Plan of Union
1763 — End of French and English Wars
1765 — Stamp Act
Boone
1775 — Lexington and Concord
July 4, 1776 — Declaration of Independence
1777 — Saratoga
Yorktown
1789 — Constitution
1800

Time Chart — Unit V

Proceed as on page 304.

1. The man who surrendered at Yorktown was _ _ _ _.
2. The man who told Boston not to take the tea was _ _ _ _   _ _ _ _.
3. A great American general in the south was _ _ _ _   _ _ _ _.
4. A noble Frenchman who helped the Americans was _ _ _ _.
5. The man who surrendered at Saratoga was _ _ _ _   _ _ _ _.
6. The man who said "Give me liberty or give me death" was _ _ _ _   _ _ _ _.
7. The Northwest was won by _ _ _ _   _ _ _ _   _ _ _ _.

Test on Historical Terms. The teacher prepares descriptions such as the following, which may have been used previously as the subject of drill games.

I. Here is a list of words:

Yankee	Tory
Constitution	Fourth of July
tax	Continental Congress
Articles of Confederation	surrender

Put each word in its right place in the sentences below:

1. A citizen of the United States was called a _ _ _ _.
2. When men of one army give themselves up to another army, we say they _ _ _ _.
3. The name of the weakest government we ever had was the _ _ _ _ _ _ _ _ _ _ _ _.
4. The day on which the Declaration of Independence was signed was the _ _ _ _ _ _ _ _ _ _ _ _.
5. Money which must be paid to support the government is a _ _ _ _.
6. An American who sided with England during the Revolution was called a _ _ _ _.
7. The most important law of the United States is its _ _ _ _.
8. Representatives from all the colonies met and made up the _ _ _ _ _ _ _ _. It carried on the war.

II. Here is a list of words:

retreat	revolution
the north	expedition
traitor	high seas
Declaration of Independence	"swamp fox"

Do the same as above.

1. The paper in which the representatives said that they were no longer part of England is the _ _ _ _   _ _ _ _   _ _ _ _.
2. Marion was called the _ _ _ _   _ _ _ _ because he would hide in the forests and swamps when the British came after him.

3. A great change in the kind of government a country has is called a _ _ _ _.

4. A man who helps the enemies of his country is a _ _ _ _.

5. The waters of the oceans are called the _ _ _ _ _ _ _ _.

6. The part of the United States east of New York was called _ _ _ _ _ _ _ _.

7. To go back from before an enemy is to _ _ _ _.

8. When many persons make a journey together for a certain purpose, they make an _ _ _ _ _.

COMPREHENSION TEST ON UNIT V

1. *Check the best answer:*

    a. The government which we have in the United States today is based on the

         _ _ _ Continental Congress
         _ _ _ Articles of Confederation
         _ _ _ Constitution

    b. The colonies and the mother country quarreled

         _ _ _ because the colonies wanted to trade as they pleased
         _ _ _ because the colonies wanted to make a new country
         _ _ _ because England made them pay too much money

    c. The early governments failed

         _ _ _ because the states were afraid of Washington
         _ _ _ because the states would not let the United States government have any real power
         _ _ _ because the states did not have enough money

    d. The war in the north resulted in a victory for

         _ _ _ England
         _ _ _ the United States
         _ _ _ neither

    e. When the war began, the colonies were fighting

         _ _ _ because they wanted the rights of Englishmen
         _ _ _ because they wanted to make a new country
         _ _ _ because England started the fighting

    f. After the British had failed at Saratoga

         _ _ _ America decided she was going to win
         _ _ _ England decided to give up the war
         _ _ _ France decided to help the United States

    g. The first president of the United States was

         _ _ _ Samuel Adams
         _ _ _ George Washington
         _ _ _ John Hancock

h. The United States began

    _ _ _ when France agreed to help us

    _ _ _ when the war was over

    . _ _ _ when the Declaration of Independence was signed

i. The United States claimed the Northwest

    _ _ _ because George Rogers Clark had won it

    _ _ _ because the colonists had settled it

    _ _ _ because the king had given it to them

j. The British navy did not decide the war in favor of England

    _ _ _ because John Paul Jones won many victories

    _ _ _ because the French fleet was helping the Americans

    _ _ _ because England did not have many ships

2. *What is the title of the fifth unit?*

ORGANIZATION OF THE UNIT AS A WHOLE

The children give coöperatively a list of the stories comprising the unit. The teacher records this list on the board.

RECITATION OF THE UNIT AS A WHOLE

Each child chooses which of the stories he prefers to tell. Go through the entire list with one set of story-tellers, then another, until all have taken part.

UNIT VI

HOW THE UNITED STATES MADE ITSELF RESPECTED AMONG THE NATIONS

I. The New Nation made a Good Start at Home.
1. Washington was the first president.
2. Alexander Hamilton made the new nation pay its debts.
3. A new capital was selected.
4. The first American ship circumnavigated the globe.
   Captain Gray.
5. Thomas Jefferson was the first great Democrat.
6. The new nation produced painters and writers.
   a. Benjamin West was the first great painter from America.
   b. Bryant, Cooper, and Washington Irving were the first great American writers.
II. The New Nation made itself respected in Europe.
1. The new nation kept out of war with France.
2. The Barbary pirates learned a lesson.
3. The second war for independence from England was called the War of 1812.
   a. The war on land.
   b. The war at sea.
   c. Tecumseh's conspiracy.
   Extra — for advanced group only : How Stephen Girard helped his country.

PREPARATION FOR THE OVERVIEW

"If a new student joins your class in school, what are some of the things you must know about him before you think much of him? What other things ought he to be able to do besides fight? What things might a new nation have to do before the other nations would think much of it?

"Who was Magellan? Drake? We shall read in our new unit about an American who circumnavigated the globe also.

"Have you ever heard of the city of Washington? What do you know about it?"

PRESENTATION OR OVERVIEW

Just as a new boy in a school must earn the respect of his classmates, so the United States needed to earn the respect of all the other nations. It was a new nation — poor, weak,

309

inexperienced, and very young. How did the proud old nations of Europe regard it? Naturally, they were going to wait to see whether its people behaved well, and whether the president could manage the country's business well, before they decided to welcome the United States into the family of nations.

One of the first problems of the new nation was its heavy debt. It had cost a great deal of money to carry on the Revolutionary War so many long years, and much of this money the United States had had to borrow. Now some of the Americans said: "We are so poor, and our new nation is so small and weak, that we had better not pay back any of the money which we borrowed. Let us tell the people who lent it to us that we cannot pay it back, and will not."

But other Americans were much wiser. They said: "No, indeed; that is not honest. We borrowed the money and promised to pay it back. Now pay it back we must — every penny of it. Who has any respect for a man or a nation that goes back on promises?" The European nations, which were watching to see what America would do, were much pleased. They said to each other: "Perhaps this new United States government will prove to be a success after all. At least it is making an honest start."

After that the United States grew very slowly, but it grew steadily. George Washington was president. He selected land along the Potomac River, and there a new capital was begun. It was not very large nor very grand at first, but it grew until it became the great city which it is today.

American ships began going about the seas to trade with other people, and one of them even went around the world, as Magellan and Drake had done.

You must not suppose, however, that the only things in which the new nation had any interest were money and trade and buildings. There were men who painted beautiful pictures, and men who wrote inspiring poems and stories. It was clear that the people of the United States had minds and souls, as well as willingness to work.

After the United States had been going about its business peaceably for a number of years, again dark war clouds rose above it. France was carrying on war in Europe and said: "When you were in trouble I helped you. Now you should come and help me." Some Americans were much troubled. They felt that they really ought to help France. But where was money for an army and a navy to come from? The United States had none, for it was, you remember, a very poor nation. It did not help France, and France was very angry.

Then things in Europe went from bad to worse. England went to war as well as France, and as usual they were fighting each other. A moment ago I told you that the ships of the United States had begun to sail the seas as traders; they took to Europe lumber and fish from New England and sugar from the West Indies. Now that France and England were at war our ships found themselves in a bad situation indeed. If they took goods to England a French fleet would stop them, because they did not want England to have any supplies. And if our American ships went to France, then the British fleet would stop them, because England did not want France to have any supplies. The United States lost, either way.

Our people were very angry. They said, "We really ought to make war on both England and France, for they are both capturing our ships." However, we could not quite forget that France had once been our friend; and, then, how could we attack France, which was far away across the ocean? We could not, for we had few war vessels. But Canada, our northern neighbor, belonged to the British: it would be very easy to send armies up to Canada. So we started war with the British instead of with the French.

The war lasted only two years, and was not a very great one. By the time it was over, Europe had come to respect the United States, and the other countries had decided that this new nation had come to stay.

PRESENTATION TEST

Check the best answer:

a. One thing that made the older nations respect the United States was

_ _ _ that it fought many wars

_ _ _ that it paid its debts

_ _ _ that it talked a great deal about itself

b. The first president was

   _ _ _ George Washington   _ _ _ Thomas Jefferson
   _ _ _ Benjamin Franklin

c. The new capital was built along which river?

   _ _ _ Mississippi   _ _ _ Hudson
   _ _ _ Potomac

d. Some of our ships began

   _ _ _ to sail for adventure   _ _ _ to fight
   _ _ _ to trade

e. Europe decided that some of the men of America had good minds

   _ _ _ because they could write stories and paint pictures
   _ _ _ because they could make long journeys
   _ _ _ because they did not pay their debts

f. At first the United States did not help France in its war

   _ _ _ because it did not want to
   _ _ _ because it was tired
   _ _ _ because it was so poor

g. Later the United States became very angry at both England and France

   _ _ _ because they both borrowed money from us
   _ _ _ because they both captured our ships
   _ _ _ because they both made fun of us

h. We went to war with England instead of France

   _ _ _ because we loved France
   _ _ _ because we hated England
   _ _ _ because we could get at England and not France

i. After this war

   _ _ _ Europe respected the United States more
   _ _ _ Europe did not like the United States
   _ _ _ Europe made fun of the United States

I. The New Nation made a Good Start at Home
1. Washington was the first president

No additional preparation and presentation are needed.

Assimilation
Readings

Upper Group

BAILEY. Boys and Girls of Colonial Days, 151–160.
EGGLESTON. A First Book in American History, 125–126.
GILMAN. The Making of the American Nation, 101–102, 104, 105.
GORDY. Leaders in Making America, 240–246.
GORDY. Stories of Later American History, 151–157, 163.
GUERBER. Story of the Great Republic, 31–37, 48–49, 51–55.
LEFFERTS. American Leaders, I: 87–88, 90–92.

PERRY and PRICE. American History, II : 72–74.
Compton's Pictured Encyclopedia (Washington).
World Book (Washington).

Average Group

BARNES. Elementary History of the United States, 208–210, 212.
BEARD and BAGLEY. A First Book in American History, 154–155, 158.
COE. Makers of the Nation, 181–185.
ELSON and MACMULLAN. Story of our Country, II : 9–11, 12–15.
FORMAN. First Lessons in American History, 167–169, 170–171, 173.
GORDY. Elementary History of the United States, 190.

Lower Group

BARNES. Primary History of the United States, 120–121.
BLAISDELL and BALL. American History Story Book, 86–91.
BLAISDELL and BALL. Short Stories from American History, 104–110.
DAVIS. Stories of the United States, 173–175.
PRATT. Stories of Colonial Children, 220–221.

Teachers

BASSETT. The Federalist System, 3–26.
CHANNING. History of the United States, IV : 29–56.
CONKLIN. American Political History, 145–152.
FORD. Washington and his Colleagues, 1–25.
HART. Formation of the Union, 136–146, 151–153, 164–166.
JOHNSTON. History of American Politics, 19–26.
LAMPREY. Days of the Commanders, 287–297.
MUZZEY. An American History, 157–158.
MUZZEY. The United States of America, I : 147–152.
SCHOULER. History of the United States, I : 79–140.
Baltimore County Course of Study, 519.

Minimal Essentials

Name of Place: **Philadelphia** (review)
Historical Terms: **president; inauguration; administration**
Things to Remember

George Washington was the first president of the United States.
He served for eight years.

Illustrative Material

PYLE. Book of the American Spirit, 271, 273, 274, 275, 277, 279, 287.
Keystone Views: 94, Subtreasury, New York City (where Washington was inaugurated);
    322, Washington inaugurated First President (slide only).
World Book (Washington).

Procedure during Assimilation

Reading as described on pages 24–29.
Picture study based on the illustrative material listed above.
Stage the scene of Washington's inauguration in the toy theater.[1]
Dress a doll in the costume of 1789 to show how Washington appeared at his
    inauguration.
Give the speech Washington might have given.

[1] See page 256.

Bring to class copies of the newspapers containing the most recent inaugural ad-
    dress. Show pictures of the most recent inauguration.
Sing "Mount Vernon Bells."
Use the phonographic record of Washington's Farewell Address.
Drill on minimal essentials.
Objective test.

Organization

The teacher puts on the board the following outline and the
children write two or three main points under each.

GEORGE WASHINGTON AS OUR FIRST PRESIDENT

1. Election of George Washington
2. His journey to New York
3. The inauguration
4. Washington as president

Recitation

Each child prepares his recitation on the whole outline,
though not all can be called on for all the points.

> 2. Alexander Hamilton made the new nation pay its debts

Preparation

"Read the following: $52,000,000. That is the amount of
the debt which the United States had borrowed during the
Revolution, with interest. From what foreign country had we
borrowed money? We had borrowed $40,000,000 from our
own people. How much had we borrowed from Europe?"

Presentation

Almost everybody agreed that we must pay back the
$12,000,000 we had borrowed from Europe; the question was
about the money we had borrowed from our own people. Besides the debt which the United States had borrowed, the
states had borrowed much money also to carry on the war.
Virginia had borrowed money to send George Rogers Clark
into the West, and Massachusetts had borrowed enormous
sums to send her armies down to the middle states. Besides
the United States debts, then, there were these state debts.
Should the United States pay these also?

Some people said: "All these states were fighting for the United States as a whole. They were not fighting for themselves. Therefore the United States ought to pay the state debts too." But some of the southern states said: "No. We have worked hard and paid our own state debts. Let Connecticut and Massachusetts and the rest do the same; let them work hard and pay their debts instead of asking the United States to pay these debts for them."

The quarrel went on. One of the wisest men of the United States government, Alexander Hamilton (*pointing to his name on the board*), said: "I am sorry that we do not all think the same. I am sorry that the southern states think it would not be fair to ask the United States to pay the state debts also. But we must be perfectly honest. We must pay every penny we owe — not only the debt to Europe, which was borrowed by the whole United States, but also the debts which the states themselves owe. The states are the children of the United States, and we must pay their debts as well as our own. That is the only honest way."

The southern states grumbled: "We think that is not fair. It is right to pay back the money which the United States borrowed, but some of the states have paid their own state debts. Why can't the rest do the same?" Hamilton was firm. "No," he said; "all debts must be paid — United States debts and state debts alike."

At last the southern states agreed, although they still grumbled. Then the United States could look the whole world in the face, for it had paid back its honest debts, both those of the states and of the United States. Much of the credit for the United States having acted honestly in the payment of her debts belongs to Alexander Hamilton.

PRESENTATION TEST

Check the best answer:

a. All the states agreed right away

_ _ _ that we should pay back the state debts

_ _ _ that we should pay back the money which the United States had borrowed

_ _ _ that we should not pay back any of our debts

b. The question about which they could not agree was this:

_ _ _ Should the United States pay the state debts also?

_ _ _ Should the United States pay its own debt?

_ _ _ Should they pay back any money at all?

c. Some of the southern states did not want the United States to pay the state debts

_ _ _ because they did not want to spend the money

_ _ _ because they did not want to pay any debts at all

_ _ _ because they had already paid their own state debts

d. Alexander Hamilton said that the United States must pay the state debts

_ _ _ because it would not take much money

_ _ _ because the states are the children of the United States

_ _ _ because the states wanted it

e. The United States proved that it was honest

_ _ _ by paying all the debts, both of the states and of the United States

_ _ _ by saying that it was an honest nation

_ _ _ by paying part of the debt

Assimilation
Readings

Upper Group

BURNHAM. Hero Tales from History, 301–309.
FOOTE and SKINNER. Makers and Defenders of America, 129–139.
GORDY. Stories of Later American History, 157.
GUERBER. Story of the Great Republic, 37.
LEFFERTS. American Leaders, I: 193–216.
OLCOTT. Good Stories for Great Birthdays, 154–161.
PERRY and PRICE. American History, II: 75–77.
TURPIN. Brief Biographies from American History, 193–200.
Compton's Pictured Encyclopedia (Hamilton).
World Book (Hamilton).

Average Group

BARNES. Elementary History of the United States, 236–237.
BEARD and BAGLEY. A First Book in American History, 155–158.
BURTON. Four American Patriots, 71–130.
COE. Makers of the Nation, 187.
ELSON and MACMULLAN. Story of our Country, II: 11–12, 31–32.
FORMAN. First Lessons in American History, 169–170.
GORDY. Elementary History of the United States, 192–193.
MORRIS. Primary History of the United States, 187–188.
MOWRY. First Steps in the History of our Country, 168–175.
SOUTHWORTH. Builders of our Country, II: 97–107.
UHRBROOK and OWENS. Famous Americans, 134–149.

Lower Group

Try FORMAN and SOUTHWORTH.

Teachers

BASSETT. The Federalist System, 27–41, 190–203.
CHANNING. History of the United States, IV: 60–115.

COMAN. Industrial History of the United States, 154–156.
CONKLIN. American Political History, 152–156.
FORD. Washington and his Colleagues, 26–79.
FRYER. Book of Boyhoods, 117–126.
HART. Formation of the Union, 146–151.
LODGE. Alexander Hamilton.
MCMASTER. History of the People of the United States, II: 25–32, 35–41, 81–82.
MUZZEY. An American History, 159–162.
MUZZEY. The United States of America, I: 149–150, 152–161.
SCHOULER. History of the United States, I: 143–149, 173–177, 197–198, 203–205.
Baltimore County Course of Study, 520–521.

Minimal Essentials

Name of Person: **Alexander Hamilton**
Historical Terms: **debts; treasurer; Secretary of the Treasury**
Things to Remember
    Alexander Hamilton was the first Secretary of the Treasury.
    The United States paid its debts.
    It paid the debts of the states too.

Illustrative Material

Chronicles of America Photoplays, Yale University Press: Alexander Hamilton.

Procedure during Assimilation

Reading as described on pages 24–29.
Picture study based on the illustrative material listed above.
Show the class a United States government bond (which is one form in which the public debt is represented today).
Graph the amounts and kinds of debts assumed.[1]
Find a picture of the present Secretary of the Treasury.
Carry on a classroom project which will necessitate the appointment of a treasurer.
Drill on minimal essentials.
Objective test.

Organization

The teacher and the class together work out an outline somewhat similar to the following. The children tell what belongs under each point.

ALEXANDER HAMILTON

    1. Early life in the West Indies
    2. As a soldier
    3. His part in the payment of the debt

---

[1] Muzzey, D. S., *The United States of America*, I: 154–155.

Recitation

Invite members of the senior economics class to hear the recitations based on the outline.

---

3. A new capital was selected

Preparation

"In what city was the Constitution written?

"In what city was George Washington inaugurated?

"What is the capital of the United States today?

"Which states had not wanted the United States to pay the state debts? Why?"

Presentation

Alexander Hamilton and many of the other men of the north were very sorry that the southern states had been angry. They wanted all the children of the new constitution to get along well together. So they said to each other: "Here is a good plan. We have to have a capital city for our new nation. Let us put it somewhere in the south. Then the southern states will know that we intend to be fair to them."

The southern states were pleased. They said: "We should be very happy to have the capital located in the south. Let us put it somewhere along the Potomac River." One of them suggested: "George Washington is a southerner; he lives in Virginia. To show how much we all love and respect him, let him select the exact place to put the new city, and let us name it after him, *Washington.*" This idea pleased everybody, so it was carried out. From that day to this Washington has been our capital city.

PRESENTATION TEST

Check the best answer:

The capital city was put in the south

_ _ _ because Washington lived in the south

_ _ _ to please the southern states, which had felt so bad about the United States paying the state debts

_ _ _ because it was warmer in the south

Assimilation

Readings

Upper Group

CHAMBERLAIN. North America, 53–60.
FARIS. Where our History was Made, Book II : 325–333.
LEFFERTS. American Leaders, I : 88–90.
LEFFERTS. Our Own United States, 84–90.
LOGIE. From Columbus to Lincoln, 171–174.
PERRY and PRICE. American History, II : 74.
Compton's Pictured Encyclopedia (Washington).
St. Nicholas, XX : Part II, 572–578.
World Book (Washington, History ; District of Columbia, History).

Average Group

COE. Makers of the Nation, 186, 187–189.
ELSON and MACMULLAN. Story of our Country, II : 21–22.
FORMAN. First Lessons in American History, 176.
INGRAHAM. The Story of Democracy, 243–257.
McMASTER. Primary History of the United States, 150–152.

Lower Group

CARROLL and CARROLL. Around the World, III : 47–53.
DAVIDSON and ANDERSON. Lincoln Readers, V : 200–209.

Teachers

HART. American History told by Contemporaries, III : 331–333.
McMASTER. History of the People of the United States, II : 483–489.
MUZZEY. An American History, 174.
SPARKS. The Expansion of the American People, 175–187.
Baltimore County Course of Study, 520.

Minimal Essentials

Names of Places: **Washington, D. C.** (explanation of D. C.) ; **Potomac** (pǒ tō′măk)
   River; District of Columbia; Pennsylvania Avenue
Date: **nineteenth century**
Historical Terms: **White House; capitol; capital**
Things to Remember
   A stretch of land ten miles square was selected as the District of Columbia.
   The capital city was built in the District of Columbia.
   The capital city was named Washington.

Illustrative Material

BROWN. Famous Pictures : 43, The Capitol, Washington, D. C., 1897 ; 44, White House.
GABRIEL (ED.). Pageant of America, XIII : 116–122.
Detroit Publishing Company. Little Phostint Journeys : Washington, D. C., Parts I and II.
Ford Educational Library (films) : 42, The Nation's Capital, Washington, D. C.

Procedure during Assimilation

Reading as described on pages 24–29.
On the sand table represent the city of Washington as it is at present, placing the important government buildings. Divide the class into committees, each being responsible for one building.

Read to the class the letter of Abigail Adams describing the capital.[1]
Someone who has visited Washington describes it to the class.
Children find on a large map the District of Columbia, the city of Washington, the
state of Washington.
Show a map of the District of Columbia.[2]
Drill on minimal essentials.
Objective test.

Organization

The teacher puts the following outline on the board. The
children hear others tell what points come under each, appeal-
ing to the teacher if necessary.

THE CAPITAL OF THE UNITED STATES

1. The early capitals of the United States
2. Washington as the capital

Recitation

The same children who heard each other's outlines now hear
the recitations based on the outlines.

> 4. The first American ship circumnavigated the globe
>   Captain Gray

Preparation

"Who was the first man to sail around the world?
"Had he touched the western coast of North America?
"Who was the first Englishman to sail along the Pacific
coast of North America?
"Do you know where Oregon is?"

Presentation

Now that the United States was a nation by itself, it naturally had to look out for its own trade. It could not depend on
British ships any longer to supply it with sugar from the West
Indies, tea from China, wines from Spain, and so on. American merchants built their own ships and began sending them
over all the seas to bring back the goods which the people

[1] Hart, A. B., *American History told by Contemporaries*, III : 331–333.
[2] Sparks, E. E., *Expansion of the American People*, p. 178.

wanted. We are going to read today about one captain who went to China for tea. Then he made another voyage and came along here (*showing the Oregon coast*), where he discovered a beautiful large river. The ship in which he was sailing was named the *Columbia*, so he named the river after his ship.

You will remember, however, that Francis Drake had claimed this land for England two centuries ago. Now both England and the United States claimed the land. Rival claims usually lead to trouble, and did in this case, but the trouble did not come until a long time afterwards.

PRESENTATION TEST

1. *Check the best answer:*

 a. When the United States became a separate country

 _ _ _ it had to depend on England for its goods
 _ _ _ it had to supply itself with goods
 _ _ _ it had to go without goods, except those it could make

 b. An American captain discovered a great river which he named

 _ _ _ the Mississippi
 _ _ _ the Colorado
 _ _ _ the Columbia

2. *Check two answers:*

 The Oregon country was then claimed by two nations:

 _ _ _ England   _ _ _ France
 _ _ _ Spain   _ _ _ United States

Assimilation

Readings

Upper Group

 DAKIN. Great Rivers of the World, 105–108.
 JUDSON. Early Days in Old Oregon, 25–30.
 MONTGOMERY. Beginners' American History, 209–212.
 MORRIS. Heroes of Discovery in America, 288–295.
 PERRY and PRICE. American History, II: 88.
 World Book (Oregon, History).

Average Group

 McMASTER. Primary History of the United States, 165–166.
 MORRIS. Primary History of the United States, 210–211.

Lower Group

 Try McMASTER.

Teachers

 McMASTER. History of the People of the United States, II: 633–635.
 SKINNER. Adventurers of Oregon, 18–26.
 SPARKS. Expansion of the American People, 211.

Minimal Essentials

Names of Places: **Oregon** (ŏr'ĕ gŏn) ; **Columbia River**
Things to Remember
　　Captain Gray was the first American to circumnavigate the globe.
　　He discovered the Columbia River.
　　The United States claimed the Oregon country because of his voyage.

Procedure during Assimilation

Reading as described on pages 24–29.
Read to the class selections from Skinner's *Adventurers of Oregon.*
Draw a picture of Captain Gray's ship, the *Columbia*, arriving in Boston in 1790
　　with a cargo of tea from China; arriving at the mouth of the Columbia
　　River in Oregon.
Model in clay the medal struck for the voyage of the *Columbia.*[1]
Who was the first man to circumnavigate the globe? the first Englishman?
Drill on minimal essentials.
Objective test.

Organization

The drawing of the pictures mentioned above.

Recitation

Explaining the pictures.

---

5. Thomas Jefferson was the first great Democrat

Preparation

"At election time you hear a great deal about Democrats
and Republicans. Do you know whether your father is a
Democrat or a Republican?"

Show children a printed ballot, with the names *Republican*
and *Democrat* above the party columns. Explain how it is
decided which man has been elected.

"Both parties have had great men in United States history.
The Republican party is much newer than the Democratic.
Lincoln was a Republican.

"Our story today is of a time when there was no Republican
party and when the Democratic party was just beginning.

[1] Sparks, E. E., *Expansion of the American People,* p. 211.

Thomas Jefferson was the man who started the Democratic party, and he was the first president of the United States who belonged to that party."

Presentation

You know that all people do not agree about any one matter. In religion some are Catholics and some are Protestants; in time of war some believe in fighting and some would rather talk things over; some think the United States ought to build more ships, and others think that we need more airplanes. And we could name many other cases. In all lines of work or play people believe different things.

You may be sure that when it comes to such a difficult matter as running the business of a great nation like the United States, people are not going to think alike either. Some people will think that the United States should go to war with its neighbors when its trade has been hurt, and some people will think that it should not.

All the people who agree in their ideas come together and form a political party (*pointing to the words written on the board*). They vote for one of their own men who thinks as they do. If there are enough of them they elect him, and he runs the government as they think it should be run. Thomas Jefferson was one of the first men in the United States to form a political party. His was the Democratic party. It is one of our great parties today.

PRESENTATION TEST

Check the best answer:

 a. The reason why there are political parties is

    _ _ _ because there always have been parties
    _ _ _ because men do not agree about how things should be done
    _ _ _ because men like to vote

 b. Members of each political party try

    _ _ _ to elect a man who believes as they do
    _ _ _ to kill members of the other party
    _ _ _ to harm the other party

 c. The party which was formed by Thomas Jefferson was

    _ _ _ the Republican party
    _ _ _ the Labor party
    _ _ _ the Democratic party

Assimilation

Readings

Upper Group

BURNHAM. Hero Tales from History, 309–314.
CHANDLER and CHITWOOD. Makers of American History, 176–182.
DAVIDSON. Founders and Builders of our Nation, 109–114.
EGGLESTON. A First Book in American History, 127–133.
ELLIS. Makers of our Country, 127–131.
EVANS. America First, 236–240.
FARIS. Where our History was Made, Book II, 292–296.
FOOTE and SKINNER. Makers and Defenders of America, 117–125.
GORDY. Leaders in Making America, 251–255.
GORDY. Stories of Later American History, 164–169.
GUERBER. Story of the Great Republic, 55–57.
LEFFERTS. American Leaders, I : 94–109.
MONTGOMERY. Beginners' American History, 162–168, 170.
OLCOTT. Good Stories for Great Birthdays, 304–313.
PERRY and PRICE. American History, II : 77–78, 83–84.
TURPIN. Brief Biographies from American History, 186–193.
WOODBURN and MORAN. Makers of America, 189–195.
Compton's Pictured Encyclopedia (Jefferson).
St. Nicholas, XXXI : Part II, 861; XLII : Part II, 791–792.
World Book (Jefferson).

Average Group

BARNES. Elementary History of the United States, 229–231, 233–238.
COE. Makers of the Nation, 213–216.
EGGLESTON. Stories of Great Americans, 87–90.
ELSON and MACMULLAN. Story of Our Country, II : 22–26.
FORMAN. First Lessons in American History, 182.
GORDY. American Leaders and Heroes, 241–243.
GORDY. Elementary History of the United States, 195–196.
MORRIS. Primary History of the United States, 183–186.
MOWRY. First Steps in the History of our Country, 176–179.
SOUTHWORTH. Builders of our Country, II : 108–113.
UHRBROCK and OWENS. Famous Americans, 72–80.

Lower Group

BALDWIN. Fifty Famous People, 54–57.
BARNES. Primary History of the United States, 122–123.
WAYLAND. History Stories for Primary Grades, 119–121.

Teachers

BASSETT. The Federalist System, 42–55, 136–162.
CHANNING. History of the United States, IV : 150–157.
CHANNING. The Jeffersonian System, 3–35.
CONKLIN. American Political History, 139, 157–158, 187–191, 193–196.
EGGLESTON. American Immortals, 66–95.
FISH. Development of American Nationality, 86–95, 99–102.
FORD. Washington and his Colleagues, 164–194.
HART. American History told by Contemporaries, III : 344–362.
HART. Formation of the Union, 155–157, 177–183, 188–191.
JOHNSON. Jefferson and his Colleagues, 1–188.

JOHNSTON. History of American Politics, 26–29, 55–57.
McMASTER. History of the People of the United States, II: 49–50, 87–88, 289–307.
MUZZEY. The United States of America, I: 161–167.
SCHOULER. History of the United States, I: 180–192, 219–230; II: 1–16, 22–27.
TURNER. Rise of the New West, 3–66.
Baltimore County Course of Study, 521.

Minimal Essentials

Name of Person: **Thomas Jefferson**
Historical Terms: **Democrat; Democratic party; political party**
Things to Remember
    Thomas Jefferson was the first Democratic president.
    Political parties began in America at this time.

Illustrative Material

BROWN. Famous Pictures: 1786, Thomas Jefferson.
Educational Posters of the National Child Welfare Association: Freedom through Democracy: Thomas Jefferson.
Mentor, XIII: 37–44 (October, 1925).
Perry Pictures: 116, Thomas Jefferson; 116-B, His Home, "Monticello."

Procedure during Assimilation

Reading as described on pages 24–29.
Picture study based on the illustrative material listed above.
Find the name of Thomas Jefferson among the signers of the Declaration of Independence.
On the sand table construct Monticello.
In the index of a large atlas find places which are named for Thomas Jefferson. Is anything in your city named for him?
The class divides into two parties, decides on a platform, and votes for candidates.
Drill on minimal essentials.
Objective test.

Organization

The teacher writes the following points on the board. Each child in class is to give one point that belongs under each of the topics.

THOMAS JEFFERSON THE FIRST DEMOCRATIC PRESIDENT

    1. Jefferson elected by the Democratic party
    2. Jefferson as president.

Recitation

The class is divided into two parts, each part preparing a full recitation on one of the topics.

> 6. The new nation produced painters and writers
>   *a*. Benjamin West was the first great painter from
>   America

Preparation and Presentation

"So far the United States has shown that it is honest in money matters. How? It has started trade on the seas. Mention instances. But it has not yet produced anything beautiful or artistic to show that it is interested in other things besides making money.

"What things should you like to see Americans doing now to produce a national art?

"We are going to read today about the first great American painter. He later lived in England, but he was born and reared here, so we claim him as an American.

"After the United States produced great painters and great writers, Europe had more respect for the new nation."

PRESENTATION TEST

Check the best answer:

Europe began to respect the United States more when it produced

  _ _ _ great crops
  _ _ _ great soldiers
  _ _ _ great painters and writers

Assimilation

Readings

Upper Group

BACON. Pictures Every Child should Know, 354, 372–376.
World Book (Benjamin West).

Average Group

EGGLESTON. Stories of Great Americans, 56–60.

Lower Group

BALDWIN. Fifty Famous People, 71–75.
CALMERTON and WHEELER. Wheeler's Graded Readers, II : 116–119.

Teachers

CARPENTER. Stories Pictures Tell, Book VIII : 1–15 (discussion of West's "Death of General Wolfe").
HARTMANN. History of American Art, I : 21–26.
McFALL. History of Painting, VII : 205–208.
Cyclopedia of Painters and Paintings, IV : 424–425 (West).

Minimal Essentials

Name of Person: **Benjamin West** [1]

Things to Remember

Benjamin West spent his youth in America.

He lived in England most of the time when he was a man.

Illustrative Material

BROWN. Famous Pictures: 1421, Death of Wolfe.

Perry Pictures: 1382, Death of General Wolfe; 1395-A, Penn's Treaty with the Indians.

School Arts Magazine, XXIV: 521 (May, 1925): Elijah and the Widow's Son.

Procedure during Assimilation

Reading as described on pages 24–29.

Study with the children the following paintings of Benjamin West: "Christ Healing the Sick"; "Death of General Wolfe"; [2] "Penn's Treaty with the Indians."

Drill on minimal essentials.

Objective test.

Organization

Children themselves make an outline of the principal points in the story, somewhat as follows:

BENJAMIN WEST, THE FIRST GREAT PAINTER FROM AMERICA

1. His youth in America
2. His studies in Italy
3. His life in England
4. His pictures

Recitation

Each child tells the story based on his own outline.

> *b.* Bryant, Cooper, and Washington Irving were the first great American writers

No additional preparation and presentation are needed.

Assimilation

Readings

Bryant

Works

BAKER and THORNDIKE. Everyday Classics, IV: 143–146; V: 190–193.

HARTWELL. Story-Hour Readings, IV: 174–176, 278–281.

SMITH. Easy Road to Reading, V: 257–259.

[1] Not included in the studies of personages referred to on page 5.

[2] See the reading from Carpenter under references for teachers, above.

"The Planting of the Apple Tree." *Poems Teachers Ask For* (F. A. Owen Publishing Company), 164–165.
"Robert of Lincoln." Ibid. 189–190.
"Song of Marion's Men." Ibid. 54–55.
"White-Footed Deer." Smith, *Easy Road to Reading*, IV : 281–285.

Life

BOLENIUS. Fifth Reader, 289–296.
CODY. Four American Poets, 9–68.
EGGLESTON. Stories of Great Americans, 120.
ELSON. Readers, V : 297–298.
ELSON and MACMULLAN. Story of our Country, II : 147–148.
Compton's Pictured Encyclopedia (Bryant).
St. Nicholas, IV : 99–103 ; XXII : 15–19.
World Book (Bryant).

Teachers

BIGELOW. William Cullen Bryant.
HART. Seven Great American Poets, 5–46.
PATTEE. Sidelights on American Literature, 293–326.
TASSIN and MAURICE. Child's Story of American Literature, 63–71.
WARNER. Library of the World's Best Literature, VI : 2623–2642.

Cooper

Works

"At the Helm." Hartwell, *Story-Hour Readings*, VI : 81–87.
"The Flight across the Lake." Ibid. V : 206–220.
"Long Rifle." Smith, *Easy Road to Reading*, V : 48–61.
"Washington and the Spy." Ibid. 250–257.

Life

ELSON and MACMULLAN. Story of our Country, II : 145–147.
Compton's Pictured Encyclopedia (Cooper).
St. Nicholas, XXI : Part II, 872–878.
World Book (James Fenimore Cooper).

Teachers

LOUNSBURY. James Fenimore Cooper.
MUZZEY. An American History, 200–201.
TASSIN and MAURICE. A Child's Story of American Literature, 94–105.
VAN DOREN. The American Novel, 24–50.
WARNER. Library of the World's Best Literature, X : 3985–4039.

Irving

Works

"Adventure of the Mason." Elson, *Readers*, V : 316–321.
"Capturing the Wild Horse." Ibid. 311–316.
"Rip Van Winkle." Free and Treadwell, *Reading-Literature, Fourth Readers*, 321–342.
"Rip Van Winkle." David McKay Company, Wyeth Illustrations.
"The Schoolmaster." Baldwin, *Fifty Famous Rides and Riders*, 169–182.
"The Schoolmaster." Ettinger, Shimer, and O'Regan, *Progressive Road to Silent Reading*, IV : 24–27.

Life

EGGLESTON. Stories of Great Americans, 101–104.
ELSON and MACMULLAN. Story of our Country, II : 142–145.

Compton's Pictured Encyclopedia (Irving).
St.¦ Nicholas, XXI : Part I, 630–636 ; XXXVIII : Part II, 454–455; XL : Part II, 583–591.
World Book (Washington Irving).

Teachers

BOLTON. Famous American Authors, 58–81.
BOYNTON. Washington Irving.
EGGLESTON. American Immortals, 287–302.
MABIE. Backgrounds of Literature, 99–131.
TASSIN and MAURICE. A Child's Story of American Literature, 84–93.
WARNER. Library of the World's Best Literature, XX : 7991–8045.
WARNER. Washington Irving.

Minimal Essentials

Names of Persons: Washington Irving; James Fenimore Cooper; William Cullen Bryant [1]
Things to Remember
Bryant was our first great poet.
Cooper wrote long storybooks.
Washington Irving wrote histories and stories.

Illustrative Material

GABRIEL (ED.). Pageant of America, XI : 101–112, 116–122, 128–133.
Perry Pictures: 1, Washington Irving; 2, His Home, "Sunnyside"; 3, James Fenimore Cooper; 4, His Home; 5, William Cullen Bryant; 6 and 7, His Home.

Procedure during Assimilation

Reading as described on pages 24–29.
Picture study based on the illustrative material listed above.
Read to the class certain of the most stirring selections from *The Spy, The Last of the Mohicans*, etc.
The children read the selections from one author, then his biography. As a result of this work a short article may be written for the school newspaper characterizing the work and the author.
Drill on minimal essentials.
Objective test.

Organization

Children choose one organization sentence about each author mentioned.

Recitation

The class is divided into three groups. Each group selects one author about whom to give a three-minute speech. The speech includes biography and works. It may be illustrated by pictures.

A drill lesson on section I of Unit VI should be given here.

---

[1] Not included in the studies of personages referred to on page 5.

II. The New Nation made itself respected in Europe
  1. The new nation kept out of war with France

Preparation

"When had France helped us? How?"

Explain the sending of ambassadors, ministers, and consuls from one country to another. Explain that ministers in this sense have nothing to do with the church.

"What minister went from the United States to France during the Revolution?"

Presentation

Not long after we had our revolution here in America, France had a revolution in Europe. She threw down the French government which had helped us, and which had made the treaty with us during the war. Things went from bad to worse. France treated the American ministers who were in Paris very badly, and some French people tried to make America pay them a great sum of money. The United States government grew angry and declared it would never send another man to represent it in France unless the French promised to treat our representatives better.

In fact, we might as well admit that we were at war with France for two years. They captured some of our ships, and we captured some of theirs. We built a small navy to help to protect us. Neither nation, however, really wanted to fight the other, so after a while France promised to treat our representatives courteously. The United States was glad to stop fighting, and thus we avoided a real war with France, though we had been dangerously near to it. One of our most popular songs was written during this period of trouble with France. It was "Hail, Columbia!"

PRESENTATION TEST

Check the best answer:

  a. The government of France which had made the treaty with us

 _ _ _ was kept
 _ _ _ was overthrown
 _ _ _ was forgotten

b. The United States ships captured French ships

_ _ _ because France had treated our representatives badly, and captured our ships

_ _ _ because France did not have as many ships as we had

_ _ _ because we hated France

c. After a while France promised

_ _ _ to give back our ships

_ _ _ to help us fight England

_ _ _ to treat our representatives better

Assimilation
Readings

Upper Group

GUERBER. Story of the Great Republic, 40–42, 49–51.

PERRY and PRICE. American History, II : 76–77, 79–80.

TAPPAN. Elementary History of our Country, 173–174.

Average Group

BARNES. Elementary History of the United States, 210–211.

ELSON and MACMULLAN. Story of our Country, II : 19–21.

FORMAN. First Lessons in American History, 171–172.

GORDY. Elementary History of the United States, 194.

MCMASTER. Primary History of the United States, 152–153.

SEAWELL. Little Jarvis.

Lower Group

BARNES. Primary History of the United States, 124–125.

BLAISDELL and BALL. American History Story Book, 98–105.

Teachers

BASSETT. The Federalist System, 84–100, 218–275.

CHANNING. History of the United States, IV : 116–140, 142–147, 176–209.

CONKLIN. American Political History, 162–177.

FORD. Washington and his Colleagues, 115–163.

HART. American History told by Contemporaries, III : 302–326.

HART. The Formation of the Union, 157–164, 166–168.

JOHNSTON. History of American Politics, 30–46.

MCMASTER. History of the People of the United States, II : 89–143, 213–235, 285–289.

MUZZEY. An American History, 164–167, 170–172.

MUZZEY. The United States of America, I : 167–184.

SCHOULER. History of the United States, I : 260–286, 304–313, 332–341.

Minimal Essentials

Historical Term: **neutral**

Things to Remember

Washington wanted the United States to keep out of European wars.

Many people thought we ought to help France.

We remained neutral.

Illustrative Material

GRANT. The Story of the Ship: the *Terrible.*

Procedure during Assimilation

Reading as described on pages 24–29.

Teach children to sing "The Marseillaise" and "Hail, Columbia."

Why did France think we should help her? Why did the United States think we should not? In what war did we fight on the same side as France? What did one of our soldiers in the World War mean when he said before a statue in France, "Lafayette, we are here"?

Give examples from the wars with the French and from the Revolution to show what is meant by a neutral country.

Drill on minimal essentials.

Objective test.

Organization

The teacher and the class working together make an outline somewhat as follows:

WE KEPT OUT OF WAR WITH FRANCE

1. France thought we should help her
2. For several years we were almost at war with France

Recitation

Each child writes two paragraphs on the points above.

> ### 2. The Barbary pirates learned a lesson

Preparation

"About what pirates have we studied so far?

"In our story of Captain Robert Gray we found that American ships had begun to trade with the Orient. In what different directions could our ships sail, in order to secure goods from the Far East?" (Across the Pacific; across the Atlantic and around the Cape of Good Hope; through the Mediterranean to Asia.) (*These routes are pointed out on the map.*)

"The Mediterranean route was a paradise for pirates. If you were a pirate, where would you hide your ships, in order to attack other sailing vessels?

"Has anyone ever read of a man's being captured and held for ransom?" Write on the board *held for ransom*. Explain *paying tribute*.

Presentation

The northern coast of the Mediterranean (*showing on the map*) was an ideal place for pirates. They would hide here along the coast, and then suddenly pounce down upon an unsuspecting sailing vessel and rob it. By the time any war vessels could arrive to punish the pirates, they would be far away. Therefore many of the nations of Europe decided that it would be easier to buy them off. They paid the rulers of the pirate states a large sum of money each year, and then the pirates promised not to attack them. The United States did not like to do this, but to protect our commerce we had to! You can well imagine that Americans were ashamed.

The pirates decided later that if the goods carried on a ship were valuable, the men must be even more valuable. When they captured a ship they not only sold the goods but they also put the sailors in prison. They would write letters to the sailors' families, stating that the prisoners would not be sent home until a great sum of money was paid as ransom.

Then the pirates declared war on us. The United States became thoroughly tired of the whole affair, and sent out a fleet to punish them. We shall read today how it was done. After we had defeated the pirates Europe had more respect for us.

PRESENTATION TEST

Check the best answer:

  a. The pirates lived along the
      _ _ _ Mediterranean Sea   _ _ _ North Sea
      _ _ _ Black Sea

  b. The nations of Europe protected themselves against the pirates
      _ _ _ by fighting
      _ _ _ by talking to the rulers of the pirates
      _ _ _ by paying money so that the pirates would not attack them

  c. The pirates robbed the ships and
      _ _ _ let the men go   _ _ _ killed all the men
      _ _ _ held the men for ransom

  d. At first the United States
      _ _ _ kept their ships at home   _ _ _ fought the pirates
      _ _ _ paid money to the pirates

  e. At last the United States decided
      _ _ _ to keep their ships at home   _ _ _ to fight the pirates
      _ _ _ to pay money to the pirates

Assimilation

Readings

Upper Group

AUSTIN. Uncle Sam's Secrets, 235–236.
BLAISDELL. The Story of American History, 323–325.
BLAISDELL and BALL. Hero Stories from American History, 156–173.
CHANDLER and CHITWOOD. Makers of American History, 192–195.
EVANS. America First, 240–244.
GUERBER. Story of the Great Republic, 61–68.
LANIER. The Book of Bravery, 336–341.
LEFFERTS. American Leaders, I : 217–222.
LODGE and ROOSEVELT. Hero Tales from American History, 103–113 (difficult).
MORRIS. Heroes of the Navy in America, 126–141.
MORRIS. Historical Tales : American, 233–244.
PERRY and PRICE. American History, II : 88–92.
SEAWELL. Decatur and Somers.
STEVENS. Story of our Navy, 28–30, 38–52.
TAPPAN. Elementary History of our Country, 174–175.
WRIGHT. Children's Stories of American Progress, 41–52.

Average Group

EGGLESTON. Stories of Great Americans, 83–87.
ELSON and MACMULLAN. Story of our Country, II : 36–41.
MOWRY. First Steps in the History of our Country, 192–194, 198–200.
SOUTHWORTH. Builders of our Country, II : 146–148.
UHRBROCK and OWENS. Famous Americans, 167–171.

Lower Group

BARNES. Primary History of the United States, 126–127, 139.

Teachers

HART. The Formation of the Union, 184–185.
LAMPREY. Days of the Commanders, 300–307.
MCMASTER. History of the People of the United States, II : 170–171, 588–594, 601–603.
MUZZEY. An American History, 138–139, 179.

Minimal Essentials

Name of Place: **Tripoli**
Historical Terms: **Barbary** (bär′bà rĭ) ; **ransom; paying tribute**
Things to Remember
Some pirates lived in northern Africa.
They would stop ships that went by, rob them, and hold people for ransom.
An American fleet made them agree to let our ships alone.

Procedure during Assimilation

Reading as described on pages 24–29.
Show flags of the Barbary states.[1]
Dramatize the attack on Tripoli.
Give modern instances of people being held for ransom. Children tell of examples from the moving pictures.

[1] *The National Geographic Magazine,* XXXII : 358 (October, 1917).

Discuss whether we should support this statement by Decatur: "Our country! In her dealings with other nations may she always be in the right; but our country, right or wrong."

Drill on minimal essentials.

Objective test.

Organization

The teacher and the children together make an outline of the principal points, such as:

THE BARBARY PIRATES

1. The pirates of northern Africa
2. Work of the United States fleet

Recitation

Invite the children's parents to hear the stories.

> 3. The second war for independence from England was called the War of 1812
>
> *a.* The war on land

Preparation and Presentation

"When France was at war with England, why would she not want American ships to go to England?

"When England was at war with France, why would she not want American ships to go to France?

"Then with whom could America trade?

"Is it always wrong to fight?

"To protect our rights as a neutral to trade with any country that we wanted to, we went to war.

"Why did we fight England instead of France?" (Told in the overview.)

"We must remember that there were no railroads in those days and very few roads. How could we approach Canada easily?" (*Turn to a map and point to the danger spots: Lake Champlain, the Niagara River, the Detroit River.*) "We shall read how the United States tried to take these places.

"Where could Great Britain best attack the United States?" (At the coast towns and at the mouth of the Mississippi.) "We shall also read how Great Britain tried to take some of these towns.

"If Great Britain should fail to defeat the United States, what would that decide about our right to trade?

"In what way would that make the new nation respected in Europe?"

PRESENTATION TEST

Check the best answer:

a. We had good reason to go to war with

_ _ _ only France

_ _ _ only England

_ _ _ both France and England

b. We went to war

_ _ _ to protect our right to trade

_ _ _ to get even with England

_ _ _ to help France

c. The easiest place for us to attack Great Britain was

_ _ _ England

_ _ _ Canada

_ _ _ India

d. Great Britain could attack us best at

_ _ _ the capital

_ _ _ Cuba

_ _ _ the coast towns

Assimilation

Readings

Upper Group

AUSTIN. Uncle Sam's Secrets, 231–235.

BLAISDELL. The Story of American History, 325–327, 336–338.

DAVIDSON. Founders and Builders of our Nation, 121–124.

EVANS. America First, 274–278.

FARIS. Where our History was Made, Book II, 32–38.

FOOTE and SKINNER. Makers and Defenders of America, 149–151.

GUERBER. Story of the Great Republic, 75–77, 83–91.

HORTON. A Group of Famous Women, 13–24 (Dolly Madison).

LODGE and ROOSEVELT. Hero Tales from American History, 139–147.

MONTGOMERY. Beginners' American History, 193–194.

MOWRY. American Pioneers, 230–238 (Madison).

PERKINS. American Twins of 1812.

PERRY and PRICE. American History, II: 94–96, 103–106.

TAPPAN. Elementary History of our Country, 176–177, 179–182.

TOMLINSON. Fighters Young Americans want to Know, 148–163, 164–181.

WRIGHT. Children's Stories of American Progress, 130–131, 132–134, 137–144.

Compton's Pictured Encyclopedia (War of 1812).

World Book (War of 1812: Story of the War).

Average Group

BARNES. Elementary History of the United States, 240–242, 265–267.

EGGLESTON. Stories of Great Americans, 107–111.

ELSON and MacMULLAN. Story of our Country, II: 47–50, 55–56, 64–75.

FORMAN. First Lessons in American History, 182–184, 186–187.

GORDY. Elementary History of the United States, 207–208, 209–210, 211–212, 213–216.

MCMASTER. Primary History of the United States, 154–158, 159–160.

MORRIS. Primary History of the United States, 193, 196–199.

TAPPAN. American Hero Stories, 224–230, 231–236 (Dolly Madison).

Lower Group

BARNES. Primary History of the United States, 129–130, 131–133, 135–136, 137–139.

BLAISDELL and BALL. American History Story Book, 121–125.

BLAISDELL and BALL. Short Stories from American History, 111–121.

WAYLAND. History Stories for Primary Grades, 195–199 (the Star-Spangled Banner).

Teachers

BOGART. Economic History of the United States, 120–126, 126–127.

CALLENDER. Economic History of the United States, 240–260.

CHANNING. The Jeffersonian System, 36–47, 169–270.

COMAN. Industrial History of the United States, 175–179, 179–183, 189–191.

CONKLIN. American Political History, 196–205, 208–219.

FISH. Development of American Nationality, 102–106, 108–126.

HART. American History told by Contemporaries, III : 385–388.

HART. The Formation of the Union, 191–198, 200–215.

JOHNSON. Jefferson and his Colleagues, 144–188.

LAMPREY. Days of the Commanders, 309–323, 350–368.

MUZZEY. An American History, 180–186.

OGG. The Old Northwest, 151–172.

Baltimore County Course of Study, 522.

Minimal Essentials

Names of Persons: **James Madison; Andrew Jackson**

Name of Place: **New Orleans** (ôr′lê ănz)

Dates: 1812 — second war with England ; **half-century before Civil War**

Historical Terms: **"the Star-Spangled Banner"; War of 1812; Uncle Sam**

Things to Remember

The War of 1812 was a second war for independence.

On land the British were generally successful.

Washington was burned.

The battle of New Orleans was fought after the treaty of peace had been signed.

Illustrative Material

MCKINLEY. Illustrated Topics for American History : S. 20, The Capitol after the Fire.

Keystone Views : 326, James Madison (slide only) ; 327, Impressment of American Seamen (slide only) ; 328, Detroit in 1815 ; 329, Surrender of General Hull (slide only) ; 332 Where "The Star-Spangled Banner" was Written (slide only) ; 333, Battle of New Orleans.

Procedure during Assimilation

Reading as described on pages 24–29.

Picture study based on the illustrative material listed above.

Use the following dramatizations : "The Star-Spangled Banner." Hubbard, *Little American History Plays*, pp. 101–108 ; "Dolly Madison." Bird and Starling, *Historical Plays for Children*, pp. 247–270 ; "Dolly Madison." Hague and Chalmers, *Dramatic Moments in American History*, pp. 129–151.

Sing "The Star-Spangled Banner."
Give a special report on flag etiquette.[1]
Make a map, "The Second War between the United States and Great Britain."
Show the scenes of the battles mentioned; color red if a British victory, blue if an American victory.
Drill on minimal essentials.
Objective test.

Leave organization and recitation until after the next story has been finished; include the two in one organization.

> *b.* The war at sea

No additional preparation and presentation are needed.

Assimilation
Readings
Upper Group

BLAISDELL. The Story of American History, 327–336.
BLAISDELL and BALL. Hero Stories from American History, 174–184.
CHANDLER and CHITWOOD. Makers of American History, 195–199.
EVANS. America First, 265–269.
FARIS. Where our History was Made, Book II, 24–32.
FOOTE and SKINNER. Makers and Defenders of America, 152–160.
GUERBER. Story of the Great Republic, 69–70, 77–83.
LEFFERTS. American Leaders, I : 222–226, 227–236.
LODGE and ROOSEVELT. Hero Tales from American History, 117–126, 129–136.
MORRIS. Heroes of the Navy in America, 210–238.
PERRY and PRICE. American History, II : 92–94, 96–103.
STEVENS. Story of our Navy, 53–117.
TAPPAN. Elementary History of our Country, 176–179.
TOMLINSON. Boy Sailors of 1812.
TURPIN. Brief Biographies from American History, 204–212.
WRIGHT. Children's Stories of American Progress, 131–132, 134–137.
Compton's Pictured Encyclopedia (War of 1812).
World Book (War of 1812 : Story of the War).

Average Group

BEARD and BAGLEY. A First Book in American History, 181–186.
ELSON and MacMULLAN. Story of our Country, II : 50–51, 56–64.
FORMAN. First Lessons in American History, 184–186.
GORDY. Elementary History of the United States, 208–209, 210–211, 212–213.
GORDY. Our Patriots, 132–135.
MOWRY. First Steps in the History of our Country, 194–198.
SOUTHWORTH. Builders of our Country, II : 140–146.
TAPPAN. American Hero Stories, 218–223.
UHRBROCK and OWENS. Famous Americans, 178–184.

Lower Group

BARNES. Primary History of the United States, 133–135.
GROVE. American Naval Heroes, 14–19.

[1] *The National Geographic Magazine*, XXXII : 404–413 (October, 1917).

Teachers
    BABCOCK. Rise of American Nationality, 106–128.
    JOHNSON. History of American Politics, 68–88.
    JOHNSON. War of 1812, 61–148, 194–222, 290–325.
    LAMPREY. Days of the Commanders, 324–348.
    MCMASTER. History of the People of the United States, III : 253–264.
    MUZZEY. An American History, 187.
    PAINE. The Fight for a Free Sea, 1–22, 46–63, 108–125, 126–184.
    The Literary Digest, LXXXVII : 44–49 (December 5, 1925).

Minimal Essentials

Name of Person: **Oliver Hazard Perry**
Name of Place: **Lake Erie**
Things to Remember
    England and France were at war.
    If American ships went to France, England captured them; if American ships went to England, France captured them.
    We had cause for war with both countries, but we could not get at France very easily, so we fought England instead.
    At sea the Americans were generally successful.

Illustrative Material

GRANT. Story of the Ship: the *Constitution*, the *Victory*, the *Niagara*.
MCKINLEY. Illustrated Topics for American History : S. 20, the *Constitution* and the British Ships *Cyane* and *Levant*.
Keystone Views : 99, *Old Ironsides*; 102, Powder on the Way to Commodore Perry at Lake Erie; 330, Commodore O. H. Perry (slide only) ; 331, *Chesapeake* and *Shannon* (slide only).

Procedure during Assimilation

Reading as described on pages 24–29.
Picture study based on the illustrative material listed above.
Show pictures of Perry's flag.[1]
Explain the cartoon in Knowlton's *Making History Graphic*, p. 22.
The boys construct a replica of *Old Ironsides* to place in the school museum.
Add the scenes of the naval battles to the map "The Second War between the United States and Great Britain."
Drill on minimal essentials.
Objective test.

Organization

Children work out, with as little help from the teacher as possible, an outline somewhat similar to the following. Children then write the principal subheads under each point.

THE WAR OF 1812

1. Causes of the war
2. The events at sea
3. The events on land
4. The treaty of peace

[1] *The National Geographic Magazine*, XXXII : 338 (October, 1917).

Recitation

Give the recitations at a Parent-Teacher Association meeting.

---

c. Tecumseh's conspiracy

Preparation

"Which great Indians had already tried to keep the land from the clutches of the white people? With what results?" (Philip, Pontiac.)

Study with the children a population map [1] based on the census of 1790, noticing the center of population and the number of inhabitants to the square mile. Call attention to the movement into the back-country.

Presentation

For years the westward movement of the white people had been worrying one of the Indians' greatest leaders, Tecumseh. Again and again he had led uprisings against them, and always he had been defeated. Then he had gone to the British in Canada and received help in the form of arms and ammunition, and had traveled away down to the land of the southern Indians to persuade them to join him.

When the War of 1812 came on, of course Tecumseh joined with the British, hoping that they would win and that the land-hungry Americans would be driven back. We shall read today how his efforts succeeded.

PRESENTATION TEST

1. *Check two answers:*

    Tecumseh wanted to get help from
      _ _ _ the Indians of the South
      _ _ _ the Americans
      _ _ _ the British
      _ _ _ the French

2. *Check one answer:*

    When the War of 1812 came, Tecumseh took the side of the
      _ _ _ British
      _ _ _ Americans

[1] Such as map 12 of the Sanford American History Maps.

Assimilation
Readings

Upper Group

EGGLESTON. A First Book in American History, 147–152.
EVANS. America First, 270–274.
MONTGOMERY. Beginners' American History, 179–184, 191.
WRIGHT. Children's Stories of American Progress, 121–129.
Compton's Pictured Encyclopedia (Tecumseh).
World Book (War of 1812 : Harrison's Indian Campaign, Tecumseh).

Average Group

BARNES. Elementary History of the United States, 264–265.
ELSON and MACMULLAN. Story of our Country, II : 51–55.
FORMAN. First Lessons in American History, 190–192.
MORRIS. Primary History of the United States, 189–193.

Lower Group

BLAISDELL and BALL. American History Story Book, 126–136.
BLAISDELL and BALL. Child's Book of American History, 138–143.

Teachers

EGGLESTON and SEELYE. Tecumseh and the Shawnee Prophet.
JOHNSON. A History of the War of 1812, 38–45.
JOHNSTON. Famous Indian Chiefs, 309–337.
MCMASTER. History of the People of the United States, III : 529–536.

Minimal Essentials

Names of Persons : **Tecumseh** (tê kŭm'sĕ) ; **William Henry Harrison**
Name of Place : **Tippecanoe** (tĭp'ê kà nōō')
Historical Terms : **defeat; uprising**
Things to Remember

Tecumseh had been making attacks on the Americans in the Northwest.
People believed that the British were helping him.
William Henry Harrison defeated the Indians at Tippecanoe.

Procedure during Assimilation

Reading as described on pages 24–29.
Give a speech which Tecumseh might have given to his people to incite them to war against the Americans.
What other great Indians had made similar attempts?
Why was Harrison called Old Tippecanoe?
Drill on minimal essentials.
Objective test.

Organization

The teacher puts the following points on the board. Children tell what belongs under each.

TECUMSEH'S CONSPIRACY

1. Tecumseh's early attempts
2. His journey to the south
3. Tecumseh in the War of 1812

Recitation

The complete story told by each child.

A drill lesson on section II of Unit VI should be given at this point.

MINIMAL ESSENTIALS OF UNIT VI

PERSONS	PLACES	TERMS	DATES
William Cullen Bryant James Fenimore Cooper Alexander Hamilton William Henry Harrison Washington Irving Andrew Jackson Thomas Jefferson James Madison Oliver Hazard Perry Tecumseh Benjamin West	Columbia River District of Columbia Lake Erie New Orleans Oregon Potomac River Tippecanoe Tripoli Washington, D.C.	administration Barbary capital capitol debt defeat Democrat Democratic party inauguration neutral president treasurer Uncle Sam War of 1812 White House	*1812.* Second war with England Nineteenth century Half-century Drill on the peaks of the time chart. What does 1812 mean when used as a date?

TESTS[1] ON THE ENTIRE UNIT

(To be given after all the stories are completed)

Test of Place-Sense. Pass double-sized outline maps of the United States. Give the following directions:

1. Draw a square where the District of Columbia is.
2. Put the figure 1 where Washington, D.C., is.
3. Draw a wavy line to represent the Potomac River.
4. Put the letter *O* where Oregon is.
5. Draw another wavy line to represent the Columbia River.
6. Put the initials *N O* where New Orleans is.
7. Write the word *Erie* in Lake Erie.
8. Pass to the wall map of the world and show where Tripoli is.

[1] Penell, Olivia C., " Research Tests in United States History." *Historical Outlook,* XV : 128–143.

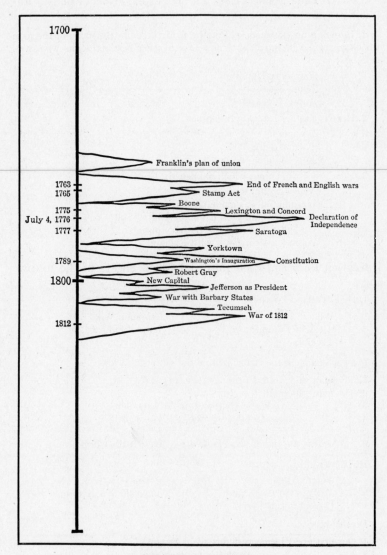

1700

Franklin's plan of union

1763 — End of French and English wars
1765 — Stamp Act
Boone
1775 — Lexington and Concord
July 4, 1776 — Declaration of Independence
1777 — Saratoga

Yorktown
1789 — Washington's Inauguration — Constitution
Robert Gray
1800 — New Capital
Jefferson as President
War with Barbary States
Tecumseh
War of 1812
1812 —

Time Chart — Unit VI

Test of Time-Sense. Pass mimeographed sheets of the following :

1. Here is a list of persons. Put the figure 1 before the name of the man who lived or did his great work first, the figure 2 before the one who lived next, and so on.

_ _ _ Alexander Hamilton
_ _ _ James Madison
_ _ _ Andrew Jackson

2. Here is another list. Do the same.

_ _ _ Tecumseh
_ _ _ Thomas Jefferson
_ _ _ James Fenimore Cooper

3. Here is a list of things which happened. Do the same.

_ _ _ A new capital was selected.
_ _ _ Washington was made president.
_ _ _ Alexander Hamilton made the United States pay its debts.
_ _ _ We had a war with the Barbary pirates.
_ _ _ We had a second war with England.

Test on Persons. Pass mimeographed sheets of the following :

I. Here is a list of people :

William Henry Harrison	Benjamin West
Alexander Hamilton	James Madison
Tecumseh	Washington Irving

Put each name in the right blank in the sentences below :

1. The man who wrote stories and histories was _ _ _ _ _ _ _ _.
2. The man who painted pictures was _ _ _ _ _ _ _ _.
3. _ _ _ _ _ _ _ _ made the United States pay its debts.
4. _ _ _ _ _ _ _ _ was president during the War of 1812. ¹
5. _ _ _ _ _ _ _ _ _ _ _ _ defeated the Indians.
6. _ _ _ _ was the Indian who wanted to drive out the white people.

II. Here is a list of people :

Thomas Jefferson	Andrew Jackson
William Cullen Bryant	James Fenimore Cooper
Oliver Hazard Perry	

Do the same.

1. Our first great Democratic president was _ _ _ _ _ _ _ _.
2. _ _ _ _ _ _ _ _ _ _ _ _ wrote stories about Indians.
3. _ _ _ _ _ _ _ _ defeated the British at New Orleans.
4. Our first great poet was _ _ _ _ _ _ _ _ _ _ _ _.
5. The man who defeated the British on Lake Erie was _ _ _ _ _ _ _ _ _ _ _ _.

Test on Historical Terms. The teacher prepares descriptions such as the following, which may have been used previously as the subject of drill games.

I. Here is a list of words:

president   Uncle Sam
defeat   administration
War of 1812   Barbary
inauguration   debt

Put each word in the right place in the sentences below:

1. Money which is owed is a _ _ _ _.
2. The chief officer of the nation is the _ _ _ _.
3. Some countries on the northern coast of Africa were called the _ _ _ _ States.
4. The years during which a man is president are his _ _ _ _.
5. The second war with England was the _ _ _ _ _ _ _ _ _ _ _ _.
6. When one side overthrows the other in a battle, we say that the side which loses has met a _ _ _ _.
7. The _ _ _ _ is the occasion when a man begins to act as president.
8. The United States government is sometimes called _ _ _ _ _ _ _ _.

II. Here is a list of words:

neutral   Democrat
treasurer   capital
Democratic party   capitol
White House

Do the same.

1. The city from which the government of a country is carried on is the _ _ _ _.
2. A man who takes care of the money for a society or a nation is the _ _ _ _.
3. People who do not take either one side or the other in a quarrel are _ _ _ _.
4. The house in which the president lives is the _ _ _ _ _ _ _ _.
5. The party of Thomas Jefferson was the _ _ _ _ _ _ _ _.
6. The building in which the lawmakers of the United States have their meetings is called the _ _ _ _.
7. A man who belongs to the Democratic party is a _ _ _ _.

COMPREHENSION TEST ON UNIT VI

1. *Check the best answer:*

   a. Tecumseh's conspiracy was

     _ _ _ an attempt to keep the white men from taking the Indians' land
     _ _ _ an attempt to help the British
     _ _ _ an attempt to get even with the Americans

b. The first president of the United States was

     _ _ _ Thomas Jefferson

     _ _ _ Benjamin Franklin

     _ _ _ George Washington

c. We fought England instead of France in 1812

     _ _ _ because we could not get at France

     _ _ _ because we had nothing against France

     _ _ _ because we wanted to fight England

d. The greatest thing that Alexander Hamilton did was

     _ _ _ to fight with Aaron Burr

     _ _ _ to act as treasurer

     _ _ _ to make the new nation pay its debts

e. The War of 1812 was really

     _ _ _ a war to gain more land

     _ _ _ a war to gain sea power

     _ _ _ a second war for independence

f. The capital of the United States was placed in

     _ _ _ New York

     _ _ _ Washington, D. C.

     _ _ _ Philadelphia

g. The claim of the United States to the Oregon country was based on the work of

     _ _ _ Captain Robert Gray

     _ _ _ Francis Drake

     _ _ _ George Rogers Clark

h. The war with the Barbary pirates was fought because

     _ _ _ they robbed our ships

     _ _ _ they took our lands

     _ _ _ they impressed our sailors

i. The first president to belong to the Democratic party was

     _ _ _ George Washington

     _ _ _ John Adams

     _ _ _ Thomas Jefferson

j. We did not want a war with France

     _ _ _ because we liked the French people

     _ _ _ because France had helped us in the Revolution

     _ _ _ because France had a larger navy than we had

2. *Here is a list of words: painter, poet, history writer, story writer. Select one word at a time and write it in the right blank below:*

     Benjamin West was a _ _ _ _.

     James Fenimore Cooper was a _ _ _ _ _ _ _ _.

     Washington Irving was a _ _ _ _ _ _ _ _.

     William Cullen Bryant was a _ _ _ _.

3. *What is the title of the sixth unit?*

ORGANIZATION OF THE UNIT AS A WHOLE

The teacher writes on the board the names of the stories in the unit, changing the order. The children are to number them correctly.

RECITATION OF THE UNIT AS A WHOLE

The children prepare to tell orally any of the stories above. In class one child tells the first story. If his story is unacceptable the teacher calls on someone else; if his story is acceptable he may call on another child to tell the next story, and so on to the end of the outline.

UNIT VII

HOW THE UNITED STATES MOVED WESTWARD
TO THE PACIFIC

I. The First Great Addition was the Land just West of the Mississippi.
  1. Very early, people had begun to go over the mountains.
  2. The vast Louisiana country was bought.
  3. Roads and canals were necessary to reach unsettled parts of the country.
  4. Steamboats made travel easier and faster.
  5. Railroads reached parts of the country which steamboats could not.
  6. Huge farms in the new lands demanded new machinery and methods.
  7. Life in the new regions was full of adventure.
  8. Andrew Jackson was the first great man from the West.
  9. Florida was bought from Spain.
II. In Reaching the Pacific Trouble arose with Other Nations.
  1. Texas became part of the United States.
  2. There was war with Mexico over the question of Texas.
  3. Gold was discovered in California.
  4. Oregon became part of the United States.
  5. Alaska was added later.

PREPARATION FOR THE OVERVIEW

"Have you ever traveled on a steamboat? In what way does it differ from a sailboat? Why would it, then, be better for trading purposes?

"Have you ever seen a pack horse? Why would traveling by pack horses be slow work?

"What is a reaper and binder? Does a man have to help to operate one, or will it run entirely by itself? Then in what way is it a labor saver?"

Recall the main points in the story of Daniel Boone.

"Show on the map the western boundary of the United States at the close of the Revolution. Do you know how far the United States extends today?

"Our story for today is the story of how the United States obtained all the land from the Mississippi to the Pacific Ocean and what things helped people to settle the countless square miles of this new territory."

348

PRESENTATION OR OVERVIEW

You remember from our study of the early days of the colonies that a few people had already gone west of the mountains. Some went by land through the gaps in the mountains, but their progress was very slow. They had to travel on foot or on horseback and to cut their roads through the forest as they advanced. Others went by way of the Ohio River, but traveling on a raft in a wide, swift river is dangerous. Nevertheless people kept coming and coming until some of them lived even as far away as the banks of the Mississippi River. They were few in number, however, and lived many miles apart.

There was one great difficulty which these people met. Another nation owned the mouth of the Mississippi River (*showing at the map*). Sometimes they would let the Americans come down the river in their boats (*illustrating the route*) and sometimes they would not. Not being able to ship their goods out of the interior troubled the western Americans very much. What could be done about it? At last America decided to buy the land which the other nation owned west of the Mississippi (*show on a map*). We had a great deal of land of our own and did not need more, but we did need to own all the territory along both sides of the river.

Then we had more land that we could use. How could our people ever travel into the new country? At first we began to build roads and canals, but that was slow work and very expensive. An American inventor then had a brilliant idea: he would make a boat which would run by steam, which could go up rivers as well as down, and which would not have to wait, as sailboats do, for a favorable wind. And he did. All the country which was near to rivers could be settled easily after that.

All lands, however, are not near rivers and lakes. What could be done to settle the great plains, far from the water? Other Americans said, "Let us put rails down on the ground and run an engine on them, just as the steamboat runs in the water." Almost everyone believed that it couldn't be done, but the inventors tried their plan, and it worked. Soon railroads were built which reached many parts of the country.

Then any man could go West and take up as large a farm as he wanted. Many did. But to take up a huge farm is one thing, and to find men to work it is another thing altogether. There were no men to be hired in the new land. Who would do the work? Again Americans racked their brains to solve the problem. At last one of them said, "Since we can't get workmen, let us make a machine that will do a man's work." Others asked, "How can a machine work like a man?" But reapers and binders, which were invented, did work, not only as well as a man but as well as twenty men. Thus immense quantities of food could be raised, and lands were settled faster.

By this time the United States was near to the region we today call Texas (*showing at the map*). Texas belonged to Mexico, but many Americans from the surrounding country (*pointing to the states of the South*) wanted to go on into Texas and take up land there too. So they went, even though the land belonged to Mexico. They didn't get along very well with the Mexicans. War followed. Texas became independent of Mexico, and soon afterwards was added to the United States. How the country was spreading out!

Naturally, Mexico did not like to lose Texas, and a war broke out between her and the United States. We were much stronger than she was. Therefore we won. At the close of the war Mexico had to give us still more land (*illustrating at the map*). At last we had reached the Pacific coast.

Instead of remaining a struggling nation of thirteen states hugging the Atlantic, we had swept clear across the continent to the Pacific. Not only had we added territory, but we knew how to build steamboats and railroads by means of which to travel to the new lands. We had machines to work for us, so that we could farm in that vast territory. All that we needed was people, and soon they came in a great rush from all the corners of the earth. We call this onsweep of people toward the west the westward movement.

PRESENTATION TEST

1. *Check the two best answers:*

The early ways of traveling west of the mountains were
_ _ _ by railway
_ _ _ by automobile
_ _ _ by way of the Ohio River
_ _ _ through gaps in the mountains

2. *Check the one best answer:*

We had to buy the land west of the Mississippi
_ _ _ because another nation owned the mouth of the river
_ _ _ because we needed more land
_ _ _ because our president wanted it

3. *Check the two best answers:*

In order to travel into the new country, Americans had to invent
_ _ _ railways   _ _ _ canals
_ _ _ roads   _ _ _ steamboats

4. *Check the one best answer:*

a. The binder was invented
_ _ _ because men did not like to do farm work
_ _ _ because the farms were too big for a few men to work
_ _ _ because inventors needed money

b. Texas had belonged to
_ _ _ France
_ _ _ the United States
_ _ _ Mexico

c. After the war with Mexico
_ _ _ Mexico had to give the United States much land
_ _ _ the United States had to give Mexico much land
_ _ _ no land changed owners

I. THE FIRST GREAT ADDITION WAS THE LAND JUST WEST OF THE MISSISSIPPI

1. *Very early, People had begun to go over the Mountains*

Preparation

Show the Wilderness Road. Show what parts of the country could be reached by way of the Ohio.

Show pictures of a flatboat. "What disadvantages were there in traveling on this kind of boat?"

Show how far westward settlement had progressed by the close of the French and Indian War [1]; by 1790.[2]

No additional presentation is needed.

---

[1] Sanford American History Map No. 5.   [2] Ibid. No. 12.

Assimilation

Readings

Upper Group

BLAISDELL. The Story of American History, 314–316, 339–340.
BRIGHAM. From Trail to Railway, 67–70.
CATHERWOOD. Rocky Fork.
GORDY. Stories of Later American History, 187.
HART. How our Grandfathers Lived, 97–98, 109–113.
LOGIE. From Columbus to Lincoln, 114–122.
MCMURRY. Pioneers of the Mississippi Valley, 150–169.
MARSHALL. The Story of Human Progress, 237–240 (difficult).
MOWRY. American Inventions and Inventors, 187–206.
OTIS. Benjamin of Ohio.
PERRY and PRICE. American History, II : 113–114, 235–236.
TAPPAN. Elementary History of our Country, 185–186, 189.
VOLLINTINE. The Making of America, 14–16, 75–91, 106–115, 120–130.

Average Group

BARNES. Elementary History of the United States, 215–220.
BEARD and BAGLEY. A First Book in American History, 163–164.
BEEBY. How the World grows Smaller, 20–32, 98–107.
FORMAN. First Lessons in American History, 189, 192–193.
GORDY. Elementary History of the United States, 196–198, 217.
INGRAHAM. The Story of Democracy, 215–221.
MORRIS. Primary History of the United States, 204.
NIDA. Following Columbus, 282–283.
NIDA. Following the Frontier, 39–48, 52–53, 55–62, 191–195.
SOUTHWORTH. Builders of our Country, II : 135–136.
STONE and FICKETT. Days and Deeds a Hundred Years Ago, 16–35, 68–77.

Lower Group

EDSON-LAING. Readers, IV : 109–113.
FAIRGRIEVE and YOUNG. The World, 16–20.
MCMASTER. Primary History of the United States, 161–163, 169–170.

Teachers

BOGART. Economic History of the United States, 156–158, 189–195.
GARRISON. Westward Extension, 3–21.
HART. American History told by Contemporaries, II : 383–393.
HULBERT. Paths of Inland Commerce, 44–53.
MUZZEY. An American History, 191–193.
MUZZEY. The United States of America, I : 290–294.
RUGG and SCHWEPPE. The Westward Movement and the Growth of Transportation, 16–24.
SKINNER. Pioneers of the Old Southwest, 1–30.
TURNER. Rise of the New West, chaps. v, vi.

Minimal Essentials

Name of Place: **Wilderness Road**
Historical Terms: **"dark and bloody ground"; flatboat; frontier; pack horse**
Things to Remember

Some early pioneers traveled by way of the Ohio River.
Others went through gaps in the mountains, and settled in the valleys.

Illustrative Material

Chronicles of America Photoplays, Yale University Press: The Frontier Woman.
Society for Visual Education. Picturol: The First Westward Movement.
Society for Visual Education. Schoolfilm: Breaking through the Appalachians; Settling the Ohio Valley.

Procedure during Assimilation

Reading as described on pages 24–29.
Picture study based on the illustrative material listed above.
Make a picture collection of flatboats, rafts, keel boats; of stagecoaches and Conestoga wagons.
The teacher may read to the class some of the source materials listed under references for teachers.
A special report is given to the class by children who have read Otis's *Benjamin of Ohio.*
Illustrate on the sand table the construction of a corduroy road.
The boys in manual training may make a flatboat.
Make a map showing the Wilderness Road[1]; the Ohio River route.[2]
Drill on minimal essentials.
Objective test.

Organization

The teacher and the pupils working together make an outline somewhat as follows:

The First Wave of the Westward Movement

1. By way of the Wilderness Road
2. By way of the Ohio River
3. Other routes
4. Methods of travel

Recitation

Children tell what points belong under each heading and then give three-minute talks on each.

2. *The Vast Louisiana Country was Bought*

Preparation

Show the boundaries of the United States at the end of the Revolution.

"Who was George Rogers Clark?

"What country had owned the land west of the Mississippi and at the mouth of the river?

---

[1] Muzzey, D. S., *An American History*, p. 195.
[2] Woodburn, J. A., and Moran, T. F., *Elementary American History and Government*, p. 91.

"Why would the Americans in the new land west of the mountains have to send out their products by boat? Trace the routes they would use.

"Why would they not like to have Spain own the mouth of the Mississippi? Sometimes Spain made our goods pay a tax at New Orleans in order to pass through, and sometimes she did not."

Presentation

Just at this time, while the Americans were very bitter toward Spain because our boats could not pass down the Mississippi whenever they wanted to, Spain gave all this vast tract of land (*illustrating at the map*) to France. Then things were worse than ever. We had never really been afraid of Spain as a neighbor, but we were afraid of France. Her ruler was a very strong and powerful man who had conquered most of Europe. Therefore the United States was troubled. Would he try to conquer us too, now that he was so near us?

President Jefferson sent a man to France to see if we might not buy the land at the mouth of the Mississippi. We already had all the territory we needed, but if we owned both sides of the mouth of the river (*illustrating at the map*) we could then control it and decide who could and who could not go up and down the river.

The ruler of France did not want to sell what we might call just the front yard of his American territory (*illustrating*), because the back yard (*illustrating*) would be of little value to him if its people could not get out to the sea. So he said to us: "If you want any of this land, you will have to buy it all. The northern part alone is of no use to me." We replied: "So much land as that would be only a burden to us; we don't need it and haven't enough money to pay for it. We want only the southern part." But France was firm: "All or none."

We bought it all, and found that the new land was as large as all that we had had before. Our story today tells us of some men who explored the new region, guided by an Indian woman, and of their thrilling adventures. One of them was a brother of George Rogers Clark.

PRESENTATION TEST

Check the best answer:

a. In the early days the land west of the Mississippi belonged to

    _ _ _ Spain
    _ _ _ France
    _ _ _ England

b. She gave it to

    _ _ _ Spain
    _ _ _ France
    _ _ _ England

c. We did not like to have any other country own the land at the mouth of the river

    _ _ _ because they could keep our boats from going up and down the river
    _ _ _ because they would have more land than we did
    _ _ _ because they would make war on us

d. We wanted to buy

    _ _ _ the land east of the river
    _ _ _ all the land
    _ _ _ the land at the mouth of the river

e. We had to buy

    _ _ _ the land east of the river
    _ _ _ all the land
    _ _ _ the land at the mouth of the river

Assimilation

Readings

Upper Group

BLAISDELL. The Story of American History, 340–342.
BURNHAM. Hero Tales from History, 247–258.
COE. Makers of the Nation, 198–212.
DAKIN. Great Rivers of the World, 78–79, 108–110.
DAVIDSON. Founders and Builders of our Nation, 114–115.
EVANS. America First, 244–259.
FAIRBANKS. The Western United States, 151–161.
FARIS. Real Stories from our History, 100–109.
FARIS. Real Stories of the Geography Makers, 248–255.
GORDY. Leaders in Making America, 255–263.
GORDY. Stories of Later American History, 170–180.
LEFFERTS. American Leaders, I: 276–288.
LOGIE. From Columbus to Lincoln, 175–180.
MONTGOMERY. Beginners' American History, 168–170.
PERRY and PRICE. American History, II: 85–88.
ROOSEVELT. Stories of the Great West, 69–94.
TAPPAN. Elementary History of our Country, 175–176.
VOLLINTINE. The Making of America, 130–144.
WOODBURN and MORAN. Makers of America, 195–207.
Compton's Pictured Encyclopedia (Louisiana Purchase, Lewis and Clark Expedition).
Southern Stories retold from *St. Nicholas*, 28–33.
World Book (Louisiana Purchase, Lewis and Clark Expedition).

Average Group

BARNES. Elementary History of the United States, 238–239.
BEARD and BAGLEY. A First Book in American History, 164–179.
EGGLESTON. Stories of Great Americans, 90–96.
ELSON and MACMULLAN. Story of our Country, II : 26–31.
FORMAN. First Lessons in American History, 202–205.
GORDY. Elementary History of the United States, 202–206.
MACE. Primary History, 278–280, 324–329.
MOWRY. First Steps in the History of our Country, 179–184.
NIDA. Following the Frontier, 217–237.
SOUTHWORTH. Builders of our Country, II : 113–114.
TAPPAN. American Hero Stories, 207–216.
UHRBROCK and OWENS. Famous Americans, 158–166.

Lower Group

BARNES. Primary History of the United States, 127–128.
MCMASTER. Primary History of the United States, 163–165.

Teachers

CHANNING. The Jeffersonian System, 60–99.
COMAN. Industrial History of the United States, 170–174.
HART. American History told by Contemporaries, III : 363–384.
HART. Formation of the Union, 185–187.
HOCKETT. Political and Social History of the United States, 187–190, 278–286.
JOHNSON. Jefferson and his Colleagues, 58–75.
MUZZEY. An American History, 175–178.
MUZZEY. The United States of America, I : 212–221.
RUGG and SCHWEPPE. The Westward Movement and the Growth of Transportation, 66–71.
Elementary School Journal, XVII : 627, 637–640, 644–645.
Public School Methods, V : 263–273. (The Methods Co., Chicago.)

Minimal Essentials

Names of Persons: **Lewis** and **Clark**; **Thomas Jefferson**
Names of Places: **Missouri River**; **Rocky Mountains**
Date: **1803** — purchase of Louisiana
Historical Terms: **purchase**; **territory**
Things to Remember

We wanted only the land at the mouth of the Mississippi.
The Louisiana Purchase was as large as all the rest of the United States put together.
The West became as important as the older East.

Illustrative Material

Society for Visual Education. Picturol : The Louisiana Purchase.
Society for Visual Education. Schoolfilm : Louisiana Purchase and Lewis and Clark Expedition.

Procedure during Assimilation

Reading as described on pages 24–29.
Picture study based on the illustrative material listed above.
Write coöperatively a class diary of Sacajawea, the "Bird Woman."[1]

[1] Schultz, J. W., *The Bird Woman.*

Trace on the map the route of the Lewis and Clark expedition.[1]
Begin to make a map entitled "Territorial Growth of the United States." Show the states that have since been made from the Louisiana purchase.[2]
Children cut out the exercise suggested on pages 187–189 of Eggleston's *First Book in American History.*
Drill on minimal essentials.
Objective test.

Organization

The class makes a coöperative outline with as little help from the teacher as possible.

THE LOUISIANA PURCHASE

1. Why we wanted to buy the land
2. Why France decided to sell
3. Extent and importance of the purchase
4. Exploring expeditions

Recitation

The stories are told before the entire school assembly on Jefferson's birthday, April 13.

3. *Roads and Canals were necessary to reach Unsettled Parts of the Country*

Preparation

Show the children a map of the roads in 1800.[3] Notice what parts of the country were untouched. Call attention to the National (or Cumberland) Road.[4]

"Suppose a road were to be built from the upper Ohio River to Lake Erie through the new lands. Who would pay for it?" (Question of improvements at national or state expense.)

"Do you know which is cheaper: to transport heavy goods a long way by land or by water?"

Have modeled in the sand table the region from New York to Lake Erie, showing the Mohawk River valley. Children

---

[1] Woodburn, J. A., and Moran, T. F., *Elementary American History and Government,* p. 266; Stephenson, N. W., *An American History,* pp. 272–273.
[2] Muzzey, D. S., *An American History,* pp. 178–179.
[3] Sanford American History Map No. 11.
[4] Lawler, T. B., *Essentials of American History,* p. 285.

decide where a canal should be dug to connect the Hudson River and Lake Erie. Then verify by a map.[1]
No additional presentation is needed.

Assimilation
Readings
Upper Group

BRIGHAM. From Trail to Railway, 40–52, 87–97.
COE. Makers of the Nation, 241–245.
EVANS. America First, 278–282.
FARIS. Real Stories from our History, 110–115, 134–168.
FOOTE and SKINNER. Makers and Defenders of America, 219–223.
GORDY. Leaders in Making America, 275–278.
GORDY. Stories of Later American History, 194–198.
HART. How our Grandfathers Lived, 102–104.
LEFFERTS. American Leaders, II : 38–51.
MARSHALL. The Story of Human Progress, 240–246 (difficult).
MOWRY. American Inventions and Inventors, 215–222.
PERRY and PRICE. American History, II : 111–114.
ROCHELEAU. Great American Industries : Transportation, 31, 34–41, 125–129.
ROCHELEAU. Primitive Travel and Transportation.
TAPPAN. Elementary History of our Country, 189–191.
TAPPAN. Travelers and Traveling, 89–93.
VOLLINTINE. The Making of America, 151–162.
WOODBURN and MORAN. Makers of America, 211–212, 215–220.
Compton's Pictured Encyclopedia (Roads, Canals).

Average Group

BEARD and BAGLEY. A First Book in American History, 212–213, 224–227.
BEEBY. How the World grows Smaller, 74–80.
ELSON and MacMULLAN. Story of our Country, II : 78–80, 94–98.
FORMAN. First Lessons in American History, 214–218.
GORDY. American Leaders and Heroes, 246–252.
GORDY. Elementary History of the United States, 190–192, 219–221.
NIDA. Following the Frontier, 149–153, 164–178, 201–203.
SOUTHWORTH. Builders of our Country, II : 176–179.
STONE and FICKETT. Days and Deeds a Hundred Years Ago, 94–102.
UHRBROCK and OWENS. Famous Americans, 223–229.

Lower Group

DAVIDSON and ANDERSON. Lincoln Readers, IV : 51–57, 181–187.
FAIRGRIEVE and YOUNG. The World, 20–27.
McMASTER. Primary History of the United States, 170–171.

Teachers

BOGART. Economic History of the United States, 205–216.
COMAN. Industrial History of the United States, 166–170, 216–222.
DUNBAR. History of Travel in America, II : 691–716.
HART. Formation of the Union, 227–229.

[1] Gordy, W. F., *History of the United States*, p. 243; Stephenson, N. W., *An American History*, p. 292.

Hockett. Political and Social History of the United States, 347–353.
Hulbert. Paths of Inland Commerce, 53–80.
Muzzey. An American History, 194–197.
Muzzey. The United States of America, I : 294–300.
Rugg and Schweppe. The Westward Movement and the Growth of Transportation, 58–62, 139–167, 180–190.
Turner. Rise of the New West, 96–106, 224–235.
Elementary School Journal, XVII : 641–642.
Normal Instructor and Primary Plans, pp. 38–39 (May, 1918) (lesson plan for teaching the Erie Canal).

Minimal Essentials

Name of Person: **De Witt Clinton**
Names of Places: **Erie Canal; National Road**
Historical Terms: **canal; turnpike**
Things to Remember

Roads had to be built so that the people of the East could send their products to the West, and the people of the West could send their products to the East.

Canals made it possible to travel faster, and thus made the price of goods cheaper.

Illustrative Material

Canal Map of the State of New York, State Engineer and Surveyor, Albany, New York. (Free map and accompanying booklet, *Story of New York State Canals.*)
Ford Educational Library : 34, A Century of Progress, Part I.
Mentor, XIII : 39–42 (September, 1925).
Society for Visual Education. Picturol : Canals.
Society for Visual Education. Schoolfilm : Canals in United States History.
World Book (Canals).

Procedure during Assimilation

Reading as described on pages 24–29.
Picture study based on the illustrative material listed above.
The teacher may read to the class some of the accounts of early travelers. (See references for teachers.)
The children themselves suggest means that could be provided to solve the transportation difficulties.[1]
Make a sand-table representation of a canal, showing how locks operate.
Show graphs of the movements of population.[2]
Show on a map the National Road [3] and the Erie Canal.[4]
How did the expression "low bridge" originate.
Drill on minimal essentials.
Objective test.

[1] Parker, S. C., *Types of Elementary Teaching and Learning*, p. 208.
[2] Rugg, H., and Schweppe, E., *The Westward Movement and the Growth of Transportation*, pp. 60–61.
[3] Gordy, W. F., *History of the United States*, p. 238; Lawler, T. B., *Essentials of American History*, p. 285.
[4] Woodburn, J. A., and Moran, T. F., *Elementary American History and Government*, p. 251; Stephenson, N. W., *An American History*, p. 292.

Organization

The teacher gives the class the following outline:

HOW TO REACH THE NEW COUNTRY

1. The building of roads
2. The making of canals
   The Erie Canal

Recitation

Each child chooses one of the topics above and prepares a speech, illustrating his talk by pictures or construction work.

4. *Steamboats made Travel Easier and Faster*

Preparation

Turn to a map of the United States, showing the original forested area.[1] "Why would it be very slow work to wait for the building of roads before settling this area? Even if a canal were made, for example, from Lake Michigan to the Des Plaines River, how would the boats have to be moved? What is the quickest way to travel by water? What advantages would a steamboat have over a sailboat?"

Presentation

For years people in different parts of the world had been playing with the idea of making a boat that would run by steam. Men in France, England, and other countries had made steamboats, but always something happened to them. Sometimes the machinery would be so heavy that the boat would sink; sometimes it would make the ship break in two. But even those steamships worked well enough each time they failed so that some other man would say: "The idea is right. Boats can be made to run by steam. I'm going to try to build one a different way."

The first man who made a steamboat that would work well enough to earn money was an American, Robert Fulton (*pointing to the name on the board*). Our story today tells how

[1] Sanford American History Map No. 11.

he built his boat and how people laughed at him, but how he finally succeeded.

You can see immediately what a great difference the steamboat made in the methods of traveling. No more rowing, no more waiting for a favorable wind, no more going downstream only because it was too hard work to go upstream. In a few years there were steamboats on all the rivers and on the Great Lakes.

You can see, too, how much easier it then was to settle the West. Instead of making the long weary journey overland in a wagon, or instead of running the danger of being upset from a flatboat, a pioneer could load his household goods into a steamer, sit comfortably with his family on the deck, and arrive soon at the place where he was to make his new home.

Since the journey could be made in fewer days, it no longer cost so much to move goods, and prices became cheaper.

For example, men who worked on the boat had to be paid for only one week for the same journey that had formerly taken four weeks. So the wheat and corn the boats carried could be sold cheaper.

PRESENTATION TEST

1. *Check the best answer:*

   a. Fulton

   _ _ _ was the first man who ever built a steamboat

   _ _ _ was not the first man who ever built a steamboat

   b. Fulton

   _ _ _ was the first man who built any boat

   _ _ _ was the first man who built a steamboat that would run well enough to earn money

   _ _ _ was the first man to make a steam engine

2. *Check two answers:*

   a. A steamboat was better than a sailboat because it

   _ _ _ did not have to wait for the wind to blow

   _ _ _ looked better

   _ _ _ could go upstream as well as downstream

   _ _ _ did not cost so much to build a steamboat

   b. The steamboat helped to settle the West faster

   _ _ _ because people had never liked sailboats

   _ _ _ because it was an easier method of traveling to the West

   _ _ _ because it cost less to send goods by steamer

   _ _ _ because all the people of the East moved West

Assimilation

Readings

Upper Group

BACHMAN. Great Inventors and their Inventions, 25–49.
BEARD and BAGLEY. Our Old World Background, 328–329.
BURNHAM. Hero Tales from History, 270–273.
CHANDLER and CHITWOOD. Makers of American History, 187–191.
COE. Makers of the Nation, 225–232.
DARROW. Thinkers and Doers, 67–75 (difficult).
DAVIDSON. Founders and Builders of our Nation, 130–136.
EGGLESTON. A First Book in American History, 141–145.
FARIS. Real Stories from our History, 220–249.
FOOTE and SKINNER. Makers and Defenders of America, 213–218.
GORDY. Leaders in Making America, 269–275.
GORDY. Stories of Later American History, 187–193.
HART. How our Grandfathers Lived, 99–102.
LEFFERTS. American Leaders, II : 16–37.
MARSHALL. The Story of Human Progress, 246–248 (difficult).
MONTGOMERY. Beginners' American History, 171–178.
MOWRY. American Inventions and Inventors, 207–214.
PERRY and PRICE. American History, II : 109–111.
ROCHELEAU. Great American Industries : Transportation, 65–71.
ROCHELEAU. The Story of Ships and Shipping, 18–23.
RUGG and SCHWEPPE. The Westward Movement and the Growth of Transportation, 170–179.
STIMPSON. Child's Book of American Biography, 106–115.
TOWLE. Heroes and Martyrs of Invention, 160–169.
VOLLINTINE. The Making of America, 145–150.
Compton's Pictured Encyclopedia (Fulton).
Flanagan Publishing Company. The Story of Steam, 14–18.
World Book (Fulton).

Average Group

BARNES. Elementary History of the United States, 250–258.
BEARD and BAGLEY. A First Book in American History, 220–224.
BEEBY. How the World grows Smaller, 91–97.
EGGLESTON. Stories of Great Americans, 99–101.
ELSON and MacMULLAN. Story of our Country, II : 41–46.
FORMAN. First Lessons in American History, 193–194.
GORDY. Elementary History of the United States, 217–219.
MACE. Primary History, 337–340.
McFEE. Stories of American Inventions, 14–28.
MOWRY. First Steps in the History of our Country, 186–191.
NIDA. Following the Frontier, 155–162, 179–190.
PARKMAN. Conquests of Invention, 222–241.
PERRY. Four American Inventors, 11–69.
STONE and FICKETT. Days and Deeds a Hundred Years Ago, 78–93.
SOUTHWORTH. Builders of our Country, II : 127–134.
UHRBROCK and OWENS. Famous Americans, 215–220.

Lower Group

BALDWIN. Fifty Famous People, 146–149.
CHAMBERLAIN. How we Travel, 161–170.

COLEMAN, UHL, and HOSIC. Pathway to Reading, III : 216–221.
DYER and BRADY. Merrill Readers, V : 117–121.
ETTINGER, SHIMER, and O'REGAN. Progressive Road to Silent Reading, IV : 142–146.
McMASTER. Primary History of the United States, 171–172.

Teachers

BOGART. Economic History of the United States, 195–198.
DUNBAR. History of Travel in America, II : 341–414.
GIBSON. Romance of Modern Manufacture, 299–312.
HULBERT. Paths of Inland Commerce, 100–115, 154–195.
PARKER. Types of Elementary Teaching and Learning, 204–211.
THOMPSON. Age of Invention, 57–68.
Historical Outlook, IX : 490–492.
Public School Methods, V : 285–295. (The Methods Co., Chicago.)

Minimal Essentials

Name of Person: **Robert Fulton**
Date : 1807 — Fulton's steamboat
Historical Term: Clermont (klĕr′mŏnt)
Things to Remember
Boats run by steam could go up rivers as well as down and did not have to wait for the wind.
People could reach the new land by going up the rivers in steamboats.

Illustrative Material

GABRIEL (ED.). Pageant of America, V : 85.
McKINLEY. Illustrated Topics for American History : S. 26 ; S. 30.
Keystone Views : 108, *Clermont* and Albany ; 109, Typical End-Wheeler on the Mississippi.
Society for Visual Education. Picturol : Steamboats.
Society for Visual Education. Schoolfilm : The Steamboat in United States History.

Procedure during Assimilation

Reading as described on pages 24–29.
Picture study based on the illustrative material listed above.
Use the following dramatization : "The Trial Trip of the *Clermont*." Hubbard, *Little American History Plays*, pp. 161–165.
Make a picture collection showing the development of the steamboat from Fulton's time to the present.[1]
Invite a traveler to Alaska to describe the wood-burning steamboats used on the Yukon River.
Drill on minimal essentials.
Objective test.

Organization

Children are left to themselves to work out an outline, which should include points somewhat similar to the following :

[1] Grant, Gordon, *Story of the Ship*.

THE STEAMBOAT

1. Early attempts at building a steamboat
2. Fulton's work
3. The steamboat on Western waters

Recitation

Divide the class into groups of three or four each; the members of each group tell to each other the complete story.

5. *Railroads reached Parts of the Country which Steamboats could not*

Preparation

Turn to the physical map of the United States. "What parts of our country could not be easily reached by steamboats? Would it be easy to build roads to reach them?"

Presentation

Cities which were built on rivers were very glad when steamboats were built. Their people could travel into the West cheaply, and they could buy at a low price goods that came from the West.

Other cities, however, particularly those which were not built on rivers leading into the interior, were much troubled. The steamboat was not helping them at all; in fact, they were losing their trade. One of these cities was Baltimore.

Some of its citizens said: "Have you ever seen the kind of cars they have at some of the mines and the kind they have at the ends of the canals? Let us lay some rails on the ground and run similar cars on the rails." They studied the question, and found that a Britisher had already made a steam engine that would draw cars; so they built a railroad which extended a few miles outside of Baltimore, and tried out his idea. It proved to be a success. Within a few years many more railways were built. They reached sections of the country to which steamboats could not go, and thus helped in settlement. Indeed, it is scarcely too much to say that the railroads made the settlement of the West possible.

PRESENTATION TEST

Check the best answer:

a. Cities which were not helped by the steamboat in their trade with the West were

_ _ _ the cities located on rivers
_ _ _ the cities which were not located on rivers

b. The steam engine was invented by

_ _ _ an Irishman   _ _ _ a Frenchman
_ _ _ a Britisher

c. The first important railroad in America was built near the city of

_ _ _ New York   _ _ _ Boston
_ _ _ Baltimore

d. The railroads helped in the settlement of the West

_ _ _ because they went faster than steamboats
_ _ _ because they could reach almost all parts of the country
_ _ _ because there were more railroads than steamboats

Assimilation

Readings

Upper Group

BACHMAN. Great Inventors and their Inventions, 50–71.
BEARD and BAGLEY. Our Old World Background, 323–328, 329–330.
BRIGHAM. From Trail to Railway, 53–56, 98–106.
COE. Makers of the Nation, 233–240.
DARROW. Thinkers and Doers, 57–67, 75–82 (difficult).
FARIS. Real Stories from our History, 250–282.
FARIS. Where our History was Made, Book II, 268–275.
FOOTE and SKINNER. Makers and Defenders of America, 223–229.
GORDY. Leaders in Making America, 278–281.
GORDY. Stories of Later American History, 198–201.
LEFFERTS. American Leaders, II : 52–67.
MARSHALL. The Story of Human Progress, 248–254 (difficult).
MOWRY. American Inventions and Inventors, 223–228.
PERRY and PRICE. American History, II : 114–116.
ROCHELEAU. Great American Industries : Transportation, 148–157.
STONE and FICKETT. Days and Deeds a Hundred Years Ago, 112–121.
TAPPAN. Elementary History of our Country, 191–192.
TAPPAN. Travelers and Traveling, 1–14.
TERRY. History Stories of Other Lands, VI : 191–202.
TOWLE. Heroes and Martyrs of Invention, 141–159.
UHRBROCK and OWENS. Famous Americans, 230–237.
WOODBURN and MORAN. Makers of America, 220–224.
Compton's Pictured Encyclopedia (Railroads).
Flanagan Publishing Company. The Story of Steam, 3–5, 7–11, 19–28.
World Book (Railroads: Early Railroads).

Average Group

BEARD and BAGLEY. A First Book in American History, 227–228.
BEEBY. How the World grows Smaller, 145–153.
ELSON and MACMULLAN. Story of our Country, II : 98–102.
FORMAN. First Lessons in American History, 219.
GORDY. Elementary History of the United States, 229–230.

NIDA. Following the Frontier, 205–214.
SOUTHWORTH. Builders of our Country, II : 136–139.

Lower Group

DAVIDSON and ANDERSON. Lincoln Readers, IV : 171–173.
McMASTER. Primary History of the United States, 172.
SMITH. The Railroad Book.
VAN SICKLE and SIEGMILLER. Riverside Readers, II : 107–113.

Teachers

BOGART. Economic History of the United States, 216–219.
COMAN. Industrial History of the United States, 222–225.
GIBSON. Romance of Modern Manufacture, 285–298.
HART. American History told by Contemporaries, III : 561–563.
HULBERT. Paths of Inland Commerce, 134–153.
MOODY. Railroad Builders, 1–19.
RUGG and SCHWEPPE. The Westward Movement and the Growth of Transportation, 191–205.
THOMPSON. Age of Invention, 69–83.

Minimal Essentials

Name of Place: **Baltimore**
Date: **1830** — beginning of the era of railroad building
Historical Terms: **locomotive; transportation; era; Baltimore and Ohio**
Things to Remember
Many of the Western lands were far from rivers.
To reach them, people began to build railroads.
Then the country was settled rapidly.

Illustrative Material

LEHMANN. Historical Pictures : L. H. 225, The First Railroad.
McKINLEY. Illustrated Topics for American History : S. 26.
McKINLEY. Illustrated Topics for Mediæval and Modern History : M. M. 26.
Keystone Views : 112, One of the First Railway Trains.
Society for Visual Education. Picturol : Railroads.
Society for Visual Education. Schoolfilm : Railroads in United States History.

Procedure during Assimilation

Reading as described on pages 24–29.
Picture study based on the illustrative material listed above.
Make a picture collection showing the development of the railroad from earliest times to the present. Show pictures from railway folders illustrating the luxuries of a modern transcontinental line.
Invite an old resident to tell of the changes that have occurred in railway transportation within his memory ; a European traveler to tell how trains in Europe differ from ours.
Children write a story of the early railroad.[1]
Show a railway map of your own state to find out which parts are not yet reached by a railway.
Drill on minimal essentials.
Objective test.

[1] *The Nineteenth Yearbook of the National Society for the Study of Education,* Part I, pp. 71–73.

Organization

Children make their own outlines and then choose the best to record on the board.

THE BEGINNING OF RAILROAD BUILDING

1. Early attempts to build locomotives
2. Early railroads in America
3. The effect of the railroad on the settlement of the West

Recitation

Children write for the school newspaper the story of the railroad.

6. *Huge Farms in the New Lands demanded New Machinery and Methods*

Preparation

"For what occupation was most of the land in the Middle West (*illustrating at the map*) best suited? About what farming implements did we read in our stories of the colonists?

"Have any of you seen the kinds of implements used on large farms today? Describe them. What are they called?"

Presentation

When men went West and took up tracts of land to make farms for themselves, there was so much land that they could have very large farms. However, they could not plant all their fields, because they did not have men enough to do the work. They could not hire their neighbors, because every neighbor had his own farm. How they did wish they could get help!

The cities in the East were growing amazingly too. You know that city people cannot raise their own food, so they kept calling to the farmers in the West: "Send us corn and wheat and rye. We need food." The farmers did not know what to do. There in the East, waiting for them, was a market in which they could sell a great many products, but they could not raise so much food without help.

An inventor set to work on the problem. He thought: "I cannot find workmen for the farmers, but I will try to make a machine which will do some of the hard work that men have always had to do for themselves. In this way the machine will take the place of a man."

One of the farm processes that had taken a long time to perform was the cutting of grain when it was ripe. The cutting was done by a sickle or a cradle. The inventor made a machine called a reaper which would cut in one day as much grain as many men could. This machine was equal to a large number of hired men; therefore more work could be done, and the farms became larger yet. Afterwards more and more farm work was done by machinery.

PRESENTATION TEST

Check the best answer:

a. Farmers in the West took up much land

     _ _ _ because they had much money
     _ _ _ because there was so much free land
     _ _ _ because they liked to work hard

b. They could not raise crops on all their land

     _ _ _ because they could not buy seed
     _ _ _ because part of the land was not good
     _ _ _ because they could not get enough help

c. There was not enough food grown for the farmers themselves and for the people

     _ _ _ in small towns
     _ _ _ in the big cities
     _ _ _ in the country

d. An inventor helped the farmers

     _ _ _ by making a machine to do man's work
     _ _ _ by giving them still more land
     _ _ _ by buying their crops when they were ripe

Assimilation

Readings

Upper Group

BACHMAN. Great Inventors and their Inventions, 142–160.
BURNHAM. Hero Tales from History, 279–282.
CHANDLER and CHITWOOD. Makers of American History, 251–254.
COE. Makers of the Nation, 356–360.
DARROW. Boys' Own Book of Great Inventions, 232–235.
DARROW. Thinkers and Doers, 160–170 (difficult).
DAVIDSON. Founders and Builders of our Nation, 145–151.
FOOTE and SKINNER. Makers and Defenders of America, 305–308.
LEFFERTS. American Leaders, II: 68–80.
MOWRY. American Inventions and Inventors, 111–123.

SANFORD. The Story of Agriculture in the United States, 100–123, 144–158 (difficult).
TAPPAN. Heroes of Progress, 20–29.
Compton's Pictured Encyclopedia (McCormick, Reaping Machines).
World Book (McCormick, Reaping Machines).

Average Group

BALDWIN. Fourth Reader, 55–62.
BEARD and BAGLEY. A First Book in American History, 217–218.
FORMAN. First Lessons in American History, 240–242.
McFEE. Stories of American Inventions, 29–49.
NIDA. Following the Frontier, 196–200.
PARKMAN. Conquests of Invention, 8–26.
SOUTHWORTH. Builders of our Country, II : 249–251.
UHRBROCK and OWENS. Famous Americans, 239–247.

Lower Group

Try NIDA, FORMAN, and BALDWIN.

Teachers

SANFORD. The Story of Agriculture in the United States, 100–123, 144–158.
THOMPSON. Age of Invention, 110–127.
Teachers College Record, XVI : 357–365.

Minimal Essentials

Name of Person: **Cyrus McCormick** (mȧ kôr′mĭk)
Date: **1831** — McCormick's reaper
Historical Terms: **reaper; binder**
Things to Remember
The farms in the newer parts of the country were so large that not enough men could be found to do the work.
Then machines were invented to do farm work that men used to do.

Illustrative Material

GABRIEL (ED.). Pageant of America, III : 114–141, 207–210, 216–220.
McKINLEY. Illustrated Topics for American History : S. 28.
Keystone Views : 105, Cutting Wheat with Cradle ; 106, Harvesting Wheat with Reaper and Binder ; 295, Plowing ; 296, Modern American Harvesting Machine ; 297, Modern Harvester Cutting, Threshing, and Sacking the Grain.

Procedure during Assimilation

Reading as described on pages 24–29.
Picture study based on the illustrative material listed above.
A visit to the local museum to observe early farming implements ; to an implement store to observe modern equipment ; if possible, a visit to a farm to observe the apparatus in use.
Make a picture collection showing the development of farming machinery from the earliest times to the present.
Drill on minimal essentials.
Objective test.

Organization

The teacher and the class together produce the following outline, or one similar to it:

CHANGE IN METHODS OF FARMING

1. Early methods of harvesting
2. McCormick's invention
3. The effect on the settlement of the West

Recitation

Present the talks on the outline at a Parent-Teacher Association meeting.

7. *Life in the New Regions was full of Adventure*

No additional preparation and presentation are needed.

Assimilation

Readings

Upper Group

EVANS. America First, 260–264.
FARIS. Real Stories from our History, 116–120.
FARIS. Where our History was Made, Book II, 178–182, 276–279.
GORDY. Abraham Lincoln, 7–12.
GORDY. Leaders in Making America, 221–225.
HART. How our Grandfathers Lived, 143–153, 160–163.
HILL. Community Life and Civic Problems, 114–120.
PERRY and PRICE. American History, II: 238–240.
RUGG and SCHWEPPE. The Westward Movement and the Growth of Transportation, 77–91.
VOLLINTINE. The Making of America, 115–118, 163–169.
Lessons in Community and National Life, Series A, 19–26.

Average Group

BEARD and BAGLEY. A First Book in American History, 197.
EDSON-LAING. Readers, IV: 157–162, 185–192.
FLETCHER. Old Settler Stories.
GORDY. Elementary History of the United States, 198–202.
MORRIS. Primary History of the United States, 204–206.
NIDA. Following the Frontier, 63–76, 106–148.

Lower Group

BLAISDELL and BALL. American History for Little Folks, 109–114.
BLAISDELL and BALL. Child's Book of American History, 138–143.
BLAISDELL and BALL. Log Cabin Days, 19–23.
BLAISDELL and BALL. Pioneers of America.
DAVIDSON and ANDERSON. Lincoln Readers, IV: 17–20, 165–166.
HARTWELL. Story-Hour Readings, IV: 233–237.
MCMASTER. Primary History of the United States, 166–169.

Teachers

   CALLENDER. Economic History of the United States, 271–301, 597–641.
   DUNBAR. History of Travel in America, II: 656–690.
   HART. American History told by Contemporaries, III: 459–475, 509–530.
   OGG. The Old Northwest, 110–130.
   SKINNER. Pioneers of the Old Southwest, 31–89.
   TURNER. Rise of the New West, 84–92, 107–110.

Minimal Essentials

Historical Terms: **clearing; stockade; house-raising**
Something to Remember
   Each frontier village depended on itself for almost everything it needed.

Illustrative Material

GABRIEL (ED.). Pageant of America, III: 91–97, 106–111; XIII: 141–144.
MCKINLEY. Illustrated Topics for American History: S. 19.
Keystone Views: 103, A Log House.

Procedure during Assimilation

Reading as described on pages 24–29.
Picture study based on the illustrative material listed above.
Read to the children selected portions of Hamlin Garland's *Boy Life on the Prairie, A Son of the Middle Border, A Daughter of the Middle Border, Trail Makers of the Middle Border.*
Visit the local museum to observe relics of pioneer life.
Invite pioneers in your section to tell the children incidents of pioneer life.
Dramatize some of the pictures of pioneer life.[1]
Represent on the sand table [2] a pioneer settlement.
Make an illustrated booklet on pioneer life to present to the school library. Assign such topics as the following to various committees: pioneer homes, food, farm work, home work, amusements, schools, churches, travel, etc.
Children compose original poems on any phase of expansion or of pioneer life.
Drill on minimal essentials.
Objective test.

Organization

The different committees list on the board in outline form the subjects on which they are working.

Recitation

Each committee reads to the class the section it has prepared for the booklet referred to above.

   [1] Wentzel, B. M., "Dramatized Pictures." *School Arts Magazine,* XXIV: 559–561 (May, 1925).
   [2] Yount, Ethelyn, "History of Pioneer Life." *The Twentieth Yearbook of the National Society for the Study of Education,* Part I, pp. 49–50.

8. *Andrew Jackson was the First Great Man from the West*

Preparation

Children find how many states had been admitted to the
Union up to 1820.¹ (*Do not omit Vermont.*) "How does this
number compare with the original thirteen?

"We shall expect now to find that the West will begin to
have some influence in the national elections, and particularly
it will want to elect a Western man as president. The first
president from the West was the hero of the battle of New
Orleans during the War of 1812. Who was he?"

No additional presentation is needed.

Assimilation

Readings

Upper Group

BURNHAM. Hero Tales from History, 315–320.
BURTON. Four American Patriots, 133–192.
CHANDLER and CHITWOOD. Makers of American History, 201–207.
COE. Makers of the Nation, 217–220.
DAVIDSON. Founders and Builders of our Nation, 117–127.
EGGLESTON. A First Book in American History, 153–160.
EVANS. America First, 294–298.
FARIS. Where our History was Made, Book II, 314–317.
FOOTE and SKINNER. Makers and Defenders of America, 168–177.
GORDY. Leaders in Making America, 263–268.
GORDY. Stories of Later American History, 180–186.
GUERBER. Story of the Great Republic, 101–109.
MONTGOMERY. Beginners' American History, 184–194.
WOODBURN and MORAN. Makers of America, 207–210.
Compton's Pictured Encyclopedia (Jackson).
World Book (Jackson).

Average Group

BARNES. Elementary History of the United States, 259–261.
BEARD and BAGLEY. A First Book in American History, 199–205.
ELSON and MacMULLAN. Story of our Country, II : 103–109.
FORMAN. First Lessons in American History, 219–223.
GORDY. American Leaders and Heroes, 253–262.
GORDY. Elementary History of the United States, 215.
MACE. Primary History, 293–299.
MOWRY. First Steps in the History of our Country, 201–207.
SOUTHWORTH. Builders of our Country, II : 149–157.

Lower Group

BALDWIN. Fifty Famous People, 75–78.

¹ See the list in Burnham, Smith, *Making of our Country*, p. 308.

Teachers

MacDonald. Jacksonian Democracy, 16–27, 306–315.

Ogg. The Reign of Andrew Jackson, 1–22.

Public School Methods, V : 273–283. (The Methods Co., Chicago.)

Minimal Essentials

Name of Person: **Andrew Jackson**

Historical Term: "Old Hickory"

Things to Remember

Andrew Jackson was one of the greatest of the frontiersmen

He was the first president from the West.

Illustrative Material

Keystone Views: 334, Andrew Jackson in 1812 (slide only) ; 337, President Andrew Jackson (slide only).

Procedure during Assimilation

Reading as described on pages 24–29.

Picture study based on the illustrative material listed above.

Dramatize scenes from Jackson's life.

Drill on minimal essentials.

Objective test.

Organization

The teacher puts the following outline on the board. The children are to tell what points come under each heading.

ANDREW JACKSON

1. His early life
2. His part in the War of 1812
3. As president

Recitation

Hold a special Jackson program, and invite a committee of seventh-grade children who are studying the same subject to come to hear the stories.

9. *Florida was bought from Spain*

Preparation

"Up to this time what nation owned Florida?

"Spain had also owned Louisiana once, but had sold it to what country? France had sold it to whom?"

Children step to the window and point out boundaries between city lots. "What is a boundary?" Show on the map [1] the disputed boundary between Louisiana and Florida.

Presentation

France and Spain had never been able to agree as to where the boundary line between Louisiana and Florida was. So when we bought Louisiana we could not agree with Florida on the question. The uncertainty led to an unfriendly feeling between the United States and Spain.

Also there were many Indians and runaway negroes who took refuge in the swamps of Florida and who, every once in a while, would come out and rob and burn the property of Americans. We complained to Spain, but Spain could not prevent such deeds.

Therefore we decided that the best thing to do was to buy Florida, and then we could ourselves send soldiers into the country and bring it to order. We did so, and all the land east of the Mississippi and south of Canada was then ours. Slowly we were growing toward the oceans, west and south.

PRESENTATION TEST

Check the two best answers:

The United States bought Florida
- _ _ _ because we wanted to make war on Spain
- _ _ _ because we had had trouble over the boundary line between Florida and Louisiana
- _ _ _ because negroes and Indians came from it to rob us
- _ _ _ because we could get it cheap

Assimilation

Readings

Upper Group

COE. Makers of the Nation, 217, 221–224.
DAVIDSON. Founders and Builders of our Nation, 124–125.
MONTGOMERY. Beginners' American History, 194.
PERRY and PRICE. American History, II : 122–124.
WOODBURN and MORAN. Makers of America, 209–210.
World Book (Florida : History).

Average Group

GORDY. Elementary History of the United States, 227–228.

[1] Woodburn, J. A., and Moran, T. F., *Elementary American History and Government*, p. 225; Long, W. J., *America*, p. 281.

Lower Group
   Try GORDY.

Teachers
   BABCOCK. The Rise of American Nationality, 271–289.
   HOCKETT. Political and Social History of the United States, 290–292, 356–360.
   JOHNSON. Jefferson and his Colleagues, 265–285.
   MUZZEY. An American History, 203–205.
   MUZZEY. The United States of America, I : 301–305.
   OGG. The Reign of Andrew Jackson, 45–67.

Minimal Essentials

Historical Term : **boundary line**
Something to Remember
   The United States bought Florida from Spain.

Procedure during Assimilation

Reading as described on pages 24–29.
Children cut out the exercise suggested on page 191 of Eggleston's *A First Book in American History.*
Add Florida to the map " Territorial Growth of the United States." [1]
Objective test.

Organization

The teacher and the children work out coöperatively an outline similar to the following :

THE PURCHASE OF FLORIDA

   1. Why the United States wanted to buy Florida
   2. Why Spain decided to sell it
   3. The purchase

Recitation

Each child prepares to tell the entire story.

A drill lesson on section I of Unit VII should be given at this point.

II. IN REACHING THE PACIFIC TROUBLE AROSE WITH OTHER NATIONS

1. *Texas became Part of the United States*

Preparation

"What nation had first explored and settled this part of the country?" (*Showing Texas at the map.*)

"Do you know what we call it today? To which of our other states is Texas similar in products and climate?"

[1] See page 357.

Presentation

After several centuries Mexico had made herself independent from Spain and had formed a nation of her own (*showing its extent at the map*). Many of the Southern states looked eagerly over into Texan territory. How nice it would be if they could only secure all that vast stretch of land on which to grow more cotton! But Mexico owned it.

Nevertheless many Americans went West, and lived in Texas, although they were strangers in a strange land. Naturally they did not like the way the Mexican government carried on its business, and in a short time another revolution broke out. Texas made herself independent of Mexico, just as Mexico had made herself independent of Spain.

Mexico was very angry at the Americans. She said: "What right had Americans to come into my land and settle, with the purpose of taking that land away from me later by a revolution? It is no better than stealing from me outright."

The people in Texas paid no attention. They were an independent state; so they asked to be allowed to join the United States. Permission was given, and Texas became a state of the United States instead of a country by itself.

You may be sure that Mexico was furious. "The United States wanted Texas to separate from us in order to join her," she declared. We shall see later that serious trouble arose over the matter.

PRESENTATION TEST
Check the best answer:

a. The land in Texas had first belonged to

     _ _ _ Spain   _ _ _ the United States

     _ _ _ France

b. Next a revolution made which country independent?

     _ _ _ Texas   _ _ _ Spain

     _ _ _ Mexico

c. Many Americans went to live in Texas

     _ _ _ because they could grow much cotton there

     _ _ _ because they liked Texas better than the United States

     _ _ _ because the United States sent them there

d. Then they

     _ _ _ came back to the United States

     _ _ _ became good citizens of Mexico

     _ _ _ started a revolution against Mexico

e. When Texas was independent
_ _ _ it wanted to remain a country by itself
_ _ _ it wanted to join the United States
_ _ _ it wanted to go back to Mexico

Assimilation

Readings

Upper Group

ABBOTT. David Crockett and Early Texan History.
ALTSHELER. Texan Scouts (difficult).
CHANDLER and CHITWOOD. Makers of American History, 208–215.
COE. Makers of the Nation, 253–263.
EVANS. America First, 317–324.
FARIS. Real Stories from our History, 127–133.
FARIS. Where our History was Made, Book II, 38–43.
GORDY. Leaders in Making America, 287–292.
GORDY. Stories of Later American History, 208–214.
GUERBER. Story of the Great Republic, 125–126.
LEFFERTS. American Leaders, I : 289–303.
LODGE and ROOSEVELT. Hero Tales from American History, 173–181.
MONTGOMERY. Beginners' American History, 205–208.
MOWRY. American Pioneers, 173–186.
OTIS. Philip of Texas, 144–146.
PERRY and BEEBE. Four American Pioneers, 135–194.
PERRY and PRICE. American History, II : 127–129.
ROOSEVELT. Stories of the Great West, 97–105.
TAPPAN. Elementary History of our Country, 198–199.
VOLLINTINE. The Making of America, 212–220.
WOODBURN and MORAN. Makers of America, 230–235.
Compton's Pictured Encyclopedia (Texas : History, Houston).
World Book (Texas : Americanization, Alamo, Houston).

Average Group

BARNES. Elementary History of the United States, 300–302.
BEARD and BAGLEY. A First Book in American History, 235–242.
ELSON and MACMULLAN. Story of our Country, II : 123–128.
FORMAN. First Lessons in American History, 228.
GORDY. Elementary History of the United States, 233.
MACE. Primary History, 320–324.
MOWRY. First Steps in the History of our Country, 222–224.
NIDA. Following the Frontier, 249–250.
UHRBROCK and OWENS. Famous Americans, 187–196.

Lower Group

BARNES. Primary History of the United States, 150.
BLAISDELL and BALL. American History for Little Folks, 115–121.
MCMASTER. Primary History of the United States, 178.
WAYLAND. History Stories for Primary Grades, 56–58.

Teachers

GARRISON. Westward Extension, 85–156.
HART. American History told by Contemporaries, III : 637–655.
MUZZEY. The United States of America, I : 403–421.
SCHLESINGER. Political and Social History of the United States, 97–100.
STEPHENSON. Texas and the Mexican War. 1–176.

Minimal Essentials

Name of Person: **Sam Houston** (hūs'tŭn)
Name of Place: **Texas**
Date: **1845** — annexation of Texas
Historical Terms: **annexation; Alamo** (ä'lä mō)
Things to Remember
> Texas had once belonged to Mexico, but had made itself independent.
> Then it became a part of the United States.

Illustrative Material

Keystone Views: 116, The Alamo; 119, Chapultepec.
National Geographic Magazine, XXIV: 1331, 1337 (1913).
Society for Visual Education. Schoolfilm: Trans-Mississippi Trails.

Procedure during Assimilation

Reading as described on pages 24–29.
Picture study based on the illustrative material listed above.
Use the dramatization "The Lone Star State." Hague and Chalmers, *Dramatic Moments in American History*, pp. 152–173.
Show the flag of the Alamo; the flag of Texas.[1]
Read to the class selections from Joaquin Miller's "Defense of the Alamo."
Divide the class into two groups. One group prepares a list of reasons why Texas should have been annexed to the United States; the other group, a list of reasons why it should not have been annexed.
Add Texas to the map "Territorial Growth of the United States."[2]
Children cut out the exercise suggested on page 193 of Eggleston's *A First Book in American History*.
Drill on minimal essentials.
Objective test.

Organization

The teacher puts the following outline on the board. Each child selects from the story a few of the most important points to write under each heading.

THE ANNEXATION OF TEXAS

1. The settling of Texas
2. Texas and her war for independence
3. Why Texas was annexed to the United States

Recitation

A debate on the subject *Resolved*, that Texas should have been annexed to the United States. The teacher works with the negative.

[1] *National Geographic Magazine*, XXXII: 330, 342 (October, 1917).
[2] See page 357.

2. *There was War with Mexico over the Question of Texas*

Preparation

"Tell how Texas became part of the United States.

"Why was Mexico angry at the United States?

"What is a boundary line?

"In what different ways can boundaries be marked?"

Presentation

You remember, from our story of Texas, that Mexico was very angry at what she thought was a trick the United States had played upon her. When two nations hate each other thus, it is not hard to find excuses to go to war.

The excuse in this case was the question of the boundary line between Texas and Mexico. Texas said it was here at the Rio Grande (*showing at the map*), which would give her more territory. Mexico said it was here (*showing the location at the map*), which would give her more territory.

They went to war about the boundary. Of course, the United States had more men, and more money to buy guns and supplies; so we stood a better chance. Our men attacked Mexico in three ways: (1) by sea and then across country to the City of Mexico, (2) along the Gulf coast, and (3) in California (*illustrating each at the map*).

Everything favored the United States, and she won from the first. In two years Mexico was completely defeated. At the close of the war she had to give up all this land (*illustrating at the map*). The United States had reached the Pacific. Our people had gone as far as they could go in that direction.

PRESENTATION TEST

Check the best answer:

a. The war between Mexico and the United States had this excuse:

_ _ _ the independence of Mexico

_ _ _ slaves

_ _ _ the boundary line of Texas

b. The United States won because

_ _ _ it was a larger and richer country

_ _ _ its side was right

_ _ _ it had had more wars

c. After the war

   _ _ _ everything was the same as before the war
   _ _ _ the United States had to give Mexico much land
   _ _ _ Mexico had to give the United States much land

Assimilation

Readings

Upper Group

ABBOTT. Kit Carson.
BLAISDELL. The Story of American History, 346.
BURNHAM. Hero Tales from History, 258-265.
COE. Makers of the Nation, 264–271.
FAIRBANKS. The Western United States, 106–114.
FARIS. Where our History was Made, Book II: 149–153, 160–165.
GORDY. Leaders in Making America, 292–297.
GORDY. Stories of Later American History, 214–220.
GUERBER. Story of the Great Republic, 125–131.
LEFFERTS. American Leaders, I: 304–318.
MONTGOMERY. Beginners' American History, 217–218.
OTIS. Philip of Texas, 147–149.
PERRY and BEEBE. Four American Pioneers, 197–255.
PERRY and PRICE. American History, II: 129–130, 240–242.
RUGG and SCHWEPPE. The Westward Movement and the Growth of Transportation, 74–76.
TAPPAN. Elementary History of our Country, 201–202.
WOODBURN and MORAN. Makers of America, 235–241.
Compton's Pictured Encyclopedia (Mexican War, Carson).
World Book (Mexican War, Frémont, Carson).

Average Group

BARNES. Elementary History of the United States, 302–304.
BEARD and BAGLEY. First Book in American History, 242–247.
EGGLESTON. Stories of American Life and Adventure, 166–171.
ELSON and MacMULLAN. Story of our Country, II: 132–137.
FORMAN. First Lessons in American History, 230–232.
GORDY. Elementary History of the United States, 233–234.
MACE. Primary History, 330–335.
MORRIS. Primary History of the United States, 206–207.
MOWRY. First Steps in the History of our Country, 225–226.
NIDA. Following the Frontier, 243–247, 251.
TAPPAN. American Hero Stories, 237–253.
UHRBROCK and OWENS. Famous Americans, 197–206.

Lower Group

BARNES. Primary History of the United States, 151–157.
McMASTER. Primary History of the United States, 180–181.

Teachers

GARRISON. Westward Extension, 188–253.
HART. American History told by Contemporaries, IV: 11–40.
MUZZEY. The United States of America, I: 421–442.
SCHLESINGER. Political and Social History of the United States, 102–110.
STEPHENSON. Texas and the Mexican War, 177–257.

Minimal Essentials

Names of Places: **Rio Grande** (rē'ō grän'dā) ; **City of Mexico**
Date: **1848** — end of the Mexican War
Historical Terms: **cession; Santa Fe Trail**
Things to Remember
Mexico was very angry because Texas was annexed to the United States.
There was a quarrel between Mexico and the United States over the boundary
of Texas.
The Mexican war lasted two years.
The United States gained a great deal of land in the southwest.

Illustrative Material

McKINLEY. Illustrated Topics for American History : S. 29.
Ford Educational Library : 223, The Way of the West.
Society for Visual Education. Picturol : The Pacific Coast.

Procedure during Assimilation

Reading as described on pages 24–29.
Picture study based on the illustrative material listed above.
Read to the class selections from Lowell's "Biglow Papers."
Show with three red arrows the main lines of attack : (1) along the Gulf coast,
(2) from Vera Cruz to Mexico City, (3) California.
Add to the map "Territorial Growth of the United States" [1] the Mexican Cession.
What states have since been made from the same territory ?
Children cut out the exercise suggested on page 195 of Eggleston's *First Book in
American History.*
Make a map showing the Santa Fe Trail.[2] Show the territory in dispute between
Mexico and the United States.[3]
Show the "bear flag" of California.
Drill on minimal essentials.
Objective test.

Organization

Children make their own outlines of the war, including
causes, the three main lines of attack, and results. The causes
may be made in outline form, the three main lines of attack
recorded on an outline map of North America, and the results
given in two summary sentences.

Recitation

Each child who recites successfully on one point of the outline may call on another to give the succeeding talk.

[1] See page 357.
[2] Halleck, R. P., *History of our Country*, p. 349 ; Lawler, T. B., *Essentials of
American History*, p. 335.
[3] Muzzey, D. S., *An American History*, p. 276.

3. *Gold was discovered in California*

Preparation

"Have any of you ever seen a gold mine? If so, describe it."
Turn to the statistics of the United States gold and silver
production by states [1] and let the children find which state
produces the most gold.

Presentation

Our story today is how gold came to be discovered in California. Like a great many other famous discoveries, it was
more or less by accident.

As the news spread back East, the gold fever spread like
wildfire. Men from all walks of life were seized with the desire
to go West, find a gold mine, and "strike it rich." We shall
read of what sacrifices they made, of the many who failed,
and also of the few who succeeded and became wealthy.

One of the main results of the discovery of gold was the
quick settlement of the Pacific coast. In fact, California was
thickly settled while this section (*showing Arizona, Utah,
Nevada, New Mexico*) was still the home of wild animals and
Indians. But after a while settlement from the West backed
into those territories (*illustrating the movement on the map*),
and they too were peopled by pioneers. Without the discovery
of gold in California the settlement of all this region would
have been much slower.

PRESENTATION TEST

Check the best answer:

One important result of the discovery of gold in California was
    _ _ _ that it led to war with Mexico
    _ _ _ that it helped the settlement of the West to proceed faster
    _ _ _ that it made the United States the richest country in the world

Assimilation

Readings

Upper Group

BANDINI. History of California, 147–172.
BARSTOW (ED.). The Westward Movement, 175–191.
BLAISDELL. The Story of American History, 346–349.

[1] World Almanac (Gold Produced in the United States; Mineral Products —
States They Come From).

COE. Makers of the Nation, 272–277.
EVANS. America First, 330–339.
FARIS. Real Stories from our History, 191–195.
GORDY. Leaders in Making America, 302–305.
GORDY. Stories of Later American History, 221–224.
GUERBER. Story of the Great Republic, 142–147.
HUNT. California the Golden, 187–209.
LOGIE. From Columbus to Lincoln, 183–191.
MONTGOMERY. Beginners' American History, 213–216.
MOWRY. American Pioneers, 187–195.
OTIS. Martha of California.
PERRY and PRICE. American History, II : 242–245.
RUGG and SCHWEPPE. The Westward Movement and the Growth of Trans-
portation, 100–108.
TAPPAN. Elementary History of our Country, 202–203.
VOLLINTINE. The Making of America, 221–232.
WAGNER. Pacific History Stories, 122–130.
WOODBURN and MORAN. Makers of America, 242–246.
Compton's Pictured Encyclopedia (California).
World Book (California : Discovery of Gold).

Average Group
BEARD and BAGLEY. A First Book in American History, 248–250.
EGGLESTON. Stories of American Life and Adventure, 171–177.
ELSON and MacMULLAN. Story of our Country, II : 137–142.
FORMAN. First Lessons in American History, 235–237.
GORDY. Elementary History of the United States, 234–237.
MORRIS. Primary History of the United States, 207–210.
MOWRY. First Steps in the History of our Country, 226–228.
NIDA. Following the Frontier, 253–273.
SAMUEL. Story of Gold and Silver, 21–27.
Lessons in Community and National Life, Series C, 217–222.

Lower Group
BARNES. Primary History of the United States, 157–159.
BLAISDELL and BALL. Child's Book of American History, 144–151.
CARROLL and CARROLL. Around the World, III : 133–139.
McMASTER. Primary History of the United States, 182–186.

Teachers
HART. American History told by Contemporaries, IV : 43–48.
McMASTER. History of the People of the United States, VII : 585–614.
WHITE. The Forty-Niners.

Minimal Essentials

Name of Place: **California**
Date: **1848** — discovery of gold in California
Historical Term: **"Forty-niners"**
Something to Remember
The discovery of gold in California helped to settle the Far West.

Illustrative Material

Compton's Pictured Encyclopedia (Gold, California).
Keystone Views: 340, San Francisco in 1849 (slide only).
Mentor, IX : 3–12 (January, 1922).
World Book (Gold).

Procedure during Assimilation

Reading as described on pages 24–29.
Picture study based on the illustrative material listed on page 383.
Use the dramatization "Gold in California." Hubbard, *Little American History Plays*, pp. 131–136.
Read to the class selections from Bret Harte's *Luck of Roaring Camp.*
Illustrate on the sand table how claims were marked off. Illustrate washing out the gold.
Someone who has seen a gold mine describes it to the class.
Someone who has seen the photoplay "The Covered Wagon" describes it.
Drill on minimal essentials.
Objective test.

Organization

Children work out their own organizations at the board. The class then criticizes.

DISCOVERY OF GOLD IN CALIFORNIA

1. The discovery
2. The gold rush
   Methods of travel
3. Effect on the settlement of the West

Recitation

Each row chooses a representative to give a talk on one of the points above.

4. *Oregon became Part of the United States*

Preparation

Show the class one of their own maps, "Territorial Growth of the United States," as completed to date.

"What is needed to make this map look like a present-day map of the United States?"

Review the story of Captain Robert Gray.

Presentation

During all the years that the United States had been busy about other matters our fur traders had been going quietly about their business, and had built many posts in Oregon. Some missionaries had come in, also, to work among the Indians.

Great Britain, you see (*turning to the map*), was a very near neighbor. Her fur traders also had been coming in to the same region, and for a while there was sharp disagreement between the two countries. However, they very sensibly decided to settle the question by a treaty, and for many years the land was said to belong to both. This was never very satisfactory, any more than it is for two boys to own a bicycle together; so at last they drew a line through the middle of the territory (*showing at the map*); Great Britain took the land to the north, and the United States had the land to the south. This was much better than going to war, and satisfied both nations.

PRESENTATION TEST

1. *Check the two best answers:*

   a. The early settlements in Oregon were made by

       _ _ _ fur traders   _ _ _ soldiers

       _ _ _ missionaries   _ _ _ nobles

   b. For many years the land belonged to which *two* nations?

       _ _ _ France   _ _ _ United States

       _ _ _ Great Britain   _ _ _ Spain

2. *Check the best answer:*

   a. At last they agreed

       _ _ _ to let Great Britain have all the land

       _ _ _ to let the United States have all the land

       _ _ _ to divide the land between them

   b. The question was settled

       _ _ _ by a treaty

       _ _ _ by going to war

Assimilation

Readings

Upper Group

   BLAISDELL. The Story of American History, 342–345.

   GORDY. Leaders in Making America, 297–301.

   GUERBER. Story of the Great Republic, 113–117.

   JUDSON. Early Days in Old Oregon.

   MEEKER. Ox Team Days on the Oregon Trail.

   MOWRY. American Pioneers, 196–204.

   OTIS. Antoine of Oregon.

   PERRY and PRICE. American History, II : 127.

   RUGG and SCHWEPPE. The Westward Movement and the Growth of Transportation, 102–108.

   SANFORD. Story of Agriculture in the United States, 184–187 (difficult).

TAPPAN. Elementary History of our Country, 200–201.
VOLLINTINE. The Making of America, 198–211.
Compton's Pictured Encyclopedia (Oregon).
World Book (Oregon: History).

Average Group

BEARD and BAGLEY. A First Book in American History, 252–263.
ELSON and MACMULLAN. Story of our Country, II: 128–132.
FIELD. Fifth Reader, 185–197, 202–211.
FORMAN. First Lessons in American History, 229–230.
GORDY. Elementary History of the United States, 232–233.
MORRIS. Primary History of the United States, 210–215.
MOWRY. First Steps in the History of our Country, 230–236.
NIDA. Following the Frontier, 274–279.

Lower Group

MCMASTER. Primary History of the United States, 179–180.

Teachers

GARRISON. Westward Extension, 157–174.
SCHLESINGER. Political and Social History of the United States, 100–102.
SKINNER. Adventurers of Oregon.
TURNER. Rise of the New West, 116–133.

Minimal Essentials

Names of Places: Columbia River; Oregon (ŏr'ē gŏn)
Date: during the Mexican War
Historical Terms: prairie schooners; Oregon Trail
Things to Remember

For a long time England and the United States owned the Oregon country together.
Then they divided the land.
The United States took the southern part.

Illustrative Material

GABRIEL (ED.). Pageant of America, III: 170–171.
Society for Visual Education. Schoolfilm: Across the Rockies to the Pacific.

Procedure during Assimilation

Reading as described on pages 24–29.
Picture study based on the illustrative material listed above.
Add Oregon to the map "Territorial Growth of the United States."[1]
Make a map showing the Oregon Trail.[2]
Children cut out the exercise suggested on page 191 of Eggleston's *First Book in American History.*
Drill on minimal essentials.
Objective test.

[1] See page 357.
[2] Halleck, R. P., *History of our Country*, p. 328; Lawler, T. B., *Essentials of American History*, p. 335.

Organization

The teacher works with the group whose last organizations were unsatisfactory.[1] The other children make their outlines independently.

THE ANNEXATION OF OREGON

1. Early exploration and settlement in Oregon
2. Troubles with Great Britain
3. The question settled

Recitation

Each child writes a few summary sentences on each of the points above.

5. *Alaska was added Later*

No additional preparation and presentation are needed.

Assimilation
Readings

Upper Group

FARIS. Where our History was Made, Book II, 203–207.
LOGIE. From Lincoln to Coolidge, 112–119.
PERRY and PRICE. American History, II: 251–252.
RYDELL. On Pacific Frontiers, 120–197.
TAPPAN. Elementary History of our Country, 231–232.
Compton's Pictured Encyclopedia (Alaska: History).
World Book (Alaska: History).

Average Group

EGGLESTON. Stories of American Life and Adventure, 207–214.
ELSON and MACMULLAN. Story of our Country, II: 255–256.
GEORGE. Little Journeys to Alaska and Canada, 9–11.
GORDY. Elementary History of the United States, 290–291.

Lower Group

Try ELSON and MACMULLAN.

Teachers

HART. American History told by Contemporaries, IV: 547–550.

Minimal Essentials

Name of Place: **Alaska**
Historical Term: **"Seward's Ice Box"** (sū'ĕrdz)
Things to Remember
    We bought Alaska from Russia.
    At first people thought it was of little value, but later it proved to be a rich country.

[1] See page 381.

Illustrative Material

Compton's Pictured Encyclopedia (Alaska).
Keystone Views: 187, On the Dyea Trail; 188, Main Street, Wrangel; 189, Main Street of Sheep Camp; 190, Gold Miners at Work in the Klondike Country; 191, Arctic Dog Team; 192, First Train over the White Pass to the Yukon.
National Geographic Magazine, XX: 315–333, 586–607 (1909); XXI: 6–53 (1910).

Procedure during Assimilation

Reading as described on pages 24–29.
Picture study based on the illustrative material listed above.
A traveler to Alaska describes the country to the class.
List the products we obtain from Alaska. (See any geography text.)
Find out the value of Alaska's exports last year.[1]
Compare the purchase price per acre of Alaska, the Gadsden purchase, Florida, Louisiana.
Add Alaska to the map "Territorial Growth of the United States."[2]
Drill on minimal essentials.
Objective test.

Organization

Members of the slower group again try to make their own outlines; brighter groups continue independently.

THE PURCHASE OF ALASKA

1. Why Russia wanted to sell
2. Why the United States decided to buy
3. What we have obtained from Alaska

Recitation

Each child prepares the entire story.

A drill lesson on section II of Unit VII should be given at this point.

Drill on the minimal essentials of the entire unit (see pages 40–43).

Certain parts of standard tests may be used, such as questions 10–14, inclusive, in Test III, and questions 12–20, inclusive, in Test IV of the *Informational Tests in United States History* to accompany Beard and Bagley's *History of the American People.*

---

[1] World Almanac (Alaska: Exports and Imports; United States: Gold and Silver Production by States.)

[2] See page 357.

MINIMAL ESSENTIALS OF UNIT VII

PERSONS	PLACES	TERMS	DATES
William Clark	Alaska	Alamo	*1803.* Purchase of
De Witt Clinton	California	annexation	Louisiana
Robert Fulton	City of Mexico	Baltimore and	*1807.* Fulton's
Sam Houston	Columbia River	Ohio	steamboat
Meriwether Lewis	Erie Canal	binder	*1830.* Beginning of
Cyrus McCormick	Missouri River	boundary line	era of railroad
	Oregon	canal	building
	Rio Grande	cession	*1831.* McCormick's
	Rocky Mountains	clearing	reaper
	Texas	*Clermont*	*1845.* Annexation
	Wilderness Road	"dark and bloody	of Texas
		ground"	*1848.* End of the
		era	Mexican War
		flatboat	*1848.* Discovery of
		"forty-niners"	gold in Califor-
		frontier	nia
		house-raising	
		locomotive	Drill on the peaks
		"Old Hickory"	of the time chart
		Oregon Trail	
		pack horse	
		prairie schooner	
		purchase	
		reaper	
		"Seward's Ice	
		Box"	
		territory	
		transportation	
		turnpike	

TESTS ON THE ENTIRE UNIT

(To be given after all the stories are completed)

Test of Place-Sense. Pass double-sized outline maps of North America. Lists of the words to be spelled may be placed on the board to assist the children in writing. Give the following directions:

1. Put the letter *C* where the Columbia River is.
2. Write the word *Alaska* in the right place.
3. Write the word *California* in the right place.
4. Draw two parallel lines where the Erie Canal is.

5. Put the letter *M* where the City of Mexico is.
6. Write the words *Missouri River* in the right place.
7. Draw with green crayon a line to represent the Wilderness Road.
8. Write the word *Texas* in the right place.
9. Write the words *Rio Grande* in the right place.
10. Write the word *Oregon* in the right place.
11. Pass to the map and show the Rocky Mountains.

Test of Time-Sense. Pass mimeographed sheets of the following:

1. Here is a list of persons. Put the figure 1 before the name of the man who lived or worked first, the figure 2 before the one who lived next, and so on.

     _ _ _ Clark
     _ _ _ McCormick
     _ _ _ Sam Houston
     _ _ _ De Witt Clinton

2. Here is another list. Do the same.

     _ _ _ Robert Fulton
     _ _ _ Lewis
     _ _ _ Andrew Jackson
     _ _ _ Thomas Jefferson

3. Here is a list of things which happened. Do the same.

     _ _ _ End of the Mexican War
     _ _ _ Fulton's steamboat invented
     _ _ _ Beginning of railroads
     _ _ _ Purchase of Louisiana
     _ _ _ Annexation of Texas
     _ _ _ McCormick's reaper invented

Test on Persons. Pass mimeographed sheets of the following:

Here is a list of people:

Jefferson	Andrew Jackson
De Witt Clinton	Clark
Lewis	Robert Fulton
Cyrus McCormick	Sam Houston

Put each name in the right blank space in the sentences below:

1. _ _ _ _ and _ _ _ _ explored the Louisiana territory.
2. _ _ _ _ _ _ _ _ was the first president from the West.
3. The reaper was invented by _ _ _ _ _ _ _ _.
4. The steamboat was built by _ _ _ _ _ _ _ _.
5. _ _ _ _ _ _ _ _ built the Erie Canal.
6. _ _ _ _ _ _ _ _ was a hero in the early history of Texas.
7. _ _ _ _ was president when Louisiana was purchased.

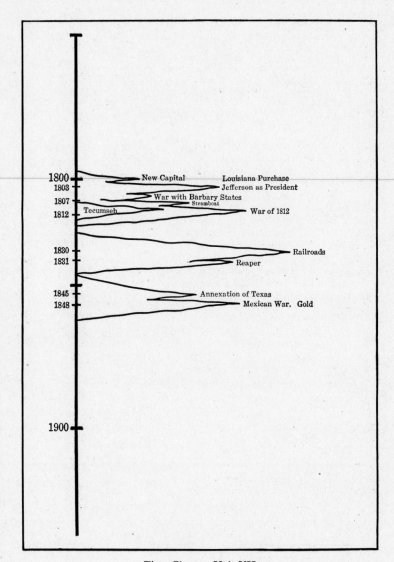

Time Chart — Unit VII

Test on Historical Terms. The teacher prepares descriptions such as the following, which may have been used previously as the subject of drill games.

I. Here is a list of words:

Alamo   stockade
turnpike   binder
annexation   reaper
transportation   boundary line
Baltimore and Ohio   purchase

Put each in the right place in the sentences below:

1. Anything that is bought with money is a _ _ _ _.
2. The first successful railroad in the United States was the _ _ _ _ _ _ _ _ _ _ _ _.
3. Adding new territory to a country is _ _ _ _.
4. A line of upright posts that make a fence used for protection is a _ _ _ _.
5. A _ _ _ _ is a machine for cutting grain.
6. The _ _ _ _ was a mission in Texas.
7. The line which divides one country from another is a _ _ _ _ _ _ _ _.
8. A machine that ties grain in bunches is a _ _ _ _.
9. Moving persons or goods from one place to another is _ _ _ _.
10. A road on which there are tollgates is a _ _ _ _.

II. Here is another list:

canal   "dark and bloody ground"
prairie schooner   cession
Clermont   era
territory   pack horse
"Seward's Ice Box"   clearing

Do the same.

1. An animal used for carrying burdens is a _ _ _ _ _ _ _ _.
2. Alaska was called _ _ _ _ _ _ _ _ _ _ _ _.
3. The first successful steamboat was the _ _ _ _.
4. Kentucky was called the _ _ _ _ _ _ _ _ _ _ _ _ _ _ _ _.
5. A large ditch used for transporting goods within a country is a _ _ _ _.
6. Land that has been surrendered by one country to another is a _ _ _ _.
7. A large stretch of land is a _ _ _ _.
8. The large covered wagon used in early days was called a _ _ _ _ _ _ _ _.
9. A period of time counted from some important event is an _ _ _ _.
10. A piece of forest land after the trees are cut down is a _ _ _ _.

III. Here is another list:

house-raising   flatboat
"Old Hickory"   frontier
locomotive   "forty-niners"

Do the same.

1. Men who rushed to California soon after the discovery of gold were called _ _ _ _.

2. A steam engine that travels on wheels is a _ _ _ _.

3. The part of a country that is near the border is called the _ _ _ _.

4. Andrew Jackson was called _ _ _ _ _ _ _ _.

5. A boat with a flat bottom was called a _ _ _ _.

6. Putting up the frame of a house was called a _ _ _ _.

COMPREHENSION TEST ON UNIT VII

1. *Check the two best answers:*

Early settlers in the West went

_ _ _ by way of the Ohio River
_ _ _ by sailing around South America
_ _ _ by the Panama Canal
_ _ _ by gaps through the mountains

2. *Check the best answer:*

a. People thought Alaska was not worth much

_ _ _ because we bought it from Russia
_ _ _ because it was so cold
_ _ _ because we had so much land already

b. We bought Florida from

_ _ _ England
_ _ _ France
_ _ _ Spain

c. The Louisiana Purchase was important

_ _ _ because it made it possible for Americans to move westward
_ _ _ because the land no longer belonged to Spain
_ _ _ because it made the map of the United States larger

d. The settling of the Oregon question kept the peace with

_ _ _ Spain
_ _ _ France
_ _ _ England

e. Andrew Jackson's election as president showed the power of the

_ _ _ East
_ _ _ West
_ _ _ South

f. Good roads and canals were needed in order

_ _ _ to save the wagons from wearing out
_ _ _ to ride comfortably
_ _ _ to make it cheaper to send goods to the West

g. California was settled before the other Pacific-coast states

     _ _ _ because people liked California better

     _ _ _ because gold was discovered in California

     _ _ _ because it was nearer

h. Farming machinery was invented

     _ _ _ because Western farms were too large for a few men to work

     _ _ _ because men preferred to work by machinery

     _ _ _ because inventors had to have work

i. Steamboats and railroads helped to settle the West

     _ _ _ because they were easy to build

     _ _ _ because people liked to go fast

     _ _ _ because they made it quicker and cheaper to transport men
          and goods

j. When the Mexican War was over

     _ _ _ the United States had learned how to fight

     _ _ _ the United States had won a great deal of land

     _ _ _ the United States had made Mexico give us our rights

k. The United States thought it had a right to annex Texas

     _ _ _ because the United States is larger than Mexico

     _ _ _ because Texas no longer belonged to Mexico

     _ _ _ because Americans in Texas asked for annexation

3. *What is the title of the seventh unit?*

ORGANIZATION OF THE UNIT AS A WHOLE

Children should be able to give in outline form the titles of the stories comprising the subject matter of the unit.

RECITATION OF THE UNIT AS A WHOLE

Each child should be able to give a résumé of all the stories, illustrating his talk at the map.

UNIT VIII

HOW ONE MACHINE CALLED FOR ANOTHER, UNTIL ALL OUR METHODS OF LIVING WERE CHANGED

I. One Field of Invention was in the Clothing Industry.
1. An Englishman made a machine that would spin thread.
2. So much thread called for a machine that would weave.
3. These huge machines were hard to run by hand.
4. Machines used so much cotton that a new way of cleaning it had to be found.
5. Sewing-machines helped in making cloth into garments.
6. All these machines were put into great buildings called factories.
7. Factories needed many working people; so towns began to grow into great cities.

II. Men had to find Ways of Sending News to People in Distant Parts.
1. In early days messengers and letters were the chief ways of sending news.
2. The railroads carried letters faster.
3. The telegraph sent messages in an instant.
4. Telegraphing across the ocean was made possible by the cable.
5. Newspapers could then gather news quickly.

III. Review briefly the Stories of the Development of Transportation and Farm Machinery to the Civil War Period. Add also:
America led the world in her clipper ships.

IV. A New Metal Industry was Begun.
1. New ways of working iron were found.
2. We began to use coal instead of wood to run our machines.

PREPARATION FOR THE OVERVIEW

Have ready for use several small pieces of cloth whose threads will pull easily. Call attention to the fact that cloth is made of two threads, one going one way, and the other the other way. Children draw threads out of the cloth and un-twist each to ascertain how thread is made. Show samples of embroidery floss; of darning cotton. Children find of how many strands each is composed.

"If you wanted to send some friend in a far-away state a message to come to you immediately, how would you send the message? In the days of the Indians how would you have sent it? What inventions have made the difference?

"Our story today tells how all our ways of living have been changed since colonial times. What has caused this great change? Machinery."

PRESENTATION OR OVERVIEW

You remember that in colonial days spinning was done by means of a spinning-wheel, which made only one thread at a time. Therefore not much thread could be produced by one person, and it was scarce and costly. This had been true for many hundreds of years. Not only the kind of thread with which we sew was expensive, but also the kind you pulled out of the cloth a few minutes ago.

After many centuries, however, a man, through an accident, found out that many threads could be spun at one time; so he made a machine which would do that work. Then there was all the thread that anybody could use and more too. The spinning-machines turned out great quantities of thread. One problem had been solved.

Now we shall find out about a second problem. Long before the time of the Crusades men had known how to weave threads together on a hand loom, some threads going one way and some another, thus making cloth. If the threads were of wool they made good cloth, but if of cotton it was very poor.

Now that so much thread was being manufactured, the men and women who did the weaving could not keep up. No matter how hard or how late they worked, there was always a great deal of thread left over. Again some men who were better thinkers than the rest said: "There is only one way to keep up with the machine which spins, and that is to make a machine which weaves. Then people will not have to weave by hand. As fast as one machine spins thread, the other will weave it into cloth." So a weaving-machine was made, and then cloth was more plentiful than it had ever been before in the history of the world.

So much cloth called for the invention of another machine to help make garments, since such yards and yards of goods could not be sewed by hand. And so the story went. One machine called for another, until today practically all the work of the world is done by these willing steel and iron friends of man, which we call machines.

The machines were very large, however, and very expensive. No longer could each cottage or farmhouse have in one corner of the kitchen its own loom for weaving and its own spinning-wheel. Instead, the machines were brought together in one place, and a huge building was built to house them. That is how we came to have factories. We shall find out in our reading how many changes in our lives these factories have made.

In addition to the question of manufacturing, there was another very hard problem for our people to solve because of the great size of our country. Suppose that a fur merchant in New York, just after the Louisiana Purchase, wanted to send some directions to his fur traders in Oregon (*illustrating at the map*). Can you imagine how long it would have taken for the news to reach them and the messenger to return? It would have taken almost two years! [1] When Andrew Jackson was elected president in 1828, the news did not reach him, even in Tennessee (*illustrating at the map*), until a full month later.

Many people did not believe that so large a territory (*showing at the map with a sweeping gesture*) could ever hold together as one country. There were grave fears that it must break up into two or three different nations. But it did not. Some of the reasons we have already studied. The building of roads and the coming of railroads and steamships meant that a man in far-away California could step into a railway coach and in less than a week arrive in New York. Another thing that helped to keep the country together instead of allowing it to break into small pieces was the invention of a way to send news faster than a railway express travels, faster than steamboats, as fast as lightning itself. What was this way of sending messages? (Telegraph.)

We must remember then that railroads, steamboats, and the telegraph helped to keep our country *one*.

[1] Based on the time consumed by the Lewis and Clark expedition.

PRESENTATION TEST

1. *Check the best answer:*
   a. Before the invention of new machinery for spinning
   _ _ _ no thread was spun
   _ _ _ as much could be done as with machines
   _ _ _ only one thread could be spun at a time

   b. When thread could be made in great quantities, we immediately needed also
   _ _ _ a machine to weave the thread into cloth
   _ _ _ a sewing machine
   _ _ _ a machine for picking cotton

   c. As soon as an inventor invented one machine, we needed
   _ _ _ money to buy it
   _ _ _ another machine to use up the product of the first
   _ _ _ railroads to carry the goods away

2. *Check two answers:*
   Machines had to be placed in big buildings called factories because
   _ _ _ they were too big to work on at home
   _ _ _ people liked to work in large groups
   _ _ _ they cost too much money for the workers to own their machines
   _ _ _ factories needed large machines

3. *Check the best answer:*
   Many people used to think that our country would fall apart into several different countries
   _ _ _ because the people did not like each other
   _ _ _ because it took so long to send news from one part to another
   _ _ _ because we had too much poor land

4. *Check as many answers as are right:*
   The following inventions helped keep the country together:

_ _ _ telegraph	_ _ _ cotton gin
_ _ _ sewing-machine	' _ _ _ steamboat
_ _ _ railroad	_ _ _ spinning-machinery

I. ONE FIELD OF INVENTION WAS IN THE CLOTHING INDUSTRY

1. *An Englishman made a Machine that would spin Thread*

No additional preparation and presentation are needed.

Assimilation

Readings

Upper Group

BACHMAN. Great Inventors and their Inventions, 87–93.
BEARD and BAGLEY. The History of the American People, 289–290.
BEARD and BAGLEY. Our Old World Background, 323–325, 330–331, 332–334.
BROOKS. Story of Cotton, 84–89.
DARROW. Masters of Science and Invention, 41–47.

DARROW. Thinkers and Doers, 83–92 (difficult).
HOLLAND. Historic Inventions, 84–95.
MARSHALL. Story of Human Progress, 127–128, 133–134 (difficult).
ROCHELEAU. The Story of King Cotton, 15–18.
SMITH. Industrial History, 115–116 (difficult).
TOWLE. Heroes and Martyrs of Invention, 71–83.
TURPIN. Cotton, 53–56.
Compton's Pictured Encyclopedia (Spinning, Hargreaves).
World Book (Spinning, Spinning Jenny, Hargreaves).

Average Group
CARPENTER. How the World is Clothed, 40–42.
PARKMAN. Conquests of Invention, 38–48, 49–53.

Lower Group
CHAMBERLAIN. How we are Clothed, 154–156.

Teachers
BOGART. Economic History of the United States, 148–152.
CALLENDER. Economic History of the United States, 260–264.
CHEYNEY. Industrial and Social History of England, 203–210.
GIBSON. Romance of Modern Manufacture, 34–46.
HALL. Weavers and Other Workers, 162–164.
OSGOOD. History of Industry, 256–259.
Baltimore County Course of Study, 522–523, 554–555, 559.

Minimal Essentials

Date: about the middle of the eighteenth century
Historical Terms: spin; spinning jenny; spindle
Things to Remember
For hundreds of years people had spun one thread at a time.
The new machine spun many threads at once.
Great quantities of thread were then produced.

Illustrative Material

GABRIEL (ED.). Pageant of America, V: 15–16, 29–31, 153, 155–157.
MCKINLEY. Illustrated Topics for Mediæval and Modern History: M.M. 21, Development of Spinning Machinery.
Compton's Pictured Encyclopedia (Cotton).

Procedure during Assimilation

Reading as described on pages 24–29.
Picture study based on the illustrative material listed above.
If there is spinning-machinery in the household-economics or industrial departments, take the class to see it in operation. If not, try to find someone in the community to demonstrate the use of a spinning wheel.
Some person who has visited a great spinning mill may describe it.
Ask for a volunteer committee of boys to rig up a simple type of spinning jenny with the help of the teacher of industrial arts (see " Cotton-Spinning Machinery " in the Encyclopædia Britannica).
Drill on minimal essentials.
Objective test.

Organization

The teacher and the pupils working together produce an outline somewhat similar to the following :

INVENTION OF SPINNING-MACHINERY

1. Old methods of spinning
2. The spinning jenny invented
3. Effect

Recitation

The children write a paragraph on each of the points above.

2. *So Much Thread called for a Machine that would Weave*

Children try to tell which are the warp and which the woof threads in their own clothing.

"What is the next step in the manufacture of clothing, after the cotton or wool is spun into thread?

"When so much thread was manufactured by the spinning machines, what problem arose?"

No additional presentation is needed.

Assimilation
Readings

Upper Group

BACHMAN. Great Inventors and their Inventions, 94–98.
BEARD and BAGLEY. Our Old World Background, 331–332.
DARROW. Masters of Science and Invention, 49–50.
DARROW. Thinkers and Doers, 92–95 (difficult).
FORMAN. Stories of Useful Inventions, 116–119.
ROCHELEAU. Story of King Cotton, 19–22.
SMITH. Industrial History, 116–117 (difficult).
TURPIN. Cotton, 56–61.
Compton's Pictured Encyclopedia (Spinning and Weaving).
World Book (Weaving).

Average Group

CARPENTER. How the World is Clothed, 42–43.
PARKMAN. Conquests of Invention, 54–62.

Lower Group

SHILLIG. Four Wonders, 51–52.

Teachers

BOGART. Economic History of the United States, 149–150.
COMAN. Industrial History of the United States, 184–187.
GIBSON. Romance of Modern Manufacture, 47–59.
HALL. Weavers and Other Workers, 151–157.

Minimal Essentials

Historical Terms: **weave; loom; shuttle; textile**
Things to Remember
 Weaving had formerly been done by hand.
 Weaving-machines worked the shuttles without hand labor.
 Weaving-machinery wove into cloth the great quantities of thread that the
   spinning jenny made.

Illustrative Material

GABRIEL (ED.). Pageant of America, V: 32, 158.
Child's World Pictures: Weaver at her Loom.
Keystone Views: 293, Close View of a Modern Loom; 294, Weaving Room in a Cotton Mill.

Procedure during Assimilation

Reading as described on pages 24–29.
Picture study based on the illustrative material listed above.
If possible visit a weaver of rag rugs. Perhaps there is a loom in the household-
   economics or the industrial-arts department which can be used for a demonstration.
Children weave mats of paper, slats, or raffia. Then they make a simple loom and
   weave doll's rugs from yarn (see Encyclopædia Britannica under "Weaving").
If there is any kind of textile factory in the vicinity, visit it.
Make a list of the things we would have to go without, if there were no spinning-
   machinery and weaving-machinery.
Drill on minimal essentials.
Objective test.

Organization

Children make an outline for this story similar to the
preceding outline.

Recitation

Each child prepares to tell the whole story. The teacher
calls on one to begin; after he has proceeded at some length,
another takes up the story and goes on.

3. *These Huge Machines were Hard to run by Hand*

Preparation and Presentation

"Have you ever seen a washing-machine that is run by
hand? How does it work? Is there any other way to work
a machine? We call that way of running it 'running machinery
by *power*'" (*writing the word on the board*).

"Are there any other kinds of power besides electricity?
Name them.

"Our story today tells how power first began to be used for
running machines."

Assimilation

Readings

Upper Group

BEARD and BAGLEY. Our Old World Background, 332–334.
DARROW. Masters of Science and Invention, 50–53.
DARROW. Thinkers and Doers, 95–97 (difficult).
FORMAN. Stories of Useful Inventions, 119–120.
MARSHALL. Story of Human Progress, 107–113 (difficult).
ROCHELEAU. The Story of King Cotton, 22–23.
SMITH. Industrial History, 122–127 (difficult).
TOWLE. Heroes and Martyrs of Invention, 89–93.
TURPIN. Cotton, 61.
Compton's Pictured Encyclopedia (Spinning and Weaving, Cartwright).
World Book (Weaving: Power Loom, Cartwright).

Average Group

CARPENTER. How the World is Clothed, 43–44.

Lower Group

Read BEARD and BAGLEY with the children.

Teachers

BOGART. Economic History of the United States, 149–150.
GIBSON. Romance of Modern Manufacture, 59–62.
OSGOOD. History of Industry, 260.

Minimal Essentials

Historical Terms: **power; power loom; application of power to machinery**
Things to Remember

Running machines by hand is hard work; it also is a very slow method of manufacture.
Applying power to machinery makes the manufacturing process much faster; therefore more goods are produced.

Illustrative Material

GABRIEL (ED.). Pageant of America, V: 44.
Illustrate the application of power by several of the methods suggested in "Procedure during Assimilation."
World Book (Weaving).

Procedure during Assimilation

Reading as described on pages 24–29.
Demonstrate the use of power by showing (1) the type of phonograph that must be wound and one that is run electrically, (2) a sewing-machine that must be treadled by the feet and one run by a motor, (3) a rotary mimeograph that runs by hand and one run by electricity, (4) a washing-machine that must be turned by hand and one run by electricity, (5) a pump that must be worked by hand and one that is run by a gasoline engine.
Has any member of the class seen a mill wheel turned by water power? If so, describe it; if not, show a picture.
Make a list of machines that are ordinarily run by power; of those that are run by hand.

How many different kinds of power are used to run machines?
What is the derivation of the word *manufacture*? Does it apply today?
Drill on minimal essentials.
Objective test.

Organization

The teacher puts the outline on the board. Children tell what belongs under each point.

THE APPLICATION OF POWER TO MACHINERY

1. Running machines by hand
2. Application of different kinds of power
3. Results of the use of power

Recitation

The class makes a coöperative booklet to leave in the room library. Each row prepares and illustrates one point. The booklet is read at a Parent-Teacher Association meeting.

4. *Machines used so Much Cotton that a New Way of Cleaning it had to be Found*

Preparation

"Have you ever seen or read about the way cotton grows? Describe it."

Show cotton bolls. The children try to pick out the seeds.

Show a map of cotton-growing areas [1] of the United States.

Presentation

Since spinning-machines and weaving-machines had been invented, they could do much more work than men alone had been able to do before; therefore they could make much more cotton cloth.

The mills kept calling to the cotton-planter: "Send us more raw cotton. We need more cotton. Our machines work so fast that we can't supply them with enough material. *We want more cotton.*"

[1] Brigham, A. P., and McFarlane, C. T., *Essentials of Geography*, Book II, pp. 105–106; Atwood, W. W., *New Geography*, Book II, p. 282; Smith, J. R., *Human Geography*, Book II, p. 24; McMurry, F. M., and Parkins, A. E., *Advanced Geography*, p. 100.

The cotton-planters planted more fields and raised more plants. But when they picked the ripe bolls a serious problem arose. How could the seeds be removed from such huge quantities of cotton? The mills could not use it until the seeds were taken out, and there weren't enough laborers in all the South to do the work. How unhappy the planters were! There was a splendid chance for them to make a great deal of money if only they could remove the seeds more quickly.

Living among them at the time was a young Yankee school-teacher. A woman who knew him said: "Ask my young friend if he can't help you. He is so bright that I am sure he could plan a machine to do the work you want."

You may well believe that they were glad to visit the young school-teacher and ask him to make a machine for them. He worked for a while, and then did invent an engine that could remove the seeds.

After that the planters could raise all the cotton that their lands would produce and send it to the mills, for the seeds could be removed quickly.

PRESENTATION TEST

Check the best answer:

a. The mills needed more raw cotton

    _ _ _ because a great deal of the raw cotton was not very good

    _ _ _ because the machines worked so much faster than men had

    _ _ _ because there was so much wasted

b. It would not be of any use to raise more cotton

    _ _ _ unless the spinning mills really wanted it

    _ _ _ unless they were quite sure they could sell it all

    _ _ _ unless the seeds could be taken out more quickly than by hand

Assimilation

Readings

Upper Group

BACHMAN. Great Inventors and their Inventions, 105–120.
BEARD and BAGLEY. The History of the American People, 291–293.
BROOKS. Story of Cotton, 89–99.
BURNHAM. Hero Tales from History, 266–269.
DARROW. Thinkers and Doers, 97–103 (difficult).
DAVIDSON. Founders and Builders of our Nation, 137–144.
ELLIS. Makers of our Country, 122–125.
EVANS. America First, 232–235.
FOOTE and SKINNER. Makers and Defenders of America, 205–209.

GORDY. Leaders in Making America, 246–247.
GORDY. Stories of Later American History, 158–159.
GUERBER. Story of the Great Republic, 45–48.
HOLLAND. Historic Inventions, 96–110.
LEFFERTS. American Leaders, II : 1–14.
MONTGOMERY. Beginners' American History, 156–162.
MOWRY. American Inventions and Inventors, 148–158.
PERRY. Four American Inventors, 73–130.
PERRY and PRICE. American History, II : 143–144.
ROCHELEAU. Story of King Cotton, 23–28.
RUGG and SCHWEPPE. The Westward Movement and the Growth of Transportation, 94–98.
SANFORD. The Story of Agriculture in the United States, 124–129 (difficult).
STONE and FICKETT. Days and Deeds a Hundred Years Ago, 53–67.
TAPPAN. Elementary History of our Country, 172–173.
TOWLE. Heroes and Martyrs of Invention, 93–102.
TURPIN. Cotton, 76–86.
WOODBURN and MORAN. Makers of America, 181–187.
Compton's Pictured Encyclopedia (Cotton, Whitney).
World Book (Whitney, Cotton, Cotton Gin).

Average Group

BARNES. Elementary History of the United States, 243–249.
BEARD and BAGLEY. A First Book in American History, 213–217.
CARPENTER. How the World is Clothed, 29–33.
COE. Makers of the Nation, 190–197.
ELSON and MACMULLAN. Story of our Country, II : 15–18.
FORMAN. First Lessons in American History, 196–198.
GORDY. Elementary History of the United States, 193–194.
McFEE. Stories of American Inventions, 1–13.
PARKMAN. Conquests of Invention, 63–79.
SOUTHWORTH. Builders of our Country, II : 123–126.
UHRBROCK and OWENS. Famous Americans, 208–214.

Lower Group

CHAMBERLAIN. How we are Clothed, 46–49.
CHASE and CLOW. Stories of Industry, II : 13–15.
McMASTER. Primary History of the United States, 174–175.
SHILLIG. Four Wonders, 10–11, 15–20.

Teachers

BOGART. Economic History of the United States, 133–135, 167–170, 181–182.
COMAN. Industrial History of the United States, 239, 259.
THOMPSON. Age of Invention, 32–52.

Minimal Essentials

Name of Person: **Eli Whitney**
Date: **1793** — invention of the cotton gin
Historical Term: **cotton gin**
Things to Remember
Separating the seeds from the cotton was slow work.
The new textile machinery needed much cotton.
Eli Whitney invented the cotton gin, which removed the seeds quickly.
Then cotton-growing spread very fast through the South.

Illustrative Material

GABRIEL (ED.). Pageant of America, III: 143–144.
Child's World Pictures: Picking the Cotton.
Keystone Views: 96, First Cotton Gin; 97, A Modern Cotton Gin.

Procedure during Assimilation

Reading as described on pages 24–29.
Picture study based on the illustrative material listed above.
If cotton bolls can be procured, children try to separate the seeds by hand; they rig up a crude combing device to see whether time can be saved in separating the seeds.
Use the dramatization "Eli Whitney." *The Historical Outlook*, XVI: 130–131.
Find in the World Almanac (under "Cotton Production") the statistics showing the increase in cotton production in the United States from 1800 to 1920.[1] Make a graph to illustrate. How has the cotton gin influenced this increase? What does the word *gin* mean?
The class may make a booklet about cotton.[2]
Drill on minimal essentials.
Objective test.

Organization

The teacher and the children working together produce an outline somewhat similar to the following:

THE INVENTION OF THE COTTON GIN

1. The great demand for cotton
2. Invention of the cotton gin
3. Effect on the South

Recitation

A socialized recitation following the outline given above.

5. *Sewing-Machines helped in Making Cloth into Garments*

Preparation

"When the spinning-machines had turned out so much thread that workers couldn't handle it by the old methods, what had men done?

"When the machines for making cloth had turned out so much that raw cotton couldn't be supplied fast enough, what had men done?"

[1] An increase in bales of 500 pounds each from 73,222 bales in 1800 to 12,987,000 bales in 1920.

[2] "A Booklet about Cotton." *The Twentieth Yearbook of the National Society for the Study of Education*, Part I, p. 65; Lutz, Gertrude, "Booklets that are not Forgotten." *School Arts Magazine*, XXIV: 48–50.

Presentation

Our story today tells us what happened when cloth began to be very plentiful. The old ways of sewing by hand were too slow to use up the material. So what do you expect to find that men did about it?

Assimilation

Readings

Upper Group

BACHMAN. Great Inventors and their Inventions, 121–141.
BEARD and BAGLEY. The History of the American People, 294–295.
BURNHAM. Hero Tales from History, 282–285.
DARROW. Thinkers and Doers, 148–159 (difficult).
FOOTE and SKINNER. Makers and Defenders of America, 209–212.
HOLLAND. Historic Inventions, 206–214.
MORRIS. Heroes of Progress in America, 159–165.
TOWLE. Heroes and Martyrs of Invention, 180–189.
Compton's Pictured Encyclopedia (Sewing-Machine, Howe).
World Book (Sewing-Machine, Howe).

Average Group

BEARD and BAGLEY. A First Book in American History, 218–220.
CARPENTER. How the World is Clothed, 327–328.
FORMAN. First Lessons in American History, 243–245.
McFEE. Stories of American Inventions, 74–83.
PARKMAN. Conquests of Invention, 87–103.

Lower Group

CHAMBERLAIN. How we are Clothed, 163–166.

Teachers

COCHRANE. Romance of Industry and Invention, 72–80.
COMAN. Industrial History of the United States, 260–261.
GIBSON. Romance of Modern Manufacture, 114–122.

Minimal Essentials

Name of Person: **Elias** (ē lï′ăs) **Howe**
Date: **a year after the annexation of Texas**
Historical Term: **clothing industry**
Things to Remember
    Clothing was formerly sewed by hand.
    The sewing-machine was invented by Elias Howe.
    Women's work in the home was made much lighter by sewing-machines.

Procedure during Assimilation

Reading as described on pages 24–29.
Two girls conduct an experiment in the sewing class. One sews a certain seam by hand; another equally skillful sews a seam of the same length on a machine. A timekeeper records the time used by each. The seams and the records are presented to the class as evidence of the value of the machine.

Send a committee to observe the working of a hand sewing-machine. How does it
  differ from a modern machine?
What have women done with the time saved for them by the sewing-machine?
Drill on minimal essentials.
Objective test.

Organization

The teacher selects certain children to put their own outlines on the board. The class criticizes.

INVENTION OF THE SEWING-MACHINE

  1. Disadvantages of hand sewing
  2. The invention of the sewing-machine
  3. Effects

Recitation

Each child tells the story to his mother and brings from her
a written statement as to his work.

6. *All these Machines were put into Great Buildings called Factories*

Preparation

"Are there any factories in this town?

"Have you ever been inside one?

"In what ways do they look different from the colonial
kitchens, in which most of the work was done during the
colonial period?

"Name different kinds of manufactured goods."

Presentation

As more of the manufacturing of the world began to be
done by machines, the machines themselves grew larger and
larger. They took up so much room that people could no
longer have them in their kitchens nor anywhere else in their
houses.

As the machines grew larger they naturally cost more
money also. At last they became so expensive that it was
impossible for each spinner to own a spinning-machine and
for each weaver to own a weaving-machine. How was the
work to be carried on, then?

The system that was finally worked out was as follows: A wealthy man would buy up a number of machines, build a large building for them, and then let his neighbors come into the building and work the machines. He would pay them a small sum of money regularly for their work, but would keep the goods himself. This was very different from the old method, by which the workers owned their own tools and sold the goods they made. The new system was called the *factory system* (*pointing to the expression written on the board*). It is the method by which almost all goods are made today.

Just about the same time that factories were beginning, the War of 1812 came on. We could no longer buy manufactured goods from England, and her warships roving the seas kept us from buying from anyone else.

How were we to secure our manufactured goods? America answered, "We will make our own manufactured goods in these new factories that are just starting up." And we did. So, although war is always a terrible thing, this war had at least one good effect: it helped us to begin to manufacture goods for ourselves.

PRESENTATION TEST

1. *Check the two best answers:*

Workers could no longer do the work in their own homes
_ _ _ because the machines were too big
_ _ _ because they had forgotten how
_ _ _ because the machines were too heavy to move
_ _ _ because the machines cost too much money

2. *Check the best answer:*

a. The only way in which all the necessary machinery for manufacturing could be brought together was
_ _ _ for one worker to buy one piece and another worker another piece
_ _ _ for a rich man to buy enough machinery for the whole process
_ _ _ for the government to buy the machinery

b. In the old days the workers were paid
_ _ _ by the money they got from selling their product
_ _ _ by wages

c. Under the factory system the workers were paid
_ _ _ by the money they got from selling their product
_ _ _ by wages

d. The War of 1812
_ _ _ helped the United States in manufacturing
_ _ _ did not help the United States in manufacturing
_ _ _ did not make any difference in our manufacturing

Assimilation

Readings

Upper Group

BEARD and BAGLEY. The History of the American People, 312–317.
BEARD and BAGLEY. Our Old World Background, 337–340.
BROOKS. Story of Cotton, 109–125, 253–254.
MOWRY. American Inventions and Inventors, 153–157.
ROCHELEAU. The Story of King Cotton, 28–31.
SMITH. Industrial History, 109–112 (difficult).
TURPIN. Cotton, 61–65, 71–74.
Compton's Pictured Encyclopedia (Factories).
World Book (Factory and Factory System).

Average Group

CARPENTER. How the World is Clothed, 329–333.

Lower Group

SHILLIG. Four Wonders, 13–15.
WAYLAND. History Stories for Primary Grades, 41–43.

Teachers

BOGART. Economic History of the United States, 150–155, 162–165.
CHEYNEY. Industrial and Social History of England, 185–189, 212–213.
OSGOOD. History of Industry, 260–261, 265–271.
SCHLESINGER. Political and Social History of the United States, 5–10, 79–80.
THOMPSON. Age of Invention, 84–109.
American Citizenship Course in United States History, IV: 75–108.
Teachers College Record, XVI: 354–357.

Minimal Essentials

Name of Person: **Samuel Slater** [1] (slāt′ĕr)
Historical Terms: **factory system; quantity production**
Things to Remember
 Goods were formerly made by hand in people's homes.
 The newer machines were too large and too expensive for each home to own.
 Factories made great quantities of goods and sold them.

Illustrative Material

GABRIEL (ED.). Pageant of America, V: 35–41, 149–150.
Pictures of modern factories: exterior and interior views.

Procedure during Assimilation

Reading as described on pages 24–29.
Make a picture collection of advertisements showing modern manufacturing plants.
Take children on a trip through a local factory to show them the methods of division
 of labor and quantity production. If possible choose a factory working in tex-
 tiles, so that the class may see the types of machines for sewing.
Children list the factories in the town (consult the local Chamber of Commerce).
Explain the cartoon in Knowlton's *Making History Graphic*, p. 31.

---

[1] Not included in the list of minimal essentials referred to on page 5.

The teacher puts on the board the statistics of the increase in the number of factories in the United States from 1850 to the present time.[1] Children graph the numbers.

Drill on minimal essentials.

Objective test.

Organization

The teacher puts the outline on the board. Children write a summary sentence for each point.

Coming of the Factory System

1. Hand manufacture at home
2. The beginning of the factory system
3. Effect

Recitation

Each child tells the complete story to his father and brings from him a written statement as to the work.

7. Factories needed Many Working People; so Towns began to grow into Great Cities

Preparation

"Where do the laborers at (the largest local factory) live? Do most of them live in any particular part of the city?

"If so, how many houses do they occupy? How many grocery stores are needed to supply them with food? How many drug stores, hardware stores, etc.?

"How many doctors and dentists have their offices in that section? How many lawyers?

"How many teachers are there in the schools of that section?

"How many churches are needed?"

(*These questions may be given out as subjects for investigation.*)

Presentation

From the results of our study you may see that as soon as factories are put up in a town, the town must grow to meet the needs of the factory workers. In this way, places which used to be small villages began to grow into towns when fac-

---

[1] *Fourteenth Census of the United States* (1920), Vols. VIII–X (Manufactures).

tories were built. And places that had been towns grew into cities. And places which had been cities grew to be enormous cities. That is one reason why there are so many large cities in the United States now, while there were few large cities years ago.

PRESENTATION TEST

Check the best answer:

Cities began to grow with the introduction of the factory system

___ because people liked to live where there were crowds

___ because factories needed workers, and workers needed supplies

___ because if one person moved to town, others followed his example

Assimilation

Readings

Upper Group

BEARD and BAGLEY. The History of the American People, 325–326, 490–491.
BEARD and BAGLEY. Our Old World Background, 340–341.
BROOKS. Story of Cotton, 125–131.
BURNHAM. The Making of our Country, 292–293.
GORDY. History of the United States, 547–548.
MARSHALL. The Story of Human Progress, 129–132, 136–137 (difficult).
PERRY and PRICE. American History, II : 121–122.
SMITH. Industrial History, 130–131 (difficult).
Compton's Pictured Encyclopedia (Cities : Rise of our Giant Cities).
World Book (City — *use the graphs*).

Average Group

FORMAN. First Lessons in American History, 267.
GORTON. Elementary Civics, 10–13.

Lower Group

MCMASTER. Primary History of the United States, 233–234.

Teachers

BOGART. Economic History of the United States, 256–257, 258–259.
COMAN. Industrial History of the United States, 233.
OSGOOD. History of Industry, 271–272.
Baltimore County Course of Study, 559–560.

Minimal Essentials

Historical Term: **growth of cities**
Things to Remember

To be near the factories, people began to crowd into the towns.
The towns grew to be large cities.
Nowadays more people in the United States live in cities than on farms.

Illustrative Material

MCKINLEY. Illustrated Topics for American History : S. 21.
ROBBINS. School History of the American People, 531 (graph).
Keystone Views : 336, Chicago in 1831 (slide only) ; 340, San Francisco in 1849 (slide only).

Procedure during Assimilation

Reading as described on pages 24–29.

Name places in the vicinity which grew from villages to towns and others which grew from towns into cities with the introduction of factories.

On an outline map of the United States, record with a yellow dot all cities [1] of 100,000 to 500,000 population; with a blue dot all cities of 500,000 to 750,000 population; with green, those from 750,000 to 1,000,000; and with red, those of 1,000,000 or more.

Children graph the growth of cities, following the figures given in the World Almanac (Population: Growth of United States Cities) or the graph mentioned under "Illustrative Material."

Why do we now wish that many people would move back to the farms? Why don't they?

The class makes coöperatively a list of the ways in which the people of the United States have to live differently if they live in large cities than if they live on farms.

Drill on minimal essentials.

Objective test.

Organization

The teacher writes the following outline on the board. Children are to tell which points belong under each subhead.

THE GROWTH OF CITIES

1. Need for more workmen
2. Need for supplies of food and raw material
   Transportation facilities
3. Problems of city life

Recitation

The points are divided, each child choosing one on which to make a three-minute speech.

A drill lesson on section I of Unit VIII should be given at this point.

II. MEN HAD TO FIND WAYS OF SENDING NEWS TO PEOPLE IN DISTANT PARTS

1. *In Early Days Messengers and Letters were the Chief Ways of Sending News*

Preparation

"In our study of colonial life we found that people sent word to distant parts by what means?"

No additional presentation is needed.

[1] Statesman's Yearbook (United States: Cities), or World Almanac (Cities: Population).

Assimilation

Readings

Upper Group

BACHMAN. Great Inventors and their Inventions, 208–210.

BLAISDELL. The Story of American History, 312–316.

DARROW. Thinkers and Doers, 133–135 (difficult).

FINCH. Every Day Civics, 148–149.

FORMAN. Stories of Useful Inventions, 226–228.

HILL. Community Life and Civic Problems, 381–388.

LOGIE. From Columbus to Lincoln, 169–171.

MARSHALL. The Story of Human Progress, 218–225, 260–262 (difficult).

MONTGOMERY. Beginners' American History, 197.

MOWRY. American Inventions and Inventors, 258–260.

ROCHELEAU. Carrying the United States Mail, 3–16.

RUGG and SCHWEPPE. The Westward Movement and the Growth of Transportation, 6–7.

TAPPAN. Elementary History of our Country, 189.

ZIEGLER and JAQUETTE. Our Community, 86–87.

Average Group

BEEBY. How the World grows Smaller, 247–254.

EGGLESTON. Stories of American Life and Adventure, 137–147.

GORDY. Elementary History of the United States, 190–192.

LARGE. Every Day Wonders, 106–108.

REINSCH. The Young Citizen's Reader, 113.

TURPIN. Brief Biographies from American History, 232–233.

Lower Group

BAILEY. What to do for Uncle Sam, 121.

CHAMBERLAIN. How we Travel, 18–23, 193–199.

HARTWELL. Story Hour Readings, IV: 251–255.

Teachers

Baltimore County Course of Study, 524.

Minimal Essentials

Historical Terms: postrider; communication

Things to Remember

To send news by messengers was very slow and costly.

Letters had to travel by stagecoach, by boat, or by postrider.

Therefore there was little communication between one part of the country and another.

Procedure during Assimilation

Reading as described on pages 24–29.

If possible show a copy of an old letter, folded to serve as an envelope. The local museum may possess examples.

In what way is the poem "Paul Revere's Ride" an example of our topic?

Show a map of the early postroads.[1]

Read to the class Browning's "How they brought the Good News from Ghent to Aix"[2] and "Pheidippides."

[1] Sparks, E. E., *The Expansion of the American People*, p. 250.

[2] Baldwin, James, *Fifty Famous Rides and Riders*, pp. 224–226.

Boy Scouts illustrate wigwagging.
Each child is to report to the class one interesting fact from his outside reading.
Drill on minimal essentials.
Objective test.

Organization

Each child makes his outline, the teacher criticizing and helping those who need help.

EARLY METHODS OF COMMUNICATION

1. By messenger; how the messenger traveled
2. By letter; how letters traveled

Recitation

The class is divided into two parts, each of which makes a complete booklet on one of the above points to leave in the school library.

2. *The Railroads carried Letters Faster*

Preparation

"You have seen postmen collecting letters from the post boxes in various places in the city. What is done with the letters in the post office? What is done with the mail after it is put on the train?"

(*If children do not know the answers to these questions, the questions are written down and serve as the basis for investigation or a trip.*)

No additional presentation is needed.

Assimilation

Readings

Upper Group

AUSTIN. Uncle Sam's Secrets, 21–23.
HILL. Community Life and Civic Problems, 390–391.
ROCHELEAU. Carrying the United States Mail, 16–28.
ROCHELEAU. Great American Industries: Transportation, 252–258.
ROLT-WHEELER. The Boy with the United States Mail.
TAPPAN. Travelers and Traveling, 15–19.
Compton's Pictured Encyclopedia (Post Office).
St. Nicholas, XVIII: Part I, 252–259.
World Book (Post Office: Railway Post Office).

Average Group

BEEBY. How the World grows Smaller, 191–216.
REINSCH. Young Citizen's Reader, 115–116.

Lower Group
   BAILEY. What to do for Uncle Sam, 123–124.

Teachers
   COCHRANE. Romance of Industry and Invention, 260–268.

Minimal Essentials

Historical Terms: **railway mail clerk; railway mail car; Post Office Department**
   (of the United States government)
Things to Remember
   Railway trains traveled much faster than messengers or stagecoaches.
   A special kind of car was built to carry the mail.
   Communication was much swifter afterwards.

Illustrative Material

Compton's Pictured Encyclopedia (Post Office).
Ford Educational Library: 12, Some of Uncle Sam's Workshops.

Procedure during Assimilation

Reading as described on pages 24–29.
Picture study based on the illustrative material listed above.
Children keep a record for a week of all incoming letters. From the postmark and
   the date of the letter find how much time was consumed in the journey.
Children go to the local post office to see how incoming mail is handled; outgoing
   mail.
Invite a railway mail clerk to address the class on how the mail is handled and on
   the time saved by modern methods.
Drill on minimal essentials.
Objective test.

Organization

   The teacher and the children working together make an
outline somewhat similar to the following:

UNITED STATES RAILWAY MAIL

   1. How the mail is handled
   2. Time saved
   3. Influence in making people think about the same questions

Recitation

   A child recites on one point, then calls on another to recite
on the second, and so on.

3. *The Telegraph sent Messages in an Instant*

Preparation

"If you wanted to send the reports of today's baseball game immediately to a newspaper in San Francisco, what would be the quickest way to do it?

"Has any one of you ever been inside a telegraph office? Did you see how the messages were sent? Could you understand the messages that came in?"

No additional presentation is needed.

Assimilation

Readings

Upper Group

BACHMAN. Great Inventors and their Inventions, 210–227.
BURNHAM. Hero Tales from History, 274–278.
BURTON. Builders of our Nation, 224–235.
CHANDLER and CHITWOOD. Makers of American History, 247–251.
DARROW. Thinkers and Doers, 135–147 (difficult).
EGGLESTON. A First Book in American History, 161–170.
ELLIS. Makers of our Country, 141–149.
EVANS. America First, 325–330.
FARIS. Real Stories from our History, 290–294.
FOOTE and SKINNER. Makers and Defenders of America, 309–314.
FORMAN. Stories of Useful Inventions, 235–239.
GORDY. Leaders in Making America, 281–286.
GORDY. Stories of Later American History, 201–207.
GUERBER. Story of the Great Republic, 124–125.
HILL. Community Life and Civic Problems, 386.
HOLLAND. Historic Inventions, 168–188.
LEFFERTS. American Leaders, II: 82–97.
MARSHALL. Story of Human Progress, 262–264 (difficult).
MONTGOMERY. Beginners' American History, 197–204.
MORRIS. Historical Tales: American, 255–269.
MOWRY. American Inventions and Inventors, 270–277.
PERRY. Four American Inventors, 133–201.
PERRY and PRICE. American History, II: 118–119.
STIMPSON. The Child's Book of American Biography, 155–163.
STONE and FICKETT. Days and Deeds a Hundred Years Ago, 121–130.
TAPPAN. Elementary History of our Country, 199–200.
WOODBURN and MORAN. Makers of America, 224–228.
WRIGHT. Children's Stories of American Progress, 209–229.
Compton's Pictured Encyclopedia (Morse, Telegraph).
Lessons in Community and National Life, Series B, 85–87.
World Book (Morse, Telegraph).

Average Group

BARNES. Elementary History of the United States, 273–282.
BEARD and BAGLEY. A First Book in American History, 228–231.

BEEBY. How the World grows Smaller, 228–246, 254–259.
COE. Makers of the Nation, 246–252.
DRESSEL, ROBBINS, and GRAFF. New Barnes Readers, V: 235–246.
ELSON and McMULLAN. Story of our Country, II: 116–122.
FORMAN. First Lessons in American History, 242–243.
GORDY. American Leaders and Heroes, 273–281.
GORDY. Elementary History of the United States, 230–232.
MACE. Primary History, 341–344.
McFEE. Stories of American Inventions, 50–73.
MORRIS. Primary History of the United States, 236.
MOWRY. First Steps in the History of our Country, 237–242.
NIDA. Following the Frontier, 295–300.
PARKMAN. Conquests of Invention, 350–378.
SOUTHWORTH. Builders of our Country, II: 180–183.
TURPIN. Brief Biographies of American History, 233–236.
UHRBROCK and OWENS. Famous Americans, 249–256.

Lower Group

CHAMBERLAIN. How we Travel, 204–211.
TATE, WITHERS, and BROWNE. Child's World, Fifth Reader, 332–342.

Teachers

COCHRANE. Romance of Industry and Invention, 269–279.
COMAN. Industrial History of the United States, 251–252.
Baltimore County Course of Study, 523.

Minimal Essentials

Name of Person: **Samuel F. B. Morse**
Date: **1844** — the sending of the first message by the telegraph
Historical Terms: **telegraph; Morse code**
Things to Remember

Samuel F. B. Morse invented the telegraph.
The telegraph sent messages which were received almost instantly.
Then news could be spread quickly.
Quick communication is a great help in making people think about the same
  questions.

Illustrative Material

Compton's Pictured Encyclopedia (Telegraph).
Keystone Views: 335, Samuel F. B. Morse (slide only).
World Book (Telegraph).

Procedure during Assimilation

Reading as described on pages 24–29.
Picture study based on the illustrative material listed above.
Show children the forms, and explain day letter, night letter, etc.
Take the children to the telegraph office to observe the sending of messages.
Use the dramatization "Samuel Morse's Telegraph." Hubbard, *Little American
  History Plays*, pp. 166–169.
Using the code given in McFee's *Stories of American Inventions*, p. 60, or in the
  World Book (under "Telegraph"), children write short messages to each other,
  or sign their names.
Drill on minimal essentials.
Objective test.

Organization

Each child makes his own outline, somewhat as follows:

INVENTION OF THE TELEGRAPH

1. Early efforts
2. Morse's struggles
3. Final success
4. Effects of the telegraph on communication

Recitation

A socialized recitation.

4. *Telegraphing across the Ocean was made Possible by the Cable*

Preparation

"Why do we call certain poles along the side of the road telegraph poles?

"What do the workers do when they come to a very broad river? a lake?

"What great difficulties would be encountered in telegraphing across the ocean?"

No additional presentation is needed.

Assimilation

Readings

Upper Group

EVANS. America First, 396–401.
FOOTE and SKINNER. Makers and Defenders of America, 314–316.
FORMAN. Stories of Useful Inventions, 238–239.
MORRIS. Heroes of Progress in America, 153–158.
MOWRY. American Inventions and Inventors, 278–285.
PERRY and PRICE. American History, II: 252–254.
TAPPAN. Elementary History of our Country, 231.
Compton's Pictured Encyclopedia (Cables, Submarine).
World Book (Cables, Field).

Average Group

BARNES. Elementary History of the United States, 282.
ELSON and MACMULLAN. Story of our Country, II: 153–160.
GORDY. Elementary History of the United States, 289–290.
MACE. Primary History, 345–347.
MOWRY. First Steps in the History of our Country, 242–244.
SOUTHWORTH. Builders of our Country, II: 184–185.

Lower Group

BARNES. Primary History of the United States, 214.
CHAMBERLAIN. How we Travel, 219–227.

Teachers

COCHRANE. Romance of Industry and Invention, 279–283.

Minimal Essentials

Name of Person: **Cyrus W. Field**
Date: **just after the Civil War**
Historical Term: **Atlantic cable**
Things to Remember

Somebody had to find a way to telegraph across the ocean.
The best way was to lay a cable on the bottom of the ocean.
Cyrus W. Field laid the first Atlantic cable.

Illustrative Material

Compton's Pictured Encyclopedia (Cables).
Mentor, X: 29–31 (July, 1922).
World Book (Cable).

Procedure during Assimilation

Reading as described on pages 24–29.
Children trace on a slated map the principal cable routes [1] of the world.
From the local telegraph office find the cost of sending cables to various foreign ports.
Drill on minimal essentials.
Objective test.

Organization

The children make their own outlines, the teacher working especially with those who had difficulty the last time.[2]

Laying of the Atlantic Cable

1. Difficulties
2. Final success
3. Effect

Recitation

Continue the socialized recitation.[3]

5. *Newspapers could then gather News quickly*

Preparation

Show a copy of the morning newspaper. Call attention to articles from London, Paris, etc. "How do you suppose the news came to us so quickly?

"Who sent the cable?"

---

[1] *Journal of Geography*, I: 317–320; Shepherd, W. R., *Historical Atlas*, pp. 179–180; World Book (Cable); Goode, J. P., *School Atlas*, p. 13.
[2] See page 419.
[3] Whitney, W. T., *The Socialized Recitation*.

Presentation

Our story today tells us how the great newspapers of the country have organized a tremendous business army of people who gather the news in every out-of-the-way corner of the globe and send it home.

At the breakfast tables of the world every morning Englishmen, Americans, Frenchmen, and Spaniards are all reading in their newspapers about the same topics. Thus we are helped to know what the rest of the world is doing, and thus people are made to think about the same world questions.

Assimilation
Readings

Upper Group

BLAISDELL. The Story of American History, 311–312.
DARROW. Thinkers and Doers, 113–115 (difficult).
HILL. Community Life and Civic Problems, 393.
HUGHES. Community Civics, 429–430.
MARSHALL. The Story of Human Progress, 326–328 (difficult).
MORRIS. Heroes of Progress in America, 287–295 (Greeley).
PARTON. Captains of Industry, 49–58 (Greeley).
PERRY and PRICE. American History, II : 117.
ROCHELEAU. Story of Newspapers and Books, 4–17.
WILLIAMS. Some Successful Americans, 55–77 (Greeley).
World Book (Newspaper).

Average Group

BEEBY. How the World grows Smaller, 260–284.
EGGLESTON. Stories of Great Americans, 145–152 (Greeley).
LANE (ED.). Industries of Today, 127–137.

Lower Group

HARTWELL. Story Hour Readings, IV : 220–224.

Teachers

THOMPSON. Age of Invention, 146–149.
Encyclopædia Britannica (Newspapers : Journalism).
New International Encyclopædia (Press Associations and Agencies).

Minimal Essentials

Name of Person: **Horace Greeley**
Historical Terms: New York Tribune ; **the press**
Things to Remember

Telegraphs made it easy for newspapers to collect news while it was still new.
Therefore newspapers became popular.
Then all people in the United States read the same news, and so thought about the same questions.

Illustrative Material

Mentor IX: 8, 11, 12–28, 30 (June, 1921).

Procedure during Assimilation

Reading as described on pages 24–29.

Collect clippings from the front pages of morning newspapers, especially of those from foreign countries. Post on the bulletin board.

Children bring to class clippings of news items sent by the Associated Press, the United Press, special correspondent, etc.

Take a trip to the local newspaper office. Arrange for an explanation of the way news is sent from distant points.

Drill on minimal essentials.

Objective test.

Organization

The teacher and the children work out coöperatively an outline somewhat like this:

EFFECT OF THE TELEGRAPH ON THE NEWSPAPERS

    1. Old ways of gathering news
    2. Modern ways of gathering news
    3. Effect of the newspapers on modern life

Recitation

Each child prepares a complete story based on the outline above. One is chosen to tell his story in the assembly.

A drill lesson on section II of Unit VIII should be given at this point.

III. REVIEW BRIEFLY THE STORIES OF THE DEVELOPMENT OF TRANSPORTATION AND FARM MACHINERY TO THE CIVIL WAR PERIOD

America led the World in her Clipper Ships

Preparation

"What do you suppose shipowners did with their sailing vessels when the steamboat was invented?"

Presentation

We must not imagine that as soon as a few steamboats began to run on our rivers and lakes, all sailing vessels were cast aside. By no means! They had cost too much money and, of course, they still sailed as well as they ever did.

Also the first steamboats were very imperfect affairs. It was a long time before they could cross the ocean.

So sailboats were still used for long voyages. The American boats were more beautiful than any of the others — long, slender, and graceful as a bird. They went so fast and cut the water so cleanly that they were called clipper ships (*pointing to the words written on the board*).

As the years went by, the time came when even these white-winged ships had to bow before the improved steamer, but for a quarter of a century at least they were the rulers of the deep.

PRESENTATION TEST

1. *Check the best answer:*

   When the steamboat was first invented

   _ _ _ all sailing ships left the ocean

   _ _ _ sailing vessels continued in use

2. *Check two answers:*

   The American clipper ships were called clippers

   _ _ _ because their sails were clipped

   _ _ _ because they went so fast

   _ _ _ because their sharp fronts cut the water

   _ _ _ because they looked like clippers

Assimilation

Readings

Upper Group

BURNHAM. The Making of our Country, 263–264.

FARIS. Where our History was Made, Book II, 250–255.

ROBBINS. School History of the American People, 289.

ROCHELEAU. Great American Industries: Transportation, 61–64.

ROCHELEAU. Story of Ships and Shipping, 14–17.

WOODBURN and MORAN. Elementary American History and Government, 263–264, 372–373.

Compton's Pictured Encyclopedia (Ships).

Standard Reference Work (Clipper).

Average Group

Read Compton's Pictured Encyclopedia with the children.

Lower Group

GRANT. Story of the Ship (picture of Clipper Ship and Sail Plan of a Full-Rigged Ship).

Teachers

INGERSOLL. The Book of the Ocean, 35, 38, 159–165.

PAINE. The Old Merchant Marine, 154–184.

Minimal Essentials

Historical Term: **clipper ships**
Things to Remember
    Clipper ships were long and narrow.
    With a good wind, they could go as fast as steamboats.
    They carried on commerce in all parts of the world.

Illustrative Material

GRANT. Story of the Ship: Clipper Ship and Sail Plan of a Full-Rigged Ship.
INGERSOLL. The Book of the Ocean, 158, 164.
McKINLEY. Illustrated Topics for American History: S. 28.

Procedure during Assimilation

Reading as described on pages 24–29.
Invite an old sailor in the community to tell the children how sailing in sailing ships
    differed from that in present-day steamships.
Boys in manual-training classes may make a model of a clipper ship.
In the art period draw or paint sailing vessels.
Compare speed records of clipper ships [1] with those of steamers.[2]

Organization

The teacher gives the class the following outline:

AMERICA'S CLIPPER SHIPS
    1. How they were built
    2. Their commerce

Recitation

Each child prepares the story of both points.

IV. A NEW METAL INDUSTRY WAS BEGUN

1. *New Ways of Working Iron were Found*

Preparation

"What do you suppose all these machines we have mentioned are made of?

"From what is iron obtained?" (*Show a piece of iron ore.*)

"How is the iron separated from the rest of the ore?

"Do you know the difference between iron and steel?"

---

[1] Compton's Pictured Encyclopedia (Ships).
[2] World Almanac (Ship Speed Records: Fast Passages).

Presentation

When so many machines of all kinds were being made, it was necessary to have great quantities of iron. Not only was more iron needed, but a much better quality was required. For example, in making locomotives a very hard tough iron had to be used, because the parts of an engine are put under great strain.

The old methods of melting iron were not very good; they left many substances in it that ought to be taken out. There, again, men set themselves to solve the problem and to fill the need. As a result much better ways of smelting and working iron were discovered.

The new material that was made was called steel.

PRESENTATION TEST

Check the best answer:

The chief thing that was needed was

_ _ _ to get more iron ore out of the ground

_ _ _ to find a way to treat iron so that it would stand great strain

_ _ _ to lower the price of iron

Assimilation

Readings

Upper Group

BACHMAN. Great Inventors and their Inventions, 161–185.

BEARD and BAGLEY. The History of the American People, 104, 295–296.

BEARD and BAGLEY. Our Old World Background, 334–335.

CHASE and CLOW. Stories of Industry, I: 63–65, 74–80.

HUSBAND. America at Work, 20–31.

MARSHALL. Story of Human Progress, 85–96 (difficult).

PARTON. Captains of Industry, 43–48.

ROCHELEAU. Great American Industries: Minerals, 96–101.

TOWLE. Heroes and Martyrs of Invention, 190–193.

Compton's Pictured Encyclopedia (Iron: How Iron is changed into Steel).

World Book (Iron: Blast Furnace).

Average Group

PARKMAN. Conquests of Invention, 298–309.

TAPPAN. Diggers in the Earth, 59–64.

Lower Group

WAYLAND. History Stories for Primary Grades, 47–49.

Teachers

BOGART. Economic History of the United States, 170–171, 182–184.

COCHRANE. Romance of Industry and Invention, 20–31.

COMAN. Industrial History of the United States, 187–189.

GIBSON. Romance of Modern Manufacture, 263–273.

OSGOOD. History of Industry, 277–283.

Baltimore County Course of Study, 529.

Minimal Essentials

Historical Terms: steel; smelting; Industrial Revolution
Things to Remember
  The use of so many machines called for much iron.
  Steel is much harder than iron.
  Better ways of making steel were found.
  All these great changes in the ways of making things are called the Industrial
    Revolution.

Illustrative Material

GABRIEL (ED.). Pageant of America, V: 176–185.
Compton's Pictured Encyclopedia (Iron and Steel).
Keystone Views: 282, Digging Iron Ore; 283, Final Rolling Mill Action.

Procedure during Assimilation

Reading as described on pages 24–29.
Picture study based on the illustrative material listed above.
The teacher may investigate the local foundries, forge works, or repair shops to
    ascertain whether their operations would serve as the subject of a class trip.
    The object is to see the general method of working in iron; no attempt should
    be made to follow the process in detail.
Sand-table construction showing the mining, transporting, and smelting of iron.[1]
Children list common articles made of iron; of steel.
Drill on minimal essentials.
Objective test.

Organization

The teacher puts the following outline on the board:

IMPROVED WAYS OF WORKING IN IRON

  1. Old methods of working iron
  2. Improved methods
  3. Effect of the improvement

Recitation

Children tell what points belong under each heading.

2. *We began to use Coal instead of Wood to run our Machines*

Preparation

"What advantages does wood have over coal as a fuel?
"What advantages does coal have over wood?
"Do you know of any other materials used as fuel?"

---

[1] "Iron Ore." *The Twentieth Yearbook of the National Society for the Study of
Education*, Part I, p. 43.

Presentation

When so much iron was being smelted you may readily see that much fuel was needed to keep up those extremely hot fires. If we had had to depend on wood, the forests would have been cut down even sooner than they were.

And besides, wood does not give a steady enough heat to smelt iron successfully. Some other fuel should be used instead.

For many long ages people had known that there was a kind of heavy black stone (coal) that would burn. In the United States some people in Pennsylvania had burned it occasionally.

But when wood proved to be not satisfactory as a fuel, coal mines were dug, stoves were built especially for burning coal, and its use became common. We have continued to use it from that day to this; it is the chief fuel of the world, although perhaps in the future oil may take its place.

PRESENTATION TEST

Check the two best answers:

Great quantities of fuel were needed

_ _ _ to keep the machines running
_ _ _ to keep people warm
_ _ _ to smelt so much iron
_ _ _ to use up our supplies of coal

Assimilation

Readings

Upper Group

CHASE and CLOW. Stories of Industry, I : 3–5.
MOWRY. American Inventions and Inventors, 44–50.
PERRY and PRICE. American History, II : 116–117.
ROCHELEAU. Great American Industries : Minerals, 8–13.
ROCHELEAU. Story of Coal.

Average Group

PERRY and PRICE. American History, II : 116–117.

Lower Group

SHEPHERD. Geography for Beginners, 45–50.
WAYLAND. History Stories for Primary Grades, 44–46.

Teachers

BOGART. Economic History of the United States, 171–172.
COMAN. Industrial History of the United States, 187–189, 241.

Minimal Essentials

Historical Terms: **Coal Age; fuel**
Things to Remember
  To manufacture so much iron demanded much fuel.
  We began to use coal as a fuel.

Illustrative Material

Gabriel (Ed.). Pageant of America, V: 58, 60, 63, 65.
Society for Visual Education. Picturol: Mining Bituminous Coal.

Procedure during Assimilation

Reading as described on pages 24–29.
Show the class the diagram of a coal mine.[1]
Invite someone who has seen a coal mine to describe it to the class.
A committee of boys who are interested examine an oil-burning engine.
Drill on minimal essentials.
Objective test.

Organization

The teacher puts the following outline on the board:

USE OF COAL AS A FUEL
  1. Use of other material as fuel
  2. Beginning of use of coal
  3. Advantages in using coal

Recitation

Children tell what points belong under each heading.

A drill lesson on the minimal essentials should be given at this point, similar to that described on pages 112–113.

Questions 22–29 of Test IV of the *Informational Tests in United States History* to accompany Beard and Bagley's *History of the American People* may be used here.

TESTS ON THE ENTIRE UNIT

(To be given after all the stories are completed)

Test of Time-Sense. Pass mimeographed sheets of the following:

I. Below are the names of some noted men. Put the figure 1 before the name of the one who did his great work first, the figure 2 before the next, and so on.

_ _ _ Cyrus W. Field   _ _ _ Samuel F. B. Morse   _ _ _ Elias Howe
_ _ _ Eli Whitney   _ _ _ Samuel Slater

[1]Frye, A. E., *New Geography*, Book I, p. 108; Atwood, W. W., *New Geography*, Book II, p. 27; Rocheleau, W. F., *Great American Industries: Minerals*, pp. 21, 23.

MINIMAL ESSENTIALS OF UNIT VIII

PERSONS	TERMS	DATES[1]
Cyrus W. Field Elias Howe Samuel F. B. Morse Samuel Slater Eli Whitney	Atlantic cable clipper ship clothing industry Coal Age communication cotton gin factory system fuel growth of cities Industrial Revolution loom	*1793.* Invention of the cotton gin *1844.* The sending of the first message by telegraph Middle of the eighteenth century Year after the annexation of Texas Just after the Civil War
	Morse code *New York Tribune* postrider power power loom the press quantity production shuttle smelting spin spindle spinning jenny steel telegraph textile weave	Drill on the peaks of the time chart

II. Here is a list of dates or time-expressions:

> just after the Civil War
> 1793
> year after the annexation of Texas
> 1844
> middle of the eighteenth century

Put each one in the right blank in the sentences below:

1. Spinning and weaving inventions were made in the _ _ _ _.
2. The cotton gin was invented in _ _ _ _.
3. The sewing-machine was invented in the _ _ _ _.
4. In _ _ _ _ the telegraph was first used.
5. The Atlantic cable was laid _ _ _ _.

[1] Showalter, B. R., "Dates and Historical Perspective." *The Historical Outlook,* XIX: 28–31.

Test on Persons. Pass mimeographed sheets of the following:

Here is a list of names of noted men:

Cyrus W. Field	Elias Howe	Samuel F. B. Morse
Eli Whitney	Samuel Slater	

Put each one in the right blank in the sentences below:

1. The man who laid the Atlantic cable was _ _ _ _ _ _ _ _ _ _ _ _ .
2. The English inventions in textile machinery were brought to America by _ _ _ _ _ _ _ _ .
3. _ _ _ _ _ _ _ _ invented the cotton gin.
4. _ _ _ _ _ _ _ _ _ _ _ _ _ _ _ _ invented the telegraph.
5. The sewing-machine was invented by _ _ _ _ _ _ _ _ .

Test on Historical Terms. The teacher prepares descriptions such as the following, which may have been used previously as the subject of drill games.

I. Below is a list of terms:

spin	spindle
fuel	Industrial Revolution
growth of cities	power
quantity production	factory system
Coal Age	smelting

Put each one in the right blank in the sentences below:

1. Matter which will burn or produce heat is _ _ _ _ _ .
2. Turning out huge lots of goods to sell is _ _ _ _ _ _ _ _ .
3. Any kind of force that can be used to do any kind of work is _ _ _ _ _ .
4. A rod which turns round and round and twists the thread is called a _ _ _ _ .
5. The great changes in methods of work and living caused by the changes in machinery are called the _ _ _ _ _ _ _ _ .
6. Melting iron ore so that the iron all runs together is _ _ _ _ _ .
7. The period of time in which coal was used as the chief fuel of the world is called the _ _ _ _ _ _ _ _ .
8. To twist material into a thread is to _ _ _ _ _ .
9. The plan of making goods in which one machine makes one part and another machine another part, until all is finished, is called the _ _ _ _ _ _ _ _ .
10. The change of little villages into very large towns is called the _ _ _ _ _ _ _ _ .

II. Here is another list:

spinning jenny	loom
steel	cotton gin
clothing industry	shuttle
weave	postrider
New York Tribune	the press

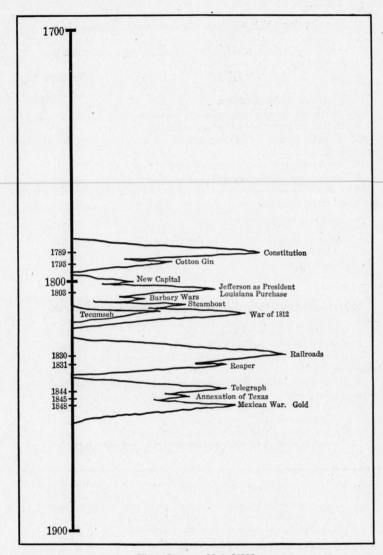

1700

1789 — Constitution
1793 — Cotton Gin
1800 — New Capital
1803 — Jefferson as President
         Louisiana Purchase
         Barbary Wars
         Steamboat
Tecumseh — War of 1812

1830 — Railroads
1831 — Reaper

1844 — Telegraph
1845 — Annexation of Texas
1848 — Mexican War. Gold

1900

Time Chart — Unit VIII

Do the same.

1. The machine which separates the seeds from the cotton is the _ _ _ _
_ _ _ _.

2. One of the earliest machines for twisting thread was called the _ _ _ _
_ _ _ _.

3. A material made partly of iron but harder and tougher than iron is
_ _ _ _.

4. A machine for weaving is a _ _ _ _ _.

5. Anyone who carries the mail on horseback is a _ _ _ _.

6. All the newspapers of a country are called _ _ _ _ _ _ _ _.

7. To make cloth by interlacing threads going one way with threads going
across them is to _ _ _ _ _.

8. The manufacture of all kinds of dress is the _ _ _ _ _ _ _ _.

9. One of our first great newspapers was the _ _ _ _ _ _ _ _ _ _ _ _.

10. A wooden needle which weaves the cross threads through the up-and-
down threads is a _ _ _ _ _.

III. Here is another list:

Atlantic cable	communication	textile
power loom	Morse code	clipper ship
telegraph		

Do the same.

1. The signals used to send messages over a telegraph wire are the _ _ _ _
_ _ _ _.

2. Any material made by weaving is a _ _ _ _ _.

3. A telegraph that goes under the sea is the _ _ _ _ _ _ _ _.

4. A weaving machine that is run in some other way than by man's
labor is a _ _ _ _ _ _ _ _.

5. An electric machine which sends signals to a distant point is a _ _ _ _ _.

6. Exchanging ideas from one person to another in any way is _ _ _ _ _.

7. A sailing vessel built for speed is a _ _ _ _ _ _ _ _.

COMPREHENSION TEST ON UNIT VIII

1. *Check the best answer:*

　a. Everywhere coal was used as a fuel

　　_ _ _ because wood was not a good fuel to melt so much iron
　　_ _ _ because the supply of coal was increased
　　_ _ _ because it takes little work to get coal

　b. Cities began to grow to a great size

　　_ _ _ because life on the farms was too hard
　　_ _ _ because the factories brought together so many people in one
　　　　place
　　_ _ _ because people would rather live in towns

c. Newspapers are important to a nation

_ _ _ because they make all the people think about the same questions

_ _ _ because they tell everybody the news

_ _ _ because they teach people to read

d. If we had not found new ways of working iron

_ _ _ our inventors would have been angry

_ _ _ the iron workers would have been out of work

_ _ _ there would not have been enough iron to make all the machines we needed

e. The Atlantic cable was important

_ _ _ because it taught us much about the bottom of the sea

_ _ _ because it helped nations to know what others were doing and thinking

_ _ _ because it was laid by an American

f. It was better to make goods in a factory than at home

_ _ _ because such great quantities could be produced in the factories

_ _ _ because machines cost too much money for workers to own them

_ _ _ because factories are big buildings

2. *Check two answers:*

Telegraphing was better than sending messages in the old way

_ _ _ because it caused much less work

_ _ _ because it could help all the people in the country to learn about news at the same time

_ _ _ because the news was still new by the time it arrived

_ _ _ because it does not cost much to telegraph

3. *Check the best answer:*

a. The chief effect of the invention of the sewing-machine was

_ _ _ the improved appearance of clothes

_ _ _ a change of style

_ _ _ the growth of the clothing industry

b. Railroads helped to send messages

_ _ _ because they carried letters free

_ _ _ because letters sent by rail traveled fast

_ _ _ because people went in trains to deliver their own messages

c. The only way to supply enough raw cotton to keep all the spinning-machines and weaving-machines busy was

_ _ _ to find a quick way of taking out the seeds

_ _ _ to send to other lands for more cotton

_ _ _ to make every farmer grow some cotton

d. The invention of spinning-machinery was important

_ _ _ because no one had ever spun thread before

_ _ _ because it could spin many threads at once

_ _ _ because men did not have to work

e. So much thread would not have been of much use

   _ _ _ if someone had not learned how to weave by machine also

   _ _ _ if someone had not bought the thread

   _ _ _ if it had not been good thread

f. The power loom did the work of many men. These men could then

   _ _ _ stay at home all day without working

   _ _ _ do work that had not been done before

   _ _ _ break the machines and get their old jobs back

4. *What is the title of Unit VIII?*

ORGANIZATION OF THE UNIT AS A WHOLE

The teacher has prepared typed slips, each bearing the name of one of the stories comprising the unit. Children are to sort and arrange them correctly.

RECITATION OF THE UNIT AS A WHOLE

One child is chosen to tell each story as a part of an assembly program. Pictures, models, or diagrams should accompany each story.

UNIT IX

HOW THE SLAVERY QUESTION ALMOST SPLIT THE
NATION INTO TWO PARTS

I. How Slavery started in this Country.
  1. Slavery had been begun during the colonial period.
  2. The slave trade was a terrible business.
  3. Gradually slavery disappeared in the North.
  4. The cotton industry made the Southerners want more slaves.
  5. How people lived on a Southern plantation.
    a. The planters.
    b. Poor whites.
    c. Negroes.

II. Should Slavery spread into the New Territories owned by the United States?
  1. In the Louisiana Purchase lands a line was drawn between slave and free.
  2. Daniel Webster was the great speaker for the North, and John Calhoun for the South.
  3. In the land received from Mexico the people were to decide for themselves.
  4. Could a slave be taken by his master into free land?
  5. Life of Abraham Lincoln (to the Civil War).
  6. The Southerners believed Lincoln would free the slaves; so they made a new nation of their own.

III. The Civil War was fought to keep the Different Parts of the Country Together.
  1. The North wanted to take the Southern capital and the South wanted to take the Northern capital.
  2. The Union ships would not let Southern ships go into or out of their harbors.
  3. The Union forces cut the South in two by opening up the Mississippi River.
  4. The North had more men and more money; so it won.

IV. During this Period the United States did Some Work that helped Mankind.
  1. The wounded were cared for better than ever before.
  2. Poets wrote on slavery and other subjects.
    a. Longfellow.   *c.* Holmes.
    b. Whittier.   *d.* Lowell.
  3. Great novels and stories were written.
    a. Harriet Beecher Stowe: *Uncle Tom's Cabin.*
    b. Poe.
    c. Hawthorne.
  4. Horace Mann helped to improve the school system.
  5. Some advances were made in science.
    a. Ether.
    b. Audubon: birds.
    c. Photography.
  6. Temperance societies were formed.
  7. Perry opened the ports of Japan to trade.

PREPARATION FOR THE OVERVIEW

"In what war did the old soldiers that we see on Memorial Day fight? What was the name of their army? How does their uniform differ from that of the soldiers of today? Whom did they fight? Do you know what the war was about?"

Review by use of a wall map the successive territorial acquisitions to the United States. List them on the board as the answers are given. Then ask in regard to each acquisition, "Was slavery allowed here?" The children will probably find that they do not know.

"Who was president of the United States during the Civil War? Do you know any of the names of generals on either side? Who won the war? What was decided by the war?

"How many of you had forefathers who fought in the Civil War? If any of them are yet living, ask them to tell you some stories about the war, which you can retell to the class."

PRESENTATION OR OVERVIEW

You remember from our study of colonial life that negroes had been brought from Africa by slave traders almost as soon as our country was settled. Practically from the beginning we had slaves here. These slaves were in North and South alike; but as time went on, it became clear that they were not of much use in the North. They were too ignorant to be used in fishing, shipbuilding, or commerce. Therefore little by little they began to disappear in the North, where they could not make much money for their masters.

In the South, however, the case was different. Negroes could work in the fields: they could plant and hoe and they could pick cotton. So their masters kept them and bought more. When the great increase in cotton production came, which we studied in our last unit, the result was that masters wanted more and more slaves to take care of their larger and larger fields. Instead of disappearing as they did in the North, the negroes in the South grew ever more numerous.

When the United States gained all this new land (*showing at the map with a sweeping gesture*) the cotton planters were very glad. They said: "Here is a good opportunity for us. Instead of fertilizing (*pointing to the word written on the board*) our old fields, which are almost worn out, we will go over into the new lands, take up new farms, and grow cotton there. Then we will not have to spend our money for fertilizers."

The people in the North had begun by this time to feel anxious. They asked, "Do you intend to take your slaves with you into the new territories?" "Of course," replied the planters; "how else could we raise our cotton?"

The answer did not please the Northerners. So long as the slaves were kept in the slave states they said little, but they did not want the new lands taken up by owners of negroes. So they declared: "The slaves must stay where they are. They cannot be taken over into the new lands."

You may well imagine how angry the South became. A quarrel broke out which soon grew fierce; it lasted almost half a century. Neither side wanted to give in, but neither side wanted to be blamed as the cause of the trouble. Many halfway measures were tried, which people thought might perhaps settle the difficulty. For example, once they said, "Let's draw a line here (*illustrating at the slated map*) and let all lands north of that be free; and all south, slave lands." That calmed the angry spirits for a while, but not for long. Then somebody else said: "Let's leave it to the people who come to live in the new territory. They may decide for themselves whether or not they want to allow slavery." So this plan was tried; but it, too, failed to make the different interests agree. Each side always thought that the other was getting the best of it.

Thus the country drifted along for half a century; and as one plan after another was tried out and failed, it began to be clear that war would come, as the only means of settling the question of slavery.

War did come — the great Civil War. It lasted for four long years, and cost the lives of many hundreds of thousands of our young men, both in the North and in the South. Each side fought bravely and well, but as the North had so many more people and so much more money, it won at last.

Then the nation decided that it would have no more slavery; so there could never again be any quarrel about it. From that day to this America has been really the "home of the free," as it had been called long before.

You might think from this story that our country had had no thought for any other subject than slavery during the long half-century of quarreling. However, we shall find in our reading that during those years great poets were composing poems, great story writers were writing stories, and great scientists were making discoveries that made life easier and more pleasant. There was some progress, then, even though our country lost a great deal of time, money, and effort by having to stop to fight a war.

PRESENTATION TEST

Check the best answer:

  a. Slavery began in our history

  _ _ _ in the colonial period
  _ _ _ before the period of exploration
  _ _ _ after the colonial period

  b. As time went on, slaves made a profit for their masters

  _ _ _ only in the South
  _ _ _ only in the West
  _ _ _ only in the North

  c. The cotton planters wanted to raise cotton in the new territories

  _ _ _ because they liked to move
  _ _ _ because the new land was smoother than theirs
  _ _ _ because they would not have to fertilize the soil

  d. The opinion of the North in regard to slavery was

  _ _ _ that slavery should end immediately
  _ _ _ that slavery should not spread to the territories
  _ _ _ that all the country should be open to slaves

  e. After the war it was decided

  _ _ _ that all slavery should end
  _ _ _ that slaves should stay in the slave states
  _ _ _ that the new territories should be open to slaves

> I. How Slavery started in this Country
> 1. Slavery had been begun during the colonial period

No additional preparation and presentation are needed.

Assimilation
Readings

Upper Group

BLAISDELL. The Story of American History, 358.
GORDY. Leaders in Making America, 314.
GORDY. Stories of Later American History, 234.
PERRY and PRICE. American History, II: 135–137, 147–149.
SANFORD. The Story of Agriculture in the United States, 23, 54, 63–64, 81–84, 133 (difficult).
Compton's Pictured Encyclopedia (Slavery).
World Book (War of Secession).

Average Group

BALDWIN. Four Great Americans, 221–222.
BARNES. Elementary History of the United States, 287–288.
BEARD and BAGLEY. A First Book in American History, 265.
ELSON and MACMULLAN. Story of our Country, II: 160.
GORDY. Elementary History of the United States, 35.
MORRIS. Primary History of the United States, 224.

Lower Group

MCMASTER. Primary History of the United States, 174.
Try MORRIS and BALDWIN.

Teachers

BOGART. Economic History of the United States, 71–73.
CALLENDER. Economic History of the United States, 742–752.
HART. Slavery and Abolition, 49–53.
PHILLIPS. American Negro Slavery, 67–114.
WILSON. Division and Reunion, 123–124.
American Citizenship Course in United States History, IV: 109–111, 118.

Minimal Essentials

Date: **1619** — bringing of negro slaves into Virginia
Historical Terms: **slavery; negro**
Something to Remember
There were slaves in all the colonies, North as well as South, during the colonial period.

Procedure during Assimilation

Reading as described on pages 24–29.
Objective test.[1]

---

[1] Burton, William H., "A Contribution to the Technique of Constructing 'Best Answer' Tests," *Elementary School Journal,* XXV: 762–770.

Organization

The children make one summary sentence that adequately describes the story.

Recitation

Each child tells the story from his own summary sentence.

> **2. The slave trade was a terrible business**

Preparation

Review the story of John Hawkins.[1]

"Who had done the work before the bringing in of negroes?

"What schemes did the white people use to get the blacks on board their ships?"

Assimilation

Readings

Upper Group

SANFORD. The Story of Agriculture in the United States, 54 (difficult).
TERRY. History Stories of Other Lands, VI: 218–220.
World Book (Slavery).

Average Group

Try FAIRGRIEVE and YOUNG, and SANFORD.

Lower Group

BARNES. Primary History of the United States, 128–129.
FAIRGRIEVE and YOUNG. The World, 157–161.
SCHWARTZ. Five Little Strangers, 72–102.

Teachers

BOGART. Economic History of the United States, 70–71, 138–140.
COFFIN. Drum Beat of the Nation, 4–5.
HART. American History told by Contemporaries, III: 615–618.
HART. Slavery and Abolition, 290–295.
MUZZEY. The United States of America, I: 310–312.
PHILLIPS. American Negro Slavery, 20–45, 132–149.
STEPHENSON. An American History, 142.
TILLINGHAST. The Negro in Africa and America, 102–228.
New International Encyclopædia (Slavery).

Minimal Essentials

Name of Place: **Guinea (gĭn′ĭ) coast**
Date: **during the seventeenth and eighteenth centuries**
Historical Terms: **slave trade; "middle passage"**

[1] See pages 117–120.

Things to Remember

The slave trade from other countries to the United States was stopped very soon after we became a nation.

The slave trade was made piracy.

Buying and selling slaves within the country still went on.

Illustrative Material

McKinley. Illustrated Topics for American History: S. 23, pictures of a slave ship and slave market.

Pyle. Book of the American Spirit, 61.

Procedure during Assimilation

Reading as described on pages 24–29.

Picture study based on the illustrative material listed above.

Read to the children extracts from the source materials given under references for teachers.

On a slated map of the United States draw the land and sea routes of the slave trade.[1]

Drill on minimal essentials.

Objective test.

Organization

The teacher puts the following outline on the board.

The Slave Trade

1. How carried on
2. Why Americans objected
3. End of the foreign slave trade

Recitation

Each row prepares the discussion of one point.

---

3. Gradually slavery disappeared in the North

Preparation

"What were the chief industries of the Northern states? [2]

"Why would the negroes not be of much use in shipbuilding? whaling? spinning and weaving? sawing lumber?

"What would be the only kind of work in which they could be of much help to the Northerners?" (Housework.)

[1] Shepherd, W. R., *Historical Atlas*, pp. 206–207.
[2] See Unit III, pp. 193–194.

Presentation

Since there was very little work that the negroes could do in the North, their number kept getting smaller and smaller. And since the Northerners saw so few of them they began to think of the negroes as persons like themselves. As a result, one after another of the Northern states made laws doing away with slavery. The Southerners, who were so used to seeing thousands of them, grew to think that negroes had been created to work for the white men.

This difference of opinion does not mean that the people in the North were better than the people in the South nor more kindly by nature, but they had little work for slaves and therefore put an end to slavery. Then we had a condition that proved to be a very bad one. The country was half slave and half free.

PRESENTATION TEST

Check the best answer:

The reason that slavery disappeared in the North was

    _ _ _ because the people in the North were better than those in the South
    _ _ _ because the North had little work that slaves could do
    _ _ _ because the people in the North did not like to keep slaves

Assimilation

Readings

Upper Group

GORDY. Leaders in Making America, 314.
GORDY. Stories of Later American History, 234.
PERRY and PRICE. American History, II : 137.
World Book (War of Secession).

Average Group

BALDWIN. Four Great Americans, 221–222.
BARNES. Elementary History of the United States, 288.
BEARD and BAGLEY. A First Book in American History, 265–266.

Lower Group

McMASTER. Primary History of the United States, 174.

Teachers

ADAMS. The Power of Ideals in American History, 33–61.
BOGART. Economic History of the United States, 135–137.
COFFIN. Drum Beat of the Nation, 5.
COMAN. Industrial History of the United States, 274–276.
HART. Slavery and Abolition, 53–55, 79–91.
MACY. Anti-Slavery Crusade, 54–84.

PHILLIPS. American Negro Slavery, 118–131.
STEPHENSON. An American History, 118, 221, 234–235, 246, 329–334.
WILSON. Division and Reunion, 124.
American Citizenship Course in United States History, IV: 111–112, 118–119, 126–129.

Minimal Essentials

Name of Person: **William Lloyd Garrison**
Name of Place: **Mason and Dixon's line**
Historical Terms: **abolition; freedmen;** *Liberator*
Things to Remember
    Slavery did not profit the North.
    One after another the Northern states did away with slavery.
    Abolition societies were formed, but grew slowly.

Illustrative Material

McKINLEY. Illustrated Topics for American History: S. 27.
Educational Posters of the National Child Welfare Association: Freedom of Speech and Press: William Lloyd Garrison.

Procedure during Assimilation

Reading as described on pages 24–29.
Make a list of the different kinds of work in the North that could be done by slaves; in the South.
Children graph the following figures: in 1790 there were 40,370 slaves north of Mason and Dixon's line and 657,527 slaves south of the line.
On a slated map give the dates of the abolition of slavery in the Northern states.[1]
Find phrases in the Declaration of Independence which are not consistent with the existence of slavery.
Show that migration moved westward in parallel lines. Freedom in New England would, then, have what effect in the central plains? How does the Ordinance of 1787 prove this point?
Children locate Mason and Dixon's line.
Make an illustrated title-page for a copy of the *Liberator*.
Drill on minimal essentials.
Objective test.

Organization

Children write one summary sentence that adequately describes the whole story, and vote as to which half-dozen from the entire group are best.

Recitation

The half-dozen whose sentences were chosen may hear the rest of the group tell the story.

[1] Hart, A. B., *Slavery and Abolition*, pp. 126–127; Shepherd, W. R., *Historical Atlas*, pp. 206–207; Fox, D. R., *Harper's Atlas of American History*, p. 42.

---

4. The cotton industry made the Southerners want more slaves

Preparation

"What machines led to great demands for more cotton?

"Where could the cotton planters find new land? Why did they want new land instead of what they had? What is fertilizer?

"Why did they think they needed more slaves in order to grow more cotton?"

No additional presentation is needed.

Assimilation

Readings

Upper Group

BLAISDELL. The Story of American History, 358.
BROOKS. The Story of Cotton, 74–75, 126–127, 129–131, 137.
COE. Makers of the Nation, 196–197.
GORDY. Leaders in Making America, 247, 314.
GORDY. Stories of Later American History, 234.
ROCHELEAU. The Story of King Cotton, 12–15, 27–28.
ROLT-WHEELER. The Boy with the United States Census, 165–209.
SANFORD. The Story of Agriculture in the United States, 133–134, 200–201 (difficult).
World Book (War of Secession).

Average Group

BALDWIN. Four Great Americans, 222.
BARNES. Elementary History of the United States, 288–289.
BEARD and BAGLEY. A First Book in American History, 266–267.
GORDY. Elementary History of the United States, 194, 224.

Lower Group

FAIRGRIEVE and YOUNG. The World, 60–62.
McMASTER. Primary History of the United States, 174–175.

Teachers

BOGART. Economic History of the United States, 137–138, 199–201, 290–297.
CALLENDER. Economic History of the United States, 760–768.
COFFIN. Drum Beat of the Nation, 5–8.
COMAN. Industrial History of the United States, 272–274.
DODD. The Cotton Kingdom, 7–13.
HART. Slavery and Abolition, 55–66.
PHILLIPS. American Negro Slavery, 150–168, 205–227.
SCHLESINGER. Political and Social History of the United States, 86–88.
STEPHENSON. An American History, 299–300.
WILSON. Division and Reunion, 124–125.
American Citizenship Course in United States History, IV: 112–115.

Minimal Essentials

Names of Places: **south of Mason and Dixon's line; the cotton states**
Historical Terms: **plantation system; border states**
Things to Remember
The chief industry of the Southern states was agriculture on a large scale.
Negroes could be used for this kind of agriculture.
Negroes worked in the cotton fields.
Since the Southern states wanted more cotton, they wanted more negroes too.

Illustrative Material

LEHMANN. Geographical Pictures: L. G. 604, Cotton.
McKINLEY. Illustrated Topics in American History: S. 31, Scenes in the Slave States.
Ford Educational Library: 55, Cotton.

Procedure during Assimilation

Reading as described on pages 24–29.
Picture study based on the illustrative material listed above.
Show children an attractive edition of Stowe's *Uncle Tom's Cabin*; read one or two
    short passages, and in this way attempt to stimulate the entire group to read
    the book.
Compare land prices in North and South.[1] Why was there such a difference?
Compare prices of cotton from 1820 to 1840 [2] with the price today.
Review the statistics that you found in the World Almanac (see page 406) and graph
    them and the increase in the number of slaves in parallel columns.[3]
From the census returns find how many negroes there are in each of the Southern
    states; how many whites.[4] Graph these figures for the period 1790–1920.[5]
Drill on minimal essentials.
Objective test.

Organization

Making the graphs referred to above.

Recitation

Explaining the graphs.

---

5. How people lived on a Southern plantation
   a. The planters
   b. Poor whites
   c. Negroes

No additional preparation and presentation are needed.

[1] *American Citizenship Course in United States History,* IV : 112; Hart, A. B., *Slavery and Abolition,* p. 57.
[2] *American Citizenship Course in United States History,* IV : 113.
[3] Bogart, E. L., *Economic History of the United States,* p. 292.
[4] *Fourteenth Census of the United States: Population by States,* Vol. III : 19.
[5] *Fourteenth Census of the United States: Population, General Report,* Vol. II : 29.

Assimilation

Readings

The planters

Upper Group

BROOKS. The Story of Cotton, 157–163, 171–174.
EVANS. America First, 308–313.
GORDY. Leaders in Making America, 247–250.
HART. Romance of the Civil War, 9–13.
SANFORD. The Story of Agriculture in the United States, 189–191 (difficult).

Average Group

Try GORDY.

Lower Group

Read SANFORD to this group.

Teachers

BOGART. Economic History of the United States, 296–297, 299–301.
BURWELL. A Girl's Life in Virginia before the War.
DODD. The Cotton Kingdom, 24–47, 71–73, 76–117.
HART. Slavery and Abolition, 67–72.
MUZZEY. An American History, 340–342.
MUZZEY. The United States of America, I : 475–476.
PAGE. Social Life in Old Virginia before the War, 7–27, 32–56, 65–107.
PHILLIPS. American Negro Slavery, 228–290, 309–313, 323–330.

Poor whites

There is little available reading material on a level which children can read. The teacher should therefore prepare an oral story based on the references below, tell it to the children, and follow immediately by an objective test.

HART. Romance of the Civil War, 41–44.

Teachers

CALLENDER. Economic History of the United States, 779–785.
HART. American History told by Contemporaries, IV : 59–62.
HART. Slavery and Abolition, 72–77.
McMASTER. History of the People of the United States, VII : 236–237.
WILSON. Division and Reunion, 128.
American Citizenship Course in United States History, IV : 116–117.

Negroes

Upper Group

BROOKS. The Story of Cotton, 158, 163–165, 167–171, 174–181.
GORDY. Leaders in Making America, 248–250.
HART. Romance of the Civil War, 1–8, 13–39, 45–50.
LOGIE. From Columbus to Lincoln, 196–204.
PERRY and PRICE. American History, II : 138–143.
SANFORD. The Story of Agriculture in the United States, 189–198 (difficult).
TURPIN. Cotton, 96–98.

Average Group

FORMAN. First Lessons in American History, 248.
Let children attempt the readings of the upper group.

Lower Group

Try FORMAN, PERRY and PRICE, and GORDY.

Teachers

BOGART. Economic History of the United States, 298–299, 301–303.
CHADWICK. Causes of the Civil War, 17–36.
DODD. The Cotton Kingdom, 1–23, 73–76.
HART. American History told by Contemporaries, III: 579–588, 591–594; IV: 75–79.
HART. Slavery and Abolition, 77–78, 92–108, 123–135.
McMASTER. History of the People of the United States, VII: 237–251.
MUZZEY. The United States of America, I: 473–477.
PAGE. Social Life in Old Virginia before the War, 27–32, 57–63.
PHILLIPS. American Negro Slavery, 291–308, 313–323.
RHODES. History of the United States, I: 303–383.
SMITH. Parties and Slavery, 286–304.
STEPHENSON. An American History, 324–325.
WILSON. Division and Reunion, 125–128.
American Citizenship Course in United States History, IV: 114–117.
Baltimore County Course of Study, 565.

Minimal Essentials

Historical Terms: overseer; poor whites; "poor white trash"; field servants; house servants

Things to Remember

Most of the planters were well-to-do.
The poor whites could not afford to run large plantations, and there was little work for wages.
Negroes on the smaller plantations were generally well cared for, but their labor was slow, and costly to the owner.

Illustrative Material

GABRIEL (ED.). Pageant of America, III: 145–164; XIII: 81–91, 110–116.
Chronicles of America Photoplays, Yale University Press: Dixie.
Keystone Views: 123, Cotton is King; 124, A Negro Family at Home in the South; 125, Where Slaves were Commodities.
Travel, XXXIX: 11–14 (June, 1922); XLV: 15–18 (October, 1925). (Poor Whites.)

Procedure during Assimilation

Reading as described on pages 24–29.
Picture study based on the illustrative material listed above.
Play for the children the following records: "Deep River"; "Mammy's Song"; "Negro Folk Tunes and Spirituals"; "Old Black Joe"; "Old Folks at Home"; "Old Kentucky Home."
The teacher may add from her reading interesting details not given by the children's books.
Use the dramatization "On a Plantation." Walker, *Little Plays from American History for Young Folks*, pp. 145–155.
Find prices of slaves.[1]

---

[1] *American Citizenship Course in United States History*, IV: 115; Hart, A. B., *Slavery and Abolition*, pp. 128–129.

Construct in the sand table a typical Southern plantation. Construct and furnish
    negro quarters. Leave for the school museum.[1]
Write the letter a Northern boy might have written home to his parents about his
    Christmas visit to a friend in South Carolina.
Children compose poems on any phase of slave life.
Drill on minimal essentials.
Objective test.

Organization

Children suggest the three main headings for the outline.
Each then makes an outline of one of these main points.

Recitation

Children listen to each other's recitations on the points
selected.

A drill lesson on section I of Unit IX should be given at this
point.

II. Should Slavery spread into the New Territories
    owned by the United States?
    1. In the Louisiana Purchase lands a line was
    drawn between slave and free

Preparation

"Show the Louisiana Purchase on the map. When was it
bought?

"Who bought this land? Was it the North alone or the
South alone? Which part of the country, then, should decide
whether or not there should be any slaves there?

"Which parts would probably develop the industries that
used slaves? Why?

"Would there be any possible way of pleasing both
parties?"

On the slated map draw the outline of the Louisiana
Purchase, with the boundaries of Missouri marked out with
dotted lines. Be sure that the Mexican cession is not included.

---

[1] Colbert, Russel, "Historical Museum in a Small High School." *The Historical
Outlook*, XVI : 167.

Presentation

Since the Louisiana Purchase was made by money taken from all the states together, it would not be fair to let any one section of the country have things its own way there. Many plans were brought forward to try to please both slave and free interests. Missouri (*pointing to the map*) was ready to come into the Union as a state. She wanted to come in as a slave state. That would please the South, but not the North. Maine wanted to enter as a free state.

After a long quarrel Henry Clay (*pointing to the name written on the board*), who always hated trouble and wanted to keep the peace, brought forth his plan. He said: "Let Missouri come in as a slave state and Maine as a free state, but draw a line from Missouri's southern boundary westward as far as the Louisiana Purchase goes (*illustrating by drawing the line*). From now on, all the land north of this line (*showing it*) is to be free and all the land south of the line (*showing it*) is to be slave."

This plan seemed fair enough, and both sides agreed. For thirty years there was peace, as long a time, perhaps, as since your father was a tiny baby. The question seemed settled for good.

Then the Southerners began to see that the North was growing much faster than their own part of the country. They said, "The North received more land north of the line than we did south of it." That was true; but the North replied: "How about Texas? See what a vast stretch of land it includes! It has come into the Union as a slave state. And Texas will in time probably be divided up to make many more slave states." (*The teacher here sketches in the boundaries of Texas, as added to the Louisiana Purchase.*)

Still neither side was quite satisfied. Finally both agreed to give up the old plan of drawing a line between the sections. Instead, they allowed the people who came to live in the new land, to choose whether their territory was to be free or slave land. They could decide for themselves. So the question was settled again for a while.

PRESENTATION TEST

Check the best answer:

   a. The first way of settling the trouble between slave and free interests in the
   Louisiana Purchase was

   _ _ _ to let all the new lands become free territory
   _ _ _ to draw a line between slave and free territories
   _ _ _ to let the people of each territory decide for themselves

   b. After thirty years this plan was changed. Then it was decided

   _ _ _ to let all the new lands become slave territory
   _ _ _ to draw a line between slave and free territories
   _ _ _ to let the people of each territory decide for themselves

Assimilation
Readings

Upper Group

   BLAISDELL. The Story of American History, 358.
   BURNHAM. Hero Tales from History, 320–327.
   CHANDLER and CHITWOOD. Makers of American History 225–232 (Clay).
   COE. Makers of the Nation, 296–302 (Clay).
   EVANS. America First, 303–308.
   FOOTE and SKINNER. Makers and Defenders of America, 178–190 (Clay).
   GORDY. Leaders in Making America, 308–311 (Clay) ; 314–315.
   GORDY. Stories of Later American History, 227–231, 234–235.
   PERRY and PRICE. American History, II : 150, 160.
   TAPPAN. Elementary History of our Country, 186–187, 205.
   WOODBURN and MORAN. Makers of America, 254–257 (Clay).
   Compton's Pictured Encyclopedia (Missouri Compromise).
   World Book (Missouri Compromise, Kansas-Nebraska Bill, War of Secession).

Average Group

   BALDWIN. Four Great Americans, 223, 225.
   BARNES. Elementary History of the United States, 283–287, 289–291, 321–324.
   BEARD and BAGLEY. A First Book in American History, 274–279, 291.
   ELSON and MacMULLAN. Story of our Country, II : 80–84, 89–94, 161–162.
   FORMAN. First Lessons in American History, 210–211, 247–248, 253–257.
   GORDY. Elementary History of the United States, 222–223, 239–242.
   MACE. Primary History, 303–308 (Clay).
   MORRIS. Primary History of the United States, 202–203.
   MOWRY. First Steps in the History of our Country, 213–216.
   SOUTHWORTH. Builders of our Country, II : 158–165 (Clay).
   TURPIN. Brief Biographies from American History, 247–252 (Clay).

Lower Group

   BARNES. Primary History of the United States, 140–141, 161–162.
   McMASTER. Primary History of the United States, 175–177, 190–191.

Teachers

   MACDONALD. Documentary Source Book of American History, 315–316, 317–
   318, 403–405.
   MUZZEY. The United States of America, I : 483–492.
   RHODES. History of the United States, I : 29–38, 424–500.
   SCHOULER. History of the United States, III : 186; V : 275–289.

SMITH. Parties and Slavery, 3–27, 94–108.
STEPHENSON. An American History, 301–303.
TURNER. Rise of the New West, 149–171.
WILSON. Division and Reunion, 131–132, 182–185.
American Citizenship Course in United States History, IV : 120–124.

✓ Minimal Essentials

Name of Person: **Henry Clay**
Names of Places: **Missouri; Kansas; Nebraska**
Date: **1820** — Missouri Compromise
Historical Terms: **"the Great Peacemaker"; Missouri Compromise; compromise; Kansas-Nebraska Bill**
Things to Remember
The Missouri Compromise line cut the Louisiana Purchase lands in two.
Land north of the line was to be free; land south of the line was to be slave territory.
Later the Kansas-Nebraska Bill gave all the people in the territories on either side of the line the right to decide the slavery question for themselves.

Illustrative Material

Keystone Views: 338, Henry Clay (slide only).

Procedure during Assimilation

Reading as described on pages 24–29.
Children make up their own examples of compromises, using everyday-life situations. Be sure that the examples show each side obtaining a part of what it wants but having to give up a part also.
Make a diagram on the board, showing the following points:

THE MISSOURI COMPROMISE

THE QUESTION	WHAT THE NORTH WANTED	THE COMPROMISE	WHAT THE SOUTH WANTED

Children make a map, showing in red ink the 36° 30′ line and the southern boundary of Missouri.[1] Color black the Louisiana Purchase lands thus opened to slavery.
Make another map showing how the Kansas-Nebraska Bill [2] changed the status of slavery in the territories.
Drill on minimal essentials.
Objective test.

[1] Muzzey, D. S., *An American History*, p. 253; Burnham, Smith, *The Making of our Country*, p. 340; Woodburn, J. A., and Moran, T. F., *Elementary American History and Government*, p. 292.

[2] Muzzey, D. S., *An American History*, p. 306; Burnham, Smith, *The Making of our Country*, p. 391; Woodburn, J. A., and Moran, T. F., *Elementary American History and Government*, p. 324.

Organization

The making of the diagram referred to above and the maps illustrating the Missouri Compromise and the Kansas-Nebraska Bill.

Recitation

The explanation of the diagram and the maps.

> 2. Daniel Webster was the great speaker for the North, and John Calhoun for the South

---

Preparation

"We have said many times in our last story, 'The South declared,' 'The North replied,' etc. Now the South is a part of the country; land cannot speak. What do we mean, then, when we say 'The South demanded' etc?

"Who would speak for the North? How would such a man know what all the millions of people in the North really did want? How could they let him know?

"What is an orator?"

Presentation

Our story today is about two great American statesmen, one of whom represented the South and the other the North. Their names were John Calhoun and Daniel Webster (*pointing to the names written on the board*).

Assimilation

Readings

Upper Group

BURNHAM. Hero Tales from History, 320–324, 325–326.
BURTON. Builders of our Nation, 195–210.
CHANDLER and CHITWOOD. Makers of American History, 233–246.
COE. Makers of the Nation, 283–295.
DAVIDSON. Founders and Builders of our Nation, 181–187.
EVANS. America First, 299–303, 313–317.
GORDY. Leaders in Making America, 306–307, 311–313.
GORDY. Stories of Later American History, 225–227, 231–233, 237–238.
LOGIE. From Columbus to Lincoln, 204–209.
STIMPSON. The Child's Book of American Biography, 124–131.
WOODBURN and MORAN. Makers of America, 249–254, 258–261.
Compton's Pictured Encyclopedia (Webster, Calhoun).
World Book (Webster, Calhoun).

Average Group
> BALDWIN. Four Great Americans, 121–176 (Webster).
> BEARD and BAGLEY. A First Book in American History, 267–271, 284–288.
> EGGLESTON. Stories of Great Americans, 124–128.
> FORMAN. First Lessons in American History, 246–247.
> GORDY. Our Patriots, 143–148.
> GUERBER. Story of the Great Republic, 132–139 (Webster).
> MACE. Primary History, 309–318 (Webster, Calhoun).
> MORRIS. Primary History of the United States, 200–203.
> MOWRY. First Steps in the History of our Country, 210–213, 217–221.
> SOUTHWORTH. Builders of our Country, II : 166–175.

Lower Group
> BALDWIN. Fifty Famous People, 78–80.
> BALDWIN. Fourth Reader, 7–11.

Teachers
> EGGLESTON. American Immortals, 99–124.
> HAPGOOD. Daniel Webster.
> HART. American History told by Contemporaries, IV : 48–55.
> HUNT. John Caldwell Calhoun.
> LODGE. Daniel Webster.
> VON HOLST. John C. Calhoun.
> WARNER. Library of the World's Best Literature, VII : 3087–3100; XXXVIII : 15,725–15,757.

Minimal Essentials

Names of Persons: **John Calhoun; Daniel Webster**
Date: **the half-century before the Civil War**
Historical Term: **orator**
Things to Remember
> John Calhoun believed that the states had made the Union and could therefore unmake it.
> Daniel Webster believed that the union of all the states into one powerful country was the only good plan.

Illustrative Material

GABRIEL (ED.). Pageant of America, XI : 223–224.
Keystone Views : 339, John C. Calhoun (slide only).
Perry Pictures : 144, Daniel Webster; 144-B, His Birthplace; 144-D, John C. Calhoun's Home.

Procedure during Assimilation

Reading as described on pages 24–29.
Picture study based on the illustrative material listed above.
Use the dramatization "Daniel Webster." Hague and Chalmers, *Dramatic Moments in American History*, pp. 199–210.
Play for the children the phonograph record "Webster's Reply to Hayne."
Make biography booklets of Calhoun and Webster to leave in the room library.
Each child chooses from the readings the quotation from Webster he likes best.
Call the children's attention to the fact that it was Noah Webster, not Daniel, who compiled the dictionary.
Drill on minimal essentials.
Objective test.

Organization

Outlining the work for the booklets referred to above.

Recitation

Writing the booklets.

> 3. In the land received from Mexico the people were
>   to decide for themselves

Preparation

"What was the cause of the Mexican War?

"What lands did the United States win after the Mexican War?

"Should you expect these to be free or slave territory? Why?

"What part of this region was settled first? Why? Give the date of the discovery of gold in California.

"What was the first settlement of the slavery quarrel between North and South in the Louisiana Purchase? the second?"

Color in yellow on the slated map the Mexican cession, showing the boundaries of California by dotted lines.

Presentation

You will notice (*turning to the map*) that the Mexican cession and the Louisiana Purchase are two entirely different sections. The drawing of a line between North and South was to be done only in the Louisiana Purchase lands. That did not settle at all the question as to slavery in the Mexican cession. What should be done there?

The Mexican lands had been surrendered to us during the thirty years that the division line was in use (*pointing to map*).

Some people thought it would be a good idea to continue the same line clear to the Pacific coast (*drawing an imaginary line*). But California objected very much. Such a line would cut her in two. She was ready to ask to be admitted to the Union and wanted to come in as a free state. The line would cut her into two parts, one free and the other slave. So the question could not be settled that way.

Then our great peacemaker, Henry Clay, by this time an aged man, came forward with his last plan to prevent the two sides from quarreling. He said, "Let California come in as a free state, since she wishes to, but let all the rest of the land in the Mexican cession (*illustrating at the map*) decide for itself."

Clay's plan was followed. The rest of the people in the Mexican cession did decide for themselves. As soon as the people in the Louisiana Purchase lands found out about this plan, they too wanted to decide for themselves. That is the reason why the Missouri Compromise line was taken away. Then in all the Mexican cession and Louisiana Purchase lands the people in the territories were to decide for themselves whether their territory should be slave or free.

PRESENTATION TEST

1. *Check the best answer:*

   a. When we obtained the Mexican cession the question of slavery in the Louisiana Purchase had been settled

   _ _ _ by letting the people decide for themselves

   _ _ _ by the division line

   _ _ _ by war

   b. California wanted to come into the Union

   _ _ _ without deciding the slavery question

   _ _ _ as a slave state

   _ _ _ as a free state

2. *Check two answers:*

   Henry Clay's last plan for peace was

   _ _ _ to let California come in as a free state

   _ _ _ to let California come in as a slave state

   _ _ _ to draw the division line clear to the Pacific

   _ _ _ to let the rest of the Mexican cession land decide for itself

Assimilation

Readings

Upper Group

GORDY. Leaders in Making America, 318–322.

GORDY. Stories of Later American History, 238–242.

LEFFERTS. American Leaders, II : 144–159 (Lucretia Mott).

PERRY and PRICE. American History, II : 150–154, 156–159.

TAPPAN. An Elementary History of our Country, 195–196, 203–204.

Compton's Pictured Encyclopedia (Compromise of 1850).

World Book (Compromise of 1850, War of Secession).

Average Group

BALDWIN. Four Great Americans, 223–224.

BARNES. An Elementary History of the United States, 291–296.

BEARD and BAGLEY. A First Book in American History, 279–283.
ELSON and MACMULLAN. The Story of our Country, II : 162–163.
FORMAN. First Lessons in American History, 248–249, 250–252.
GORDY. Elementary History of the United States, 238–239.
MOWRY. First Steps in the History of our Country, 216–217.

Lower Group

BARNES. Primary History of the United States, 159–161.
MCMASTER. Primary History of the United States, 186–188.

Teachers

HART. American History told by Contemporaries, IV : 40–43, 48–58.
GARRISON. Westward Extension, 254–268, 294–332.
MACDONALD. Documentary Source Book of American History, 383–394.
MACY. The Anti-Slavery Crusade, 165–181.
MUZZEY. The United States of America, I : 443–459.
RHODES. History of the United States, I : 90, 95, 120–168, 181–198.
SCHOULER. History of the United States, IV : 544–545; V : 150–168, 175–179, 193–198.
SMITH. Parties and Slavery, 14–27, 40–58.
STEPHENSON. An American History, 369–375, 390–394.
WILSON. Division and Reunion, 165–167, 169–178.
American Citizenship Course in United States History, IV : 132–133.

Minimal Essentials

Name of Place: **the Mexican cession**
Date: **1850** — the Great Compromise
Historical Terms: **the Great Compromise; free states; slave states**
Things to Remember

California was admitted as a free state.
In all the rest of the land we obtained from Mexico the people were to decide for themselves whether their territory should be slave or free.
The Kansas-Nebraska Bill changed the Missouri Compromise, which referred only to the Louisiana Purchase lands.

Procedure during Assimilation

Reading as described on pages 24–29.
Which states were made from the Mexican cession? In how many of them would slavery be unprofitable? Why? Then, in how many could the South hope to win any extension of slavery?
Make on the board a diagram in regard to California, the rest of the land in the Mexican cession, and the fugitive-slave question, as settled by the Compromise of 1850.[1]

THE QUESTION	WHAT THE NORTH WANTED	THE COMPROMISE	WHAT THE SOUTH WANTED

Make a map showing the status of slavery in 1850.[2]
Drill on minimal essentials.
Objective test.

[1] Muzzey, D. S., *An American History*, p. 288.   [2] Ibid. p. 291.

Organization

Making the diagram referred to above.

Recitation

Explaining the diagram.

> 4. Could a slave be taken by his master into free land?

Preparation

"Why do we call certain states 'free states'?

"What would happen if a master should take his slaves from the South to a free state?" (*Children offer conjectures as to what might happen.*)

Presentation

You may be sure that every once in a while a slave would try to escape. The best place for him to go was to Canada, because the officers of the South could not very well make Canada give him up.

Canada was a long way off, and it took many months of hiding and suffering for slaves to reach there. Many times they were recaptured and taken back home to severe punishment. In our stories we shall read some interesting tales of people who helped them to escape. The South was quite sure that many Northern people helped them, and they did.

Another question about which Americans had to come to a decision was the case of a master's taking his slaves to free territory and living there. The Northerners said, "You can't bring slaves here; this is free land." The Southerners replied, "Slaves are property just as horses are; so of course we may take them with us anywhere we go."

At last they asked the courts to decide, and the courts said that the South was right: a man could take his slaves even into free territory. This made the Northerners very angry indeed. Some of them said: "What is the use of trying to make laws against slavery? The only way in which we can make land really free seems to be to make war and put an end to slavery entirely." You can see that war was coming nearer and nearer.

PRESENTATION TEST

Check the best answer:

a. The opinion of the North was

_ _ _ that it did not care whether slaves went with their masters or not

_ _ _ that no slaves might live in free land

_ _ _ that slaves might live anywhere their masters took them

b. The opinion of the South was

_ _ _ that it did not care whether slaves went with their masters or not

_ _ _ that no slaves might live in a free state

_ _ _ that slaves might live anywhere their masters took them ·

c. The court decided

_ _ _ that the North was right

_ _ _ that the South was right

Assimilation

Readings

Upper Group

EVANS. America First, 349–354.
HART. Romance of the Civil War, 51–56, 59–69.
PERRY and PRICE. American History, II : 161.
TAPPAN. An Elementary History of our Country, 204–205.
Compton's Pictured Encyclopedia (Dred Scott Decision).
World Book (Dred Scott Decision, Fugitive Slave Laws, Underground Railroad).

Average Group

BEARD and BAGLEY. A First Book in American History, 291–292.
ELSON and MacMULLAN. Story of our Country, II : 164–165.
FORMAN. First Lessons in American History, 249–250.
GORDY. Elementary History of the United States, 239, 241.
GUERBER. Story of the Great Republic, 148–151.

Lower Group

BARNES. Primary History of the United States, 163–164.

Teachers

HART. American History told by Contemporaries, III : 589–591, 630–633;
    IV : 80–83, 91–93, 122–135.
MACDONALD. Documentary Source Book of American History, 405–420.
MACY. The Anti-Slavery Crusade, 112–130 (underground railroad), 191–202.
SCHOULER. History of the United States, V : 373–377.
SMITH. Parties and Slavery, 190–208.
STEPHENSON. An American History, 395–398.
WILSON. Division and Reunion, 197–199.

Minimal Essentials

Name of Person: **Dred Scott**
Historical Terms: **underground railroad; fugitive slave; Dred Scott decision**
Things to Remember:

The law said that fugitive slaves must be returned to their masters.
Some Northern people helped them to escape.
The court decided that living in free land did not make a negro a free man.

Procedure during Assimilation

Reading as described on pages 24–29.

Show the children the routes of the underground railroad.[1]

Make imaginative drawings illustrating the work of the underground railroad.

Children compose a play based on the escape of a fugitive slave via the underground railroad.

Children select from their reading one interesting anecdote about fugitive slaves to tell to the class.

Take the children to court while a case is being tried, not to have them follow a particular case, but to show what a court is.

Put red dots over the map area that was opened to slavery by the Dred Scott decision.[2]

Drill on minimal essentials.

Objective test.

Organization

The teacher puts the following outline on the board:

SLAVES IN THE FREE LANDS

1. Fugitive slave laws
   Effect on the North
2. The Dred Scott decision
   Effect

Recitation

Each child prepares a three-minute talk on the points above.

---

5. Life of Abraham Lincoln (to the Civil War)

Preparation

"Who was president during the Civil War?"

Review what the class already knows about the life of Lincoln.

No additional presentation is needed.

Assimilation

Readings

Upper Group

BALDWIN. Abraham Lincoln, 1–207.

BLAISDELL. The Story of American History, 353–358.

BURNHAM. Hero Tales from History, 327–332.

BUTTERWORTH. In the Boyhood of Lincoln.

[1] Fox, D. R., *Harper's Atlas of American History*, p. 41; Muzzey, D. S., *An American History*, p. 293.

[2] Woodburn, J. A., and Moran, T. F., *Elementary American History and Government*, p. 324.

CHANDLER and CHITWOOD. Makers of American History, 265–269.
COE. Makers of the Nation, 303–313.
DAVIDSON. Founders and Builders of our Nation, 204–213.
EGGLESTON. A First Book in American History, 171–180.
ELLIS. Makers of our Country, 164–169.
EVANS. America First, 354–359.
GORDY. Abraham Lincoln, 1–110.
GORDY. Leaders in Making America, 323–329.
GORDY. Stories of Later American History, 243–250.
HAAREN and POLAND. Famous Men of Modern Times, 316–325.
LEFFERTS. American Leaders, II : 179–212.
LODGE and ROOSEVELT. Hero Tales from American History, 323–335.
LOGIE. From Lincoln to Coolidge, 20–22.
McMURRY. Pioneers of the Mississippi Valley, 170–184.
MONTGOMERY. Beginners' American History, 222–234.
MOORES. The Life of Abraham Lincoln for Boys and Girls, 1–67.
MOWRY. American Pioneers, 239–248.
TARBELL. Boy Scouts' Life of Lincoln.
WOODBURN and MORAN. The Makers of America, 262–268.
Compton's Pictured Encyclopedia (Lincoln).
Our Holidays, their Meaning and Spirit retold from *St. Nicholas*, 85–102.
World Book (Lincoln).

Average Group

BALDWIN. Four Great Americans, 179–220.
BARNES. Elementary History of the United States, 312–317, 320–321.
BEARD and BAGLEY. A First Book in American History, 292–299.
BROOKS. True Story of Abraham Lincoln.
CRAVENS. Story of Lincoln.
DAVIDSON and ANDERSON. Lincoln Readers, V : 1–4, 228–232.
ELSON and MacMULLAN. Story of our Country, II : 175–181.
FOOTE and SKINNER. Makers and Defenders of America, 230–244.
FORMAN. First Lessons in American History, 258–263.
GORDY. Elementary History of the United States, 244–246.
GORDY. Our Patriots, 163–178.
GUERBER. Story of the Great Republic, 161–167, 239–247.
MACE. Primary History, 360–367.
MORRIS. Primary History of the United States, 215–222.
MOWRY. First Steps in the History of our Country, 245–252.
SOUTHWORTH. Builders of our Country, II : 186–204.
TAPPAN. American Hero Stories, 254–264.

Lower Group

BALDWIN. Fifty Famous People, 7–11.
BOLENIUS. Fifth Reader, 124–130.
BOLENIUS. Fourth Reader, 114–118.
CURTIS. Why we Celebrate our Holidays, 12–17.
DAVIDSON and ANDERSON. Lincoln Readers, III : 146–148; IV : 146–149.
DAVIS. Stories of the United States, 183–202.
ELSON. Primary School Reader, III : 158–161.
HARTWELL. Story Hour Readings, IV : 177–180.
HERVEY and HIX. Horace Mann Readers, III : 82–84.
HORN and SHIELDS. Learn to Study Readers, I : 43.
LEWIS and ROWLAND. Silent Readers, V : 33–34.

SMITH. Easy Road to Reading, V: 334–339.
VAN SICKLE and SEEGMILLER. Riverside Readers, III: 93–94.
WAYLAND. History Stories for Primary Grades, 125–128, 202–204.
WILSON. History Reader, 190–191.
YOUNG and FIELD. Literary Readers, V: 261–277.

Teachers

ARNOLD. Life of Abraham Lincoln.
CHARNWOOD. Abraham Lincoln.
EGGLESTON. American Immortals, 199–220.
FRYER. A Book of Boyhoods, 173–183.
HANAFORD. Life of Lincoln.
HAPGOOD. Abraham Lincoln.
MINOR. The Real Lincoln.
MORSE. Abraham Lincoln.
NICOLAY and HAY. Abraham Lincoln: a History.
WARNER. Library of the World's Best Literature, XXIII: 9059–9076.
Public School Methods, V: 436–456. (The Methods Co., Chicago.)

Minimal Essentials

Name of Person: **Abraham Lincoln**
Date: **February 12**
Historical Term: **Honest Abe**
Things to Remember
  Lincoln came from the poor-white class in the South.
  He educated himself by his own efforts.
  He became one of the greatest Americans.

Illustrative Material

BRADLEY. Straight-Line Picture Cut-Outs: Abraham Lincoln.
Educational Posters of the National Child Welfare Association: Lincoln's Birthday.
Keystone Views: 144, Lincoln's Birthplace; 145, Earliest Portrait; 345, Lincoln studying
  before the Fire (slide only); 346, Lincoln splitting Rails (slide only).
National Posters: Story of Abraham Lincoln.
Society for Visual Education. Picturol: Abraham Lincoln.

Procedure during Assimilation

Reading as described on pages 24–29.
Picture study based on the illustrative material listed above.
Use the following dramatizations: "Abraham Lincoln." Johnston and Barnum,
  Book of Plays for Little Actors, pp. 61–65; "Abraham Lincoln." Wade, *Little
  Folks' Plays of American Heroes*; "A Little Life of Lincoln." Hubbard, *Little
  American History Plays*, pp. 139–151; "Mr. Lincoln and the Little Girl." Walker,
  Little Plays from American History for Young Folks, pp. 131–133.
Construct on the sand table Lincoln's birthplace and the Lincoln Memorial in
  Washington.
Write a paragraph on "Lincoln an Inspiration to Me."
Children prepare an assembly program for Lincoln's Birthday.
Drill on minimal essentials.
Objective test.

Organization

The children and the teacher working together prepare an outline somewhat similar to the following:

LIFE OF ABRAHAM LINCOLN (TO THE CIVIL WAR)

1. His boyhood and youth
2. His business life
3. Stories about Lincoln

Recitation

Each row prepares an oral composition on one of the points above; the three best are selected to give as part of the assembly program.

---

6. The Southerners believed Lincoln would free the slaves; so they made a new nation of their own

---

Preparation

"To what political party did Thomas Jefferson belong? In what part of the country did Jefferson live? Then what political party might we expect to find strongest in the South?"

Presentation

The Democratic party had always had many members in the South. It had elected more of its members to the presidency than had any other party. In fact, for years it was the strongest and largest party.

Since its greatest strength was in the South, naturally the Democratic party took the side of the South. It believed that slavery should be allowed to spread into the territories wherever the system could be used.

As we have seen, however, many of the people of the North objected strongly. Every attempt to please both sides had failed, because the South knew the North was much stronger and therefore thought it must spread its system into the new lands in order to protect itself.

There began in the North at this time a new political party. Its main belief was that slavery should not spread into the territories. This was the Republican party (*pointing to the words written on the board*).

When the Republican party elected Abraham Lincoln as president, the people in the South were very angry indeed. They said: "The first thing President Lincoln will do will be to prevent slavery from spreading into the territories. We will never allow that."

But what could they do about it? Lincoln was already elected. Some of their leaders said: "Since we cannot prevent Lincoln from being elected, let us withdraw from the Union. The North is so much stronger than we are that there is no use in our trying to remain one nation. We will call home all our senators and representatives from Washington, and will make an entirely new nation of our own."

Seven states agreed. What was Lincoln to do? He couldn't very well let them go, as that would have split the country into two parts. War began. Then four more states left also, because they believed that a state should be allowed to leave the Union if it wanted to. And that is how our great Civil War started.

PRESENTATION TEST

Check the best answer:

a. The Democratic party believed
 _ _ _ that slavery should be allowed to spread to the territories
 _ _ _ that slavery should not be allowed to spread to the territories

b. The Democratic party was strongest
 _ _ _ in the South
 _ _ _ in the North

c. The new Republican party believed
 _ _ _ that slavery should be allowed to spread to the territories
 _ _ _ that slavery should not be allowed to spread to the territories

d. The Republican party was strongest
 _ _ _ in the South
 _ _ _ in the North

e. The Democratic party believed that Lincoln would
 _ _ _ put an end to slavery in the South
 _ _ _ put an end to slavery in the territories
 _ _ _ put an end to the slave trade

f. The first seven states left the Union

   – – – because they did not like Lincoln

   – – – because they did not like the Republican party

   – – – because the Republican party was against the spread of slavery into
       the territories

g. The last four states left the Union

   – – – because the Republican party was against the spread of slavery into
       the territories

   – – – because they believed a state should be allowed to leave if it wanted to

Assimilation

Readings

Upper Group

BALDWIN. Abraham Lincoln, 208–231.

BLAISDELL. The Story of American History, 359–361.

BROOKS. The Story of Cotton, 184–193.

CHANDLER and CHITWOOD. Makers of American History, 255–263 (Davis).

COE. Makers of the Nation, 313–319.

EGGLESTON. A First Book in American History, 180–183.

ELLIS. Makers of our Country, 169–172.

GORDY. Abraham Lincoln, 110–142.

GORDY. Leaders in Making America, 330–335.

GORDY. Stories of Later American History, 250–252.

LEFFERTS. American Leaders, II : 212–216.

MONTGOMERY. Beginners' American History, 235–237.

PERRY and PRICE. American History, II : 154–156, 162–169.

TAPPAN. An Elementary History of our Country, 206–208.

WOODBURN and MORAN. The Makers of America, 268–271, 273–275 (Davis).

Compton's Pictured Encyclopedia (Civil War, Confederate States of America,
Davis).

World Book (Lincoln, War of Secession : Movement towards Disunion).

Average Group

BALDWIN. Four Great Americans, 225–233.

BARNES. Elementary History of the United States, 306–307, 326–328.

BEARD and BAGLEY. A First Book in American History, 299–320.

ELSON and MACMULLAN. Story of our Country, II : 182–186.

FORMAN. First Lessons in American History, 263–264, 270–272.

GORDY. Elementary History of the United States, 246–248.

MACE. Primary History, 354–359 (Douglas), 366–368.

MORRIS. Primary History of the United States, 224–225.

MOWRY. First Steps in the History of our Country, 252–253.

SOUTHWORTH. Builders of our Country, II : 206–209.

Lower Group

BARNES. Primary History of the United States, 166–167, 171–172.

DAVIS. Stories of the United States, 203–209.

MCMASTER. Primary History of the United States, 191–195.

Teachers

CHADWICK. Causes of the Civil War, 109–150.

COFFIN. Drum Beat of the Nation, 23–47.

ELSON. Side Lights on American History, II : 1–46.

HART. American History told by Contemporaries, IV : 151–172, 180–192.

MILLER (ED.). Great Debates in American History, V: 105–165.
SCHOULER. History of the United States, V: 405–412.
STEPHENSON. Abraham Lincoln and the Union, 1–18, 59–101.
STEPHENSON. An American History, 401–404, 406–415.
STEPHENSON. The Day of the Confederacy, 1–44.
WILSON. Division and Reunion, 201–218.
American Citizenship Course in United States History, IV: 134–139.

Minimal Essentials

Name of Person: **Jefferson Davis**
Name of Place: **South Carolina**
Date: **1860** — secession of South Carolina
Historical Terms: **secession; Republican party; Confederacy**
Things to Remember
    Lincoln's party believed there should be no more slave territory.
    The South was determined to spread slavery into the territories.
    When Lincoln was elected the South seceded.
    War began because of the secession.

Illustrative Material

Perry Pictures: 2536, Jefferson Davis.
Keystone Views: 128, Where the Civil War Began; 130, Statue of Jefferson Davis.
National Geographic Magazine, XXXII: 338 (October, 1917) (Confederate flags).

Procedure during Assimilation

Reading as described on pages 24–29.
Picture study based on the illustrative material listed above.
Children draw the Confederate flag.
Explain the cartoon in Knowlton's *Making History Graphic*, pp. 106–107.
The class writes two lists of arguments, one showing the Southern point of view; the other, the Union. The teacher works with the group presenting the side which the children will underestimate.
Make a map showing the United States in 1861. Color red the first secession; pink, the secession after April 15; blue, the slave states remaining loyal.[1] Which side will the territories take?
Drill on minimal essentials.
Objective test.

Organization

The teacher and the class working together select three main points. Each child then makes his own choice of subheads.

THE SECESSION OF THE SOUTHERN STATES

1. The election of 1860
2. The first secession
3. The later secession

[1] Woodburn, J. A., and Moran, T. F., *Elementary American History and Government*, p. 330; Gordy, W. F., *History of the United States*, p. 316; Burnham, Smith, *The Making of our Country*, p. 408; Muzzey, D. S., *An American History*, p. 335; Long, W. J., *America*, p. 356.

Recitation

Each child recites from his own outline.

A drill lesson on section II of Unit IX should be given at this point.

III. The Civil War was fought to keep the Different Parts of the Country Together

    1. The North wanted to take the Southern capital, and the South wanted to take the Northern capital

---

Preparation

On the slated map of the United States show with white chalk lines the two advances of the South into the North: Antietam, Gettysburg. Write these names along the lines of the arrows. Show with blue lines and arrow points the advances of the North against the South: (1) Bull Run, (2) Peninsular campaign, (3) second battle of Bull Run, (4) Fredericksburg, (5) Chancellorsville, (6) Grant's hammering campaign, and Sherman's march. Show in yellow the attempts to surround the Confederacy: (1) Chattanooga campaign and Chickamauga, (2) Lookout Mountain and Missionary Ridge.

Make no attempt to have the children remember the names of the battles; but when in their reading they come to a battle, let them locate the line of attack in which it occurred. Keep this map constantly before the class.

Explain to the class what the lines and arrows mean.

No additional presentation is needed.

Assimilation

Readings

Upper Group

BLAISDELL. The Story of American History, 361–366.
BURNHAM. Hero Tales from History, 341–346.
COE. Makers of the Nation, 325–337 (Lee), 342–345 (Jackson)
CURTIS. A Yankee Girl at Antietam.
CURTIS. A Yankee Girl at Fort Sumter.
EVANS. America First, 359–369, 374–383.
GORDY. Abraham Lincoln, 150–161, 164–172.
GORDY. Leaders in Making America, 335–341.

GORDY. Stories of Later American History, 254–261.
HART. Romance of the Civil War, 117–124, 139–144, 192–196, 220–234.
LEFFERTS. American Leaders, II : 266–283.
LOGIE. From Columbus to Lincoln, 240–243.
McSPADDEN. Boys' Book of Famous Soldiers, 51–73 (Lee).
MORRIS. Historical Tales : American, 292–319.
PERRY and PRICE. American History, II : 173–181, 185–189.
STIMPSON. The Child's Book of American Biography, 91–97 (Lee).
TAPPAN. An Elementary History of our Country, 208–212, 216–217.
WOODBURN and MORAN. The Makers of America, 282–285 (Lee), 290–292 (Jackson).
Civil War Stories retold from *St. Nicholas*.
Compton's Pictured Encyclopedia (Lee, Jackson, Civil War).
Southern Stories retold from *St. Nicholas*, 102–107.
World Book (War of Secession : Progress of the War).

Average Group

BARNES. Elementary History of the United States, 297–300, 303, 304–305, 307–309.
BEARD and BAGLEY. A First Book in American History, 320–324, 326–327, 336–340.
ELSON and MacMULLAN. The Story of our Country, II : 186–188, 195–201, 205–209, 212–214.
FOOTE and SKINNER. Makers and Defenders of America, 274–287.
FORMAN. First Lessons in American History, 272–275, 279–280, 282.
GORDY. Elementary History of the United States, 248–250, 262–265.
GUERBER. Story of the Great Republic, 167–183, 193–200, 247–252.
MACE. Primary History, 380–386.
MORRIS. Primary History of the United States, 226, 227–228.
MOWRY. First Steps in the History of our Country, 257–263.
SOUTHWORTH. Builders of our Country, II : 209–210, 229–235.
TURPIN. Brief Biographies from American History, 277–282 (Lee).

Lower Group

BAKER and THORNDIKE. Everyday Classics, V : 146–149 (Lee).
BALDWIN. Fifty Famous People, 11–13 (Lee).
BARNES. Primary History of the United States, 172–176, 179–181, 184–192.
DAVIDSON and ANDERSON. Lincoln Readers, IV : 234–240.
DYER and BRADY. Merrill Fifth Reader, 199–200 (letter from Lee).
McMASTER. Primary History of the United States, 195–197.
WAYLAND. History Stories for Primary Grades, 122–124.

Teachers

HART. American History told by Contemporaries, IV : 228–289.
HOSMER. The Appeal to Arms, 3–111, 125–200.
STEPHENSON. An American History, 417–443.
WILSON. Division and Reunion, 218–226.
WOOD. Captains of the Civil War, 1–83, 168–192.
American Citizenship Course in United States History, IV : 139–141, 145–146, 148–149.
Public School Methods, V : 179–183, 412–435. (The Methods Co., Chicago.)
The Century Co. (ED.). Famous Adventures and Prison Escapes of the Civil War.

Minimal Essentials

Names of Persons: **Robert E. Lee; "Stonewall" Jackson**
Names of Places: **Richmond, Virginia**
Dates: **1861–1865** — the Civil War
Historical Terms: **the Blue and the Gray; the Civil War; the South, Confederate; the North, "the Union," Federal**
Things to Remember
    The Northern armies made six different attempts to take Richmond.
    The Southern armies tried twice to come up into the North.
    The North tried to surround the South.
    For three years it was hard to tell which would win.

Illustrative Material

Coffin. Drum-Beat of the Nation (many small pictures).
Ford Educational Library (films): 33, Civil War Period.
Keystone Views: 131, Confederate Capitol; 135, Robert E. Lee's Old Home, Arlington; 342, General Robert E. Lee (slide only).
Society for Visual Education. Picturols: Battle Hymn of the Republic; Dixie.

Procedure during Assimilation

Reading as described on pages 24–29.
Picture study based on the illustrative material listed above.
Use the dramatization "Barbara Frietchie." Hubbard, *Little American History Plays*, pp. 152–157.
Play on the phonograph the following records: "Dixie"; Civil War songs.
Read to the children the following from Persons's *Our Country in Poem and Prose*: Baker, "The Black Regiment," pp. 151–153; Lathrop, "Keenan's Charge," pp. 149–151; Shepherd, "Roll Call," pp. 173–175; Stedman, "Cavalry Song," p. 175.
Use a large-sized paper wall-map of the United States. Make a red dot on the map each time that the class reads of a battle that was a Southern victory, and a blue dot for each Northern victory. Make no attempt to remember the names of battles.
Drill on minimal essentials.
Objective test.

Organization

The teacher puts the following outline on the board:

Progress of the War

    1. Attempts of the North to take the Southern capital
    2. Attempts of the South to take the Northern capital

Recitation

By consulting the map referred to above, children prepare a very brief recitation on the points.

> 2. The Union ships would not let Southern ships go into or out of their harbors

Preparation

Children model in the sand table an outline map of the United States. Mark all the important seaports in the seceding states.

"How do you suppose the South planned to earn money to carry on the war? What country was their best customer in the cotton market? Could the North do anything to prevent the Confederacy from earning this money? If the South could no longer earn money, what must the result be in time?"

No additional presentation is needed.

Assimilation

Readings

Upper Group

AUSTIN. Uncle Sam's Secrets, 219–224, 237.
BLAISDELL. The Story of American History, 387–405.
BLAISDELL and BALL. Heroic Deeds of American Sailors, 129–143.
EVANS. America First, 383–387.
FOOTE and SKINNER. Makers and Defenders of America, 294–297.
HART. Romance of the Civil War, 347–366.
MORRIS. Historical Tales: American, 270–278.
PERRY and PRICE. American History, II: 181–184.
TAPPAN. An Elementary History of our Country, 212–213.
TURPIN. Cotton, 109–110, 113–114.
WORDEN. The *Monitor* and the *Merrimac*.
Compton's Pictured Encyclopedia (Blockade, *Monitor*).

Average Group

BEARD and BAGLEY. A First Book in American History, 324–326.
ELSON and MACMULLAN. Story of our Country, II: 202, 204–205, 239–240.
FORMAN. First Lessons in American History, 281.
GORDY. Elementary History of our Country, 251–258.
GUERBER. Story of the Great Republic, 189–193, 226–231.
MORRIS. Primary History of the United States, 227.
SOUTHWORTH. Builders of our Country, II: 210–211, 238–248.

Lower Group

BARNES. Primary History of the United States, 176–179, 181–184.
MCMASTER. Primary History of the United States, 206–212.

Teachers

HART. American History told by Contemporaries, IV: 330–333, 336–338, 356–358, 363–368.

HOSMER. Outcome of the Civil War, 163–185.
STEPHENSON. An American History, 427–428.
WILSON. Division and Reunion, 229–230.
WOOD. Captains of the Civil War, 84–115, 307–326.
American Citizenship Course in United States History, IV: 141–145.

Minimal Essentials

Name of Person: **John Ericsson** (ĕr'ĭk sŭn)
Name of Place: the seaboard
Historical Terms: **blockade**; **"cheese box on a raft"**; **ironclad**; *Merrimac*; *Monitor*
Things to Remember
　　Almost all the navy had remained in the hands of the Union.
　　The South had expected that her cotton exports would provide the money necessary to carry on the war.
　　The blockade of the Southern ports by the navy bottled up the South.
　　The use of ironclad vessels was begun.

Illustrative Material

Keystone Views: 134, The *Monitor* in Hampton Roads

Procedure during Assimilation

Reading as described on pages 24–29.
Read to the children Baker's "Cruise of the *Monitor*," in Persons's *Our Country in Poem and Prose*, pp. 143–146.
On the sand-table model of the Atlantic and Gulf coasts, station toy ships to guard the entrances to the important harbors.
Show figures of the cotton exportations as affected by the blockade.[1]
Invite someone who has served in the navy to explain to the children how a vessel can be covered with steel plates.
Drill on minimal essentials.
Objective tests.

Organization

Children decide what the two main points are.

THE WAR AT SEA

　　1. The blockade
　　　 Effect on the South
　　2. The ironclads

Recitation

Short paragraphs are written on each of the points above.

---

[1] *American Citizenship Course in United States History*, IV: 144.

> 3. The Union forces cut the South in two by opening up the Mississippi River

Preparation

To the sand-table model add specific marking of the strategic points along the Mississippi and its branches: Columbus, Island No. 10, New Madrid, Forts Henry and Donelson, Shiloh, Memphis, New Orleans, Port Hudson, Vicksburg.

As children read they find on the sand table the places mentioned.

"Why would the North want to cut the Confederacy in two?"

No additional presentation is needed.

Assimilation

Readings

Upper Group

BLAISDELL. The Story of American History, 373–377.
BURNHAM. Hero Tales from History, 346–352.
HART. Romance of the Civil War, 177–179.
LANIER. The Book of Bravery, 349–360.
LODGE and ROOSEVELT. Hero Tales from American History, 303–322.
MILLER. My Book House, IV: 354–362.
MORRIS. Heroes of the Navy in America, 273–293.
PAGE. Two Little Confederates.
PERRY and PRICE. American History, II: 189–192, 206.
TAPPAN. Elementary History of our Country, 213–216, 220–221.
Compton's Pictured Encyclopedia (Farragut).

Average Group

BEEBE. Four American Naval Heroes, 133–192.
ELSON and MACMULLAN. Story of our Country, II: 203–204.
FOOTE and SKINNER. Makers and Defenders of America, 288–294.
FORMAN. First Lessons in American History, 277–279.
GORDY. Elementary History of the United States, 259–261.
GUERBER. Story of the Great Republic, 183–188.
MOWRY. First Steps in the History of our Country, 273–279.
TURPIN. Brief Biographies from American History, 282–289.

Lower Group

BARNES. Primary History of the United States, 181.
GROVE. American Naval Heroes, 19–27.
MCMASTER. Primary History of the United States, 213.

Teachers

COFFIN. Drum-Beat of the Nation, 443–456.
HART. American History told by Contemporaries, IV: 336–338, 368–371, 416–418.

HOSMER. The Appeal to Arms, 112–124, 265–280.
WILSON. Division and Reunion, 223–224.
WOOD. Captains of the Civil War, 116–167, 260–286.
American Citizenship Course in United States History, IV: 145, 146–148.

Minimal Essentials

Name of Person: **Admiral Farragut**
Name of Place: **New Orleans** (ôr'lê ănz)
Historical Term: **admiral**
Things to Remember
 The South held several important points along the Mississippi River.
 If the North could take these, it could split the Confederacy into two parts.

Illustrative Material

GRANT. Story of the Ship: *Monitor, Hartford.*
McKINLEY. Illustrated Topics for American History: S. 32.
Keystone Views: 343, Admiral Farragut at the Battle of Mobile (slide only).
Perry Pictures: 1422, An August Morning with Farragut.

Procedure during Assimilation

Reading as described on pages 24–29.
Study naval uniforms. How many admirals have there been in United States
 history?
Model in the sand table the lower Mississippi Valley. Mark with little Confederate
 flags the chief river ports held by the Confederacy. Remove each flag when the
 class has read the story of its capture.
Is there any similarity between this plan (see the title of the story) and Burgoyne's
 plan during the Revolution?
On the paper wall-map mentioned on page 468 use red-headed pins to show the
 important points along the Mississippi River held by the Confederacy. Replace
 by blue-headed pins when these points are taken by Union forces.
Drill on minimal essentials.
Objective test.

Organization

The teacher puts on the board an outline somewhat similar
to the following:

THE WAR ALONG THE MISSISSIPPI

 1. Points held by the Confederacy
 2. Admiral Farragut's work
 3. Effect on the South

Recitation

Children prepare summary sentences for each point.

> 4. The North had more men and more money; so it won

Preparation

Continue the use of the sand table and the wall-map.
No additional presentation is needed.

Assimilation

Readings

Upper Group

BLAISDELL. The Story of American History, 366–373, 377–386.

BROOKS. The Story of Cotton, 194–197.

BURNHAM. Hero Tales from History, 332–340.

CHANDLER and CHITWOOD. Makers of American History, 269–286.

COE. Makers of the Nation, 319–324 (Lincoln), 338–342 (Grant), 345–348 (Sheridan).

ELLIS. Makers of our Country, 173–182 (Grant).

EVANS. America First, 391–396.

GORDY. Abraham Lincoln, 162–261.

GORDY. Leaders in Making America, 341–356.

GORDY. Stories of Later American History, 252–254, 261–280.

HART. Romance of the Civil War, 179–183, 189–191, 277–282.

LEFFERTS. American Leaders, II : 220–256.

LOGIE. From Columbus to Lincoln, 248–262.

LOGIE. From Lincoln to Coolidge, 5–14, 23–24.

McSPADDEN. Boys' Book of Famous Soldiers, 26–49 (Grant).

MONTGOMERY. Beginners' American History, 237–239.

MOWRY. American Pioneers, 239–255.

PERRY and PRICE. American History, II : 193, 197–214.

STIMPSON. Child's Book of American Biography, 62–74.

TAPPAN. Elementary History of our Country, 217–228.

WOODBURN and MORAN. Makers of America, 272–273, 275–282 (Grant), 285–287 (Sherman), 288–290 (Sheridan), 293–295.

Compton's Pictured Encyclopedia (Grant, Sherman, Sheridan, Civil War).

World Book (War of Secession: Events of 1863, The Year 1864, End of War, Cost of War).

Average Group

BALDWIN. Four Great Americans, 233–235.

BARNES. Elementary History of the United States, 310–311, 328–341.

BEARD and BAGLEY. A First Book in American History, 326–335, 340–341.

BLAISDELL. Stories of the Civil War.

BROOKS. True Story of U. S. Grant.

ELSON and MacMULLAN. Story of our Country, II : 188–195, 209–212, 215–229.

FOOTE and SKINNER. Makers and Defenders of America, 258–273.

FORMAN. First Lessons in American History, 276–277, 283–288.

GORDY. Elementary History of the United States, 264–277.

GUERBER. Story of the Great Republic, 200–226, 233–236.

MACE. Primary History, 369–370, 372–379 (Grant).

MORRIS. Primary History of the United States, 228–229.

MOWRY. First Steps in the History of our Country, 253–256, 265–272.
SOUTHWORTH. Builders of our Country, II : 212–228.
TURPIN. Brief Biographies from American History, 267–277 (Grant).
Southern Stories retold from *St. Nicholas*, 3–17.

Lower Group

BAKER and THORNDIKE. Everyday Classics, V : 139–145 (Grant).
BALDWIN. Fifty Famous Rides and Riders, 160–162.
BARNES. Primary History of the United States, 192–208.
BLAISDELL and BALL. American History for Little Folks, 122–127.
McMASTER. Primary History of the United States, 197–205, 213–216.

Teachers

HART. American History told by Contemporaries, IV : 390–415, 422–444.
HOSMER. The Appeal to Arms, 281–322.
HOSMER. Outcome of the Civil War, 2–144, 186–306.
STEPHENSON. An American History, 453–464.
WILSON. Division and Reunion, 226–238.
WOOD. Captains of the Civil War, 193–259, 287–306, 327–396.
American Citizenship Course in United States History, IV : 150–159.

Minimal Essentials

Names of Persons : **General Sherman; General Ulysses** (û lĭs'ēz) **S. Grant**
Names of Places : **Gettysburg; Atlanta, Georgia; Ford's Theater**
Dates : **1863** — Emancipation Proclamation; **1865** — Lee's surrender
Historical Terms : **Emancipation Proclamation; draft; march through Georgia; assassination**
Things to Remember

The Emancipation Proclamation declared that all the slaves in the seceding states were free.

The battle of Gettysburg showed that the South could not hope to take the Northern capital.

At last the South became so worn out that it had to surrender, and the war was over.

Since then our country has been united.

Illustrative Material

McKINLEY. Illustrated Topics for American History : S. 33, Emancipation Proclamation.
Keystone Views : 136, General Lee's Headquarters ; 137–138, From Little Round Top ; 141, Monument where Lincoln's Famous Gettysburg Address was Made ; 149, Ford's Theater ; 151, Lincoln Memorial ; 341, U. S. Grant (slide only) ; 344, Lee's Surrender to Grant (slide only).
National Posters : The Story of U. S. Grant.
Society for Visual Education. Picturols : Uncle Tom's Cabin, Dixie, Battle Hymn of the Republic.

Procedure during Assimilation

Reading as described on pages 24–29.
Picture study based on the illustrative material listed above.
Use the dramatization : "A House Divided." Hague and Chalmers, *Dramatic Moments in American History*, pp. 246–294.
Read to the children from Persons's *Our Country in Poem and Prose*: Harte's "John Burns of Gettysburg," pp. 154–157 ; Lincoln's "Address at Gettysburg," p. 159 ;

Robbins's "Soldier's Reprieve," pp. 162–168 ; Read's "Sheridan's Ride," pp. 168–170 ; Byers's "Sherman's March to the Sea," pp. 176–177 ; Whitman's "O Captain! my Captain!", pp. 179–180.
Children sing the Civil War songs.
Play the record "Lincoln's Gettysburg Address."
Continue placing the battles on the paper wall-map as described on page 468.
Show to the class copies of the newspapers announcing the death of Lincoln.
Drill on minimal essentials.
Objective test.

Organization

The teacher puts the following outline on the board. Children tell what points belong under each heading.

THE LAST YEARS OF THE WAR

1. The Emancipation Proclamation
2. The last attempt of the South to invade the North
3. The march to the sea
4. The end of the Confederacy

Recitation

A child tells the story of one point, then calls on another to continue, and so on.

A drill lesson on section III of Unit IX should be given at this point.

> IV. During this Period the United States did Some Work that helped Mankind
>   1. The wounded were cared for better than ever before

Preparation

"During the World War what organization did much in caring for the wounded? Is the Red Cross an American organization?

"How were the wounded cared for during the Revolution?"

Presentation

Our story today tells about the beginning of the Red Cross in America.

Assimilation

Readings

Upper Group

BURNHAM. Hero Tales from History, 358–364.
CABOT. A Course in Citizenship and Patriotism, 208–210.
DAVIDSON. Founders and Builders of our Nation, 222–229.
EVANS. America First, 409–414.
FOOTE and SKINNER. Makers and Defenders of America, 298–301.
GORDY. Leaders in Making America, 445–449.
HART. Romance of the Civil War, 381–390, 395–406, 416–418.
LEFFERTS. American Leaders, II : 311–319 (Clara Barton).
LOGIE. From Columbus to Lincoln, 244–247.
MOWRY. American Heroes and Heroism, 189–195.
PERRY and PRICE. American History, II : 270–271.
SANFORD and OWEN. Modern Americans, 65–71.
STIMPSON. Child's Book of American Biography, 75–80.
SWEETSER. Ten American Girls from History, 143–173.
TAPPAN. Heroes of Progress, 140–146.
WADE. The Light Bringers, 64–111.
Compton's Pictured Encyclopedia (Barton, Red Cross).
World Book (Barton, Red Cross Societies).

Average Group

BEARD and BAGLEY. A First Book in American History, 401–407.
GORDY. Our Patriots, 154–162.
HORTON. A Group of Famous Women, 165–171.
MOWRY. First Steps in the History of our Country, 295–298, 302–303.
SOUTHWORTH. Builders of our Country, II : 252–255.

Lower Group

FAULKNER. Red Cross Stories for Children, 33–42.
MOORE. When they were Girls, 37–44.

Teachers

EPLER. Life of Clara Barton.
HUMPHREY. Women in American History, 189–206.

Minimal Essentials

Name of Person: **Clara Barton** [1]
Date: **during the Civil War**
Historical Term: **Red Cross**
Something to Remember

Clara Barton started the American branch of the Red Cross.

Illustrative Material

BROWN. Famous Pictures : 70, Clara Barton.
Educational Posters of the National Child Welfare Association : Service of the Suffering : Clara Barton.
Keystone Views : 240, Clara Barton.
Society for Visual Education. Schoolfilm : In Florence Nightingale's Footsteps.

[1] Not in the lists of personages referred to on page 5.

Procedure during Assimilation

Reading as described on pages 24–29.
Invite a Civil War veteran to tell the children how the wounded were cared for.
Drill on minimal essentials.
Objective test.

Organization

The teacher and the pupils working together produce an outline somewhat similar to the following:

THE AMERICAN RED CROSS

1. How the wounded were cared for during the early wars
2. The work of Clara Barton in the Civil War

Recitation

Two paragraphs are written on the above points.

> 2. Poets wrote on slavery and other subjects
>   *a.* Longfellow   *c.* Holmes
>   *b.* Whittier   *d.* Lowell

Preparation

"What poet did we study about in Unit VI, 'How the United States made itself Respected among the Nations'?

"What other American poets do you know? Which do you like best?"

Presentation

We are now going to read some of the works of four of America's greatest poets: Longfellow, Whittier, Holmes, and Lowell.

Assimilation

Readings

Longfellow

Works
  The Arrow and the Song
    CRANE and WHEELER. Wheeler's Graded Literary Readers, V: 209–211.
    DYER and BRADY. Merrill Fifth Reader, 63.
    SMITH. Easy Road to Reading, V: 196.
  The Bell of Atri
    BAKER and THORNDIKE. Everyday Classics, V: 172–177.

The Children's Hour
  BAKER and THORNDIKE. Everyday Classics, V: 212–213.
  CRANE and WHEELER. Wheeler's Graded Literary Readers, V: 203–208.
Christmas Bells
  DYER and BRADY. Merrill Fourth Reader, 86.
  McMANUS. Natural Method Readers, V: 33–34.
A Group of Poems
  FREE and TREADWELL. Reading-Literature, IV: 76–86.
The Launching of the Ship
  EDSON-LAING. Readers, V: 355.
  McMANUS. Natural Method Readers, V: 237–239.
A Letter from Longfellow
  FIELD. Fourth Reader, 254–256.
The Lighthouse
  ELSON and BURRIS. Child-Library Readers, V: 122–126.
The Old Clock on the Stairs
  BOLENIUS. Fifth Reader, 267–270.
  SMITH. Easy Road to Reading, V: 68–72.
Paul Revere's Ride
  BAKER and THORNDIKE. Everyday Classics, V: 201–207.
A Psalm of Life
  HARTWELL. Story Hour Readings, V: 166–167.
Rain in Summer
  BOLENIUS. Fifth Reader, 270–274.
  HARTWELL. Story Hour Readings, V: 251–252.
  SMITH. Easy Road to Reading, III: 314–315.
The Village Blacksmith
  BAKER and THORNDIKE. Everyday Classics, IV: 265–267.
  HARTWELL. Story Hour Readings, IV: 217–219.
  YOUNG and FIELD. Literary Readers, IV: 63–70.
Windmill
  CRANE and WHEELER. Wheeler's Graded Literary Readers, IV: 126–129.

Life

  BAKER and THORNDIKE. Everyday Classics, IV: 201–203.
  BALDWIN. Fifty Famous People, 18–21.
  BOLENIUS. Fifth Reader, 256–264.
  BURNHAM. Hero Tales from History, 365–371.
  CODY. Four American Poets, 71–130.
  DAVIDSON. Founders and Builders of our Nation, 171–178.
  EGGLESTON. Stories of Great Americans, 140–142.
  HART. Seven Great American Poets, 151–187.
  MILLER. My Book House, VI: 129–130.
  O'SHERIDAN. A Longfellow Booklet, 5–30.
  STIMPSON. Child's Book of American Biography, 197–203.
  Compton's Pictured Encyclopedia (Longfellow).
  Our Holidays retold from *St. Nicholas*, 123–138.
  World Book (Longfellow).

Teachers

  EGGLESTON. American Immortals, 317–323.
  HIGGINSON. Henry Wadsworth Longfellow.
  PERRY. The American Spirit in Literature, 152–157.

Whittier

Works

The Barefoot Boy
> BAKER and THORNDIKE. Everyday Classics, IV: 119–124.
> EDSON-LAING. Readers, IV: 122–123.
> SMITH. Easy Road to Reading, V: 62–64.

The Corn Song
> SEARSON and MARTIN. Studies in Reading, IV: 138–143.

The Fish I Didn't Catch
> BAKER and THORNDIKE. Everyday Classics, IV: 64–67.
> BOLENIUS. Fifth Reader, 240–245.
> DYER and BRADY. Merrill Fourth Reader, 129–130.

The Frost Spirit
> BOLENIUS. Fifth Reader, 62–64.
> YOUNG and FIELD. Literary Readers, IV: 310–316.

How the Robin Came
> BOLENIUS. Fifth Reader, 252–255.

In School-Days
> SMITH. Easy Road to Reading, V: 37–39.

King Solomon and the Ants
> CRANE and WHEELER. Wheeler's Graded Literary Readers, V: 254–258.

Red Riding-Hood
> YOUNG and FIELD. Literary Readers, V: 363–365.

The Three Bells
> FIELD. Fifth Reader, 102–104.

A Winter Fireside
> McMANUS. Natural Method Readers, V: 162.

Life

> BAKER and THORNDIKE. Everyday Classics, IV: 116–118.
> BOLENIUS. Fifth Reader, 233–240.
> CODY. Four American Poets, 133–192.
> ELSON and MacMULLAN. Story of our Country, II: 170–173.
> HART. Seven Great American Poets, 193–237.
> MILLER. My Bookhouse, VI: 168.
> RIDEING. Boyhood of Famous Authors, 92–110.
> Compton's Pictured Encyclopedia (Whittier).
> Our Holidays retold from *St. Nicholas*, 35–50.
> World Book (Whittier).

Teachers

> CARPENTER. John Greenleaf Whittier.
> PERRY. The American Spirit in Literature, 157–163.

Holmes

Works

Grandmother's Story of Bunker Hill
> HOLMES. Complete Poetical Works.

The Height of the Ridiculous
> HARTWELL. Story Hour Readings, V: 240–241.
> SMITH. Easy Road to Reading, V: 195–196.

The Heritage
> EDSON-LAING. Readers, V: 18–20.

Old Ironsides
> BAKER and THORNDIKE. Everyday Classics, IV: 160–161.
> DYER and BRADY. Merrill Fifth Reader, 207–208.
> McMANUS. Natural Method Readers, V: 226–227.

Scribblers
> SMITH. Easy Road to Reading, IV: 260.

To a Katydid
> YOUNG and FIELD. Literary Readers, V: 216–220.

Life
> CODY. Four American Poets, 195–253.
> EGGLESTON. Stories of Great Americans, 122–124.
> HART. Seven Great American Poets, 243–274.
> RIDEING. Boyhood of Famous Authors, 1–15.
> Compton's Pictured Encyclopedia (Holmes).
> World Book (Holmes).

Teachers
> CROTHERS. Oliver Wendell Holmes.
> MORSE. Life and Letters of Holmes.
> PERRY. The American Spirit in Literature, 163–168.

Lowell

Works

Aladdin
> BAKER and THORNDIKE. Everyday Classics, V: 299.
> EDSON-LAING. Readers, V: 194.

The First Snow Fall
> EDSON-LAING. Readers, V: 128–130.
> SMITH. Easy Road to Reading, V: 140–142.
> YOUNG and FIELD. Literary Readers, V: 362.

The Fountain
> BAKER and THORNDIKE. Everyday Classics, IV: 110–111.
> YOUNG and FIELD. Literary Readers, IV: 178–184.

Life
> HART. Seven Great American Poets, 279–306.
> RIDEING. Boyhood of Famous Authors, 140–154.
> Compton's Pictured Encyclopedia (Lowell).
> World Book (Lowell).

Teachers
> GREENSLET. James Russell Lowell.
> PERRY. The American Spirit in Literature, 168–174.

Minimal Essentials

Names of Persons: Henry Wadsworth Longfellow; John Greenleaf Whittier;
Oliver Wendell Holmes; James Russell Lowell
Historical Term : "the Children's Poet"
Things to Remember
> Longfellow, Whittier, Holmes, and Lowell are among the greatest American
> poets.
> They lived in New England.

Illustrative Material

BROWN. Famous Pictures: 1494, Longfellow's Study, Cambridge.
GABRIEL (ED.). Pageant of America, XI: 154–181.
Perry Pictures: 15, Henry Wadsworth Longfellow; 16, His Birthplace, Portland; 17, His Home, Portland; 18, His Home, Cambridge; 19, His Daughters; 25, John Greenleaf Whittier; 26, Birthplace; 28, His Home, Amesbury; 29, His Home, "Oak Knoll"; 35, Oliver Wendell Holmes; 36, His Birthplace, Cambridge; 37, His Home, Boston; 38, Holmes and the *Constitution*; 45, James Russell Lowell; 46, His Home; 47, His Study.

Procedure during Assimilation

Reading as described on pages 24–29.
Picture study based on the illustrative material listed above.
After the general silent reading, each child chooses one selection to read aloud to the class.
Children make drawings to illustrate any one of the poems they have read.
Drill on minimal essentials.
Objective test.

Organization

Each child chooses one biography to outline.

Recitation

Invite the high-school teacher of English to listen to the stories.

> 3. Great novels and stories were written
>   *a.* Harriet Beecher Stowe: *Uncle Tom's Cabin*
>   *b.* Poe
>   *c.* Hawthorne

Preparation

"About what story writers did we read in Unit VI, 'How the United States made itself Respected among the Nations'?

"Have any of you ever seen the play *Uncle Tom's Cabin*? Tell us about it."

Presentation

We are now going to read about three of America's great story tellers: Harriet Beecher Stowe, Edgar Allan Poe, and Nathaniel Hawthorne.

Assimilation

Readings

Harriet Beecher Stowe

Works

Uncle Tom's Cabin. (Try to induce every child to read this story.)

Historical account of her work

LOGIE. From Columbus to Lincoln, 209–221.
MOWRY. First Steps in the History of our Country, 293.
PERRY and PRICE. American History, II : 159–160.
TAPPAN. Elementary History of Our Country, 204.

Life

BOLTON. Girls who became Famous, 1–17.
ELSON and MacMULLAN. Story of our Country, II : 173–175.
HORTON. A Group of Famous Women, 83–96.
LEFFERTS. American Leaders, II : 160–177.
MOORE. When they were Girls, 163–169.
Compton's Pictured Encyclopedia (Stowe).
World Book (Stowe).

Teachers

HUMPHREY. Women in American History, 132–153.
WARNER. Library of the World's Best Literature, XXXV : 14,067–14,106.

Poe

Work

Tell the children the story of "The Gold Bug."

Life

HART. Seven Great American Poets, 91–146.
Compton's Pictured Encyclopedia (Poe).
World Book (Poe).

Teachers

PAINTER. Poets of the South, 29–47.
PERRY. The American Spirit in Literature, 187–196.
WARNER. Library of the World's Best Literature, XXIX : 11,651–11,700.
WOODBERRY. Life of Edgar Allan Poe.

Hawthorne

Works

The Wonder Book and Tanglewood Tales. Illustrated by Maxfield Parrish
    (Duffield & Company). (Try to induce every child to read this work.)
Baucis and Philemon
    FREE and TREADWELL. Reading-Literature, IV : 103–123.
    SMITH. Easy Road to Reading, V : 197–222.
Dragon's Teeth
    DYER and BRADY. Merrill Fourth Reader, 202–226.

The Golden Fleece
  SMITH. Easy Road to Reading, V: 340–349.
A Group of Greek Myths
  FREE and TREADWELL. Reading-Literature, IV: 148–174.
Hercules
  DYER and BRADY. Merrill Fifth Reader, 218–230.
Little Daffy-Down-Dilly
  BAKER and THORNDIKE. Everyday Classics, IV: 321–331.
  CRANE and WHEELER. Wheeler's Graded Literary Readers, IV: 103–117.
  HARTWELL. Story Hour Readings, V: 60–65.
  SMITH. Easy Road to Reading, V: 25–35.
An Old-fashioned School
  BAKER and THORNDIKE. Everyday Classics, V: 11–16.
  McMANUS. Natural Method Readers, V: 195–200.
The Paradise of Children
  CRANE and WHEELER. Wheeler's Graded Literary Readers, V: 219–250.
  FREE and TREADWELL. Reading-Literature, IV: 87–102.
  HARTWELL. Story Hour Readings, V: 373–376.
  SMITH. Easy Road to Reading, III: 119–131.
The Pine-Tree Shillings
  BAKER and THORNDIKE. Everyday Classics, V: 69–76.
  DYER and BRADY. Merrill Fifth Reader, 213–218.
The Pygmies
  ELSON and BURRIS. Child-Library Readers, V: 382–406.
Sunken Treasure
  BAKER and THORNDIKE. Everyday Classics, V: 77–87.

Life

  BOLENIUS. Fifth Reader, 275–281.
  DYER and BRADY. Merrill Fifth Reader, 209–212.
  MILLER. My Bookhouse, VI: 118–120.
  Compton's Pictured Encyclopedia (Hawthorne).
  World Book (Hawthorne).

Teachers

  EGGLESTON. American Immortals, 303–316.
  HAWTHORNE. Nathaniel Hawthorne and his Wife.
  PERRY. The American Spirit in Literature, 143–152.
  VAN DOREN. The American Novel, 77–108.
  WOODBERRY. Nathaniel Hawthorne.

Minimal Essentials

Names of Persons: **Harriet Beecher Stowe; Edgar Allan Poe; Nathaniel Hawthorne**[1]
Historical Term: Uncle Tom's Cabin
Things to Remember
  Harriet Beecher Stowe wrote *Uncle Tom's Cabin* to give Northern people a picture of slavery.
  Poe wrote mystery stories and many beautiful poems.
  Hawthorne was a great writer of stories.

[1] Not included in the lists of personages referred to on page 5.

Illustrative Material

BROWN. Famous Pictures: 19, 2130, [Nathaniel Hawthorne; 31, Harriet Beecher Stowe;
  1647, Her Home; 1249, Edgar Allan Poe.
GABRIEL (ED.). Pageant of America, XI: 150–154, 182–189, 211–213.
Mentor, X: 1–12 (September, 1922): Poe.
Perry Pictures: 11, Nathaniel Hawthorne.
Society for Visual Education. Picturol: *Uncle Tom's Cabin.*

Procedure during Assimilation

Reading as described on pages 24–29.
Picture study based on the illustrative material listed above.
Each child makes a book report on one story he has been reading, selecting from it
  an interesting incident to tell to the class.
Drill on minimal essentials.
Objective test.

Organization

Each child chooses one biography to outline.

Recitation

Invite a teacher of English to listen to the stories.

---

4. Horace Mann helped to improve the school system

Preparation

"What kind of schools did the early colonies have?
"What do we mean when we speak nowadays of our 'public
school' system? Why do we call it public?"

Presentation

The New England colonies started out very well indeed in
education, but soon slowed down in their efforts. They had
so many other things to do, such as fighting the Indians, the
French, and the king, that they had not much time or money
left for schools.

Just about the time that railroads were being built everywhere east of the Mississippi, Horace Mann (*pointing to the
name written on the board*) came forward in New England and
showed everybody the very bad condition of the schools, and
what was needed to improve them.

He wanted schools enough so that every child could attend. The only way to have so many was to tax everybody, and, of course, many people objected.

Then also he wanted new methods of teaching, so that children would be interested in their lessons. In order to do this, he saw that it was necessary to have normal schools for training teachers. He built the first public normal school in the United States.

For many years he worked hard and faithfully to make the schools better, and by the time he died so much had been accomplished through his efforts that he is called the "father of the public-school system" in America.

PRESENTATION TEST

Check the best answer:

a. Horace Mann began his work about the same time

    _ _ _ that the Revolution was fought
    _ _ _ that railroads were first being built
    _ _ _ that the telegraph was invented

b. He believed that the way to get money enough for schools for everybody was

    _ _ _ to ask the pupils to pay
    _ _ _ to ask rich men for money
    _ _ _ to tax everybody

c. He believed that the way to make the teaching better was

    _ _ _ to build normal schools to train teachers
    _ _ _ to pay the teachers more money
    _ _ _ to hire more teachers

Assimilation

Readings

Upper Group

MOWRY. American Pioneers, 266–278.
WINSHIP. Great American Educators, 15–51.
World Book (Mann).

Average Group

MOWRY. First Steps in the History of our Country, 280–287.

Lower Group

Read MOWRY to this group.

Teachers

EGGLESTON. American Immortals, 380–384.
SLOSSON. The American Spirit in Education, 124–140.

Minimal Essentials

Name of Person: **Horace Mann**
Date: **during the era of railroad-building**
Historical Term: **common schools**
Things to Remember
> Horace Mann started our common-school system.
> He also started the first public normal school.

Illustrative Material

McKinley. Illustrated Topics for American History: S. 28, Early Text Books.
Educational Posters of the National Child Welfare Association: Education for All: Horace Mann.

Procedure during Assimilation

Reading as described on pages 24–29.
Show children copies of textbooks used before the Civil War. The local museum may contain copies. Some of the children may be able to bring books from home.
List the names of schools in your vicinity which are not public schools.
Examine a real-estate tax receipt to see for what purposes the tax was levied.
Children list the normal schools in their own state.
Drill on minimal essentials.
Objective test.

Organization

The teacher puts the following outline on the board:

Horace Mann's Work for the Schools

1. Bad condition of schools before the time of Horace Mann
2. Life of Horace Mann
3. Changes in the schools

Recitation

Invite the principal to hear the stories based on the outline.

> 5. Some advances were made in science
>   *a*. Ether
>   *b*. Audubon : birds
>   *c*. Photography

Preparation

"Do you know anybody who has taken ether for an operation? How did it affect him? Why was the discovery of ether a blessing to mankind?

"Do you have an Audubon society in your school? Why is it so called?"

Presentation

Most of the improvements that we have mentioned so far have been either in writing or in education. But while some people were writing, others were making wonderful discoveries in science. We are now going to read stories of three lines of discovery in science which have helped to make life easier and more pleasant.

Assimilation

Readings

Ether

PIERCY. Great Inventions and Discoveries, 147–153.
TAPPAN. Heroes of Progress, 39–46 (Morton).
Compton's Pictured Encyclopedia (Anæsthetics).
World Book (Ether, Anæsthetics, Morton).

Audubon

Works

The Baltimore Oriole
    YOUNG and FIELD. Literary Readers, VI : 343–354.
A Forest on Fire
    HARTWELL. Story Hour Readings, V : 26–30.
A Journey in Florida
    FIELD. Fifth Reader, 314–319.

Life

BOLTON. Famous Men of Science, 167–201.
EGGLESTON. Stories of Great Americans, 111–117.
FIELD. Fifth Reader, 319–320.
STIMPSON. Child's Book of American Biography, 98–105.
TAPPAN. Heroes of Progress, 1–10.
WEED. Bird Life Stories.
World Book (Audubon).

Teachers

BEARD. Our Foreign-Born Citizens, 20–29.
EGGLESTON. American Immortals, 413–417.
HERRICK. Audubon the Naturalist.
WARNER. Library of the World's Best Literature, III : 956–961.

Photography

DARROW. Thinkers and Doers, 171–182 (difficult).
EVERETT and REED. When they were Boys, 45–52.
JENKS. Photography for Young People.
PIERCY. Great Inventions and Discoveries, 177–181.
Compton's Pictured Encyclopedia (Photography).
World Book (Photography : Progress in Photography).

Teachers
    SPARKS. National Development, 46–47.
    STORY. The Story of Photography.
    THOMPSON. The Age of Invention, 153–156.

Minimal Essentials

Name of Person : Audubon [1] (ô′dōō bŏn)
Historical Terms: ether; photography
Things to Remember
    Ether was a great help to doctors.
    Audubon was a great student of birds.
    Men learned to take photographs.

Illustrative Material

REED. Bird Guide : Land Birds East of the Rockies.
REED. Western Bird Guide.
Compton's Pictured Encyclopedia (Anæsthetics, Photography).
Mentor, XIII : 22–24 (June, 1925), Audubon.

Procedure during Assimilation

Reading as described on pages 24–29.
Take the children on a bird trip to see how many birds they can recognize.[2]
Dramatize Longfellow's "Birds of Killingworth."
Form an Audubon club.[3] Give an entertainment and buy a bird bath with the
    proceeds.
Consult Arbor Day and Bird Day annuals.
Children who can obtain the use of a camera form a camera club, and learn how to
    take, develop, and print snapshots.
Drill on minimal essentials.
Objective test.

Organization

Children will suggest the main points in the following
outline :
    SOME DISCOVERIES IN SCIENCE

        1. Ether
        2. Audubon's work on birds
        3. Photography

Recitation

Invite a high-school teacher of science to hear the stories.

    [1] Not included in the lists of personages referred to on page 5.
    [2] Reed, C. A., *Bird Guide: Land Birds East of the Rockies* ; Reed, C. A., *Western
Bird Guide.*
    [3] *Elementary School Journal*, XXVI : 486–487.

6. Temperance societies were formed

Preparation

"What is the prohibition law?

"Before we had the prohibition law, was there any attempt to make people temperate?

"Do you know what the W. C. T. U. is?

"Why do you suppose women have always been so much interested in temperance?"

Presentation

Today we are going to read of the beginnings of the temperance movement in the United States, long before there was any prohibition law.

Assimilation

Readings

Upper Group
> DAVIDSON. Founders and Builders of our Nation, 230–235.
> GORDY. Leaders in Making America, 441–444.
> LEFFERTS. American Leaders, II : 320–328.
> SANFORD and OWEN. Modern Americans, 139–146.
> WILLIAMS. Some Successful Americans, 89–97.
> Compton's Pictured Encyclopedia (Temperance, Willard).
> World Book (Temperance, Willard).

Average Group
> BEARD and BAGLEY. A First Book in American History, 407–409.
> GORDY. Our Patriots, 150–153.
> HORTON. A Group of Famous Women, 199–205.
> MOWRY. First Steps in the History of our Country, 295.
> TAPPAN. Heroes of Progress, 132–139.

Lower Group
> MOORE. When they were Girls, 178–185.

Teachers
> GORDON. The Beautiful Life of Frances E. Willard.
> WOOLLEY and JOHNSON. Temperance Progress in the Nineteenth Century.

Minimal Essentials

Name of Person: **Frances E. Willard** [1]
Historical Terms: **temperance movement; prohibition; "white ribbon"**
Things to Remember
> Frances E. Willard was one of the first women to be known by the whole nation. She worked very hard for the temperance movement.

[1] Not in the lists of personages referred to on page 5.

Illustrative Material

Educational Posters of the National Child Welfare Association: War against Alcoholism: Frances E. Willard.
Perry Pictures: 152, Frances Willard; 153, Her Home, Evanston, Illinois.

Procedure during Assimilation

Reading as described on pages 24–29.
Readings on the effect of alcohol on the body are: Jewett, *The Body and its Defenses*, pp. 96–104, 136–142; Jewett, *Health and Safety*, pp. 77–79, 121–130; O'Shea and Kellogg, *The Body in Health*, pp. 269–275; O'Shea and Kellogg, *Health Habits*, pp. 135–139; Winslow, *Healthy Living*, Book I, pp. 150–154.
After reading from hygiene books, children make a list of reasons why one should not drink liquor.
Invite a physician to tell the children the bad effects of alcohol.
Drill on minimal essentials.
Objective test.

Organization

The teacher and the children working together produce an outline somewhat similar to the following:

TEMPERANCE MOVEMENT

1. Drinking in the early days
2. Work of Frances E. Willard
3. Temperance societies

Recitation

Children give a temperance program in assembly.[1]

---

7. Perry opened the ports of Japan to trade

Preparation

Review the story of Captain Robert Gray.[2]
Review the story of the clipper ships.[3]
"Who was Oliver Hazard Perry?"

Presentation

We had been trading with China for some time but not with Japan. We should have been glad to trade with Japan, but she had had some unhappy experiences with strangers and so

[1] Holmes, C. W., "Assemblies for the Elementary School." *Elementary School Journal*, XXVI: 30–35.
[2] See pages 320–322.   [3] See pages 422–424.

kept all foreign people out of her country. At last the President sent Commodore Perry, a brother of Oliver Hazard Perry, to see if Japan would not let our ships come to some of her ports to trade. Our story today is about Commodore Perry in Japan.

Assimilation
Readings

Upper Group
> BRAIN. All about Japan, 131–148.
> GRIFFIS. Japan in History, 209–215.
> MORRIS. Heroes of the Navy in America, 261–272.
> VAN BERGEN. Story of Japan, 191–206.
> WHEELER and HOLMES. Burton Holmes Travel Stories: Japan, 7–10.
> World Book (Perry).

Average Group
> Read WHEELER and HOLMES to the children.

Lower Group
> Read WHEELER and HOLMES to the children.

Teachers
> HART. How our Grandfathers Lived, 265–270.

Minimal Essentials

Name of Person: **Commodore Perry** [1]
Name of Place: **Japan**
Date: **about the same time as the Kansas-Nebraska Bill**
Historical Term: **opening the ports; commodore**
Things to Remember
> Japan had refused to have anything to do with strangers.
> Commodore Perry made a treaty of commerce with Japan.
> Since then Japan has made great progress.

Illustrative Material

BRADLEY. Village Series of Cut-Outs: Japanese Village.
McKINLEY. Illustrated Topics for Mediæval and Modern History: M. M. 32.

Procedure during Assimilation

Reading as described on pages 24–29.
The teacher may tell the children the story as given in Hart's *How our Grandfathers Lived*, pp. 265–270.
List all the articles which came from Japan that are to be found in the town's largest department store. Inspect the Oriental department of the local museum.
Find statistics as to the amount of trade between Japan and the United States.[2] Show how it has grown. Graph the figures.
Drill on minimal essentials.
Objective test.

---

[1] Not in the lists of personages referred to on page 5.
[2] World Almanac: Japan (Trade with the United States).

Organization

The teacher puts the following outline on the board :

OPENING THE PORTS OF JAPAN

1. Why Japan wanted to keep to herself
2. How Perry won the treaty
3. Japan's growth and progress

Recitation

Each child tells the entire story.

A drill lesson on section IV of Unit IX should be given at this point, similar to that described on pages 112-113.

Children see what they can do with Test V of the *Informational Tests in United States History* to accompany Beard and Bagley's *History of the American People.*

Give the *Van Wagenen Information Scale F1* for Grades 5 and 6, "The Revolutionary War to the Civil War."

TESTS ON THE ENTIRE UNIT

(To be given when all the stories are completed)

Test of Place-Sense. Pass outline maps of the United States showing the state boundaries by dotted lines. Give the following directions :

1. Put the letter *K* in the state of Kansas.
2. Put the letter *M* in the state of Missouri.
3. Put the letter *N* in the state of Nebraska.
4. Put the letter *S* in the state of South Carolina.
5. Draw Mason and Dixon's line in red.
6. Color the Mexican cession yellow.
7. Place a * where Richmond, Virginia, is.
8. Place an O where New Orleans is.
9. Place a V where Atlanta is.
10. Draw a blue line along the eastern seaboard.
11. Place a square where Gettysburg is.
12. On the map of the world at the front of the room, show the Guinea coast and Japan.

MINIMAL ESSENTIALS OF UNIT IX

PERSONS	PLACES	TERMS	DATES
Audubon	Atlanta, Georgia	*Liberator*	*1619.* Bringing of negro slaves into Virginia
Clara Barton	Ford's Theater	march through Georgia	
John C. Calhoun	Gettysburg	*Merrimac*	*1820.* The Missouri Compromise
Henry Clay	Guinea coast	"middle passage"	
Jefferson Davis	Japan	Missouri Compromise	*1850.* The Great Compromise
John Ericsson	Kansas	*Monitor*	February 12
Admiral Farragut	Mason and Dixon's line	negro	*1860.* Secession of South Carolina
William Lloyd Garrison	Mexican cession	the North	
General U. S. Grant	Missouri	opening the ports	*1861–1865.* The Civil War
Nathaniel Hawthorne	Nebraska	orator	
Oliver Wendell Holmes	New Orleans	overseer	*1863.* The Emancipation Proclamation
"Stonewall" Jackson	Richmond, Virginia	photography	
Robert E. Lee	seaboard	plantation system	*1865.* Lee's surrender
Abraham Lincoln	South Carolina	poor whites	During the seventeenth and eighteenth centuries
Henry Wadsworth Longfellow		prohibition	
James Russell Lowell		Red Cross	The half-century before the Civil War
Horace Mann		Republican party	
Commodore Perry		secession	During the Civil War
Edgar Allan Poe		slave states	During the era of railroad-building
Dred Scott		slavery	
General Sherman		the South	Drill on the peaks of the time chart
Harriet Beecher Stowe		temperance movement	
Daniel Webster		*Uncle Tom's Cabin*	
John Greenleaf Whittier		"underground railroad	
Frances E. Willard		"the Union," Federal	
		"white ribbon"	

PERSONS (cont.)		TERMS (cont.)	
abolition	ether		
admiral	field servants		
assassination	free states		
the Blue and the Gray	freedmen		
border states	fugitive slave		
"cheese box on a raft"	Great Compromise		
"Children's Poet"	"Great Peacemaker"		
Civil War	Honest Abe		
commodore	house servants		
common schools	ironclad		
compromise	Kansas-Nebraska Bill		
Confederacy			
cotton states			
draft			
Dred Scott decision			
Emancipation Proclamation			

Test of Time-Sense. Pass mimeographed sheets of the following:

I. Here is a list of names. Put the figure 1 before the name of the person who lived first or whose great work was done first, the figure 2 before the name of the person who lived next, and so on.

    _ _ _ Abraham Lincoln
    _ _ _ Henry Clay
    _ _ _ Horace Mann

II. Here is another list. Do the same.

    _ _ _ John C. Calhoun
    _ _ _ Robert E. Lee
    _ _ _ Frances E. Willard

III. Here is another list. Do the same.

    _ _ _ General U. S. Grant
    _ _ _ Commodore Perry
    _ _ _ Daniel Webster

IV. Here is another list. Do the same.

    _ _ _ Dred Scott
    _ _ _ William Lloyd Garrison
    _ _ _ Jefferson Davis

V. Here is another list. Do the same.

    _ _ _ Harriet Beecher Stowe
    _ _ _ "Stonewall" Jackson
    _ _ _ Nathaniel Hawthorne

VI. Here is another list. Do the same.

    _ _ _ John Ericsson
    _ _ _ Henry Wadsworth Longfellow
    _ _ _ Clara Barton

VII. Here is a list of dates or time expressions:

    during the era of railroad-building
    1619
    1865
    during the seventeenth and eighteenth centuries
    1820
    during the Civil War

Put each in its right place in the sentences below:

1. Horace Mann made great changes in the school system _ _ _ _.
2. The Missouri Compromise was made in _ _ _ _.
3. Clara Barton did her great work _ _ _ _.
4. Lee surrendered in _ _ _ _.
5. Slaves were first brought into Virginia in _ _ _ _.
6. The slave trade was carried on _ _ _ _.

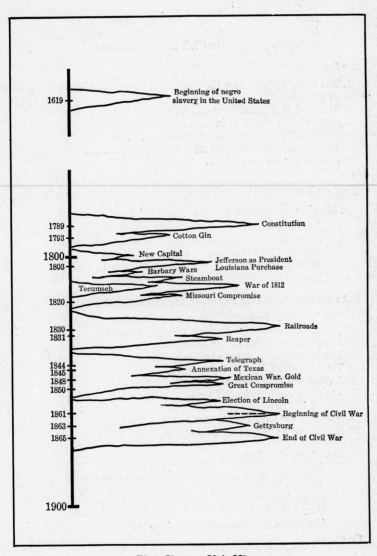

1619	Beginning of negro slavery in the United States
1789	Constitution
1793	Cotton Gin
1800	New Capital
1803	Jefferson as President
	Louisiana Purchase
	Barbary Wars
	Steamboat
Tecumseh	War of 1812
1820	Missouri Compromise
1830	Railroads
1831	Reaper
1844	Telegraph
1845	Annexation of Texas
1848	Mexican War. Gold
1850	Great Compromise
	Election of Lincoln
1861	Beginning of Civil War
1863	Gettysburg
1865	End of Civil War
1900	

Time Chart — Unit IX

VIII. Here is another list:

1850	1860
1863	1861–1865
half-century before the Civil War	February 12

Do the same.

1. The years during which the North and the South tried to make compromises were the _ _ _ _.
2. The Civil War lasted from _ _ _ _.
3. South Carolina seceded in _ _ _ _.
4. The Great Compromise was made in _ _ _ _.
5. The Emancipation Proclamation was made in _ _ _ _.
6. Lincoln was born on _ _ _ _.

Test on Persons. Pass mimeographed sheets of the following:

I. Here is a list of names:

John Ericsson	Henry Clay
Henry Wadsworth Longfellow	"Stonewall" Jackson
William Lloyd Garrison	Audubon
Admiral Farragut	Robert E. Lee
Frances E. Willard	Harriet Beecher Stowe

Put each name in the right blank in the sentences below:

1. The "Great Peacemaker" was _ _ _ _ _ _ _ _.
2. _ _ _ _ _ _ _ _ built the ironclad ship for the Union.
3. *Uncle Tom's Cabin* was written by _ _ _ _ _ _ _ _ _ _ _ _.
4. The greatest hero of the South was _ _ _ _ _ _ _ _ _ _ _ _.
5. The "Children's Poet" was _ _ _ _ _ _ _ _ _ _ _ _.
6. A great worker for temperance was _ _ _ _ _ _ _ _ _ _ _ _.
7. The great leader of abolition was _ _ _ _ _ _ _ _ _ _ _ _.
8. Robert E. Lee's greatest general was _ _ _ _ _ _ _ _.
9. A hero of the navy during the Civil War was _ _ _ _ _ _ _.
10. _ _ _ _ was a great authority on birds.

II. Here is another list:

John C. Calhoun	Nathaniel Hawthorne
Jefferson Davis	James Russell Lowell
Edgar Allan Poe	Commodore Perry
Daniel Webster	Horace Mann
General U. S. Grant	Dred Scott

Do the same.

1. _ _ _ _ _ _ _ _ _ _ _ was a great New England poet.
2. The president of the Confederacy was _ _ _ _ _ _ _ _.
3. _ _ _ _ _ _ _ _ opened up the ports of Japan.
4. _ _ _ _ _ _ _ _ was a slave who lived for a while in a free state.

5. The great orator for the Union was _ _ _ _ _ _ _ _.
6. _ _ _ _ _ _ _ _ _ _ _ wrote mystery stories.
7. The great orator for the South was _ _ _ _ _ _ _ _ _ _ _ _.
8. _ _ _ _ _ _ _ _ wrote *The Wonder Book.*
9. _ _ _ _ _ _ _ _ made the schools better.
10. The greatest Union general was _ _ _ _ _ _ _ _ _ _ _ _ _ _ _ _.

III. Here is another list:

> Abraham Lincoln
> General Sherman
> John Greenleaf Whittier
> Oliver Wendell Holmes
> Clara Barton

Do the same.

1. _ _ _ _ _ _ _ _ made the famous march to the sea.
2. The Quaker poet was _ _ _ _ _ _ _ _ _ _ _ _.
3. Another great New England poet was _ _ _ _ _ _ _ _ _ _ _ _.
4. _ _ _ _ _ _ _ _ started the American Red Cross.
5. _ _ _ _ _ _ _ _ made the Emancipation Proclamation.

Test on Historical Terms. The teacher prepares descriptions such as the following, which may have been used previously as the subject of drill games.

I. Here is a list of terms:

admiral	"middle passage"
compromise	Republican party
"cheese box on a raft"	photography
"Great Peacemaker"	*Uncle Tom's Cabin*
Liberator	Confederacy

Put each one in the right blank in the sentences below:

1. The _ _ _ _ was a league among the Southern states.
2. Taking pictures is _ _ _ _.
3. The *Monitor* was called a _ _ _ _ _ _ _ _ _ _ _ _ _ _ _ _ _ _ _ _.
4. The great newspaper of abolition was the _ _ _ _.
5. The highest officer in the navy is the _ _ _ _.
6. Henry Clay was the _ _ _ _ _ _ _ _.
7. The party that believed there should be no slavery in the territories was the _ _ _ _ _ _ _ _.
8. A settlement of a question by which each side gains something but has to give up something is a _ _ _ _.
9. The part of the Atlantic between Africa and the West Indies which was used by the slave ships was called the _ _ _ _ _ _ _ _.
10. A famous story about slaves was _ _ _ _ _ _ _ _ _ _ _ _.

II. Here is another list:

slavery   Missouri Compromise
common schools   Red Cross
field servants   plantation system
Honest Abe   the South
ironclad   underground railroad

Do the same.

1. A vessel covered with iron or steel is an _ _ _ _ _.
2. The raising of one crop on a very large farm, usually by negro labor, is the _ _ _ _ _ _ _ _.
3. Public schools are _ _ _ _ _ _ _ _.
4. The states that seceded were _ _ _ _ _ _ _ _.
5. The settlement of the question about Missouri was the _ _ _ _ _ _ _ _.
6. Slaves who worked in agriculture were _ _ _ _ _ _ _ _.
7. Lincoln was called _ _ _ _ _ _ _ _.
8. The _ _ _ _ _ _ _ _ was formed to help the wounded and sick in war time.
9. The system of helping slaves to escape to Canada was the _ _ _ _ _ _ _ _.
10. The condition of a human being who is the property of another is _ _ _ _.

III. Here is another list:

assassination   ether
cotton states   opening the ports
free states   poor whites
house servants   temperance movement
Civil War   "white ribbon"

Do the same.

1. The war between the states was the _ _ _ _ _ _ _ _.
2. The _ _ _ _ _ _ _ _ was the sign of the temperance movement.
3. _ _ _ _ is a drug that helps in operations.
4. Killing a great person in public life is _ _ _ _ _.
5. Slaves who did work around the house were _ _ _ _ _ _ _ _.
6. States in which the growing of cotton was a chief industry were called _ _ _ _ _ _ _ _.
7. Securing the right to trade with certain coast towns is _ _ _ _ _ _ _ _ _ _ _ _.
8. The attempt to do away with the habit of drinking is called the _ _ _ _ _ _ _ _.
9. States in which no slavery was allowed were _ _ _ _ _ _ _ _.
10. Southerners who did not have slaves or large plantations were _ _ _ _ _ _ _ _.

IV. Here is another list:

abolition	*Merrimac*
draft	orator
"Children's Poet"	secession
Kansas-Nebraska Bill	commodore
march through Georgia	the Blue and the Gray

Do the same.

1. The Confederate ironclad was the _ _ _ _.
2. Longfellow is called the _ _ _ _ _ _ _ _.
3. Putting an immediate end to slavery is _ _ _ _.
4. Forcing people to serve in an army or navy is a _ _ _ _.
5. Sherman's advance to Atlanta is called the _ _ _ _ _ _ _ _ _ _ _ _.
6. A great public speaker is an _ _ _ _.
7. The act of Congress which said that the Louisiana Purchase lands could decide the slavery question for themselves instead of keeping to the Missouri Compromise line was the _ _ _ _ _ _ _ _ _ _ _ _.
8. The naval officer next above the captain used to be the _ _ _ _.
9. The withdrawing of states from the Union, or the attempt to withdraw, is _ _ _ _.
10. Because of the colors they wore, the Union and Confederate soldiers were called _ _ _ _ _ _ _ _ _ _ _ _ _ _ _ _ _ _ _ _.

V. Here is another list:

border states	overseer	negro
slave states	Emancipation Proclamation	freedmen
Great Compromise	the North	fugitive slave
prohibition	*Monitor*	

Do the same.

1. A slave who ran away was a _ _ _ _ _ _ _ _.
2. The five slave states that were next to the free states of the North were the _ _ _ _ _ _ _ _.
3. Forbidding the manufacture or sale of drinks containing alcohol is _ _ _ _.
4. A black man is a _ _ _ _.
5. One who had charge of slaves at work was an _ _ _ _.
6. The paper in which President Lincoln declared that the negroes in the seceding states were free is the _ _ _ _ _ _ _ _.
7. The act of Congress which allowed the people in the lands we got from Mexico (except California) to choose for themselves whether the territory should be slave or free was the _ _ _ _ _ _ _ _.
8. The states north of the slave states were called _ _ _ _ _ _ _ _.
9. The states in which slavery existed were _ _ _ _ _ _ _ _.
10. Slaves who were given their freedom were called _ _ _ _.
11. The ironclad vessel that sat very low on the water and had a round turret was the _ _ _ _.

COMPREHENSION TEST ON UNIT IX

1. *Check the best answer:*

    a. Slavery in America was begun

        _ _ _ during the American Revolution
        _ _ _ in the colonial period
        _ _ _ after the Constitution was adopted

    b. The result of opening the ports of Japan was

        _ _ _ the growth of trade with Japan
        _ _ _ a bitter feeling toward Japan
        _ _ _ much travel to Japan

    c. The slave trade was the name given especially

        _ _ _ to the selling of slaves inside the state
        _ _ _ to the selling of negroes from the border states to the far South
        _ _ _ to the securing of negroes in Africa and selling them in America

    d. In the Civil War each side wanted

        _ _ _ to wait at home until the other attacked it
        _ _ _ to take the capital and the government of the other
        _ _ _ to starve the other out

    e. One attempt during this period to make our people live a different kind of life was

        _ _ _ the building of churches
        _ _ _ the writing of books
        _ _ _ the temperance movement

    f. By 1800 slavery had almost disappeared

        _ _ _ in the North
        _ _ _ in the South
        _ _ _ in the territories

    g. The reason why the Union fleet blockaded the Southern ports was

        _ _ _ to cut off trade with Europe
        _ _ _ to prevent armies being sent from port to port
        _ _ _ to burn the Southern ports

2. *Check as many as are right:*

The following advances were made in science during this period:

    _ _ _ photography   _ _ _ ether
    _ _ _ the telephone   _ _ _ bird study
    _ _ _ printing   _ _ _ radio

3. *Check the best answer:*

    a. The main reason why the South wanted more slaves was

        _ _ _ because the Southerners did not like to work
        _ _ _ because they wanted to grow more cotton
        _ _ _ because the negroes made their population greater

b. The reason why the Federal forces wanted to have all the cities along the Mississippi was

_ _ _ to cut the Confederacy in two
_ _ _ to travel by water instead of by land
_ _ _ to own the largest cities

c. Horace Mann's chief work was

_ _ _ to start normal schools
_ _ _ to start our public-school system
_ _ _ to write new books

d. Should slavery be spread into the new territories? The first settlement of the question in the Louisiana Purchase lands was

_ _ _ to draw a line, north of which was to be free soil, and south, slave
_ _ _ to let the people decide for themselves
_ _ _ to allow no slavery at all

e. Later in the same lands it was decided

_ _ _ to draw a line, north of which was to be free soil, and south, slave
_ _ _ to let the people decide for themselves
_ _ _ to allow no slavery at all

f. The reason why the North won in the Civil War was

_ _ _ because its soldiers were braver
_ _ _ because its side was right
_ _ _ because it had more men and more money

4. *Check as many as are right:*

Great writers of stories were

_ _ _ Horace Mann
_ _ _ Nathaniel Hawthorne
_ _ _ Harriet Beecher Stowe
_ _ _ Henry Clay
_ _ _ Clara Barton
_ _ _ Edgar Allan Poe

5. *Put the letter S before the name of the man who was the speaker for the South, a U before the name of the man who was the speaker for the Union, and a C before the name of the man who was for compromise:*

_ _ _ Henry Clay
_ _ _ Daniel Webster
_ _ _ John C. Calhoun

6. *Check the best answer:*

In the lands we got from Mexico, all but California were

_ _ _ to decide for themselves whether they would be slave or free
_ _ _ to draw the Missouri Compromise line farther west
_ _ _ not to try to settle the slavery question

7. *Check as many as are right:*

Great American poets were

_ _ _ Henry Wadsworth Longfellow
_ _ _ Oliver Wendell Holmes
_ _ _ Frances E. Willard
_ _ _ Clara Barton
_ _ _ John Greenleaf Whittier
_ _ _ James Russell Lowell
_ _ _ Nathaniel Hawthorne
_ _ _ Jefferson Davis

8. *Check the best answer:*

a. The Dred Scott decision said

_ _ _ that a slave was free if he went into free territory
_ _ _ that Congress could not prevent a master from taking his slaves into United States territory
_ _ _ that slaves must stay in the slave states

b. The person who founded the American Red Cross was

_ _ _ Harriet Beecher Stowe
_ _ _ Clara Barton
_ _ _ Frances E. Willard

c. The South seceded after the election of Lincoln

_ _ _ because they did not like Lincoln
_ _ _ because Lincoln's party stood for "no more slavery in the territories"
_ _ _ because they believed Lincoln would free their slaves

9. *What is the title of Unit IX?*

ORGANIZATION AND RECITATION OF THE UNIT AS A WHOLE

Plan the organization as a school fair.[1] Each story is allotted a booth. The recitation is given in the form of an explanation to visitors regarding the contents of each booth.

[1] "A School Fair." *The Twentieth Yearbook of the National Society for the Study of Education*, Part I, p. 98.

UNIT X

HOW THE UNITED STATES BECAME REALLY UNITED IN SPIRIT

I. The South had to be brought back as a Working Member of the Union.
   1. The South was left in a very bad condition at the end of the war.
   2. The North did not treat the South well.
   3. The South at last took matters into its own hands.
II. North, South, East, and West were bound together by Improved Transportation and Communication.
   1. Lands were given to settlers.
   2. The pony express carried the mails.
      Travel by stagecoach was exciting.
   3. Railroads and telegraphs were built from coast to coast.
   4. The telephone was invented.
   5. The Indians were conquered so completely that they were no longer a danger.
   6. The cattle and sheep businesses became great industries in the West.
   7. The frontier disappeared.
III. People in Different Parts of the Country learned to understand Each Other Better.
   1. The same writers were read in all parts of the country.
      a. Walt Whitman.
      b. Mark Twain.
   2. Painters and sculptors showed forth the American spirit.
      a. John Singer Sargent (painter).
      b. Augustus Saint-Gaudens (sculptor).
   3. America began to create music: Edward MacDowell.
   4. Great exhibitions showed what all the world was making.
   5. Great parks helped people to realize what a wonderful country we have.
IV. Efforts were made to help the Less Fortunate Members of Society.
   1. Education of the negroes was begun.
   2. Labor of women and children was lessened.
   3. Work was begun to better the conditions in prisons and asylums.

PREPARATION FOR THE OVERVIEW

"What had the Southern states tried to do in the Civil War? Had they succeeded? When the war was over, what would have to be done with the Confederate government?

"Bringing the South back into the Union as an active member was a long step toward making the United States *one* in spirit. But there was still the West to be considered.

Do you remember why some people at the time of the Louisiana Purchase feared the addition of land so far away? Would
the same reasons apply to land acquired later?"

PRESENTATION OR OVERVIEW

Up to the time that we have now reached in our story the
United States has usually been divided into sections, and these
sections have not always got along well together. Many times
the East was against the West, and the North against the
South. After the war the nation faced the great task of trying
to bind all parts together, so that people would think of themselves first as belonging to the United States as a whole, and
only afterwards as belonging to North, South, East, or West.
How was such a thing to be done?

Surely one point that was necessary was for all parts to be
under the same government. Since the South had tried to
set up a nation of its own, the first step toward binding all
the nation together was to bring the South back to share in
the same government as the rest of the country. Nobody
knew just how the bringing back should be done, as it had
never happened before. One man had one plan; other men,
other plans. Some people were very sure that the South
should be punished; others thought it had already been punished enough. In the meantime things in the South were in a
terrible condition. However, after some years had gone by,
the plans were fully worked out, and the Southern representatives again sat in Congress. Ever since it has been as loyal
a part of the United States as has the North. And because
there were no more slaves, the South was no longer so different
from the North. The two sections began to grow together.

Even if two sections do have the same kind of government,
they cannot very well be *one* in spirit unless their people can
travel easily from one part to another. You remember that
in earlier days it had taken almost two years to make a round
trip from coast to coast. A country never could have remained one nation under such conditions. The railroad and
the steamship came just in time.

After the Civil War the railroads were built clear to the Pacific coast. People could move freely from place to place, settlers could reach their lands more easily, and products from the West could be shipped out to the markets in the East. The shining steel rails did more than offer a path for the locomotives to travel over: they gripped firmly all the land they crossed and bound it together into one nation. Telegraphs and telephones followed, and helped the railroad in its work. The Indians were conquered, and settlers no longer needed to fear. So, while measured in miles, the country was as large as before, nevertheless, measured in days it took to travel from one part to another, the United States had grown smaller. All parts had been bound together by improved transportation and communication. Now we have mentioned two ways in which the country had been made *one*: first, by being brought under one government; secondly, by the improvement of transportation and communication.

As a result we find different parts of the country beginning to understand each other better. The same news was read in all sections. If a Brooklyn writer produced a good book, it was read in Maine and California. If a Missouri man printed a funny story, people in Washington and Florida laughed at it. A man in Seattle could telephone to a man in Baltimore, and statues in parks in Chicago were made by artists who lived in New York. We may say that the mind of the United States began to be *one* mind, rather than many sectional, warring minds.

Since the different states were united in government, in transportation, and in mind, it was not so hard to become *one* in spirit. Instead of leaving every person to look out for himself, we began to care for our unfortunates — the blind, the deaf, the orphans and widows, the feeble-minded and insane, prisoners, and the poor. Schools were established for the negroes and the Indians. We began to realize that we were all one people, that those who were more fortunate should aid those who had less; that what helped one class helped all.

In these ways the different parts and sections began to grow together, and for the first time it was evident that this country was going to endure as one nation.

PRESENTATION TEST

1. *Check the best answer:*

    a. Before the Civil War the different parts of the United States

        _ _ _ had been a united nation

        _ _ _ had been sections jealous of each other

        _ _ _ had been completely independent of each other

    b. It was necessary for the South to be brought back as a working part of the Union

        _ _ _ so that all parts would be under the same government

        _ _ _ so that the North could punish it

        _ _ _ so that the war might end

    c. The reason why the West remained a part of the United States was

        _ _ _ because it was afraid of another civil war

        _ _ _ because it was afraid of Canada

        _ _ _ because it was closely bound to the East by improved transportation and communication

    d. A sign that the United States was becoming *one* in spirit was

        _ _ _ caring for the unfortunates

        _ _ _ wanting to fight the rest of the world

        _ _ _ making all states just alike

    e. Because of improved means of transportation and communication the people of the United States

        _ _ _ began to earn more money

        _ _ _ began to understand each other better than ever before

        _ _ _ began to separate into sections

2. *Check four answers:*

    The four ways in which the United States became really united after the Civil War were

    _ _ _ in government   _ _ _ in body

    _ _ _ in transportation and communication   _ _ _ in spirit

    _ _ _ in hating other nations   _ _ _ in mind

    _ _ _ in adopting the same customs

I. The South had to be brought back as a Working Member of the Union

    1. The South was left in a very bad condition at the end of the war

---

Preparation

"When the war was over, why would it be hard for Southern men to go back to their old work?

"What things had the war destroyed?

"Why was there little money in the South?

"Why would it be hard for Southerners to earn money?"

Assimilation
Readings

Upper Group

BROOKS. The Story of Cotton, 197, 199–202.
GUERBER. Story of the Great Republic, 252–253.
LOGIE. From Lincoln to Coolidge, 36–42.
PERRY and PRICE. American History, II : 223–226, 229–231.
WOODBURN and MORAN. Makers of America, 293–295.
WRIGHT. Children's Stories of American Progress, 328–330.
World Book (War of Secession : Cost of War).

Average Group

BARNES. Elementary History of the United States, 340–341.
ELSON and MACMULLAN. Story of our Country, II : 228–229.
GORDY. Elementary History of the United States, 280.

Lower Group

CURTIS. Why we celebrate our Holidays, 81–85.
SMITH. Easy Road to Reading, IV : 123, 271–272.

Teachers

FLEMING. The Sequel of Appomattox, 1–33.
HART. American History told by Contemporaries, IV : 445–458.
HOSMER. Outcome of the Civil War, 269–289.
STEPHENSON. An American History, 468–471, 474–481.
American Citizenship Course in United States History, IV : 162–163.

Minimal Essentials

Date: **the decade following the Civil War**
Historical Term: **reconstruction**
Things to Remember
Many Southern men had died in the war.
Roads and railways in the South had been destroyed during the war.
Money and supplies had all been used up.
The labor system was completely changed.

Illustrative Material

Educational Posters of the National Child Welfare Association : Memorial Day.

Procedure during Assimilation

Reading as described on pages 24–29.
Go back to one of the pictures of a Southern plantation studied in Unit IX. Children point out which features of Southern life the war has changed.
Use the following dramatizations : "Memorial Day." Hubbard, *Little American History Plays*, pp. 173–177 ; "Heart's Ease and Rue." McElroy, *A Dramatic and Musical Program for the School Grades* (American Book Company series ; free).
Read to the children Mayo's "The Blue and the Gray." Consult Memorial Day annuals of the Department of Education of your state.
If there is a Confederate soldier in the community, ask him to describe the homecoming of the Southern troops. /
Drill on minimal essentials.
Objective test.

Organization

Children make a list of the most important ways in which the condition of the South was bad.

Recitation

Oral paragraphs are given about the effect of each of the points above on Southern life.

---

2. The North did not treat the South well

Preparation

"In what ways had the South really been out of the Union during the Civil War?

"Why would some people not like to see her come back too easily? How could they punish the South, now that the war was over?

"We shall read today how the North punished the South." No additional presentation is needed.

Assimilation

Readings

Upper Group

GUERBER. Story of the Great Republic, 253–256.
PERRY and PRICE. American History, II : 226–228.
TAPPAN. Elementary History of our Country, 229–230.
WRIGHT. Children's Stories of American Progress, 330–332.
Compton's Pictured Encyclopedia (Civil War : Reconstruction, Carpetbaggers).
World Book (Reconstruction).

Average Group

BARNES. Elementary History of the United States, 341–342.
ELSON and MACMULLAN. Story of our Country, II : 234–236.
FORMAN. First Lessons in American History, 289–293, 296–297.
GORDY. Elementary History of the United States, 278–280.

Lower Group

MCMASTER. Primary History of the United States, 216–219.

Teachers

BURGESS. Reconstruction and the Constitution, 1–194.
DUNNING. Reconstruction, Political and Economic, 3–17, 35–84, 109–123, 174–189, 203–237.
FLEMING. The Sequel of Appomattox, 34–53, 118–139, 221–242.

HART. American History told by Contemporaries, IV: 459–485, 497–500.
MACDONALD. Documentary Source Book of American History, 482–487, 494–
500, 508–511, 514–518.
STEPHENSON. American History, 481–483.
American Citizenship Course in United States History, IV: 164–175.
Baltimore County Course of Study, 569.

Minimal Essentials

Historical Terms: **amendment; carpetbaggers; citizen; voter**
Things to Remember
  Lincoln believed that the South had been punished enough.
  Congress believed that the South should be punished still more.
  Negroes were made free, made citizens, and given the right to vote.
  In many Southern states the negroes ruled for a while.

Illustrative Material

BURNHAM. The Making of our Country, 458: A Carpetbagger Legislature in Session.

Procedure during Assimilation

Reading as described on pages 24–29.
Read to the children the description of a negro legislature as given in Thomas
  Dixon's *Leopard's Spots*.[1]
Dramatize a session of a carpetbaggers' legislature.[2]
"Are you a citizen? How can you tell?" (Read the first part of the Fourteenth
  Amendment.) "Is your baby brother a citizen?"
"Are you a voter? Then do the terms *citizen* and *voter* mean the same?"
Show a copy of the Constitution, and let the children point to the amendments. (Do
  not attempt to read them.)
Drill on minimal essentials.
Objective test.

Organization

The teacher puts on the board the following outline:

RECONSTRUCTION

  1. The President's plan
  2. The plan of Congress
  3. The carpetbaggers
  4. The Thirteenth, Fourteenth, and Fifteenth amendments

Recitation

Each child prepares to give orally four summary sentences
explaining the points above.

---

[1] Chap. xvi.
[2] Burnham, *The Making of our Country*, p. 458.

> ### 3. The South at last took matters into its own hands

Preparation

"If the people in the South did not like the things done by their carpetbaggers' legislatures, why did they not elect different men?

"Then what was left for them to do?

"Our readings today will tell us how they solved their problem." No additional presentation is needed.

Assimilation
Readings

Upper Group

LOGIE. From Lincoln to Coolidge, 42–59.
PERRY and PRICE. American History, II: 228–229.
TURPIN. Cotton, 115–122.
World Book (Ku-Klux Klan).

Average Group

BEARD and BAGLEY. A First Book in American History, 360.
ELSON and MacMULLAN. The Story of our Country, II: 236–239.
FORMAN. First Lessons in American History, 297–298.

Lower Group

Try FORMAN

Teachers

DUNNING. Reconstruction, Political and Economic, 121–123, 266–280.
FLEMING. The Sequel of Appomattox, 243–304.
HART. American History told by Contemporaries, IV: 495–497.
STEPHENSON. An American History, 483–485, 489–491.
THOMPSON. The New South, 9–30.
American Citizenship Course in United States History, IV: 174–175.

Minimal Essentials

Historical Term: **Ku-Klux Klan**
Things to Remember

For a while the white people in the South frightened the negroes to make them behave.
At last many of the white people again gained their right to vote.
Then they made laws that only people who had property or were educated could vote.
In this way the white people once more got control.

Illustrative Material

McKINLEY. Illustrated Topics for American History: S. 34.

Procedure during Assimilation

Reading as described on pages 24–29.

Has anyone ever seen a Ku-Klux Klan meeting? If so, describe how the members were dressed; how they burned their fiery crosses.

Is the Ku-Klux Klan of Civil War times the same as the Ku-Klux Klan of today?

Set two miniature stages, one to show a Ku-Klux visit to a negro's cabin, the other to show the educational test being applied at the polls.

Drill on minimal essentials.

Objective test.

Organization

The teacher writes the heading on the board and the children supply the subheads in sequence.

METHODS OF REGAINING WHITE CONTROL

1. Ku-Klux Klan
2. Control by law
   a. Tests of education
   b. Property tests

Recitation

Children prepare three-minute speeches as to which of the two methods mentioned above was better for the Southern people.

A drill lesson on section I of Unit X should be given at this point.

II. North, South, East, and West were bound together by Improved Transportation and Communication
   1. Lands were given to settlers

Preparation

"Did any of your grandparents come into this state from older sections and take up land? What did they have to do to secure their land?" (*Topics for investigation at home.*)

"How much is land in the same districts worth today?" (*Investigation.*)

Reports on the topics.

No additional presentation is needed.

Assimilation

Readings

Upper Group

GORDY. Leaders in Making America, 382–383.
GUERBER. Story of the Great Republic, 262–263.
OTIS. Seth of Colorado, 33–38, 101–104.
PERRY and PRICE. American History, II : 247–248.
SANFORD. The Story of Agriculture in the United States, 209 (difficult).
VOLLINTINE. The Making of America, 237–238.
Compton's Pictured Encyclopedia (Lands).
World Book (Homestead Laws, Lands : Disposal of Public Lands).

Average Group

GORDY. Elementary History of the United States, 282.

Lower Group

Try GORDY.

Teachers

BOGART. Economic History of the United States, 263–268, 286–288, 308.
COMAN. Economic Beginnings of the Far West, II : 361–365.
COMAN. Industrial History of the United States, 294–297.
DUNBAR. A History of Travel in America, IV : see "Land" in the Index.
HOUGH. The Passing of the Frontier, 151–173.
SPARKS. National Development, 256–258.
Baltimore County Course of Study, 572.

Minimal Essentials

Name of Persons: homesteaders
Names of Places: the Middle West; the West
Date: during the Civil War
Historical Terms: free land; Homestead Act; land office
Things to Remember

At first land was sold to settlers at rather high prices.
Later the government gave land away to settlers.
Free land made America a country of opportunity.

Illustrative Material

BURNHAM. The Making of Our Country, 186: diagrams explaining public land system.
GABRIEL (ED.). Pageant of America, III : 190–191.
McKINLEY. Illustrated Topics for American History : S. 35.

Procedure during Assimilation

Reading as described on pages 24–29.
Invite an old settler to tell the children how he took up land from the government under the Homestead Act.
Show copies of a deed to land.
Does the land that has not yet been taken up belong to the state or to the United States?
Where is the nearest branch of the Federal Land Office?
Drill on minimal essentials.
Objective test.

Organization

The teacher and the children working together produce an outline somewhat similar to the following:

LAND SYSTEM OF THE UNITED STATES

1. Early policy of the United States
2. Homestead Act
3. Influence of free land on American life

Recitation

Invite the local register of deeds to hear the complete story.

---

2. The pony express carried the mails
Travel by stagecoach was exciting

Preparation

"When did the era of railroad-building begin?

"All these early railroads, however, were east of the Mississippi River." (*Children point out the region on the map.*)

"When was gold discovered in California?

"Then there must have been many people in the West who would like to write letters to their friends back home. How do you suppose such letters would be carried?

"Have you ever heard of 'Buffalo Bill'? We shall read today how he helped to carry the mail.

"Suppose people wished to travel from the East to the West. In what different ways might they travel?

"Have you seen stagecoaches in the moving pictures?

"Our story today tells us how the mail was carried and how passengers traveled."

No additional presentation is needed.

Assimilation

Readings

Upper Group

BARSTOW (ED.). The Westward Movement, 46–55.
CODY. Adventures of Buffalo Bill.
EVANS. America First, 339–344.
FAIRBANKS. The Western United States, 198–204.

FARIS. Real Stories from our History, 169–190, 196–212.
FARIS. Where our History was Made, Book II, 165–174, 190–194.
GORDY. Leaders in Making America, 364–372.
HART. How our Grandfathers Lived, 85–87.
MOWRY. American Inventions and Inventors, 200–206.
TAPPAN. Elementary History of our Country, 232–233.
VOLLINTINE. The Making of America, 238–240.
WILSON and DRIGGS. The White Indian Boy, 139–156, 167–175.
Lessons in Community and National Life, Series C, 221–224.

Average Group

GORDY. Elementary History of the United States, 284–285.
NIDA. Following the Frontier, 288–294.

Lower Group

McMASTER. Primary History of the United States, 221–222.

Teachers

BRADLEY. The Story of the Pony Express.
DUNBAR. History of Travel in America, IV: see "Stagecoaches" in the Index, especially pages 1318–1319.
McMASTER. History of the People of the United States, VIII: 402–404.
PARRISH. Great Plains, 192–224.
PAXSON. The Last American Frontier, 174–191.
THOMPSON. The Age of Invention, 144–145.

Minimal Essentials

Name of Person: "Buffalo Bill" Cody [1]
Historical Terms: overland stage; pony express; scout
Things to Remember
The pony express carried the mail to sections where there was no railroad.
The overland stage made regular trips to carry passengers and baggage.

Illustrative Material

GABRIEL (ED.). Pageant of America, III: 113.

Procedure during Assimilation

Readings as described on pages 24–29.
Play a relay game, so that children may understand how the horses were used in relays.
Read to the children extracts from Bradley's *Story of the Pony Express*.
Write an imaginary diary of Buffalo Bill in the days when he was a pony express-man.
Illustrate the stories on the blackboard.[2]
Make a series of drawings representing Indians attacking an overland stage.
Drill on minimal essentials.
Objective test.

[1] Not in the lists of personages referred to on page 5.
[2] *The Twentieth Yearbook of the National Society for the Study of Education*, Part I, p. 55.

Organization

The children suggest a title for the organization and the names of the two subheads.

Recitation

Invite the fourth grade to hear the stories.

---

3. Railroads and telegraphs were built from coast to coast

Preparation

"When were railroads first built in the United States? Where?

"When was the telegraph invented?

"Why would it be more difficult to build railroads west of the Mississippi than east of it?

"What reason was there for building railroads through to the Pacific coast?

"Why did the railroad-builders think that their railroads to the Pacific coast would earn money for them?"

No additional presentation is needed.

Assimilation

Readings

Upper Group

BROOKS. The Story of Cotton, 236–238.

CRUMP. Boys' Book of Railroads.

DARROW. Thinkers and Doers, 213–223 (difficult).

EVERETT and REED. When they were Boys, 98–104 (James J. Hill).

FARIS. Real Stories from our History, 283–289.

GORDY. Leaders in Making America, 373–378.

GUERBER. Story of the Great Republic, 261–262.

LOGIE. From Lincoln to Coolidge, 109–112.

MOWRY. American Inventions and Inventors, 235–244.

PERRY and PRICE. American History, II : 245–247.

ROCHELEAU. Great American Industries: Transportation, 157–204.

SANFORD. The Story of Agriculture in the United States, 212–213 (difficult).

TAPPAN. Elementary History of our Country, 233.

TAPPAN. Heroes of Progress, 168–178.

VOLLINTINE. The Making of America, 240–242, 246–249.

Compton's Pictured Encyclopedia (Railroads).

Lessons in Community and National Life, Series B, 225–232.

World Book (Railroads: Transcontinental, Telegraph).

Average Group

BEEBY. How the World grows Smaller, 120–129.
FORMAN. First Lessons in American History, 299.
GORDY. Elementary History of the United States, 285–286.
LARGE. Everyday Wonders, 134–144.
MORRIS. Primary History of the United States, 236.
NIDA. Following the Frontier, 304–310.

Lower Group

BARNES. Primary History of the United States, 214–215.
McMASTER. Primary History of the United States, 222–224.

Teachers

BOGART. Economic History of the United States, 350–356.
COMAN. Industrial History of the United States, 297–301.
DEWEY. National Problems, 91–111.
DUNBAR. History of Travel in America, IV: 1320–1356.
DUNNING. Reconstruction, Political and Economic, 144–150.
HART. American History told by Contemporaries, IV: 513–517.
MOODY. The Railroad Builders, 121–241.
OSGOOD. A History of Industry, 397–401.
PARRISH. Great Plains, 326–334.
PAXSON. The Last American Frontier, 211–224.
SPARKS. National Development, 53–67, 254–256.
Baltimore County Course of Study, 570–571.

Minimal Essentials

Name of Person: **James J. Hill**
Historical Terms: **Great Northern Railroad; transcontinental; Union Pacific Railroad**
Things to Remember

Building railroads across the continent cost a great deal of money.
The United States helped the railroads by giving them land on both sides along the tracks.
The railroads helped to settle the West.

Illustrative Material

McKINLEY. Illustrated Topics for American History: S. 36.
SPARKS. National Development, 54: map of railroads of the United States in 1880.
Keystone Views: 152, Railroad in Platte Canyon; 153, Boulder Canyon.

Procedure during Assimilation

Reading as described on pages 24–29.
Picture study based on the illustrative material listed above.
Write to the leading railway companies for advertising material on the luxuries of modern railway service. Show on the bulletin board pictures of dining-cars, sleeping-cars, club cars, observation cars, maid and valet service, shower baths, etc.
Make a picture collection showing the development of the locomotive from 1830 to the present.
Children who have seen the photoplay *The Iron Horse* tell the story.
Use the dramatization "The Tie that Binds." Hague and Chalmers, *Dramatic Moments in American History*, pp. 175–198.

Children who have traveled to either coast describe their travel experiences.
Show a railway map of the United States. Make a map of the principal trunk
systems.
Drill on minimal essentials.
Objective test.

Organization

Children outline their own stories. The best outline is
selected to record on the board.

Recitation

Each row chooses one member to represent it in telling the
story.

> 4. The telephone was invented

Preparation

"What is the difference between the telephone and the telegraph? Why do we need both? Wouldn't the telegraph alone
be sufficient for our needs?"

No additional presentation is needed.

Assimilation

Readings

Upper Group

BACHMAN. Great Inventors and their Inventions, 228–246.
CHANDLER and CHITWOOD. Makers of American History, 294–296.
DARROW. Thinkers and Doers, 237–252 (difficult).
EVANS. America First, 401–404.
FARIS. Real Stories from our History, 295–301.
GORDY. Leaders in Making America, 409–412.
HOLLAND. Historic Inventions, 215–232.
HUSBAND. America at Work, 89–95.
LEFFERTS. American Leaders, II : 99–115.
MARSHALL. The Story of Human Progress, 265–268 (difficult).
MOWRY. American Inventions and Inventors, 286–291.
PERRY and PRICE. American History, II : 289–290.
PIERCY. Great Inventions and Discoveries, 74–77.
SANFORD and OWEN. Modern Americans, 29–35.
TAPPAN. Heroes of Progress, 115–121.
Compton's Pictured Encyclopedia (Telephone, Bell).
Lessons in Community and National Life, Series B, 81–85.
World Book (Telephone).

Average Group

BEEBY. How the World grows Smaller, 157–190.
FORMAN. First Lessons in American History, 309–310.

LARGE. Everyday Wonders, 56–70.
McFEE. Stories of American Inventions, 84–104.
NIDA. Following the Frontier, 301–302.
PARKMAN. Conquests of Invention, 379–395.
UHRBROCK and OWENS. Famous Americans, 259–267.

Lower Group
CHAMBERLAIN. How we Travel, 212–218.
EVERETT and REED. When they were Boys, 15–23.
TATE, WITHERS, and BROWNE. Child's World, V: 343–351.

Teachers
BOGART. Economic History of the United States, 380–382.
HENDRICK. The Age of Big Business, 86–118.
SMITH. Industrial History, 215–216.

Minimal Essentials

Name of Person: **Alexander Graham Bell**
Date: **1876** — invention of the telephone
Things to Remember
    Alexander Graham Bell invented the telephone in 1876.
    It has helped people in different parts of the country to carry on business
    speedily.

Illustrative Material

Ford Educational Library: 228, Number, Please.
National Geographic Magazine, XLII: 302.
Society for Visual Education. Schoolfilm: Speeding the Spoken Word.

Procedure during Assimilation

Reading as described on pages 24–29.
Picture study based on the illustrative material listed above.
Take the class to the local telephone exchange. Notice how calls come in, how the
    connection is made, how long-distance calls are handled. How many different
    kinds of work are represented in the telephone system?
On the bulletin board post pictures showing "People who help us to make a Tele-
    phone Call."
Class discussion of telephone courtesy.
Use and explain the graph in Marshall's *Story of Human Progress*, p. 341.
Explain the diagram in the World Book, p. 5742.
Drill on minimal essentials.
Objective test.

Organization

The teacher works with all children who had difficulty in
making out the last outline. Of the others, one is chosen as
chairman, and they make out a coöperative outline of their
own.

Recitation

The chairman calls on different children from each group to
tell the story from their outlines.

> 5. The Indians were conquered so completely that they
> were no longer a danger

Preparation

"In what way had the Indians slowed up the westward movement?

"Now that the railroad had gone through to the West, the passengers amused themselves shooting buffaloes from the trains. What effect must this have had upon the Indians?

"Are there any Indians today?

"Does the United States government do anything for them?"

Assimilation

Readings

Disappearance of the buffalo

Upper Group

DOUBLEDAY. From Cattle Ranch to College.
GORDY. Leaders in Making America, 390–391.
GRINNELL. Jack among the Indians.
LAUT. The Story of the Trapper, 65–80.
LOGIE. From Lincoln to Coolidge, 195–197.
OTIS. Antoine of Oregon, 95–99, 111–113.
WILSON and DRIGGS. The White Indian Boy, 28–32.
Compton's Pictured Encyclopedia (Bison).
Western Frontier Stories retold from *St. Nicholas*, 84–98.

Average Group

EGGLESTON. Stories of American Life and Adventure, 191–194.
NIDA. Letters of Polly the Pioneer, 51–56.

Lower Group

Read GORDY to this group.

Teachers

HORNADAY. Our Vanishing Wild Life.
Encyclopedia Americana (Bison).
New International Encyclopædia (Bison).

Indian wars: Custer's last stand

Upper Group

BROOKS. Master of the Stronghearts.
CUSTER. The Boy General.
EVANS. America First, 344–349.
FARIS. Where our History was Made, Book II, 66–70.
GORDY. Leaders in Making America, 388–390.

GUERBER. Story of the Great Republic, 267–268.
HOWARD. Famous Indian Chiefs I have Known, 298–312, 353–364 (difficult).
LANIER. The Book of Bravery, 231–239.
LOGIE. From Lincoln to Coolidge, 149–162.
PERRY and PRICE. American History, II : 249–251.
ROOSEVELT. Stories of the Great West, 203–218.
SABIN. Boys' Book of Indian Warriors, 182–201, 292–308.
STODDARD. Little Smoke.
TAPPAN. Elementary History of our Country, 238–239.
WADE. Ten Big Indians, 199–256.
WAGNER. Pacific History Stories, 146–156.
WILSON and DRIGGS. The White Indian Boy, 128–138, 157–166.
Compton's Pictured Encyclopedia (Indians : Indian Wars).
World Book (North American Indians, p. 2968).

Average Group

EGGLESTON. Stories of American Life and Adventure, 194–201.
FORMAN. First Lessons in American History, 298–299.
MORRIS. Primary History of the United States, 229–230.

Lower Group

BARNES. Primary History of the United States, 217–218.
DAVIS. Stories of the United States, 223–225.
HARTWELL. Story Hour Readings, IV : 256.
McMASTER. Primary History of the United States, 224–227.
WILLIAMS. Boys' Book of Indians and the Wild West.

Teachers

HOUGH. The Passing of the Frontier, 112–136.
PAXSON. The Last American Frontier, 14–32, 119–137, 243–283, 304–323, 358–371.
SPARKS. National Development, 265–266, 272–275.

Opening the Indian lands to settlement: the reservation system

Upper Group

GUERBER. Story of the Great Republic, 265–267, 294–295.
LEFFERTS. Our Own United States, 138–140.
TAPPAN. Elementary History of our Country, 239.
WILSON and DRIGGS. The White Indian Boy, 202–206.
Compton's Pictured Encyclopedia (Oklahoma Indians, p. 1774).
Western Stories retold from *St. Nicholas*, 192–198.
World Book (Indians, pp. 2968–2970; Oklahoma : History, History of the Indian Country).

Average Group

GORDY. Elementary History of the United States, 294–295.

Lower Group

McMASTER. Primary History of the United States, 227.

Teachers

HART. American History told by Contemporaries, IV : 649–651.
PAXSON. The Last American Frontier, 340–357, 372–386.
SPARKS. National Development, 266–272, 275–281.

Minimal Essentials

Names of Persons: **Sitting Bull**[1]; **General Custer**
Names of Places: **the Little Big Horn; Oklahoma**
Historical Terms: **government Indian schools; reservation**
Things to Remember

When the number of buffaloes became smaller the Indians' chief food supply was gone.

Gradually soldiers and forts made the Indians no longer a danger.

The Indians were put on reservations.

As they became civilized, many left the reservations and lived like other people.

Illustrative Material

GABRIEL (ED.). Pageant of America, I: 37–39; III: 172–174.
SPARKS. National Development, 266: map of Indian reservations of 1880 compared with those of 1840.
Ford Educational Library: 232, Wards of a Nation.
National Geographic Magazine, XXVII: 73–87 (1915).

Procedure during Assimilation

Reading as described on pages 24–29.

Picture study based on the illustrative material listed above.

Children who have seen buffaloes in circuses or the zoo describe them.

Read to the children Vachel Lindsay's "Ghosts of the Buffaloes." Field, *Fifth Reader*, pp. 198–201.

Play these records on the phonograph: "By the Waters of Minnetonka"; "Death of Custer"; "Indian Lament"; "Indian Life"; "Natoma"; "Three Sioux Scouts."

Each child selects from his reading on Indian wars one incident to tell to the class.

Secure pictures of the nearest government Indian school.

Drill on minimal essentials.

Objective test.

Organization

The children suggest a title and three subheads for the outline.

Recitation

Each row writes a paragraph on one point.

---

6. The cattle and sheep businesses became great industries in the West

---

Preparation

"You probably have seen cowboys in the moving pictures. What is their work? How can they tell their cattle from other people's? Do you know what a sheep-herder is?

"Have you heard of the stockyards?"

[1] Not in the lists of personages referred to on page 5.

Assimilation

Readings

Upper Group

ALLEN. United States, 209–251.
BARROWS and PARKER. United States and Canada, 75–83.
CANFIELD. The Boys of the Rincon Ranch, 24–59, 116–132, 165–179.
CARPENTER. How the World is Fed, 73–98.
CHAMBERLAIN. North America, 119–122.
DOUBLEDAY. From Cattle Ranch to College, 229–272, 289–303.
FAIRGRIEVE and YOUNG. The World, 132–142.
GORDY. Leaders in Making America, 379–381.
GORDY. Stories of Later American History, 286–288.
GRINNELL. Jack the Young Ranchman.
HUSBAND. America at Work, 96–102.
LEFFERTS. Our Own United States, 218–222, 253–257.
LOGIE. From Lincoln to Coolidge, 191–195.
MONROE and BUCKBEE. Our Country and its People, 78–84.
OTIS. Philip of Texas.
ROCHELEAU. The Meat-Packing Industry.
ROOSEVELT. Ranch Life and the Hunting Trail.
ROOSEVELT. Stories of the Great West, 109–119, 123–148, 151–199.
SANFORD. The Story of Agriculture in the United States, 235–245.
VOLLINTINE. The Making of America, 235–237.
Compton's Pictured Encyclopedia (Meat-Packing).
World Book (Cattle: the Great Cattle Ranges, Meat-Packing).
Youth's Companion series: Our Country, West, 217–239.

Average Group

BRIGHAM and McFARLANE. Essentials of Geography, I: 20–21, 137–138.
GORDY. Elementary History of the United States, 283.
LANE (ED.). Industries of Today, 12–18.
PITKIN and HUGHES. Seeing America: Farm and Field, 213–224.
SMITH. Human Geography, I: 83.
TAPPAN. The Farmer and his Friends, 83–85.
TARR and McMURRY. New Geographies, I: 148.

Lower Group

ALLEN. How and Where we Live, 26–30, 36–37.
CARPENTER and CARPENTER. The Foods we Eat, 35–45.
CARROLL and CARROLL. Around the World, III: 81–85, 139–141.
CHAMBERLAIN. How we are Clothed, 59–71.
CHAMBERLAIN. How we are Fed, 18–31.
FAIRBANKS. Home Geography for Primary Grades, 194–197.
KNOWLTON. First Lessons in Geography, 112–117.
McMASTER. Primary History of the United States, 228–229.
SHEPHERD. Geography for Beginners, 69–75, 138–141.
WINSLOW. The Earth and its People, 77–78.

Teachers

HOUGH. The Passing of the Frontier, 11–56, 137–150.
PARRISH. Great Plains, 314–325.
SPARKS. National Development, 251–254.

Minimal Essentials

Historical Terms: **brand; cowboys; rodeo; round-up; sheep-herder; stockyards**
Things to Remember

Long ago the great herds grazed out on the open range.

The sheep-herders and the cattlemen did not like each other, because both wanted the sources of water supply and because cattle cannot graze on land that sheep have grazed on.

Now most of the cattlemen and sheepmen own or rent their grazing land.

The cattle and the sheep are taken to the stockyards to be killed.

Illustrative Material

Gabriel (Ed.). Pageant of America, III: 166-167, 175-190, 202-205; V: chap. xii.
Ford Educational Library: 29, Meat-Packing; 31, Cattle Ranch; 223, The Way of the West.
Little Phostint Journeys: Scenes of Western Life.
Society for Visual Education. Schoolfilm: Great Plains.
Travel, XL: 5-10 (April, 1923); XLIII: 14-17 (June, 1924).

Procedure during Assimilation

Reading as described on pages 24-29.

Picture study based on the illustrative material listed above.

Children tell of moving pictures in which they have seen cowboys.

Someone who has seen a rodeo describes it to the children.

Children design their own brands for cattle.

Make a sand-table representation of a round-up.

See the article "Learning about Beef," in *The Twentieth Yearbook of the National Society for the Study of Education*, Part I, p. 62.

Each child asks at his local meat market the source of the meat supply.

Drill on minimal essentials.

Objective test.

Organization

The planning of the sand table.

Recitation

Explaining the sand table to visitors from the lower grades.

---

7. The frontier disappeared

Preparation

"What is a frontier?

"Does the same place always remain the frontier?

"How many different frontiers have we studied about so far?"

Presentation

The teacher tells the story based on the references which follow. A presentation test is given immediately afterwards.

Assimilation
Readings
All Groups [1]
VOLLINTINE. The Making of America, 243.

Teachers
HOUGH. The Passing of the Frontier.
OSGOOD. A History of Industry, 417, 418–419.
PAXSON. The Last American Frontier.
TURNER. The Frontier in American History.

Minimal Essentials
Things to Remember
The frontier constantly moved westward.
At last it disappeared entirely.
American life is becoming more like the life in older countries since the frontier has disappeared.

Procedure during Assimilation [2]
The teacher asks the following questions :
"Is there free land anywhere in the United States today?
"Why do we not call this the frontier?
"How does life on the frontier differ from life in older sections?
"Why did people leave their homes and go to live in a wild country?
"Has the disappearance of the frontier made any difference in the opportunities open to the poor of today?"
Objective test.

Organization

The teacher puts the following outline on the board :

DISAPPEARANCE OF THE FRONTIER

1. The westward movement of the frontier
2. Disappearance of the frontier
3. Effect of the disappearance

Recitation

Each child prepares summary sentences for the points above.

A drill lesson on section II of Unit X should be given at this point.

---

[1] Little reading material is available on this phase for intermediate-grade children.
[2] The next day.

III. PEOPLE IN DIFFERENT PARTS OF THE COUNTRY LEARNED
   TO UNDERSTAND EACH OTHER BETTER
  1. The same writers were read in all parts of the country
    a. Walt Whitman
    b. Mark Twain

Preparation

"Has anyone read the stories of Tom Sawyer and Huckleberry Finn? Tell us what the stories were about. Did you like them? Do you know who wrote them?" (*Explain how the name "Mark Twain" came to be used.*)

"In reading of the death of Lincoln did anyone find mention of a great poem written about it?" ("O Captain! my Captain!")

"We are going to read now about two very different authors. One wrote stories like *Tom Sawyer* and the other wrote great poems."

No additional presentation is needed.

Assimilation
Readings
Walt Whitman

Works

"O Captain! my Captain!"
  Leaves of Grass.
"Pioneers" (three stanzas)
  FIELD. Fifth Reader, 171–173.

Life

Compton's Pictured Encyclopedia (Whitman).
World Book (Whitman).

Teachers

BAZALGETTE. Walt Whitman: The Man and his Work.
BURROUGHS. Whitman: a Study.
MABIE. Backgrounds of Literature, 197–243.
PERRY. The American Spirit in Literature, 196–205.
PERRY. Walt Whitman.
WARNER. Library of the World's Best Literature, XXXIX: 15,885–15,910.

Mark Twain

Works

The Adventures of Huckleberry Finn (illustrated by Hatherell). Harper & Brothers.
The Adventures of Tom Sawyer. Same edition.

The Prince and the Pauper.   Same edition.
"New England Weather"
      HARTWELL. Story Hour Readings, V : 242–247.

Life
      BEARD and BAGLEY. A First Book in American History, 387–399.
      PAINE. Boys' Life of Mark Twain, 365–386.
      SANFORD and OWEN. Modern Americans, 212–219.
      STIMPSON. Child's Book of American Biography, 181–187.
      Compton's Pictured Encyclopedia (Clemens).
      World Book (Clemens).

Teachers
      BOLTON. Famous American Authors.
      HOWELLS. My Mark Twain.
      PERRY. The American Spirit in Literature, 236–240.
      VAN DOREN. The American Novel, 157–187.
      WARNER. Library of the World's Best Literature, IX : 3787–3820.

Minimal Essentials

Names of Persons: **Mark Twain; Walt Whitman** (hwĭt′măn)
Historical Term: **the greatest American humorist**
Things to Remember
      Mark Twain (Samuel L. Clemens) was the greatest American humorist.
      Walt Whitman was one of the greatest poets America ever produced.

Illustrative Material

GABRIEL (ED.). Pageant of America, XI : 190–193, 237–241.
Perry Pictures : 48, Walt Whitman ; 2515, Mark Twain.
Mentor XI : 1–14 (September, 1923) : Walt Whitman ; XII : 3–44 (May, 1924) : Mark Twain.

Procedure during Assimilation

Reading as described on pages 24–29.
Read aloud to the children Whitman's "O Captain! my Captain!" Have a copy
      left on the board for several days, and give children time to read it over several
      times, or supply each pupil with a mimeographed copy. Read aloud also "I
      hear America singing" and the first stanzas of "Song of the Open Road."
Assign the stories of Tom Sawyer and Huckleberry Finn early in the year, so that
      by this time every child has had an opportunity to read them. A Mark Twain
      program may be given, as follows :

                    My favorite character
                    A place described
                    A funny story
                    An exciting incident
                    A sad scene
                    Description of a picture
                    The author

Organization
Planning the program.

Recitation
Giving the program.

2. Painters and sculptors showed forth the American spirit
   a. John Singer Sargent (painter)
   b. Augustus Saint-Gaudens (sculptor)

Preparation

Show children some of Sargent's pictures. Tell the story of "Carnation, Lily, Lily, Rose"; of one of Saint-Gaudens's statues. "What is a sculptor? We are going today to read about one of the greatest American painters and one of the greatest American sculptors."
No additional presentation is needed.

Assimilation
Readings
Sargent

Compton's Pictured Encyclopedia (Sargent).
World Book (Sargent).

Teachers

BRYANT. American Pictures and their Painters, 157–163.
CAFFIN. American Masters of Painting, 55–67.
CAFFIN. How to Study Pictures, 441–456.
COX. Old Masters and New, 145, 255–265.
EMERY. How to enjoy Pictures, 187–196.
HARTMANN. History of American Art, II : 213–222, 236.
ISHAM. American Painting, 428–438. (See Index also.)

Saint-Gaudens

EVERETT and REED. When they were Boys, 170–176.
STIMPSON. Child's Book of American Biography, 132–140.
TAPPAN. Heroes of Progress, 157–167.
Compton's Pictured Encyclopedia (Saint-Gaudens).
World Book (Saint-Gaudens).

Teachers

BEARD. Our Foreign-Born Citizens, 227–234.
HUSBAND. Americans by Adoption, 121–139.
STURGIS. The Appreciation of Sculpture, 196–197.

Minimal Essentials

Names of Persons: **Sargent** (sär'jĕnt) ; **Saint-Gaudens** (sånt gô'dĕnz)
Historical Terms: **sculptor; sculpture**
Things to Remember
John Singer Sargent was a great American painter.
Augustus Saint-Gaudens was a great American sculptor.

Illustrative Material

BROWN. Famous Pictures: 842–846 (inclusive), The Prophets (Sargent).
Perry Pictures: 1421, Lincoln Statue (Saint-Gaudens); 1421-B, Shaw Memorial (Saint-Gaudens); 1421-C, The Puritan (Saint-Gaudens); 1031, Hosea (Sargent); 1032, Isaiah (Sargent); 1033–1037, The Prophets (Sargent).
Mentor, XII: 3–29 (October, 1924): Sargent.

Procedure during Assimilation

Reading as described on pages 24–29.
Use the study of Sargent's Frieze of the Prophets, as given in Carpenter's *Stories Pictures Tell*, VIII: 29–55.
If at all possible take the children to see an artist working on his canvases; to the studio of a sculptor. Show how a cast is made. The art department will coöperate.
Children attempt to create something from clay or to carve from white soap. Make a frieze representing one of the stories studied in this unit.
Study Saint-Gaudens's The Puritan, President Lincoln, Memorial to Robert Gould Shaw, Admiral Farragut, General Sherman, General Logan.

Organization

The teacher puts the following outline on the board:

ART IN AMERICA

1. Sargent and his painting
2. Saint-Gaudens and his sculpture

Recitation

Children choose the topic they prefer for a three-minute speech.

> 3. America began to create music: Edward MacDowell

See a stenographic report of this story as taught to a class of fifth-grade children by Miss Lila M. Rose of the State Teachers College, Oshkosh, Wisconsin.[1]

For a list of music suitable for use in American History see *The Historical Outlook*, XVII: 333 (November, 1926).

Assimilation

Readings

MacDowell

BROWER. Story-Lives of Master Musicians, 348–360.
EVERETT and REED. When they were Boys, 163–169.
FORSYTH. Progressive Series History of Music, 163.
FRYER. Book of Boyhoods, 291–302.

[1] See text, pp. 707–709.

STIMPSON. Child's Book of American Biography, 236–242.
STONE. Music Appreciation, 141.
TAPPAN. Heroes of Progress, 189–198 (Theodore Thomas).
Victor Talking Machine Company. Music Appreciation with the Victrola, 253–255.
World Book (MacDowell).

Teachers
PORTE. Edward MacDowell.
Literary Digest, LXXXVII: 49–50 (December 5, 1925).
Music and Youth, I: 45–46.

Minimal Essentials

Name of Person: **Edward MacDowell** (măk dou′ĕl)

Procedure during Assimilation

See lesson on pages 707–709.

---

4. Great exhibitions showed what all the world was making

Preparation

"What is the object of having a county fair each year? What good does it do one farmer to know that his neighbor raised a larger pumpkin than he did?

"Have any of you ever attended the state fair? Tell us about it. What good do you think it accomplished?

"Have you ever heard of a fair in which different states and different nations took part? How would it help each of the exhibitors?"

No additional presentation is needed.

Assimilation

Readings

Upper Group
EGGLESTON. A First Book in American History, 186–196.
GUERBER. Story of the Great Republic, 271–273, 301–303.
MONTGOMERY. Beginners' American History, 240–241.
PERRY and PRICE. American History, II: 287–306.
TAPPAN. Elementary History of our Country, 233–234, 240.
World Book (Exposition, Centennial Exposition, World's Columbian Exposition).

Average Group
FORMAN. First Lessons in American History, 300, 314.
GORDY. Elementary History of the United States, 291–292, 295–296.
MORRIS. Primary History of the United States, 233–236.

Lower Group
BARNES. Primary History of the United States, 217, 234.

Minimal Essentials

Historical Terms: **Centennial Exposition; World's Fair**
Things to Remember
   Expositions in which different nations take part help them to exchange ideas.
   They help in making nations respect each other.

Illustrative Material

GABRIEL (ED.). Pageant of America, XIII: 232-235.
Children look at home for illustrated books on the World's Fair etc.

Procedure during Assimilation

Reading as described on pages 24-29.
Each child selects one great exposition to study in detail, reads about it, and collects pictures to illustrate his topic when he gives it to the class. Results of this study are exchanged.

Organization

Preparing the story referred to above. .

Recitation

Giving the story.

> 5. Great parks helped people to realize what a wonderful
>   country we have

Preparation

"Why does our city have a park?

"It costs a great deal of money to keep up the parks.
(*Give the figures from the last city report.*) Do you think they
are worth that much money?

"Are there any state parks in ____ (*name of your state*)?

"Do you know of any national parks? What are their
names?" No additional presentation is needed.

Assimilation

Readings

Upper Group

   BARROWS and PARKER. United States and Canada, 45-46.
   CARROLL and CARROLL. Around the World, IV: 108-111, 144-146.
   CHAMBERLAIN. North America, 142-149.
   FAIRBANKS. The Western United States, 294-302.
   FARIS. Real Stories of the Geography Makers, 265-281.

LEFFERTS. Our Own United States, 242–247, 249, 273–276, 287–292, 312–313.
Compton's Pictured Encyclopedia (National Parks: Yellowstone, Yosemite, Glacier, Grand Canyon).
World Book (Yellowstone, Yosemite, Glacier, Grand Canyon).

Average Group
BRIGHAM and McFARLANE. Essentials of Geography, I : 139–140.
REINSCH. The Young Citizen's Reader, 103–104.
SMITH. Human Geography, I : 95.
TARR and McMURRY. New Geographies, I : 156–157.

Lower Group
ALLEN. How and Where we Live, 262–273.
WINSLOW. The Earth and its People, 112–113.

Teachers
United States Department of the Interior. National Parks Portfolio.

Minimal Essentials

Name of Place: **Yellowstone National Park**
Historical Terms: **national park; state park**
Things to Remember
The United States government has set aside some of its chief beauty spots as playgrounds for the nation.
They belong to all of us, so we should take good care of them.

Illustrative Material

Ford Educational Library: 12, Grand Canyon; 18, Yosemite Valley; 28, Yellowstone National Park; 39, Niagara Falls; 44, Mount Rainier; 52, Playgrounds for the People.
Little Phostint Journeys: The Yellowstone.
Perry Pictures: 1399-C, Entrance to Golden Gate Canyon, Yellowstone; 1399-D, Old Faithful Geyser; 1399-E, Bee Hive Geyser; 1399-M, The Three Brothers, Yosemite; 1401, Yosemite; 1424, Niagara Falls; 1425, Niagara Falls; 1425-B, Rock of Ages, Niagara; 1425-C, Niagara Falls by Moonlight; 1425-G, Niagara Falls in Winter; 7000, Sentinel Rock, Yosemite; 7001, El Capitan; 7002, Mirror Lake, Yosemite; 7003, North and South Domes; 7004, Nevada Falls; 7005, Bridal Veil Falls; 7006, Yosemite Falls; 7050, Golden Gate Canyon, Yellowstone; 7051, Golden Gate Canyon; 7052, Pulpit Terrace; 7053, Castle Geyser; 7054, Crater of Excelsior Geyser; 7055, Grand Canyon.
Society for Visual Education. Picturols: National Park Scenes — Lafayette, Yellowstone, Mount Rainier, Glacier, Grand Canyon, Mesa Verde, Hawaii, Rocky Mountain.
Society for Visual Education. Schoolfilm: A Study of Niagara.
United States Department of the Interior. National Parks Portfolio.

Procedure during Assimilation

Reading as described on pages 24–29.
Picture study based on the illustrative material listed above.
If any of the children have visited the national parks, they give the descriptions; if not, people who have visited them talk to the class.
Each child chooses from the *National Parks Portfolio* one of the national parks to describe to the class. He locates it on the map and illustrates his talk by a few well-chosen pictures.

Organization

Planning the talk referred to above.

Recitation

Giving the talk. This exercise makes a good assembly program. Pictures may be projected by use of the lantern.

A drill lesson on section III of Unit X should be given at this point.

IV. Efforts were made to help the Less Fortunate
Members of Society
1. Education of the negroes was begun

Preparation

"Why were the negroes not educated in the South during the slavery period? What was the law in this matter?

"After the war who would have to act as their teachers at first? Why? Later how could this be changed?

"Do negroes and white children go to the same schools in your city?" No additional presentation is needed.

Assimilation
Readings
Upper Group

LOGIE. From Lincoln to Coolidge, 162–171, 212–224.

MOWRY. American Pioneers, 306–317.

SANFORD. The Story of Agriculture in the United States, 328–329 (difficult).

Compton's Pictured Encyclopedia (Negro, pp. 2434–2435).

World Book (Negro: Education, Hampton Institute, Tuskegee, Booker T. Washington).

Average Group

TAPPAN. Heroes of Progress, 147–156.

Lower Group

Read TAPPAN to this group.

Teachers

HART. American History told by Contemporaries, IV: 652–654, 663–665.

MILLER and Others. From Servitude to Service.

TILLINGHAST. The Negro in Africa and America, 209–216.

WASHINGTON. The Story of the Negro, II: 114–149.

WASHINGTON. Up from Slavery.

WASHINGTON and Others. The Negro Problem, 9–29.

WOODSON. The Negro in our History, 260–304.

United States Bureau of Education. Negro Education, Bulletin 39 (1916), Vols. I and II.

Minimal Essentials

Name of Person: **Booker T. Washington**
Name of Place: **Tuskegee** (tŭs kē′gē)
Historical Terms: **industrial schools; the negro problem**
Things to Remember
  At first white people taught the negroes.
  Later they had their own schools and teachers.
  First they were taught to work; then they were taught school subjects also.
  Now there are many educated and prosperous negroes.

Illustrative Material

Keystone Views: 214, Booker T. Washington and Distinguished Guests; 215, An Arithmetic Class, Tuskegee; 216, Colored Students Plowing.

Procedure during Assimilation

Reading as described on pages 24–29.
List the things which an ex-slave would have to learn in order to earn his living and manage his household affairs.
A child who has read Booker T. Washington's *Up from Slavery* reports on it to the class.
Invite someone who has visited negro schools to describe them to the children.
Drill on minimal essentials.
Objective test.

Organization

The teacher and the children working together produce an outline somewhat similar to the following:

EDUCATION OF THE NEGROES

1. What the negro needed to learn first
2. Schools for negroes
3. The condition of the negroes today

Recitation

A written composition of three paragraphs.

---

2. Labor of women and children was lessened

Preparation

"If somebody has to work twelve hours a day, who is most able to do it: men, women, or children? Why?
"Ought anybody to have to work so long? Why not?

"Can factories in our state make their women employees work as many hours as they want them to? Our reading today will tell us."

No additional presentation is needed.

Assimilation
Readings

Upper Group

BEARD and BAGLEY. Our Old World Background, 404.
LOGIE. From Lincoln to Coolidge, 334–338.
ROLT-WHEELER. The Boy with the United States Census, 105–126.
SMITH. Industrial History, 241, 259–266 (difficult).
Lessons in Community and National Life, Series B, 233–240.
World Book (Child Labor: Regulation, Children's Bureau).

Average Group

Try Lessons in Community and National Life.

Lower Group

Read SMITH to this group.

Teachers

BOGART. Economic History of the United States, 476–478.

Minimal Essentials

Historical Term: **child labor**
Things to Remember

Children need to be protected against too long hours of work or too hard work, because they should be in school learning to be good citizens.

Women should be protected, because the health of a mother affects the health of her children.

Illustrative Material

Sample copies of the placard of the law regarding the labor of women and children. (From the State Industrial Commission.)

Procedure during Assimilation

Reading as described on pages 24–29.

Children form committees. One goes to the continuation school to find out the state law regulating the labor of children. Another visits factories, department stores, etc. to find out the state law regulating the labor of women. Are placards posted stating the hours?

Read to the class parts of Elizabeth Barrett Browning's "The Cry of the Children."

Show the table of children at labor in Smith's *Industrial History*, p. 264.

Objective test.

Organization

Children suggest the two subheads into which the study falls; then select a title.

Recitation

Children tell the state law on each point above and why a law was needed.

> 3. Work was begun to better the conditions in prisons and asylums

---

Preparation

"How were prisoners punished during the colonial period?
"What is the object of sending people to prison?" (Reform.) "What things, then, should prisoners learn?
"What public homes for unfortunate people are there in your city?"

Assimilation

Readings

Upper Group

HORTON. A Group of Famous Women, 61–72.
MOWRY. American Heroes and Heroism, 181–188 (Dix).
MOWRY. American Pioneers, 292–305 (Samuel G. Howe), 337–346 (Dix).
STIMPSON. Child's Book of American Biography, 54–61 (Dix).

Average Group

Try HORTON and STIMPSON.

Lower Group

EGGLESTON. Stories of Great Americans, 153–155.

Teachers

TIFFANY. Life of Dorothea Lynde Dix.
New International Encyclopædia (Dix).

Minimal Essentials

Name of Person: **Dorothea Dix**
Historical Term: **asylum; dependent; prison reform**
Things to Remember
  Dependent children are now cared for in homes or asylums which are supported by taxes.
  Prisons have been made better places.
  Homes or schools have been provided for the deaf, blind, feeble-minded and insane, and for the aged and poor.

Illustrative Material

Ford Educational Library: 34, A Century of Progress, Part I.

Procedure during Assimilation

Reading as described on pages 24–29.

List the local institutions for the care of the unfortunate.

Collect pictures of the local asylums and homes for the dependent.

Committees from the class take presents to the Old Ladies' Home, the Orphans' Home, and the County Poor Farm.

The teacher reports to the class the provisions for health, sanitation, and reform in the local prisons.

Someone who has visited a modern prison system describes the work done among prisoners.

How are these public institutions supported? Why should all of us pay taxes for things we ourselves may never use?

Drill on minimal essentials.

Objective test.

Organization

The teacher puts the following outline on the board:

CARE OF THE UNFORTUNATE

1. Homes for children
2. Homes for the aged and the poor
3. Schools for the blind and the deaf
4. Homes for the feeble-minded and the insane

Recitation

Children choose those of the points above that they wish to use for their stories.

A drill lesson should be given at this point similar to that described on pages 40–43.

TESTS ON THE ENTIRE UNIT

(To be given after all the stories are completed)

Test of Place-Sense. Pass outline maps of the United States on which the state boundaries are shown by dotted lines. Give the following directions:

1. Print in the right place *Middle West*.
2. Print in the right place *The West*.
3. Put the letters *L B H* in the state in which the battle of the Little Big Horn was fought.
4. Put the letter *O* in Oklahoma.
5. Put the letter *T* in the state in which Tuskegee is located.
6. Draw a little square, thus (□), where the Yellowstone National Park is.

Minimal Essentials of Unit X

Persons	Places	Terms	Dates
Alexander Graham Bell	Little Big Horn	amendment	*1876.* Invention of the telephone
"Buffalo Bill" Cody	Oklahoma	asylum	Decade following the Civil War
General Custer	Tuskegee	brand	During the Civil War
Dorothea Dix	Yellowstone National Park	carpetbagger	
James J. Hill		Centennial Exposition	
homesteaders		child labor	
Edward MacDowell		citizen	Drill on the peaks of the time chart
Saint-Gaudens		cowboy	
Sargent		dependent	
Sitting Bull		free land	
Mark Twain		government Indian schools	
Booker T. Washington		Great Northern Railroad	
Walt Whitman		Homestead Act	
		humorist	
		industrial schools	
		Ku-Klux Klan	
		land office	
		national park	
		negro problem	
		overland stage	
		pony express	
		prison reform	
		reconstruction	
		reservation	
		rodeo	
		round-up	
		scout	
		sculptor	
		sculpture	
		sheep-herder	
		state park	
		transcontinental	
		Union Pacific Railroad	
		voter	
		World's Fair	

Test of Time-Sense. Pass mimeographed sheets of the following :

1. Here is a list of names. Put the figure 1 before the name of the person who did his great work first, the figure 2 before the name of the person who came next, and so on.

_ _ _ Alexander Graham Bell

_ _ _ General Custer

_ _ _ Samuel F. B. Morse

2. Here is another list. Do the same.

_ _ _ Paul Revere

_ _ _ "Buffalo Bill" Cody

_ _ _ Mark Twain

3. Here is another list. Do the same.

_ _ _ Harriet Beecher Stowe

_ _ _ Priscilla Alden

_ _ _ Dorothea Dix

4. Here is another list. Do the same.

_ _ _ James J. Hill

_ _ _ Robert Fulton

_ _ _ Cyrus McCormick

5. Here is another list. Do the same.

_ _ _ Sargent

_ _ _ Booker T. Washington

_ _ _ Walt Whitman

6. Here is a list of events which took place. Put the figure 1 before the event which took place first, the figure 2 before the event which took place next, and so on.

_ _ _ invention of the telephone

_ _ _ Homestead Act

_ _ _ reconstruction

Test on Persons. Pass mimeographed sheets of the following :

I. Here is a list of names :

homesteaders	Saint-Gaudens
Walt Whitman	Edward MacDowell
Alexander Graham Bell	Dorothea Dix
Sitting Bull	

Put each name in the right blank in the sentences below :

1. The Indian in charge of the forces that defeated General Custer was _ _ _ _ _ _ _ _ .

2. A great American musician was _ _ _ _ _ _ _ _ .

3. The poet who wrote "O Captain! my Captain!" was _ _ _ _ _ _ _ _ .

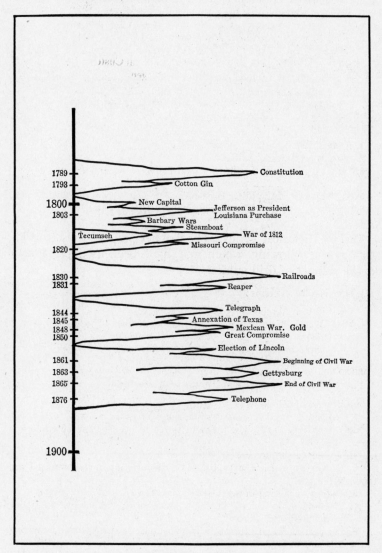

Time Chart — Unit X

4. People who went to take up free government land were called _ _ _ _.
5. The man who invented the telephone was _ _ _ _ _ _ _ _ _ _ _ _.
6. _ _ _ _ _ _ _ _ began work for reform of prisons and asylums.
7. _ _ _ _ was a great American sculptor.

II. Here is another list:

Booker T. Washington   General Custer
Mark Twain   Sargent
James J. Hill   "Buffalo Bill" Cody

Do the same.

1. A great American painter was _ _ _ _.
2. A great negro leader was _ _ _ _ _ _ _ _ _ _ _ _.
3. _ _ _ _ _ _ _ _ _ _ _ _ built the Great Northern Railroad.
4. _ _ _ _ _ _ _ _ _ _ _ _ was a rider for the pony express.
5. At the battle of the Little Big Horn _ _ _ _ _ _ _ _ was defeated.
6. _ _ _ _ _ _ _ _ wrote *Tom Sawyer* and *Huckleberry Finn*.

Test on Historical Terms. The teacher prepares descriptions such as the following, which may have been used previously as the subject of drill games.

I. Here is a list of terms:

industrial schools   voter
World's Fair   land office
rodeo   dependent
carpetbagger   child labor
amendment   sculpture

Put each one in the right blank in the sentences below:

1. A change made in our Constitution is an _ _ _ _.
2. People who need support from outside sources are _ _ _ _.
3. Anyone who has by law the right to record his choice in an election is a _ _ _ _.
4. Driving cattle together to be branded is a _ _ _ _.
5. Schools in which the processes of manufacture and commerce are taught are _ _ _ _ _ _ _ _.
6. The art of carving in wood, stone, clay, etc. is _ _ _ _.
7. The showing in Chicago in 1893 of many articles of interest and value from all over the world was the _ _ _ _ _ _ _ _.
8. The part of our government which has charge of the sale and managing of the government lands is the _ _ _ _ _ _ _ _.
9. A Northern man who settled in the Southern states at the close of the Civil War was called a _ _ _ _.
10. Work regularly done for money if the worker is not grown up is _ _ _ _ _ _ _ _.

II. Here is another list:

asylum
Union Pacific Railroad
cowboy
scout
transcontinental

brand
Homestead Act
reconstruction
reservation
state park

Do the same.

1. A person sent out to observe and get information about the enemy in time of war is a _ _ _ _.

2. A territory set apart for a certain public use is a _ _ _ _.

3. A home for a certain class of unfortunate persons is an _ _ _ _.

4. A piece of land set apart by the state as an ornament and playground is a _ _ _ _ _ _ _ _.

5. The first railroad to the Pacific coast was the _ _ _ _ _ _ _ _ _ _ _ _.

6. The law which allowed any citizen twenty-one years of age or more to take up one hundred and sixty acres of public land was the _ _ _ _ _ _ _ _.

7. A mark burned upon cattle with a hot iron is a _ _ _ _.

8. Anything passing across a whole continent is called _ _ _ _.

9. A man who rides horseback and cares for cattle is a _ _ _ _.

10. The process by which the seceding states were brought back into the Union was _ _ _ _.

III. Here is another list:

Centennial Exposition
sheep-herder
prison reform

Ku-Klux Klan
free land

Do the same.

1. A secret society in many Southern states after the Civil War was the _ _ _ _ _ _ _ _.

2. Improving conditions in prisons is _ _ _ _ _ _ _ _.

3. The great fair held on the hundredth birthday of the United States was the _ _ _ _ _ _ _ _.

4. One who cares for a flock of sheep is a _ _ _ _.

5. Land given by the government to an individual is _ _ _ _ _ _ _ _.

IV. Here is another list:

humorist
national park
negro problem
pony express
Great Northern Railroad

overland stage
sculptor
round-up
government Indian schools
citizen

Do the same.

1. The gathering together of herds of cattle for counting, branding, and selecting for sale is a _ _ _ _.

2. The system of sending the mail across the continent by relays of horses was the _ _ _ _ _ _ _ _.

3. Schools set up for Indians only and supported by the United States are _ _ _ _ _ _ _ _ _ _ _ _ _.

4. A member of the Republic who must obey its laws and whom it must protect is a _ _ _ _ _.

5. A piece of land set apart by the nation as an ornament and playground is a _ _ _ _ _ _ _ _.

6. A person who speaks or writes funny things is a _ _ _ _ _.

7. The carriage which made regular trips across country, especially in the West, was called the _ _ _ _ _ _ _ _.

8. The difficult question of how negroes and white people are to live in the same country, and how they are to treat each other, is the _ _ _ _ _ _ _ _.

9. One who carves statues is a _ _ _ _ _.

10. The railroad built by James J. Hill was the _ _ _ _ _ _ _ _ _ _ _ _.

COMPREHENSION TEST ON UNIT X

1. *Check the best answer:*

   a. What the United States decided to do with its public land was

       _ _ _ to sell it at a high price
       _ _ _ to give it to settlers
       _ _ _ to keep it all

   b. Great parks are helpful to the United States

       _ _ _ because they make us feel an interest in different parts of the country
       _ _ _ because the United States can make money from them
       _ _ _ because they are more beautiful than those of other countries

   c. At the close of the war, which was left in worse condition:

       _ _ _ the North?   _ _ _ the South?

   d. Dorothea Dix began work to better the conditions

       _ _ _ in prisons and asylums
       _ _ _ in the Red Cross
       _ _ _ in the army and navy

   e. Mails were carried in the West just after the Civil War

       _ _ _ by the pony express
       _ _ _ by railroads
       _ _ _ by steamboats

   f. Passengers were carried at the same time

       _ _ _ by railroads
       _ _ _ by the overland stage
       _ _ _ by automobiles

   g. There are laws to better the working conditions and hours

       _ _ _ of negroes
       _ _ _ of Southerners
       _ _ _ of women and children

h. Great fairs help the different nations of the world

   _ _ _ because they show the new ideas of each

   _ _ _ because they show how much better we are than the others

   _ _ _ because it is fun to see them

i. After the Civil War the North

   _ _ _ was very good to the South

   _ _ _ paid no attention to the South

   _ _ _ treated the South harshly

j. One of our greatest American composers of music was

   _ _ _ MacDowell

   _ _ _ Sargent

   _ _ _ Saint-Gaudens

k. A great American painter was

   _ _ _ MacDowell

   _ _ _ Sargent

   _ _ _ Saint-Gaudens

l. A great American sculptor was

   _ _ _ MacDowell

   _ _ _ Sargent

   _ _ _ Saint-Gaudens

m. The way in which affairs in the South were improved at last was

   _ _ _ that the South let the negroes run the states

   _ _ _ that the North sent soldiers to the South

   _ _ _ that the South took matters into its own hands

n. Education of the negroes was greatly helped by the work of

   _ _ _ Booker T. Washington

   _ _ _ George Washington

   _ _ _ Washington Irving

o. One thing that bound the West to the East was

   _ _ _ the transcontinental railroads

   _ _ _ the discovery of gold

   _ _ _ the defeat of the Indians

2. *Check two answers:*

   a. Two great writers of this period were

      _ _ _ Longfellow

      _ _ _ Walt Whitman

      _ _ _ Mark Twain

      _ _ _ Harriet Beecher Stowe

      _ _ _ Theodore Roosevelt

   b. Two great results of the defeat of the Indians were

      _ _ _ that it showed how strong the United States was

      _ _ _ that settlement of the West could go on faster

      _ _ _ that the Indians had to give up their lands

3. *Check the best answer:*

   a. One of the greatest effects of the disappearance of the frontier was

       _ _ _ that there was little free land left

       _ _ _ that the people became lazy

       _ _ _ that no one could live a life of adventure any more

   b. A great effect of the invention of the telephone was

       _ _ _ that people could talk more

       _ _ _ that people did not have to wait for letters from their families

       _ _ _ that business could be carried on more quickly

   c. A great business for which much of the land of the West could be used was

       _ _ _ the growing of rice

       _ _ _ the manufacturing of cotton

       _ _ _ the cattle-raising business

4. *What is the title of Unit X?*

ORGANIZATION OF THE UNIT AS A WHOLE

Children are supplied with mimeographed or hectographed sheets containing the name of the Unit and the names of the stories comprising the Unit.

They are to decide what bearing each story has upon the Roman-numeraled subhead under which it stands, and what bearing each story and subhead have upon the title of the Unit as a whole.

RECITATION OF THE UNIT AS A WHOLE

Telling the relationships mentioned above.

UNIT XI

HOW THE UNITED STATES BECAME A GREAT INDUSTRIAL NATION

I. The United States became the Leading Manufacturing Country of the World.
  1. There was a great increase in mining: coal, copper, gold, oil.
  2. Iron and steel industries multiplied in the North and in the South.
  3. The textile industries in New England and in the South supplied the whole country.
  4. A way to use rubber was discovered.
  5. The use of electricity began: lights, power, X rays.
  6. The United States produced so many manufactured goods that it began to look about the world for markets.
  7. Steamships had to be greatly improved to carry so many goods.

II. Many New Inventions and Discoveries were Made.
  1. The inventions and discoveries.
    a. Trolley car.
    b. Phonograph.
    c. Wireless telegraphy; radio.
    d. Typewriter.
    e. Moving pictures.
    Extra — for advanced group only: telescope.
  2. Machines of one kind were made with interchangeable parts.
  3. The Patent Office kept the records of inventions.

III. A New Class of Workers grew up in the United States.
  1. A great many immigrants came to America.
  2. The workers became machine workers and were paid wages.
  3. The workers formed labor unions.
  4. The employers formed big corporations.
  5. Cities grew larger yet.

IV. Scientific Agriculture was Necessary to provide Food for our Huge Population.
  1. Further improvements in farm machinery were made.
  2. Crops were planned more wisely.
  3. Work of Luther Burbank.
  4. Flour mills were improved.

V. We began to realize that our Natural Resources had been Sadly Wasted.
  1. Forests and mineral resources were protected.
  2. Fisheries and game were protected.
  3. Irrigation was begun in the West.

PREPARATION FOR THE OVERVIEW

"What was the title of Unit VIII?

"Name some of the machines which were invented during that period."

PRESENTATION OR OVERVIEW

We have found that even before the Civil War the United States had learned to use machinery to lighten men's labors, that the number of these machines had increased beyond belief, and that with their help people had begun to work and live very differently.

For a long time afterwards the nation's attention was occupied in getting used to these changes. Rather than having only a few railroads, they were building railroads everywhere; not only were factories built in a few large cities, but most industries everywhere were being carried on in factories. This growth took a good many years, and just to look at the surface of things, you would have said that there had not been much change for fifty years.

The time came when railroads and factories had gone everywhere; they no longer could spread out into new territory. But a growing nation cannot stand still. So instead of building more factories, people began to build larger factories. The larger the factories became, the more iron and steel and wool and cotton they needed. Therefore the mines had to employ more men, more sheep had to be raised, and more cotton had to be planted. Instead of changing industry completely, as the earlier inventions had done, most of the changes now were in size or volume. Business began to grow to tremendous proportions.

Soon these huge factories were producing a quantity of goods so great that, large as the United States was, it could not use all that was turned out. It had to try to sell goods to the other countries. It had become the greatest industrial country in the world, and had to have customers and markets.

In one way it is very pleasant to think that our country is the greatest country industrially, but greatness of any kind always brings with it a number of problems.

One of these problems was labor. Where could we get people enough to do all the work for our railroads, factories, and farms? So much could not be done by Americans alone. Therefore we let a great many people from other countries come here to live — Russians, Germans, Irish, Italians, etc. They helped us in our work and solved our labor problem; but they did not understand our ways and we did not understand their ways, so we had another problem on our hands.

A second question was how to get food enough to feed all our people. Our own laborers had been for years flocking into the cities to work in factories. Fewer and fewer were left on the farms to raise the crops. Our agricultural industry, therefore, had to try to produce more food with fewer laborers. The task was not easy.

And finally we began to realize that in our hurry to build up and to grow great we had formed some very wasteful habits. We had cut down too many trees, wasted our coal, and killed off our birds, game, and fish. How could we help to repair the damage we had done? Even yet we do not know the answer to this problem very well.

You can see, then, that although we became the greatest industrial country in the world the pathway to greatness was not a smooth one. Our growth brought us many problems, some of which we do not even yet know how to solve.

PRESENTATION TEST

Check the best answer:

a. The changes in our ways of living caused by the increased use of machinery began
 _ _ _ before the Civil War
 _ _ _ during the Civil War
 _ _ _ after the Civil War

b. For many years afterwards the attention of the nation was occupied
 _ _ _ in making still more changes
 _ _ _ in fighting against the changes
 _ _ _ in getting used to the changes

c. After railroads and factories had spread everywhere, the next change was
 _ _ _ for them to disappear
 _ _ _ for them to grow larger
 _ _ _ for them to stay as they were

d. Increased production of the factories demanded
 _ _ _ selling our products to other countries
 _ _ _ using up all our own products
 _ _ _ making poorer goods

e. To make so many products we secured workers
 _ _ _ from our own cities
 _ _ _ from other countries
 _ _ _ from our slave population

f. Those workers did not understand our ways
   _ _ _ because they did not like us
   _ _ _ because we did not like them
   _ _ _ because they were from other countries

g. Our farmers had to
   _ _ _ produce more food with fewer laborers
   _ _ _ produce less food than before
   _ _ _ go to the cities to find work

h. We have to learn to care for our bird life and trees now
   _ _ _ because now we know how to do it
   _ _ _ because we have wasted so many of them in the past
   _ _ _ because other nations will get them away from us

I. The United States became the Leading Manufacturing
   Country of the World
   1. There was a great increase in mining: coal, copper,
      gold, oil

Preparation

"What fuel was used during the colonial period? When was wood found to be not satisfactory as a fuel? Then the more machines we have the more fuel we shall need. What was the effect of the great increase in railroad-building on the coal and iron industries?

"Up to this time we have found gold mines mentioned in only one instance. Where? When was gold discovered in California? What other precious metal do you know of?

"What was the reason that there was such a great need of iron?

"Our story today tells us how our whole mining industry developed after the Civil War."

Assimilation

Readings

Upper Group

ALLEN. United States, 138–208.
BARROWS and PARKER. United States and Canada, 38–41, 117–119, 141–142.
CHASE and CLOW. Stories of Industry, I: 13–30, 39–80.
FAIRBANKS. The Western United States, 215–248.
GORDY. Leaders in Making America, 358–360 (Clarence King), 360–364.
GORDY. Stories of Later American History, 288–292.

JACKSON. Nelly's Silver Mine.
LEFFERTS. Our Own United States, 49–52, 59–64, 174–177.
MOWRY. American Inventions and Inventors, 77–84.
NIXON-ROULET. Our Little Alaskan Cousin, 111–118.
OTIS. Seth of Colorado.
PERRY and PRICE. American History, II : 248–249, 251–252.
ROCHELEAU. Great American Industries : Minerals, 39–74, 92–104, 177–188.
SAMUEL. The Story of Gold and Silver.
SAMUEL. The Story of Iron.
TAPPAN. Diggers in the Earth, 43–56, 65–75, 84–94.
VOLLINTINE. The Making of America, 233–235.
WINSLOW. The United States, 61–70, 148–155, 176–180.
WOODBURN and MORAN. Makers of America, 298–300.
Compton's Pictured Encyclopedia (Coal, Copper, Gold : Mines and Mining).
World Book (Coal, Copper, Gold, Klondike, Petroleum, Mining).

Average Group

BRIGHAM and McFARLANE. Essentials of Geography, I : 24–27, 144.
EGGLESTON. Stories of American Life and Adventure, 207–214 (Alaska).
FRYE. New Geography, I : 107–111.
GEORGE. Little Journeys to Alaska and Canada, 49–50 (Alaska).
GORDY. Elementary History of the United States, 283–284, 306.
SMITH. Human Geography, I : 86–90, 140–141.
TARR and McMURRY. New Geographies, I : 111–112, 135–136, 150.

Lower Group

ALLEN. How and Where we Live, 97–102.
CARROLL and CARROLL. Around the World, III : 53–62, 75, 122–131.
CHAMBERLAIN. How we are Clothed, 222–225.
DAVIDSON and ANDERSON. Lincoln Readers, V : 116–121, 150–152.
DYER and BRADY. Merrill Readers, V : 126–132.
KNOWLTON. First Lessons in Geography, 172–177, 194–197.
SHEPHERD. Geography for Beginners, 51–55.
WINSLOW. The Earth and its People, 91–97.

Teachers

BOGART. Economic History of the United States, 170–172, 323–324, 445.
COMAN. Industrial History of the United States, 288–292.
SMITH. Industrial History, 252–255.

Minimal Essentials

Names of Places: **Yukon** (yōō′kŏn); **Klondike**
Historical Terms: **claim; prospector**
Things to Remember
The United States has the greatest mineral resources of any country in the world.
Mines of all kinds have been opened up.

Illustrative Material

GABRIEL (ED.). Pageant of America, V : 64–81, 95–96, 103–105, 109.
McKINLEY. Illustrated Topics for American History : S. 35.
WOODBURN and MORAN. Makers of America, 301 (map).
Ford Educational Library : 22, Anthracite Coal Mining ; 45, Safety in the Mine.
Society for Visual Education. Picturols : Mining Bituminous Coal ; Petroleum Refining.

Procedure during Assimilation

Reading as described on pages 24–29.

Picture study based on the illustrative material listed on page 549.

For sand-table suggestions see *The Twentieth Yearbook of the National Society for the Study of Education*, Part I, p. 43.

An adult who has seen oil wells shooting describes the process to the class.

After the general reading and picture study, each child chooses one kind of mining on which he reads. He collects pictures to illustrate his talk to the class.

Use the graph on "Mining Operations in the United States," World Book, p. 3820.

Drill on minimal essentials.

Objective test.

Organization

Each child lists the chief points he intends to bring out in his talk to the class.

Recitation

Giving the descriptions of mining referred to above.

> 2. Iron and steel industries multiplied in the North and in the South

---

Preparation

"What would the people of the country do with so much iron after they had it? with so much gold? silver? oil? copper? Of all these products which do you suppose is worth the most money?" (Children usually say "gold.") Show the figures [1] comparing the value of the gold, silver, and iron output. Illustrate by a diagram or graph.

No additional presentation is needed.

Assimilation

Readings

Upper Group

DARROW. Thinkers and Doers, 196–212 (difficult).

HUSBAND. America at Work, 20–31.

LEFFERTS. Our Own United States, 55–56, 103–104.

MONTGOMERY. Beginners' American History, 240.

ROCHELEAU. The Story of Iron.

---

[1] "Mines and Quarries." *Fourteenth Census of the United States* (1920), p. 20, diagram on page 21.

SANFORD and OWEN. Modern Americans, 169–175.
TAPPAN. Heroes of Progress, 228–236 (Carnegie).
WOODBURN and MORAN. Makers of America, 302–304.
Compton's Pictured Encyclopedia (Iron and Steel, Carnegie).
World Book (Iron, Steel, Carnegie).

Average Group

BARNES. Elementary History of the United States, 368.
BRIGHAM and McFARLANE. Essentials of Geography, I : 93–94, 129–130.
GORDY. Elementary History of the United States, 306.
SMITH. Human Geography, I : 136–139.
SOUTHWORTH. Builders of our Country, II : 266–269 (Carnegie).
TARR and McMURRY. New Geographies, I : 151–152.
TURPIN. Brief Biographies from American History, 297–299.
Lessons in Community and National Life, Series C, 81–88.

Lower Group

TATE, WITHERS, and BROWNE. Child's World, V : 283–295.

Teachers

BOGART. Economic History of the United States, 163–165, 182, 412–414, 440–444.
HENDRICK. The Age of Big Business, 58–85.

Minimal Essentials

Name of Person: **Andrew Carnegie** [1] (kär nĕg′ĭ)
Historical Terms: **age of steel; United States Steel Corporation**
Things to Remember
Steel is the foundation of modern industry.
It is more important to us than any other metal product.

Illustrative Material

GABRIEL (ED.). Pageant of America, V : 186–212.
Ford Educational Library : 13, Iron and Steel.
Keystone Views : 283, Final Rolling Mill Action ; 286, Steel Mills.

Procedure during Assimilation

Reading as described on pages 24–29.
Picture study based on the illustrative material listed above.
The teacher and a committee of students visit a local foundry or machine shop and list the articles made of steel. Another committee visits hardware stores and implement shops and makes a similar list. Other children list steel articles they find in their own homes.
After the general reading, each child chooses a particular article made of steel and prepares to tell the class about its manufacture.
Graph the tabulation given in Burnham's *Making of our Country*, p. 481.
Graph figures for the production of iron as given in Bogart's *Economic History of the United States*, pp. 183–184.
Drill on minimal essentials.
Objective test.

[1] Not included in the lists of personages referred to on page 5.

Organization

Each child makes a list of the most important points he intends to bring out in his story.

Recitation

Giving the stories.

> 3. The textile industries in New England and in the South supplied the whole country

---

Preparation

"We found that the factory system began in the United States in what industry?

"Anything woven is a textile. Name some of the textiles found in your own home."

Presentation

During our early history Great Britain was the great textile manufacturer. We imported what we needed from her. Of late years, however, the United States not only has produced what it needs, but even exports much cloth to other countries. The mills used to be located only in the North, but now there are many in the South also.

Assimilation

Readings

Upper Group

BARROWS and PARKER. United States and Canada, 138.
BROOKS. The Story of Cotton, 230–236, 242–248, 254–264.
CARPENTER. How the World is Clothed, 34–44, 44–50, 329–335.
CHASE and CLOW. Stories of Industry, II : 17–76.
CURTIS. Story of Cotton, 112–123.
LEFFERTS. Our Own United States, 12–15, 98–100.
World Book (Textiles : Importance of the Industry).

Average Group

BRIGHAM and McFARLANE. Essentials of Geography, I : 93, 112.
FRYE. New Geography, I : 97.
GORDY. Elementary History of the United States, 280–281.

Lower Group

CHAMBERLAIN. How we are Clothed, 72–79.

Teachers

BOGART. Economic History of the United States, 167–170, 181–182, 410–412, 437–440.

COMAN. Industrial History of the United States, 311–312.

American Citizenship Course in United States History, IV : 178–179.

Minimal Essentials

Historical Terms: **export; import; the New South**
Things to Remember

At first most of the textile manufactories were located in New England and in the middle states.

Of late years much cotton is manufactured in the same regions in which it is grown.

Illustrative Material

BROOKS. The Story of Cotton, 218–219 (map) ; 257 (tabulation).
GABRIEL (ED.). Pageant of America, V : chap. viii.
Ford Educational Library : 204, To "Suit" Man.
Keystone Views : 293, Close View of a Modern Loom ; 294, Weaving Room in a Cotton Mill.

Procedure during Assimilation

Reading as described on pages 24–29.
Picture study based on the illustrative material listed above.
Visit a local textile plant.
From the advertising materials collected, each child chooses the story of a particular textile — for example, rugs, woolen cloth, silk, etc. — and prepares to tell the story of its manufacture to the class.
Graph the figures of the tabulation showing the increase in the number of textile factories in the South from 1840 to 1910 [1] or the increase in number of Southern cotton factories. [2]
Children compare the number of trade centers in the South in 1850 with the number in 1910. [3]
Drill on minimal essentials.
Objective test.

Organization

Each child lists the points he is to tell in his story.

Recitation

The giving of the stories.

---

[1] Brooks, E. C., *The Story of Cotton*, p. 257.
[2] Coman, K., *The Industrial History of the United States*, p. 312 ; Bogart, E. L., *Economic History of the United States*, p. 429.
[3] Brooks, E. C., *The Story of Cotton*, pp. 218–219.

> ## 4. A way to use rubber was discovered

Preparation and Presentation

"Of what is rubber made? Where does it come from? As it comes to us from Brazil and other places it is very sticky. It cracks when it becomes cold and runs together when it is heated. What must be done before it can be used?

"Our story today is about the man who gave up years of his life in order to find out for us how to make rubber usable."

Assimilation

Readings

Upper Group

BROWNE. Peeps at Industries: Rubber.
CHASE and CLOW. Stories of Industry, II: 89–113.
DARROW. Thinkers and Doers, 183–195 (difficult).
NIXON-ROULET. Our Little Brazilian Cousin, 33–39.
PIERCY. Great Inventions and Discoveries, 156–163.
TAPPAN. Heroes of Progress, 30–38.
TAPPAN. Makers of Many Things, 6–15.
TOWLE. Heroes and Martyrs of Invention, 170–179.
Compton's Pictured Encyclopedia (Rubber).
World Book (Goodyear, Rubber).

Average Group

EGGLESTON. Stories of Great Americans, 128–131.
PARKMAN. Conquests of Invention, 110–131.

Lower Group

ALLEN. How and Where we Live, 103–106.
CHAMBERLAIN. How we are Clothed, 107–128.
FAIRGRIEVE and YOUNG. The World, 110–114.

Teachers

FREEMAN and CHANDLER. World's Commercial Products, 278–297.
GEER. The Reign of Rubber.
MILLS. Searchlights on Some American Industries, 131–164.
PEARSON. Rubber Country of the Amazon.
SLOSSON. Creative Chemistry, 145–163.

Minimal Essentials

Name of Person: **Charles Goodyear** [1]
Historical Term: **vulcanization**
Things to Remember

Before the time of Goodyear, rubber goods became stiff in winter and soft and sticky in summer.

Goodyear heated a mixture of rubber and sulphur and found how to make it usable. The process was called vulcanization.

[1] Not included in the lists of personages referred to on page 5.

Illustrative Material

Compton's Pictured Encyclopedia (Rubber).
Ford Educational Library: 14, Making Rubber Tires.
Travel, XXX: 18–23 (March, 1918).

Procedure during Assimilation

Reading as described on pages 24–29.
Picture study based on the illustrative material listed above.
Children at their homes list articles made of rubber.
Graph figures of the world output of rubber [1] and of America's rubber imports.[2]
  How might America supply her own rubber?
Drill on minimal essentials.
Objective test.

Organization

Children and teacher working together produce an outline
somewhat similar to the following:

GOODYEAR'S DISCOVERY OF VULCANIZATION

1. Early difficulties in working with rubber
2. Goodyear's attempts
3. His success
4. Rubber in industry today

Recitation

Invite a local automobile dealer to hear the stories.

---

5. The use of electricity began: lights, power, X rays

Preparation

"What kind of lighting was used in the homes of the
colonists? In what way were lamps an improvement? In
what way was gas an improvement over oil lamps? In what
way is electricity an improvement over gaslighting?

"What do we mean when we say a machine is run by
power? [3] Give examples of machines run by electric power.
What great American do you know who made electrical
inventions?

[1] World Almanac.
[2] American Yearbook or World Almanac.
[3] Referring to Unit VIII, section I, lesson 3, p. 401.

"Have any of you ever heard of an X-ray machine? For what is it used?

"Our story today is about the wonders of electricity and about one of the greatest American inventors."

No additional presentation is needed.

Assimilation

Readings

Electricity

Upper Group

BAKER. Boys' Book of Inventions, 173–203.

CHANDLER and CHITWOOD. Makers of American History, 292–294.

DARROW. Thinkers and Doers, 25–41, 253–270, 284–287 (difficult).

DAVIDSON. Founders and Builders of our Nation, 165–167.

FORMAN. Stories of Useful Inventions, 36–37.

GROVE. The Story of Electricity, 3–17.

HOLLAND. Historic Inventions, 233–260.

LEFFERTS. American Leaders, II : 134–137.

MEADOWCROFT. Boys' Life of Edison, 183–196, 208–218.

MOWRY. American Inventions and Inventors, 85–89.

PERRY. Four American Inventors, 251–254.

PIERCY. Great Inventions and Discoveries, 78–91.

STOUT. Boys' Book of Mechanical Models, 111–121.

Compton's Pictured Encyclopedia (Electricity : Electric Lighting, Electric Motor, X Rays).

World Book (Electricity : Uses of Electricity, Electric Light).

Average Group

BEARD and BAGLEY. A First Book in American History, 344, 348–350.

FORMAN. First Lessons in American History, 307–308.

GORDY. Elementary History of the United States, 306–309.

MACE. Primary History, 349–352.

McFEE. Stories of American Inventions, 105, 117–142.

PARKMAN. Conquests of Invention, 168–182.

Lower Group

DAVIDSON and ANDERSON. Lincoln Readers, V : 174–179.

SHEPHERD. Geography for Beginners, 56–59.

Teachers

LANE and HILL. American History in Literature, 167–168.

SPARKS. National Development, 39–44.

THOMPSON. The Age of Invention, 194–203, 212–219.

Life of Edison

Upper Group

BACHMAN. Great Inventors and their Inventions, 247–248.

BURNHAM. Hero Tales from History, 285–291.

CHANDLER and CHITWOOD. Makers of American History, 289–292.

DAVIDSON. Founders and Builders of our Nation, 160–168.
ELLIS. Makers of our Country, 183–192.
EVANS. America First, 405–408.
GORDY. Leaders in Making America, 404–408.
GROVE. The Story of Electricity, 21–27.
GUERBER. Story of the Great Republic, 273–274.
LEFFERTS. American Leaders, II : 116–129, 139–142.,
MEADOWCROFT. The Boys' Life of Edison.
PERRY. Four American Inventors, 205–251.
ROLT-Wheeler. Thomas Alva Edison.
SANFORD and OWEN. Modern Americans, 17–27.
STIMPSON. The Child's Book of American Biography, 243–251.
TAPPAN. Heroes of Progress, 199–207.
Compton's Pictured Encyclopedia (Edison).
World Book (Edison).

Average Group

BARNES. Elementary History of the United States, 368.
BEARD and BAGLEY. A First Book in American History, 344–348.
DAVIDSON and ANDERSON. Lincoln Readers, V : 71–77.
FORMAN. First Lessons in American History, 306–307.
GORDY. Elementary History of the United States, 310.
MACE. Primary History, 348–349.
McFEE. Stories of American Inventions, 105–117.
PARKMAN. Conquests of Invention, 158–168.
SOUTHWORTH. Builders of our Country, II : 260–265.
TATE, WITHERS, and BROWNE. Child's World, V : 352–362.
UHRBROCK and OWENS. Famous Americans, 269–279.

Lower Group

EVERETT and REED. When they were Boys, 15–22.
LEWIS and ROWLAND. Silent Readers, IV : 136.

Teachers

THOMPSON. The Age of Invention, 203–212.

Minimal Essentials

Name of Person: **Thomas A. Edison**
Date: 1879 — invention of the electric light
Historical Terms: **"Wizard of Menlo Park"; age of electricity**
Things to Remember
Electricity was found better for lighting than gas.
Electricity is useful as power, because the power can be sent a long distance.
X rays are useful to physicians in finding out the condition of the body.
Thomas A. Edison improved the electric light and invented the phonograph as well as many other machines.

Illustrative Material

GABRIEL (ED.). Pageant of America, V : 139–140, 143–145.
Ford Educational Library : 187, Making an Electric Light Bulb.
Keystone Views : 211, Thomas A. Edison in his Laboratory.
Perry Pictures : 2513, Thomas A. Edison.

Procedure during Assimilation

Reading as described on pages 24–29.

Picture study based on the illustrative material listed on page 557.

Perform some simple experiments with electricity. The high-school teacher of science can probably supply the apparatus.

If there is an X-ray machine in town in a doctor's or dentist's office or in a shoe store, take the children to see it. If not, show them X-ray pictures.

Are there power lines running into or out of your city? Show pictures of power lines and poles; point out differences between these and telegraph poles.

Take those children who wish to go, to the local electric-light plant to see the dynamo. Make no attempt to explain the process in detail.

Drill on minimal essentials.

Objective test.

Organization

Children suggest subheads for the outline, then a name for the story.

Recitation

Invite the high-school teacher of science to hear the stories.

---

6. The United States produced so many manufactured goods that it began to look about the world for markets

---

Preparation

" When the time came that the United States manufactured more phonographs and reaping-machines and locomotives than our own people could use, what do you suppose the manufacturers did with their articles? We call goods sent out of the country exports " (*pointing to the word written on the board*).

Have prepared on the board a list of the chief countries which take America's exports, in the order of quantity consumed.[1] A slated map of the world is also ready. Children place the figure 1 on the map of the country which is our best customer, the figure 2 on the map of the country which is our next best customer, and so on. "We call the places where we sell our goods our markets."

Presentation

Countries which manufacture very little for themselves are naturally good markets. Why? In some few cases why

[1] World Almanac (Imports and Exports: United States).

are they not? (*Show on the map some countries we should like to have as markets: China, Brazil, Argentina, etc.*) Since we should like to have them as markets, you may be sure that other manufacturing countries also would like to have them as their markets. Therefore many quarrels have arisen between the great manufacturing countries of the world over their markets. Sometimes this has even led to war. It was one of the important causes of the World War.

The United States uses its islands, such as the Philippines and Porto Rico, as markets and as centers from which to distribute its goods among other peoples (*illustrating how the islands may serve as centers of radiation*).

PRESENTATION TEST

Check the best answer:

a. When countries manufacture more goods than their own people need, they must
 _ _ _ import them
 _ _ _ export them
 _ _ _ stop making them

b. We call the places where we sell our goods our
 _ _ _ customers
 _ _ _ exports
 _ _ _ markets

c. Some good markets are
 _ _ _ countries which have no products at all
 _ _ _ countries which manufacture little for themselves
 _ _ _ countries which are our friends

d. Much trouble arises between manufacturing countries
 _ _ _ because they want the same markets
 _ _ _ because they make the same things
 _ _ _ because they will not buy each other's goods

Assimilation
Readings

Upper Group

BLAICH. Three Industrial Nations, 332–333, 341.
MARSHALL. The Story of Human Progress, 273–283.
WERTHNER. How Man makes Markets, 9–14.

Average Group

McMURRY-PARKINS. Elementary Geography, 303–309.

Lower Group

Read and explain MARSHALL to this group.

Teachers

Muzzey. The United States of America, II : 295, 348–350.
Schlesinger. Political and Social History of the United States, 280–285, 407–409.

Minimal Essentials

Historical Terms: **colonial markets; markets; surplus**
Things to Remember

If a nation manufactures more goods of any one kind than it can use, it must sell the surplus to other nations.

The places where we regularly sell our goods are our markets.

Many nations are jealous of each other's markets; this jealousy often leads to war.

Procedure during Assimilation

Reading as described on pages 24–29.
Graph the figures given for the exports of the United States [1] by ten-year periods. Drill on minimal essentials.

Organization

The teacher puts the following outline on the board :

ATTEMPT OF THE UNITED STATES TO SECURE MARKETS

1. Need of markets
2. Chief markets
3. Causes of trouble

Recitation

Each child prepares to tell the complete story.

---

7. Steamships had to be greatly improved to carry so many goods

---

No additional preparation and presentation are needed.

Assimilation

Readings

Upper Group

Beard and Bagley. Our Old World Background, 348–350.
Doubleday. Stories of Inventors, 87–96.
Mowry. American Inventions and Inventors, 229–234.
Rocheleau. Great American Industries : Transportation, 70–79.
Rocheleau. Ocean Routes and Navigation.
Rocheleau. The Story of Ships and Shipping, 23–32.
Tappan. Travelers and Traveling, 95–107.
Compton's Pictured Encyclopedia (Ships, pp. 3212–3220).
World Book (Steamships).

[1] World Almanac (Imports and Exports : United States).

Average Group
AITCHISON and UTTLEY. Across Seven Seas to Seven Continents, 287–296.
BEEBY. How the World grows Smaller, 62–97.
BRIGHAM and MCFARLANE. Essentials of Geography, I: 42–43.
LARGE. Everyday Wonders, 23–34.

Lower Group
CHAMBERLAIN. How we Travel, 165–170.

Teachers
BOGART. Economic History of the United States, 378–380.
COMAN. Industrial History of the United States, 333–335.

Minimal Essentials

Historical Terms: **Canadian Pacific Line; Cunard** (kủ närd′) **Line; merchant marine; White Star Line**
Things to Remember
Modern passenger steamships are floating palaces.
United States ships carry on comparatively little commerce at sea; other nations carry our goods for us.
The United States is trying to build up its merchant marine.

Illustrative Material

GRANT. Story of the Ship: Unloading Machinery, Navigation, Whalebacks.
Compton's Pictured Encyclopedia (Ships).
Keystone Views: 245, The Leviathan.

Procedure during Assimilation

Reading as described on pages 24–29.
Picture study based on the illustrative material listed above.
Write to the great transatlantic and transpacific companies for advertising material describing their ships: Cunard, Anchor, Canadian Pacific, Hamburg-American, Holland-America, North German Lloyd, Red Star, Royal Mail, United States, White Star, American Oriental Mail, Dollar, Nippon Yusen Kaisha, etc. Each child chooses one line to describe, tracing its routes on a map of the world.
Travelers on transoceanic liners describe the ships and the life on shipboard.
Children write an imaginary diary of a voyage to whatever port they choose.
Use the diagram showing the increase in size of ships, in Rocheleau's *Great American Industries: Transportation*, p. 74.
Find the number of ships in the merchant marine of the United States.[1]
Drill on minimal essentials.
Objective test.

Organization

Writing the diaries referred to above.

Recitation

Reading the diaries.
A drill lesson on section I of Unit XI should be given at this point.

[1] World Almanac (World's Merchant Shipping).

> II. Many New Inventions and Discoveries were Made
>   1. The inventions and discoveries
>   *a.* Trolley car
>   *b.* Phonograph
>   *c.* Wireless telegraphy; radio
>   *d.* Typewriter
>   *e.* Moving pictures

Preparation

"The time about which we are now studying is sometimes called the age of invention. What does the term mean? Let us read to find out why it is so called."

No additional presentation is needed.

Assimilation
Readings
Trolley car

Upper Group

ROCHELEAU. Great American Industries: Transportation, 229–233.
ROCHELEAU. Navigating the Air: Electric Railways, 13–17.
SMITH. Industrial History, 208 (difficult).
TAPPAN. Travelers and Traveling, 54–62.

Average Group

BEARD and BAGLEY. A First Book in American History, 350–352.
BEEBY. How the World grows Smaller, 109–119.

Lower Group

KNOWLTON. First Lessons in Geography, 210–211.

Teachers

BOGART. Economic History of the United States, 374.
HENDRICK. The Age of Big Business, 119–124, 147–148.
SPARKS. National Development, 37–39.

Phonograph

Upper Group

BACHMAN. Great Inventors and their Inventions, 249–251.
BAKER. The Boys' Book of Inventions, 251–280.
DARROW. Thinkers and Doers, 292–298 (difficult).
DAVIDSON. Founders and Builders of our Nation, 164.
LANE and HILL. American History in Literature, 168–169.
LEFFERTS. American Leaders, II: 131–134.
MEADOWCROFT. Boys' Life of Edison, 175–182.
PERRY. Four American Inventors, 255–260.
Compton's Pictured Encyclopedia (Phonograph).
World Book (Talking Machine).

Average Group
> BEARD and BAGLEY. First Book in American History, 348.
> FORMAN. First Lessons in American History, 308–309.
> LARGE. Everyday Wonders, 112–123.
> McFEE. Stories of American Inventions, 143–165.
> PARKMAN. Conquests of Invention, 182–185.

Lower Group
> Try FORMAN.

Teachers
> SPARKS. National Development, 45.
> THOMPSON. The Age of Invention, 152–153.

Wireless telegraphy; radio

Upper Group
> BAKER. The Boys' Book of Inventions, 79–117.
> DARROW. Thinkers and Doers, 341–354 (difficult).
> DOUBLEDAY. Stories of Inventors, 3–26.
> GORDY. Leaders in Making America, 412–413.
> GROVE. The Story of Electricity, 27–32.
> HOLLAND. Historic Inventions, 261–272.
> MARSHALL. The Story of Human Progress, 268–270 (difficult).
> WADE. The Light Bringers, 172–195.
> Compton's Pictured Encyclopedia (Wireless Telegraph and Telephone).
> Lessons in Community and National Life, Series B, 87–88.
> World Book (Wireless Telegraph, Wireless Telephone).

Average Group
> GORDY. Elementary History of the United States, 307–308.
> LARGE. Everyday Wonders, 97–106.
> NIDA. Following the Frontier, 317–319.
> PARKMAN. Conquests of Invention, 396–408.

Lower Group
> Read and explain MARSHALL to this group.

Teachers
> SMITH. Industrial History, 216–219.

Typewriter

Upper Group
> DARROW. Thinkers and Doers, 224–236 (difficult).
> PERRY and PRICE. American History, II : 289.
> PIERCY. Great Inventions and Discoveries, 164–168.
> Compton's Pictured Encyclopedia (Typewriter).
> World Book (Typewriter).

Average Group
> Try PERRY and PRICE.

Lower Group
> Read PERRY and PRICE to this group.

Teachers
> THOMPSON. The Age of Invention, 149–152.

Moving pictures

Upper Group

BACHMAN. Great Inventors and their Inventions, 251–253.
DARROW. Thinkers and Doers, 298–304 (difficult).
DOUBLEDAY. Stories of Inventors, 115–130.
LUBSCHEZ. Story of the Motion Picture.
Compton's Pictured Encyclopedia (Motion Pictures).
World Book (Moving Pictures).

Average Group

LARGE. Everyday Wonders, 84–96.
McFEE. Stories of American Inventions, 206–225.

Lower Group

Read DOUBLEDAY aloud to this group.

Teachers

LESCARBOURA. Behind the Motion Picture Screen.
MOSES. The American Dramatist, 200–226.
MÜNSTERBERG. The Photoplay.
REYNOLDS. Motion Pictures and Motion Picture Equipment.

Minimal Essentials

Name of Person: **Marconi** (mär kō′nē)
Historical Terms: **moving pictures; phonograph; trolley car; typewriter; wireless telephone**
Things to Remember

The trolley car helped to increase the size of cities.
It also helped to settle rural districts.
Edison invented the phonograph.
The phonograph helped to educate America in music.
The radio is an amusement that can be enjoyed at home.
It is not an American discovery.
The typewriter is a great aid to American business.
Moving pictures soon became the chief amusement of the American people.

Illustrative Material

Compton's Pictured Encyclopedia (Motion Pictures, Phonograph, Wireless, Telegraph and Telephone).
Ford Educational Library: 35, A Century of Progress, Part II.
Keystone Views: 212, Marconi.
Perry Pictures: 123-B, Marconi.
World Book (Moving Pictures, Wireless Telegraph, Wireless Telephone).

Procedure during Assimilation

Reading as described on pages 24–29.
Picture study based on the illustrative material listed above.
Make a map of the local community, placing all street-car and interurban lines.
Arrange for a radio concert.
Children report whether typewriters are used in conducting the business of their local grocery and meat markets, bakeries, and dairies.
If possible, secure an old roll of moving-picture film to show to the children.
Drill on minimal essentials.
Objective test.

Organization

Children list the inventions and discoveries studied.

Recitation

A summary sentence is written about each of the points above.

---

2. Machines of one kind were made with interchangeable parts

Preparation

"If you should break the clamp on one of your skates, would you have to throw the pair away? Why not? How do you know that the new clamp will fit?" Show the class the works of an alarm clock, and parts they could replace if broken.

Divide the class into committees. Each committee investigates at a different store what spare parts are kept for the repair of skates, express wagons, clocks, fountain pens, automobiles, washing-machines, pumps, stoves, etc. Committees report to the class.

Presentation

Years ago it was the custom for one man to make all of an article; an armchair, for example. He made the rungs, the seat, the back, and then put them all together. Other things were made the same way, one at a time: one watch, one wagon, etc. The workman knew his craft thoroughly and turned out a very good article. But when the owner broke a rung of his chair and wanted to replace it, or when one of his wagon shafts was broken and another was needed, then there was difficulty.

Since each wagon had been made independently of the others, no two were apt to be exactly alike. One would be a little longer, the next a little heavier, etc. About the only way, then, to have repairs made was to build another new part exactly like the old one. This was hard work, took a good deal of time, and was expensive.

To solve the difficulty the factories decided that from that time on they would make all the articles of one kind exactly alike. For example, the dining-room tables of Class A No. 102 would all be exactly alike : legs the same length and the same distance around, tops exactly the same size, etc. All these pieces would be made separately and then brought together at last, when any top would fit any pairs of legs. We call this putting-together process "assembling" (*pointing to the word written on the board*). How much easier and faster this was than the old process! After the parts were made separately and assembled, if somebody burned his table top badly he could write back to the factory (or the store would write for him) that he wanted another table top for a dining-room table of Class A No. 102. When the new top came it would fit exactly.

Other goods were manufactured in the same way : automobile parts, parts of clocks and watches, electric irons, washing-machines; in fact, almost every piece of machinery of any kind. Therefore today repairs are much cheaper and articles can be used much longer.

Since these parts we have been describing are all exactly alike, we call them standard parts (*pointing to the words written on the board*), or since the parts of any one machine can be changed with the parts of another similar machine we also call them interchangeable parts (*pointing to the words on the board*). Standard parts made the manufacturing process move so much faster that more goods could be made than ever before.

Making machines of standard parts is one reason why the United States has become such a great manufacturing nation.

PRESENTATION TEST

1. *Check the best answer:*

   Years ago most articles were manufactured
   _ _ _ by one man making the entire article
   _ _ _ by many men making one article
   _ _ _ by many men working under a boss

2. *Check two answers:*

   The chief trouble with the old system was
   _ _ _ that repairs were not needed
   _ _ _ that no repairs could be made at all
   _ _ _ that repairs had to be made to order
   _ _ _ that the work was slow

3. *Check the best answer:*

   a. Factory owners decided that a better way would be

      _ _ _ to make parts that could be changed from one article to another like it

      _ _ _ to make only one kind of article

      _ _ _ to make parts that would not break

   b. Putting standard parts together to make a whole article is called

      _ _ _ making standard parts

      _ _ _ assembling the article

      _ _ _ making goods by the factory system

4. *Check two answers:*

   Parts which are all alike in similar articles are called

      _ _ _ machine parts

      _ _ _ standard parts

      _ _ _ factory parts

      _ _ _ interchangeable parts

Assimilation

Minimal Essentials

Historical Terms: **assembling; interchangeable parts; standard parts**
Things to Remember
   Articles of one kind are made of standard parts.
   Putting these parts together to make a whole article is called assembling.

Procedure during Assimilation

Take children to a local automobile shop to see a motor car assembled; to an implement shop to see farm machinery assembled; to a jeweler's shop to see a clock assembled.
"Can parts of one automobile be interchanged with parts of all other automobiles? Why not?
"What do we mean when we say that a certain article was 'made to order'? How does it differ from a similar article made of standard parts?"
Children make at home, with the assistance of their parents, a list of household goods made of standard parts.
Drill on minimal essentials.
Objective test.

Organization

Each child plans a paragraph on "Quantity Production by turning out Standard Parts."

Recitation

Reading the paragraphs.

> 3. The Patent Office kept the records of inventions

Preparation and Presentation

The teacher shows the children the inscription on her fountain pen, "Reg. U. S. Pat. Off." "Does anyone know what it means?" Write the words on the board.

Have children find the records of patents of the heating apparatus, parts of the printing set, the metal wastebasket, certain keys, and other articles about the schoolroom. "The expression sometimes used is 'Pat. Appl'd For.' What does this mean?

"Why does an inventor want a patent? Where and how would he get it? Our reading today tells just what he must do.

"One cannot get a patent on a book or on a piece of music. How are an author's rights protected?" Children open all their books to see if each contains a copyright.

"Sometimes instead of just a patent or a copyright, people use trade-marks. Have you ever seen one?" The teacher has ready at hand certain advertisements showing trade-marks. Children name others they have seen.

Children find in their dictionaries the definition of a patent and write it on the board.

Assimilation

Readings

Upper Group
> ROLT-WHEELER. The Boy with the United States Inventors.
> Compton's Pictured Encyclopedia (Patents).
> World Book (Patent).

Average Group
> Lessons in Community and National Life, Series C, 97–104.

Lower Group
> The teacher reads the World Book to this group.

Teachers
> BOGART. Economic History of the United States, 176–178, 419–420, 436–437.

Minimal Essentials

Historical Terms: copyright; patent; Patent Office; trade-mark
Things to Remember
> People who have made new things should be protected in their rights.
> The United States gives patents, copyrights, and the use of trade-marks.

Procedure during Assimilation

Reading as described on pages 24–29.

The class is divided into three committees. One makes at home a list of articles patented, with the exact inscription on each; one cuts out of magazines pictures showing trade-marks or brings the articles themselves; the third makes at home a list of the copyright dates on books, calendars, pictures, and music.

Does anyone in your town hold a patent? a copyright?

Why should an inventor be allowed to take out a patent? Why shouldn't it last forever?

Visitors to the United States Patent Office describe it to the children.

Drill on minimal essentials.

Objective test.

Organization

The teacher puts the following outline on the board:

WORK OF THE PATENT OFFICE

1. The use of patents
2. The use of copyrights
3. The use of trade-marks
4. Work of the United States Patent Office

Recitation

Each child prepares an oral story of all four points.

A drill lesson on section II of Unit XI should be given at this point.

III. A New Class of Workers grew up in the United States
1. A great many immigrants came to America

Preparation

The teacher asks the children the following questions, recording the results in the table:

"Are there any children here who were not born in the United States? If so, in what country were you born?

"Were your fathers and mothers born outside the United States? If so, where?

"Where were your four grandfathers and grandmothers born?"

(*Arrange the following figures in order, to show what countries are represented the greatest number of times in the ancestry of the class. Explain that the tabulation does not count native Americans.*)

FOREIGN ANCESTRY OF OUR CLASS [1]

	BIRTHPLACE													
	Germany	Norway	Sweden	Denmark	Scotland	England	Ireland	Canada	Austria	Hungary	Wales	France	Holland	Switzerland
Children										2				
Fathers and mothers .	12	4	2				5	1		2	3	3		
Grandfathers and grandmothers	22	9	3	6	1	1	16	2	2	5	6	7	1	3
Total.	34	13	3	8	1	1	21	3	2	9	9	10	1	3

"What do we call people who come from some foreign country to the United States to live?" (*Write the word "immigrant" on the board.*)

"Our diagram shows that most of our forefathers were immigrants here only one or two generations ago."

No additional presentation is needed.

Assimilation

Readings

Upper Group

ROLT-WHEELER. The Boy with the United States Census, 127–164.
TAPPAN. An Elementary History of our Country, 237.
VOLLINTINE. The Making of America, 170–186.
WADE. Pilgrims of Today (biographies of noted immigrants).
Compton's Pictured Encyclopedia (Immigration).
World Book (Emigration and Immigration).

Average Group

GORDY. Elementary History of the United States, 293–294, 310–312.
INGRAHAM. The Story of Democracy, 231–233.
Lessons in Community and National Life, Series C, 249–256.

Lower Group

McMASTER. Primary History of the United States, 229–231.
MIRICK and HOLMES. Home Life around the World, 156–159.
SCHWARTZ. Five Little Strangers, 103–136.

Teachers

BOGART. Economic History of the United States, 473–475.
COMAN. Industrial History of the United States, 369–374.
MACDONALD. Documentary Source Book of American History, 616–618, 630–635.
SMITH. Industrial History, 256–259.
SPARKS. National Development, 229–250.
American Citizenship Course in United States History, IV : 221–226.

[1] Figures from one Wisconsin class of sixteen members. Some children did not know the ancestry of their grandparents.

Minimal Essentials

Historical Terms: **Chinese Exclusion Act; immigrant; immigration**
Things to Remember
    At first the United States allowed almost anybody to enter.
    Now we allow only a small number of immigrants to enter each year.
    We should try to make the immigrants good Americans.

Illustrative Material

McMASTER. Primary History of the United States, 229 (diagram).
WOODBURN and MORAN. Elementary American History and Government (Revised Edition), 513.
Compton's Pictured Encyclopedia (United States, p. 358: diagram).
Keystone Views: 276, Emigrants leaving for America; 277, Immigrants just Arrived; 278,
    United States Inspectors; 279, Admitted Immigrants.
Perry Pictures: 7691, In the Immigrant Station; 7692, In the Immigrant Station.
Society for Visual Education. Schoolfilms: Immigration to the United States; Father Knicker-
    bocker's Children.

Procedure during Assimilation

Reading as described on pages 24–29.
Picture study based on the illustrative material listed above.
Dramatize a phase of the immigration story.[1]
Invite naturalized foreigners to tell the children about their trips across the ocean
    and the examinations at Ellis Island or elsewhere.
Use the outline on immigration given in Vollintine's *Making of America*, pp. 186–187.
Drill on minimal essentials.
Objective test.

Organization

Children make their own outlines, the teacher giving only
such help as is needed.

Recitation

Reciting from the individual outlines.

---

2. The workers became machine workers and were paid wages

Preparation and Presentation

"Why did our people first begin to build factories?[2] Who
did all the work in these large buildings? How could the
factory owner persuade his neighbors to work in his building
and at his machines? How had they earned their living previously? What kinds of machines had they had experience
with before?

---

[1] "A Travel Club." *The Twentieth Yearbook of the National Society for the Study
of Education*, Part I, p. 70.
[2] Referring to Unit VIII, p. 408.

"We find that instead of almost everybody's working on a farm and being his own master, as was true in colonial times, in 1920 [1] 39.4 per cent of our people were wage earners." (*Have prepared on the board a diagram to show the proportions of wage earners to the total population.*)

"Now we can see what the title of our story for today means: The workers became machine workers and were paid by wages, instead of by selling their product."

Assimilation

Readings

Upper Group

BEARD and BAGLEY. Our Old World Background, 338–340.
SMITH. Industrial History, 237 (difficult).
World Book (Wages: Unions).

Average Group

Try the World Book.

Lower Group

The teacher reads SMITH to this group.

Teachers

BOGART. Economic History of the United States, 166, 473.

Minimal Essentials

Historical Terms: machine workers; wages
Things to Remember

During our early history most people worked for themselves and sold their own products.

With the coming of the factory system, workers became machine workers and were paid wages.

The number of wage workers is constantly increasing.

Illustrative Material

GABRIEL (ED.). Pageant of America, V: 150–159.

Procedure during Assimilation

Reading as described on pages 24–29.

Each child makes at home with the assistance of his parents a survey of the number of men and women living in his block who are working for wages.

Why is it possible that a man working for wages may not take as much interest in his work as he would if he owned the business?

Ascertain from the local Chamber of Commerce the number of wage workers in your city; the total population. Make a diagram to show the proportions.

Drill on minimal essentials.

Objective test.

[1] World Almanac (Wage Earners in the United States).

Organization

The teacher and the children working together produce an outline somewhat similar to the following:

WAGE WORKERS

1. The old system of carrying on work
2. The factory system
3. Effect on the workers

Recitation

Each row chooses a representative to tell its story. A judge decides which of the representatives tells the best story.

---

3. The workers formed labor unions

Preparation

Tell children the fable of the old man and the bundle of sticks.[1] Ask them what the story teaches.

Presentation

Suppose that Smith Brothers' factory employed five hundred men and paid them all very low wages. If John Jones did not think the wages were fair he could quit work, and Mr. Smith could easily find another man.

But if John Jones could persuade all five hundred men to quit at once, Mr. Smith would have a hard time to find so many more, and therefore might be willing to raise their wages.

Many workers saw this truth, and years ago they began to form societies of their own, called *labor unions* (*pointing to the words written on the board*). Each labor union tried to help its own members in every way. There came into being a barbers' union, a steamfitters' union, a musicians' union, a brotherhood of railway trainmen, etc.

The chief things these unions worked for were higher wages, shorter hours of labor, and better working conditions, such as better light, cleaner factories, safe machinery, etc. The unions have helped to improve the condition of the working men.

[1] *Æsop's Fables* (Stickney edition, p. 140); Edson-Laing, *Readers*, IV: 193.

PRESENTATION TEST

1. Check the best answer:

Labor unions were formed

_ _ _ because the workers wanted to get ahead of the factory owners

_ _ _ because many men together are stronger than each one alone

_ _ _ because they liked to talk things over

2. Check three answers:

The chief things that the labor unions wanted were

_ _ _ shorter hours of work

_ _ _ more officers

_ _ _ better-looking buildings to work in

_ _ _ higher wages

_ _ _ better working conditions

_ _ _ better transportation to their work

Assimilation

Readings

Upper Group

Compton's Pictured Encyclopedia (Labor Organizations, Samuel Gompers).

Lessons in Community and National Life, Series B, 241–248.

World Book (Labor Organizations, Gompers, Eight-Hour Day, Factory and Factory System, Wages).

Average Group

BEARD and BAGLEY. A First Book in American History, 422–424.

Lower Group

Read BEARD and BAGLEY to this group.

Teachers

BOGART. Economic History of the United States, 253–255, 478–480, 488–497.

COMAN. Industrial History of the United States, 276–278, 304–305, 361–367.

DEWEY. National Problems, 40–56, 288–296.

ORTH. The Armies of Labor.

OSGOOD. A History of Industry, 409–412.

SPARKS. National Development, 68–83.

American Citizenship Course in United States History, IV: 200–208.

Minimal Essentials

Name of Person: **Samuel Gompers** (gŏm'pĕrz)

Historical Terms: **American Federation of Labor; United States Department of Labor; strike**

Things to Remember

Labor unions were formed to help to secure higher wages, shorter hours of labor, and better working conditions.

When there is trouble, representatives of the labor unions talk things over with the factory owners.

Sometimes, when the trouble cannot be settled, they strike.

Illustrative Material

GABRIEL (ED.). Pageant of America, V: 279, 290, 294, 299–301.

Educational Posters of the National Child Welfare Association: Labor Day.

Procedure during Assimilation

Reading as described on pages 24–29.

Children list all the different kinds of labor unions they can find out about at home.

The teacher makes arrangements with a local labor union for a committee of children and herself to attend a meeting of the union.

Post on the bulletin board newspaper clippings about labor unions.

Show children a union card.

Children describe strikes they have heard of or seen.

Drill on minimal essentials.

Objective test.

Organization

The teacher puts the following outline on the board:

LABOR UNIONS

1. Purpose of a labor union
2. What it does for its members
3. How it works

Recitation

Children tell what points belong under each heading.

---

4. The employers formed big corporations

Preparation

"You have noticed that there are some stores and factories which use the word *company* in their trade name, such as the Morgan Company, the Standard Oil Company, the Ford Motor Company." Children list the local businesses conducted by companies.

"Another way of doing business is for two men to go into partnership." Children list local partnerships.

"And some men go into business by themselves without help from anybody." List these.

Children may add to these lists later.

"What is an employer?"

Presentation

We notice that the list of companies is much longer than the list of partnerships or individuals. Let us see why people prefer to do business as a company.

Have you ever been a member of a baseball team which wanted a mask, a ball, some bats, mitts, and gloves, but nobody could afford to buy all of them? How might the problem be solved? (Each one putting in what money he has.) To whom would the equipment belong then? (To the whole team.)

That is just the way people do business nowadays. It costs so much to run a big factory that one man seldom has enough money; even two men may not have enough. So a number of men come together, and each puts in what money he wishes to. This is a company, or, more correctly, a *corporation* (*pointing to the word on the board*). Then, if one man puts in half the money, he receives half the profits; if another man puts in one fourth of the money, he gets one fourth of the profits; and if two other men each put in one eighth of the money, they each get one eighth of the profits. If they lose, they lose in the same proportion.

Most modern business is conducted by corporations.

We found in our last story that the workers joined together and formed labor unions. So we will not be surprised now to learn that factory owners, store owners, bankers, corporations, etc. had done the same thing. They had long ago formed unions for the employers. Some of these were the Merchants' Association, The National Association of Manufacturers of the United States of America, and the various chambers of commerce.

We can see then that employers and laborers alike have found that they can do better when they work together than when they work alone.

PRESENTATION TEST

Check the best answer:

    a. A corporation is

         _ _ _ any group of people who work together

         _ _ _ a body composed of people who unite according to law to do a certain kind of business

         _ _ _ a club

    b. Employers formed unions or associations of their own

         _ _ _ because they could work together better than separately

         _ _ _ because they were afraid of the labor unions

         _ _ _ because there were so many of them

Assimilation

Readings

Upper Group

MARSHALL. The Story of Human Progress, 402–406 (difficult).
TAPPAN. An Elementary History of our Country, 246–247.
Compton's Pictured Encyclopedia (Corporations).
World Book (Corporations).

Average Group

Try TAPPAN.

Lower Group

Read and explain MARSHALL to this group.

Teachers

BOGART. Economic History of the United States, 257, 452–469, 497–498.
COMAN. Industrial History of the United States, 354–359, 367–369.
HENDRICK. The Age of Big Business, 1–57.
MOODY. Masters of Capital.
OSGOOD. A History of Industry, 404–406.
SMITH. Industrial History, 271–276, 278–281.
Baltimore County Course of Study, 571.

Minimal Essentials

Historical Terms: **corporation; employee; employer**
Things to Remember

Most modern business is done by corporations.
Employers have associations, just as the workers have labor unions.
Representatives of the employers' associations meet representatives of the labor
unions and talk over their problems.

Procedure during Assimilation

Reading as described on pages 24–29.
Complete and verify the lists of local corporations and partnerships.
Children ask their local grocers, butchers, bakers, and milkmen whether their
businesses are conducted by corporations, partnerships, or individual ownership.
A committee from the class visits the local Chamber of Commerce.
Cut out from newspapers and post on the bulletin board the names of different well-
known corporations in the United States.
Drill on minimal essentials.
Objective test.

Organization

The teacher puts the following outline on the board:

MODERN BUSINESS ORGANIZATIONS

1. Corporations
2. Associations of employers

Recitation

Children write a paragraph on each point.

---
5. Cities grew larger yet

Preparation

"Why did the growth of cities come at the same time as the factory system?

"What problems does living in cities present which living in villages or in the country does not?

"Since we have found that after the Civil War the products of our factories increased so greatly, what shall we expect to find true of the size of American cities?"

Assimilation

Readings

Upper Group

SMITH. Industrial History, 238–239 (difficult).
VOLLINTINE. The Making of America, 249–253.
Compton's Pictured Encyclopedia (Cities, p. 770).
World Book (City: Fifty Largest Cities in the United States).

Average Group

GORDY. Elementary History of the United States, 312–313.

Lower Group

Try GORDY.

Teachers

BOGART. Economic History of the United States, 256–257.
American Citizenship Course in United States History, IV: 181–185.

Minimal Essentials

Things to Remember

Cities grew larger as the factory system spread.
Today we are a nation of city dwellers.

Illustrative Material

Ford Educational Library: 44, New York City; 26, Dynamic Detroit.
Society for Visual Education. Picturols: New York City, Boston, Cleveland, Detroit, Chicago, Minneapolis, New Orleans, Los Angeles, San Francisco, Seattle.

Procedure during Assimilation

Reading as described on pages 24–29.
Picture study based on the illustrative material listed above.
Read aloud to the children Walt Whitman's "Song of the Broad-Axe."
Use the diagram in the *American Citizenship Course in United States History*, IV: p. 181, on city growth to 1915; Sparks's *Expansion of the American People*, p. 427, shows a graph of city growth from 1790 to 1890.
Children choose from the list of United States cities given in the World Almanac ten to graph for the period from 1860 to 1920.

Organization

Making the graph referred to above.

Recitation

Explaining the graph.
A drill lesson on section III of Unit XI should be given at this point.

> IV. Scientific Agriculture was Necessary to provide Food for our Huge Population
>   1. Further improvements in farm machinery were made

Preparation

"Who was the great inventor of farm machinery of whom we learned in Unit VII? What did he invent? What work did the reaper do?

"You may be sure that invention did not stop with the reaper as McCormick first made it. One man saw an improvement here, another saw an improvement there, still another invented a machine to do a different kind of farm work, until today we have a surprising number of machines doing a wide variety of work on our modern farms.

"Let us make a list of machines you have seen working on farms."

The list is begun here, and is completed during the step of assimiliation.

No additional presentation is needed.

Assimilation

Readings

Upper Group

BROOKS. The Story of Cotton, 224–230.
DARROW. Thinkers and Doers, 167–170 (difficult).
FORMAN. Stories of Useful Inventions, 84, 93–96.
MOWRY. American Inventions and Inventors, 111–123.
SANFORD. The Story of Agriculture in the United States, 210–212, 246 (difficult).
SMITH. Industrial History, 243–246 (difficult).
WOODBURN and MORAN. Makers of America, 302.
World Book (Agriculture: Causes of Progress — Machinery).

Average Group

> BRIGHAM and McFARLANE. Essentials of Geography, I : 16.
> GORDY. Elementary History of the United States, 282–283.
> Lessons in Community and National Life, Series C, 89–96.

Lower Group

> Try GORDY, and BRIGHAM and McFARLANE.

Teachers

> BOGART. Economic History of the United States, 277–283, 310–311, 332–334.
> HENDRICK. The Age of Big Business, 149–169.
> THOMPSON. The Age of Invention, 118–127.

Minimal Essentials

Historical Terms: **harvester; tractor; twine binder**
Things to Remember [1]
> Machinery saved labor and time.
> It made possible much greater crops.
> Farmers now do not have to work so hard.
> The farmer has become a business man.

Illustrative Material

GABRIEL (ED.). Pageant of America, III : 211–215, 220–228, 229–234.
Keystone Views: 295, Plowing on a Prairie Farm; 296, Modern American Harvesting
  Machine; 297, Modern Harvester; 298, Orchard Tractor Drawing Spring Tooth Harrow;
  299, Digging Potatoes.
Perry Pictures: 7510, Harvester at Work, Prairies.
Society for Visual Education. Picturol: Farm Conveniences.

Procedure during Assimilation

Reading as described on pages 24–29.
Picture study based on the illustrative material listed above.
Complete the list of farm machinery referred to on page 579.
Cut from farm magazines and farm-implement catalogues the pictures of different
  kinds of farm machinery. Post on the bulletin board.
Invite a farm boy from the upper grades to talk to the children on the care of farm
  machinery.
Take the children to a farm-implement store to see the different implements. If
  possible visit a farm to see these in operation.
Use the diagram in the World Book, p. 95.
Drill on minimal essentials.
Objective test.

Organization

Each child prepares to explain the work of one type of farm
machine.

Recitation

The explanations of the different machines.

---

[1] From Sanford's *Story of Agriculture in the United States*, pp. 210–212, 246.

> 2. Crops were planned more wisely

Preparation

"Is it a good thing to plant always the same crop in the same field? Why not?"

Draw on the board three identical diagrams of a farm containing five large fields. Children tell what crops the farm might contain the first year. These are recorded on the board. Then they arrange a different order for the second and third years. These are recorded also.

"Will anything else help to increase the crops grown here this year (*referring to the first diagram*)?"

"In our reading today we shall find how it became possible to plan crops more wisely."

Assimilation
Readings
Upper Group

BARROWS and PARKER. United States and Canada, 94–95.
BROOKS. The Story of Cotton, 280–290, 302–313, 317–328.
PERRY and PRICE. American History, II : 248.
SANFORD. The Story of Agriculture in the United States, 282–322 (difficult).
SMITH. Our Neighborhood, 84–94, 211–228.
WOODBURN and MORAN. Makers of America, 297–298, 300–302.
Compton's Pictured Encyclopedia (Agriculture).
World Book (Scientific Agriculture).

Average Group

Try PERRY and PRICE.

Lower Group

Read PERRY and PRICE to this group.

Teachers

BOGART. Economic History of the United States, 284, 340–341.
COMAN. Industrial History of the United States, 395–398.
SMITH. Industrial History, 246–248.

Minimal Essentials

Historical Terms: **codling moth; United States Department of Agriculture; fertilizer; rotation of crops**
Things to Remember

Fertilization is necessary so that land may not be worn out.
Rotation of crops helps, because different crops do not take the same things from the soil.
Spraying helps to keep down insect pests.
Science has helped farming.

Illustrative Material

Compton's Pictured Encyclopedia (Agriculture, p. 45: diagram; United States, p. 3591: Relative Value of Farm Products in the United States (diagram)).

Procedure during Assimilation

Reading as described on pages 24–29.
Picture study based on the illustrative material listed above.
Invite a farm boy from the upper grades to give an illustrated talk on how his father rotates crops.
Show samples of commercial fertilizers.
Plan to fertilize the school flower gardens.
Use the exercises suggested in Smith's *Our Neighborhood*, pp. 84–94, 211–229.
Send to the United States Department of Agriculture for a list of their bulletins on planning crops; select and send for those which are easiest to understand.
Drill on minimal essentials.
Objective test.

Organization

The teacher and the children working together produce an outline somewhat similar to the following:

SCIENCE AS A HELP TO AGRICULTURE

> 1. Fertilization
> 2. Rotation of crops
> 3. Spraying

Recitation

Children tell what points belong under each heading.

---

3. Work of Luther Burbank

Preparation

"Did any of you ever hear of grafting one plant on another?
"Did you ever hear of Luther Burbank?
"Our story today is about a man who produced new plants that the world had never seen before: white blackberries, seedless oranges, spineless cactuses. His name was Luther Burbank."
No additional presentation is needed.

Assimilation

Readings

Upper Group

GORDY. Leaders in Making America, 424–429.
SANFORD and OWEN. Modern Americans, 57–64.

SLUSSER and Others. Stories of Luther Burbank and his Plant School.
STIMPSON. Child's Book of American Biography, 229–235.
TAPPAN. Heroes of Progress, 106–115.
Compton's Pictured Encyclopedia (Burbank).
World Book (Burbank).

Average Group

TATE, WITHERS, and BROWNE. Child's World, V: 308–313.
WADE. The Wonder Workers, 1–33.

Lower Group

EVERETT and REED. When they were Boys, 128–134.
MIRICK and HOLMES. Home Life around the World, 128–133.

Teachers

HARWOOD. New Creations in Plant Life.
WHITSON (ED.). Luther Burbank : his Methods and Discoveries.

Minimal Essentials

Name of Person: **Luther Burbank** (bûr′băŋk)
Historical Terms: **grafting; "the plant wizard"**
Things to Remember

Burbank improved old plants and produced new ones.
He added as much to the national wealth as men who make new machines.

Illustrative Material

Compton's Pictured Encyclopedia (Burbank).
Ford Educational Library : 34, Luther Burbank.
Mentor, XI : 3–16 (August, 1923) : Burbank.

Procedure during Assimilation

Reading as described on pages 24–29.
Picture study based on the illustrative material listed above.
Look through seed catalogues for Burbank products.
Visit the local greenhouse to see new varieties of plants.
Ask the high-school teacher of botany to demonstrate grafting plants.
Drill on minimal essentials.
Objective test.

Organization

The teacher and the children working together produce an outline somewhat similar to the following :

WORK OF LUTHER BURBANK

1. Early struggle
2. Success with plants

Recitation

Half the class prepares to recite on one point, and half on the other.

---
4. Flour mills were improved

Preparation

Show the children some grains of wheat. They try to remove the colored bran coats with a pin.

"How did the Indians grind their corn?

"How did the old water mills work?

"What is bran? What are middlings?

"Can you see why it is difficult to produce pure-white flour?

"Why do Americans want pure-white flour? Which is more healthful: white bread or whole-wheat bread?

"We are going to read today about the way flour is made in the most up-to-date mills."

No additional presentation is required.

Assimilation
Readings
Upper Group

CARPENTER. How the World is Fed, 37–43.

FORMAN. Stories of Useful Inventions, 108.

HUSBAND. America at Work, 79–88.

LEFFERTS. Our own United States, 207–209.

ROCHELEAU. The Story of Wheat.

SANFORD. The Story of Agriculture in the United States, 213–218 (difficult).

Compton's Pictured Encyclopedia (Flour and Flour Milling).

World Book (Flour: How Flour is Made).

Average Group

FRYE. New Geography, I: 100–101.

Washburn-Crosby Co., Minneapolis. Wheat and Flour (free booklet).

Lower Group

CARROLL and CARROLL. Around the World, III: 76–79.

CHAMBERLAIN. How we are Fed, 7–17.

Teachers

VULTÉ and VANDERBILT. Food Industries, 64–78.

Encyclopædia Britannica (Flour and Flour Manufacture).

New International Encyclopædia (Flour and Flour Milling).

Minimal Essentials

Historical Terms: **gristmills; roller mills**

Things to Remember

In former times the whole wheat kernel was ground into flour.

Now the outside coverings are removed.

The white part is ground between many rollers.

Then the flour is sifted.

Illustrative Material

Compton's Pictured Encyclopedia (Flour and Flour Milling).
Ford Educational Library: 40, Wheat and Flour.

Procedure during Assimilation

Reading as described on pages 24–29.
Picture study based on the illustrative material listed above.
An educational exhibit of charts etc. may sometimes be obtained from a flour-milling company and used as a basis for classroom study.
Exhibit on the bulletin board all the stages in the manufacture of flour.[1]
If possible take the children to visit a flour mill.
Drill on minimal essentials.
Objective test.

Organization

Children make their own outlines, the teacher supplying only the two headings:

IMPROVEMENTS IN MILLING

1. Old ways of grinding wheat
2. Present-day methods

Recitation

Children explain the exhibit as an assembly exercise.

V. We began to realize that our National Resources had
    been Sadly Wasted
  1. Forests and mineral resources were protected

Preparation and Presentation

"What is the Boy Scout rule about putting out camp fires? Why was it made?

"Have you seen in the moving pictures incidents about forest rangers? What is their work?

"Most of the coal fields in Alaska belong to the government. Those in older parts of the country are owned usually by corporations. Why was a different policy followed in Alaska? Who paid for Alaska? Then to whom should the wealth belong?

[1] *The Twentieth Yearbook of the National Society for the Study of Education*, Part I, pp. 40–41.

"Can you name any ways in which trees were wasted in the early days? It is easy to see how forests can be protected against waste now. Mention some ways.

"It is not so easy to see how mineral resources can be protected against waste. Can anyone think of a way? Let us read to find out."

Assimilation

Readings

Upper Group

ALLEN. United States, 282–283.
CHAMBERLAIN. North America, 282–287.
CRUMP. Boys' Book of Forest Rangers.
FAIRBANKS. Conservation Reader, 89–95, 112–138, 155–161.
FAIRBANKS. The Western United States, 290–294.
MARSHALL. The Story of Human Progress, 180–188, 195–204 (difficult).
PARSONS. The Land of Fair Play, 88.
ROLT-WHEELER. The Boy with the United States Foresters.
Compton's Pictured Encyclopedia (Conservation, pp. 869–870).
World Book (Conservation, Coal, Forests and Forestry).

Average Group

BEARD and BAGLEY. A First Book in American History, 422.
GORDY. Elementary History of the United States, 313–314.
MORRIS. Primary History of the United States, 231.
REINSCH. Young Citizens' Reader, 97–101.
Lessons in Community and National Life, Series C, 49–56.

Lower Group

BAILEY. What to do for Uncle Sam, 163–169.
MIRICK and HOLMES. Home Life around the World, 134–146.

Teachers

COMAN. Industrial History of the United States, 378–381, 384–386, 398–400.
ELY and Others. Foundations of National Prosperity.
TOWNE. Social Problems, 307–331.
American Citizenship Course in United States History, IV: 210–211.

Minimal Essentials

Name of Person: Gifford Pinchot (gĭf'ẽrd pĭn'shō)
Historical Terms: conservation; forest rangers; natural resources
Things to Remember

Our forests protect the land from floods.
They are sources of supply for lumber.
New trees should be grown when trees are cut down.
Our minerals should be used carefully.
Owners should not be allowed to mine only the part on which they can make a big profit.

Illustrative Material

Ford Educational Library: 224, Timberlust.
Keystone Views: 254, Navy Coal Reservation in Alaska.

Procedure during Assimilation

Reading as described on pages 24–29.

Picture study based on the illustrative material listed above.

Children who have read stories of forest rangers report on them.

Write to the State Conservation Commission for information on forest reserves, or government forest lands.

Report on tree surgery. Arrange for a demonstration, if possible.

Drill on minimal essentials.

Objective test.

Organization

Prepare a conservation program for Arbor Day.

Recitation

The program.

> 2. Fisheries and game were protected

Preparation

"Can a man hunt in this state any time of year that he wants to? Why not? What are some of the game laws?

"Can a man fish any time of year that he wants to? Can he catch as many fish as he wants to? Are there any laws protecting the fish?

"Have you ever heard of the Izaak Walton League?"

No additional presentation is needed.

Assimilation

Readings

Upper Group

ALLEN. United States, 313–317.

FAIRBANKS. Conservation Reader, 162–170, 176–212.

ROLT-WHEELER. The Boy with the United States Fisheries.

SMITH. Our Neighborhood, 181–198.

World Book (Birds: Bird Reservations).

Average Group

Read SMITH.

Lower Group

BAILEY. What to do for Uncle Sam, 56–62, 160–162, 166.

Teachers

COMAN. Industrial History of the United States, 375–378, 389–390.

TOWNE. Social Problems, 345–349.

VAN HISE. Conservation of Natural Resources in the United States.

Public School Methods, V: 483–505. (The Methods Co., Chicago.)

Minimal Essentials

Historical Terms: **closed season; fish hatchery; game laws**
Things to Remember

Game is protected by a closed season.
Fish are protected by laws as to the kind, number, and size that can be taken.
Certain birds may not be shot; for others there is a closed season; others may
be shot at any time.
Game preserves and fish hatcheries have been set up by the government.

Illustrative Material

GABRIEL (ED.). Pageant of America, III: 311–314.

Procedure during Assimilation

Reading as described on pages 24–29.
Some states issue with the hunting license a little pamphlet on the game and fish
laws. If your state does so, secure a copy to show to the children.
A visitor to a state fish hatchery describes it to the children.
If possible arrange for a committee of children to attend a meeting of the local
Izaak Walton League.
Use the tabulation as to the work of birds given in Bailey's *What to do for Uncle Sam*,
pp. 161–162.
Write to the State Conservation Commission for information on the game laws in
your state.
Drill on minimal essentials.
Objective test.

Organization

Add this story to the Arbor Day program suggested on
page 587.

Recitation

The Arbor Day program.

---

3. Irrigation was begun in the West

Preparation

"Our geographies tell us that an average of twenty inches
of rainfall a year is necessary to grow crops."

Show a rainfall map of the United States.[1] Children point
out which regions have less than twenty inches.

"Then is it true that no crops at all can be grown here?
Have you ever heard of irrigation?

[1] Such as in Brigham, A. P., and McFarlane, C. T., *Essentials of Geography*,
Book II, p. 42; Atwood, W. W., *New Geography*, Book II, p. 82; McMurry, F. M.,
and Parkins, A. E., *Advanced Geography*, p. 28.

"Let us read to find out how crops may be grown in some regions of less than twenty inches' average rainfall."
No additional presentation is needed.

Assimilation

Readings

Upper Group

BARROWS and PARKER. United States and Canada, 55–57, 83.
CHAMBERLAIN. North America, 290–295.
FAIRBANKS. The Western United States, 259–267.
FARIS. Where our History was Made, II : 207–222.
GORDY. Leaders in Making America, 385–388 (Powell).
LEFFERTS. Our Own United States, 223–227.
SANFORD. The Story of Agriculture in the United States, 338–342 (difficult).
Compton's Pictured Encyclopedia (Irrigation).
World Book (Irrigation).

Average Group

BEARD and BAGLEY. A First Book in American History, 421–422.
GORDY. Elementary History of the United States, 286–288.
REINSCH. Young Citizen's Reader, 101–102.
SMITH. Human Geography, I : 93–94.
TARR and McMURRY. New Geographies, I : 147.
Lessons in Community and National Life, Series C, 41–48.

Lower Group

ALLEN. How and Where we Live, 71–72.
DAVIDSON and ANDERSON. Lincoln Readers, V : 236–240.
WINSLOW. The Earth and its People, 75–76.

Teachers

BOGART. Economic History of the United States, 341–344.
COMAN. Industrial History of the United States, 401–405.
American Citizenship Course in United States History, IV : 208–210.

Minimal Essentials

Names of Persons: **Brigham Young; Mormons**
Names of Places: **Great Salt Lake; the Great American Desert**
Historical Term: **irrigation**
Things to Remember
In many of our deserts the soil is good, and only water is needed.
Water can be brought from long distances and distributed by irrigation ditches.
Much land has been reclaimed for use by irrigation.

Illustrative Material

GABRIEL (ED.). Pageant of America, III : 234–238.
McKINLEY. Illustrated Topics in American History : S. 39.
SANFORD. Story of Agriculture in the United States, 339 (map).
Ford Educational Library : 35, Irrigation.

Society for Visual Education. Picturol: Irrigation.
Society for Visual Education. Schoolfilm: Reclaiming Arid Land by Irrigation; Making the
　Desert Blossom.
United States Bureau of Reclamation. Motion Picture Reels: Making the Desert Blossom
　(general reclamation reel).

Procedure during Assimilation

Reading as described on pages 24–29.
Picture study based on the illustrative material listed above.
For suggestions on the teaching of irrigation see Charles A. McMurry's *Teaching
　by Projects*, pp. 189–236, and Charles A. and Frank M. McMurry's *Method of
　the Recitation*, pp. 257–269.
In the sand table set up an irrigation system that will work.
Study a map of "Irrigation Projects of the United States Government."[1]
Drill on minimal essentials.
Objective test.

Organization

The teacher puts the following outline on the board:

IRRIGATION IN THE UNITED STATES

　　1. Method of irrigating
　　2. Work of the Mormons
　　3. Work of the government

Recitation

Each child prepares to tell the entire story.

A drill lesson on sections IV and V of Unit XI should be
given at this point similar to that described on pages 40–43.

TESTS ON THE ENTIRE UNIT

(To be given after all the stories are completed)

Test of Place-Sense. Pass outline maps of North America.
Give the following directions:

　　1. Print *Great American Desert* in the right place.
　　2. Put a cross (X) in the Great Salt Lake.
　　3. Print the word *Klondike* in the right place.
　　4. Trace the Yukon River in yellow crayon.

[1] Sanford, A. H., *The Story of Agriculture in the United States*, p. 339.

MINIMAL ESSENTIALS OF UNIT XI

PERSONS	PLACES	TERMS		DATES
Luther Burbank	Great American Desert	age of electricity	merchant marine	1879. The electric light first used
Andrew Carnegie	Great Salt Lake	age of steel	moving pictures	
Thomas A. Edison	Klondike	American Federation of Labor	natural resources	Drill on the peaks of the time chart
Samuel Gompers	Yukon	assembling	New South	
Charles Goodyear		Canadian Pacific Line	patent	
Marconi		Chinese Exclusion Act	Patent Office	
Mormons		closed season	phonograph	
Gifford Pinchot		codling moth	"plant wizard"	
Brigham Young		conservation	prospector	
		copyright	roller mills	
		corporation	rotation of crops	
		Cunard Line	standard parts	
		employee	strike	
		employer	surplus	
		export	tractor	
		fertilizer	trade-mark	
		fish hatchery	trolley car	
		forest rangers	typewriter	
		game laws	twine binder	
		grafting	United States Department of Agriculture	
		gristmills	United States Department of Labor	
		harvester	United States Steel Corporation	
		immigrant	vulcanization	
		immigration	wages	
		import	White Star Line	
		interchangeable parts	"Wizard of Menlo Park"	
		irrigation		
		machine workers		
		markets		

Test of Time-Sense. Pass mimeographed sheets of the following:

1. Here is a list of persons. Put the figure 1 before the name of the man who did his great work first, the figure 2 before the name of the one who was next, and so on.

       _ _ _ Marconi
       _ _ _ Charles Goodyear
       _ _ _ Samuel Gompers

2. Here is another list. Do the same.

       _ _ _ Luther Burbank
       _ _ _ Mormons
       _ _ _ Cyrus McCormick

3. Here is another list. Do the same.

       _ _ _ Brigham Young
       _ _ _ Andrew Carnegie
       _ _ _ Alexander Hamilton

4. Here is another list. Do the same.

       _ _ _ Thomas A. Edison
       _ _ _ Robert Fulton
       _ _ _ James J. Hill

5. Here is another list. Do the same.

       _ _ _ Andrew Jackson
       _ _ _ Gifford Pinchot
       _ _ _ Audubon

6. Here is a list of events. Put the figure 1 before that which came first, the figure 2 before that which came next, and so on.

       _ _ _ invention of the telegraph
       _ _ _ invention of the telephone
       _ _ _ invention of the phonograph

Test on Persons. Pass mimeographed sheets of the following:

Here is a list of names:

Samuel Gompers	Luther Burbank
Marconi	Mormons
Gifford Pinchot	Charles Goodyear
Andrew Carnegie	Thomas A. Edison
Brigham Young	

Put each name in the right blank in the sentences below:

1. _ _ _ _ _ _ _ _ _ _ _ _ made the electric light usable.
2. _ _ _ _ _ _ _ _ was a leader for conservation.
3. The man who vulcanized rubber was _ _ _ _ _ _ _ _.

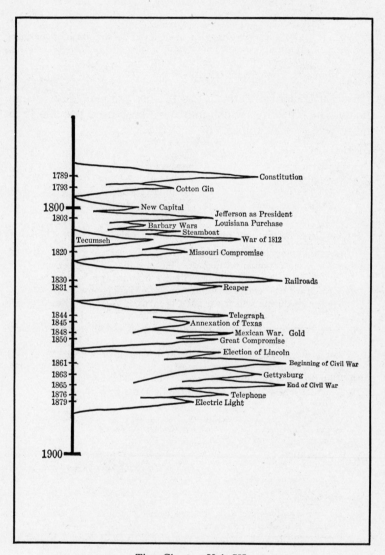

Time Chart — Unit XI

4. A great labor leader was _ _ _ _ _ _ _ _.

5. The " plant wizard " was _ _ _ _ _ _ _ _.

6. _ _ _ _ discovered the use of the wireless.

7. _ _ _ _ _ _ _ _ earned a great deal of money in the steel business and gave much of it to libraries.

8. The _ _ _ _ began irrigation in the West.

9. _ _ _ _ _ _ _ _ was their leader.

Test on Historical Terms. The teacher prepares descriptions such as the following, which may have been used previously as the subject of drill games.

I. Here is a list of terms:

patent	prospector
immigrant	irrigation
corporation	age of electricity
White Star Line	"Wizard of Menlo Park"
import	markets

Put each term in the right blank in the sentences below:

1. Edison is sometimes called the _ _ _ _ _ _ _ _ _ _ _ _ _ _ _ _.

2. A _ _ _ _ is a company which does business like a single person.

3. That which is brought into one country from another is an _ _ _ _.

4. A foreigner who enters a country to settle there is an _ _ _ _.

5. The years during which we have been using so much electricity are called the _ _ _ _ _ _ _ _ _ _ _ _.

6. A government grant to an inventor which gives only to him the right to sell his invention is a _ _ _ _.

7. The places where our products are in demand are our _ _ _ _.

8. One who searches for minerals is a _ _ _ _.

9. Watering land by ditches is _ _ _ _.

10. A famous line of vessels on the Atlantic is the _ _ _ _ _ _ _ _ _ _ _ _.

II. Here is another list:

vulcanization	employer
strike	claim
Patent Office	age of steel
machine workers	United States Steel Corporation
interchangeable parts	surplus

Do the same.

1. Anyone who uses the work of other people whom he pays is an _ _ _ _.

2. A tract of land which a miner has a right to call his own is a _ _ _ _.

3. One of the largest companies engaged in making steel is called the _ _ _ _ _ _ _ _ _ _ _ _ _ _ _ _.

4. The quitting of work by a body of laborers is a _ _ _ _.

5. The part of the government which attends to the giving of patents is the _ _ _ _ _ _ _ _.

6. The process of heating rubber and treating it with sulphur is _ _ _ _.

7. Anything that remains over and above what is used or needed is a _ _ _ _.

8. Parts of one machine which can be changed for similar parts of a similar machine are called _ _ _ _ _ _ _ _.

9. Laborers who work at machines are called _ _ _ _ _ _ _ _.

10. The time during which much steel is used is called the _ _ _ _ _ _ _ _ _ _ _ _.

III. Here is another list:

assembling	merchant marine
Cunard Line	phonograph
exports	standard parts
immigration	tractor
twine binder	wireless telephone

Do the same.

1. The entrance of settlers from a foreign country is called _ _ _ _.

2. An engine which pulls farm machinery is a _ _ _ _.

3. Any goods sent out of one country to another are _ _ _ _.

4. A machine which records and then gives forth sounds is a _ _ _ _.

5. Joining together the parts of a machine is called _ _ _ _.

6. A machine which ties up grain with heavy cord is a _ _ _ _ _ _ _ _.

7. Ships used for commerce and trade on the high seas are the _ _ _ _ _ _ _ _.

8. A famous line of ships on the Atlantic is the _ _ _ _ _ _ _ _.

9. Similar parts which are of exactly the same size and material are _ _ _ _ _ _ _ _.

10. An instrument which sends sounds through the air without wires is called the _ _ _ _ _ _ _ _.

IV. Here is another list:

wages	gristmills
rotation of crops	United States Department of Labor
trade-mark	Canadian Pacific Line
New South	Chinese Exclusion Act
fish hatchery	moving pictures

Do the same.

1. Rapidly changing pictures thrown on a screen are _ _ _ _ _ _ _ _.

2. A place where fish eggs are hatched is a _ _ _ _ _ _ _ _.

3. A famous line of vessels on both the Pacific and the Atlantic is the _ _ _ _ _ _ _ _ _ _ _ _.

4. The particular mark used by a manufacturer to show that certain goods were made by him is a _ _ _ _.

5. Mills which grind grain by crushing it between two stones are called _ _ _ _.

6. Since the South has started many industries, it is often called the _ _ _ _ _ _ _ _.

7. The law of Congress which forbids Chinese to come into our country to live or to work is the _ _ _ _ _ _ _ _ _ _ _ _.

8. The certain fixed sum of money paid to laborers is called _ _ _ _.

9. The part of the government which attends particularly to the interests of laboring people is the _ _ _ _ _ _ _ _ _ _ _ _ _ _ _ _ _ _ _ _.

10. Changing crops about by turns is called _ _ _ _ _ _ _ _ _ _ _ _.

V. Here is another list:

American Federation of Labor natural resources
conservation "plant wizard"
codling moth roller mills
employee trolley car
forest ranger fertilizer

Do the same.

1. Burbank was often called the _ _ _ _ _ _ _ _.

2. One who works for wages or a salary in the service of another is an _ _ _ _.

3. Keeping or protecting natural resources from injury is _ _ _ _.

4. Material to make land more productive is _ _ _ _.

5. All the trade unions in the United States and Canada together make up the _ _ _ _ _ _ _ _ _ _ _ _ _ _ _ _.

6. Mills which grind grain by passing it between heavy rollers are _ _ _ _ _ _ _ _.

7. A street car is a _ _ _ _ _ _ _ _.

8. The advantages that nature has supplied a country are its _ _ _ _ _ _ _ _.

9. A man who guards tracts of woods for the state is a _ _ _ _ _ _ _ _.

10. A great pest of apple orchards is the _ _ _ _ _ _ _ _.

VI. Here is another list.

closed season United States Department of
copyright Agriculture
harvester grafting
typewriter game laws

Do the same.

1. A machine used to take the place of writing with a pen or pencil is a _ _ _ _.

2. The time when it is against the law to shoot certain game is the _ _ _ _ _ _ _ _.

3. The part of the government which attends particularly to the business of farming is the _ _ _ _ _ _ _ _ _ _ _ _ _ _ _ _ _ _ _ _.

4. To fasten a shoot from one tree into another so that it will grow is called _ _ _ _.

5. Laws to protect game are _ _ _ _ _ _ _ _.

6. A machine used in reaping or gathering crops is a _ _ _ _.

7. The right that the government gives to an author so that only he may sell his works is called a _ _ _ _.

COMPREHENSION TEST ON UNIT XI

1. *Check the best answer:*

 a. Much land in the West was made useful for agriculture by

  ___ buying it from Canada

  ___ irrigation

  ___ inventing new machinery

 b. An improvement in method of grinding wheat was

  ___ to pass it between heavy rollers

  ___ to grind it between an upper and a lower stone

  ___ to grind it by chopping

 c. As the factory system spread, cities

  ___ grew worse

  ___ grew smaller

  ___ grew larger

 d. A record of all inventions is kept

  ___ in the Patent Office

  ___ in the United States Department of Labor

  ___ in the United States Department of Agriculture

 e. Steamships had to be greatly improved

  ___ because it was so far to go to the other continents

  ___ because other countries improved their ships

  ___ because they had to carry so many more goods for export

2. *Check five answers:*

 We learned that we must pass laws to protect from waste

  ___ our forests

  ___ our soil

  ___ our air

  ___ our birds

  ___ our minerals

  ___ our water

  ___ our game

  ___ our smoke

  ___ our fish

3. *Check the best answer:*

 a. The man who did most to improve plants was

  ___ Thomas A. Edison

  ___ Luther Burbank

  ___ Marconi

 b. Just as the laborers formed unions, the employers

  ___ destroyed the labor unions

  ___ joined the labor unions

  ___ formed associations of their own

c. One of the greatest improvements in making machines was

_ _ _ to make them with interchangeable parts

_ _ _ to make them of better materials

_ _ _ to make more of them

d. We had to find new markets

_ _ _ because the old ones were worn out

_ _ _ because we did not want any other country to have them

_ _ _ because we produced such great quantities of goods

e. One of the greatest improvements in agriculture was

_ _ _ to plan the crops more wisely

_ _ _ to build larger barns

_ _ _ to buy more land

f. Workers formed labor unions

_ _ _ because the employers formed associations of their own

_ _ _ because they could elect officers and have a club of their own

_ _ _ because, all together, they could accomplish more than each man working alone

4. *Check five answers:*

The following inventions were made during this period:

_ _ _ the locomotive   _ _ _ the photograph

_ _ _ the typewriter   _ _ _ the automobile

_ _ _ the cotton gin   _ _ _ moving pictures

_ _ _ the phonograph   _ _ _ the trolley car

_ _ _ wireless telegraphy

5. *Check the best answer:*

a. A new kind of power that we began to use was

_ _ _ steam

_ _ _ electricity

_ _ _ hand power

b. Most workers were paid at this time

_ _ _ by wages

_ _ _ by selling their own product

_ _ _ by working land

c. A new material that we learned to use was

_ _ _ cotton

_ _ _ rubber

_ _ _ wool

d. Our population increased faster than it ever had before

_ _ _ because more children were born

_ _ _ because fewer people died

_ _ _ because many immigrants came

6. *Check* **three** *answers:*

The following industries grew to a huge size during this period:

_ _ _ embroidering
_ _ _ mining
_ _ _ sewing by hand
_ _ _ textile manufactures
_ _ _ painting
_ _ _ iron and steel manufactures
_ _ _ making pottery
_ _ _ lumbering

7. *What is the title of Unit XI?*

ORGANIZATION OF THE UNIT AS A WHOLE

Children are supplied with mimeographed or hectographed sheets containing the name of the Unit and the names of the stories comprising the Unit.

They are to decide what bearing each story has upon the Roman-numeraled subhead under which it stands, and what bearing each story and subhead have upon the title of the Unit as a whole.

Hold a "stunt day," when original plays, dramatizations, and other projects worked out during the Unit are presented. The teacher has nothing to do with the planning of the program, which is the class's surprise for its guests.

RECITATION OF THE UNIT AS A WHOLE

Telling the relationships mentioned above.
Giving the "stunts."

UNIT XII

HOW THE UNITED STATES BECAME A WORLD POWER

I. During its Early History the United States had Little to do with Other Countries.
The Monroe Doctrine made it the guardian of the Western Hemisphere.

II. When the Nation obtained Lands far from Home, it had to become a World Power.
1. Hawaii was annexed.
2. The war with Spain added the Philippines and Porto Rico.
  a. The causes of the war.
  b. The Spanish-American War.
  c. The Philippines.
  d. Porto Rico.
  e. The United States helped Cuba to become a republic.
3. The United States helped to secure the "open door" in China.
4. The United States obtained the Canal Zone and built the Panama Canal.
5. Life of Theodore Roosevelt.
6. The United States bought the Virgin Islands.
7. The policy with regard to Mexico was "watchful waiting."

III. The United States joined the Allies in the World War.
1. Causes of the war.
2. The war from 1914 to 1917.
3. Entrance of the United States into the war and her part in it.
4. End of the war.
5. Refusal of the United States to enter the League of Nations.

IV. At Home also the United States had been growing more Powerful.
1. It led the world in the manufacture of automobiles.
2. In aircraft it made a good beginning.
3. Submarines were invented.
4. It had made two amendments to the Constitution.
5. It had taken part in polar exploration.
6. It called a disarmament conference.

V. Our Unsolved Problems.
1. What to do with subject races.
2. How to make our own citizens obey our laws.
3. The relations between capital and labor.

PREPARATION FOR THE OVERVIEW

"Since the United States had become a nation, how many wars had we had with other countries?" (Only two.) "In how many years?" (Up to 1898.) (*The teacher turns to the*

600

*board and puts the figures down: 1898 minus 1783. Some child
tells the remainder.)* "Only two wars in one hundred and fifteen
years is not a bad record.

"Can you see any reason why we had had little to do with
other countries?" (Geographical location.)

"Which do you think is better: to have a country hold one
territory, like the United States *(illustrating at the map)*, or
territory scattered about, like the British Empire?" *(Illustrating.)* Give arguments on both sides.

PRESENTATION OR OVERVIEW

As we have just seen, during its early history the United
States had little to do with other countries. Our people were
busy cutting down the forests and making homes for themselves; they had little time to travel. They made their own
clothes and furniture and traded little. For these reasons it
was very easy for them to stay by themselves. George Washington thought that was the best thing to do.

As the years went by, conditions changed greatly. Americans did not have to work all the time: they traveled and
became interested in other people. Foreigners also came here
in great numbers — some to travel, others to live. We were
no longer a lonely nation.

The greatest reason for the change, however, was the huge
production of our factories. We had to sell some of our goods
that we couldn't use, and therefore had to become interested
in lands far away. One cannot "stay at home and mind his
business," and at the same time sell his goods at the corners
of the earth. Selling his goods becomes his business.

We no longer, then, stayed by ourselves. We had to mingle
with European countries. What hurt them hurt us too, because when they were poor they couldn't buy our goods.

Americans began to own property in all parts of the world
— sugar fields in Cuba, herds of cattle in Argentina, gold
mines in Australia, tobacco crops in Turkey.

When our little neighbor Cuba *(illustrating at the map)* was
badly used by Spain, we felt very sorry for her and wanted

to do something about it. Americans who owned property there were losing money, too. In consequence we went to war with Spain, for Spain owned Cuba. The war did not last long. When it was over, we found ourselves owning some of these islands in the Caribbean and some away over here near China (*illustrating at the map*).

Now, whenever a war breaks out in China, we fear for the safety of these islands (*showing the Philippines at the map*); and when a war breaks out between Germany and England, we fear that one of them will want to go through the Panama Canal (*map*). If Japan threatens us our minds turn to these islands (Hawaii). No longer can we say, "Let the other countries do what they please; it is none of our business." The United States had always been a power in North America; now she has become a world power.

To prove how true these statements are, let me tell you what happened next. You have heard about the World War. Some of your fathers and brothers fought in it. At the beginning Germany and England and France and most of the other countries were fighting in Europe. Of course we could have kept all our ships and all our people at home and have taken no part in it. But who would have bought our goods? We either had to sell our goods, or many factories would close their doors, and their working people would go hungry. We kept sending out our trading ships as before, and the warring countries blew them up by means of their submarines, or captured them.

Then America entered the war, and showed once more that she was a world power. The problems of the rest of the world, even though they are not our problems, have a direct effect on us, because today people all over the world are our customers.

PRESENTATION TEST

1. *Check the best answer:*

    a. During our early history the United States

        _ _ _ was a world power

        _ _ _ had little to do with other countries

        _ _ _ kept quarreling with other countries

b. The reason why we changed was

    _ _ _ because we had to sell our goods to other nations
    _ _ _ because we decided we wanted more land
    _ _ _ because we wanted to be a world power

2. *Check two answers:*

The reasons why we went to war with Spain were

    _ _ _ because Spain bothered us
    _ _ _ because Spain used Cuba badly
    _ _ _ because Americans owned property in Cuba
    _ _ _ because we wanted to show that we were stronger than Spain

3. *Check the best answer:*

a. After the Spanish-American War we had to be a world power whether we
    wanted to or not

    _ _ _ because we wanted to interfere with Europe
    _ _ _ because we owned land all over the world
    _ _ _ because we had beaten Spain

b. America had to enter the World War

    _ _ _ because Germany was beating the Allies
    _ _ _ because Germany stopped our trade
    _ _ _ because Germany made war on us

c. World problems have an effect on us

    _ _ _ because we want to rule the world
    _ _ _ because we interfere where we do not have to
    _ _ _ because the world is our customer

I. During its Early History the United States had Little
to do with Other Countries
The Monroe Doctrine made it the guardian of the
Western Hemisphere

Preparation

"Which European nation had taken the lead in exploring and settling South America? Which nation had settled Brazil? Do you remember how Spain treated her colonies?

"How do you suppose the Spanish colonies would feel when they saw the English colonies win their independence? What kind of government did most of the European nations have?

"What do we mean when we say a certain child has a guardian?"

Show on the map the Western Hemisphere; the Eastern Hemisphere.

Presentation

After many years the Spanish and Brazilian colonies had a revolution, and under leaders who helped them as George Washington helped us they became independent. Spain wished to get her colonies back again, since they were valuable lands. Several European countries planned to go together and help her, and they would all get back their colonies.

President Monroe wrote a letter to Congress and said that the United States ought not to allow European countries to come into the Western Hemisphere to colonize or to set up governments like their own. His policy would prevent Spain from getting back her former colonies. Naturally she did not like it; but England said President Monroe was right, so the other European countries had to agree.

From that time on, the United States has acted as a sort of guardian for the Western Hemisphere. If a European country and a South American country get into trouble, the United States steps in and helps to settle the problem. If European countries send an army and a ruler into Mexico, as they once did, the United States tells them they must go back home.

The policy of making the United States the guardian of the Western Hemisphere is known as the Monroe Doctrine (*pointing to the word written on the board*) because President Monroe first stated it. Many of the South American countries do not like it, because they think they do not need a guardian.

PRESENTATION TEST

1. *Check two answers:*

   The chief countries which had colonized in South America were

   _ _ _ Portugal   _ _ _ Spain

   _ _ _ Africa   _ _ _ France

   _ _ _ England

2. *Check the best answer:*

   a. After many years these colonies had

   _ _ _ fought each other

   _ _ _ all joined as one country

   _ _ _ won their independence

   b. Several European countries together had planned

   _ _ _ to make war on the United States

   _ _ _ to get back their colonies

   _ _ _ to get out of the Western Hemisphere entirely

c. President Monroe's letter to Congress said

_ _ _ that European countries should keep out of the affairs of the Western Hemisphere

_ _ _ that European countries should not trade in the Western Hemisphere

_ _ _ that the United States would keep out of the Eastern Hemisphere

d. From that time on, the United States has been

_ _ _ the enemy of all the European countries

_ _ _ the guardian of the Western Hemisphere

_ _ _ the ruler of all the South American countries

e. The countries of South America

_ _ _ like the Monroe Doctrine

_ _ _ do not like the Monroe Doctrine

Assimilation

Readings

Upper Group

BEARD and BAGLEY. Our Old World Background, 419–423.

HUMPHREY. Stories of the World's Holidays, 207–222 (Bolivar).

JONES and SLEMAN. Modern World Setting for American History, **161–171.**

PERRY and PRICE. American History, II : 124–125.

TAPPAN. An Elementary History of our Country, 184.

Compton's Pictured Encyclopedia (Monroe Doctrine).

World Book (Monroe Doctrine).

Average Group

BEARD and BAGLEY. A First Book in American History, 193–194.

ELSON and MACMULLAN. Story of our Country, II : 76–77.

FORMAN. First Lessons in American History, 211–212.

GORDY. Elementary History of the United States, 228–229.

Lower Group

Try FORMAN.

Teachers

COOLIDGE. The United States as a World Power, 95–120.

DEWEY. National Problems, 304–313.

FISH. The Path of Empire, 1–18, 79–89.

HART. American History told by Contemporaries, IV : 625–628.

JOHNSON. Jefferson and his Colleagues, 286–307.

LATANÉ. America as a World Power, 255–268.

SHEPHERD. The Hispanic Nations of the New World, 30–55 (see Index).

TURNER. Rise of the New West, 199–223.

Baltimore County Course of Study, 574.

Minimal Essentials

Date: **1823** — Monroe (mŭn rō′) Doctrine

Historical Term: **Monroe Doctrine**

Things to Remember

Bolivar (bŏl′ĭ vär *or* bô lē′vär) had helped the Spanish-American countries to secure their independence from Spain.

European powers were planning to get their colonies back.

President Monroe wrote a letter which said that European countries ought not to colonize nor to set up in America governments like their own.

Illustrative Material

Mentor, XIII: 21–23 (November, 1925).
Perry Pictures: 2020, Bolivar Statue.

Procedure during Assimilation

Reading as described on pages 24–29.

Picture study based on the illustrative material listed above.

For a lesson on our relations with Latin America see *The Nineteenth Yearbook of the National Society for the Study of Education*, Part I, pp. 117–132.

Show Bolivar's flag, the flag of the Army of the Andes, and San Martín's flag.

Dramatize the story of Simon Bolivar or of San Martín.

On an outline map of South America, color yellow all the countries which won their independence from Spain; color orange those which won their independence from Portugal.[1]

Drill on minimal essentials.

Objective test.

Organization

Teacher and pupils working together produce an outline somewhat similar to the following:

THE MONROE DOCTRINE

1. Independence of the South American republics
2. Plans of the European powers
3. President Monroe's letter
4. Effects

Recitation

Children tell what facts belong under each heading.

II. When the Nation obtained Lands far from Home, it had to become a World Power
1. Hawaii was annexed

Preparation

"How did we get the Louisiana territory? Florida? Texas? Oregon? the Mexican cession? Alaska?

"What do you think is the best way to win new territory? Why?

"Of all the additions of territory which we mentioned, which one is separated from the rest of the United States? Is it better to have our territory all together or scattered about the earth?" Review the arguments on both sides.

[1] Shepherd, W. R., *Historical Atlas*, pp. 136, 179–180, 214–215.

"We shall read today the story of how we obtained our first island possessions."

No additional presentation is needed.

Assimilation

Readings

Upper Group

BRAIN. Transformation of Hawaii.
GUERBER. Story of the Great Republic, 323–331.
KROUT. Alice's Visit to the Hawaiian Islands.
LAWRENCE. Old Time Hawaiians.
MOWRY. American Heroes and Heroism, 168–175.
PERRY and PRICE. American History, II: 275.
Compton's Pictured Encyclopedia (Hawaiian Islands, p. 1605).
World Book (Hawaii: History).

Average Group

BARROWS and PARKER. Geography: United States and Canada, 249–251.
GEORGE. Little Journeys to Hawaii and the Philippines, 11–14.
GORDY. Elementary History of the United States, 299–300.
WADE. Our Little Hawaiian Cousin.
WINSLOW. Our American Neighbors, 92–98.

Lower Group

BRIGHAM and McFARLANE. Essentials of Geography, I: 151–152.
CARROLL and CARROLL. Around the World, III: 228–240.
DAVIS. Stories of the United States, 235–236.
FAIRGRIEVE and YOUNG. The World, 199–204.
McMASTER. Primary History of the United States, 237.
SMITH. Human Geography, I: 178–179, 181.
TARR and McMURRY. New Geographies, I: 162–163.

Teachers

DEWEY. National Problems, 297–304.
FISH. The Path of Empire, 74–78.
RHODES. The McKinley and Roosevelt Administrations, 112–114.

Minimal Essentials

Names of Places: **Hawaii** (hä wī'ē) ; **Honolulu** (hō′nô lōō′lōō)
Date: **1898**—annexation of Hawaii
Historical Term: **"crossroads of the Pacific"**
Things to Remember
    The native queen of Hawaii was overthrown.
    Some of the people asked to be annexed to the United States.
    Hawaii was annexed by a treaty in 1898.

Illustrative Material

Ford Educational Library: 85, Hawaiian Islands.
Hawaii Tourist Bureau, San Francisco (advertising material).
Keystone Views: 181, Honolulu's Executive Building; 182, Everyday Business on Fort Street, Honolulu; 183, Pounding Poi.
National Parks Portfolio, United States Department of the Interior: Hawaii National Park.
Society for Visual Education. Picturol: The Hawaiian Islands.
Travel, XXVIII: 22–25 (November, 1916); XLIII: 13–16 (October, 1924).

Procedure during Assimilation

Reading as described on pages 24–29.

Picture study based on the illustrative material listed above.

Children make a picture collection of Hawaiian scenes and mount them on the bulletin board.

Invite a traveler who has visited Hawaii to describe it to the children.

Give a Hawaiian entertainment.[1]

Show why Hawaii is called the "crossroads of the Pacific."[2]

Begin here to make a map entitled "America as a World Power." Locate Hawaii. Add other territorial acquisitions as they are studied.

Drill on minimal essentials.

Objective test.

Organization

Children make their own outlines, the teacher giving help only to those who need it.

Recitation

Each recites from his own outline.

---

2. The war with Spain added the Philippines and Porto Rico
   a. The causes of the war

Preparation

"We had wanted Cuba before the Civil War. Why? Many Americans had bought land in Cuba. For what purpose? Why then would America be interested in Spain's treatment of Cuba?"

No additional presentation is needed.

Assimilation

Readings

Upper Group

BLAISDELL. The Story of American History, 406–410.

CHANDLER and CHITWOOD. Makers of American History, 299–300.

FOOTE and SKINNER. Makers and Defenders of America, 323–325.

GORDY. Leaders in Making America, 396–399.

GUERBER. The Story of the Great Republic, 305–310.

MONTGOMERY. Beginners' American History, 241–245.

PERRY and PRICE. American History, II : 263–266.

STUCKEY. William McKinley.

[1] "A Hawaiian Entertainment." *The Twentieth Yearbook of the National Society for the Study of Education*, Part I, pp. 78–79.

[2] Goode, J. P., *School Atlas*, pp. 14–15.

TAPPAN. An Elementary History of our Country, 241–242.
Compton's Pictured Encyclopedia (Spanish-American War).
World Book (Spanish-American War).

Average Group

BEARD and BAGLEY. A First Book in American History, 367–372.
BRYANT. I am an American, 89–90.
ELSON and MACMULLAN. Story of our Country, II : 258–260.
FORMAN. First Lessons in American History, 317–318.
GORDY. American Leaders and Heroes, 314–317.
GORDY. Elementary History of the United States, 296–297.
MORRIS. Primary History of the United States, 238–239.

Lower Group

DAVIS. Stories of the United States, 236–237.
MCMASTER. Primary History of the United States, 237–238.

Teachers

COOLIDGE. The United States as a World Power, 121–133.
FISH. The Path of Empire, 90–115.
HART. American History told by Contemporaries, IV : 557–561, 573–575.
LATANÉ. America as a World Power, 3–28.
LODGE. The War with Spain, 1–44.
PAXSON. Recent History of the United States, 242–245.
RHODES. The McKinley and Roosevelt Administrations, 41–67.
WILSON. Division and Reunion, 328–332.
Baltimore County Course of Study, 573.

Minimal Essentials

Name of Person: **William McKinley**
Name of Place: **Cuba**
Historical Term: **"Remember the *Maine*"**
Things to Remember
We had sympathy with Cuba in her attempts to free herself from Spain.
Many Americans owned property in Cuba.
Interfering with Spain in Cuba was a different policy for the United States;
formerly we had attended strictly to our own business and expected other
nations to attend to theirs.

Illustrative Material

BROWN. Famous Pictures: 3, William McKinley; 2136, Mr. and Mrs. McKinley; 2146, Mrs.
McKinley.
Keystone Views: 163, Morro Castle and Entrance to Havana Harbor; 164, United States
Battleship *Maine*; 165, "Remember the *Maine*."

Procedure during Assimilation

Reading as described on pages 24–29.
Picture study based on the illustrative material listed above.
Write two editorials for newspapers: one for a European newspaper declaring that
the United States should not have gone to war with Spain; one for an American
newspaper favoring war with Spain.
Drill on minimal essentials.
Objective test.

Organization

The outline consists of a list of the causes.

Recitation

Give the recitation of all of section II of Unit XII, pp. 606–627, as an assembly program, "How our Flag reached the Corners of the Earth."

---

b. The Spanish-American War

Preparation

"Would the United States probably send its army to Spain? Why not? Fighting on land would be done where, then?

"Where might the Spanish navy be stationed besides in the Caribbean?" (Philippines.)

No additional presentation is needed.

Assimilation
Readings

Upper Group

AUSTIN. Uncle Sam's Soldiers.
BARSTOW. Progress of a United People, 70–77, 93–106.
BLAISDELL. The Story of American History, 410–423.
BROOKS. The American Soldier, 289–308.
CHANDLER and CHITWOOD. Makers of American History, 300–307.
EVANS. America First, 414–422.
FOOTE and SKINNER. Makers and Defenders of America, 323–327.
GORDY. Leaders in Making America, 399–403.
GUERBER. Story of the Great Republic, 310–323.
LEFFERTS. American Leaders, II : 297–310.
LOGIE. From Lincoln to Coolidge, 241–259, 261–267.
MONTGOMERY. Beginners' American History, 245–255.
MORRIS. Heroes of the Navy in America, 302–320.
MOWRY. American Heroes and Heroism, 78–83.
PERRY and PRICE. American History, II : 266–273.
TAPPAN. An Elementary History of our Country, 242–244.
TOMLINSON. Fighters Young Americans want to Know, 217–224.
Compton's Pictured Encyclopedia (Spanish-American War).
World Book (Spanish-American War).

Average Group ⸁

BEARD and BAGLEY. A First Book in American History, 372–375.
BRYANT. I am an American, 90–93.
ELSON and MacMULLAN. The Story of our Country, II : 260–262.

FORMAN. First Lessons in American History, 318–322.
GORDY. American Leaders and Heroes, 317–326.
GORDY. Elementary History of the United States, 297–299.
MACE. Primary History, 388–393.
MORRIS. Primary History of the United States, 239–242.
SOUTHWORTH. Builders of our Country, II : 256–259.
TURPIN. Brief Biographies from American History, 292–297.
UHRBROCK and OWENS. Famous Americans, 337–346.

Lower Group

BARNES. Primary History of the United States, 235–237.
DAVIS. Stories of the United States, 237–241.
GROVE. American Naval Heroes, 27–31.
McMASTER. Primary History of the United States, 238–242.

Teachers

FISH. The Path of Empire, 116–197.
HART. American History told by Contemporaries, IV: 576–590.
LATANÉ. America as a World Power, 29–81.
LODGE. The War with Spain, 45–236.
PAXSON. Recent History of the United States, 240–259.
RHODES. The McKinley and Roosevelt Administrations, 68–98.
WILSON. Division and Reunion, 332–338.
Baltimore County Course of Study, 573–574.

Minimal Essentials

Name of Person: **George Dewey** (dū′ĭ)
Names of Places: **Havana; Manila**
Date: **1898** — Spanish-American War
Historical Terms: **Spanish-American War; Rough Riders; hundred days' war with Spain**
Things to Remember
Many countries thought the United States ought not to fight Spain.
At sea the principal battles were at Manila and Santiago.
On land the principal battle was at San Juan.
We lost many men through disease.

Illustrative Material

BROWN. Famous Pictures: 66, Admiral Dewey.
Keystone Views: 166, Admiral Dewey on his Flagship; 167, The *Yucatan* carrying the "Rough Riders" to Cuba; 169, Wheeler, Wood, Roosevelt, Brodie, Dunn, Brown; 171, Embarkation of Spanish Troops, Santiago, Cuba.

Procedure during Assimilation

Reading as described on pages 24–29.
Picture study based on the illustrative material listed above.
Invite a veteran of the Spanish-American War to tell his experiences.
Compare the uniforms of the Spanish-American War and the Civil War.
On a slated map of the world, mark with red crosses the principal battles fought.
A sand-table representation of the Caribbean region may show by yellow flags the location of the Spanish forces. Replace by small American flags when the places are conquered.

List the terms of the treaty of peace.
Children write cablegrams for home newspapers, describing the principal battles.
Drill on minimal essentials.
Objective test.

Organization

Children suggest three main subheads and a title for the story.

Recitation

Give as part of the assembly program.[1]

---

c. The Philippines

Preparation

"Why should the Philippines be given to the United States at the close of the war? Why should we want them? In what ways would they present difficulties to us?
"Locate the Philippines."
No additional presentation is needed.

Assimilation

Readings

Upper Group

Du Puy. Uncle Sam's Modern Miracles, 15–27.
Guerber. Story of the Great Republic, 331–334.
Perry and Price. American History, II : 273–275.
Tomlinson. Fighters Young Americans want to Know, 225–238.
Compton's Pictured Encyclopedia (Philippine Islands).
World Book (Philippine Islands : Spanish Days, Awakening, Americans Arrive,
    A New Way to Colonize, American Rule.)

Average Group

Barrows and Parker. Geography : United States and Canada, 252–254.
Beard and Bagley. A First Book in American History, 378–380.
Blaisdell and Ball. Heroic Deeds of American Sailors, 156–166.
Carroll and Carroll. Around the World, III : 241–266.
George. Little Journeys to Hawaii and the Philippines, 10–15.
Winslow. Our American Neighbors, 99–110.

Lower Group

Allen. How and Where we Live, 193–197.
Brigham and McFarlane. Essentials of Geography, I : 152–153
Burks. Barbara's Philippine Journey.
Carpenter. Around the World with the Children, 74–81.
Carroll and Carroll. Around the World, II : 196–207.

[1] See page 610.

CHANCE. Little Folks of Many Lands, 83–93.
DAVIS. Stories of the United States, 241–242.
FAIRGRIEVE and YOUNG. Homes Far Away, 133–142.
FAIRGRIEVE and YOUNG. The World, 197–199, 204.
McMASTER. Primary History of the United States, 242.
PERKINS. Filipino Twins.
SCHWARTZ. Five Little Strangers, 137–176.
SMITH. Human Geography, I : 172–176, 182.
TARR and McMURRY. New Geographies, I : 161–162.

Teachers

COOLIDGE. The United States as a World Power, 148–171.
FISH. The Path of Empire, 204–217.
HART. American History told by Contemporaries, IV : 594–597.
LATANÉ. America as a World Power, 82–99, 153–174.
PAXSON. Recent History of the United States, 259–260, 289–290.
RHODES. The McKinley and Roosevelt Administrations, 102–112, 183–217.
WILSON. Division and Reunion, 338–342.
WORCESTER. The Philippines, Past and Present.

Minimal Essentials

Name of Place: **Philippines** (fĭl'ĭ pĭnz *or* pēnz *or* pĭnz)
Historical Term: **Philippine independence**
Things to Remember
  Many people did not want territory in the Old World.
  Land so far away is hard to protect.
  Getting territory so far away made the United States a world power.
  The Filipinos speak a different language from ours and are of a different race.
  They want to be independent.
  We have promised them independence as soon as they are ready for it.

Illustrative Material

BRADLEY. Straight-Line Picture Cut-Outs: Filipino Village.
Compton's Pictured Encyclopedia (Philippine Islands).
Keystone Views: 173, Filipino Farmers; 174, Primitive Method of Cleaning Rice, Philippines; 175, Homes of Many in the Philippines; 176, Aguinaldo; 179, Filipino School Girls.
Travel, XXXV: 13–17 (July, 1920) ; XXXIX: 11–14 (July, 1922).

Procedure during Assimilation

Reading as described on pages 24–29.
Picture study based on the illustrative material listed above.
Children make a picture collection of Philippine scenes, and mount them on the bulletin board.
Begin to make a museum of recent additions to United States territory.[1]
A traveler to the Philippines describes his experiences.
Locate the Philippines on the map "America as a World Power."[2]
Drill on minimal essentials.
Objective test.

[1] "A Museum of Nations." *The Twentieth Yearbook of the National Society for the Study of Education,* Part I, p. 88.
[2] See page 608.

Organization

THE PHILIPPINES AS A UNITED STATES POSSESSION

1. How we obtained possession
2. War in the Philippines
3. Difficulties in our new possession
4. The future of the Philippines

Recitation

Give as part of the assembly program.[1]

---

d. Porto Rico

Preparation

"Have we heard of Porto Rico in any other story than that of the Spanish-American War?" (Ponce de Leon was governor there.)

Locate Porto Rico.

Review the terms of the treaty of 1898.

No additional presentation is needed.

Assimilation

Readings

Upper Group

WADE. Our Little Porto Rican Cousin.

Compton's Pictured Encyclopedia (Porto Rico).

World Book (Porto Rico: History).

Average Group

BARROWS and PARKER. Geography: United States and Canada, 254–257.

CARROLL and CARROLL. Around the World, III: 223–227.

GEORGE. Little Journeys to Cuba and Porto Rico, 5–7 (Porto Rico).

WINSLOW. Our American Neighbors, 80–85.

Lower Group

BRIGHAM and McFARLANE. Essentials of Geography, I: 149.

CARROLL and CARROLL. Around the World, II: 188–195.

DAVIS. Stories of the United States, 240–241.

SMITH. Human Geography, I: 176–178, 181.

Teachers

COOLIDGE. The United States as a World Power, 134–147.

FISH. The Path of Empire, 203–204.

HART. American History told by Contemporaries, IV: 597–601.

LATANÉ. America as a World Power, 133–152.

PAXSON. Recent History of the United States, 288.

RHODES. The McKinley and Roosevelt Administrations, 176–177.

[1] See page 610.

Minimal Essentials

Name of Place: **Porto Rico** (pōr′tō rē′kō)
Historical Term: **island possession**
Things to Remember
Porto Rico was given to the United States after the Spanish-American War.
For a while it was ruled by soldiers.
Gradually it was allowed to help in its own government.
The Porto Ricans are citizens of the United States.
The United States does not know whether or not to allow Porto Rico to become
a state.

Illustrative Material

Keystone Views: 180, Columbus Monument and Cristóbal Colón Fort, Porto Rico.
National Geographic Magazine, XLVI: 599–651.
Perry Pictures: 7641, City Home, San Juan, Porto Rico; 7642, In a Patio; 7643, Porto
Rican Babies; 7644, A "Lightning Express"; 7655, A Village Street in Porto Rico.
Travel, XXXVI: 22–25 (January, 1921); XLII: 10–11 (December, 1923); XLIV: 43–46
(November, 1924); XLVI: 22–23 (November, 1925).

Procedure during Assimilation

Reading as described on pages 24–29.
Picture study based on the illustrative material listed above.
Add a Porto Rican scene to the museum of recent additions to United States
territory.[1]
A traveler to Porto Rico describes his experiences.
The class may exchange correspondence with schools in San Juan, Ponce, or
Mayagüez, Porto Rico.
Locate Porto Rico on the map "America as a World Power." [2]
Drill on minimal essentials.
Objective test.

Organization

The class divides into groups and each prepares its own
outline.

Different groups criticize each other's outlines.

Recitation

Give as part of the assembly program.[3]

---

e. The United States helped Cuba to become a republic

Preparation

Review the terms of the treaty of 1898.
"Does the United States own Cuba now?
"Why didn't we keep Cuba as well as Porto Rico?
"What is a republic?

[1] See page 613.   [2] See page 608.   [3] See page 610.

"Why is it hard for a very small country to keep its position as a republic?"

No additional presentation is needed.

Assimilation

Readings

Upper Group

LOGIE. From Lincoln to Coolidge, 267–269.
WADE. Our Little Cuban Cousin, 81–106.
Compton's Pictured Encyclopedia (Cuba: How Uncle Sam set Cuba Free).
World Book (Cuba: History).

Average Group

CARROLL and CARROLL. Around the World, III: 215–222.
GEORGE. Little Journeys to Cuba and Porto Rico, 5–7 (Cuba).
WINSLOW. Our American Neighbors, 73–79.

Lower Group

Try CARROLL and CARROLL.

Teachers

FISH. The Path of Empire, 198–203.
HART. American History told by Contemporaries, IV: 601–603.
LATANÉ. America as a World Power, 175–191.
PAXSON. Recent History of the United States, 288–289, 302.
RHODES. The McKinley and Roosevelt Administrations, 177–183, 364–366.
WILSON. Division and Reunion, 342–344.

Minimal Essentials

Historical Term: **protectorate**
Things to Remember

The United States had wanted Cuba for a long time.
We had told the European countries that we did not go into the Spanish-American War to take Cuba for ourselves.
Therefore we gave it its independence.
We stand ready to help Cuba if it gets into trouble.

Illustrative Material

Keystone Views: 172, Cuban Republic's Birth.
National Geographic Magazine, XXXVIII: 1–33.
New Standard Dictionary: Flags of America.
Travel, XXXVI: 23–24 (February, 1921); XL: 11–14 (December, 1922); XLII: 5–9 (December, 1923); XLIV: 27–29 (November, 1924); XLVI: 7–9 (November, 1925).

Procedure during Assimilation

Reading as described on pages 24–29.
Picture study based on the illustrative material listed above.
Plan a class trip to Cuba. Write about routes, fares, etc. Different children choose the portions of the journey for which they wish to act as guides.

A traveler to Cuba describes the people and their customs.
Impress on the children's minds the fact that the United States does not own Cuba.
Locate Cuba on the map.
Drill on minimal essentials.
Objective test.

Organization

The teacher provides the following outline:

THE REPUBLIC OF CUBA

1. Cuba in the treaty of 1898
2. The work of the United States in Cuba
3. Making Cuba a republic

Recitation

Give as part of the assembly program.[1]

---

3. The United States helped to secure the "open door" in China

---

Preparation

"Do you remember why Spain had been so angry at John Hawkins's sale of negroes in the West Indies?

"What were the navigation laws? Why had the colonies objected to them?

"It was common, then, for nations not to allow their colonies to trade with anyone else. Suppose, however, that Great Britain should send some of her traders over to live in a Chinese city. Should she, then, make a law that the Chinese city could trade only with Great Britain? Why not? Who, if anyone, should make such a law?"

Presentation

China's government was not very strong, and she did not have modern guns, submarines, aëroplanes, etc. As a result, gradually her whole coast line (*illustrating at the map*) was settled by foreigners. The French lived here (*showing the extreme south*), the Portuguese here (*showing Macao*), the British here (*showing Hongkong*), the Germans here (*showing the Shantung peninsula*), the Russians here (*showing Port Arthur*),

[1] See page 610.

and the Japanese here (*northeast*). Of course they did not really own all these lands (China did), but no one of them would let any other foreigner carry on trade within his settlement.

The United States had taken no part in this dividing up of China's trade, probably because we were so far away. After we had the Philippines (*illustrating at the map*), however, China was our next-door neighbor. We should have liked to trade with her, but (*illustrating at the map as each place is mentioned*) France's door was closed here, Portugal's here, England's here, Germany's here, Russia's here, Japan's here. We could not get in to trade with China.

A great American named John Hay then wrote notes to all those countries and said that each one of them ought to open up her doors and allow anybody who wished to come in and trade with China. None of the countries wanted to seem selfish; so all agreed.

Ever since then there has been what we call the "open door" in China. That means that all countries can trade in any part.

PRESENTATION TEST

Check the best answer:

a. The foreigners could come into China easily
   _ _ _ because China was not strong enough to keep them out
   _ _ _ because China was so near to them
   _ _ _ because China wanted them to come

b. Each one of the foreign countries we named
   _ _ _ owned part of the land in China
   _ _ _ went to war with China
   _ _ _ made settlements along the coast

c. Then they would not allow any other foreign people
   _ _ _ to buy land in China
   _ _ _ to trade with China in their settlements
   _ _ _ to come into China at all

d. The United States wanted to trade with China
   _ _ _ after we had the Philippines
   _ _ _ after we had Porto Rico
   _ _ _ after we had Hawaii

e. The "open door" means
   _ _ _ that the United States must have China's trade
   _ _ _ that all nations have equal trading rights in China
   _ _ _ that nobody shall trade with China

Assimilation

Readings

Upper Group

BEARD and BAGLEY. Our Old World Background, 401–402, 412–413.
MOWRY. American Heroes and Heroism, 160–167.
PERRY and PRICE. American History, II : 275–276.
WINSLOW. Distant Countries : Asia, Africa, Australia, 76–78.
Compton's Pictured Encyclopedia (China, p. 748).

Average Group

BEARD and BAGLEY. A First Book in American History, 380–384.
GORDY. Elementary History of the United States, 301–302.
MOWRY. First Steps in the History of our Country, 317–321.
SMITH. Human Geography, II : 329–330.

Lower Group

DAVIS. Stories of the United States, 243–246.
McMASTER. Primary History of the United States, 242–243.

Teachers

COOLIDGE. The United States as a World Power, 327–340.
FISH. The Path of Empire, 218–239.
HART. American History told by Contemporaries, IV : 616–622.
LATANÉ. America as a World Power, 100–102.
PAXSON. Recent History of the United States, 283–285.
RHODES. The McKinley and Roosevelt Administrations, 120–131, 319–321.
WILSON. Division and Reunion, 344–346.
Baltimore County Course of Study, 574.

Minimal Essentials

Name of Person: John Hay
Names of Places: China; Peking (pē′kĭng′)
Historical Terms: Boxer rebellion; "open door"; partition of China
Things to Remember

Many nations had made settlements along the coast of China.
They would not let other foreign countries trade in their settlements.
John Hay stated the policy of the "open door" in China.
The "open door" meant that all nations had equal trading rights.

Illustrative Material

Keystone Views: 184, Some of China's Trouble Makers; 185, Gatling Gun on City Wall of Tientsin; 186, Li Hung Chang.

Procedure during Assimilation

Reading as described on pages 24–29.
Picture study based on the illustrative material listed above.
Make a trip to the local museum to see the Chinese exhibit.
With the help of the geographies make a list of things we import from China.
On the slated map of Asia show the foreign spheres of influence.[1]
A traveler to China describes the things that the Chinese make.
Drill on minimal essentials.
Objective test.

[1] Webster, H., *Modern European History*, p. 412; Robinson, J. H., and Beard, C. A., *Outlines of European History*, Part II, pp. 476, 610; Harding, S. B., *New Mediæval and Modern History*, pp. 692–693; Shepherd, W. R., *Historical Atlas*, pp. 170–171.

Organization

The teacher and the pupils working together produce an outline somewhat similar to the following:

THE "OPEN DOOR" IN CHINA

1. Foreign settlements in China
2. The United States desire to trade
3. The "open door"
4. Modern movements in China

Recitation

Give as part of the assembly program.[1]

---

4. The United States obtained the Canal Zone and built the Panama Canal

---

Preparation

Review the principle of the lock canal.[2]

"What is the largest canal you ever heard of?

"Why should the United States want to build a canal in territory so far away from home?

"We did not own that land. How, then, could we build a canal through it?

"We shall read today to find *first* how we obtained the land; *secondly*, how the canal was built."

No additional presentation is needed.

Assimilation

Readings

Upper Group

BABSON. A Central American Journey, 43–56.
BARSTOW. The Progress of a United People, 107–124.
CHANDLER and CHITWOOD. Makers of American History, 308.
GORDY. Leaders in Making America, 438–440.
HALL. Panama and the Canal.
LEFFERTS. American Leaders, II: 339–342.
LOGIE. From Lincoln to Coolidge, 229–240.
NIDA. Panama and its Bridge of Water.
PERRY and PRICE. American History, II: 277–278.
PIKE. Our Little Panama Cousin, 71–118.

[1] See page 610.   [2] See page 359.

SANFORD and OWEN. Modern Americans, 73–80.
TAPPAN. Heroes of Progress, 237–244, 254–263.
Compton's Pictured Encyclopedia (Panama Canal).
World Book (Panama Canal).

Average Group

BARROWS and PARKER. Geography: United States and Canada, 254.
BEARD and BAGLEY. A First Book in American History, 424–427.
ELSON and MacMULLAN. Story of our Country, II : 263–264.
EVERETT and REED. When they were Boys, 77–90.
FORMAN. First Lessons in American History, 327–328.
GORDY. Elementary History of the United States, 302–306.
MORRIS. Primary History of the United States, 248–249.
MOWRY. First Steps in the History of our Country, 323.
NIDA. Following the Frontier, 312–315.
WINSLOW. Our American Neighbors, 66–71.

Lower Group

BRIGHAM and McFARLANE. Essentials of Geography, I : 149.
DAVIS. Stories of the United States, 247–248.
McMASTER. Primary History of the United States, 244.
SMITH. Human Geography, I : 110.

Teachers

COOLIDGE. The United States as a World Power, 267–280.
DEWEY. National Problems, 117–126.
FISH. The Path of Empire, 240–258.
LATANÉ. America as a World Power, 204–223.
PAXSON. Recent History of the United States, 285–286, 351–352, 383.
RHODES. The McKinley and Roosevelt Administrations, 263–278.
WILLIAMS. The Romance of Modern Engineering, 267–291.
WILSON. Division and Reunion, 349–350.
Baltimore County Course of Study, 574.

Minimal Essentials

Names of Persons: **Goethals** (gō'thălz); **Gorgas**
Names of Places: **Panama; Canal Zone**
Date: **1914** — opening of the Panama Canal
Historical Term: **Panama Canal**
Things to Remember
 Panama won its liberty from Colombia.
 Panama then sold to the United States a strip of land ten miles wide from coast
  to coast. This is the Canal Zone.
 Gorgas made it possible to live in the zone.
 Goethals was the engineer who dug the canal.

Illustrative Material

McKINLEY. Illustrated Topics for American History: S. 40, Roosevelt's Administration.
Educational Posters of the National Child Welfare Association: The War against Disease:
 General William C. Gorgas.
Ford Educational Library: 9, Panama Canal.
Keystone Views: 197, Abandoned French Machinery near Cristóbal; 200, Colonel Goethals;
 201, Gorgas; 203, A Landslide; 204, A View down the Panama Canal.
Mentor, XIII : 40–50 (February, 1925).

National Geographic Magazine, XXV: 133–183; XXVIII: 159; XLI: 131–146.
The Panama Canal, Washington, D. C. (free booklet).
Society for Visual Education. Schoolfilm: The Panama Canal and its Historical Significance.
Travel, XXVIII: 32–36 (March, 1917).

Procedure during Assimilation

Reading as described on pages 24–29.
Picture study based on the illustrative material listed above.
Add a Panama Canal Zone scene to the museum of recent additions to the territory
of the United States.[1]
Visitors to the Canal describe their experiences.
Construct the Canal and the railway on the sand table.
Use the dramatization "Manifest Destiny." Hague and Chalmers, *Dramatic Moments in American History*, pp. 212–245.
Show how the world trade routes have been affected by the building of the Canal.[2]
Locate the Canal Zone on the map "America as a World Power."[3]
List the number of nations that used the Canal last year.[4]
Graph the number of ships of each nation that passed through the Canal last year.[5]
Drill on minimal essentials.
Objective test.

Organization

The teacher and the pupils working together produce an
outline somewhat similar to the following:

THE PANAMA CANAL

1. Panama's revolt from Colombia
2. Sale of the Canal Zone
3. Building of the Canal
4. Effect of the Canal

Recitation

Giving the assembly program.[6]

---

5. Life of Theodore Roosevelt

Preparation

Children tell what they already know about the life and
work of Roosevelt.
No additional presentation is needed.

[1] See page 613.
[2] Goode, J. P., *School Atlas*, pp. 14–15; Brigham, A. P., and McFarlane, C. T., *Essentials of Geography*, II: 248; Atwood, W. W., *New Geography*, II: Appendixes VI and VII; Beard, C. A., and Bagley, W. C., *History of the American People*, p. 593.
[3] See page 608.   [4] World Almanac.   [5] World Almanac.   [6] See page 610.

Assimilation

Readings

Upper Group

BURNHAM. Hero Tales from History, 352–358.
DAVIDSON. Founders and Builders of our Nation, 245–254.
FARIS. Real Stories of the Geography Makers, 185–189.
FRYER. A Book of Boyhoods, 280–290.
GORDY. Leaders in Making America, 430–438, 440–441.
HAGEDORN. Boys' Life of Theodore Roosevelt (difficult).
LEFFERTS. American Leaders, II : 330–345.
PEARSON. Theodore Roosevelt.
ROOSEVELT. Theodore Roosevelt's Letters to his Children.
SANFORD and OWEN. Modern Americans, 37–42.
Compton's Pictured Encyclopedia (Roosevelt).
World Book (Roosevelt).

Average Group

BEARD and BAGLEY. A First Book in American History, 416–420, 432–433.
ELSON and MacMULLAN. Story of our Country, II : 262–263.
FORMAN. First Lessons in American History, 325–327.
INGRAHAM. The Story of Democracy, 233–241.
MORRIS. Primary History of the United States, 243–251.
TAPPAN. American Hero Stories, 265–278.
UHRBROCK and OWENS. Famous Americans, 348–366.

Lower Group

ELSON and BURRIS. Child Library Readers, V : 159–165.
EVERETT and REED. When they were Boys, 53–59.
LEWIS and ROWLAND. Silent Readers, V : 234–236.

Teachers

ABBOTT. Theodore Roosevelt.
HOWLAND. Theodore Roosevelt and his Times.
LEWIS. Life of Theodore Roosevelt.
ROBINSON. My Brother, Theodore Roosevelt.
ROOSEVELT. Theodore Roosevelt : an Autobiography.

Minimal Essentials

Name of Person: **Theodore Roosevelt** (rō'zē vĕlt)
Historical Term: **Progressive party**
Things to Remember

Roosevelt was a sickly child, but made himself strong and healthy.
He was great along many lines : author, naturalist, statesman, warrior, traveler.
He was President when the Panama Canal was dug.

Illustrative Material

Educational Posters of the National Child Welfare Association : Justice to Every Citizen :
    Theodore Roosevelt.
National Posters : Story of Theodore Roosevelt.
Travel, XXXII : 34–35 (February, 1919).

Procedure during Assimilation

Reading as described on pages 24–29.
Picture study based on the illustrative material listed above.
Dramatize incidents in Roosevelt's life.[1]
Is Roosevelt's name commemorated in any way in your city?
Read aloud to the children some of *Theodore Roosevelt's Letters to his Children.*
Plan a program for Roosevelt's birthday, October 27.
Drill on minimal essentials.
Objective test.

Organization

The teacher puts the following outline on the board. Children choose one topic on which to write a paragraph.

THEODORE ROOSEVELT

1. His fight for health
2. His life in the West
3. His work in the Spanish-American War
4. His work as President

Recitation

Giving the assembly program.[2]

---

6. The United States bought the Virgin Islands

Preparation

Show children a large map of the Caribbean region. Locate Porto Rico; the Canal Zone.

"If the United States should want to defend Porto Rico and the Canal Zone from a hostile navy, it ought to have an island away out in the Atlantic. Then it could station our warships there and prevent the enemy from coming any farther.

"Do you see any such islands on this map?

"They all belonged to other countries, however. How could the United States obtain them?

"We shall read today which islands the United States obtained and how it obtained them."

No additional presentation is needed.

[1] See the illustrative lesson on pages 664–689.
[2] See page 610.

Assimilation
Readings
Upper Group
Compton's Pictured Encyclopedia (Virgin Islands).
World Book (Virgin Islands).

Average Group
FORMAN. First Lessons in American History, 337.
GORDY. Elementary History of the United States, 300.

Lower Group
DAVIS. Stories of the United States, 270–271.

Teachers
HARTLEY. Census of the Virgin Islands of the United States. (Department of Commerce, Bureau of the Census.)

Minimal Essentials
Name of Place: **Virgin Islands**
Date: **1917** — purchase of the Virgin Islands
Historical Terms: **"Gibraltar of America"; Danish (dān′ĭsh) West Indies**
Things to Remember
We bought the Danish West Indies and renamed them the Virgin Islands.
They are useful to us only in case of war.

Illustrative Material
National Geographic Magazine, XXX: 89–96.
Travel, XXVII: 36–37 (October, 1916); XXXI: 39–40 (October, 1918).

Procedure during Assimilation
Reading as described on pages 24–29.
Picture study based on the illustrative material listed above.
Add a scene in the Virgin Islands to the museum of recent additions to United States territory.[1]
A traveler to the Virgin Islands describes his experiences.
Locate the Virgin Islands on the map "America as a World Power."[2]
What other name in our history was given to honor the same person for whom the Virgin Islands were named?
Drill on minimal essentials.
Objective test.

Organization
The teacher writes the title and the children suggest two main subheads.
PURCHASE OF THE VIRGIN ISLANDS
1. Why the United States wanted them
2. Terms of the purchase

Recitation
Giving the assembly program.[3]

[1] See page 613.   [2] See page 608.   [3] See page 610.

> 7. The policy with regard to Mexico was "watchful waiting"

Preparation

"What did the other countries think was the United States' real reason for making war on Spain? How did the United States prove that this was not true?

"Why would Mexico have been very ready to believe the worst of the United States?

"So when there was a great revolution in Mexico, and Americans in Mexico suffered, what did the Mexicans fear that the United States would do? What did the European nations think that the United States would do?

"Why didn't the United States seize Mexico?

"Our President said that we should adopt a policy of 'watchful waiting.' What would 'watchful waiting' be?"

No additional presentation is needed.

Assimilation

Readings

Upper Group

CHANDLER and CHITWOOD. Makers of American History, 311–312.
LOGIE. From Lincoln to Coolidge, 295–301.
TAPPAN. Elementary History of our Country, 249–250.
World Book (United States: History, p. 5992).

Average Group

FORMAN. First Lessons in American History, 333–334.
GORDY. Elementary History of the United States, 314–317.

Lower Group

DAVIS. Stories of the United States, 256–259.

Teachers

FISH. The Path of Empire, 275–277.
HACKETT. The Mexican Revolution and the United States (World Peace Foundation Pamphlets, Vol. IX, No. 5, 1926).
PAXSON. Recent History of the United States, 423–432.
SHEPHERD. The Hispanic Nations of the New World, 196–212

Minimal Essentials

Name of Place: **Mexican border**
Historical Term: **"watchful waiting"**
Things to Remember

American troops were sent into Mexico to protect Americans there.
The presence of our troops in Mexico made Mexicans believe that we were only waiting to conquer them.
Our President withdrew the troops and waited to see what Mexico would do next.

Illustrative Material

Keystone Views: 223, United States Army Camp doing Outpost Duty.
New Standard Dictionary: Flags of America.
Travel, XXVII: 28–32 (May, 1916).

Procedure during Assimilation

Reading as described on pages 24–29.
Picture study based on the illustrative material listed above.
Invite veterans who served on the Mexican border to tell their experiences.
Make two lists of points: one headed "Why we should have seized Mexico," the other headed "Why we did not seize Mexico."
Drill on minimal essentials.
Objective test.

Organization

The teacher puts the following outline on the board:

OUR DEALINGS WITH MEXICO

1. The revolution in Mexico
2. Experiences of American troops in Mexico
3. "Watchful waiting"

Recitation

Giving the assembly program.[1]

A drill lesson on sections I and II of Unit XII should be given at this point.

III. The United States joined the Allies in the World War
   1. Causes of the war

Preparation

"How many of you had relations in the World War? (*Give an opportunity to relate what each did.*) What countries were fighting on the same side as the United States? (*List as the countries are named.*) What countries were fighting on the other side?

"Do you know what they were all fighting about? (*Children tell what they know of the causes.*)

"What are markets? We learned in Unit XI that nations sometimes quarrel about their markets. Why?"

[1] See page 610.

On a slated map of the world before 1914, color red all the colonies and dependencies, and the mother countries themselves, of the Allied Powers;[1] color the Central Powers yellow. Call children's attention to the vast extent covered by the Allied territory. "What was left for Germany's markets? Why did she feel that this situation was unfair?

"One great cause of the war was, then, the struggle for markets. We shall now read to find other causes."

No additional presentation is needed.

Assimilation

Readings

Upper Group

BEARD and BAGLEY. Our Old World Background, 426–431.
GORDY. Causes and Meaning of the Great War, 1–72 (difficult).
PERRY and PRICE. American History, II : 309–312.
World Book (War of the Nations : Causes of the War).

Average Group

BRYANT. I am an American, 94–105.
MORRIS. Primary History of the United States, 252.

Lower Group

DAVIS. Stories of the United States, 259–261.

Teachers

BENEZET. The World War and What was behind It, 144–268.
BEVERIDGE. What is Back of the War.
DAVIS. Roots of the War.
HAYES. A Brief History of the Great War, 1–20.
McKINLEY. Collected Materials for the Study of the War, 27–44, 66–76.
McKINLEY, COULOMB, and GERSON. A School History of the Great War, 5–66.
PAXSON. Recent History of the United States, 433–444.

Minimal Essentials

Name of Place: **Belgium**
Date: **1914** — beginning of the World War
Historical Terms: **kaiser**; **World War**; *Lusitania* (lū′sĭ tā′nĭ *à*) ; **alliances**
Things to Remember

Many European countries wanted to be greater than their neighbors in territory and markets.

The chief European countries were divided into two groups, each group jealous of the other.

Each group wanted greater armies and navies than the other.

At last their jealousy led to war.

[1] Shepherd, W. R., *Historical Atlas*, pp. 179–182; Brigham, A. P., and McFarlane, C. T., *Essentials of Geography*, II : 240–241; Bartholomew, J. G., *School Economic Atlas*, pp. 14–15, 16–17; Tarr, R. S., and McMurry, F. M., *New Geographies*, II : 274, 308.

Illustrative Material

McKINLEY. Illustrated Topics for Mediæval and Modern History: M. M. 35, Table — comparison of great powers in armies, navies, wealth, population.

Procedure during Assimilation

Reading as described on pages 24–29.

Make a list of all the causes of war mentioned in any of the books.

Children write editorials for an English newspaper as to the causes of the war; for a German newspaper.

On a slated map of Europe color red the members of the Entente Cordiale; color yellow the Triple Alliance. Why would Italy not fight on the side of the Triple Alliance? Change the color of the map of Italy from yellow to red when reading about its entrance into the war.

Drill on minimal essentials.

Objective test.

Organization

The teacher and the pupils together work out an outline like the following:

CAUSES OF THE WORLD WAR

1. Scramble for territory and markets
2. Long-standing quarrel between Germany and France
3. The two armed camps in Europe
4. Competition in armaments
5. The occasion of the war

Recitation

Each child gives the entire story.

---

2. The war from 1914 to 1917

Preparation

Have ready for use a slated map of Europe. Trace in red crayon the western front,[1] in yellow crayon the eastern front,[2] and in green crayon the southern and Balkan fronts.[3]

[1] Woodburn, J. A., and Moran, T. F., *Elementary American History and Government* (Revised Edition), p. 445; Halleck, R. P., *History of our Country*, p. 508; McKinley, A. E., Coulomb, C. A., and Gerson, A. J., *School History of the Great War*, p. 80; Lawler, T. B., *Essentials of American History*, p. 459.

[2] Robinson, J. H., and Beard, C. A., *History of Europe, our Own Times*, pp. 549, 550; Harding, S. B., *New Mediæval and Modern History*, p. 763; Davis, W. S., *History of Mediæval and Modern Europe*, pp. 547 f.; McKinley, A. E., Coulomb, C. A., and Gerson, A. J., *School History of the Great War*, p. 85.

[3] Harding, S. B., *New Mediæval and Modern History*, p. 763; McKinley, A. E., Coulomb, C. A., and Gerson, A. J., *School History of the Great War*, p. 124.

"We are now going to read to see which side was winning on each front up to 1917."

No additional presentation is needed.

Assimilation
Readings
Upper Group

BEARD and BAGLEY. Our Old World Background, 431–433.

EVANS. America First, 428–433.

GORDY. Causes and Meaning of the Great War, 72–92.

GREENE (Chairman of Board). War Readings, 5–181.

McSPADDEN. Boys' Book of Famous Soldiers, 185–237.

PARKMAN. Fighters for Peace, 3–27, 27–47, 47–75, 75–99, 99–123, 257–282 (difficult).

PERRY and PRICE. American History, II : 312–317.

SANFORD and OWEN. Modern Europeans, 9–20, 21–31, 32–41, 51–58, 59–71, 89–98, 99–109, 121–131, 149–157, 165–176, 177–185.

THOMPSON and BIGWOOD. Lest we Forget, 1–227.

Compton's Pictured Encyclopedia (World War, pp. 3789–3798).

World Book (War of the Nations : First Weeks, Battle Fronts, Land Operations in 1915, 1916, 1917, War on the Sea, War in the Air, Tanks, Submarines).

Average Group

BRYANT. I am an American, 106–116.

CURTIS. Why we celebrate our Holidays, 117–119.

MORRIS. Primary History of the United States, 252–255.

Lower Group

DAVIS. Stories of the United States, 261–262.

Teachers

BENEZET. The World War and What was behind It, 231–303.

HAYES. A Brief History of the Great War, 21–200.

McKINLEY. Collected Materials for the Study of the War, 44–49, 76–80.

McKINLEY, COULOMB, and GERSON. A School History of the Great War, 67–117.

PAXSON. Recent History of the United States, 434–455.

Minimal Essentials

Names of Persons: **Foch** (fōsh) ; **Hindenburg** (hǐn′dĕn boͦoͬrK)

Names of Places: **Marne** (märn) ; **Verdun** (vĕr′dŭN′)

Historical Terms: **the Allies** (ă līz′) ; **Central Powers; western front; submarine war zone; tanks**

Things to Remember

Western front : Germany planned to take Paris, surprising it by marching through Belgium.

At the first battle of the Marne, her onrush was stopped.

For a long time neither side could push the other back.

Eastern front : Russia had a revolution and could not carry on the war.

Southern front : Italy kept the Austrians from the sea.

Great Britain failed to take Constantinople.

At sea : the German fleet was defeated by the Allies.

Illustrative Material

McKinley. Illustrated Topics for American History: S. 45.
McKinley. Illustrated Topics for Mediæval and Modern History: M. M. 36, M. M. 37, M. M. 38.
Society for Visual Education. Picturol: War-Time Serbia and her Refugees.
Society for Visual Education. Schoolfilm: Serbia Victorious.

Procedure during Assimilation

Reading as described on pages 24–29.
Picture study based on the illustrative material listed above.
Children make a picture collection of the progress of the war up to 1917; mount it on the bulletin board.
Children make a complete list of all the countries which fought with the Allies; with the Central Powers.
Special topics are given on new methods and implements of warfare. Illustrate the talks by pictures.
On the slated map of the Eastern Hemisphere show the submarine war zone.[1]
Visit the local museum to see war relics.
Drill on minimal essentials.
Objective test.

Organization

Children make their own outlines, using one subhead for each of the military fronts mentioned.

Recitation

Children choose one subhead to describe in detail.

---

3. Entrance of the United States into the war and her part in it

---

Preparation

"Since the United States had stayed out of the war for nearly three years, why did she enter at all?
"What would our nation have to do to get ready to carry on war against the Central Powers?
"How did the people at home help?
"What was the draft?
"Did the American troops take part in any real battles?"
No additional presentation is needed.

[1] Woodburn, J. A., and Moran, T. F., *Elementary American History and Government* (Revised Edition), p. 451; McKinley, A. E., Coulomb, C. A., and Gerson, A. J., *School History of the Great War*, p. 128; Stephenson, N. W., *An American History*, p. 569.

Assimilation
Readings
Upper Group

BEARD and BAGLEY. Our Old World Background, 433–434.

EVANS. America First, 433–447.

GORDY. Causes and Meaning of the Great War, 92–131 (difficult).

GORDY. Leaders in Making America, 454–466.

GREENE. (Chairman of Board). War Readings, 127–265.

LOGIE. From Lincoln to Coolidge, 319–328.

MCSPADDEN. Boys' Book of Famous Soldiers, 239–260.

PARKMAN. Fighters for Peace, 229–254, 285–311 (difficult).

PERRY and PRICE. American History, II : 307–309, 317–328.

SANFORD and OWEN. Other Soldiers.

STUDEBAKER. Our Country's Call to Service.

SYNON. My Country's Part.

THOMPSON and BIGWOOD. Lest we Forget, 228–344.

TOMLINSON. Fighters Young Americans want to Know, 239–256, 257–265, 266–275.

Compton's Pictured Encyclopedia (World War, pp. 3798–3808).

World Book (War of the Nations: Events on Land in 1918, America in the War).

Average Group

BEARD and BAGLEY. A First Book in American History, 435–447.

BRYANT. I am an American, 117–148.

CURTIS. Why we celebrate our Holidays, 119–120.

FORMAN. First Lessons in American History, 334–343.

GORDY. Elementary History of the United States, 317–325.

MORRIS. Primary History of the United States, 253–255.

UHRBROCK and OWENS. Famous Americans, 368–376.

Lower Group

BOLENIUS. Fifth Reader, 130–137.

DAVIS. Stories of the United States, 263–267.

EVERETT and REED. When they were Boys, 65–70, 116–122, 123–127.

SMITH. Easy Road to Reading, IV : 152–153.

Teachers

BENEZET. The World War and What was behind It, 304–327.

HAYES. A Brief History of the Great War, 201–325.

MCKINLEY. Collected Materials for the Study of the War, 9–26, 49–56.

MCKINLEY, COULOMB, and GERSON. A School History of the Great War, 118–166.

PAXSON. Recent History of the United States, 467–521, 543–553.

Minimal Essentials

Names of Persons: Woodrow Wilson; Pershing

Date: 1917 — entrance of the United States into the World War

Historical Terms: Liberty Loans; draft; blockade

Things to Remember

The United States entered the war because German submarines kept attacking our merchant vessels.

It took the United States several months to get ready.

The Allies, with American help, began to drive the Germans back on the western front.

Illustrative Material

McKINLEY. Illustrated Topics for American History: S. 46.
Keystone Views: 229, President marching in First Liberty Loan Parade; 231, Pack Inspection; 232, Soldiers about to enter Tear-Gas Trench; 235, "Feeding Grannie"; 236, French Soldiers; 238, In Belleau Wood; 239, Huge Tanks.
Perry Pictures: 130-D, John J. Pershing; 132-F, Woodrow Wilson.
Society for Visual Education. Schoolfilms: Heroes All; The Spirit of Service.
Travel, XXXI: 16–18 (October, 1918): Liberty Loan Posters.

Procedure during Assimilation

Reading as described on pages 24–29.
Children make a collection of pictures of the World War after July, 1917, and of America's part in the war. Mount it on the bulletin board.
Use records of war music.
Invite World War veterans to tell their experiences.
Make a sand-table representation of the western front, marking places where American troops fought.
Write cablegrams describing the progress of the war from the summer of 1917 to November, 1918.
On the slated map used for the previous story, show the advances on the western front up to November, 1918.[1] Mark scenes of battles in which Americans participated.[2]
Show the class a Liberty Bond.
Drill on minimal essentials.
Objective test.

Organization

The teacher and the pupils working together produce an outline somewhat similar to the following:

AMERICA'S PART IN THE WORLD WAR

    1. Why America entered the war
    2. How she got ready to fight
    3. American troops in Europe

Recitation

Invite a World War veteran to hear the recitation of this story and of that following (pp. 634–635).

---

[1] Halleck, R. P., *History of our Country*, p. 508; Schlesinger, *Political and Social History of the United States*, p. 526; Lawler, T. B., *Essentials of American History*, p. 459.
[2] Montgomery, D. W., *Leading Facts of American History*, p. 417; Long, W. J., *America*, p. 495.

---
4. End of the war

Preparation

Place on the board the table from McKinley mentioned on page 629.

"From this diagram which side seems almost certain to win? Why? Why, then, did it take so long?

"On which front can the final attack on Germany best be made? Why?"

No additional presentation is needed.

Assimilation

Readings

Upper Group

BEARD and BAGLEY. Our Old World Background, 434–439.
GORDY. Causes and Meaning of the Great War, 131–141 (difficult).
LOGIE. From Lincoln to Coolidge, 331–334, 339–342.
Compton's Pictured Encyclopedia (World War, pp. 3808–3812).
World Book (War of the Nations).

Average Group

BEARD and BAGLEY. A First Book in American History, 447–449.
BRYANT. I am an American, 149–156.
FORMAN. First Lessons in American History, 343–344.
GORDY. Elementary History of the United States, 325–330.
MORRIS. Primary History of the United States, 255–256.

Lower Group

CURTIS. Why we celebrate our Holidays, 120–123.
DAVIS. Stories of the United States, 267–269.

Teachers

HAYES. A Brief History of the Great War, 365–411.
McKINLEY. Collected Materials for the Study of the War, 57–62.
McKINLEY, COULOMB, and GERSON. A School History of the Great War, 167–180.
PAXSON. Recent History of the United States, 522–542, 553–554.

Minimal Essentials

Name of Place: **Versailles** (vĕr'sä′y' *or* vĕr sälz')
Date: **November 11, 1918** — armistice signed
Historical Terms: **armistice; peace conference; Treaty of Versailles**
Things to Remember

The Central Powers at length became worn out.
The last great German drive westward failed.
Germany became a republic.
The armistice was signed on November 11, 1918.
According to the terms of the treaty of peace Germany had to give up much territory and to pay huge sums of money.
Many new countries were created.

Illustrative Material

Educational Posters of the National Child Welfare Association: Armistice Day.
Keystone Views: 241, Drafting the Armistice Terms; 242, Plenary Session of Peace Conference; 243, Clemenceau, Wilson, and Lloyd George; 244, Gallery of Mirrors; 246, American Army of Occupation on the Rhine; 350, German Envoys on their Way to meet the Armistice Commission (slide only).

Procedure during Assimilation

Reading as described on pages 24–29.
The class makes a collection of poems of the World War.[1]
They write original verses.
On a slated map of Europe draw the new boundary lines created by the treaty. Compare with a pre-war map.[2]
Graph the figures for the war losses; for war costs.[3]
Ask a World War veteran to describe the reception accorded to the armistice by the troops.
Drill on minimal essentials.
Objective test.

Organization

The teacher writes the title and the children work out the subheads somewhat as follows:

END OF THE WAR

1. The last drive
2. The armistice
3. Terms of the Treaty of Versailles

Recitation

Unite with the preceding recitation.

---

5. Refusal of the United States to enter the League of Nations

Preparation

"When two boys quarrel over a bicycle, is fighting the only way to settle the question? How else might they settle it?

"How have nations settled their quarrels in the past? Does war decide which nation is right?

---

[1] "Editing Poems of the Great War." *The Twentieth Yearbook of the National Society for the Study of Education*, Part I, pp. 96–97.
[2] *The Literary Digest Atlas of the New Europe and the Far East*.
[3] Halleck, R. P., *History of our Country*, pp. 516–517.

"Suppose a question came up which was of interest to seven great nations. Six of the nations were willing to settle the question peaceably, but the seventh would not agree. Is there any way in which the six could force the seventh not to go to war?

"We are going to read today about a plan to prevent wars in the future, and what the United States has done about it."

No additional presentation is needed.

Assimilation

Readings

Upper Group

Compton's Pictured Encyclopedia (League of Nations).
World Book (League of Nations).

Average Group

BEARD and BAGLEY. A First Book in American History, 444–445.
FORMAN. First Lessons in American History, 344–345.
GORDY. Elementary History of the United States, 330.

Lower Group

Try FORMAN.

Teachers

BRAILSFORD. League of Nations.
JOHNSEN. League of Nations.
PAXSON. Recent History of the United States, 555–565.
PHELPS. Selected Articles on a League of Nations.

Minimal Essentials

Name of Place: **Geneva**
Historical Term: **League of Nations**
Things to Remember

The members of the League of Nations agree to settle their quarrels without fighting.
If any country will not agree, all the others will join against it.
The United States does not belong to the League.

Procedure during Assimilation

Reading as described on pages 24–29.
Make a picture collection of meetings of the League.
What is a baseball league? a basketball league? In what ways are they similar to a league of nations?
Use the dramatization "World Concord." Hague and Chalmers, *Dramatic Moments in American History*, pp. 296–314.
List the countries which belong to the League of Nations; list those which do not.[1]
List reasons why the United States should join the League; reasons why it should not.
Drill on minimal essentials
Objective test.

[1] World Almanac.

Organization

The teacher puts the following outline on the board:

LEAGUE OF NATIONS

1. Need of an agency for world peace
2. The plan of the League
3. Countries which joined
4. Why the United States did not join

Recitation

Children write a paragraph on each point.
A drill lesson on section III of Unit XII should be given at this point.

IV. At Home also the United States had been growing more Powerful
   1. It led the world in the manufacture of automobiles

Preparation

Children name and list different makes of automobiles.
"Where is each made? Do you know any foreign makes? Who is the greatest man that the automobile world has produced?"
No additional presentation is needed.

Assimilation
Readings
Upper Group

ADAMS. Harper's Machinery Book for Boys, 295–315.
BAKER. The Boys' Own Book of Great Inventions, 212–231 (difficult).
DARROW. Thinkers and Doers, 305–315.
DOUBLEDAY. Stories of Inventors, 69–84.
FORMAN. Stories of Useful Inventions, 161–163.
GORDY. Leaders in Making America, 414–418.
MARSHALL. The Story of Human Progress, 254–257 (difficult).
ROCHELEAU. Great American Industries: Transportation, 46–49.
SANFORD and OWEN. Modern Americans, 125–130.
TAPPAN. Travelers and Traveling, 74–81.
Compton's Pictured Encyclopedia (Automobile).
World Book (Automobile).

Average Group

LARGE. Everyday Wonders, 71–83.
NIDA. Following the Frontier, 315–316.
PARKMAN. Conquests of Invention, 310–324.

Lower Group

CHAMBERLAIN. How we Travel, 131–136.

Teachers

WILDMAN. Famous Leaders of Industry, 131–143.
New International Encyclopædia (Automobiles: Modern Period of Development).

Minimal Essentials

Name of Person: **Henry Ford**
Name of Place: **Detroit** (dē troit′)
Date: **1894** — coming of the automobile
Historical Term: **good roads**
Things to Remember
The United States leads the world in the number of automobiles.
The automobile has led to the building of good roads all over the country.
Much commerce is carried on by means of trucks.

Illustrative Material

Children's collection of pictures (see below).
Compton's Pictured Encyclopedia (Automobile).
National Geographic Magazine, XLIV : 337–414.
World Book (Automobile).

Procedure during Assimilation

Reading as described on pages 24–29.
Children make a picture collection of different makes of automobiles and mount it on the bulletin board. Make a collection showing the evolution of types since 1894.
If there is a local automobile or accessories factory, take the children to visit it.
A visitor to the Ford plant describes the methods used.
Graph the automobile census of the principal countries of the world.[1]
Drill on minimal essentials.
Objective test.

Organization

Children make their own outlines, the teacher helping only those who had difficulty with the last that they made alone.[2]

Recitation

Invite an automobile dealer to hear the stories.

---

[1] World Almanac.   [2] See page 631.

> 2. In aircraft it made a good beginning

Preparation

"Have you ever seen an aëroplane? For what is it used?
"Are all aëroplanes alike?
"Do you know where any of them are made?
"Is the United States ahead of or behind other countries in aircraft production? Let us read to find out."
No additional presentation is needed.

Assimilation

Readings

Upper Group

BACHMAN. Great Inventors and their Inventions, 253–261.
BAKER. The Boys' Book of Inventions, 321–354.
BARSTOW. The Progress of a United People, 125–134.
BOND. Inventions of the Great War, 123–208.
DARROW. Boys' Own Book of Great Inventions, 134–155.
DARROW. Masters of Science and Invention, 315–325.
DARROW. Thinkers and Doers, 326–340.
DOUBLEDAY. Stories of Inventors, 29–50.
FORMAN. Stories of Useful Inventions, 163–165.
GORDY. Leaders in Making America, 419–421.
HOLLAND. Historic Inventions, 273–295.
MARSHALL. The Story of Human Progress, 257–258.
PERRY and PRICE. American History, II : 281.
PIERCY. Great Inventions and Discoveries, 203–206.
ROCHELEAU. Great American Industries : Transportation, 264–275.
ROCHELEAU. Navigating the Air : Electric Railways, 1–12.
SANFORD and OWEN. Modern Americans, 99–107.
TAPPAN. Heroes of Progress, 217–227.
WADE. The Light Bringers, 112–141.
Compton's Pictured Encyclopedia (Airplane).
World Book (Flying Machine, Wright).

Average Group

LARGE. Everyday Wonders, 17–22.
McFEE. Stories of American Inventions, 226–251.
NIDA. Following the Frontier, 316–317.
PARKMAN. Conquests of Invention, 325–343.
Lessons in Community and National Life, Series C, 9–16.

Lower Group

EVERETT and REED. When they were Boys, 38–44.
CHAMBERLAIN. How we Travel, 182–187.
TATE, WITHERS, and BROWNE. Child's World, V : 363–369, 375–383.

Teachers

THOMPSON. The Age of Invention, 220–245.
WILDMAN. Famous Leaders of Industry, 327–338.

Minimal Essentials

Name of Persons: **Wright brothers**
Date: **1903** — coming of the aëroplane
Historical Terms: **aëroplane** (ā′ēr ŏ plān′) ; **airship**
Things to Remember
The Wright brothers made a successful flying machine in 1903.
Aëroplanes are useful both in peace and in war.
The United States has not progressed so fast in building aëroplanes for war as some other countries have.

Illustrative Material

McKINLEY. Illustrated Topics for Mediæval and Modern History: M. M. 36.
Keystone Views: 227, Wright Aëroplane.
National Geographic Magazine, XLIX: 1–61 (January, 1926).

Procedure during Assimilation

Reading as described on pages 24–29.
Children make a picture collection of different types of aircraft, and mount it on the bulletin board.
Newspaper clippings as to the work of aircraft are displayed on the bulletin board.
Someone who has made an airship journey describes the experience.
A member of the American flying forces during the war tells of his experiences.
Show children an air-mail stamp.
The class collects pictures of Lindbergh.
Drill on minimal essentials.
Objective test.

Organization

Children who made good outlines for the last story are allowed to help those whose work needed correction.

Recitation

Children who received help recite from their own outlines.

---

3. Submarines were invented

Preparation

"In the World War where else was fighting carried on besides on land and in the air?

"What is an assassin? Why was the submarine called the 'assassin of the sea'?

"Which nation would find submarines more helpful: Great Britain or Germany? Why?

"Are submarines useful during peace times?

"What nation invented submarines? Let us read to find out."
No additional presentation is needed.

Assimilation
Readings

Upper Group
BAKER. Boys' Book of Inventions, 1–39.
BISHOP. Story of the Submarine.
BOND. Inventions of the Great War, 232–275.
BOND. With the Men who do Things, 197–213.
COLLINS. Boys' Book of Submarines.
DARROW. The Boys' Own Book of Great Inventions, 173–193.
DARROW. Masters of Science and Invention, 306–314.
DARROW. Thinkers and Doers, 316–325.
DOUBLEDAY. Stories of Inventors, 155–179.
INGERSOLL. The Book of the Ocean, 152–154.
Compton's Pictured Encyclopedia (Submarine).
World Book (Submarine).

Average Group
McFEE. Stories of American Inventions, 166–205.

Lower Group
TATE, WITHERS, and BROWNE. Child's World, V: 384–390.

Teachers
LAKE. Submarine in War and Peace.
New International Encyclopædia (Torpedo Boat, Submarine).

Minimal Essentials

Historical Term: **submarine**
Things to Remember
Submarines can cross the ocean.
They are of little value in peace times.

Illustrative Material

McKINLEY. Illustrated Topics for Mediæval and Modern History: M. M. 36.
Keystone Views: 226, Submarines and Great Steel Cranes.

Procedure during Assimilation

Reading as described on pages 24–29.
Make a picture collection of submarines and mount it on the bulletin board.
A veteran of the navy who has seen submarine duty describes his experiences.
The class draws illustrations of the work of submarines in war time.
Drill on minimal essentials.
Objective test.

Organization

The teacher puts the following outline on the board:

THE SUBMARINE
1. The submarine itself
2. Its work during the war
3. Its value to the world

Recitation

Children who did not recite the last time give the stories.

> 4. It had made two amendments to the Constitution

Preparation

"What is prohibition? Has the United States always had prohibition? Why do we have it now?

"When election time comes does your mother vote? Have women always voted? Why does the United States allow women to vote now?" Explain the term "woman suffrage."

Show the children the Eighteenth and Nineteenth amendments to the Constitution.[1] "These are the laws which have given to the United States prohibition and woman suffrage."

No additional presentation is needed.

Assimilation

Readings

Upper Group

GORDY. Leaders in Making America, 449–454.
PERRY and PRICE. American History, II : 278–279.
SANFORD and OWEN. Modern Americans, 177–185.
Compton's Pictured Encyclopedia (Women's Rights, p. 3778; Prohibition, p. 2921).
World Book (Woman Suffrage, Prohibition).

Average Group

BEARD and BAGLEY. A First Book in American History, 407–414.
MOORE. When they were Girls, 30–36, 155–162.

Lower Group

YOUNG and FIELD. Literary Readers, V : 295–303.

Teachers

PAXSON. Recent History of the United States, 464–465, 578–579.
Dial, LXVI : 541–543.
Independent, XCV : 397; CI : 24–26.
Living Age, CCCIV : 134–146.
Outlook, CXXI : 180–181, 212–213; CXXIII : 527–528.
Review of Reviews, LXII : 380–384.
Survey, XXXVII : 128–130.
World's Work, XXXIX : 225–226.

---

[1] Gordy, W. F., *Elementary History of the United States*, p. 363; Perry, A. C., and Price, G. A., *American History*, II : 363; Robbins, C. L., *School History of the American People*, p. 570; Woodburn, J. A., and Moran, T. F., *Elementary American History and Government* (Revised Edition), Appendix, p. xxv; Montgomery, D. W., *Leading Facts of American History*, Appendix, p. xxiv; Long, W. J., *America*, Appendix, p. xxi.

Minimal Essentials

Historical Terms: **woman suffrage; prohibition**

Things to Remember

The temperance movement had been growing for a long time.

Prohibition was adopted because money spent for liquor is wasted.

When women were allowed to vote, the United States took another step toward democracy.

Illustrative Material

Educational Posters of the National Child Welfare Association: Justice to Women: Susan B. Anthony.

Keystone Views: 221, Dr. Anna Howard Shaw; 222, A Suffragette Parade.

Procedure during Assimilation

Reading as described on pages 24–29.

Children phrase for themselves the Eighteenth and Nineteenth amendments.

Children list arguments as to why it was right to allow women to vote; why it was not wise.

Should we obey laws of which we disapprove?

Drill on minimal essentials.

Objective test.

Organization

Children suggest two main subheads and a title for the outline.

Recitation

The class divides into two parts. Each recites on one of the points.

---

5. It had taken part in polar exploration

Preparation

Show on a globe the north pole; the south pole.

"Why would it be very difficult to reach the poles?

"Why would anyone want to reach the poles?

"In which one would the United States be more interested?

"Do you know who was the first man to reach the north pole? Let us read to find out how he accomplished the feat."

No additional presentation is needed.

Assimilation

Readings

Upper Group

CRUMP. Boys' Book of Arctic Exploration.

FARIS. Real Stories of the Geography Makers, 289–302.

HORTON. The Frozen North, 32–58, 81–103, 133–148, 158–169.

McLEAN. Heroes of the Farthest North and Farthest South, 154–173.
PERRY and PRICE. American History, II : 282–283.
SANFORD and OWEN. Modern Americans, 109–116.
WADE. The Light Bringers, 1–63.
Compton's Pictured Encyclopedia (Polar Exploration, Peary).
World Book (Polar Exploration, Peary, Frederick Cook).

Average Group
TAPPAN. Heroes of Progress, 245–253.

Lower Group
BARROWS and PARKER. Geography : Journeys in Distant Lands, 122–123.
PEARY. Snow Baby.

Teachers
PEARY. The North Pole.
National Geographic Magazine, XXI : 536 ff. (1910) ; XXXVII : 319 ff. (1920).
New International Encyclopædia (Polar Research).

Minimal Essentials

Name of Person: **Robert E. Peary** (pē′rĭ)
Names of Places: **Arctic; north pole**
Historical Term: **polar exploration**
Things to Remember
Polar exploration is difficult and dangerous work.
Peary had given his whole life to polar exploration.
Peary reached the north pole.

Illustrative Material

Compton's Pictured Encyclopedia (Polar Exploration, Peary).
National Geographic Magazine, XXXVII : 293–322; XLI : 639–646; XLVII : 673–722.
World Book (Polar Exploration).

Procedure during Assimilation

Reading as described on pages 24–29.
Picture study based on the illustrative material listed above.
Use the record "Discovery of the North Pole." [1]
Children write an imaginary diary of a polar trip.
Drill on minimal essentials.
Objective test.

Organization

The teacher and the children working together produce an
outline somewhat similar to the following :

THE UNITED STATES IN POLAR EXPLORATION

1. Difficulties of a polar trip
2. Peary's trip to the north pole

Recitation

A written paragraph on each of the points above.

[1] *Graded List of Victor Records for Home and School,* p. 123.

6. It called a disarmament conference

Preparation

"Have you any idea how much a modern battleship costs? About $20,000,000.[1] The United States possesses eighteen of these ships,[2] Great Britain twenty-two, Japan ten, France nine, Italy seven, and so on.

"Here is a picture of the relative amounts of money spent by the United States government for war, and the amounts spent for peace.[3]

"Explain this cartoon.[4]

"Every time a great nation builds an expensive new battleship, what do you suppose the other countries do? So it is a continual race to get ahead of each other.

"Can you see any way in which such an expensive and hopeless race might be avoided? Let us read to find out."

No additional presentation is needed.

Assimilation
Readings

Upper Group
> BEARD and BAGLEY. Our Old World Background, 464–465.
> SANFORD and OWEN. Modern Americans, 9–15.

Average Group
> GORDY. Elementary History of the United States, 331–333.

Lower Group
> Read BEARD and BAGLEY to this group.

Teachers
> *Forum*, LXVII: 54–63.
> *Independent*, CVII: 257–258, 320–321; CVIII: 169–171.
> *Literary Digest*, LXXI: 7–9; LXXII: 7–10.
> *Nation*, CXIII: 746–747; CXIV: 37–38, 184–185.
> *Outlook*, CXXIX: 465–467, 595; CXXXII: 649–650.
> *Political Science Quarterly*, XXXIX: 201–217.
> *Review of Reviews*, LXIV: 599–605; LXV: 33–41, 261–271.

[1] World Almanac.
[2] Ibid.
[3] Graph, *Literary Digest*, LXXXVII: 7 (December 26, 1925). Color red the sections representing war expenditures.
[4] Cartoon, *Literary Digest*, LXXXVIII: 13 (January 9, 1926).

Minimal Essentials

Historical Terms: **Washington Conference; disarmament; limitation of armaments; 5:5:3**

Things to Remember

President Harding invited many nations to come to Washington to talk about cutting down armaments.

They agreed to cut down their battleships to a certain number.

Any question about islands in the Pacific was to be settled peaceably.

No attempt was made at that time to cut down the size of armies or the number of submarines and aircraft.

Illustrative Material

Cartoons in: *Literary Digest*, XCII: 1 (March 26, 1927); 11 (April 30, 1927); XCIII: 13 (January 14, 1928); *World's Work*, LV: 429, 431.

Ford Educational Library: 10, Presidents of the United States.

Keystone Views: 249, World Disarmament Conference.

World's Work, LV: 350, 429, 431.

Procedure during Assimilation

Reading as described on pages 24–29.

Dramatize a meeting of the disarmament conference. A representative of Great Britain tells why competition in armaments is harmful; and a representative of the United States tells how this competition may be avoided. The conference decides which countries need the largest navies.[1]

Cablegrams of the proceedings are written for the newspapers.

Draw a diagram to illustrate the 5: 5: 3 ratio.

Design a series of borders to illustrate factors in warfare which many countries wish to limit or prohibit the use of, for example, submarines, cruisers, large land forces, poison gas, etc. A useful model may be found in the *School Arts' Magazine*, XXVII: 404 (1928).

Drill on minimal essentials.

Objective test.

Organization

The teacher and the children working together produce an outline somewhat similar to the following:

DISARMAMENT CONFERENCE

1. The armament race
2. Calling the disarmament conference
3. Its work

Recitation

Invite the high-school teacher of history to hear the stories.

[1] Based on population, foreign trade, and present size of naval forces.

V. Our Unsolved Problems
  1. What to do with subject races
  2. How to make our own citizens obey our laws
  3. The relations between capital and labor

Preparation

"What are some of the problems which the United States has solved during its history?

"What problems have we mentioned which have not yet been solved?" (Philippine independence, capital and labor, limitation of land armaments, etc.)

"Do you suppose these are all the problems that the United States ever will have? Who will have to solve the future problems? Why have we studied history for two years?"

No additional presentation is needed.

Assimilation

Readings

Upper Group

GORDY. Leaders in Making America, 467–472.
MARSHALL. The Story of Human Progress, 534–535, 537–539.
MONTGOMERY. Beginners' American History, 253–254, 257–258.

Average Group

BRYANT. I am an American, 160–162.
GORDY. Elementary History of the United States, 334–335.
GORDY. Our Patriots, 180–186.
MACE. Primary History, 395–396.
MOWRY. First Steps in the History of our Country, 326–327.

Lower Group

Try MACE and GORDY.

Teachers

ADAMS. The Power of Ideals in American History, 65–94 (Manifest Destiny).
HART. National Ideals historically Traced, 47–67 (Dependent Races).

Procedure during Assimilation

Reading as described on pages 24–29.
Read with the children, as the last lesson, the reference from Marshall's *Story of Human Progress* (see above).

Tests at the end of the unit: *Van Wagenen Information Scale K 1*, "The Civil War to the Present."

MINIMAL ESSENTIALS OF UNIT XII

PERSONS	PLACES	TERMS	DATES
George Dewey	Arctic	aëroplane	*1823.* Monroe Doctrine
General Foch	Belgium	airship	
Henry Ford	Canal Zone	alliances	*1894.* Coming of the automobile
Colonel Goethals	China	allies	
Colonel Gorgas	Cuba	armistice	*1898.* Annexation of Hawaii
John Hay	Detroit	blockade	
General Hindenburg	Geneva	Boxer rebellion	*1898.* Spanish-American War
William McKinley	Havana	Central Powers	
Robert E. Peary	Hawaii	"crossroads of the Pacific"	*1903.* Coming of the aëroplane
General Pershing	Honolulu	Danish West Indies	
Theodore Roosevelt	Manila	disarmament	*1914.* Beginning of the World War
Woodrow Wilson	Marne	draft	
Wright brothers	Mexican border	5:5:3	*1914.* Opening of the Panama Canal
	north pole	good roads	
	Panama	hundred days' war with Spain	*1917.* Purchase of Virgin Islands
	Peking	island possessions	*1917.* Entrance of the United States into the World War
	Philippines	kaiser	
	Porto Rico	League of Nations	
	Verdun	Liberty Loans	*November 11, 1918.* The armistice
	Versailles	limitation of armaments	
	Virgin Islands	*Lusitania*	Drill on the peaks of the time chart
		Maine	
		Monroe Doctrine	
		"open door"	
		Panama Canal	
		partition of China	
		peace conference	
		Philippine independence	
		polar exploration	
		Progressive party	
		protectorate	
		Rough Riders	
		Spanish-American War	
		submarine war zone	
		submarine	
		tank	
		Treaty of Versailles	
		Washington Conference	
		"watchful waiting"	
		western front	
		woman suffrage	
		World War	

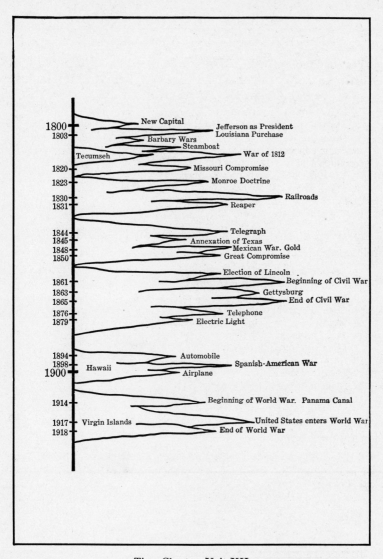

1800	New Capital
1803	Jefferson as President
	Louisiana Purchase
	Barbary Wars
	Steamboat
Tecumseh	War of 1812
1820	Missouri Compromise
1823	Monroe Doctrine
1830	Railroads
1831	Reaper
1844	Telegraph
1845	Annexation of Texas
1848	Mexican War. Gold
1850	Great Compromise
	Election of Lincoln
1861	Beginning of Civil War
1863	Gettysburg
1865	End of Civil War
1876	Telephone
1879	Electric Light
1894	Automobile
1898	Spanish-American War
Hawaii	
1900	Airplane
1914	Beginning of World War. Panama Canal
1917	Virgin Islands United States enters World War
1918	End of World War

Time Chart — Unit XII

TESTS ON THE ENTIRE UNIT

(To be given after all the stories are completed)

Test of Place-Sense. I. Pass double-sized outline maps of North America, and crayon. Give the following directions:

1. Place the letter *C* in Cuba.
2. Make a dot where Havana is.
3. Make a cross (X) in Porto Rico.
4. Draw two lines (====) where the Canal Zone is.
5. Color Panama yellow.
6. Make a circle (O) around the Virgin Islands.
7. Trace the Mexican border in green.
8. Make a blue dot for Detroit.
9. Place a star (*) over the north pole.
10. Color the Arctic brown.

II. Pass double-sized outline maps of the world. Give the following directions:

1. Make a dot where Honolulu is.
2. Color the Hawaiian Islands green.
3. Make a cross (+) where Manila is.
4. Color the Philippines yellow.
5. Write the word *China* in the right place.
6. Make a blue dot for Peking.
7. Put the letter *B* in Belgium.
8. Show the Marne by a wavy line (〰).
9. Make a circle (O) for Verdun.
10. Make a brown dot for Geneva.
11. Draw a little arrow (→) from Paris to Versailles.

Test of Time-Sense. Pass mimeographed sheets with the following directions:

I. Here is a list of names. Put the figure 1 before the name of the man who did his great work first, the figure 2 before the name of the man who came next, and so on.

　　　　　_ _ _ William McKinley
　　　　　_ _ _ General Pershing
　　　　　_ _ _ Theodore Roosevelt
　　　　　_ _ _ President Monroe

II. Here is another list. Do the same.

　　　　　_ _ _ General Sherman
　　　　　_ _ _ Colonel Gorgas
　　　　　_ _ _ General Hindenburg
　　　　　_ _ _ George Dewey

III. Here is another list. Do the same.

   _ _ _ Wright brothers
   _ _ _ John Hay
   _ _ _ Robert E. Peary
   _ _ _ Woodrow Wilson

IV. Here is another list. Do the same.

   _ _ _ Colonel Goethals
   _ _ _ General Foch
   _ _ _ Henry Ford

V. Here is a list of events. Put the figure 1 before that which happened first, the figure 2 before that which happened next, and so on.

   _ _ _ the coming of the aëroplane
   _ _ _ the Monroe Doctrine
   _ _ _ the Spanish-American War
   _ _ _ the armistice

VI. Here is another list. Do the same.

   _ _ _ annexation of Hawaii
   _ _ _ the opening of the Panama Canal
   _ _ _ United States enters the World War
   _ _ _ coming of the automobile

VII. Here is another list. Do the same.

   _ _ _ beginning of the World War
   _ _ _ the United States gets possession of the Philippines
   _ _ _ purchase of the Virgin Islands

VIII. Here is a list of dates:

1914	1917
November 11, 1918	1894
1898	

Place each one in the right blank in the sentences below:

1. The Panama Canal was finally opened in _ _ _ _.
2. The first really successful automobile was built in _ _ _ _.
3. The Virgin Islands were purchased in _ _ _ _.
4. The armistice was signed on _ _ _ _.
5. The Spanish-American War took place in _ _ _ _.

IX. Here is another list of dates:

1898	1823
1917	1914
1903	

Do the same.

1. The World War began in _ _ _ _.
2. The first really successful aëroplanes were built in _ _ _ _.
3. Hawaii was annexed in _ _ _ _.
4. The United States entered the World War in _ _ _ _.
5. The Monroe Doctrine was written in _ _ _ _.

Test on Persons. Pass mimeographed sheets of the following:

I. Here is a list of names:

Theodore Roosevelt	George Dewey
General Foch	John Hay
Colonel Gorgas	Wright brothers
Henry Ford	

Place each name in the right place in the sentences below:

1. The first people to build a really successful aëroplane were the _ _ _ _ _ _ _ _.
2. _ _ _ _ _ _ _ _ was the President who had the Panama Canal dug.
3. _ _ _ _ _ _ _ _ won a great naval victory in the Spanish-American War.
4. The "open door" was suggested by _ _ _ _ _ _ _ _.
5. The man who made the Panama Canal Zone a healthful place in which to live was _ _ _ _ _ _ _ _.
6. The world's greatest builder of automobiles is _ _ _ _ _ _ _ _.
7. The supreme commander of the Allied forces during the World War was _ _ _ _ _ _ _ _.

II. Here is another list:

Colonel Goethals	William McKinley
Woodrow Wilson	General Hindenburg
General Pershing	Robert E. Peary

Do the same.

1. _ _ _ _ _ _ _ _ _ _ _ _ discovered the north pole.
2. _ _ _ _ _ _ _ _ was President during the Spanish-American War.
3. _ _ _ _ _ _ _ _ was President during the World War.
4. _ _ _ _ _ _ _ _ was commander of the American forces during the World War.
5. The man who dug the Panama Canal was _ _ _ _ _ _ _ _.
6. _ _ _ _ _ _ _ _ was a commander of the German forces during the World War.

Test on Historical Terms. The teacher prepares descriptions such as the following, which may have been used previously as the subject of drill games.

I. Here is a list of terms:

Monroe Doctrine	*Maine*
prohibition	"crossroads of the Pacific"
limitation of armaments	Spanish-American War
polar exploration	airship
5:5:3	kaiser

Place each in the right blank in the sentences below:

1. _ _ _ _ means that for every five battleships which the United States and Great Britain have, Japan may have 3.
2. The German title for their emperor was _ _ _ _ _.
3. The _ _ _ _ was an American warship that was blown up.
4. Forbidding the manufacture or sale of liquor is _ _ _ _.
5. Cutting down land or naval forces is called _ _ _ _ _ _ _ _ _ _ _ _.
6. A large vessel sailing through the air and depending on gases to make it float is an _ _ _ _ _.
7. The war for the liberation of Cuba was the _ _ _ _ _ _ _ _ _ _ _ _.
8. Searching through unknown regions near the poles is _ _ _ _ _ _ _ _.
9. Hawaii is called the _ _ _ _ _ _ _ _ _ _ _ _ _ _ _.
10. The principle that European countries should not interfere in the affairs of the Western Hemisphere nor colonize there is the _ _ _ _ _ _ _ _.

II. Here is another list:

Washington Conference	disarmament
woman suffrage	submarine
World War	aëroplane
hundred days' war with Spain	"watchful waiting"
good roads	Rough Riders

Do the same.

1. The recent war between the Central and Allied powers was the _ _ _ _ _ _ _ _.
2. A boat that can travel beneath the surface of the water is a _ _ _ _ _.
3. The act of greatly reducing land or naval forces is _ _ _ _ _.
4. Our policy to wait and see what would happen in Mexico was _ _ _ _ _ _ _ _.
5. Roads which have been given a hard surface are _ _ _ _ _ _ _ _.
6. The Spanish-American War is sometimes called the _ _ _ _, _ _ _ _ _ _ _ _ _ _ _ _.
7. A flying machine supported by wings is an _ _ _ _ _.
8. The meeting to talk about limitation of armaments was the _ _ _ _ _ _ _ _.
9. A special troop of cavalry in the Spanish-American War was called the _ _ _ _ _ _ _ _.
10. Women's right to vote at elections is _ _ _ _ _ _ _ _.

III. Here is another list:

League of Nations	armistice
Danish West Indies	*Lusitania*
Philippine independence	allies
peace conference	protectorate
Progressive party	"open door"

Do the same.

1. The meeting to talk over the terms by which the war should be ended was the _ _ _ _ _ _ _ _.

2. A great ship blown up by the Germans was the _ _ _ _.

3. Countries leagued with each other are _ _ _ _.

4. Before we bought the Virgin Islands they were the _ _ _ _ _ _ _ _ _ _ _ _ _.

5. An agreement to stop fighting for a little while is an _ _ _ _.

6. The political party organized by Theodore Roosevelt was the _ _ _ _ _ _ _ _.

7. The protection and part control which a stronger nation has over a weaker is a _ _ _ _.

8. The alliance which attempts to prevent war is the _ _ _ _ _ _ _ _ _ _ _ _.

9. Giving all nations the right to trade on equal terms in China is the _ _ _ _ _ _ _ _.

10. The problem of whether or not to allow the Philippines to become a nation is the problem of _ _ _ _ _ _ _ _.

IV. Here is another list:

Treaty of Versailles	island possessions
Boxer rebellion	alliances
blockade	partition of China
draft	Panama Canal
Liberty Loans	tank

Do the same.

1. The shutting in of a line of coast by enemy ships is a _ _ _ _.

2. Compelling men to enroll for military or naval service is a _ _ _ _.

3. Connections formed between states to aid each other in war are _ _ _ _.

4. The great waterway dug between the Atlantic and the Pacific is the _ _ _ _ _ _ _ _.

5. The money raised by the United States to carry on the World War was raised largely by _ _ _ _ _ _ _ _.

6. An armored gasoline engine traveling on a caterpillar tread is a _ _ _ _.

7. The terms which ended the World War made up the _ _ _ _ _ _ _ _ _ _ _ _.

8. Our possessions in the Philippines and Porto Rico are often called our _ _ _ _ _ _ _ _.

9. An uprising against foreigners in China was the _ _ _ _ _ _ _ _.

10. The dividing up of China's trade and territory among other powers was called the _ _ _ _ _ _ _ _ _ _ _ _.

V. Here is another list:

> submarine war zone
> western front
> Central Powers

Do the same

1. The part of the seas surrounding the British Isles was declared a
_ _ _ _ _ _ _ _ _ _ _ _ by Germany.

2. Where the armies of the Allies and the armies of the Central Powers
came together in western Europe was called the _ _ _ _ _ _ _ _ _.

3. Germany, Austria, Turkey, and Bulgaria were the chief _ _ _ _ _ _ _ _ _.

COMPREHENSION TEST ON UNIT XII

1. *Check the best answer:*

a. The United States

 _ _ _ has solved all its problems
 _ _ _ still has many problems to solve

b. The United States did not join the League of Nations

 _ _ _ because it was afraid of being mixed up in the troubles of Europe
 _ _ _ because it did not want to help any other nation
 _ _ _ because President Washington had told us to stay at home

c. When there was trouble on the Mexican border the United States

 _ _ _ thought this was a good chance to seize Mexico's land
 _ _ _ helped Mexico to settle the trouble
 _ _ _ waited to see what would happen

d. During recent years the United States

 _ _ _ has explored many new lands
 _ _ _ has kept all her explorers at home
 _ _ _ has discovered the north pole

e. When Germany was quite worn out, and failed in the last westward
    drive, she

 _ _ _ gave up all the land she had conquered
 _ _ _ asked for an armistice
 _ _ _ got Russia to help her

f. We bought the Virgin Islands

 _ _ _ because they would help us to protect the Panama Canal
 _ _ _ because they were valuable
 _ _ _ because we wanted more territory

g. The Monroe Doctrine stated

 _ _ _ that European powers must not come to America at all
 _ _ _ that European powers must not colonize in nor interfere with
    the Western Hemisphere
 _ _ _ that America would keep out of Asia and Europe

2. *Check two answers:*

The last two amendments to our Constitution were about

_ _ _ prohibition   _ _ _ the income tax

_ _ _ negro votes   _ _ _ woman suffrage

3. *Check the best answer:*

   a. The United States entered the World War

_ _ _ because she hated Germany

_ _ _ because she thought the Allies were going to lose

_ _ _ because Germany interfered with her shipping

   b. We wanted to build a canal at Panama

_ _ _ to be ahead of the other nations

_ _ _ to save the long journey around South America

_ _ _ to get Panama away from Colombia

4. *Check the* ***three*** *best answers:*

Three great inventions during this period were

_ _ _ the telegraph   _ _ _ the automobile

_ _ _ the submarine   _ _ _ the railroad

_ _ _ the telephone   _ _ _ the aëroplane

5. *Check the best answer:*

   a. The World War was caused chiefly

_ _ _ by the struggle for markets

_ _ _ by Germany's wickedness

_ _ _ by the kaiser

   b. The United States wanted the "open door" in China

_ _ _ because she was so near to China

_ _ _ because she was not so selfish as the other countries

_ _ _ because she did not have any section to trade with in China

   c. We secured Hawaii

_ _ _ by purchase

_ _ _ by annexation

_ _ _ by the Spanish-American War

6. *Check two answers:*

   a. Ever since the Spanish-American War we have kept

_ _ _ Cuba   _ _ _ the Philippines

_ _ _ Porto Rico   _ _ _ the British Isles

   b. The Spanish-American War was caused

_ _ _ by our desire to obtain Cuba

_ _ _ by the fact that Americans had property in Cuba

_ _ _ by our sympathy with Cuba

_ _ _ by our hatred of Spain

7. *What is the title of Unit XII?*

ORGANIZATION OF THE UNIT AS A WHOLE

A skeleton outline of the Unit is placed on the board, thus:

I.
  1.
II.
  1., etc.

The class is divided into two parts, and each child is supplied with a narrow slip of paper containing the name of one story. A child on one side calls out the name of his story and designates a child on the other side to place the name in the outline. He is the judge as to whether or not the answer is correct. The teacher may keep the score and act as referee.

RECITATION OF THE UNIT AS A WHOLE

Each child prepares the detailed story of one subject, and illustrates his talk by the construction projects already completed.

REVIEW. DRILL WORK ON THE UNITS AS A WHOLE

Teach children how to read the centuries; for example, that 1000 is the eleventh century. The diagram on page 660 may help. This diagram may be put on the board.

The teacher gives drill exercises, such as asking children to locate as to century the following years: *1453, 1498, 1300, 1000*, etc. Each child tells in what century[1] the given year is, and why it is always named in advance of the index figures.[2]

In this connection, also teach what *1498* means as a date;[3] that is, that one thousand four hundred ninety-eight years have elapsed since the birth of Christ (approximately). Also teach the meaning of A. D. (anno Domini, "in the year of our Lord").

Use the parts of exercises suitable for intermediate grades in F. E. Moyer's *Self-Testing Review Book of American History and Government.*

[1] For proof that fourth-grade children have the concept "century," see Kelty, M. G., "Time Expressions comprehended by Children of the Elementary School," *The Elementary School Journal*, XXV: 615–616.
[2] Ibid. pp. 616–617.   [3] Ibid. pp. 617–618.

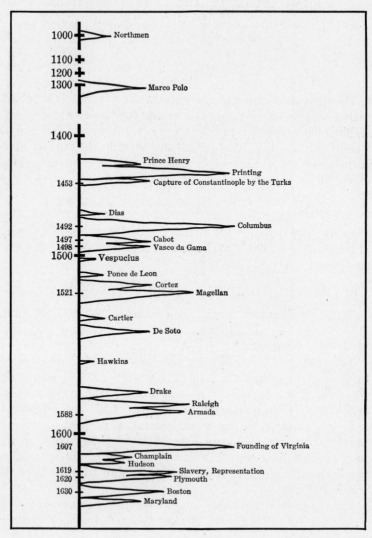

Time Chart of American History

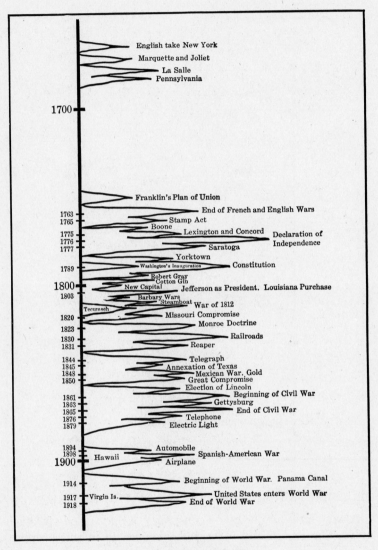

English take New York
Marquette and Joliet
La Salle
Pennsylvania

1700

Franklin's Plan of Union
End of French and English Wars
1763
1765   Stamp Act
            Boone
1775   Lexington and Concord   Declaration of
1776   Independence
1777   Saratoga
            Yorktown
1789   Washington's Inauguration   Constitution
            Robert Gray
            Cotton Gin
1800   New Capital   Jefferson as President. Louisiana Purchase
1803
            Barbary Wars
            Steamboat   War of 1812
Tecumseh
1820   Missouri Compromise
1823   Monroe Doctrine
1830   Railroads
1831   Reaper
1844   Telegraph
1845   Annexation of Texas
1848   Mexican War. Gold
1850   Great Compromise
            Election of Lincoln
1861   Beginning of Civil War
1863   Gettysburg
1865   End of Civil War
1876   Telephone
1879   Electric Light

1894   Automobile
1898   Hawaii   Spanish-American War
1900   Airplane

1914   Beginning of World War. Panama Canal

1917   Virgin Is.   United States enters World War
1918   End of World War

Time Chart of American History

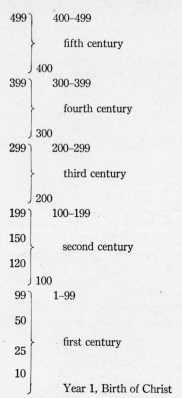

TESTS OVER THE WHOLE FIELD

Van Wagenen American History Scales:

Information Scale R 1
Information Scale S 1
Information Scale U 1

ORGANIZATION AND RECITATION OF THE ENTIRE WORK

A pageant [1] may be given consisting of one episode for each unit. The fourth and fifth grades coöperate in this exercise.

---

[1] "The Pageant — 'End of the School Year.'" *The Twentieth Yearbook of the National Society for the Study of Education,* Part I, p. 52. See also McElroy, "The Mother Speaks" and "The Children of Old Glory," in *Dramatic and Musical Programs for School Grades.*

PART III. ILLUSTRATIVE LESSONS

LESSON I

A DRILL LESSON IN HISTORY

[Planned by Miss Nelle E. Moore, State Normal School, Bloomsburg, Pennsylvania]

Teacher's Purpose. To give the pupils practice in associating names of important characters with correct events in history, so that recall is prompt and accurate, and to give each pupil specific help with the names of characters he has not been able to remember.

SUBJECT MATTER	PROCEDURE
1. *a.* Individual sets of flash cards containing individual difficulties. (See Chart I, p. 41, for each child's individual difficulties.)	1. *a.* Individual sets of cards are passed to pupils having made errors on the tests. Each is asked to choose from the group who have made perfect scores some child to help him go over his list and help him correct his mistakes. (Names of those having perfect scores are found on Chart I.)
b. List of characters on the board:[1] Americus Vespucius John Cabot Cartier Champlain Cortez De Soto Francis Drake John Hawkins Henry Hudson Magellan Ponce de Leon Walter Raleigh	*b.* Children not chosen as helpers are given these instructions: "Look over the list of characters on the board and word one good question you might ask your classmates about each. If you cannot think of a good question, take your text and look for that man's name in the index, find the page, read what your text says about him, and then make a question. You may use these questions in a game[2] we shall play in a few minutes."

c. Texts.

[1] Taken from Unit II, p. 153.
[2] Woodburn, J. A., and Moran, T. F., *Introduction to American History*, p. 298.

2. The same as *b* above.

2. A pupil from those having made a perfect score in the test is selected to be the leader in the game "Guess who I Am." The leader selects a name from the list, whispers it to the teacher, then says: "I am thinking of one of the characters we have studied. Who is it?" Other pupils question him as follows: "Are you thinking of the man who —" (*telling one thing the character did*). The leader answers, "No, I am not thinking of —" (*names character*), or, "Yes, I am thinking of —" (*names character*). A pupil remains in the lead until the correct character is named or until he makes a mistake. New leaders will be chosen from the group having made perfect scores in the test as they are needed. (*Continue the game for about five minutes*.) Pupils having sets of cards on their desks are asked to keep these cards in sight as the game goes on, and to question about those characters which they are having the hardest time to remember.

3. Same list of characters.   (See chart of errors, p. 41.)

3. One child who made errors on the test is sent from the room. The teacher reads to the class the names this child missed on the test. They select one of these names to use in the game. The pupil returns to the room and questions the class as pupils were questioned in step 2. The class replies in concert as the leader replied in step 2.

Different pupils are sent from the room. The teacher selects them so that all characters are reviewed (see Chart I; about five minutes are needed for this step).

4. Statements for the board:

_ _ _ _ _ _ _ discovered the Mississippi River.
_ _ _ _ discovered the St. Lawrence River.

4. Statements telling important things done by these characters have been written on the board (one on each section of the board). Pupils having sets of flash cards are asked

_ _ _ _ was the first man to sail around the world.

_ _ _ _ _ _ _ _ _ _ _ _ discovered Florida.

_ _ _ _ _ _ _ _ discovered the mainland of North America.

America was named for _ _ _ _ _ _ _ _.

_ _ _ _ built Quebec.

_ _ _ _ _ _ _ _ discovered the Hudson River.

_ _ _ _ _ _ _ _ began the English slave trade.

_ _ _ _ _ _ _ _ tried to plant colonies in America for England but failed.

_ _ _ _ _ _ _ _ was the first Englishman to sail around the world.

_ _ _ _ conquered the natives of Mexico.

to go to the board and place each card, face to the board, under the statement that tells what he did. Pupils having no cards to place are then sent to look these cards over and correct the mistakes made. This exercise serves as a test of the day's drill.[1]

---

[1] See pages 40–43 for a description of this type of lesson as worked out with a fourth-grade class.

LESSON II

COMPOSING A DRAMATIZATION

This series of lessons was taught by Miss Clara A. Trotter, Director of the Intermediate Department in the Oshkosh State Teachers College. Eight children in the advanced reading group of the fifth grade constituted the special class. Their reading scores follow:

NATIONAL INTELLIGENCE SCALE B, FORM I

Test, June 2, 1926

NAME	C. A.	SCORE	M. A.	I. Q.	R. A.	R. Q.	
Gilbert . .	10–7	114	12–9	120	14–7	137	
Hamilton .	11–2	117	13–0	116	13–9	123	
Clarence . .	10–5	86	10–11	105	10–8	102	Stanford
Melvin. . .	10–11	115	12–10	116	13–11	127	Achieve-
Virginia . .	9–8	103	12–0	124	14–9	152	ment Test
Garner . .	10–7	123	13–6	127	14–9	139	
Eleanor . .	10–4	119	13–2	127	13–1	126	
Helen . . .	10–6	117	13–0	123	13–0	123	

The lessons, including the reading, extended over eight days, of which only three are described in detail.

INTRODUCTORY LESSON

On the board were written, before class, the following words used in the study:

frontispiece
autobiography

MISS TROTTER. You have been invited to make a play, to be really printed in a book. Should you like to do that?

GARNER. Yes.

MISS TROTTER. How many would like to make up a play to be printed in a book? You may raise your hands. (*Everyone does.*) Miss Kelty is writing a book, a history book, that will be used in the fifth grade, and she would like very much to have a play in that history book made up by children. (*Expres-*

sions of pleasure) She wants the play to be about Theodore Roosevelt. Do you know anything interesting about Theodore Roosevelt? (*Five volunteers*)

MELVIN. He was the president of the United States once upon a time.

GARNER. Didn't he build the Panama Canal?

MISS TROTTER. He oversaw the building of the Canal.

GILBERT. He was the first president to go across the ocean on a boat when he was president, wasn't he?

MISS TROTTER. No; that was President Wilson. Roosevelt did go across the ocean, but not while he was president of the United States. Do you know anything else interesting about Theodore Roosevelt?

GARNER. Didn't he go hunting in Africa?

MISS TROTTER. Do you know whether he did or not?

GARNER. Yes.

ELEANOR. I think it is some relation to him who is hunting in Africa. (*Shows a rather confused idea of present-day events.*)

MISS TROTTER. You think it is not Theodore Roosevelt?

ELEANOR. No.

MISS TROTTER. If you were to make up a play about Theodore Roosevelt, what should you need to do?

MELVIN. We must think it out in our heads, to think what we are going to have — not all details; some important parts.

VIRGINIA. We must read about him to find out things.

MISS TROTTER. (*To the class*) Do you agree with Virginia? Do you remember how you made up the play for the puppet show?

GARNER. We all coöperated to think out the words.

MISS TROTTER. And why were you able to make up the play about Goldilocks?

VIRGINIA. We knew the story.

MISS TROTTER. Exactly. You do not yet know the story of Roosevelt, and you must learn some interesting things. That is what we are going to do this morning. Do you all think it would be interesting to make a play?

CHILDREN. Yes. (*Smile and nod.*)

MISS TROTTER. (*Showing a group of books*) This is a pretty big book, isn't it? We are not going to attempt to read it all, but there are certain parts of this big book that we can use. (GILBERT *remarks that he will read all of it.*) All these books except one are drawn from the city library by grown people, but much of the material you can read. In each book you will find a sheet of typed directions. Go through all the directions before you begin any reading at all. As soon as you have finished what you are to read, close the book and come forward to get another. How many of you know what the frontispiece in a book is? (*Three children do.*)

GILBERT. I think it is a picture of something about the book — right in the front (*picks up a book*). This book has it.

MISS TROTTER. Find the frontispiece in another book. (GILBERT *does so.*) Hold it up for all the children to see. How many know what an autobiography is? (*No one does.*) An autobiography is a book that a man writes about himself — the story of his own life. You will find here Theodore Roosevelt's autobiography (*showing the book*). Who wrote this book?

GARNER. Theodore Roosevelt (*mispronouncing the name*).

MISS TROTTER. I looked up the pronunciation of that word, and I find that it is Roosevelt — a long *o*. As soon as I give each one of you a book, read the directions and proceed.

GILBERT. Is this really going to be printed in a book and published?

MISS TROTTER. Really printed and published, and people all over the United States will read this play. (*Gives him another book.*) This book is Hamilton's; but you may use it today if you want it, and these are extras. One more thing before you begin. I have listed all the references which we are to read. Each time you finish reading one will you record your initial just below it? Eventually everyone will have read all the material.

The teacher then gave out the books, assigning each first to the child to whom it would make a particular appeal. The book list and the guiding study-questions follow:

ROOSEVELT. African Game Trails.
ROOSEVELT. Theodore Roosevelt : an Autobiography.
ROOSEVELT. Theodore Roosevelt's Letters to his Children.
ROOSEVELT. Through the Brazilian Wilderness.
ROOSEVELT. The Wilderness Hunter, 299–302.
Scribner's Magazine, XLVI: 385–406, 513–539, 652–669; XLVII: 1–16, 129–143, 257–277.

The selected group read, in addition to the above, as many of the titles given in Unit XII of the text (p. 623) as they have time for. The rest of the class read only the titles given in the text.

ROOSEVELT, AFRICAN GAME TRAILS

1. Who wrote this book?
   Is this an interesting thing for a man to do?

2. Look at the frontispiece. Does the picture tell you anything interesting about Theodore Roosevelt?

3. Look at the pictures on the following pages to see if they tell you any interesting thing that Roosevelt has done: 138, 143, 217, 244, 252, 256, 266, 343, 358, 360, 364, 380, 452.

4. Read about the elephant hunt (pp. 251–254).

5. Be ready to tell about Roosevelt's interesting experience in shooting an elephant.

6. Do you find any material at the bottom of page 253 that could be used for a scene in a play? If so, how would you arrange the scene? What do you think the characters would talk about? Plan the conversation.

THEODORE ROOSEVELT: AN AUTOBIOGRAPHY

1. Do you know what an autobiography is?
2. Read, beginning on page 34. What interesting things does Roosevelt say about killing elephants in Africa?
3. Roosevelt had an interesting experience hunting another animal. What was it?
4. What animal was Roosevelt hunting when he had his most narrow escape? Read about it. In another book you will find pictures of this.

THEODORE ROOSEVELT'S LETTERS TO HIS CHILDREN

1. Study the frontispiece. As you read a letter you may want to turn back to this picture to see the child to whom the letter is addressed.
2. Read the Introduction, p. 3, and the first paragraph on page 4. Read more if it seems interesting.
3. As you read each letter, notice to whom the letter is addressed.
4. After you have read the letters select four of the most interesting.
5. The letters on the following pages are very interesting: 98, 99, 100, 101, 105 (The Picture Letter), 121, 148, 153, 155, 157, 167, 199, 209, 216, 228.
6. Do these letters help you to know what kind of man Roosevelt was? What do they tell you about him?

ROOSEVELT, THROUGH THE BRAZILIAN WILDERNESS

1. Who wrote this book?
2. Do you know where Brazil is? Find it on a map of South America. There is a map at the back of the book showing Brazil.
3. On this map do you find a river named for Roosevelt? Why do you suppose it was named for him?
4. The river was known as the River of Doubt. The pictures on pages 244, 249, 250, 252, 254, 259, 262, 266, will tell you of the dangers in exploring this river.
5. Perhaps you will want to read parts of this chapter.

ROOSEVELT, THE WILDERNESS HUNTER

1. Who wrote this book?
2. If you will read from page 299 to page 302, you will get a very interesting story about a grizzly bear.

Scribner's Magazine, XLVI. Study the pictures on the following pages: 385–406, 513–539, 652–669.

Scribner's Magazine, XLVII. Study the pictures on the following pages: 1–16, 129–143, 257–277.

Some children examined the frontispieces before starting to read. All read the guiding questions or directions first, and then occasionally during their reading went back to them for specific points.

Concentration of attention on the reading was so intense that when the stenographer left the room (as she did when the reading had begun) only one child looked up. The thirty-six observers drew not one glance. When chairs were moved to allow for conference between teacher and pupils, no one looked up.

Melvin and Gilbert had books in which no reading was asked for, but both read, Gilbert using the entire period on the story of the River of Doubt.

Melvin finished first, having read about three minutes. He came to the desk, left his book, signed his initials, and sat down to confer with the teacher. Each child followed the same procedure.

Some of the questions which the teacher asked during the conference periods were these:

Did you read anything interesting?
What was the most interesting part?
Who were the characters? Which pictures did you like?
Could we use this story in a dramatization?

In answer to the last question some of the answers were as follows:

It's pretty hard, but I'll think about it.

Yes, you could have somebody writing letters or reading them.

The boys could have a lion hunt. The scene could be in Africa, and the characters Roosevelt and his son.

After twenty-five minutes Miss Trotter said: "You may close your books now. Tomorrow you will have another opportunity to read. What titles can we apply to Roosevelt?"

MELVIN. He was a great hunter. (MISS TROTTER *writes on the board* "1. Great Hunter.")

VIRGINIA. If he didn't succeed the first time, he tried again.

GARNER. He was patient and ambitious.

MISS TROTTER. Those are qualities. We will use titles only.

ELEANOR. He was a lover of children.

MISS TROTTER. How do you know?

ELEANOR. Because he wrote letters to his children almost all of the time, from the dates almost every two or three days. And because he told them he loved them. (MISS TROTTER *writes on the board* "2. Lover of Children.")

GILBERT. He was a great explorer.

MISS TROTTER. Did you know that before? (MISS TROTTER *writes on the board* "3. Great Explorer.")

GILBERT. I didn't know whether it was Roosevelt or his sons.

A pause ensued here. The teacher showed a book Roosevelt had written; children examined their books to see how many were written by him.

Five children volunteered, as another title, "A Great Writer."

Miss Trotter wrote on the board "4. An Interesting Writer." Garner read the list of four points from the board.

MISS TROTTER. We shall read more about each of these points later, since each person is to read all the books on the list. I shall post this list in your room, and, as you read, please record your initials under the name of the book. We shall discuss the material more in detail later. As you read, keep in mind how you could work the material over into a play.

THE SUCCEEDING READING PERIODS

For four days the reading was continued. On the second day Hamilton (who had been absent) joined the group. The class told him what had been done so far. Miss Trotter said: "There was a question I was going to ask the class yesterday, but I forgot. Shall we say 'Roosevelt is a great hunter or Roosevelt was a great hunter'"?

HAMILTON. Oh, no! Roosevelt died in 1919.

At intervals children were sent back to re-read points on which their ideas were hazy.

On the third day, at the end of the period, Melvin remarked, "I'd rather read about Theodore Roosevelt than even draw pictures on the board, and I'd rather draw pictures than anything else I know of." Eleanor volunteered to give material that she had read in *Scribner's*, not being satisfied with merely looking at pictures.

On the fourth day children reported that they had seen in the Sunday paper pictures of a Roosevelt hunting expedition. The teacher asked if this was the same hunting expedition as that described in *African Game Trails*. The class explained the difference. Gilbert contributed from the book he had been reading a funny story about Theodore Roosevelt and his mice. At the end of the period the teacher announced that on the next day they would begin to plan the play. Four children stated that they already had plans in mind.

CHILDREN'S COMPLETE READING RECORD

(See list on page 666. Books from the list in the text are not included.)

Clarence	Nos. 2, 3, 4, 5.
Eleanor	Nos. 1, 2, 3, 4, 5.
Garner	Nos. 1, 2, 5, 6.
Gilbert	Nos. 3, 4 (spent three days on it).
Hamilton . . . . , .	Nos. 1, 2, 3, 4, 5, 6.
Helen	Nos. 1, 2, 3, 5, 6.
Melvin	Nos. 1, 2, 3, 4, 5, 6.
Virginia	Nos. 1, 2, 3, 5, 6.

PLANNING THE DRAMATIZATION

This class had never before composed a history play, and therefore the suggestions for the first two days were quite at random. After that they began to feel the situation and learned how to proceed.

On the board was written the list of points referred to on page 669.

SCENE I

MISS TROTTER. You have been reading for a number of days about Theodore Roosevelt, and I wonder if you have decided which phase of his life you want to show in your play? (*Three volunteers*)

MELVIN. His life as president. That would be one point. Another would be as a lover of children and as a writer. Maybe we could put on a play "The Great Explorer."

MISS TROTTER. Is it your idea to have four plays?

MELVIN. Four scenes. One scene as president directing his men. Next he could be writing letters to his children. In the next one he could be exploring, and in the next he could be sitting around with his children and telling them stories.

MISS TROTTER. You want to make his whole life the play and divide it into scenes?

GILBERT. One scene could be about a great hunter. We could make grass easily enough — take a lot of green cloth.

MISS TROTTER. We will talk now just about the phases of his life. Let's see if we can work this out.

GILBERT. In the beginning, when he was just a little boy, and then the next scene — we would have four or five scenes — he would probably be just a young man, and the next one older, probably next hunting. Have it just the way it came in his life. Begin when he was just a little boy.

ELEANOR. But in the books we read we didn't read much about his boyhood. (*Two children object.*) Gilbert's was a good idea, but — (GILBERT *indicates that he has read much about Roosevelt's boyhood.*)

MISS TROTTER. Pick out for us the book you read, Gilbert. I think I know the difficulty. Eleanor read the books I assigned; Gilbert did more. He hunted up something else very interesting in that book.

GILBERT. (*Finding the book he had read*) Right in the beginning of this.

MISS TROTTER. I did not assign anything on Theodore Roosevelt's childhood, but there is much of interest. Suppose you tell them what you found of interest.

GILBERT. In the beginning he was always collecting animals and things. Once he and another boy found some toads. They didn't have any place to put them, so they took off their caps and put them in their caps. Then they met some lady they knew, and they had to take off their caps.

MISS TROTTER. You haven't told why they were collecting these toads.

GILBERT. He and another boy had a museum called — (*he hesitates and* GARNER *prompts him*) the "Roosevelt Museum of Natural History." They collected all kinds of things. He had some white mice. He had some baby ones and put them in the ice box. His mother found them and threw them out. He said he didn't care, but it was a loss to science.

MISS TROTTER. What does that mean? (*Two volunteers*)

GARNER. They lost something they could experiment on.

MISS TROTTER. Was he experimenting?

GARNER. Yes; he was experimenting by putting them in the ice box.

MISS TROTTER. Yes; and he did not have the opportunity to study his results.

GILBERT. He went to Europe when he was just a boy to see if he could not help his health. He was very weak. He went to all the museums. He didn't like the pictures. All he liked was to see the skeletons and birds.

MELVIN. I read *The Boy's Life of Theodore Roosevelt*. It said he went to Europe once when he was a little boy, but he didn't like it. He was so young he couldn't enjoy half the things he wanted to. He went again when he was a little older, and saw all the things he wanted to see. After he was president of the United States he went to Africa.

MISS TROTTER. Suppose we decide on a beginning. What do you think of Gilbert's suggestion that we begin with Roosevelt's boyhood?

GARNER. The only trouble we would have would be we'd have to take the parts of people bigger than we are. (*Three children are ready to meet this objection.*)

GILBERT. We could have grown-up clothes on.

MISS TROTTER. Yes. I should think your audience might use their imagination. Suppose then we decide on Roosevelt's early life as your first scene. Do you feel you have read enough about his early life to work that scene out? ("Yes.") Well, what would be your plan for working that out?

MELVIN. Well, first we could have him when he was small, just a baby, and then when he starts for Europe, and then he could come back, and we could let him go again. We could make believe he was on a big ship, going across to Europe twice. Put down the second time the things he couldn't see the first time.

MISS TROTTER. Has anyone else a suggestion for telling your audience all of his life in a few interesting incidents? Perhaps you might let me list the points of interest. (*All but two have in mind incidents to suggest.*)

VIRGINIA. We could start it out where he was just getting ready to go.

MISS TROTTER. Melvin read about the interesting incidents. The rest of us will have to refer to that book. What did you find, Melvin?

MELVIN. He liked to go to Europe.

MISS TROTTER. Wouldn't your audience like to know why he wanted to go to Europe?

MELVIN. He wanted to go to see the wild animals and for his health.

MISS TROTTER. That was his real reason. Isn't it interesting to you that Theodore Roosevelt was not a healthy child? (*Writes on the board:*

"1. Early Life
"*a.* Health")

CHILDREN. Yes. (*Four children are consumed with eagerness to tell about the significance of this point.*)

MISS TROTTER. Why?

MELVIN. The important part is that that is why he went to Europe. He would not have gone to Europe the first time if he had been well. Because when he was little he was so delicate, and when he grew up he was president of the United States.

MISS TROTTER. You remember the word we found when we were reading about that? You asked me what it was.

MELVIN. "Handicap." Theodore Roosevelt had a handicap.

MISS TROTTER. Is it interesting to you that he overcame a great handicap? this frail, delicate child who became all of these things we have been reading about? (*Children all nod.*) Yes, I think so. I think we had better bring in something about the health of this child.

GILBERT. We want to have something about — (*goes on to tell some details of the toad episode*).

MISS TROTTER. At least you want that incident in the play. Let us put down that incident, and take up the details a little bit later. How shall I word that? Just the name of that museum, and that would include all the things. (*Children suggest that she write Roosevelt Museum.*) Would this indicate any of his interests?

CLARENCE. Yes. When he was catching frogs for a museum he was interested.

MISS TROTTER. Would that interest carry through life — that interest in live things? Suppose we leave that, then, and begin to work out the best way to begin. Put your hands down just a minute. Now keep in mind this — that all the things which you tell your audience can't be really demonstrated in your play. You will have to convey the idea to the audience perhaps in some other way. Now you be thinking about these two incidents in his life (*referring to health and the Roosevelt Museum*). How can you plan your play so that you may tell the audience about the health of this child and about this interest which he had? Eleanor, have you a suggestion?

ELEANOR. Not about his health, but I thought it would be a good idea to have him traveling somewhere with his father or mother, and writing some letters to his friends. They could be reading these aloud, and then you wouldn't have to bring in all these things — just read about them.

MISS TROTTER. Very well. Now we have in mind what we are to include in our first scene. Where shall the scene be placed?

VARIOUS CHILDREN. White House. In the living room. (MISS TROTTER *writes on the board* "Place: White House.")

MISS TROTTER. Anything else?

CHILDREN. The date.

MISS TROTTER. What date shall we use? (*Children are not sure.*) Now we have to be careful about that date. Do you know when Theodore Roosevelt lived in the White House? (*No one knows.*) Gilbert, look in the autobiography. (*In the meantime conversation continues.*) Where was Theodore Roosevelt living when most of those letters were written?

CHILDREN. In the White House.

MISS TROTTER. Do you suppose the letters are dated?

CHILDREN. Yes.

MISS TROTTER. I appoint Melvin to find out quickly from the letters the actual dates between which Theodore Roosevelt lived in the White House.

MELVIN. (*Consulting* "Theodore Roosevelt's Letters to his Children") Here is one dated June 22, 1904, that says White House, Washington. (GILBERT *gives up looking in the autobiography.*)

MISS TROTTER. Yes. When you are writing a history play, you must be very accurate. You want to use June 22, 1904, as the date for this scene?

CHILDREN. Yes.

MISS TROTTER. Now no one reading this play can question the date. Let us move on rapidly now. You think this is sufficient for this part? (*Children agree.*) Yes, we can try that, and if it doesn't work we can change it. Whom shall we have as the characters in the play?

VARIOUS CHILDREN. Theodore Roosevelt, Ethel, Quentin, Archie, friends. (MISS TROTTER *writes these on the board.*)

MELVIN. Place: White House. Date: June 22, 1904. Where: sitting room.

MISS TROTTER. Which do you like better: sitting room or living room?

VIRGINIA. He might be in the office.

MISS TROTTER. You think Mr. Roosevelt would be more likely to be in the office than in the living room? (*Class decides on living room.*) Who is going to speak first? Remember now that what you are telling your audience is something about the health of this man when he was a child, and his interest in nature.

MELVIN. F. S.

MISS TROTTER. Who is that?

MELVIN. F. S. could stand for first speaker. It could be Archie, "Tell us a story about when you were young."

MISS TROTTER. You want Archie to speak first? What do you want him to say?

MELVIN. "Daddy, tell us a story about when you were young."

MISS TROTTER. Just how would you say that?

MELVIN. "Daddy, tell us a story about your boyhood."

MISS TROTTER. All right. Who was the next speaker?

HAMILTON. Ethel, "Yes, do, father."

ELEANOR. Theodore Roosevelt could talk next. "All right, I will tell you about the time I went to Europe," or "I will tell you about the time I caught some toads and put them in my cap."

MISS TROTTER. Remember that through this story you are going to tell your audience something about the health of the child Theodore Roosevelt. That is important, since he overcame that handicap and became all those five great things in spite of the fact that he was not a well child. Who is going to speak next?

ELEANOR. Mr. Roosevelt.

HELEN. I want the play to begin with something about his health. We could have the characters say, "Have you any pictures of yourself?" Theodore Roosevelt could get some pictures, and then when they see them they would say, "You're not very fat or well there."

MISS TROTTER. Shall the play open as Helen suggested?

CHILDREN. Yes. (*Previous conversation is erased from board.*)

MISS TROTTER. In order to get this on the board rapidly I am going to abbreviate wherever I can, and then when the play is completed we will revise to make it more highly finished. Now Helen may begin. We say here that the scene is the White House, in the living room.

ELEANOR. I think Archie could say, "Daddy, do you have any pictures of yourself when you were a little boy?"

MISS TROTTER. Now while I put this down you can be thinking of the rest of the story, so that you can do it quickly.

HAMILTON. Then Mr. Roosevelt could say, "Yes, I have." Then he could —

VIRGINIA. I shouldn't think he would have them right there in the living room. He could say, "I will go over and get them."

MELVIN. Well, he could explain to Archie where they were. Then Archie and Quentin could go and get them and bring them back, and put them in the living room.

MISS TROTTER. Very well. How would you say that?

MELVIN. "You can get them. They are upstairs, in a trunk in the attic."

MISS TROTTER. You want Quentin to get them?

CHILDREN. Yes.

MISS TROTTER. Word that.

VIRGINIA. "Quentin, go and get them. They are up in the attic."

MISS TROTTER. (*Writing on the board*) Be thinking of the next part.

VIRGINIA. Quentin could say, "Yes, father," or "Yes, daddy."

MISS TROTTER. You want Quentin to reply? What next? I just wonder if you don't want some explanation in here, so that one reading the play would know exactly what the situation is.

HAMILTON. Quentin goes up stairs and gets it.

MISS TROTTER. Can't you word that a little better?

HAMILTON. Quentin gets the pictures.

MISS TROTTER. Very well. (*Writes the direction as a parenthetical expression.*) Has anyone a suggestion now?

ELEANOR. I should think they would say something about how funny these photographs are from what ours are.

MISS TROTTER. Who is to speak?

CHILDREN. Ethel.

ELEANOR. "Oh, how funny these photographs look against the ones we have now."

MISS TROTTER. Think of the next part while I write this down.

GARNER. Miss Trotter, I should think it would sound better to say, "How different these photographs are from ours."

MISS TROTTER. That *is* better. Give it again, Garner.

GARNER. "How different these photographs are from those we have now."

MISS TROTTER. Is that better English?

CHILDREN. Yes.

MISS TROTTER. What is the next part of the conversation you want about these photographs?

MELVIN. One of them could pick up a picture and say, "Daddy, you are bigger in this one than you are in this."

MISS TROTTER. What idea is it that you want to give to your readers?

CHILDREN. About his health.

MISS TROTTER. Now how are we going to say it?

ELEANOR. You could say, "You are healthier in this than you are in the other."

MISS TROTTER. Has anyone else a suggestion about that?

GILBERT. "You look healthier in this picture than you do in the other."

MISS TROTTER. We will put it down. Maybe you will want to change it later. I have an idea you will want to when we begin to act it out. Should an explanation be put down here?

MELVIN. You could add "comparing two pictures." (MELVIN *illustrates, holding two imaginary pictures at arm's length and comparing them.*)

MISS TROTTER. Can you think of anything interesting he might say about the picture, Eleanor?

ELEANOR. He could ask, "Why, where are you going in this picture?"

VIRGINIA. My suggestion is something like Eleanor's: "Oh, father, here is a picture on a ship. I never knew you traveled across the ocean."

MISS TROTTER. Who is to say that?

VIRGINIA. Archie.

GARNER. Miss Trotter, isn't that an abbreviation for "Archibald"?

MISS TROTTER. I think it is. Isn't his father going to answer Archie?

ELEANOR. Roosevelt could say that he was not as healthy as they are, when he was small.

MISS TROTTER. Is that enough explanation?

GILBERT. He could say that because he was not as healthy as they when he was young he had to go across the ocean for his health.

MISS TROTTER. Let's have that again, and maybe we shall want to revise it.

VIRGINIA. "Yes; I went across the ocean twice. I had to go for my health."

MISS TROTTER. Suppose we use that last part too. What is the rest?

GILBERT. "I wasn't as healthy as you are, so I went over there for my health."

GARNER. "Europe."

MISS TROTTER. That would be more definite. Had we better repeat the word "health"?

GILBERT. If you did not say "for my health," they wouldn't know what he went for.

MELVIN. He was sick all the time.

MISS TROTTER. What was the matter with him?

MELVIN. Asthma.

MISS TROTTER. How many know what asthma is? (*Not many do.*) You had better explain it, Melvin. (*Four children are ready to explain.*)

MELVIN. It's a sickness in which you can hardly breathe. You could say, "I was not as healthy as you, so I went to Europe because I had asthma."

MISS TROTTER. Very well. I think at this point you had better look through all we have written, and that may give you an idea.

GARNER. Change from picture to photograph. (*The teacher does so.*)

MISS TROTTER. Now I will read all of the play to you as it stands. I still think you need more explanation in it, but you may be thinking about that.

MELVIN. Can't we have the Roosevelt Museum now?

MISS TROTTER. If you think it is rounded out sufficiently so that you have told enough of the story to your audience, we will go on.

GARNER. We didn't have any of the friends say anything.

MISS TROTTER. Yes; I thought of that. Perhaps we can find a place for them in this next scene. If Theodore Roosevelt is talking with these children about his early life and the condition of his health, do you suppose these friends contributed anything? Do you suppose they knew Theodore Roosevelt when he was a child?

MELVIN. Sure. He probably got to know them by going to school with them.

MISS TROTTER. Maybe you don't want the friends in this first scene? Would you eliminate them, and have only these characters? (*Points to the names of the members of the family.*) If you leave the play as it is now, certainly I would say that you will have to eliminate the friends. Are they needed at all?

CHILDREN. No. (MISS TROTTER *erases the word* " friends " *from the list of characters.*)

ELEANOR. I should think we need some explanation.

MISS TROTTER. What explanation would you suggest?

ELEANOR. Wouldn't you tell what was in the room?

MISS TROTTER. That would be listed in a different place — under stage properties.

MELVIN. Can't we put in something now about the museum?

HAMILTON. I thought we could go right on from where we left off. Probably Quentin would say, "What did you do, father, for amusement, since you couldn't play hard?" Then Roosevelt would say, "I had a little museum."

MISS TROTTER. What do you think of that suggestion?

MELVIN. Quentin or Archie could look at the pictures and see Theodore Roosevelt and maybe the hat or the two toads, and then Quentin could ask, "Daddy, what is this picture?"

MISS TROTTER. Your suggestion could follow Hamilton's nicely. We could work both of those in. Hamilton, did you say you wanted Quentin to ask your question?

HAMILTON. I think so, because he has only said a little.

MISS TROTTER. Very well. Now Melvin's suggestion will fit right into this (*Writes.*)

MELVIN. Archie could say, "Daddy, what is this picture of?"

MISS TROTTER. Don't you think that Theodore Roosevelt would reply to Quentin's question? He would hardly ignore it, would he?

MELVIN. Theodore Roosevelt could say, "Here are the pictures I got of my animals for our museum."

CLARENCE. We ought to tell something about the museum.

MISS TROTTER. Yes. Probably they haven't heard of that before. Shall we take Melvin's suggestion for the introduction? Any more, Clarence? (CLARENCE *tells the story of the frog episode.*)

MELVIN. Archie could pick up a picture and say: "Oh, father, what is this? Is that a picture of your museum?"

MISS TROTTER. Very well. Eleanor?

ELEANOR. "For this museum I caught animals."

MISS TROTTER. Give me the sentence just as you want it. You had a good idea.

ELEANOR. "For my museum I caught animals." (MISS TROTTER *writes.*)

MELVIN. The name of his museum was the Roosevelt Museum of Natural History. (MELVIN *needs some assistance from the class to give the correct name.*)

MISS TROTTER. I wondered why you didn't put in the name of the museum. Do you think we need to say any more about it here?

MELVIN. The story of the toads.

MISS TROTTER. What is that story, Melvin?

MELVIN. (*Tells story.*) Of how he put some toads in his cap, and when he wanted to take off his cap to a lady the toads hopped out.

VIRGINIA. "Daddy, is this the picture of it?"

MISS TROTTER. Is Archie or Quentin to say this?

VIRGINIA. Quentin.

GILBERT. I don't think we could have a picture of the toads jumping, because how could they have the camera there before the toads reached the ground?

MISS TROTTER. Gilbert is doing some thinking. Do you suppose the children say anything more to their father.

HAMILTON. I should think they would be thinking about those stories while he was telling them. Maybe they would ask questions.

MISS TROTTER. Do you suppose in this scene you could bring in a little trace of Roosevelt's later love for hunting big game?

GARNER. "I thought it was a lot of fun then, but since I went on that hunting expedition it is nothing compared to that."

MISS TROTTER. Garner, you have an excellent idea. Let's express it in such a way that we can use it here.

GARNER. "I thought that was a lot of fun then; but ever since I went on the hunting expedition for the other museum, I thought this was nothing."

GILBERT. "Yes, I had a lot of fun, but it was nothing compared to when I went on —"

MISS TROTTER. I think there is a book up there with the title of the expedition. (GILBERT *goes to look up the name.*) What was the name of it? Think of words that would mean the same thing.

VOLUNTEER. African expedition.

MISS TROTTER. That was exactly what it was called. Virginia, will you read the play to us? (VIRGINIA *does so. In the meantime* MISS TROTTER *goes to the front of the room and selects a reference.*) Now before we take any suggestions, there is part of a page in this book I have asked Helen to read to you, and after you listen to this I want you to see if you have made a historical error at any place in the play. (HELEN *reads.*) Virginia, did you detect a historical error?

VIRGINIA. Yes. He hadn't gone on his hunting trip until after he was president, and we have him president when he was telling about it.

MISS TROTTER. What part must we change?

GARNER. Change the place and the time.

MISS TROTTER. Would that be the easiest change — to change the time and place of the whole play, or to make your revision here? Had he been on the African expedition? Hamilton?

HAMILTON. Not yet.

MISS TROTTER. Do you suppose he had ever thought anything about it?

CHILDREN. Yes.

VIRGINIA. "I thought that was a lot of fun, but now I am thinking of making a different museum and going to Africa."

MISS TROTTER. Is he really going to make a museum? Is that correct?

VIRGINIA. No; but he could say, "But now I am thinking of going to Africa."

MISS TROTTER. Do you suppose he said anything about why he was going to Africa?

HAMILTON. He was going to Africa for a museum.

MISS TROTTER. Put it in words Theodore Roosevelt would have used in this situation.

MELVIN. He was going to hunt animals for the museum.

MISS TROTTER. What museum?

MELVIN. The Roosevelt Museum of Natural History.

GARNER. I think it was the Field Museum.

MISS TROTTER. You read the word, Helen. Do you remember? Look for it quickly.

HELEN. Is this it? (*Shows the name in the book.*)

MISS TROTTER. Yes. What is the name?

HELEN. Smithsonian Institution.

MISS TROTTER. That is a big museum in Washington.

MELVIN. Are the animals he caught still there?

MISS TROTTER. Yes. That was the purpose of his trip — not just to kill animals, but to contribute to science. Even when he was a child he had that desire, and it stayed with him.

GARNER. I think when he was in Africa he didn't want to kill any more than he had to.

MISS TROTTER. Yes. Was someone else with him?

CHILDREN. Kermit.

MISS TROTTER. You want him to speak of Kermit? What shall I put down?

MELVIN. "I was thinking of taking Kermit along because —"

MISS TROTTER. There must have been some reason why Kermit was chosen. What was he interested in?

CHILDREN. Hunting.

MISS TROTTER. Be thinking about what you want next.

MELVIN. "I was thinking of taking Kermit along because he likes to hunt better than Theodore."

GILBERT. "I think it would be better to take Kermit with me because he seems most interested in the wilds."

VIRGINIA. Quentin could ask, "When are you going, daddy?"

MISS TROTTER. Do you want to continue the conversation here?

VIRGINIA. Yes.

MISS TROTTER. Do you want his father to answer him?

CLARENCE. You could say he was going in a year or two.

VIRGINIA. After his presidency was over.

MISS TROTTER. What do you think of Virginia's suggestion? Is her answer true to history?

CHILDREN. Yes.

MISS TROTTER. Let's put that down. I should think that would be a good place to end your scene. By whom was Theodore Roosevelt succeeded? Helen, you read it.

HELEN. Taft.

MISS TROTTER. Taft was elected, and inaugurated on the fourth of March. Then Roosevelt was free from all responsibilities of the presidency, and could take his trip. If we have finished here, let's go on to the next scene. What phase of his life are you going to represent in the next scene? (*Referring to the outline of points previously made*)

HELEN. His hunt.

MISS TROTTER. Look at the outline of his life. Is there any other phase that must be represented in the White House?

ELEANOR. He was a great president and an interesting writer.

MISS TROTTER. Is there any other phase?

MELVIN. A lover of children.

HAMILTON. A great explorer.

MISS TROTTER. Do you think that would be the logical one? The only one you want to show?

HAMILTON. A great hunter. We could have him in a tent showing some of the game he shot.

MISS TROTTER. Which of these two do you think ought to follow, Clarence?

CLARENCE. In Africa. A great hunter.

MISS TROTTER. Melvin has read about the great hunt. Are there any suggestions about where the scene might be laid? Before you suggest that, you ought to think out your plan for telling the audience about this great hunt. (*Four volunteers*)

VIRGINIA. We couldn't have the hunting party in Africa very well. We couldn't make the animals very easily.

GILBERT. You could have them in the tent after dark, probably just before they went to bed. They could be talking about it — getting in just about everything that happened.

MISS TROTTER. Where is this scene laid?

GILBERT. In the tent.

MISS TROTTER. What country?

GARNER. Africa or Brazil probably. He shot a lot of animals there.

MISS TROTTER. Where was the hunt? Had we best emphasize the hunt or the exploration? I think we will have to do some more reading. There are two books I think everyone should examine before we make the last scene. In *African Game Trails* read the references that are assigned, and in *The Wilderness Hunter*. You can't make a play unless you have some information. These are two very fine books, and I believe you had better read thoroughly so that your information is accurate.

ELEANOR. I don't think we ought to have it in the tent. It would be sort of hard to make the tent.

MISS TROTTER. Do your reading before you make suggestions. You know, when you are making a history play you must be very careful so that your readers can't say, "Why, that isn't true about Theodore Roosevelt."

MELVIN. Where are we going to get all the people to act? There are only eight in the class, and we have to have more than eight.

GILBERT. This is going in a book, and probably the other schools would have more.

MISS TROTTER. Aren't we going to play it?

CHILDREN. Yes.

MISS TROTTER. Would any of you object to taking two parts?

CHILDREN. No.

MELVIN. Are those books going to be here all the time?

MISS TROTTER. Yes.

MELVIN. That top one about his boy's life?

ELEANOR. That doesn't mean he was a little boy. It is his life for boys to read.

HAMILTON. I was going to say what she said. This is the boys' book of Roosevelt.

The following day was devoted to reading. After the reading had been completed the dramatization was continued.

Scene II

MISS TROTTER. Now we are better prepared to go on with our second scene. What incidents shall we include?

CLARENCE. The hunt.

MISS TROTTER. What is the place?

HELEN. Near Mt. Kenya.

MISS TROTTER. Where is that?

HELEN. Way over on the eastern part of Africa near the equator.

MISS TROTTER. Who are the characters?

VARIOUS CHILDREN. Theodore Roosevelt, Kermit, Cuninghame, Heller, Natives.

MISS TROTTER. After an interesting hunt, what do you suppose they would talk about in the evening when they assembled? Decide what the conversation is to be.

ELEANOR. I think they would talk about the elephant hunt.

MISS TROTTER. Tell me exactly what you want them to say.

ELEANOR. I should think Theodore Roosevelt would speak first.

MISS TROTTER. What would he say?

ELEANOR. He can say, "That was a narrow escape I had from that big bull elephant."

MISS TROTTER. Be thinking of what you want next.

HAMILTON. I was thinking Kermit could say something and Mr. Roosevelt answer him. "Gee, daddy, I didn't have any breath left when that elephant went after you."

MISS TROTTER. Let's make it interesting.

HAMILTON. Mr. Roosevelt could say "Neither did I."

GILBERT. To make it shorter, he could say "Ditto."

Miss Trotter. Remember your audience wants to know what happened. That will do Hamilton. Garner?

Garner. I was raising my hand before you got started. I was going to say, "That was quite a successful day."

Miss Trotter. Who is to say that?

Garner. Theodore Roosevelt.

Miss Trotter. Can't we say it now?

Garner. I think it would be better to say it before.

Miss Trotter. What do you want?

Garner. "That was quite a successful day."

Miss Trotter. What was it that was a success? Your audience hasn't read about this hunt. You will have to tell your story so clearly that they will get the idea.

Garner. "The elephant hunt was quite a success today."

Miss Trotter. Very well. Is this the way you want it?

Garner. Yes.

Miss Trotter. That will fit in very nicely there. Then let's go on with the rest.

Virginia. "If I had not shot that big elephant I would not be here."

Miss Trotter. You want Theodore Roosevelt to tell that?

Gilbert. Kermit could say, "I wasn't looking for that other elephant right after you shot the first one." Then he could say —

Miss Trotter. Aren't you going to have any of these other characters say anything?

Gilbert. Cuninghame could say it. He hasn't said anything.

Miss Trotter. What is Cuninghame to say?

Gilbert. "I wasn't looking for that other big bull elephant after you shot the first one."

Miss Trotter. There is a better word than "looking" there.

Gilbert. Mr. Roosevelt could say, "I wish I had shot that other elephant too, but I guess I couldn't."

Miss Trotter. But can't you put in a better word there than "looking"?

Garner. He wasn't expecting.

Miss Trotter. Wouldn't that be a better word? I can see that would be a great surprise to them. Do you suppose they made any conversation about the ivory?

Clarence. Heller could say something about the big tusks. "The tusks were —"

Miss Trotter. How much would they weigh? Remember you are telling this to your audience. They haven't read the book at all. Do you remember how much the tusks weighed?

Clarence. I thought they weighed three hundred pounds.

Garner. The tusks of that elephant weighed three hundred pounds a pair. They wouldn't know but what they weighed three hundred pounds apiece. I should think it would be better for Theodore Roosevelt to say that about the narrow escape and to have Cuninghame, Kermit, or Heller say the next.

Melvin. I agree with Garner that it doesn't look right to have Theodore Roosevelt say all those things while the rest of them sit there and don't say anything.

MISS TROTTER. You think he is saying too much? We will keep that in mind from now on. What else do you suppose they discussed?

HAMILTON. One of the skinners could say: "I wonder about how much stuffing it would take to fill that elephant. It was quite a job this evening, and we will have some of it left for the morning."

MELVIN. Then one of the guides could say, "We are going to have an awful job stuffing that elephant."

MISS TROTTER. You want the native guide to say that? I wonder if that would be the thing he would be interested in?

MELVIN. Yes; because he had to guide Theodore Roosevelt, and maybe stuff it for him.

MISS TROTTER. Do you remember how one day when Helen read to you she said a very hard word?

VOLUNTEERS. Taxidermist.

GILBERT. They stuff things. There must be one at Percey's fur house, because they have stuffed animals there.

MISS TROTTER. Yes; they stuff animals. They would have to have a trained taxidermist.

ELEANOR. I should think Kermit would say something about where they are going tomorrow. The guide could say, "To follow the elephant we wounded."

MISS TROTTER. You want Kermit to say that?

ELEANOR. Yes. Kermit has said hardly anything.

MISS TROTTER. What are you going to have him say?

ELEANOR. "Where are we going tomorrow?" One of the guides could say, "Let's follow the elephant we wounded."

MISS TROTTER. Had they wounded one?

ELEANOR. Yes; the bull elephant. It said that Cuninghame shot the elephant.

MISS TROTTER. That is true. They wounded the elephant that came out behind them. Do you suppose they had any conversation about the elephant meat?

CLARENCE. They could say it was good.

MISS TROTTER. Tell me just who is to say it, and what words you want to put in.

MELVIN. Theodore Roosevelt.

MISS TROTTER. What is he to say?

MELVIN. He could be tasting the heart, and could say, "My, this heart is delicious."

MISS TROTTER. Is that true of the story of his hunt?

MELVIN. Yes.

MISS TROTTER. Do you suppose any of the other characters could hold any conversation about the taste of this elephant's heart?

CLARENCE. Do people eat elephant hearts like chicken hearts?

VARIOUS CHILDREN. Yes.

MISS TROTTER. Any other conversation?

HAMILTON. The natives ate the meat raw. We could give the natives names. "Joe, I can't see how you can eat that meat raw."

Miss Trotter. Who is to say that?

Hamilton. Kermit. The guide could say, "It is good," and keep right on eating.

Gilbert. "I think it is about time for going to bed now."

Miss Trotter. Who shall suggest it?

Hamilton. Heller. He hasn't said much.

Miss Trotter. All right. We must give him a fair chance.

Garner. Cuninghame could say, "Don't you think we had better keep a watch or have shifts on the watch?"

Miss Trotter. Do you want Cuninghame to tell the audience why that would be necessary?

Garner. "I think we had better keep a watch to see if any lions will come around to get a drink."

Hamilton. The natives sleep close to the fire. Kermit could say, "Don't you fellows sleep so close to the fire that you burn yourselves again tonight."

Miss Trotter. Always try to use dignified English. Are you ready to have them go to bed?

Hamilton. One of the guides could say, "Yes; but I am afraid of the lions."

Miss Trotter. Who is to speak?

Hamilton. A skinner.

Miss Trotter. What is his reply about sleeping so close to the fire?

Hamilton. "We'll try not to, but we are afraid of the lions." Cuninghame could say, "I don't believe there will be any lions around tonight."

|Miss Trotter. Is that a good place to end that scene? What do you have the characters do then?

Virginia. Go to bed.

Garner. They go to sleep in sleeping-bags.

Virginia. On the ground.

Garner. On the ground in sleeping-bags. But I should think that sleeping-bags would be kind of unhandy if lions should come.

Virginia. Theodore Roosevelt could say, "Get the blankets ready, and let's go to bed."

At this point the class went back to the beginning of Scene II for revision. The following changes were made:

A parenthetical expression, (*to the guide*), was inserted before "I don't see how you can eat that meat raw," and the same before "Don't sleep so close to the fire that you will burn yourselves."

To the phrase "lions come down to get a drink" was added "or to eat the elephant's carcass. If they do, we'll get a good shot at them."

The class now decided that they had suggested all the important phases of Roosevelt's life except that of great explorer, and that they could not take the time to write more.

PRACTICING THE DRAMATIZATION

In the meantime mimeographed copies of Scenes I and II had been made.

Miss Trotter. I will pass out copies of Scene I of your play. We are going to read the scene aloud first. (*Assigning the characters*) This is for the first reading. We will do as real actors do. Real actors assemble with their manuscripts, and different people read the different parts. Then the people who do them well are chosen to take the parts. Try your very best. (*The reading of the scene follows. Suggestions as to improvement are called for.*)

Garner. When he said about the toads, he didn't have them both in his cap. He should have said that he had his pockets all full, and his hands full, and he put one in his cap, and the boy with him put one in his cap. He could make up a name for the other boy. I should think after he tells the story of the mice someone could say, "Do you know any other stories?" Then Roosevelt could say, "Oh, yes; I forgot to tell you this one." Then he could tell the story of the toads.

Miss Trotter. Very well, you can make that change when you tell it.

The scene was read twice by different sets of characters, and the stage was set.

Miss Trotter. Suppose now we have the play. Can you remember the parts? Let's try. We will have the first set of characters tried out. The people who did the reading the first time may come up and try their parts. (Miss Trotter *reminds the characters of action, and* Garner *suggests that they pretend to pass the pictures.*) How many pictures do you suppose Quentin found?

Children. About ten or eleven. About five or six.

Miss Trotter. He might have. (*Children go through their parts once without the manuscript.*) We will try this again a little later with the other group. Now we will try Scene II. I will give you copies. Let's have the same group who read Scene II act it first. What was the hunting party doing around the fire?

Children. Talking.

Miss Trotter. They were talking, but they were doing something.

Gilbert. Eating. (*Children decide to use long sticks and pretend to roast meat over a fire.*)

Miss Trotter. Will you go through the second act without your notes and as naturally as you can? (*Scene II is acted twice.*) Now when we consider that first scene, what are you going to need? We will call them stage properties (*writing this on the board*).

Melvin. Living room, some chairs, fireplace, pictures.

Gilbert. Some clothes like they used to have.

Miss Trotter. You are going to dress up differently?

Children. Yes.

Miss Trotter. Is there any item of dress very characteristic of Theodore Roosevelt?

Garner. A swallowtail coat.

Miss Trotter. I didn't notice that; but glasses — did you ever notice any picture of him without glasses?

Hamilton. Out West he couldn't wear them very well — when he was riding. (*The children look for a picture of Roosevelt without glasses but do not find one.*)

Miss Trotter. Is there anything else characteristic of him?

Garner. A mustache.

Miss Trotter. What else shall we need?

Garner. Some rugs and carpets.

Gilbert. We could make a fireplace look as though it had a fire in it by using an extension cord and some red paper.

Miss Trotter. Could you manage that for us?

Gilbert. Yes; if I can get a long enough extension cord.

Children assumed the responsibility for securing the various stage properties, a committee assuming general charge. For Scene II the following properties were listed:

> khaki costumes
> toy guns
> camp fire
> canvas for a tent
> forked sticks for roasting the meat
> blankets

They then decided to have an announcer to give the setting and the list of characters for each scene. At the end the characters were to roll themselves up in blankets and lie down by the fire, the natives remaining on guard.

DRESS REHEARSAL

Helen suggested two plans for the announcer, one in which she should tell how and by whom the play was written, and the other in which she should give only the names of the characters. She suggested that the class give the play a name. *The Life of Theodore Roosevelt, President Theodore Roosevelt, Theodore Roosevelt as a Great Man, Theodore Roosevelt*, were suggested. *The Life of Theodore Roosevelt* was chosen. The class decided that the announcement should include only the place, the time, and the characters for each scene.

One set of characters went through Scene I.

Different characters went through Scene II. They found it necessary to rehearse a second time and then to study the lines before going on with the practice. They read through twice with the manuscript; then, looking away from the papers as much as possible; then, quite without papers. A new child who came into the group at this point was assigned by the group to be a dorobo, or native, since she would not have time to learn anything to say.

The teacher found it necessary to speed up the action after the lines were learned perfectly, and to see that cues were picked up promptly.

At the last rehearsal the class went through both scenes consecutively, with an announcement before Scene I and another before Scene II.

Children set the stage for Scene I before the first announcement was made, and shifted all the scenery between acts themselves.

GIVING THE PLAY

For the first performance the rest of the children in the room served as the audience. The stage (one corner of the room) was set at noon; there was no curtain. The play was repeated three times: once for a class of observers, once for the sixth grade, and once for the fourth grade.

The play follows:

THE LIFE OF THEODORE ROOSEVELT

SCENE I

PLACE: *White House living room*
TIME: *June 22, 1904*

CHARACTERS

QUENTIN ROOSEVELT	THEODORE ROOSEVELT
ARCHIE ROOSEVELT	ETHEL ROOSEVELT

ARCHIE. Oh, daddy, have you any pictures of yourself when you were a little boy?

THEODORE ROOSEVELT. Yes, I have. Quentin, go and get them. They are in the attic.

QUENTIN. Yes, daddy. (QUENTIN *gets the photographs and distributes them among the children.*)

ETHEL. How different these photographs are from ours! You look healthier in this one than you do in the other (*comparing two pictures*).

THEODORE ROOSEVELT. Yes; I had to work hard to make my body as strong as it is now.

ARCHIE. Daddy, here is a picture of you on a ship. I didn't know you traveled across the ocean when you were little.

THEODORE ROOSEVELT. I was not as healthy as you, so I went to Europe because I had asthma.

QUENTIN. Well, father, what did you do for amusement since you couldn't play hard?

THEODORE ROOSEVELT. I had a museum. Its name was "The Roosevelt Museum of Natural History." For my museum I caught animals. Once another boy and I went out to get some animals. We got several toads. We put some of the toads into our pockets, but they were pretty full, so there wasn't much room. There were only two left, so I took one and put it in my hat, and the other boy put one into his hat. Then a lady came along. We had to take off our hats, and the toads jumped out.

QUENTIN. Oh, that's a good one. Do you know any more stories?

THEODORE ROOSEVELT. Yes. I had some baby white mice once. I put them in the ice box to see what would happen. After a while my mother came along and found the mice and threw them out. I didn't care so much myself, but I said it was a loss to science. I thought that was a lot of fun, but now I am thinking of going to Africa to hunt animals for the Smithsonian Institution. I am going to take Kermit with me, because he is most interested in hunting animals.

QUENTIN. When are you going, daddy?

THEODORE ROOSEVELT. After my presidency is over.

SCENE II

PLACE: *Outside a tent in Africa near Mt. Kenya*
TIME: *In the evening after an elephant hunt*

CHARACTERS

THEODORE ROOSEVELT	CUNINGHAME
KERMIT ROOSEVELT	HELLER

Natives: skinners, guides

(*Characters sitting around a fire toasting elephant meat on forked sticks*)

THEODORE ROOSEVELT. The elephant hunt was quite a success today. That was a narrow escape I had from the bull.

KERMIT. I did not have any breath left when that elephant went after you.

THEODORE ROOSEVELT. If I had not shot him I would not be here now.

CUNINGHAME. I was not expecting that big bull elephant after you shot the first.

THEODORE ROOSEVELT. I wish I might have shot that one that got away.

HELLER. The tusks of this one you did kill must weigh three hundred pounds.

NATIVE SKINNER. We had quite a job of skinning that elephant and it isn't all done yet.

NATIVE GUIDE. The one who stuffs him will have an awful job.

KERMIT. Where are we going tomorrow?

NATIVE GUIDE. I should think that we would follow that elephant that we wounded.

THEODORE ROOSEVELT. (*Eating*) My, but this heart is delicious!

KERMIT. (*To the natives*) I don't see how you natives can eat that meat raw.

NATIVE GUIDE. It's good that way.

HELLER. Isn't it about time to go to bed?

CUNINGHAME. I think that we had better keep watch to see whether any lions will come to get a drink or to eat the elephant's carcass. If they do, then we'll get a good shot at them.

KERMIT. (*To the natives*) Don't sleep so close to the fire that you burn yourselves again tonight.

NATIVES. We will try not to, but we are so afraid of the lions.

THEODORE ROOSEVELT. All right. Let us get the blankets ready and go to bed.

(*All secure blankets, wrap themselves up, and lie down on the ground*)

NATIVES : We will keep watch.

END

LESSON III

THEME ILLUSTRATION

The following lesson was taught by Miss Ethel Bouffleur, Chairman of the Art Department of the Oshkosh State Teachers College.[1] The 5-A class of the training department carried out the project, which centered around the general topic of making portages.[2]

INTRODUCTION TO THE READING

TEACHER. Name some of the French explorers around the Great Lakes region (*review work*).
GARNER. La Salle, Marquette, Joliet.
TEACHER. Any others?
HAMILTON. Champlain.
MELVIN. Some of them went down the Fox River, right past Oshkosh.
TEACHER. Did they travel mainly by land or by water?
JOSEPH. By water.
TEACHER. (*Illustrating at the physical map*) When they came to the upper waters of the Fox, how did they get over here to the Wisconsin River?
GILBERT. I'll show you on the map (*going to the front of the room*). When they got up this far, they went across by land to the Wisconsin.

At this point several children interjected, "That's a portage." The teacher had believed that this would be a new term to them and had planned to introduce the word.

TEACHER. What do you mean by a portage? (*Writing the word on the board*)
KENNETH. A portage is a place where you walk across the land and carry the canoes.
MELVIN. How would they manage if they were traveling on a big boat?

Several children at once explained that most of the voyages were made, not in large sailing vessels, but in canoes.

TEACHER. Some of these exploring trips lasted as long as two years. What would they have to take with them?

[1] With the assistance of Miss Mildred Glaeser, a student teacher.
[2] See page 230.

690

SEVERAL CHILDREN. (*At once*) Ammunition, blankets, food supplies, articles with which to trade with the Indians.

TEACHER. What people made up these small trading and exploring parties?

JACK. Priests and traders.

HAMILTON. They had Indian guides with them too.

TEACHER. We have here some books which will tell us much more about portages.

THE READING

The reading was organized about five points:

MAKING A PORTAGE

1. The goods carried
2. How a portage was made
3. Different kinds of portages: geographic setting
4. Costumes of traders, priests, Indian guides
5. Description of canoes

Procedure followed the process described on pages 24–29. The study question for point one was written on the board:

List on your paper all the goods that were carried on the journeys.

Lists were read and compared. For the other points, question slips similar to the illustrations on page 25 were used. Individual conferences tested the reading. In three days' time the children had exhausted the reference list.

UNDIRECTED FIRST ATTEMPT AT DRAWING

TEACHER. You have now read all that the books give us about our story. Did the pictures help in any way to give the story?

CHILDREN. Yes.

TEACHER. Do you notice the pictures in magazines and newspapers when you are reading them?

GILBERT. Yes. Sometimes I look at the pictures first, and they make me want to read the story.

TEACHER. Pictures are a means of expressing oneself graphically. Do pictures ever tell a story by themselves, without any reading?

JACK. Yes. Sometimes the teacher shows us a picture and we have to make up a story about it.

TEACHER. Are there other ways that you could tell a story besides pictures?

SEVERAL CHILDREN. (*At once*) Telling it orally, writing it, making up a poem, making up your own drawing.

TEACHER. Dramatization also. Have you read anything lately that you could express in drawing?

VARIOUS CHILDREN. Pictures of Indians, tools, canoes, dress, Marquette and Joliet going down the river, portages.

TEACHER. Can you think of anything from those stories that you could draw quickly?

JACK. Marquette and Joliet in the canoes.

KENNETH. Trading for furs, trinkets, etc.

GARNER. The camps at night.

LLOYD. Pulling a canoe out of the water at a portage.

TEACHER. Think for a few minutes of a definite picture you could make that would have some connection with our story of portages. Raise your hands when ready.

While the children were thinking, supplies (pencil, paper, crayons) were passed. When most of the children had raised their hands, indicating that they had a picture in mind, they were directed to begin to draw. The teacher passed among them, answering questions. The most common question was "May I put so-and-so into my picture?" The teacher answered, "Put into it whatever you wish, provided that it is about portages."

About twenty minutes were spent in this exercise. No help in drawing was given. Specimens of the undirected first attempts appear at the left in each case on page 231 and in the frontispiece.

When the time limit was reached, children brought their pictures to the front of the room and stood them up in the chalk trays. Above each one the teacher wrote a number by which to designate it during the class criticism.

TEACHER. Study the pictures for a moment. Pick out one you like.

BETTY. I like Number 9 because it shows the story that they are carrying their canoes from the Fox to the Wisconsin. (*Most of the class agree.*)

TEACHER. Which have Indians?

KENNETH. Number 10, but they are rather small. Number 1 has.

TEACHER. In which picture is the canoe most carefully drawn?

ALL. Number 9.

TEACHER. Is there another good one?

VERNON. Number 14.

TEACHER. Yes; but it is too light in value. In how many pictures are there trees?

LLOYD. In five.

TEACHER. The trees in Number 3 have no leaves. Are there any other types of trees between the Fox and the Wisconsin?

ELEANOR. I don't know.

MELVIN. All the trees aren't without leaves in winter. There are some evergreens.

TEACHER. That is a subject about which we do not seem to know much. We shall have to read more about it. Did anyone represent in his picture any other portage than that between the Fox and the Wisconsin?

KENNETH. Yes. I had a portage around falls in mine. I didn't know how to make them either.

TEACHER. About what other things do we need to read?

SEVERAL CHILDREN. The dress of the Indians.

TEACHER. Should we represent any other people besides Indians? And how?

HAMILTON. Marquette was a priest, so he'll have to have a priest's dress, and Joliet was a trader, so he'll have to have a trader's dress.

TEACHER. It is evident that the pictures can be improved, especially the canoes, dress, and the landscapes. They need more color, more contrast between sky, land, and figures, and, in general, they should be darker in value. Here are some pictures from which you may get a more correct idea.

PICTURE STUDY

On the board were written lists of pictures in books, classified as to subject; tools and supplies, canoes, people — traders, priests, Indians. Mounted pictures and specimens of work from other classes were included. Each child saw every picture, passing it, when he had finished looking at it, to the person back of him. Several commented on points which had been criticized in their own drawings. The purpose of the exercise was to study the particular points which the children wished to represent in their drawings.

VISIT TO THE MUSEUM

The class now made a trip to the local museum to see the construction of the canoes, the dress of the Indians, and samples of wild rice. In the lecture room of the museum a small canoe about three feet long was given to the children for examination. They looked minutely at its structure and decoration, and several children practiced carrying it to study the position of the body and the angle in which the canoe rested. Different views above and below the eye level were compared.

DIRECTED DRAWING

TEACHER. After having seen these pictures and made a trip to the museum, you should now have a very different idea of how to represent a portage. There are several different ways in which you can plan your final sketch. One way is to list all the things you wish to put into your composition. We call this a graphic vocabulary. Or, you may make a series of small sketches of what you wish to include. You may refer to any of the books or pictures you have seen. This attempt is not final.

Materials were distributed, and the children began to plan their compositions. Several had trouble representing water, whereupon the teacher illustrated at the board four possible methods. She passed among the pupils, making suggestions as to composition, variety, completeness of graphic vocabularies, and as to methods of representing specific objects, and reviewing principles previously taught which should be applied here. At intervals she sent children back to the pictures and books to correct inaccuracies. Many others referred to the references of their own accord.

All the class had difficulty in drawing the canoe, so the teacher asked them to stop work while she illustrated at the board.

Class criticism of the first draft followed. Each child passed to the front of the room and held up his picture. Other children gave suggestions as to how to improve the drawings, such as a more definite line between land and water, the addition of figures, the grouping of trees, the coloring, angle of carrying the canoes, proportions of different objects, etc. Many times the teacher added to the points to be commended and criticized spacing and arrangement. She suggested that each child study his own particular difficulties before beginning his last drawing.

FINAL COMPOSITION

Children now began work on the final sketch. In many cases the teacher had to remind them of the class criticisms they had received. Outlines were sketched first; these had to be approved by the teacher before color could be applied.

When the drawings were nearly finished, they were arranged again in a row on the chalk trays to receive the last constructive criticism. The teacher told the class that this was the last chance for improvement, and asked them to study the pictures carefully, especially as to values, coloring, and arrangement.

TEACHER. Can you suggest improvements?

KENNETH. In Number 7 the space ought to be filled better. One man would not be alone in a canoe. And the trees are too small.

As each picture was criticized, its owner removed it to his desk.

VERNON. There should be trees in Number 9.

HELEN. In Number 8 the trees would be better if they didn't look so much like the ground. (*The teacher suggests the use of brown.*)

ELEANOR. The branches are too big too.

MELVIN. In Number 11 the figures are good. They are smaller in the distance. But the canoe shouldn't be up on land unless it was night. And the tepee is too big for the people.

AVIS. In Number 3 the trees are nice, but not dark enough. The figures are not dark enough. You couldn't tell whether they were men or what.

HAMILTON. Number 1. The man looks as if he was rowing the canoe. They didn't row; they paddled. And the sun is too high up in the sky to be so red.

JOSEPH. Number 8 is good because the figures are well drawn and the shore looks real. But the Indians are too big. The wigwam ought to be bigger.

GARNER. Number 2. There are no figures. Too much smoke is coming out of the wigwam.

TEACHER. Yes; it would be better if there were figures.

MELVIN. And the shadow is too big for the wigwam.

JACK. Number 12. The canoe is quite big for the men, and the bird looks like a kite.

TEACHER. I might add that the figures are too near this side of the picture. Something should be added over here at the other side.

BETTY. In Number 13, if there was a sun, there would be a shadow too.

ELMER. And that thing hanging up in the tree looks more like a bee's nest than a papoose.

JACK. Number 14. Why would one boat have to be carried across land while there are two boats going around by the river?

LLOYD. Anyway, that water back there looks as if it were going up hill, and water doesn't go up hill.

Children now attempted to correct the points criticized. After each had improved his to the best of his ability, he subjected it to the teacher's criticism. If she considered that he had done all he could, she directed him to stand it again in the chalk trays. When all had finished, they discussed the success of each one in carrying out the suggestions. In final criticism they told what each one liked about each picture and what in it was good.

The pictures on page 231 and in the frontispiece give at the left in each case the child's undirected first attempt, and at the right his final composition.

LESSON IV

TEACHING AN HISTORICAL TERM

THE WORD *GOVERNMENT* [1]

We have said many times in our stories: "The United States paid the soldiers," "The United States asked France to help us," "The United States signed the treaty of peace." But the United States is a vast country (*showing at the map*). This land could not sign a treaty, neither could all the people living in all these states. Who, then, would actually sign the paper for the United States? (*Children offer suggestions.*) Then our President with all his helpers, and the people who make our laws for us, are the ones who really attend to the affairs of the nation. We call them the *government* (*writing the word on the board*). *The government*, then (*writing the definition on the board as given*), *consists of those who make our laws and those who put them into force.* What are the two things which that sentence tells us? Can you give them without looking at the board?

Here are some sentences using the word *government*:

1. The government of the United States does the nation's business.

2. The affairs which interest all the states are taken care of by the United States government.

3. Our government has changed many times since we were colonies of England.

At this point show the flash card which will be used in later drill work.

One Side	Other Side
GOVERNMENT	THE BODIES WHICH MAKE OUR LAWS AND PUT THEM INTO FORCE ARE THE _ _ _ _

[1] See page 298, in the list of minimal essentials.

The following blanks are to be filled with the word *government*, if it makes the right meaning:

1. The _ _ _ _ paid the debts of the United States.
2. The beginning of our present _ _ _ _ was in the eighteenth century.
3. Mount Vernon was the home of the _ _ _ _.
4. George Rogers Clark took the Western lands for the United States _ _ _ _.
5. The _ _ _ _ printed *Poor Richard's Almanac.*
6. Congress, the president, and his helpers make up the _ _ _ _.

Children compose sentences using the word *government*.

The following day include the flash card on page 697 with those used for a few minutes' drill.

LESSON V

PICTURE STUDY[1]

[Taught by Mrs. Laura T. Johnson, Critic Teacher in
Oshkosh State Teachers College]

MRS. JOHNSON. Take seats near the center of the room. (*Children group themselves as near as possible to the center of the room.*) What are some of the sources that we may use to study history?

VARIOUS CHILDREN. Reading, illustrations, maps, outlines, charts, stories.

MRS. JOHNSON. Today we are going to use a picture to study history, as Durwood suggested — illustrations. I will put the picture up without showing the caption to you. (*Places picture. Picture is mounted with thumb tacks on an easel in the front of the room, the caption concealed by cardboard attached with clips.*) Can you see the picture from where you sit? I believe the other day at the library you studied something about pictures. Can you look at this and tell me the type of picture it is?

JOHN D. It looks like war. I think I know what it is (*referring to the subject*).

MRS. JOHNSON. What materials were used in making the picture? Durwood?

DURWOOD. Oil paints.

MRS. JOHNSON. The texture shows that oil paints were used instead of water colors. Can you tell whether it is an original picture or a copy?

SUSAN. Original.

MRS. JOHNSON. How many agree? (*None do.*) How many disagree?

WILLIAM. (*Going up and feeling the surface*) I know it is a copy, because a regular original is rougher.

MRS. JOHNSON. Where can you find the name of the artist?

JUNIOR. Probably in the corner.

MRS. JOHNSON. Come up to see if you can find it.

JUNIOR. (*Goes to front of room and points to corner of picture.*) H. G. Ford.

MRS. JOHNSON. I think you learned something about every picture having a center of interest. Can you pick it out in this one? Georgia? (*GEORGIA cannot.*)

ELIZABETH. I believe it's the ships.

MRS. JOHNSON. Put your hand on the point.

ELIZABETH. These two ships (*points to two foremost in left-hand corner*).

WILLIAM. Right between these two ships it looks as though something is happening. (*Points to smoke screen between the two ships.*)

[1] See pages 127–130.

MRS. JOHNSON. What means did the artist use to emphasize the center of interest?

MARTHA. He has made it larger.

MRS. JOHNSON. What do you mean?

MARTHA. Placed it in the foreground and the other things in the background.

FRANCES. He used color to emphasize.

DURWOOD. Red always stands out in pictures.

MRS. JOHNSON. Come up and point out your center of interest. (DURWOOD's *is the same as* WILLIAM'S.)

MRS. JOHNSON. What lines bring out the center of interest?

JOHN T. Black lines.

MRS. JOHNSON. All important lines curve down toward the center of interest.

CATHERINE. My eyes traveled down the curves straight to the center of interest. It looks like excitement: people in a rush; water aroused.

MRS. JOHNSON. True. Can you look at that picture and tell what time of day the scene takes place?

GEORGIA. In the afternoon, because you see the sun in different colors.

WILLIAM. Dawn. When dawn comes, the sky is different colors just as at sunset.

FRANCES. I agree with William.

MRS. JOHNSON. That is right. How does an artist show the time of day?

MARTHA. The kind of sky tells.

MRS. JOHNSON. Can you tell anything about the condition of the sea?

ALFRED. Calm. In the foreground it's wavy, but not back farther.

FRANCES. It looks as though it isn't so very calm — just enough to make it interesting.

MRS. JOHNSON. Is there anything else in the picture that would indicate the condition of the weather?

MARJORIE. The sky would not be that color in the winter time.

JUNE. Water would be a little frozen in the winter time. It looks like a warm day because the water is exploding into little waves.

SUSAN. It looks as though the sails were blowing.

JOHN D. It looks windy. The flags and sails look as though they were moving.

GENEVIEVE. When it is windy the clouds move across the sky.

MRS JOHNSON. Any other suggestions about the weather?

WILLIAM. The waves all seem to come toward the point of interest.

MRS. JOHNSON. That is interesting. Can you tell any other thing that seems to bring out interest in the ships?

MARTHA. The ships are —

FRANCES. (*Interrupting*) It is interesting to look at the flags.

MRS. JOHNSON. I think so too. I should like to have you look at the flags, and see the different kinds. Come up and point to the different kinds, Georgia.

GEORGIA. (*Coming to picture*) Some are long and narrow, some are wide, and this looks as though it might be a white one.

MARTHA. This flag called my attention most (*points to upper left-hand corner*) because it is shaped like a kite. And this one looks different and interesting. It shows the wind.

MRS. JOHNSON. There are different kinds floated as royal standards of the countries. Can you point out a royal standard? (*About two thirds of the class volunteer to come to the front.*)

CATHERINE. I think this one is, because it is the largest, but the other flags on the same boat stand for something in the country.

MRS. JOHNSON. Each ship has a royal standard of its own.

JOHN D. (*Goes up and points to the flag that is a royal standard.*)

MRS. JOHNSON. Did you ever see one before, John?

JOHN D. No; but that just looks like it.

MRS. JOHNSON. I will show you some. Royal standards are very interesting. John picked out the royal standard in the picture. Can you find those in this book? (*The teacher comes a little way down each aisle while showing the royal standards from a book. Various children raise their hands.*)

JUNE. (*Points out two.*)

MRS. JOHNSON. They are both royal standards of the same country. Are they alike?

CHILDREN. No. (*Seven out of sixteen answer.*)

MRS. JOHNSON. Why would a country change its royal standard?

WILLIAM. Which of these is the latest?

DURWOOD. While they were Catholic they might have one, and change when they became Protestant.

FRANCES. They might not have a king and queen any more, and change.

MARTHA. This one is for the country's independence.

MRS. JOHNSON. Martha was pretty nearly right. How many provinces do you think England had conquered when she had that standard?

CATHERINE. Five or six.

MRS. JOHNSON. This was the royal standard of England when she had France (*pointing to one*). Did she own France when this one was her standard (*showing another*)?

CHILDREN. No.

MRS. JOHNSON. Did she at the time of this picture?

CHILDREN. Yes.

WILLIAM. You can see the lily.

MRS. JOHNSON. Down here we have England, Scotland, and Ireland. What other kinds of flags do you see in the picture? Come up and draw the shape of a flag you see there.

JUNIOR. (*Draws flag.*) Here is a pennon.

WILLIAM. That is what I was thinking of, but I couldn't fit the name in right.

MRS. JOHNSON. Can you see another, John?

JOHN T. There is another one, only it is longer. It has a few curlicues.

MRS. JOHNSON. Come and point. (JOHN *goes to the picture.*) Do you see that this pennon has been slashed? There is an interesting story attached to that. Those pennons are some which were given to knights on board the ship. When a man became a knight, the monarch usually gave him a silken pennon, and it was usually swallowtailed. When the knight was very brave on the field of battle, the king demanded the knight's pennon and cut away those streamers until he had what was a knight banneret, shaped like this. (*She demonstrates at the blackboard.*) Can you see other decorations?

ELIZABETH. There are pictures on the sails of dragons and crosses — probably Catholic.

MRS. JOHNSON. What do you think they mean? Do you know what the dragon means?

JUNIOR. It is the emblem of England.

MRS. JOHNSON. A particular man in England was given that emblem when he was made knight. (*Children make some suggestions as to the name of the knight.*) It was the dragon of the sea, Sir Francis Drake. He was so notorious that mothers mentioned him when they wished to frighten their children. Here we have a cross on almost all the English flags. Do you know anything about this?

GENEVIEVE. I think it stands for the Catholic religion.

MRS. JOHNSON. Was England Catholic?

GENEVIEVE. No. I don't believe they are English ships.

MRS. JOHNSON. They are English ships. They are fighting for their religion. The cross of St. George is often used here as well as Drake's dragon. All the private pennons of the knights have the cross of St. George on them.

JUNIOR. (*Volunteering*) They still have that same cross on their flag. (*In order to get on with the lesson the teacher occasionally ignores the hands of children who want to ask still more questions.*)

MRS. JOHNSON. The cross is in the most prominent place to show that the knight is, first and foremost, a subject of the king of England. What about the other ship? Can you tell to whom it belongs by the colors?

JUNE. Spain.

MRS. JOHNSON. What are the colors of the Spanish flag?

JUNE. I don't know.

MARTHA. I do not know.

JOHN T. Red, white, and yellow.

MRS. JOHNSON. Red and yellow. Here are Spanish flags. Can you point to the royal standards? You will also find on the Spanish ships crosses and designs. Those crosses have been put there because this ship is out on a religious duty. Those red crosses were used at the time of the Crusades. To whom do those ships belong?

Children now begin to anticipate the point, and to show by their expressions that they are ready to locate the picture in point of time and to bring in the question of the Armada.

WILLIAM. Was it one of those privateers?

CATHERINE. Isn't it the Armada? The English had many small boats; most of the small ones were easier to fight with. It looks like war because men are in the water.

MRS. JOHNSON. How many think it is a time of peace? (*No reaction.*) A time of war?

GENEVIEVE. War.

MRS. JOHNSON. Can you place this picture according to time in history? About the right century? (*Eight out of sixteen volunteer.*)

JUNIOR. The sixteenth.

MRS. JOHNSON. How many agree? Near the beginning or the end?

CHILDREN. Beginning.

SUSAN. Around 1875. (*Class disagree vehemently.*)

WILLIAM. 1580 to 1590.

MRS. JOHNSON. William is right. That is close enough. It was in the latter part of the sixteenth century.

Can you go to the map and point to the place this scene took place? (*All but four volunteer.*)

DURWOOD. (*Points to the English Channel.*)

WILLIAM. Around Dover.

MRS. JOHNSON. Point to the two countries engaged in war.

DURWOOD. (*Points to Spain and England.*)

MRS. JOHNSON. Can you make a title for this picture, — or, as we say, a caption? What would you suggest, Catherine?

CATHERINE. The Spanish Armada.

FRANCES. The Defeat of the Spanish Armada.

WILLIAM. The Defeat of the Spanish Armada in the English Channel. Otherwise you would not know where it was.

JOHN D. When I first looked at it I thought it might be the Spanish Armada. (*See page 699 :* JOHN *says,* "I think I know what it is.")

MRS. JOHNSON. Why?

JOHN D. Well, it suggested to me fighting, and we studied about the Spanish Armada and little English ships. (*The class had already read the story; hence the wealth of detail in their possession.*)

MRS. JOHNSON. Point to the ships England owned.

JOHN D. (*Points to the little ones for England and the big one for Spain.*)

MRS. JOHNSON. (*Removes the cardboard covering the caption.*) "Armada in the Channel; Sir Francis Drake capturing Don Pedro's Ship." Point to the ship that belongs to Sir Francis Drake.

GENEVIEVE. The smallest one. (*Points.*) The largest one is Don Pedro's.

MRS. JOHNSON. How many can tell the name of that type of ship?

DURWOOD. Galleon.

MRS. JOHNSON. How did it happen to have that name? Does anyone know?

JOHN T. Because of galley slaves.

WILLIAM. See the big holes. The galley slaves used them for their oars.

MRS. JOHNSON. Did Sir Francis Drake use galley slaves?

CHILDREN. No.

MRS. JOHNSON. They were not generally used at this time, although they were not prohibited by law until later. What do you think this boat depended upon for moving?

VARIOUS CHILDREN. Oars.

JOHN D. The wind. With so many sails the wind can carry it, and when it can't they can use oars.

MRS. JOHNSON. What were all these flags used for? Just for decoration?

ALFRED. They stood for brave deeds of men.

MRS. JOHNSON. Did these ships want to appear conspicuous to the enemy?

DURWOOD. The Spanish had such a lot of ships they weren't figuring on much fighting.

MARTHA. King Philip decided he would show Sir Francis Drake that he was sure he could capture the ships, and make them afraid right away.

JOHN D. Maybe that was one of Don Pedro's boats. He had a lot of pennons.

MRS. JOHNSON. Some of those flags were used for signaling.

WILLIAM. Now they have them on the deck. They don't keep them up. When they signal they use a big long rope. Wasn't that the custom?

MRS. JOHNSON. Yes. Signaling is very interesting to read about. The code was in the possession of only two men on board the ship. The flag signals were kept very closely guarded; and if a ship was damaged, the signals were thrown overboard into the sea with an anchor, and one of the first things the enemy tried to do was to obtain the code of war signals. Can you see anything that suggests a code of war signals?

GEORGIA. The little boat looks as though it had been wrecked.

JUNE. That small boat is waving for something.

MRS. JOHNSON. Do they show any signs of encounter? (*Class looks uncomprehending.*) Do they look as though they had been in a battle with one another? Come up and look at the picture.

GEORGIA. The sail on this little English ship looks as though it had.

MRS. JOHNSON. Examine it closely. You may all move up and see it. (*The class goes to the bulletin board. A general bevy of comment follows:* "You can see them falling overboard." "You can see them in the water.")

JOHN T. This is a mast that belongs up.

MRS. JOHNSON. Do you think those two ships were engaged in battle?

CATHERINE. I think this ship is throwing its signals overboard. They are so small. We can see the people look excited, and you can see this anchor they have on their signals. The boat had been shot at, and it looks as though it was going down.

ALFRED. It looks as though it is after the war now, and the ships are at peace. Back farther it looks like war, but right there it looks as though the Spanish Armada is captured.

MRS. JOHNSON. What is your suggestion, William?

WILLIAM. It looks like war. There is smoke, and soldiers seem to be sinking. There are shattered places in the ships.

DURWOOD. Isn't this the crow's nest? There are quite a few on the English ships. There are some all along here. This looks like one that was shot away from the Spanish ship.

MRS. JOHNSON. Possibly.

WILLIAM. They had sharpshooters up on top of the ships.

JOHN D. The other English ships have been captured. Francis Drake and Don Pedro are fighting it out. The other ships don't look as though they were fighting.

MRS. JOHNSON. Any other suggestions?

FRANCES. (*One of the most advanced readers in the group, who had read much more than most of the others*) Don Pedro wasn't a very good commander. He didn't want to come this time, but the king thought he should come because he was old; but he didn't know how to make his men act.

Mrs. Johnson. I am now going to tell you the story of the picture. The characters in the story are King Philip II of Spain, the commander of the Spanish fleet, Don Pedro, the commander of the *Capitana*, Queen Elizabeth of England, and Sir Francis Drake. King Philip prepared the Spanish Armada, which was equipped as one of the best fleets of that time. During the period that the Armada was being equipped a very able commander was in charge, but just before it was ready to sail he was overcome from fatigue and died. A duke was put in his place. The duke did not want to take the post, but Philip insisted, and he assumed the command. He knew nothing about naval warfare. He was perhaps one of the poorest men King Philip could have selected. On one of the ships was a very able commander, Don Pedro. The Spanish Armada sailed up into the English Channel. The English were two miles astern. One of the Spanish ships got into some difficulty, and Don Pedro left the rest of the fleet to go to its assistance. Just as Don Pedro was leaving the rest of the fleet, he happened to turn suddenly and rammed his ship against another Spanish ship. So the Spanish ship *Capitana* was not damaged in a fight. Don Pedro realized he could not go to the aid of the other Spanish ship. Neither could he follow the Spanish fleet when it was given the order to retreat, and he was left without assistance. The English had been witness to this affair. Francis Drake saw that Don Pedro was disabled, watched all night, and in the morning sailed out to ask Don Pedro to surrender. Don Pedro was very brave and decided he would go down fighting, but when he found out that Francis Drake, "dragon of the sea," was the opposing commander he decided it was more of an honor to surrender to him than to defend a fleet which had deserted him. The *Capitana* had a great deal of treasure, and Francis Drake had it taken into a port on the English Channel. After the end of the war Queen Elizabeth proclaimed a day of thanksgiving, and the flags that had been taken in the defeat of the Spanish Armada were hung by Sir Francis Drake in one of the cathedrals in London. Today you may see eleven banners taken by Sir Francis Drake in one of the cathedrals.

Durwood. (*Describes his own reading habits as follows:* "I don't read as fast as some people do, but I know what I read.") The English ships were not very well equipped. They did not have enough powder for more than one battle, and they had three good battles. Queen Elizabeth was always changing her mind. (William *evidently does not believe this point. He takes out his book, looks up the reference, and then, apparently satisfied, puts it back again and resumes attention to the discussion.*) She disarmed the navy, and when the Armada was only a little way away Drake had to find his own men — any he could get. The queen gave him only enough rations for one month and enough powder for two battles. I don't know exactly, but I think it was two. When the Armada came he had only two or three rations left.

Mrs. Johnson. That is interesting. Any other suggestions?

Frances. What became of Don Pedro after this?

Mrs. Johnson. Can anyone answer? (*No one can.*) I think that would be a very good thing for you to read. I will get you a reference for that. Any other questions you would like to look up?

MARTHA. When Don Pedro surrendered to Drake, some of the soldiers did not want to go under his command to help. So he decided that instead of fighting he would surrender, because he would rather do that than fight for men who weren't willing to help him.

MRS. JOHNSON. Yes. Are there any other questions?

JOHN D. Which boats are in the background, English or Spanish?

MRS. JOHNSON. Which do you think?

JOHN D. This one over here looks like a Spanish one.

MRS. JOHNSON. It looks like a Spanish flag.

WILLIAM. What is that red flag?

MRS. JOHNSON. How many would like to look at this book with different flags? (*Everyone responds.*)

MRS. JOHNSON. Any other questions?

DURWOOD. Isn't this true? The Spanish ships were too large to be worth anything. One reason they had the banners was that they thought the English would be afraid right away.

MRS. JOHNSON. Perhaps. Any other questions?

SUSAN. Did Spain become Protestant or stay Catholic?

MRS. JOHNSON. That is a good question to look up.

MARTHA. Did Don Pedro have codes on his ship, and did he throw them in the water? I thought at first he had thrown his codes in the water.

MRS. JOHNSON. That may have been the artist's idea. Do you think that Ford was present at the time this battle was fought?

JOHN D. No.

MRS. JOHNSON. Where did he get the material?

GEORGIA. He may have looked in the history book.

MARJORIE. He might have got it from a copy.

MRS. JOHNSON. He did. The original of this is copied from a piece of tapestry (*five in the class do not know what tapestry is*) made at the time of the Spanish Armada, and hanging in Westminster Abbey at this time. We will have to draw our lesson to a close now. If you have other questions we will take a little time during tomorrow's history time. You may use these books to locate other material. How many liked the picture? (*Everyone is enthusiastic.*)

The following references were given the children to help them find answers to the points they had raised. A specific page reference was given in each case.

HULME. *Flags of the World.*
WOOD. *Elizabethan Sea Dogs.*
CORBETT. *Drake and the Tudor Navy.*

LESSON VI

MACDOWELL [1]

Miss Lila M. Rose, of the Music Department, State Teachers College, Oshkosh, Wisconsin, taught the following as a demonstration lesson, using as subjects the fifth grade of the training department. The A and B sections were thrown together for this exercise, although they had had somewhat different backgrounds. Of the twenty-four children in the group, there were only nine girls. The regular music period of twenty minutes was devoted to the lesson, which served as the summary of a series of foregoing lessons. All the compositions referred to had been taught previously as separate studies. One group of children had not had all the compositions.

Before the period began the following was written on the board :

EDWARD MacDOWELL

To a Wild Rose	From Uncle Remus
To a Water Lily	Indian Suite
Of a Tailor and a Bear	From Dwarf Land
From an Indian Lodge	Witches' Dance
Sea Pieces	

MISS ROSE. We have so much enjoyed hearing MacDowell's music, I thought you might like to hear it once more. The best listeners are those who have nothing in their hands. (*General clearing of desks.*) Which one in this list would you like to hear? (*Referring to the list at the left*) We do not have those listed at the right.

ELEANOR. "Tailor and the Bear."

KENNETH. I wish we had the "Witches' Dance."

MISS ROSE. We shall have "Of a Tailor and a Bear." You remember that this is the type of music which tells a story.

At this point she played the record "Of a Tailor and a Bear." It took about two minutes. Some boys smiled appreciatively at the point where the bear struggled with his keeper.

[1] See pages 528–529. *Music Appreciation in the Schoolroom* of the Music Education Series (Ginn and Company) may be useful.

JIMMIE. (*Raises hand as soon as the music ceases.*) You can just hear the tapping of the drums in the middle of the piece.

OTHERS. (*Correcting him*) That's the bear growling when he fights.

MISS ROSE. MacDowell has written another composition of the same type, "From Uncle Remus."

BETTY. I'd like to hear the story of "The Tailor and the Bear."

MISS ROSE. Again? Garner, you may tell it.

GARNER. The tailor was in his shop. I don't just remember all of it, but anyhow he had a fiddle. There was a trained bear that broke away, and he heard the music and began to dance.

AVIS. I thought the tailor was in the shoe shop. When the bear came along he looked in. The tailor was afraid, so he thought the bear might like to dance.

MISS ROSE. Do you think it was a true story?

CHILDREN. No.

MISS ROSE. What kind of man would compose this type of music?

VARIOUS CHILDREN. Jolly, cheerful, merry.

MISS ROSE. Do you know what we can call that quality? (*Children look thoughtful, but no one replies.*) We call it a sense of —

HAMILTON. Humor.

MISS ROSE. (*Writes on board* "Sense of Humor.") What would you like to hear next from our list?

CLARENCE. "Indian Lodge."

This record required about three minutes to play.

MISS ROSE. MacDowell has written other pieces based on Indian legends. There is this one called "Indian Suite." Is there anyone who knows what "suite" means? (*No one does.*) It means a group, and this is a group of five or six compositions based upon Indian tunes. What would you say that MacDowell must have been interested in to write music like this?

Boys responded to this question more readily than girls, five boys and one girl volunteering *lodges, wigwams.*

KENNETH. Indian music. If he hadn't known about Indian music, he wouldn't have known how it went. He studied their ways.

MISS ROSE. Yes. Then he must also have been interested in their history. Let us write it down as "Interest in History." (*Does so.*)

HELEN. May we have "To a Water Lily"?

Miss Rose played the record, which took about three minutes. It was very interesting to observe the change in facial expression, giving evidence of the appreciation of the change in mood.

MISS ROSE. Do you remember the group of instruments that play "To a Water Lily"?

VARIOUS CHILDREN. The flute, violin, cello, and harp.

BETTY. May we have "To a Wild Rose"?

MISS ROSE. In just a moment. This composition and "To a Wild Rose" belong to a suite called "Woodland Sketches," some of which are based on nature. MacDowell believed this kind of music could best be written when out in the woods, close to nature. He bought a farm in New England, and all around built little log cabins, where he invited his friends who were interested in painting, poetry, and music to spend their vacations. The settlement was called Peterboro. There are many famous artists and poets who have spent vacations at the Peterboro Colony, which was what MacDowell called his farm in New England. "To a Wild Rose" and "To a Water Lily" show which one of MacDowell's interests?

JACK. His interest in nature. (*Teacher writes on the board* "Love of Nature.")

MISS ROSE. You know "To a Wild Rose" so well that while you listen I am going to show you some pictures.

She put on the record, and during the three minutes in which it was being played books containing the pictures were quietly passed from one to another.

JAMES. Miss Rose, how long ago was this music written?

MISS ROSE. About thirty years ago. Will you please read for us the three points about MacDowell which we discovered today from his works?

DOROTHY. Sense of humor, interest in history, love of nature.

MISS ROSE. I am going to leave these books here,[1] and I should like to have you write for next Friday a little paragraph on MacDowell.

Two of the compositions follow:

5-B MUSIC

(MacDowell)

He was a great composer. He was eight years old when he started writing music. He had a sense of humor in music. He took music lessons from his father's friend. He loved nature very much. He is one of the greatest American composers. He wrote very much music.   [James]

5-B MUSIC

(MacDowell)

MacDowell was born in New York and started to study music when he was about eight years old. He is an American composer. From what I know about him he must have liked history and nature. He certainly had a sense of humor to write a piece about a tailor and a bear. He had a music apartment in New England. After a while his health broke down and he became an invalid and died.   [Helen]

[1] See list on pages 528–529.

APPENDIX A

BOOK LISTS

1. FOURTH-GRADE BOOKS

In addition to the book list given on pages 30–31, the following books were used more than ten times in fourth-grade stories:

Upper Group

	Times Used
PRATT. Early Colonies	23
GORDY. Colonial Days	20
MORRIS. Heroes of Discovery in America	18
CROWE. Studies in American History, I	14
WRIGHT. Children's Stories in American History	14

Average Group

HART. Colonial Children	15
SHAW. Discoverers and Explorers	14
PRATT. Exploration and Discovery	10

2. FIFTH-GRADE BOOKS

In addition to the book lists given on pages 31–32 the following books were used more than ten times in fifth-grade stories:

Upper Group

FOOTE and SKINNER. Makers and Defenders of America	22
MONTGOMERY. Beginners' American History	21
BURNHAM. Hero Tales from History	19
CHANDLER and CHITWOOD. Makers of American History	19
MARSHALL. Story of Human Progress	19
MOWRY. American Inventions and Inventors	17
TAPPAN. Heroes of Progress	17
DAVIDSON. Founders and Builders of our Nation	16
SANFORD. Story of Agriculture in the United States	16
SANFORD and OWEN. Modern Americans	15
BACHMAN. Great Inventors and their Inventions	14
BROOKS. Story of Cotton	14
VOLLINTINE. Making of America	14
STIMPSON. Child's Book of American Biography	13
EGGLESTON. First Book in American History	11

TIMES
USED

Logie. From Columbus to Lincoln 11
Barrows-Parker. Geography: United States and Canada 10
Forman. Stories of Useful Inventions 10
Rocheleau. Great American Industries: Transportation 10
Smith. Industrial History 10

Average Group

Eggleston. Stories of Great Americans for Little Americans 15
Parkman. Conquests of Invention 15
Beeby. How the World grows Smaller 12
McFee. Stories of American Inventions 12
Turpin. Brief Biographies from American History 12
Carroll. Around the World, III 10
Everett and Reed. When they were Boys 10

3. SUPPLEMENTARY READING LISTS

Recommendations as to supplementary-reading lists for fourth grade, with number of times each book is used in the unit given (in addition to the lists given on pages 30–31 and in Appendix A above):

Unit I

Woodburn and Moran. Introduction to American History 7
Bourne and Benton. Introductory American History 6
Harding. Our Old World Background 6
Woodburn and Moran. Beginners' History of the United States 3
Colum. Children of Odin 1
Hall. Viking Tales 1
Johnston. Our Little Viking Cousin of Long Ago 1
Stein. Our Little Crusader Cousin of Long Ago 1
Wilson. A History Reader 1

Unit II

Chandler and Chitwood. Makers of American History 8
Turpin. Brief Biographies from American History 8
Woodburn and Moran. Beginners' History of the United States 8
McMurry. Pioneers on Land and Sea 7
Wilson. A History Reader 6
Lawler. Story of Columbus and Magellan 5
Tappan. American Hero Stories 5
Pyle. Book of Pirates 1
Schwartz. Five Little Strangers 1
Snedden. Docas, the Indian Boy 1

Unit III

Woodburn and Moran. Beginner's History of the United States 10
Mowry. First Steps in the History of our Country 8
Tappan. Letters from Colonial Children 8

TIMES
USED

WILSON. A History Reader 8
HAZARD and DUTTON. Indians and Pioneers 7
STONE and FICKETT. Everyday Life in the Colonies 6
MOWRY. American Pioneers 5
USHER. Story of the Pilgrims for Children 5
WARREN. Little Pioneers 5
BALDWIN. Stories of Old New England 4
EGGLESTON. Stories of Great Americans for Little Americans 4
WELSH. Colonial Days 3
OTIS. Calvert of Maryland 1
OTIS. Mary of Plymouth 1
OTIS. Peter of New Amsterdam 1
OTIS. Richard of Jamestown 1
OTIS. Ruth of Boston 1
OTIS. Stephen of Philadelphia 1
PUMPHREY. Pilgrim Stories 1

UNIT IV

PRATT. Later Colonial Period 9
VOLLINTINE. The Making of America 9
TAPPAN. American Hero Stories 7
CHANDLER and CHITWOOD. Makers of American History 6
BALDWIN. Four Great Americans 5
GORDY. American Leaders and Heroes 5
WOODBURN and MORAN. Beginners' History of the United States 5
EGGLESTON. Stories of Great Americans for Little Americans 4
WILSON. A History Reader 4
DAVIDSON. Founders and Builders of our Nation 3

UNIT V

(Many may be borrowed from fifth grade)

COE. Makers of the Nation 9
GORDY. Stories of Later American History 8
MOWRY. First Steps in the History of our Country 7
BLAISDELL and BALL. Hero Stories from American History 6
DICKINSON. Children's Book of Patriotic Stories 6
LEFFERTS. American Leaders, I 6
PRATT. Foundations of the Republic 6
WOODBURN and MORAN. Makers of America 6
SOUTHWORTH. Builders of our Country, II 5
BALDWIN. Fifty Famous Rides and Riders 4
BLAISDELL and BALL. American History Story Book 4
DICKSON. Pioneers and Patriots in American History 4
EGGLESTON. Stories of Great Americans for Little Americans 4

Recommendations as to supplementary-reading lists for fifth grade, with number of times each book is used in the unit given (in addition to the lists given on pages 31–32 and in Appendix A above) :

Unit VI

TIMES
USED

LEFFERTS. American Leaders, I 7
BLAISDELL and BALL. American History Story Book 4
WRIGHT. Children's Stories of American Progress 4
ROOSEVELT and LODGE. Hero Tales from American History 3

Unit VII

RUGG and SCHWEPPE. Westward Movement and Growth of Transportation 5
HART. How our Grandfathers Lived 4
STONE and FICKETT. Days and Deeds a Hundred Years Ago 4
BRIGHAM. From Trail to Railway 3
EGGLESTON. Stories of American Life and Adventure 3
MOWRY. American Pioneers 3
ROOSEVELT. Stories of the Great West 3
OTIS. Philip of Texas 2
OTIS. Antoine of Oregon 1
OTIS. Benjamin of Ohio 1
OTIS. Martha of California 1

Unit VIII

CARPENTER. How the World is Clothed 6
TOWLE. Heroes and Martyrs of Invention 5
HOLLAND. Historic Inventions 4
CHAMBERLAIN. How we are Clothed 3
CHAMBERLAIN. How we Travel 3
CHASE and CLOW. Stories of Industry, I 3
DARROW. Masters of Science and Invention 3
MORRIS. Heroes of Progress in America 3
SHILLIG. Four Wonders 3
BAILEY. What to do for Uncle Sam 2
RUGG and SCHWEPPE. Westward Movement and Growth of Transportation 2

Unit IX

BALDWIN. Four Great Americans 9
HART. Romance of the Civil War 9
HART. Seven Great American Poets 5
BALDWIN. Fifty Famous People 4
GORDY. Our Patriots 4
CODY. Four American Poets 3
HORTON. Group of Famous Women 3
MOORE. When they were Girls 3
MOWRY. American Pioneers 3
RIDEING. Boyhood of Famous Authors 3
SCHWARTZ. Five Little Strangers 1

Unit X

WILSON. White Indian Boy 4
Lessons in Community and National Life, Series B 4
LEFFERTS. Our Own United States 3
ROOSEVELT. Stories of the Great West 2

Unit XI

	Times Used
Lessons in Community and National Life, Series C	6
LEFFERTS. Our Own United States	5
ALLEN. How and Where we Live	3
ALLEN. United States	3
BAKER. Boys' Book of Inventions	3
CHAMBERLAIN. How we are Clothed	3
DOUBLEDAY. Stories of Inventors	3
FAIRBANKS. Western United States	3
MIRICK and HOLMES. Home Life around the World	3
PIERCY. Great Inventions and Discoveries	3
OTIS. Seth of Colorado	1

Unit XII

BRYANT. I am an American	7
TOMLINSON. Fighters Young Americans want to Know	4
WINSLOW. Our American Neighbors	4
BAKER. Boys' Book of Inventions	3
CURTIS. Why we Celebrate our Holidays	3
DOUBLEDAY. Stories of Inventors	3
MOWRY. American Heroes and Heroism	3

APPENDIX B

ILLUSTRATIVE MATERIAL

Addresses of firms supplying material referred to in the text

American Citizenship Course in United States History, IV
    Charles Scribner's Sons, 597 Fifth Avenue, New York
Arnold Historical Pictures
Arnold Season Series
    Denoyer-Geppert Co., 5235–5237 Ravenswood Avenue, Chicago
Bradley's Modern Trade Pictures
Bradley's Straight-Line Cut Outs
Bradley's Village Series of Cut Outs
    Milton Bradley Company, Springfield, Massachusetts
    Thomas Charles Co., 2249–2253 Calumet Avenue, Chicago
BROOKS, EUGENE C. Story of Cotton
    Rand McNally & Company, 538 South Clark Street, Chicago
Brown's Famous Pictures
    George P. Brown and Co., 38 Lovett Street, Beverly, Massachusetts
BURNHAM, SMITH. Making of our Country
    John C. Winston Co., 1006–1016 Arch Street, Philadelphia
Busy Bee Packets
    Davis Press, 44 Portland Street, Worcester, Massachusetts
Child's World Pictures
    Thomas Charles Co., 2249–2253 Calumet Avenue, Chicago
Chronicles of America Photoplays
    Yale University Press Film Service, Yale University, New Haven, Connecticut
COFFIN, CHARLES C. Drum Beat of the Nation
COFFIN, CHARLES C. Freedom Triumphant
    Harper & Brothers, Franklin Square, New York
Compton's Pictured Encyclopedia
    F. E. Compton Co., 58 East Washington Street, Chicago
DALTON, JACK
    537 South Clark Street, Chicago. (From him may be obtained replicas of newspapers announcing the death of Washington and of Lincoln.)
DIEZ, WILHELM. Zur Geschichte der Costüme
    Braun und Schneider, Munich, Germany
EARLE, ALICE M. Two Centuries of Costume in America, I, II
    The Macmillan Company, 66 Fifth Avenue, New York ; Prairie Avenue and 25th Street, Chicago
Educational Posters of the National Child Welfare Association
    70 Fifth Avenue, New York
Ford Educational Library
    Ford Motion Picture Laboratories, 14310 Woodward Avenue, Detroit, Michigan

GABRIEL, R. H. (ED.). Pageant of America, I–III, V, XI, XIII
  Yale University Press, New Haven, Connecticut
GRANT, GORDON. Story of the Ship
  McLoughlin Brothers, 74 Park Street, Springfield, Massachusetts
HALLECK, REUBEN P. History of our Country
  American Book Company, 100 Washington Square, New York; 330 East
  22d Street, Chicago
INGERSOLL, ERNEST. Book of the Ocean
  The Century Co., 353 Fourth Avenue, New York
Keystone Views
  Keystone View Company, Inc., Meadville, Pennsylvania
Lehmann Animal Pictures
Lehmann Geographical Pictures
Lehmann Historical Pictures
  Denoyer-Geppert Co., 5235–5237 Ravenswood Avenue, Chicago
  A. J. Nystrom Co., 2249–2253 Calumet Avenue, Chicago
LEMOS, PEDRO. School Posters
  Davis Press, 44 Portland Street, Worcester, Massachusetts
"Lincoln Logs": building material and book of designs
  John L. Wright, 232 East Erie Street, Chicago
Literary Digest
  Funk & Wagnalls Company, 354–360 Fourth Avenue, New York
Little Phostint Journeys
  Detroit Publishing Company, Detroit, Michigan
Longman's Historical Illustrations
Longman's Historical Wall Pictures
  Longmans, Green & Co., 55 Fifth Avenue, corner of 12th Street, New York.
McKinley's Illustrated Topics
  McKinley Publishing Co., 1623 Ranstead Street, Philadelphia. (Wall outline
  maps may be obtained also.)
McMASTER, JOHN B. Primary History of the United States
  American Book Company, 100 Washington Square, New York; 330 East
  22d Street, Chicago
Mentor
  Crowell Publishing Company, Springfield, Ohio
National Geographic Magazine
National Geographic Society Series of Pictures
  National Geographic Society, Hubbard Memorial Hall, Washington, D. C.
National Parks Portfolio
  Department of the Interior, Washington, D. C.
National Posters
  801 South Wells Street, Chicago
New Standard Dictionary
  Funk & Wagnalls Company, 354–360 Fourth Avenue, New York
Old South Leaflets Series
  Directors of the Old South Work, Old South Meeting-House, Boston,
  Massachusetts
Outline Maps
  A. J. Nystrom Co., 2249–2253 Calumet Avenue, Chicago
  Denoyer-Geppert Co., 5235–5237 Ravenswood Avenue, Chicago
  Rand McNally & Company, 538 South Clark Street, Chicago
  McKinley Publishing Co., 1623 Ranstead Street, Philadelphia
  Ginn and Company, 15 Ashburton Place, Boston, Massachusetts

Perry Pictures
  The Perry Pictures Company, Malden, Massachusetts
Picturol
  Society for Visual Education, 327 South LaSalle Street, Chicago
Public School Methods, V
  Bellows-Hanson Co., 104 South Michigan Avenue, Chicago
PYLE, HOWARD. Book of the American Spirit
  Harper & Brothers, Franklin Square, New York
ROBBINS, CHARLES L. School History of the American People
  World Book Company, 2126 Prairie Avenue, Chicago
St. Nicholas
  The Century Co., 353 Fourth Avenue, New York
SANFORD, ALBERT H. Story of Agriculture in the United States
  D. C. Heath & Co., 231–245 West 39th Street, New York; 1815 Prairie
    Avenue, Chicago
School Arts Magazine
  Davis Press, 44 Portland Street, Worcester, Massachusetts
School Studies in Agriculture: Charts
  A. J. Nystrom Co., 2249–2253 Calumet Avenue, Chicago
Schoolfilm
  Society for Visual Education, 327 South LaSalle Street, Chicago
SPARKS, E. E. National Development
  Harper & Brothers, Franklin Square, New York
Travel
  Robert M. McBride & Co., 7 West 16th Street, New York
Victor Records: A Graded List of Victor Records for Home and School
  Victor Talking Machine Co., Camden, New Jersey
Wheeler Natural History Charts
  A. J. Nystrom Co., 2249–2253 Calumet Avenue, Chicago
WOODBURN, JAMES A., and MORAN, THOMAS F. Elementary American History
    and Government
WOODBURN, JAMES A., and MORAN, THOMAS F. Makers of America
  Longmans, Green & Co., 55 Fifth Avenue, corner of 12th Street, New York
World Book
  W. F. Quarrie and Co., 154 East Erie Street, Chicago

Additional material may often be obtained in the form of free advertising folders and pamphlets. These sometimes contain information and illustrations of historic interest. For addresses of firms supplying such material, see advertisements in magazines and newspapers.

APPENDIX C

COMPLETE LIST OF MINIMAL ESSENTIALS IN AMERICAN HISTORY FOR THE ELEMENTARY SCHOOL

[Based on the Minimal Essentials for each story]

Persons (160)

Adams, Samuel
Algonquin
Appleseed, Johnny
Audubon
Aztec

Baltimore, Lord
Barton, Clara
Bell, Alexander Graham
Boone, Daniel
Braddock, General
Bradford, Governor William
British
Bryant, William Cullen
Burbank, Luther
Burgoyne, General

Cabot, John
Calhoun, John
Carnegie, Andrew
Cartier
Catholics
Champlain
Clark, George Rogers
Clark, William
Clay, Henry
Clinton, De Witt
Cody, "Buffalo Bill"
Columbus
Cooper, James Fenimore
Cornwallis
Cortez
Custer, General

Davis, Jefferson
De Soto
Dewey, George
Dias
Dix, Dorothea

Drake, Sir Francis
Dutch

Edison, Thomas A.
Elizabeth, Queen
English
Ericson, Leif
Ericsson, John

Farragut, Admiral
Ferdinand
Field, Cyrus W.
Foch
Ford, Henry
Franklin, Benjamin
French
Fulton, Robert

Gama, Vasco da
Garrison, William Lloyd
George III
Goethals
Gompers, Samuel
Goodyear, Charles
Gorgas
Governor of Virginia
Grant, General Ulysses S.
Greene, Nathanael
Gutenberg, John

Hale, Nathan
Hamilton, Alexander
Hancock, John
Harrison, William Henry
Hawkins, John
Hawthorne, Nathaniel
Hay, John
Henry, Patrick
Henry, Prince
Hill, James J.

719

Persons (continued)
Hindenburg
Holmes, Oliver Wendell
homesteaders
Houston, Sam
Howe, Elias
Hudson, Henry

Indians
Iroquois
Irving, Washington
Isabella

Jackson, Andrew
Jackson, "Stonewall"
Jefferson, Thomas
Jesuits
Johnson, Sir William
Joliet
Jones, John Paul

Lafayette
La Salle
Lee, Robert E.
Lewis, Meriwether
Lincoln, Abraham
Longfellow, Henry Wadsworth
Lowell, James Russell

McCormick, Cyrus
MacDowell, Edward
McKinley, William
Madison, James
Magellan
Mann, Horace
Marconi
Marquette
Massasoit
Montcalm, General
Mormons
Morris, Robert
Morse, Samuel F. B.

Northmen

Peary, Robert E.
Penn, William
Pershing
Perry, Oliver Hazard
Perry, Commodore
Philip, King
Pilgrims
Pinchot, Gifford
Pocahontas

Poe, Edgar Allan
Polo, Marco
Ponce de Leon
Pontiac
Powhatan
Puritans

Quakers

Raleigh, Walter
Roosevelt, Theodore

Saint-Gaudens
Sargent
Scott, Dred
Sherman, General
Sitting Bull
Slater, Samuel
Smith, John
Spaniards
Spanish
Standish, Miles
Stowe, Harriet Beecher
Stuyvesant, Peter

Tecumseh
Turks
Twain, Mark

Vespucius, Americus
Vikings

Washington, Booker T.
Washington, George
Washington, Martha
Webster, Daniel
West, Benjamin
Whitman, Walt
Whitney, Eli
Whittier, John Greenleaf
Willard, Frances E.
Williams, Roger
Wilson, Woodrow
Winthrop, John
Wolfe, General
Wright brothers

Young, Brigham

Places (150)
Africa
Alaska
America
Annapolis

Appalachian Mountains
Arctic
Asia
Atlanta, Georgia
Atlantic

Belgium
Boston
Brazil
Bunker Hill

California
Canada
Canal Zone
Canary Islands
Cape of Storms or Cape of Good Hope
Carolina
Champlain, Lake
Channel, the
China
Columbia River
Connecticut
Constantinople
Cuba

Detroit
District of Columbia
Duquesne, Fort

East Indies
Eastern coast of North America
England
Erie, Lake
Erie Canal
Europe

Florida
Ford's Theater
France

Geneva
Genoa
Georgia
Gettysburg
Great American Desert
Great Lakes
Great Salt Lake
Guinea coast

Havana
Hawaii
Holland

Holy Land
Honolulu
Hudson River

Iceland
Independence Hall
India
Indies

James River
Jamestown
Japan

Kansas
Kentucky
Klondike

Lexington
Little Big Horn, the
Louisiana

Mackinac
Manhattan
Manila
Marne
Maryland
Mason and Dixon's line
Massachusetts
Mediterranean Sea
Mexican border
Mexican cession
Mexico
Mexico, Gulf of
Mexico City
Michigan, Lake
Mississippi River
Missouri
Missouri River
Mohawk River
Montreal
Mount Vernon
Mouth of the Mississippi

Nebraska
New Amsterdam
New England
New France
New Netherland
New Orleans
New York
North America
North pole
Northwest, the

Places (continued)
Ohio River
Oklahoma
Oregon
Oregon Trail

Pacific
Pacific coast of North America
Panama
Paris
Peking
Pennsylvania
Philadelphia
Philippines
Pittsburgh (Fort Pitt)
Plains of Abraham
Plymouth
Porto Rico
Portugal
Potomac River

Quebec

Rhode Island
Richmond, Virginia
Rio Grande
Rocky Mountains

St. Augustine
St. Lawrence River
Santa Fe
Saratoga

Scotland
seaboard, the
South, the
South America
South Carolina
South Sea
Spain

Texas
Tippecanoe
Tripoli
Tuskegee

Valley Forge
Venice
Verdun
Versailles
Vinland
Virgin Islands
Virginia

Washington, District of Columbia
West, the
West coast of Africa
West Indies
West Point
Wilderness Road, the

Yellowstone National Park
Yorktown
Yukon

Dates (44)

1000. Discovery of America by the Northmen
1300. Marco Polo's return from China (approximately)
1453. Capture of Constantinople by the Turks
1492. Columbus discovered America
1497. John Cabot discovered North America
1498. Vasco da Gama reached India
1519–1522. Magellan circumnavigated the globe
1588. England defeated the Spanish Armada
1607. Founding of Jamestown
1619. Slavery introduced into Virginia
1619. Beginning of representation in America
1620. Settlement of Plymouth
1630. Settlement of Boston
1763. End of French and Indian War
1765. Stamp Act
1775. Battles of Lexington and Concord
1776. July 4, the signing of the Declaration of Independence
1777. Battle of Saratoga
1783. End of Revolution (Treaty)

1789. Constitution went into effect
1793. Invention of the cotton gin
1803. Purchase of Louisiana
1807. Fulton's steamboat
1812. Second war with England
1820. Missouri Compromise
1823. Monroe Doctrine
1830. Beginning of era of railroad-building
1831. McCormick's reaper
1844. Sending of the first message by the telegraph
1845. Annexation of Texas
1848. End of Mexican War
1848. Discovery of gold in California
1850. Great Compromise
1860. Secession of South Carolina
1861–1865. Civil War
1863. Emancipation Proclamation
1865. Lee's surrender
1876. Invention of the telephone
1879. Invention of the electric light
1894. Coming of the automobile
1898. Annexation of Hawaii
1898. Spanish-American War
1903. Coming of the aëroplane
1914. Beginning of the World War
1915. Opening of the Panama Canal
1917. Purchase of the Virgin Islands
1917. Entrance of the United States into the World War
1918. November 11, the Armistice

Historical Terms (399)

abolition
administration
admiral
aëroplane
against the law
age of electricity
age of steel
aide
airship
Alamo
alliances
allies
all-sea route
ambush
amendment
American Federation of Labor
annexation
Armada
armistice
Articles of Confederation
assassination
assembling
asylum
Atlantic cable
attack
attempt

Baltimore and Ohio
Barbary
battle
betray
binder
black flag
blockade
blockhouse
Blue and the Gray, the
border states
boundary line
Boxer rebellion
brand

Canadian Pacific Line
canal
capital

Historical Terms (continued)

capital city
capitol
capture
caravan
carpetbaggers
Centennial Exposition
Central Powers
cession
"cheese box on a raft"
child labor
Children's Poet
Chinese Exclusion Act
Church of England
circumnavigation
citizen
Civil War
claims
clearing
Clermont
clipper ships
closed season
clothing industry
coach
Coal Age
coast
codling moth
colonial period
colonists
colonization
colony, permanent
commodore
common schools
communication
company, commercial
compass
compromise
Confederacy
confer knighthood
conquer
conquest
conservation
conspiracy
Constitution of the United States
continent
Continental Congress, Second
copyright
corporation
cotton gin
cotton states, the
council
court (royal)
courtier

cowboy
"crossroads of the Pacific"
crusade
Cunard Line

Danish West Indies
"dark and bloody ground"
debtors
debts
decade
Declaration of Independence
defeat
Democrat
Democratic party
dependent
disarmament
discover
discoverer
discovery
draft
Dred Scott decision

East
Emancipation Proclamation
emperor
employee
employer
era
estates
ether
exile
expedition
exploration
explore
explorer
export

factory system
failure
Far East
Federal
fertilizer
field servants
fish hatchery
5:5:3
flatboat
fleet
forest rangers
forks of the Ohio
fort
"Forty-niners"
found a colony
Fourth of July

Historical Terms (continued)
overland stage
overseer

pack horse
Panama Canal
partition of China
patent
Patent Office
patroons
peace conference
persecution
Philippine independence
phonograph
photography
pilgrim
pillory
pioneer
pipe of peace
piracy
pirate
"plant wizard"
plantation system
plantations
plot
polar exploration
pony express
Poor Richard's Almanac
poor whites
portage
postrider
power
power loom
prairie schooners
president
press, the
prison reform
products
Progressive party
prohibition
proprietor
prospector
protectorate
purchase

quantity production

reaper
reconstruction
Red Cross
regiment
representatives

Republican party
reservation
retreat
Revolution
rodeo
roller mills
rotation of crops
Rough Riders
round-up
route

sack (of a city)
sailing charts
score of years
scout
sculptor
sculpture
sea of darkness
secession
settled
settlement
"Seward's Ice Box"
sheep-herder
shuttle
siege
slave quarters
slave states
slave trade
slavery
slaves
smelting
South, the
Spanish America
Spanish-American War
Spanish Main, the
spin
spindle
spinning jenny
stagecoach
standard parts
state
state park
steel
stockade
stocks
strike
submarine war zone
submarines
surplus
surrender
surveyor
"swamp fox"

tanks
tax
telegraph
temperance movement
territory
textile
Tory
town meeting
tractor
trade routes
trade-mark
trading posts
traitor
transcontinental
transportation
treasure fleet
treasurer
treaty
treaty of peace
trinkets
trolley car
turnpike
twine binder
typewriter

Uncle Sam
Uncle Tom's Cabin
underground railroad
"the Union," Federal
Union Pacific Railroad
unite

United States Department of Agri-
culture
United States Department of Labor
United States Steel Corporation

Versailles, Treaty of
voter
voyage
vulcanization

wages
War of 1812
war whoop
Washington Conference
"watchful waiting"
water route
weave
West, the
western front
wharf
White House
"white ribbon"
White Star Line
"Wizard of Menlo Park"
woman suffrage
woodrangers
World War
World's Fair

Yankee
"Yankee Doodle"

INDEX

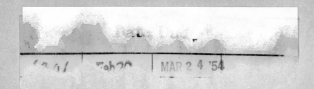